Brief Contents

W9-AAD-684

FIFTH EDITION   INSTRUCTOR'S ANNOTATED EDITION

WRITINGFIRST

with
READINGS
PRACTICE in CONTEXT

Laurie G. Kirszner
University of the Sciences

Stephen R. Mandell
Drexel University

with new technology teaching tips by
Timothy J. Jones
Oklahoma City Community College

with additional teaching tips and ESL tips by
Linda Mason Austin
McLennan Community College

Bedford/St. Martin's
Boston ◆ New York

For Bedford/St. Martin's

Executive Editor for Developmental Studies: Alexis Walker
Associate Editor: Karrin M. Varucene
Senior Production Editor: Ryan Sullivan
Senior Production Supervisor: Dennis J. Conroy
Senior Marketing Manager: Christina Shea
Copy Editor: Ginny Perrin
Indexer: Melanie Belkin
Photo Researcher: Naomi Kornhauser
Permissions Manager: Kalina K. Ingham
Art Director: Lucy Krikorian
Text Design: Jerilyn Bockorick
Cover Design: Marine Bouvier Miller
Cover Photo: Marker © Corbis/SuperStock
Composition: Cenveo Publisher Services
Printing and Binding: RR Donnelley and Sons

President: Joan E. Feinberg
Editorial Director: Denise B. Wydra
Editor in Chief: Karen S. Henry
Director of Development: Erica T. Appel
Director of Marketing: Karen R. Soeltz
Director of Production: Susan W. Brown
Associate Director, Editorial Production: Elise S. Kaiser
Managing Editor: Shuli Traub

Library of Congress Control Number: 2011943125

Manufactured in the United States of America.

6 5 4 3 2 1
f e d c b a

For information, write: Bedford/St. Martin's, 75 Arlington Street, Boston, MA 02116
    (617-399-4000)

ISBN: 978-0-312-54256-6 (Student Edition)
ISBN: 978-0-312-54307-5 (Instructor's Annotated Edition)

Preface for Instructors

In college, writing comes first. In fact, as soon as students set foot in a classroom, they are asked to write — to take notes, to complete assignments, to write papers, to take exams. For this reason, writing also comes first in *Writing First with Readings: Practice in Context*.

Our years in the classroom have taught us that students learn to write best by writing, not by completing fill-in-the-blank exercises, so unlike other books of its kind, *Writing First* makes writing integral both to the writing process chapters *and* to the grammar chapters: each of these chapters is built around a "Writing First" sequence of prompts that gets students writing on the first page and guides them in revising their writing as they move through the chapter.

Our goals in this edition of *Writing First* remain the same as they were when we wrote the first edition: to motivate students to improve their writing and to give them the tools they need to do so. With the help of feedback from instructors and students who have used past editions, we've worked to make this edition even more motivating and instructive. Specifically, we have fine-tuned the "Writing First" sequences, adding a self-reflective step and making the prompts easier to locate visually. We've added tips for instructors and students on using technology inside and outside the classroom. We've added a new first chapter that helps orient students to college life and offers tips for college success and test-taking. Perhaps most important, we've added a self-assessment tool called TEST—pioneered in our book *Focus on Writing*—that empowers students to become capable editors of their own writing.

Organization

Writing First with Readings: Practice in Context has a flexible organization that permits instructors to teach various topics in the order that works best for them and their students. The book is divided into three sections: "Writing Paragraphs and Essays," "Revising and Editing Your Writing," and "Becoming a Critical Reader." The first section is a comprehensive discussion of the writing process. The second section presents a thorough review of sentence skills, grammar, punctuation, mechanics, and spelling. The third section introduces students to critical reading skills and includes nineteen professional essays, over half of which are new to this edition, each illustrating a particular pattern of development.

Features

Central to the text is our "writing first" philosophy, which is supported by innovative features designed to make students' writing practice meaningful, productive, and enjoyable.

Writing First empowers students by teaching them essential writing skills in the context of their own writing. A three-step exercise strand (1. Write First, 2. Reflect, and 3. TEST • Revise • Edit) gets students writing immediately, asks them to reflect on what they've written, and then shows them how to revise and edit their original writing using the proven self-assessment tool TEST. By moving frequently between their own writing and workbook-style mastery exercises, students get constant practice, advice, and reinforcement of the skills they are learning.

Students get the writing and grammar help they need—in an accessible format. With five chapters on the writing process, eleven chapters on paragraph development, and a full unit on essay writing, *Writing First* provides comprehensive coverage of the process of writing paragraphs and essays. Grammar in Context boxes, cross-referenced to the book's handbook sections, integrate focused grammar coverage into the writing chapters. Four full units of grammar and mechanics coverage later in the book provide clear explanations and helpful examples essential for basic writing students. FYI (For Your Information) boxes call out additional helpful information and offer important reminders to students as they write.

Abundant opportunities for practice and review help students learn important skills and become proficient self-editors. Hundreds of practice exercises help students master the fundamentals of writing and grammar. Chapter Review activities — featuring Editing Practices, Collaborative Activities, and Review Checklists — plus Unit Reviews help students to think critically about their writing as they work on improving it.

The text helps students make the connection between reading and writing. *Writing First* treats reading and writing as linked processes, offering numerous professional and student examples throughout the text as well as nineteen engaging professional selections and guidelines for critical reading at the end of this edition.

Case studies of paragraph and essay writing in every rhetorical mode offer realistic models of student work in progress. Start-to-finish drafts in the paragraph and essay chapters allow students using *Writing First* to look over a student writer's shoulder and see how writing develops from brainstorming to final draft.

Coverage of strategies for college success and a comprehensive chapter on ESL usage address issues important to the basic writing classroom. Chapter One offers a broad range of practical skills to help students manage their time, take notes, complete homework, take exams, and adjust to college life. Additionally, a comprehensive ESL chapter addresses concerns of special interest to nonnative speakers.

New to This Edition

The fifth edition of *Writing First* now offers students a class-tested self-assessment tool—TEST. Integrated into each writing chapter, this mnemonic — standing for Topic sentence (or Thesis statement, in essay chapters), Evidence, Summary statement, and Transitions — reminds students of these four key elements of a paragraph or essay. Using TEST is a simple, easy-to-remember method that empowers students to become capable editors of their own writing. TEST boxes beside student models visually call out the model's key elements, and TEST checklists at the end of each writing chapter guide students through the process of revising their own paragraphs and essays.

A new opening chapter, "Writing and College Success," prepares students for success in the college environment, with an emphasis on academic concerns such as how to distinguish between formal and informal writing and how to perform well on writing exams. This new first chapter also offers students time management tips and homework strategies.

A revised and enhanced "Writing First" strand helps students engage more deeply with each chapter's contents. Students begin each writing chapter with a Write First activity, which is immediately followed by a new inductive exercise asking students to reflect on what they've written and discover what they already know about each pattern of writing. At the end of the chapter, with the aid of a checklist, students are guided through TESTing, revising, and editing the writing they produced.

***Writing First* provides helpful tips to students and instructors for making the most of the technology available to them.** New technology tips, included in the FYI boxes, offer students technology-related advice and direct them online for extra practice and for additional information on peer review, the finer points of doing MLA-style research papers, and similar topics. The Instructor's Annotated Edition offers instructors tips on teaching students how to avoid plagiarism, how to use wikis and blogs to continue class discussion outside of the classroom, how to help students use online databases, and much more.

Note: In response to instructors' requests, *answers to odd-numbered exercises* have been removed from the back of the print editions of *Writing First*; instead, we have made full and odd-numbered sets available in the Instructor Resources section of the free companion Web site, in formats that allow for easy printing or posting for students' use, as instructors see fit. The answer key also appears in *Classroom Resources and Instructor's Guide for Writing First with Readings*.

Support for Instructors and Students

Writing First is accompanied by comprehensive teaching and learning support that includes the following items:

Free Instructor Resources

- **The Instructor's Annotated Edition** of *Writing First with Readings* contains answers to all practice exercises, in addition to numerous teaching ideas, reminders, and cross-references useful to teachers at all levels of experience. ISBN: 978-0-312-54307-5

- *Classroom Resources and Instructor's Guide for Writing First with Readings*, **Fifth Edition**, offers advice for teaching developmental writing as well as chapter-by-chapter pointers for using *Writing First* in the classroom. It contains answers to all of the book's practice exercises, sample syllabi, additional teaching materials, and full chapters on collaborative learning. (Available in print and for download on the free companion Web site.) ISBN: 978-0-312-64568-7

- *Diagnostic and Mastery Tests for Writing First with Readings*, **Fifth Edition**, offers tests that complement the topics covered in *Writing First*. Also available for download on the instructor's side of the free companion Web site. ISBN: 978-0-312-64569-4

- **PowerPoint Slides/Transparency Masters for** *Writing First with Readings*, **Fifth Edition**, available in PowerPoint and PDF formats on the instructor's side of the companion Web site, include numerous models of student writing for group discussion and review.

- *Bedford Coursepacks* allows instructors to plug *Writing First* content into their own course management systems. For details, visit **bedfordstmartins.com/coursepacks**.

- *Testing Tool Kit: Writing and Grammar Test Bank* **CD-ROM** allows instructors to create secure, customized tests and quizzes from a pool of nearly 2,000 questions covering 47 topics. It also includes 10 pre-built diagnostic tests. ISBN: 978-0-312-43032-0

- *TeachingCentral* (**bedfordstmartins.com/teachingcentral**) offers the entire list of Bedford/St. Martin's print and online professional resources in one place. You'll find landmark reference works, source-books on pedagogical issues, award-winning collections, and practical advice for the classroom—all free for instructors.

- *Teaching Developmental Writing: Background Readings*, **Third Edition**, is a professional resource, edited by Susan Naomi Bernstein, former cochair of the Conference on Basic Writing, that offers essays on topics of interest to basic writing instructors, along with editorial apparatus pointing out practical applications for the classroom. ISBN: 978-0-312-43283-6

Student Resources

- *Writing First's* **free companion Web site** offers an abundance of resources for instructors and students, all in one convenient place. At no additional cost, you'll find diagnostic and mastery tests; supplemental exercises from *Exercise Central*; advice on avoiding plagiarism, doing research, and more from *Re:Writing Basics*; PowerPoint slides for review and in-class instruction; and much more. For a modest additional cost, you can access our innovative premium media, including *Re:Writing Plus* and *WritingClass for Writing First with Readings* (both described below). Visit **bedfordstmartins.com/writingfirst** to see all that's available.

■ **A value-priced *Writing First* e-book** is now available for use with computers, tablets, and e-readers. Visit **bedfordstmartins.com/ebooks** for more information.

■ *WritingClass for Writing First with Readings,* **Fifth Edition**, provides instructors and students with a dynamic, interactive online course space preloaded with book-specific exercises, diagnostics, video tutorials, writing and commenting tools, and more. To learn more about *WritingClass*, visit **yourwritingclass.com**. ISBN: 978-1-4576-1300-5

■ *Exercise Central 3.0* at **bedfordstmartins.com/exercisecentral** is the largest database of editing exercises on the Internet—and it's completely **free**. This comprehensive resource contains more than 9,000 exercises that offer immediate feedback; the program also recommends personalized study plans and provides tutorials for common problems. Best of all, students' work reports to a gradebook, allowing instructors to track students' progress quickly and easily.

■ *Exercise Central to Go: Writing and Grammar Practices for Basic Writers* **CD-ROM** provides hundreds of practice items to help students build their writing and editing skills. No Internet connection is necessary. **Free** when packaged with the print text. ISBN: 978-0-312-44652-9

■ *Re:Writing Basics* at **bedfordstmartins.com/rewritingbasics** is an easy-to-navigate Web site, available **free** and accessible without a password, that offers the most popular and widely used free resources from Bedford/St. Martin's, including writing and grammar exercises, model documents, help with the writing process, tips on college success, instructor resources, and more.

■ *Re:Writing Plus,* **now with** *VideoCentral: English,* gathers all of our premium digital content for the writing class into one online collection. This impressive resource includes innovative and interactive help with writing a paragraph; tutorials and practices that show how writing works in students' real-world experience; *VideoCentral: English,* with more than 140 brief videos for the writing classroom; the first-ever peer review game, *Peer Factor*; *i-cite: visualizing sources*; and hundreds of models of writing and hundreds of readings. *Re:Writing Plus* can be purchased separately or packaged with *Writing First* at a significant discount. ISBN: 978-0-312-48849-9

■ The *Make-a-Paragraph Kit* is a fun, interactive CD-ROM that teaches students about paragraph development. It also contains exercises to help students build their own paragraphs, audiovisual tutorials on four of the most common errors for basic writers, and the content from *Exercise Central to Go: Writing and Grammar Practices for Basic Writers*. **Free** when packaged with the print text. ISBN: 978-0-312-45332-9

■ *The Bedford/St. Martin's ESL Workbook,* **Second Edition**, includes a broad range of exercises covering grammatical issues for multilingual students of varying language skills and backgrounds. Answers are at the back. **Free** when packaged with the print text. ISBN: 978-0-312-54034-0

- *The Bedford/St. Martin's Planner* includes everything that students need to plan and use their time effectively, with advice on preparing schedules and to-do lists, plus blank schedules and calendars (monthly and weekly). The planner fits easily into a backpack or purse, so students can take it anywhere. **Free** when packaged with the print text. ISBN: 978-0-312-57447-5
- *Supplemental Exercises for Writing First with Readings,* **Fifth Edition**, provides students with even more practice on essential skills. **Free** when packaged with the print text. ISBN: 978-0-312-64566-3

Ordering Information

To order any of these ancillaries for *Writing First*, contact your local Bedford/St. Martin's sales representative: send an email to **sales_support@bfwpub.com** or visit our Web site at **bedfordstmartins.com**.

Use these ISBNs when ordering the following supplements packaged with your students' copy of *Writing First with Readings*:

WritingClass for Writing First with Readings, Fifth Edition, Access Card:
    ISBN: 978-1-4576-1443-9
Re:Writing Plus:
    ISBN: 978-1-4576-1410-1
The Bedford/St. Martin's ESL Workbook, Second Edition:
    ISBN: 978-1-4576-1415-6
Exercise Central to Go: Writing and Grammar Practices for Basic Writers CD-ROM:
    ISBN: 978-1-4576-1413-2
Make-a-Paragraph Kit CD-ROM:
    ISBN: 978-1-4576-1414-9
The Bedford/St. Martin's Planner:
    ISBN: 978-1-4576-1419-4
Supplemental Exercises for Writing First with Readings, Fifth Edition:
    ISBN: 978-1-4576-1425-5

Acknowledgments

In our work on *Writing First*, we have benefited from the help of a great many people.

We are grateful to Timothy Jones of Oklahoma City Community College, who used his considerable tech savvy to contribute advice for instructors and students on using technology both inside and outside the classroom. (This advice can be found in tech-specific FYI boxes and marginal annotations in the Instructor's Annotated Edition.)

We thank Laura King, who made important contributions to the exercises and writing activities in the text, and Randee Falk, who wrote and revised essential sections of the student text and the instructor's manual. Karrin Varucene and Tenyia Lee provided invaluable assistance in updating and revising the ancillary booklets.

Instructors throughout the country have contributed suggestions and encouragement at various stages of the book's development. For their collegial support, we thank Candace Boeck, San Diego State; Gwendolyne E. Bunch, Columbia College SC; Elsie M. Burnett, Cedar Valley College; Grisel Cano, Houston Community College; William Carney, Cameron University; Mary Chavarria, Pierce College; Patrick Crapanzano, Monroe College; Marjorie Dernaika, Southwest Tennessee Community College; Carol Eisenhower, Sierra College; Christina Farinacci, East Brooklyn Access; Toni Fellela, Community College of Rhode Island; Lynn Gold, Bergen Community College; Martha Goodwin, Bergen Community College; Joan M. Grupka, Moraine Valley Community College; Ava Hardiek, West Coast University; Jennifer Hill, Academic Skills Advancement; Eric Johnson, Grossmont College; Timothy J. Jones, Oklahoma City Community College; Brook Mayo, Asheville-Buncombe Technical Community College; Applewhite Minyard, College of the Desert; Aubrey Moncrieffe, Housatonic Community College; Marjorie L. Newman, Saint Augustine's College; Eva A. O'Brian, Midlands Technical College; Kelly Ormsby, Cleveland State Community College; Matthew Petti, University of the District of Columbia; Carolyn Sharer, College of the Mainland; Ann Smith, Modesto Junior College; Mary McCaslin Thompson, Inver Hills Community College; Marjorie-Anne Wikoff, St. Petersburg College; Concetta A. Williams, Chicago State University; and Jonathan Wise, Asheville-Buncombe Technical Community College.

At Bedford/St. Martin's, we thank founder and former president Chuck Christensen, president Joan Feinberg, and former editor in chief Nancy Perry, who believed in this project and gave us support and encouragement from the outset. We thank Erica Appel, director of development, for overseeing this edition. We are also grateful to Dennis Conroy, senior production supervisor, and Ryan Sullivan, senior project editor, for guiding the book ably through production, and to Lucy Krikorian, art director, for once again overseeing the book's design. Thanks also go to Christina Shea, senior marketing manager, and her team, and to our outstanding copy editor, Ginny Perrin. And finally, we thank our editors, Karrin Varucene and Alexis Walker, whose patience, hard work, and dedication kept the project moving along.

It almost goes without saying that *Writing First* could not exist without our students, whose words appear on almost every page of the book in sample sentences, paragraphs, and essays. We thank all of them, past and present, who allowed us to use their work.

We are grateful in addition for the continued support of our families—Mark, Adam, and Rebecca Kirszner and Demi, David, and Sarah Mandell. Finally, we are grateful for the survival and growth of the writing partnership we entered into when we were graduate students. We had no idea then of the wonderful places our collaborative efforts would take us. Now, we know.

Laurie G. Kirszner
Stephen R. Mandell

Contents

Unit 4 Research 299

17 Writing a Research Paper 301

REVISING AND EDITING YOUR WRITING

BECOMING A CRITICAL READER

Unit 9 Reading Essays   643

A Student's Guide to Using *Writing First*

What *Writing First* Can Do for You

It's no secret that writing will be very important in most of the courses you take in college. Whether you write lab reports or English papers, midterms or final exams, your ability to organize your thoughts and express them in writing will help to determine how well you do. In other words, succeeding at writing is the first step toward succeeding in college. Perhaps even more important, writing is a key to success outside the classroom. On the job and in everyday life, if you can express yourself clearly and effectively, you will stand a better chance of achieving your goals and making a difference in the world around you.

Whether you write as a student, as an employee, as a parent, or as a concerned citizen, your writing almost always has a specific purpose. For example, when you write an essay, a memo, a letter, or a research paper, you are writing not just to complete an exercise but to give other people information or to tell them your ideas or opinions. That is why, in this book, we do not just ask you to do grammar exercises and fill in blanks. In each chapter, we also ask you to apply the skills you are learning to a writing assignment of your own.

As teachers—and as former students—we know how demanding college can be and how hard it is to juggle assignments with work and family responsibilities. We also know that you do not want to waste your time. That is why in *Writing First* we make information easy to find and use and include many different features to help you become a better writer.

The following sections describe key features of *Writing First*. If you take the time now to familiarize yourself with these features, you will be able to use the book more effectively later on.

How to Find Information in *Writing First*

Brief table of contents.   The first page of *Writing First* shows a brief table of contents that summarizes the topics covered in this book. This feature can help you find a particular chapter quickly.

Detailed table of contents.   The table of contents that starts on page xiii provides a detailed breakdown of the book's topics. Use this table of contents to find a specific part of a particular topic.

Index.   The index, which appears at the back of the book starting on page 723, enables you to locate all the information about a particular topic. The topics appear in alphabetical order; so, for example, if you wanted to find out how to use commas, you would find the *C* section of the index and look up the word *commas*. (If the page number following a word is **boldfaced**, that tells you that on that page you can find a definition of the word.)

Easy-to-use navigational tools.   The top of each page is colored to correspond to the five parts of this book, making it easy to turn to the different sections. At the tops of most pages you will also find a unit or chapter number and title, and a number and letter (for example, "5a"). This information tells you which chapter you have turned to and which section of that chapter you are looking at. *Cross-references* (for example, "see Chapter 21") within instructional boxes such as the FYI and Grammar in Context boxes point you to other sections of the book. Together, the color-coded pages and the cross-references help you find information quickly.

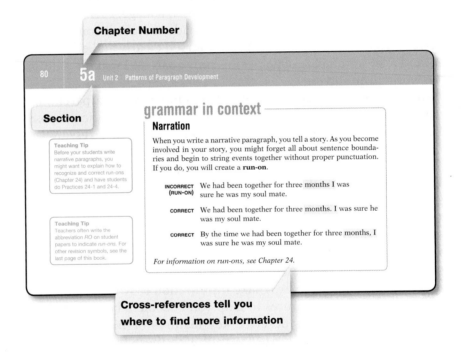

How *Writing First* Can Help You Become a Better Writer

Boxes.   Throughout the chapters, boxes highlight important information or ask you to complete specific tasks.

- **Preview boxes.**   Each chapter starts with a list of key concepts that will be discussed in the chapter. Looking at these boxes before you begin the chapter will give you an overview of it.

13 Writing an Essay

preview

In this chapter, you will learn to

- understand essay structure (13a)
- move from assignment to topic (13b)
- find ideas to write about (13c)
- state a thesis (13d)
- choose supporting points (13e)
- make an outline (13f)
- draft, TEST, revise, and edit your essay (13g–13j)
- check your essay's format (13k)

write first

Most people would agree that window washers like this one have challenging jobs. What was the hardest job you ever had? This is the topic you will be writing about as you go through this chapter. (If you have never had a job, you may write about a specific task that you disliked or about a hard job that a friend or relative has had.)

■ ***Write First* activity boxes.** Most chapters include a three-part writing activity that helps you apply particular skills to your own writing. Each chapter starts with a *Write First* activity, accompanied by a visual, that asks you to write about a topic. Later in the chapter, *Reflect* and TEST •Revise •Edit exercises guide you to fine-tune your writing.

■ **FYI boxes.** Throughout the book, purple-outlined boxes with the letters FYI (For Your Information) highlight useful information, identify key points, and explain difficult concepts.

FYI

Avoiding Sexist Language

Do not use *he* when your subject could be either male or female.

> **SEXIST**   Everyone should complete his assignment by next week.

You can correct this problem in three ways.

- *Use* he or she *or* his or her.

   Everyone should complete his or her assignment by next week.

- *Use plural forms.*

   Students should complete their assignments by next week.

- *Eliminate the pronoun.*

   Everyone should complete the assignment by next week.

- **Grammar in Context boxes.**   In Chapters 4–12 you will find boxes that identify key grammar issues in the patterns of paragraph development. Use these boxes to increase your understanding of important issues in your writing.

grammar in context

Comparison and Contrast

When you write a comparison-and-contrast paragraph, you should state the points you are comparing in **parallel** terms to highlight their similarities or differences.

> **NOT PARALLEL**   First, football is violent, and violence isn't seen very often in baseball.

> **PARALLEL**   First, football is violent, and baseball is not.

For more information on revising to make ideas parallel, see Chapter 22.

- **TEST.**   Within the writing chapters you will find examples of student writing with **TEST** boxes adjacent. **TEST** stands for **T**opic Sentence (or **T**hesis statement, for essays), **E**vidence, **S**ummary statement, and **T**ransitions. These four key elements are essential to your writing, so remembering the acronym **TEST** will help you as you write and revise your paragraphs and essays. Each letter has its own color, and sample student writing will be highlighted in these colors to point out to you each of the four key elements.

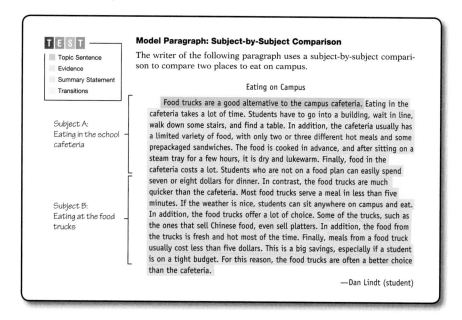

■ **Boxes in the margins.**   Word Power boxes define words that you may find useful in working with a particular writing assignment or reading selection.

Checklists.   At the end of most chapters, you will find a checklist that will help you review and apply the skills you are learning.

■ **Self-Assessment Checklists.**   Chapters 2 and 13 include Self-Assessment Checklists that give you a handy way to review your understanding of basic paragraph and essay structure.

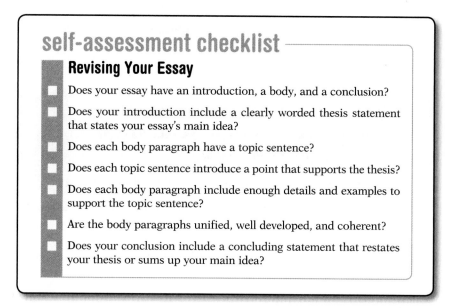

■ **Review Checklists.**   All grammar chapters and some of the writing chapters end with a summary of the most important information in the chapter. Use these checklists to review material for quizzes or to remind yourself of key points.

review checklist

Writing Complex Sentences

☐ A complex sentence consists of one independent clause (simple sentence) combined with one or more dependent clauses. (See 20a.)

☐ Subordinating conjunctions—dependent words such as *although, after, when, while,* and *because*—can join two independent clauses into one complex sentence. (See 20b.)

☐ Relative pronouns—dependent words such as *who, which,* and *that*—can also join two independent clauses into one complex sentence. The relative pronoun shows the relationship between the ideas in the two independent clauses that it links. (See 20c.)

■ **TEST Checklists.** All paragraph development chapters and each section of the essay development chapter ends with a checklist that prompts you to check your writing for the TEST elements—Topic sentence (or Thesis statement, for essays), Evidence, Summary statement, and Transitions.

TESTing an exemplification paragraph

Topic Sentence Unifies Your Paragraph

☐ Do you have a clearly worded **topic sentence** that states your paragraph's main idea?

☐ Does your topic sentence state an idea that can be supported by examples?

Evidence Supports Your Paragraph's Topic Sentence

☐ Does all your **evidence** support your paragraph's main idea?

☐ Do you need to add more examples?

Summary Statement Reinforces Your Paragraph's Unity

☐ Does your paragraph end with a **summary statement** that reinforces your main idea?

Transitions Add Coherence to Your Paragraph

☐ Do you use **transitions** to introduce each example your paragraph discusses?

☐ Do you need to add transitions to make your paragraph clearer and to help readers follow your ideas?

How to Access Additional Exercises and Resources Online

Writing First's companion Web site gives you free access to content from *Exercise Central*, a database of more than 9,000 practice exercises where you can take a diagnostic test to see the skills with which you need more help. You will also find content from *Re:Writing Basics*, a resource center with help for many issues that come up frequently in the writing classroom and in college, such as how to take good notes and how to avoid plagiarism.

Visit **bedfordstmartins.com/writingfirst** to register. It's free and you will have to register only once. Keep a record here of your username and password so that you can easily sign in on future visits.

Your Username: _____

Your Password: _____

How *Writing First* Can Help You Succeed in Other Courses

As we said earlier, writing is the key to success in college. For this reason, *Writing First* includes a new first chapter on strategies for college success and other information at the end of the book that you may find especially useful in courses you take later in college.

List of revision symbols. The chart on the last page of the book includes revision symbols that many instructors use when evaluating and grading student papers. Become familiar with these symbols so that you can get the most out of your instructor's comments on your work.

Review of the parts of speech. On the inside back cover you will find the eight major parts of speech defined with examples. Use the chart to review this essential information as often as you need.

We hope *Writing First* will help you become a better writer and student. If you have suggestions for improving this book, please send them to Laurie Kirszner and Stephen Mandell, c/o Bedford/St. Martin's, 33 Irving Place, 10th floor, New York, NY 10003.

1 Writing and College Success

write first

Most of us use writing every day to keep in touch, in a variety of different ways. Look through some of your own recent emails, Facebook posts, and texts. To whom are you writing? What reasons do you have for writing? What different styles of writing do you use? Write a few sentences analyzing your personal writing.

How Writing Can Help You Succeed

Teaching Tip
Refer students to 23b for information on concise language.

This text places writing first because writing is essential to success in college and beyond. Most people agree that the best way to learn to write is by writing. In a sense, then, you are already something of an expert when it comes to writing; after all, you have been writing for years—not just for your classes but also in your everyday life. For example, on your Facebook page, you write and update your profile, post and respond to comments, and send messages; you probably email and text every day. In these situations, you write fluently, confidently, and concisely, without self-consciousness, because you know your audience and you know what you want to say.

Of course, this informal, casual writing has its limitations. As you no doubt know, college writing is different from informal writing; "textspeak," abbreviations, and shorthand are not acceptable in college writing assignments, and spontaneous bursts of words are acceptable only in the very roughest of first drafts or in invention exercises, such as freewriting. The trick is to use the experience you have with writing informally and to make it work for you in an academic context.

Teaching Tip
Be sure students know not to call teachers by their first names—either in person or in emails—unless they are given permission to do so.

In college, writing is not just a convenience—a way to make plans, share feelings, or let off steam. College writing is more formal; it requires you to pull your thoughts together so you can develop (and support) solid ideas and opinions and express them clearly for a variety of audiences. When you write informally to someone you know well, someone just like you, there is no need to explain, give examples, or support claims; you assume your reader will understand what you mean—and often agree with you. When your audience is a college instructor or your classmates, however, you can't always count on your readers' knowing exactly what you mean or understanding the context for your remarks.

In addition, academic writing needs to be grammatically correct. You can't assume that your readers will be willing to tolerate (or ignore) errors you might make in grammar, sentence structure, punctuation, or mechanics. Your writing also has to follow certain formal conventions and formats, so you can't produce shapeless, slang-filled, punctuation-free documents and expect your readers to figure out what you mean. Much of the writing you do every day—texts, Facebook updates, blog posts, emails, and so on—use first person (*I*) and informal style, including contractions and slang. For example, if you are planning to make an appointment with your academic adviser, you might text a friend like this.

AT&T 3G   3:17 PM   100%

| Messages | manny | Edit |

Call   Contact Info

Feb 23, 2011 2:12 PM

going to appt. w/ advisor re chem. TTYL

Send

Q W E R T Y U I O P

However, college writing demands a more formal, more correct style. An email to your adviser should not use abbreviations or shorthand, and it should not omit words or punctuation to save time or space. For example, if you have concerns about a course, you might email your instructor something like this:

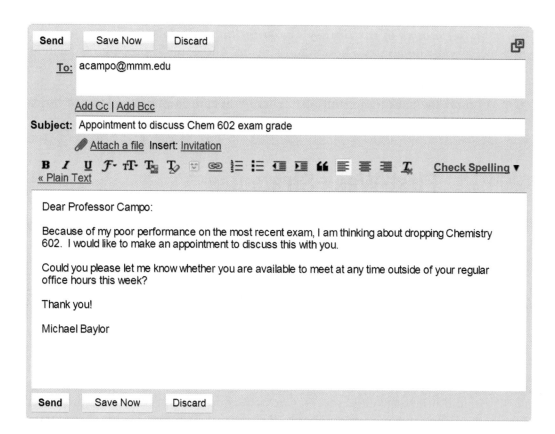

To succeed in college, you need to learn to write well—and you will learn skills and strategies for writing well as you go through this book. In the rest of this chapter, you will learn some practical strategies for making the most of your college education.

Strategies for College Success

1a Orientation Strategies

Some strategies come in handy even before school begins, as you orient yourself to life as a college student. In fact, you may already have discovered some of them.

1. ***Make sure you have everything you need:*** a college catalog, a photo ID, a student handbook, a parking permit, and any other items that entering students at your school are expected to have.

2. *Read your school's orientation materials* (distributed as handouts or posted on the school Web site) carefully. These materials will help you to familiarize yourself with campus buildings and offices, course offerings, faculty members, extracurricular activities, and so on.

3. *Be sure you know your academic adviser's name* (and how to spell it), email address, office location, and office hours. Copy this information into your personal address book.

4. *Get a copy of the library's orientation materials.* These will tell you about the library's hours and services and explain procedures such as how to use the online catalog.

5. *Be sure you know where things are*—not just how to find the library and the parking lot but also where you can do photocopying or buy a newspaper.

1b First-Week Strategies

College can seem like a confusing place at first, but from your first day as a college student, there are steps you can take to help you get your bearings.

1. *Make yourself at home.* Find places on campus where you can get something to eat or drink, and find a good place to study or relax before or between classes. As you explore the campus, try to locate all the things you need to feel comfortable—for example, ATMs, rest rooms, and vending machines.

2. *Know where you are going and when you need to be there.* Check the building and room number for each of your classes and the days and hours the class meets. Copy this information onto the front cover of the appropriate notebook. Pay particular attention to classes with irregular schedules (for example, a class that meets from 9 a.m. to 10 a.m. on Tuesdays but from 11 a.m. to noon on Thursdays).

3. *Get to know your fellow students.* Networking with other students is an important part of the college experience. Get the name, phone number, and email address of at least one student in each of your classes. If you miss class, you will need to get in touch with someone to find out what material you missed.

4. *Familiarize yourself with each course's syllabus.* At the first meeting of every course, your instructor will hand out a **syllabus**, an outline or summary of course requirements, policies, and procedures. (The syllabus may also be posted on the course's Web page.) A syllabus gives you three kinds of useful information.

- Practical information, such as the instructor's office number and email address and what books and supplies to buy

- Information that can help you plan a study schedule—for example, when assignments are due and when exams are scheduled

- Information about the instructor's policies on absences, grading, class participation, and so on

Read each syllabus carefully, ask questions about anything you do not understand, refer to all your course syllabi regularly—and do not lose them.

5. ***Buy books and supplies.*** When you buy your books and supplies, be sure to keep the receipts, and do not write your name in your books until you are certain that you are not going to drop a course. (If you write in a book, you will not be able to return it for a full refund.) If your schedule of courses is not definite, wait a few days to buy your texts. You should, however, buy some items right away: a separate notebook and folder for each course you are taking, a college dictionary, and a pocket **organizer** (see 1d). In addition to the books and other items required for a particular course (for example, a lab notebook, a programmable calculator, art supplies), you may want to buy pens and pencils in different colors, paper clips or a stapler, self-stick notes, highlighter pens, and so on.

6. ***Set up your notebooks.*** Establish a separate notebook (or a separate section of a divided notebook) for each of your classes. Write your instructor's name, email address, phone number, and office hours and location on the inside front cover of the notebook; write your own name, address, and phone number on the outside, along with the class location and meeting times. (Notebooks with pocket folders can help you keep graded papers, handouts, and the class syllabus all in one place, near your notes.)

1c   Day-to-Day Strategies

As you get busier and busier, you may find that it is hard to keep everything under control. Here are some strategies to help you as you move through the semester.

1. ***Find a place to study.*** As a college student, you will need your own private place to work and study. This space should include everything you will need to make your work easier—quiet, good lighting, a comfortable chair, a clean work surface, storage for supplies, and so on.

2. ***Set up a bookshelf.*** Keep your textbooks, dictionary, calculator, supplies, and everything else you use regularly for your coursework in one place—ideally, in your own workspace. That way, when you need something, you will know exactly where it is.

3. ***Set up a study schedule.*** Try to identify thirty- to forty-five-minute blocks of free time before, between, and after classes. Set this time aside for review. Remember, studying should be part of your regular routine, not something you do only the night before an exam.

Teaching Tip
Tell students that once they establish priorities, they can use this information to help them set up a calendar and an organizer. Refer them to 1d.

FYI

Checking Your Computer Skills

Don't wait until you have an assignment due to discover that your computer skills need improvement. Be sure your basic word-processing skills are at the level you need for your work. If you need help, get it right away. Your school's computer lab should be the first place you turn for help with word processing, but writing center and library staff members may also be able to help you.

WORD POWER

priorities things considered more important than others

4. *Establish priorities.* It is very important to understand what your priorities are. Before you can establish priorities, however, you have to know which assignments are due first, which ones can be done in steps, and which tasks or steps will be most time consuming. Then, you must decide which tasks are most pressing. For example, studying for a test to be given the next day is more pressing than reviewing notes for a test scheduled for the following week. Finally, you have to decide which tasks are more important than others. For example, studying for a midterm is more important than studying for a quiz, and the midterm for a course you are in danger of failing is more important than the midterm for a course in which you are doing well. Remember, you cannot do everything at once; you need to know what must be done immediately and what can wait.

5. *Check your email.* Check your school email account regularly—if possible, several times a day. If you miss a message, you may miss important information about changes in assignments, canceled classes, or rescheduled quizzes. (If your classes have course Web pages, check those as well.)

6. *Schedule conferences.* Try to meet with each of your instructors during the semester, even if you are not required to do so. You might schedule one conference during the second or third week of the semester and another a week or two before a major exam or paper is due. Your instructors will appreciate and respect your initiative.

7. *Become familiar with the student services available on your campus.* There is nothing wrong with getting help from your school's writing center or tutoring center or from the center for disabled students (which serves students with learning disabilities as well as physical challenges), the office of international students, or the counseling center, as well as from your adviser or course instructors. Think of yourself as a consumer. You are paying for your education, and you are entitled to—and should take advantage of—all the available services you need.

Teaching Tip

Let students know if you plan to use email for class announcements and assignments. Be sure to have another method of contacting commuting students who do not have access to email. Also, be sure that students give you the email address they check regularly (which may not be their school email account).

Teaching Tip

Give students printed information about the writing lab and the tutoring center. Consider having a representative from one or both places talk to the class.

Teaching Tip

Remind students to use capitalization, correct spelling, and a formal tone when emailing their instructors.

FYI

Asking for Help

Despite all your careful planning, you may still run into trouble. For example, you may miss an exam and have to make it up; you may miss several days of classes in a row and fall behind in your work; you may have trouble understanding the material in one of your courses; or a family member may get sick. Do not wait until you are overwhelmed to ask for help. If you have an ongoing personal problem or a family emergency, let your instructors and the dean of students know immediately.

1d   Time-Management Strategies

Learning to manage your time is very important for success in college. Here are some strategies you can adopt to make this task easier.

1. ***Use an organizer.*** New electronic tools are constantly being developed to help you stay organized. For example, Schoolbinder, a free online organizer, can help you manage your time and create a study schedule. If you have trouble blocking out distractions when you are studying, a site like StudyRails can be helpful. For a small monthly fee, this site will help you plan a study schedule and alert you to when it's time to focus on schoolwork. It can also be programmed to block your go-to recreational sites during hours when you should be studying.

   If you are most comfortable with paper and pencil, purchase a "week-on-two-pages" academic year organizer (one that begins in September, not January); this format gives you more writing room for Monday through Friday than for the weekend, and it also lets you view an entire week at once.

   Carry your organizer with you at all times. At the beginning of the semester, copy down key pieces of information from each course syllabus—for example, the date of every quiz and exam and the due date of every paper. As the semester progresses, continue to write in assignments and deadlines. In addition, enter information such as days when a class will be canceled or will meet in the computer lab or in the library, reminders to bring a particular book or piece of equipment to class, and appointments with instructors or other college personnel. (If you like, you can also note reminders and schedule appointments that are not related to school—for example, changes in your work hours, a dental appointment, or lunch with a friend.) In addition to making notes on the pages for each date, some students like to keep a separate month-by-month "to do" list. Deleting completed items can give you a feeling of accomplishment—and make the road ahead look shorter.

   You can also use the calendar function on your smartphone to keep track of deadlines and appointments.

2. *Use a calendar.* Buy a large calendar, and post it where you will see it every morning—on your desk, on the refrigerator, or wherever you keep your keys and your ID. At the beginning of the semester, fill in important dates such as school holidays, work commitments, exam dates, and due dates for papers and projects. When you return from school each day, update the calendar with any new information you have entered into your organizer.

3. *Plan ahead.* If you think you will need help from a writing center tutor to revise a paper that is due in two weeks, don't wait until day thirteen to make an appointment; all the time slots may be filled by then. To be safe, make an appointment for help about a week in advance.

4. *Learn to enjoy downtime.* One final—and important—point to remember is that you are entitled to waste a little time. When you have a free minute, take time for yourself—and don't feel guilty about it.

1e　Note-Taking Strategies

Learning to take notes in a college class takes practice, but taking good notes is essential for success in college. Here are some basic guidelines that will help you develop and improve your note-taking skills.

During Class

1. *Come to class.* If you miss class, you miss notes—so come to class, and come on time. Sit where you can see the board or screen and hear the instructor. Do not feel you have to keep sitting in the same place in each class every day; change your seat until you find a spot that is comfortable for you.

2. *Develop a system of shorthand to make note taking faster and more efficient.* You can use texting abbreviations—including shorthand and symbols—here, but remember not to use such abbreviations in your college writing.

3. *Date your notes.* Begin each class by writing the date at the top of the page. Instructors frequently identify material that will be on a test by dates. If you do not date your notes, you may not know what to study.

4. *Know what to write down.* You cannot possibly write down everything an instructor says. If you try, you will miss a lot of important information. Listen carefully *before* you write, and listen for cues to what is important. For example, sometimes the instructor will tell you that something is important or that a particular piece of information will be on a test. If the instructor emphasizes an idea or underlines it on the board, you should do the same in your notes.

5. *Include examples.* Try to write down an example for each important concept introduced in class—something that will help you remember what the instructor was talking about. (If you do not have time to include examples as you take notes during class, add them when you review your notes.) For instance, if your world history instructor is explaining *nationalism*, you should write down not only a definition but also an example, such as "Germany in 1848."

6. ***Write legibly, and use helpful signals.*** Use dark (blue or black) ink for your note taking, but keep a red or green pen handy to highlight important information, jot down announcements (such as a change in a test date), note gaps in your notes, or question confusing points. Do not take notes in pencil, which is hard to read and not as permanent as ink.

7. ***Ask questions.*** If you do not hear (or do not understand) something your instructor said, or if you need an example to help you understand something, *ask!* Do not, however, immediately turn to another student for clarification. Instead, wait to see if the instructor explains further or if he or she pauses to ask if anyone has a question. If you are not comfortable asking a question during class, make a note of the question and ask the instructor—or send an email—after class.

After Class

1. ***Review your notes.*** After every class, try to spend ten or fifteen minutes rereading your notes, filling in gaps and examples while the material is still fresh in your mind.

2. ***Recopy information.*** When you have a break between classes, or when you get home, recopy important pieces of information from your notes. (Some students find it helpful to recopy their notes after every class to reinforce what they have learned, but this can be very time-consuming.)

   - Copy announcements (such as quiz dates) onto your calendar.

   - Copy reminders (for example, a note to schedule a conference before your next paper is due) into your organizer.

   - Copy questions you want to ask the instructor onto the top of the next blank page in your class notebook.

Before the Next Class

1. ***Reread your notes.*** Leave time to skim the previous class's notes just before each class. This strategy will get you oriented for the next class and will remind you of anything that needs clarification or further explanation. (You might want to give each day's notes a title so you can remember the topic of each class. This can help you find information when you study.)

2. ***Ask for help.*** Call or email a classmate if you need to fill in missing information; if you still need help, see the instructor during his or her office hours, or come to class early to ask your question before class begins.

1f Homework Strategies

Doing homework is an important part of your education. Homework gives you a chance to practice your skills and measure your progress. If you are having trouble with the homework, chances are you are having trouble with the course. Ask the instructor or teaching assistant for help *now*; do not wait until the day before the exam. Here are some tips for getting the most out of your homework.

1. ***Write down the assignment.*** Do not expect to remember an assignment; copy it down. If you are not exactly sure what you are supposed to do, check with your instructor or with another student.
2. ***Do your homework, and do it on time.*** Teachers assign homework to reinforce classwork, and they expect homework to be done on a regular basis. It is easy to fall behind in college, but trying to do three—or five—nights' worth of homework in one night is not a good idea. If you do several assignments at once, you not only overload yourself; you also miss important day-to-day connections with classwork.
3. ***Be an active reader.*** Get into the habit of highlighting your textbooks and other material as you read.
4. ***Join study groups.*** A study group of three or four students can be a valuable support system for homework as well as for exams. If your schedule permits, do some homework assignments—or at least review your homework—with other students on a regular basis. In addition to learning information, you will learn different strategies for doing assignments.

Teaching Tip
Refer students to Chapter 38 for information on active reading strategies.

Teaching Tip
You might help students establish study groups for your class by passing around a sign-up sheet. However, students may prefer to form groups without your direct involvement.

1g   Taking In-Class Essay Exams

Preparation for an exam should begin well before the exam is announced. In a sense, you begin this preparation on the first day of class.

Before the Exam

1. ***Attend every class.*** Regular attendance in class—where you can listen, ask questions, and take notes—is the best possible preparation for exams. If you do have to miss a class, arrange to copy (and read) another student's notes *before the next class* so you will be able to follow the discussion.
2. ***Keep up with the reading.*** Read every assignment, and read it before the class in which it will be discussed. If you do not, you may have trouble understanding what is going on in class.
3. ***Take careful notes.*** Take careful, thorough notes, but be selective. If you can, compare your notes on a regular basis with those of other students in the class; working together, you can fill in gaps or correct errors. Establishing a buddy system will also force you to review your notes regularly instead of just on the night before the exam.
4. ***Study on your own.*** When an exam is announced, adjust your study schedule—and your priorities—so you have time to review everything. (This is especially important if you have more than one exam in a short period of time.) Over a period of several days, review all your material (class notes, readings, and so on), and then review it again. Make a note of anything you do not understand, and keep track of topics you need to review. Try to predict the most likely questions, and—if you have time—practice answering them.
5. ***Study with a group.*** If you can, set up a study group. Studying with others can help you understand the material better. However, do not

Teaching Tip
If you give exams in your course, be sure to give students specific information about the kinds of questions you will be asking. You might even consider giving a practice exam.

come to group sessions unprepared and expect to get everything from the other students. You must first study on your own.

6. ***Make an appointment with your instructor.*** Make a conference appointment with the instructor or with the course's teaching assistant a few days before the exam. Bring to this meeting any specific questions you have about course content and about the format of the upcoming exam. (Be sure to review all your study material before the conference.)

7. ***Review the material one last time.*** The night before the exam is not the time to begin your studying; it is the time to review. When you have finished your review, get a good night's sleep.

During the Exam

By the time you walk into the exam room, you will already have done all you could to get ready for the test. Your goal now is to keep the momentum going and not do anything to undermine all your hard work.

FYI

Writing Essay Exams

If you are asked to write an essay on an exam, remember that what you are really being asked to do is write a **thesis-and-support essay**. Chapter 13 tells you how to do this.

1. ***Read through the entire exam.*** Be sure you understand how much time you have, how many points each question is worth, and exactly what each question is asking you to do. Many exam questions call for just a short answer—*yes* or *no*, *true* or *false*. Others ask you to fill in a blank with a few words, and still others require you to select the best answer from among several choices. If you are not absolutely certain what kind of answer a particular question calls for, ask the instructor or the proctor *before* you begin to write.

2. ***Budget your time.*** Once you understand how much each section of the exam and each question are worth, plan your time and set your priorities, devoting the most time to the most important questions. If you know you tend to rush through exams, or if you find you often run out of time before you get to the end of a test, you might try checking your progress when about one-third of the allotted time has passed (for a one-hour exam, check after twenty minutes) to make sure you are pacing yourself appropriately.

3. ***Reread each question.*** Carefully reread each question *before* you start to answer it. Underline the **key words**—the words that give specific information about how to approach the question and how to phrase your answer.

Remember, even if everything you write is correct, your response is not acceptable if you do not answer the question. If a question asks you to *compare* two novels, writing a *summary* of one of them will not be acceptable.

FYI

Key Words

Here are some words that can help you decide how to approach an exam question.

analyze	explain	suggest results,
argue	give examples	effects, out-
compare	identify	comes
contrast	illustrate	summarize
define	recount	support
demonstrate	suggest causes,	take a stand
describe	origins, contrib-	trace
evaluate	uting factors	

Teaching Tip
Refer students to 2c and 13c for more on brainstorming.

ESL Tip
Brainstorming may be an unfamiliar term for nonnative speakers. Make sure all students understand this concept.

Teaching Tip
Refer students to 2d for more on topic sentences and to 13d for more on thesis statements.

4. *Brainstorm to help yourself recall the material.* If you are writing a paragraph or an essay, look frequently at the question as you brainstorm. (You can write your brainstorming notes on the inside cover of the exam book.) Quickly write down all the relevant points you can think of—what the textbook had to say, your instructor's comments, and so on. The more information you can think of now, the more you will have to choose from when you write your answer.

5. *Write down the main idea.* Looking closely at the way the question is worded and at your brainstorming notes, write a sentence that states the main idea of your answer. If you are writing a paragraph, this sentence will be your **topic sentence**; if you are writing an essay, it will be your **thesis statement**.

6. *List your main points.* You do not want to waste your limited (and valuable) time making a detailed outline, but an informal outline that lists just your key points is worth the little time it takes. An informal outline will help you plan a clear direction for your paragraph or essay.

7. *Draft your answer.* You will spend most of your time actually writing the answers to the questions on the exam. Follow your outline, keep track of time, and consult your brainstorming notes when you need to—but stay focused on your writing.

8. *Reread, revise, and edit.* When you have finished drafting your answer, reread it carefully to make sure it says everything you want it to say—and that it answers the question.

Model Essay Exam

The following essay exam was written by a student in an introductory psychology class in response to the following question:

Define and explain one of the following concepts related to memory: retrieval, flashbulb memories, déjà vu, false memories. *Be sure to give examples from the text, class discussion, or your own experiences to support the points you make.*

Déjà Vu

Memory is a group of mental processes that allow us to form, store, and retrieve information. Memory concepts include retrieval, the process of recovering stored information; flashbulb memories, very specific remembered images or details of a vivid, rare, or important personal event; and false memories, recollections that are distorted or that recall things that never happened. Perhaps the most fascinating memory concept is déjà vu. Déjà vu is a French phrase meaning "already seen." Déjà vu is a feeling that one has experienced something before but is unable to remember when or where. — INTRODUCTION — Definition of term

When we experience déjà vu, we find it impossible to explain the feeling of familiarity, so many times we think it must somehow be related to the paranormal. However, déjà vu can actually be explained scientifically, through concepts related to memory. — Thesis statement

Researchers and scientists have discovered several characteristics of déjà vu. It seems to occur most commonly in young adults ages twenty to twenty-four, and the older we get, the less often we tend to have feelings of déjà vu. Researchers have found that feelings of déjà vu most commonly occur later in the day, when a person is tired or under emotional stress, and when a person is around other people. Most often a feeling of déjà vu is triggered by something we see—for example, a coffee mug in a specific place on our desk with an open book next to it. Something about the placement of the items and the specific pages of the open book seem very familiar, but we can't explain why. Sometimes déjà vu can also be triggered by something we smell, hear, or touch. For example, a case recorded by two researchers focuses on a blind man who experienced déjà vu when he zipped up his jacket while listening to a certain song. — Characteristics of déjà vu

When a feeling of déjà vu is triggered, a person is often confused by it. Something seems so familiar, but the person is unable to explain why. Because it is difficult and even impossible to give a logical explanation for the feeling of familiarity, people sometimes think the feeling must be related to the paranormal. For example, a person may think something seems very familiar because he or she has experienced it in a past life or because it is going to happen in the near future. These and other paranormal explanations may seem to make sense, but they are not grounded in science. — Misperceptions about déjà vu

Many scientific explanations for déjà vu have been proposed. For example, some scientists believe that déjà vu is a disruption in source memory. In other words, a person has forgotten the source of the memory related to the feeling of déjà vu. For example, you might experience déjà vu if you were walking down a street you had never been down before and saw a house that looked familiar to you. You are sure that you have never seen that house before, but maybe you actually saw a picture of the house in the real estate section of your local newspaper and forgot that you saw it there. Several other scientific explanations for déjà vu have been proposed, but although scientists have spent a great deal of time studying this concept, they do not agree on any one explanation for it. — Scientific explanations for déjà vu

CONCLUSION

Déjà vu is something we have all experienced. Although we know what it feels like, we find it difficult to explain. This may make us believe déjà vu is something otherworldly, but there are actually many possible scientific explanations for the feeling of déjà vu, all grounded in memory-related research.

1h Taking Standardized Assessment Tests

During your time as a student, you have probably taken a standardized test. In fact, you've probably taken several. (For example, a student in New York City takes an average of twenty-one standardized tests before graduating from high school.)

The most common standardized tests are exit exams and placement tests. **Exit exams** (like the Georgia Regents' Testing Program) determine whether you are ready to graduate from college. They can also assess whether you are ready to move higher up in a program. **Placement tests** (like the COMPASS and ASSET tests) are designed to place you in classes that are right for your skill level.

Whether you're taking an exit exam or a placement test, there are several things you can do to prepare for them. Adequate preparation will help decrease your anxiety and increase your score.

Dealing with Anxiety

Not knowing what to expect from a standardized test can make you anxious. Some amount of test anxiety is natural and can actually help you to work harder and faster. However, if you are too worried, your judgment may be impaired, or you may freeze at the first question, wasting valuable time. The best way to beat test anxiety is to know your test before you take it and then practice as much as you can.

Preparing for Standardized Tests

1. *Read.* Look at examples of previous tests so you know what the exam looks like and what kinds of questions are usually asked.
2. *Practice.* If you are taking a common exam, go to the test's Web site to look for practice tests and other materials that can help you prepare. If your test is specific to your school, ask your instructor or librarian if a practice test is available.
3. *Plan your time.* While you take the practice tests, figure out how much time you will need to complete each section, and develop a **time-plan** that tells you how much time to spend on each part of the test and how much time to spend planning and reviewing. Give yourself extra time for challenging sections, but don't spend all your time there. Then, on the day of the actual test, you can follow your plan. Remember to reserve time to review your work at the end.
4. *Be rested and ready.* On the night before the exam, relax. Don't stay up too late, and avoid cramming. Instead, prepare a few days in advance

so that you are not stressed out. In the morning, eat a good breakfast and review your time-plan. If you've done your research and taken a few practice tests, you should be ready.

Common Exit Exams and Placement Tests

The following is a list of common exit exams and placement tests. Use the resources listed below to help you prepare for your test.

ACCUPLACER

Visit **collegeboard.com/student/testing/accuplacer** for tips, general information, and sample questions.

COMPASS/ASSET

To view student guides and samples, visit **act.org/compass** and **act .org/asset**.

CATW (CUNY Assessment Test in Writing)

For information and practice exercises, visit **cuny.edu/academics**.

THEA

For information and for access to a practice test, visit **thea.nesinc.com**.

Georgia Regents' Tests

For information, a sample reading skills test, and a list of approved essay topics, go to **www2.gsu.edu/~wwwrtp**.

Tips for Multiple-Choice Questions

Multiple-choice questions measure both your ability to remember facts and your critical-thinking skills. These questions often have several answers that seem right. You are expected to find the *best* answer.

1. *Use your time-plan.* During the test, use the time-plan you developed to help you pace your work.
2. *Read the directions carefully.* The directions will tell you how to answer the questions, how much time you have for each question, and how questions will be graded. Keep these directions in mind as you work.
3. *Answer what is asked.* Be sure you know exactly what the question is asking. Read the question carefully, and be sure to highlight the question's key words. Think about how to answer the question before you answer it.
4. *Answer questions in order.* If you are taking a paper test, stay organized. Answer the questions in order, do not linger too long on any one question, and keep track of answers you have doubts about. After you have answered all the questions, recheck the ones you were uncertain of.
5. *Try to anticipate the answer.* Try to answer the question before you read through the answer choices (A, B, C, and D). Then, compare each of the possible choices to the answer you thought of. Be sure to read every word of each possible answer; often, the choices are similar.

6. ***Divide and conquer.*** If you cannot anticipate the answer, check each answer choice against the question. Eliminate any answers you know are incorrect. Of the remaining statements, pick the one that most precisely answers the question. If you are having trouble determining which one is most correct, try focusing on the differences between the remaining answers.

7. ***Consider "All of the above."*** If there is an "All of the above" answer choice and you have determined that at least two answer choices are correct, select "All of the above."

8. ***Identify negatives and absolutes.*** Underline **negative words** like *not, but, never,* and *except.* Negative words can change a question in important ways. For example, "Choose the answer that is correct" is very different from "Choose the answer that is *not* correct." Be especially alert for double (and even triple) negatives within a sentence. Work out each question's true meaning before you attempt to answer it. (For example, "He was *not unfriendly*" means that he *was* friendly.) Also underline **absolutes**, such as *always, never,* and *only.* Answers containing absolutes are often incorrect because exceptions can be found to almost every absolute statement.

9. ***Make an educated guess.*** If you're still not sure which answer to select, make an educated guess. Before guessing, eliminate as many answers as possible. Then, select an answer that uses a qualifying term, like *usually, often,* or *most.* If all else fails, choose the answer that you first thought seemed right. Your first instinct is often correct.

10. ***Understand how computer-adaptive tests work.*** If you are taking a computer-adaptive test, keep in mind that the questions get harder as you answer them correctly. Do not get discouraged if the final questions of each section are very difficult (the final questions affect your score much less than earlier questions do). Also, remember that computer-adaptive tests prevent you from returning to difficult questions. Even so, you should not spend too much time on one question; if you aren't sure, make an educated guess. Finally, be sure to have some paper handy. You will not be able to use the computer to work out answers.

Tips for Essay Questions

The essays you write on standardized tests are similar to the essays you write in class. However, test essays are often scored differently. In addition, some tests might require more than one essay—for example, one essay will assess grammar and mechanics while another will assess critical-thinking skills. Pay close attention to the instructions on your test. Review the points that follow to help you prepare:

1. ***Know how to score points.*** Before the test, find out how your essay will be scored. Ask your teacher or librarian, look at a practice test, or visit the test's Web site to find out what the test emphasizes. If this information is not available, assume that global issues (like ideas, logic, and organization) will be more important than smaller ones (like spelling and grammar)—although all of these elements count.

2. ***Know what's being asked.*** When you take the test, read through each essay question and all of the directions. Make sure you understand

them before continuing. Some standardized tests require you to write multiple essays in a limited amount of time; find out in advance if that is the case with your test.

3. ***Tackle easy questions first.*** Read all the questions, and begin with the one that seems the easiest. Starting strong will help ease your anxiety and give you momentum. In addition, you will score higher if you finish your best work before time runs out.

4. ***Make a plan.*** Quickly jot down your initial essay ideas. Then, develop a thesis, and make a rough outline of your essay. The few minutes you spend planning will improve your essay's organization and keep you on track as you work.

5. ***Get down to business.*** On standardized essay tests, keep your writing lean and efficient. Avoid long, complicated introductions. Instead, begin your first paragraph with a sentence that directly answers the essay question and states your thesis. After you've stated your thesis, keep it in mind for the rest of your essay. Look back at the question as you write, and make sure your essay is answering it.

6. ***Manage your time.*** If you run out of time before you finish writing, quickly jot down an outline of your remaining ideas. If you have time, check your essay, looking for a clear thesis, effective support, appropriate transitions, and a strong concluding statement. Finally, quickly proofread your work and correct any grammatical or mechanical errors.

1i Strategies for Maintaining Academic Honesty

Academic honesty—the standard for truth and fairness in work and behavior—is very important in college. Understanding academic honesty goes beyond simply knowing that it is dishonest to cheat on a test. To be sure you are conforming to the rules of academic honesty, you need to pay attention to the following situations.

- Don't reuse papers you wrote in high school. The written work you are assigned in college is designed to help you learn, and your instructors expect you to do the work for the course when it is assigned.

- Don't copy information from a book or article or paste material from a Web site directly into your papers. Using someone else's words or ideas without proper acknowledgment constitutes **plagiarism**, a very serious offense.

- Don't ask another student (or your parents) to help you write or revise a paper. If you need help, ask your instructor or a writing center tutor.

- Don't allow another student to copy your work on a test.

- Don't allow another student to turn in a paper you wrote (or one you helped him or her write).

- Don't work with other students on a take-home exam unless your instructor gives you permission to do so.

- Never buy a paper. Even if you edit it, it is still not your own work.

> **Teaching Tip**
> Refer students to 17d for more on avoiding plagiarism.

1j   Strategies for Staying Safe on Campus

Colleges are very concerned about student safety. You should be, too. To stay safe on campus, keep the following guidelines in mind.

- If you drive to school, be sure to lock your car, and always park in a well-lit space.

- If you live on campus, never give your room key or dorm access card to anyone else.

- Be aware of your surroundings at all times, and report strangers loitering on school property to campus police. Also report any suspicious or dangerous behavior—even by fellow students.

- If you live in a building that has buzzer access, don't buzz people in unless you know them. Get in the habit of keeping doors and windows locked.

- Don't wear valuable jewelry or bring large sums of money to class. Keep money, credit cards, and other valuables in a safe place, and don't flash them around.

- Don't walk alone at night. If you need to be out at night—to go to the library, to your dorm room, or to a public transportation stop, for example—be sure to call your school's van or escort service (even if it means you need to wait). And don't leave a party alone; if you can't get someone you know to walk with you, call for an escort.

- Get in the habit of checking your school newspaper or Web site for crime statistics. If you know what kinds of crimes are most common on your campus and where they generally occur, you will be able to protect yourself.

- Be sure you know where the emergency call stations are located on your campus—and don't hesitate to call campus police for help if you feel threatened.

- If you are stopped by strangers and feel that you are in danger, try to run away. If you can't get away, make as much noise as possible.

- If you are in a situation—for example, at a party—where trouble arises, leave. Don't get involved or try to calm things down.

- Finally, be sure you know how college officials will contact students (for example, by email or by text message) in case of a campuswide weather or crime emergency.

thinking about your writing

Look back at your response to the Write First activity on page 1. Now that you have read this chapter, what have you learned about the kinds of writing you will be doing in various situations in college? Add this information to your response.

unit
1 Focus on Paragraphs

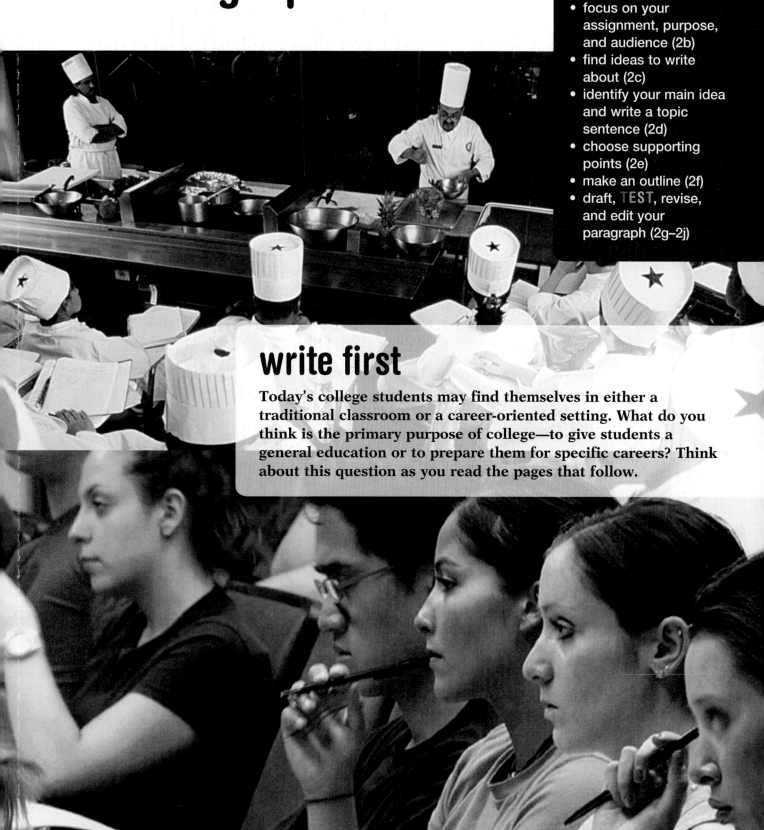

2 Writing a Paragraph

preview

In this chapter, you will learn to
- understand paragraph structure (2a)
- focus on your assignment, purpose, and audience (2b)
- find ideas to write about (2c)
- identify your main idea and write a topic sentence (2d)
- choose supporting points (2e)
- make an outline (2f)
- draft, TEST, revise, and edit your paragraph (2g–2j)

write first

Today's college students may find themselves in either a traditional classroom or a career-oriented setting. What do you think is the primary purpose of college—to give students a general education or to prepare them for specific careers? Think about this question as you read the pages that follow.

Writing is not just something you do in school; writing is a life skill. If you can write clearly, you can express your ideas convincingly to others—in school, on the job, and in your community.

Writing takes many different forms. In college, you might write a single paragraph, an essay exam, a short paper, or a long research paper. At work, you might write a memo, a proposal, or a report. In your daily life as a citizen of your community, you might write a letter or an email asking for information or explaining a problem that needs to be solved.

Writing is important. If you can write, you can communicate; if you can communicate effectively, you can succeed in school and beyond.

2a   Understanding Paragraph Structure

Because paragraphs are central to almost every kind of writing, learning how to write one is an important step in becoming a competent writer. This chapter takes you through the process of writing a paragraph. (Although a paragraph can be a complete piece of writing in itself—as it is in a short classroom exercise or an exam answer—most of the time, a paragraph is part of a longer piece of writing.)

A **paragraph** is a group of sentences that is unified by a single main idea. The **topic sentence** states the main idea, and the rest of the sentences in the paragraph provide **evidence** (details and examples) to support the main idea. The sentences in a paragraph are linked by **transitions**, words and phrases (such as *also* and *for example*) that show how ideas are related. At the end of the paragraph, a **summary statement** reinforces the main idea.

Paragraph Structure

Topic sentence —
    To write a paragraph, you need a main idea, supporting evidence, transitions, and a summary statement. First, state the main idea of the para-graph in a topic sentence. This idea unifies the paragraph. Then, add sentences to provide sup-port. In these sentences, you present evidence

Evidence (details and examples) —
    (details and examples) to help readers understand your main idea. Next, check to make sure you have linked these sentences with transitions. Finally,

Summary statement —
    write a summary statement, a sentence that rein-forces the paragraph's main idea. If you follow this general structure, you are on your way to writing an effective paragraph.

Transitions (boxed) ——————

The first letters of these four elements—**T**opic sentence, **E**vidence, **S**ummary statement, and **T**ransitions—spell **TEST**. Whenever you write a paragraph, you should **TEST** it to make sure it is complete.

Note that the first sentence of a paragraph is **indented**, starting about half an inch from the left-hand margin. Every sentence begins with a capital letter and, in most cases, ends with a period. (Sometimes a sentence ends with a question mark or an exclamation point.)

PRACTICE

2-1 Bring two paragraphs to class—one from a newspaper or magazine article and one from a textbook. Compare your paragraphs with those brought in by other students. What features do all your paragraphs share? How do the paragraphs differ from one another?

FYI

Check to see if your school's library subscribes to online research databases such as LexisNexis or ProQuest. If so, you can search a variety of newspapers online and even narrow your search by date and keywords. Of course, you could also go directly to a newspaper's Web site—for example, the *New York Times* at nytimes.com.

Step 1: Planning

2b Focusing on Your Assignment, Purpose, and Audience

In college, a writing task usually begins with an assignment that gives you a topic to write about. Instead of jumping in headfirst and starting to write, take time to consider some questions about your **assignment** (*what* you are expected to write about), your **purpose** (*why* you are writing), and your **audience** (*for whom* you are writing). Answering these questions at this point will save you time in the long run.

> **Teaching Tip**
> Refer students to 21a for information on questions and exclamations.

> **Teaching Tip**
> If you prefer, you can photocopy paragraphs for students and bring them to class. If you are teaching an online course, you can modify Practice 2-1 by supplying links that direct students to specific newspaper or magazine paragraphs.

> **Teaching Tip**
> Tell students that newspaper paragraphs usually have fewer sentences than other paragraphs because of the narrow width of the columns.

> **Teaching Tip**
> Ask students to share with the class the writing tasks they have had in the past month in school, at work, and in the community.

Questions about Assignment, Purpose, and Audience

Assignment

- What is your assignment? Is it included on your course syllabus or posted on the class Web page?

- Do you have a word or page limit?

- When is your assignment due?

- Will you be expected to work on your assignment only at home, or will you be doing some work in class?

- Will you be expected to work on your own or with others?

- Will you be allowed to revise before you hand in your assignment?

- Will you be allowed to revise after your assignment is graded?

- Will you be required to type your work?

- Does your instructor require a particular **format**?

Purpose

- Are you expected to express your personal reactions—for example, to tell how you feel about a piece of music or a news event?

- Are you expected to present information—for example, to answer an exam question, describe a process in a lab report, or summarize a story or essay you have read?

- Are you expected to argue for or against a position on a controversial issue?

Audience

- Who will read your paper—just your instructor or other students as well?

- How much will your readers know about your topic?

- Will your readers expect you to use **formal** or **informal** language?

PRACTICE

2-2   Each of the following writing tasks has a different audience and purpose. Think about how you would approach each task. (Use the Questions about Assignment, Purpose, and Audience listed above to help you decide on the best strategy.) Be prepared to discuss your ideas with your class or in a small group.

1. For the other students in your writing class, a description of your best or worst educational experience

2. For the instructor of an education course, a discussion of your first day of kindergarten

3. An email to your community's school board in which you try to convince members to make two or three changes that you believe would improve the schools you attended (or those your children might attend)

4. A thank-you note to a work supervisor—either past or current—telling what you appreciate about his or her guidance and how it has helped you develop and grow as an employee

5. A letter to a restaurant where you received poor service and were served terrible food, describing your experience and suggesting ways the service and food could be improved

2c   Finding Ideas to Write About

Once you know what, why, and for whom you are writing, you can begin the process of finding material to write about. This process is different for every writer.

In this chapter, you will be following the writing process of Stella Drew, a student in an introductory writing course who was given the following assignment:

> Should community service—unpaid work in the community—be a required part of the college curriculum? Write a paragraph in which you answer this question.

Before she drafted her paragraph, Stella used a variety of strategies to find ideas to write about. The pages that follow illustrate the four strategies her instructor asked the class to try:

- freewriting,
- brainstorming,
- clustering,
- journal writing.

WORD POWER
curriculum all the courses required by a school

Freewriting

When you **freewrite**, you write for a set period of time—perhaps five minutes—without stopping, and you keep writing even if what you are writing doesn't seem to have a point or a direction. Your goal is to relax and let ideas flow without worrying about whether or not they are related (or even make sense). Sometimes you can freewrite without a topic in mind, but at other times you will focus your attention on a particular topic. This strategy is called **focused freewriting**.

When you finish freewriting, read what you have written. Then, underline any ideas you think you might be able to use. If you find an idea you want to explore further, freewrite again, using that idea as a starting point.

Stella's focused freewriting on the topic of whether or not community service should be a required part of the college curriculum appears on the following page.

> Community service. Community service. Sounds like what you do instead of going to jail. Service to the community—service in the community. Community center. College community—community college. Community service—I guess it's a good idea to do it—but when? In my spare time—spare time—that's pretty funny. So after school and work and all the reading and studying I also have to do <u>service</u>? Right. And what could I do anyway? Work with kids. Or homeless people. Old people? Sick people? Or not people—maybe animals. Or work for a political candidate. Does that count? But when would I do it? Maybe other people have time, but I don't. OK idea, could work—but not for me.

Stella's freewriting

PRACTICE

2-3 Reread Stella's freewriting on the topic of community service for college students (above). If you were advising her, which of her ideas would you suggest she explore further? Underline these ideas in her freewriting, and be prepared to discuss your suggestions with the class or in a small group.

freewrite

Write (or type) for at least five minutes on the following topic: What is the primary purpose of college—to give students a general education or to prepare them for careers?

Don't stop writing! If you have trouble thinking of something to say, keep repeating the last word of your freewriting until something else comes to mind.

When you are finished, reread your freewriting, and underline any ideas you think you might be able to use in your paragraph. Then, choose one of these ideas, and use it as a starting point for another focused freewriting exercise.

FYI

To practice freewriting, open your word-processing program, but turn off the monitor. You can still type, but you won't be able to see what you're writing. This will help you to experience genuine freewriting.

Brainstorming

When you **brainstorm**, you record all the ideas about your topic that you can think of. Unlike freewriting, brainstorming is sometimes written in list form and sometimes scattered all over the page. You don't have to use complete sentences; single words or phrases are fine. You can underline, star, or box important points. You can also ask questions, draw arrows to connect ideas, and even draw pictures or diagrams.

Stella's brainstorming on community service appears below.

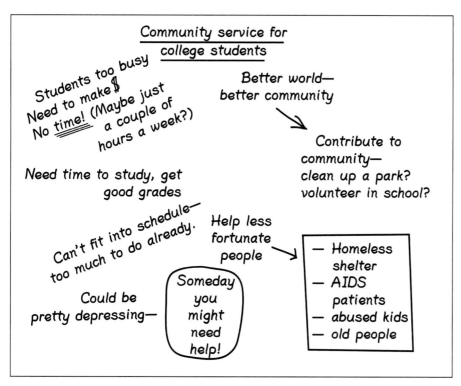

Stella's brainstorming

PRACTICE

2-4 Reread Stella's brainstorming notes on community service (above). How is her brainstorming similar to her freewriting on the same subject (p. 26)? How is it different? If you were advising Stella, which ideas would you suggest she write more about? Which ideas should she cross out? Be prepared to discuss your suggestions with the class or in a small group.

brainstorm

On paper or on your computer, brainstorm about your assignment: What do you think is the primary purpose of college—to give students a general education or to prepare them for careers? (Begin by writing your topic, "The purpose of college," at the top of the page.)

Write quickly, without worrying about using complete sentences. Try writing on different parts of the page, making lists, and drawing arrows to connect related ideas.

When you have finished, look over what you have written. Which ideas are the most interesting? Did you come up with any new ideas as you brainstormed that you did not discover while freewriting?

Usually you brainstorm on your own, but at times you may find it helpful to do **collaborative brainstorming**, working with other students to find ideas. Sometimes your instructor may ask you and another student to brainstorm together. At other times, the class might brainstorm as a group while your instructor writes down the ideas you think of. However you brainstorm, your goal is the same: to come up with as much material about your topic as you can.

PRACTICE

2-5   Working as a class or in a group of three or four students, practice collaborative brainstorming, following these steps:

- First, decide as a group on a topic for brainstorming. (Your instructor may assign a topic.)
- Next, choose one person to write down ideas on a blank sheet of paper or on the board. (If your group is large enough, you might choose two people to write down ideas, and have them compare notes at the end of the brainstorming session.)
- Then, discuss the topic informally, with each person contributing at least one idea.
- Finally, review the ideas that have been written down. As a group, try to identify interesting connections among ideas, and suggest ideas that might be explored further.

Clustering

Clustering, sometimes called *mapping*, is another strategy that can help you find ideas to write about. When you cluster, you begin by writing your topic in the center of a sheet of paper. Then, you branch out, writing related ideas on the page in groups, or clusters, around the topic. As you add new ideas, you circle them and draw lines to connect the ideas to one another and to the topic at the center. (These lines will look like a spiderweb or like spokes of a wheel or branches of a tree.) As you move from the center to the corners of the page, your ideas will get more and more specific.

Sometimes one branch of your cluster exercise will give you all the material you need. At other times, you may decide to write about the ideas from several branches, or to choose one or two ideas from each branch. If you find you need additional material after you finish your first cluster exercise, you can cluster again on a new sheet of paper, this time beginning with a topic from one of the branches.

Stella's cluster diagram on the topic of community service for college students appears below.

Teaching Tip
Tell students that for a short paragraph, where they won't be expected to go into much detail, they might not move very far from the center of their cluster diagram in selecting ideas. For longer, more complex writing assignments, however, they will need to use the more specific material generated as they moved out from the center.

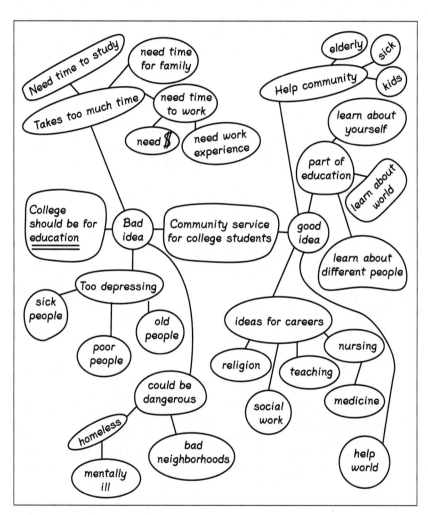

Stella's clustering

PRACTICE

2-6   Look at Stella's cluster diagram on community service. How is it similar to her brainstorming on the same subject (p. 27)? How is it different? If you were advising Stella, which branches of the cluster diagram would you tell her to develop further? Why? Would you add any branches? Be prepared to discuss your suggestions with the class or in a small group.

Teaching Tip
You might suggest that students actually write in branches and details to the cluster diagram on this page.

make a cluster diagram

Write your topic ("the purpose of college") in the center of a blank sheet of unlined paper. Circle the topic, and then branch out with specific ideas and examples, continuing to the corners of the page if you can.

When you have finished, look over what you have written. What are the most interesting ideas in your cluster diagram? Which branches seem most promising as the basis for further writing? What new ideas have you come up with that you did not get from your freewriting or brainstorming?

Use a highlighter to identify the branches and ideas that you could develop further. Then, add as many new details and branches as you can.

Keeping a Journal

A **journal** is a notebook or a computer file in which you keep an informal record of your thoughts and ideas. In a journal, you can reflect, question, summarize, or even complain. Your journal is also a place where you record ideas about your assignments and note possible ideas to write about. Here you can try to resolve a problem, restart a stalled project, argue with yourself about your topic, or comment on a draft. You can also try out different versions of sentences, list details or examples, or keep a record of interesting things you read, see, or hear.

Journal writing works best when you write regularly, preferably at the same time each day, so that it becomes a habit. Once you have started making regular entries in your journal, take the time every week or so to go back and reread what you have written. You may find material you want to explore in further journal entries—or even an idea for a paper.

FYI

Journals

Here are some subjects you can write about in your journal:

- *Your schoolwork*   You can explore ideas for writing assignments, think about what you have learned, ask questions about concepts you are having trouble understanding, and examine new ideas and new ways of seeing the world.

- *Your job*   You can record job-related successes and frustrations, examine conflicts with coworkers, or review how you handled problems on the job. Reading over these entries can help you understand your strengths and weaknesses and become a more effective employee. As an added bonus, you may discover work-related topics to write about in school.

- *Your ideas about current events*   Expressing your opinions in your journal can be a good way to explore your reactions to social or political issues. Your journal entries may encourage you to write to your local or school newspaper or to public officials—and even to become involved in community projects or political activities.

- *Your impressions of what you see*   Many writers carry their journals with them everywhere so they can record any interesting or unusual things they observe. You can later incorporate these observations into essays or other pieces of writing.

- *Aspects of your personal life*   Although you may not want to record the intimate details of your life if your instructor plans to collect your journal, writing about relationships with family and friends, personal problems, hopes and dreams—all the details of your life—can help you develop a better understanding of yourself and others.

> **Teaching Tip**
> If students are reluctant to write about personal details in their journals, you might give them the option of labeling some pages "Do not read" or even taping them closed.

Here is Stella's journal entry on the topic of community service for college students.

> I'm not really sure what I think about community service. I guess I think it sounds like a good idea, but I still don't see why we should have to do it. I can't fit anything else into my life. I guess it would be possible if it was just an hour or two a week. And maybe we could get credit and a grade for it, like a course. Or maybe it should just be for people who have the time and want to do it. But if it's not required, will anyone do it?

Stella's journal entry

PRACTICE

2-7   Buy a notebook to use as a journal. (Your instructor may require a specific size and format, particularly if journals are going to be collected at some point, or you may be asked to keep your journal in a computer file.) Set a regular time to write for fifteen minutes or so in your journal—during your lunch break, for example, or before you go to bed. Make entries daily or several times a week, depending on your schedule and on your instructor's suggestions.

> **Teaching Tip**
> You might suggest that students create blogs at blogspot.com and post their journals online regularly. This could also be done as a discussion board activity through the school's course management system (CMS).

write a journal entry

For your first journal entry, write down your thoughts about the topic you have been working on in this chapter: the primary purpose of college.

2d Identifying Your Main Idea and Writing a Topic Sentence

When you think you have enough material to write about, it's time to identify your **main idea**—the idea you will develop in your paragraph.

To find a main idea for your paragraph, begin by looking over what you have already written. As you read through your freewriting, brainstorming, clustering, or journal entries, look for the main idea that your material seems to support. The sentence that states this main idea and gives your writing its focus will be your paragraph's **topic sentence**.

The topic sentence is usually the first sentence of your paragraph. The topic sentence is important because it tells both you and your readers what the focus of your paragraph will be. An effective topic sentence has three characteristics.

1. **A topic sentence is a complete sentence.** There is a difference between a *topic* and a *topic sentence*. The **topic** is what the paragraph is about. A **topic sentence**, however, is a complete sentence that includes a subject and a verb and expresses a complete thought. This sentence includes both a topic and the writer's idea about the topic.

   TOPIC Community service for college students

   TOPIC SENTENCE Community service should be required for all students at our school.

2. **A topic sentence is more than just an announcement of what you plan to write about.** A topic sentence makes a point about the topic the paragraph discusses.

   ANNOUNCEMENT In this paragraph, I will explain my ideas about community service.

   TOPIC SENTENCE My ideas about community service changed after I started to volunteer at a soup kitchen for homeless people.

3. **A topic sentence presents an idea that can be discussed in a single paragraph.** If your topic sentence is too broad, you will not be able to discuss it in just one paragraph. If your topic sentence is too narrow, you will not be able to say much about it.

   TOPIC SENTENCE TOO BROAD Students all over the country participate in community service, making important contributions to their communities.

   TOPIC SENTENCE TOO NARROW Our school has a community service requirement for graduation.

   EFFECTIVE TOPIC SENTENCE Our school's community service requirement has had three positive results.

When Stella Drew reviewed her notes, she saw that they included two kinds of ideas: ideas about the value of doing community service and ideas about the problems it presents. She thought her paragraph could include both these ideas if she wrote about how community service requires time and commitment but is still worthwhile. She stated her main idea in a topic sentence.

> Community service takes time, but it is so important that college students should be required to do it.

When Stella thought about how to express her topic sentence, she knew it had to be a complete sentence, not just a topic, and that it would have to make a point, not just announce what she planned to write about. When she reread the topic sentence she had written, she felt confident that it did these things. Her topic sentence was neither too broad nor too narrow, and it made a statement she could support in a paragraph.

PRACTICE

2-8 Read the following items. Put a check mark next to each one that has all three characteristics of an effective topic sentence. Be prepared to explain why some items are effective topic sentences while others are not.

Examples

The common cold _____

Many people are convinced that large doses of vitamin C will prevent the common cold. ____✓____

1. Climate change, a crisis for our cities _____

2. Some strategies for reducing energy use _____

3. High school science courses should teach students about the effects of climate change. ____✓____

4. In this paragraph, I will discuss climate change. _____

5. Buying books online _____

6. College students can sometimes save money by buying their textbooks online. ____✓____

7. The advantages and disadvantages of renting textbooks _____

8. New vs. used textbooks _____

9. Our twenty-first-century world is facing many challenges. _____

10. The importance of a personal budget is the topic of this paragraph. _____

11. Setting up a budget _____

12. A budget can help students to track expenses and control spending.

   _____✓_____

PRACTICE 2-9

Read the following items. Put a check mark next to each one that has all three characteristics of an effective topic sentence. Be prepared to explain why some items are effective topic sentences while others are not.

Examples

Speaking two languages, an advantage in today's workplace _____

Our school should not abandon the foreign language requirement.

   _____✓_____

1. The new farmers' market makes it easier for people in the neighborhood to buy fresh produce. ____✓____

2. Eating a balanced diet with plenty of proteins and carbohydrates

   _____

3. In this paragraph, I will look at the disadvantages of a large high school. _____

4. The best size for high schools: not too large, not too small. _____

5. Participation in sports is important for children because it teaches them how to compete. ____✓____

6. The history of sports goes back to before the earliest civilizations.

   _____

7. Spending a quiet evening at home can have several advantages.

   _____✓_____

8. Television, the most popular leisure activity in the United States

   _____

PRACTICE 2-10

Decide whether each of the following statements could be an effective topic sentence for a paragraph. If a sentence is too broad, write *too broad* in the blank following the sentence. If the sentence is too narrow, write *too narrow* in the blank. If the sentence is an effective topic sentence, write *OK* in the blank. Be prepared to explain why a sentence is too broad or too narrow.

Example: Thanksgiving always falls on the fourth Thursday in

November. _too narrow_

1. Wireless computer networks are changing the world. _too broad_

2. There are twenty computer terminals in the campus library. _too narrow_

3. Our campus should be smoke-free. _OK_

4. Soccer is not as popular in the United States as it is in Europe. _too broad_

5. Americans enjoy watching many types of sporting events on television.
   too broad

6. There is one quality that distinguishes a good coach from a bad one.
   _OK_

7. Vegetarianism is a healthy way of life. _too broad_

8. Uncooked spinach has fourteen times as much iron as steak does.
   too narrow

9. Fast-food restaurants are finally meeting the needs of vegetarians. _OK_

10. Medical schools in this country have high standards. _too broad_

PRACTICE

2-11   Decide whether each of the following statements could be an effective topic sentence for a paragraph. If a sentence is too broad, write *too broad* in the blank following the sentence. If the sentence is too narrow, write *too narrow* in the blank. If the sentence is an effective topic sentence, write *OK* in the blank.

Example: Unfortunately, many countries in today's world are

involved in conflicts. _too broad_

1. Deciding what to do in life is a difficult task for many young people.
   too broad

2. A college career counselor can help students decide what kind of work
   they would like to do. _OK_

3. The college career counseling office has three full-time employees and
   two part-time employees. _too narrow_

4. Safe driving reduces the number of accidents and saves lives. _too broad_

5. Different countries, and even different states, have different rules of the road. _too broad_

6. Texting while driving greatly increases the chance of an accident. _OK_

7. Some students are much happier with their college experience than other students. _too broad_

8. Joining a study group is a good way for students who commute to get to know other students. _OK_

9. Flu shots are especially important for people in certain high-risk groups. _OK_

10. Flu shots occasionally result in soreness in the area where the shot was given. _too narrow_

identify your main idea and write a topic sentence

Look over the work you have done so far, and try to identify the main idea your material seems to support. Then, write a topic sentence that expresses this idea on the lines below.

Topic sentence: _Answers will vary._ _____

_____

Step 2: Organizing

2e Choosing Supporting Points

After you have stated your paragraph's main idea in a topic sentence, review your notes again. This time, look for specific **evidence** (examples and details) to **support** your main idea. Write or type your topic sentence at the top of a blank page. Then, as you review your notes, list all the points you might be able to use to support this topic sentence.

Stella chose several points from her notes to write about. After she read through her list of points, she crossed out those that she thought were not directly related to her topic or that overlapped with other points.

Topic sentence: Community service takes time, but it is so important that college students should be required to do it.

- ~~Community service helps people.~~
- ~~Some community service activities could be boring.~~
- Community service can help the world.
- Community service helps the community.
- College students are busy.
- Community service takes a lot of time.
- ~~Community service might not relate to students' majors.~~
- Community service can be upsetting or depressing.
- Community service can be part of a student's education.

choose supporting points

Reread your freewriting, brainstorming, clustering, and journal writing to find the points that can best support your topic sentence. Write your topic sentence on the lines below; then, list your supporting points.

Topic sentence: _Answers will vary._ _____

_____

Supporting points:

- _Answers will vary._ _____
- _____
- _____
- _____

Check carefully to make sure each point on your list supports your topic sentence. Cross out any points that are irrelevant or redundant.

2f Making an Outline

WORD POWER

redundant characterized by unnecessary repetition

After you have made a list of points you think you can write about, your next step is to make a short informal **outline**. You do this by arranging your points in the order in which you plan to discuss them in your paragraph.

When she read over her list of supporting points, Stella saw that she had two different kinds of points: some points identified the problems of doing community service, and other points identified the advantages of doing community service. When she arranged her points, she decided to group them in these two categories under the headings "Problems" and "Advantages."

Outline

Topic sentence: Community service takes time, but it is so important that college students should be required to do it.

Problems
- Community service takes a lot of time.
- College students are busy.
- Community service can be upsetting or depressing.

Advantages
- Community service helps the community.
- Community service can be part of a student's education.
- Community service can help the world.

Stella's informal outline

Teaching Tip
Tell students that when they arrange their points, they may find themselves deleting or combining some—or even adding one or two new points.

make an outline

Look over your supporting points, and decide which of your points are about going to college to get a general education and which are about going to college to prepare for a career. Then, make an informal outline by listing each point under one of the headings below. List your points in the order in which you plan to write about them.

Getting a general education

- *Answers will vary.* _____

- _____

- _____

- _____

Preparing for a career

- *Answers will vary.* _____

- _____

- _____

- _____

Step 3: Drafting

2g Drafting Your Paragraph

Once you have written a topic sentence for your paragraph, selected the points you will discuss, and arranged them in the order in which you plan to write about them, you are ready to write a first draft.

In a **first draft**, your goal is to get your ideas down on paper. Begin your paragraph with a topic sentence that states the paragraph's main idea. Then, following your informal outline, write or type without worrying about correct wording, spelling, or punctuation. If a new idea occurs to you, write it down. Don't worry about whether it fits with the other ideas. Your goal is not to produce a perfect piece of writing but simply to create a working draft. Later on, when you revise, you will have a chance to rethink ideas and rework sentences.

Because you will be making changes to this first draft, you should leave wide margins, skip lines, and leave extra blank lines in places where you might need to add material. (If you write by hand, feel free to be messy and to cross out; remember, the only person who will see this draft is you.)

When you have finished your first draft, don't make any changes right away. Take a break (overnight if possible), and think about something—anything—else. Then, return to your draft, and read it with a fresh eye.

Here is the first draft of Stella's paragraph on the topic of community service for college students. Note that she included a brief working title to help her focus on her topic.

ESL Tip
Remind ESL students that drafts are usually not given a grade.

Teaching Tip
Refer students to page 221 for tips on choosing a title.

Community Service

Community service takes time, but it is so important that college students should be required to do it. When college students do community service, they volunteer their time to do good for someone or for the community. Working in a soup kitchen, raking leaves for senior citizens, and reading to children are all examples of community service. Community service can require long hours and take time away from studying and jobs. It can also force students to deal with unpleasant situations, but overall it is rewarding and helpful to others. Community service is good for the community and can be more fulfilling than playing sports or participating in clubs. Community service can be an important part of a college education. Students can even discover what they want to do with their lives. Community service can also make the world a better place.

Stella's first draft

PRACTICE

2-12   Reread Stella's draft paragraph. Working in a group of three or four students, decide on a list of changes she should make. For example, what should she add? What should she cross out? Have one member of your group write all your suggestions down, and be prepared to discuss them with the class.

draft your paragraph

Write a draft of your paragraph about the purpose of a college education. Be sure to state your main idea in the topic sentence and support the topic sentence with specific evidence. If you handwrite your draft, leave wide margins and skip lines; if you type your draft, leave extra space between lines. Include a working title.

Step 4: TESTing

2h   TESTing Your Paragraph

When you have finished your draft, the first thing you should do is "test" what you have written to make sure it includes all the elements of an effective paragraph. You do this by asking yourself the following four **TEST** questions.

T ■ **Topic sentence**—Does your paragraph have a topic sentence that states its main idea?

E ■ **Evidence**—Does your paragraph include examples and details that support your topic sentence?

S ■ **Summary statement**—Does your paragraph end with a statement that reinforces its main idea?

T ■ **Transitions**—Does your paragraph include transitional words and phrases that show readers how your ideas are related?

If your paragraph includes these four **TEST** elements, you are off to a very good start. If it does not, you will need to add whatever is missing.

When Stella reread her draft, she **TEST**ed it to take a quick inventory of her paragraph.

■ She decided that her **topic sentence** clearly stated her main idea.

■ She thought she had enough **evidence** to support her topic sentence.

■ She noticed that her paragraph had no **summary statement**.

■ She realized she needed to add **transitions** to connect her ideas.

Teaching Tip
Refer students to Chapter 3 for more on TESTing paragraphs.

TEST your paragraph

TEST your draft paragraph for the four elements of an effective paragraph: **T**opic sentence, **E**vidence, **S**ummary statement, and **T**ransitions. (If any elements are missing, add them now.)

Step 5: Revising and Editing

2i   Revising Your Paragraph

Once you have TESTed your paragraph to make sure it is complete, you are ready to revise it.

    Revision is the process of reseeing, rethinking, reevaluating, and rewriting your work. Revision usually involves much more than substituting one word for another or correcting a comma here and there. Often, it means moving sentences, adding words and phrases, and even changing the direction or emphasis of your ideas. To get the most out of the revision process, begin by carefully rereading your draft, using the checklist below to guide your revision.

Teaching Tip
This might be a good time to review options students have for getting help with revising their work—for example, a student-instructor conference (face-to-face or online). Refer them to the chart in 13i.

Teaching Tip
If your students are doing **peer review**, they can also use this checklist to assess their classmates' paragraphs.

self-assessment checklist

Revising Your Paragraph

- ☐ Is your topic sentence clearly worded?

- ☐ Do you have enough ideas to support your topic sentence, or do you need to look back at your notes or try another strategy to find additional supporting material?

- ☐ Do you need to explain anything more fully or more clearly?

- ☐ Do you need to add or delete examples or details?

- ☐ Does every sentence say what you mean?

- ☐ Can you combine any sentences to make your writing smoother?

- ☐ Should you move any sentences?

- ☐ Are all your words necessary, or can you cut some?

- ☐ Should you change any words to make them more specific?

- ☐ Does your paragraph end with a summary statement that reinforces its main idea?

WORD POWER

peer someone with equal
standing; an equal

Teaching Tip
Remind students to be respectful of their classmates. Explain
how to offer constructive criticism and how to accept (and
reject) suggestions tactfully.

Sometimes you revise on your own, but at other times (with your instructor's permission), you may be able to get feedback (in the form of oral or written comments) from your classmates. The process of giving and receiving constructive feedback is called **peer review**. Peer review is most productive if you know how to make helpful comments and how to use the comments you get from others.

Giving feedback on a classmate's draft means making specific comments and pointing to particular sections of the draft. A general comment like "This is a good draft" or "Your ideas need more support" is not as helpful as more specific comments like "Your draft is convincing because you give lots of detail about your community service experience, especially in your fourth and fifth sentences" and "You need support for the point you make in sentence 6."

Using feedback means carefully evaluating the suggestions you get and deciding whether or not taking a classmate's advice will strengthen your draft. Remember, not every suggestion is worth adopting, but every one is worth considering.

Guided by the Self-Assessment Checklist on page 41 and by comments from her peer-review group, Stella revised her paragraph, writing her changes in by hand on her typed draft.

                          Why   *Should Be Required*
                    Community Service
                      ∧   ∧

    Community service takes time, but it is so important that college

    students should be required to do it. When college students do community

    service, they ~~volunteer their time to~~ do good for someone or for the
                    For example, they work   *rake*
    community. ~~Working~~ in a soup kitchen, ~~raking~~ leaves for senior citizens,
                                ∧   ∧
    or read   *. These activities* ∧
    ~~and reading~~ to children ~~are all examples of community service. Community~~
      ∧   ∧   *important things like*
    ~~service~~ can require long hours and take time away from studying and jobs.
    However, community service is worth the time it takes.   ∧
    ~~It can also force students to deal with unpleasant situations, but overall it~~
      ∧
    ~~is rewarding and helpful to others.~~ Community service ~~is good for the~~
                        also   *for students*   *other college activities, such as*
    ~~community and~~ can be more fulfilling than playing sports or participating
                      ∧   ∧   ∧
    in clubs. Community service can be an important part of a college education.
                learn about themselves, about their communities, and about their world, and
    Students can even discover what they want to do with their lives.   *they*
    Finally,   ∧   *can*
    Community service can ~~also~~ make the world a better place. *For all these*
      ∧   ∧

    reasons, community service should be a required part of the college curriculum.

Stella's revised draft

When she revised, Stella did not worry about being neat. She crossed out words, added material, and changed sentences and words. When she felt her revision was complete, she was ready to move on to edit her paragraph.

2j Editing Your Paragraph

When you **edit**, you check for correct grammar, punctuation, mechanics, and spelling. You also proofread carefully for typographical errors that your spell checker may not identify. In addition, you check to make sure that you have indented the first sentence of your paragraph and that every sentence begins with a capital letter and ends with a period. Finally, you check your essay's format to make sure it satisfies your instructor's requirements.

Remember, editing is a vital last step in the writing process. Many readers will not take your ideas seriously if your paragraph contains grammatical or mechanical errors. You can use the checklist below to guide your editing.

self-assessment checklist

Editing Your Paragraph

- Are all your sentences complete and grammatically correct?
- Do all your subjects and verbs agree?
- Have you used the correct verb tenses?
- Are commas used where they are required?
- Have you used apostrophes correctly?
- Have you used other punctuation marks correctly?
- Have you used capital letters where they are required?
- Are all words spelled correctly?

For help with grammar, punctuation, mechanics, and spelling, see Units 5–8 of this text.

When Stella edited her paragraph, she began by printing out her revised draft. Then, she checked grammar, punctuation, mechanics, and spelling and proofread for typos. The final version of her paragraph follows.

Why Community Service Should Be Required

Topic sentence [Community service takes time, but it is so important that college students should be required to do it. When college students do community service, they do good for someone or for the community. For example, they work in a soup kitchen, rake leaves for senior citizens, or read to children. These activities

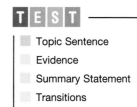

T E S T
- Topic Sentence
- Evidence
- Summary Statement
- Transitions

Evidence
(details and
examples)

can require long hours and take time away from important things like studying and jobs. However, community service is worth the time it takes. Community service can be more fulfilling for students than other college activities, such as playing sports or participating in clubs. Community service can also be an important part of a college education. Students can learn about themselves, about their communities, and about their world, and they can even discover what they want to do with their lives. Finally, community service can make

Summary
statement

the world a better place. For all these reasons, community service should be a required part of the college curriculum.

PRACTICE

2-13 Reread the final draft of Stella's paragraph about community service for college students (above), and compare it with her first draft (p. 39). Then, working in a group of three or four students, answer the following questions about her revision. (Be prepared to discuss your responses to these questions with the class.)

1. Why do you think Stella did not revise her paragraph's topic sentence? Do you agree with her decision?

2. What new material did Stella add to her paragraph? Can you think of any new points she *should* have added?

3. What did Stella cross out? Why do you think she deleted this material? Do you think she should cross out any additional material?

4. Why do you think Stella added "For example" (line 3), "However" (line 6), and "also" (line 8) to her final draft?

5. Why do you think Stella added the word "Finally" in her next-to-last sentence?

6. In her revision, Stella added a sentence at the end of the paragraph. Do you think this sentence is necessary? Why or why not?

self-assess

Use the Self-Assessment Checklist on page 41 to evaluate your draft. Can you add any details or examples to support your points more fully? Should any material be crossed out because it does not support your main idea? Can anything be stated more clearly? On the following lines, list some of the changes you might make in your draft.

Answers will vary.

revise and edit your paragraph

Revise your draft. Cross out unnecessary material and material you want to rewrite, and add new and rewritten material between the lines and in the margins. After you finish your revision, edit your paragraph, checking grammar, punctuation, mechanics, and spelling—and proofread carefully for typos. When you are satisfied with your paragraph, print it out.

review checklist

Writing a Paragraph

- [ ] Learning to write a paragraph is an important step in becoming a competent writer. (See 2a.)

- [ ] Before you start to write, consider your assignment, purpose, and audience. (See 2b.)

- [ ] Use freewriting, brainstorming, clustering, and journal writing to help you find ideas. (See 2c.)

- [ ] Identify your main idea, and write a topic sentence. (See 2d.)

- [ ] Choose points to support your main idea. (See 2e.)

- [ ] Make an informal outline by arranging your points in the order in which you plan to discuss them. (See 2f.)

- [ ] Write a first draft of your paragraph. (See 2g.)

- [ ] TEST your paragraph. (See 2h.)

- [ ] Revise your paragraph. (See 2i.)

- [ ] Edit your paragraph. (See 2j.)

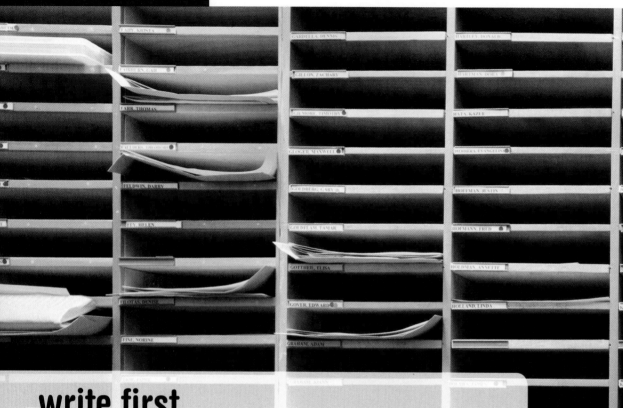

preview

In this chapter, you will learn how to **TEST** your paragraphs.

3 TESTing Your Paragraphs

write first

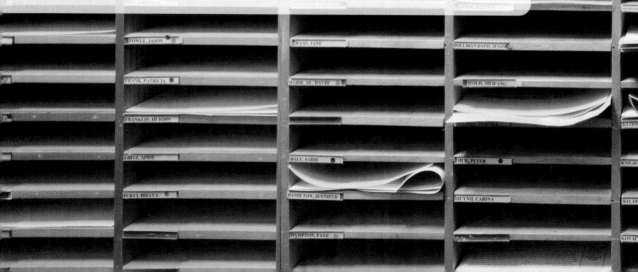

This picture shows one kind of filing system: rows of wooden mailboxes. How do you organize the papers (schoolwork, bills, important records, notes and reminders, and so on) in your life? Does everything have its place, or do you arrange papers more randomly? Write a paragraph about your system of organization.

As you learned in Chapter 2, you should TEST every paragraph as soon as you finish drafting. TESTing will tell you whether or not your paragraph includes all the elements of an effective paragraph.

T opic sentence
E vidence
S ummary statement
T ransitions

If you TEST the following paragraph, you will see that it contains all four elements of an effective paragraph.

> Although most people do not know it, the modern roller coaster got its start in Coney Island in Brooklyn, New York. First, in 1888, the Flip Flap Railway, which featured a circular loop, was built. The coaster was the first to go upside down, but it frequently injured riders' necks. Next, in 1901, the Loop-the-Loop, which was safer than the Flip Flap Railway, was built. Then, from 1884 through the 1930s, over thirty roller coasters were constructed in Coney Island. Finally, in 1927, the most famous roller coaster in history, the Cyclone, was built at a cost of over $100,000. Although it began operating over eighty years ago, it is still the standard by which all roller coasters are measured. It has steep drops, a lot of momentum, and only lap belts to hold riders in their seats. Still in operation, the Cyclone is the most successful ride in Coney Island history. It is the last survivor of the wooden roller coasters that once drew crowds to Coney Island. With their many innovations, Coney Island's roller coasters paved the way for the high-tech roller coasters in amusement parks today.

T E S T
☐ Topic Sentence
☐ Evidence
☐ Summary Statement
☐ Transitions

WORD POWER
innovation something newly invented; a new way of doing something

3a   TESTing for a Topic Sentence

The first thing you do when you TEST a paragraph is look for a **topic sentence (T)**. An effective paragraph focuses on a single main idea, and it includes a topic sentence that states that main idea.

A paragraph is **unified** when all the paragraph's sentences support the main idea stated in the topic sentence. A paragraph is not unified when its sentences wander from the main idea stated in the topic sentence. When you revise, you can make your paragraphs unified by crossing out sentences that do not support your topic sentence and, if necessary, adding sentences that do.

The following paragraph is not unified because it contains sentences that do not support the paragraph's topic sentence. (These sentences have been crossed out.)

> The weak economy has led many people to move away from the rural Ohio community where I was raised. Over the years, farmland has become more and more expensive. Years ago, a family could buy each of its children twenty-five acres on which they could start farming. Today, the price of land is so high that the average farmer cannot afford to buy this amount of land, and those who choose not to farm

Teaching Tip
Remind students that a topic sentence is not an announcement of what they plan to write about. It is a complete sentence whose idea can be discussed in a single paragraph. Refer them to 2d for more help with understanding topic sentences.

have few alternatives. ~~After I graduate, I intend to return to my town and get a job there. Even though many factories have moved out of the area, I think I will be able to get a job. My uncle owns a hardware store, and he told me that after I graduate, he will teach me the business. I think I can contribute something to both the business and the community.~~ Young people just cannot get good jobs anymore. Factories have moved out of the area and taken with them the jobs that many young people used to get after high school. As a result, many eighteen-year-olds have no choice but to move away to find employment.

The following revised paragraph is unified. It discusses only the idea that is stated in the topic sentence.

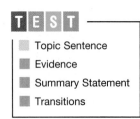

==The weak economy has led many people to move away from the rural Ohio community where I was raised.== Over the years, farmland has become more and more expensive. Years ago, a family could buy each of its children twenty-five acres on which they could start farming. Today, the price of land is so high that the average farmer cannot afford to buy this amount of land, and those who choose not to farm have few alternatives. Young people just cannot get good jobs anymore. Factories have moved out of the area and taken with them the jobs that many young people used to get after high school. As a result, many eighteen-year-olds have no choice but to move away to find employment.

PRACTICE

3-1 The following paragraphs are not unified because some sentences do not support the topic sentence. First, underline the topic sentence in each paragraph. Then, cross out any sentences in each paragraph that do not support the topic sentence.

1. <u>The one thing I could not live without is my car.</u> In addition to attending school full time, I hold down two part-time jobs that are many miles from each other, from where I live, and from school. Even though my car is almost twelve years old and has close to 120,000 miles on it, I couldn't manage without it. ~~I'm thinking about buying a new car, and I always check the ads online, but I haven't found anything I want that I can afford. If my old car breaks down, I guess I'll have to, though. I couldn't live without my digital voice recorder because I use it to record all the class lectures I attend. Then I can play them back while I'm driving or during my breaks at work.~~ Three nights a week and on weekends, I work as a counselor at a home for teenagers with problems, and my other job is in the tire department at Sears. Without my car, I'd be lost.

2. <u>Studies conducted by Dr. Leonard Eron over a period of thirty years suggest that the more television violence young boys are exposed to, the more aggressive they are as teenagers and adults.</u> In 1960, Eron questioned parents about how they treated their sons at home as well as about how much television they watched. ~~There is more violence on television today than there was then.~~ Ten years later, he interviewed these families again and discovered that whether or not teenage sons were aggressive depended

less on how they had been treated by their parents than on how much violent television programming they had watched as children. Returning in 1990, he found that these same young men, now in their thirties, were still more likely to be aggressive and to commit crimes. ~~Researchers estimate that a child today is likely to watch 100,000 violent acts on television before finishing elementary school.~~

3. Libraries today hold a lot more than just books. Of course, books still outnumber anything else on the shelves, but more and more libraries are expanding to include other specialized services. For example, many libraries now offer extensive collections of CDs, ranging from classical music to jazz to country to rock. In addition, many have large collections of vintage movies on videotape. Some libraries even stock the most recent DVDs. ~~However, most people probably get more movies from Netflix or pay-per-view than from libraries.~~ In addition, the children's section often has games and toys that young patrons can play with in the library or even check out. Most important, libraries offer free access to computerized databases, which provide much more detailed and up-to-date information than print sources. These databases enable even the smallest libraries to access as much information as large libraries do. ~~People who don't know how to use a computer are going to be out of luck.~~

PRACTICE

3-2 The following paragraph has no topic sentence. Read it carefully, and then choose the most appropriate topic sentence from the list that follows the paragraph.

Some people keep all the books they have ever read. They stack old paperbacks on tables, on the floor, and on their nightstands. Other people save magazines or newspapers. Still others save movie-ticket stubs or postcards. Serious collectors save all sorts of things—including old toys, guns, knives, plates, figurines, maps, stamps, baseball cards, comic books, beer bottles, playbills, movie posters, dolls, clocks, old televisions, political campaign buttons, and even coffee mugs. Some things—such as matchbook covers or restaurant menus—may have value only to the people who collect them. Other items—such as stamps or coins—may be worth a lot of money. A very few collectors concentrate on items that are so large that housing a collection can present some real challenges. For example, people who collect automobiles or antique furniture may have to rent a garage or even a warehouse in which to store their possessions.

Put a check mark next to the topic sentence that best expresses the main idea of the paragraph above.

1. Everyone, regardless of age or occupation, seems to have the urge to collect. _____

2. Collecting things like matchbooks and restaurant menus can be fun, but collecting jewelry or coins can be very profitable. _____

3. The things people collect are as different as the people who collect them. _____✓_____

4. In spite of the time and expense, collecting can be an interesting and fulfilling hobby. _____

5. Before you begin to collect things as a hobby, you should know what you are getting into. _____

PRACTICE

3-3 The following paragraphs do not have topic sentences. Think of a topic sentence that expresses each paragraph's main idea, and write it on the lines above the paragraphs.

Example: *Possible answer: Rock and roll originated in African-American music but was reinterpreted by white performers.*

Early 1950s African-American musicians included performers such as Johnny Ace, Big Joe Turner, and Ruth Brown. Groups like the Drifters and the Clovers were also popular. By the mid-1950s, white performers such as Bill Haley and the Comets, Jerry Lee Lewis, and Elvis Presley were imitating African-American music. Their songs had a beat and lyrics that appealed to a white audience. Eventually, this combination of black and white musical styles became known as rock and roll.

1. *Possible answer: Japan's popular comic books, known as manga, have evolved over hundreds of years.*

The Japanese word *manga* was first used in the 1700s to describe illustrated books. Early manga comics first started appearing in the late 1800s, when artists working in Europe began to influence those working in Japan. These early manga were similar to French and British political cartoons of the day. Modern-style manga, which were first produced in Japan during the U.S. occupation in the late 1940s, looked like American comic books. The first post–World War II manga focused on stereotypically male topics, such as space travel and sports. Today, there are many types of manga, including romance, horror, mystery, and comedy, and they appeal to both adults and children around the world.

2. *Possible answer: Applying for a job can be difficult, but the process can be made easier and more rewarding if you follow a few simple steps.*

First, you have to find a suitable job to apply for. Once you decide to apply, you have to put together your résumé and send it to your potential employer. Then, when you are invited in for an interview, you need to decide what you are going to wear. At the interview, you need to speak slowly and clearly and answer all questions directly and honestly. After the interview, you need to send a note to the person who interviewed you, thanking him or her. Finally, if everything goes well, you will get an email or a phone call offering you the job.

3. *Possible answer: A lot of questions remain about Native Americans who were living in North America when the Europeans arrived.*

There are no written records left by the Native Americans themselves. Most of the early European settlers in North America were more interested in staying alive than in writing about the Native Americans. In addition, as the westward expansion took place, the Europeans encountered the Native Americans in stages, not all at once. Also, the Native Americans spoke at least fifty-eight different languages, which made it difficult for the Europeans to speak with them. Most important, by the time scholars decided to study Native American culture, many of the tribes no longer existed. Disease and war had wiped them out.

PRACTICE

3-4 Choose one of the following topic sentences. Then, write a paragraph that develops the main idea that is stated in each topic sentence. After you finish, check to make sure that all the sentences in your paragraph support your topic sentence.

1. On my first day as president, I would do three things.

2. My parents prepared me for life by teaching me a few important lessons.

3. Planning a successful party is easy if you follow a few simple steps.

> **Teaching Tip**
> Remind students to use TEST to check their paragraphs.

3b TESTing for Evidence

The next thing you do when you **TEST** a paragraph is to make sure you have enough **evidence (E)**—details and examples—to support the main idea stated in your topic sentence.

A paragraph is **well developed** when it includes enough evidence to support its main idea. The following paragraph does not include enough evidence to support its main idea.

> **Teaching Tip**
> Have students discuss what makes support specific—facts, details, and anecdotes with concrete evidence, for example.

Although pit bulls have a bad reputation, they actually make good pets. Part of their problem is that they can look frightening. Actually, however, pit bulls are no worse than other breeds of dogs. Even so, the bad publicity they get has given them a bad reputation. Pit bulls really do not deserve their bad reputation, though. Contrary to popular opinion, pit bulls can (and do) make friendly, affectionate, and loyal pets.

The following revised paragraph now includes enough evidence (details and examples) to support the main idea stated in the topic sentence.

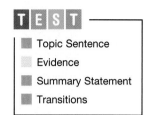

Topic Sentence
Evidence
Summary Statement
Transitions

> Although pit bulls have a bad reputation, they actually make good pets. Part of their problem is that they can look frightening. Their wide, powerful jaws, short muscular legs, and large teeth are ideally suited for fighting, and they were bred for this purpose. In addition, some pit bulls—especially males—can be very aggressive toward both people and other dogs. Actually, however, pit bulls are no worse than other breeds of dogs. As several recent newspaper articles have pointed out, the number of reported bites by pit bulls is no greater than the number of bites by other breeds. In fact, some breeds, such as cocker spaniels, bite more frequently than pit bulls. Even so, the bad publicity they get has given them a bad reputation. The problem is that whenever a pit bull attacks someone, the incident is reported on the evening news. Contrary to popular opinion, pit bulls can (and do) make friendly, affectionate, and loyal pets.

Note: Length alone is no guarantee that a paragraph includes enough supporting evidence for your main idea. A long paragraph that consists of one generalization after another will still not include enough support for the topic sentence.

PRACTICE

3-5   Underline the specific supporting evidence in each of the following paragraphs.

1. Hearing people have some mistaken ideas about the deaf community. First, some hearing adults think that all deaf people consider themselves disabled and would trade anything not to be "handicapped." Hearing people do not realize that many deaf people do not consider themselves handicapped and are proud to be part of the deaf community, which has its own language, customs, and culture. Second, many hearing people think that all deaf people read lips, so there is no need to learn sign language to communicate with them. However, lip reading—or speech reading, as deaf people call the practice—is difficult. Not all hearing people say the same words in the same way, and facial expressions can also change the meaning of the words. If hearing people make more of an attempt to understand the deaf culture, communication between them will improve.

2. In 1996, the National Basketball Association (NBA) approved a women's professional basketball league. Within fifteen months, eight teams had been formed, four in the Eastern Conference and four in the Western Conference. Next, the teams began to draft players for these teams and to select a logo and uniforms. The final logo selected, a red, white, and blue shield, showed the silhouette of a woman player dribbling the ball, with the letters "WNBA" above her. The uniforms consisted of shorts and jerseys in the colors of the different teams. That first season, games were played in the summer when the television sports schedule was lighter so they could be televised during prime time. At the end of that season, the Houston Comets became the first WNBA champions. Today, the WNBA consists of ten teams that each play thirty-four regular-season games televised to audiences worldwide.

3. One of the largest celebrations of the passage of young girls into womanhood occurs in Latin American and Hispanic cultures. <u>This event is called La Quinceañera, or the fifteenth year. It acknowledges that a young woman is now of marriageable age. The day usually begins with a Mass of Thanksgiving. The young woman wears a full-length white or pastel-colored dress and is attended by fourteen friends and relatives who serve as maids of honor and escorts. Her parents and godparents surround her at the foot of the altar. When the Mass ends, other young relatives give small gifts to those who attended, while the young woman places a bouquet of flowers on the altar of the Virgin. Following the Mass is an elaborate party, with dancing, cake, and toasts. Finally, to end the evening, the young woman dances a waltz with her favorite escort.</u> For young Hispanic women, the Quinceañera is an important milestone.

PRACTICE

3-6   Provide two or three specific examples or details to support each of the following topic sentences. *Answers will vary.*

1. When it comes to feeding a family, there are several alternatives to fast food.

   • _____

   • _____

   • _____

2. A romantic relationship with a coworker can create serious problems.

   • _____

   • _____

   • _____

3. When scheduling classes, you need to keep several things in mind.

   • _____

   • _____

   • _____

4. Consumers should take the following steps to protect themselves from identity theft.

   • _____

   • _____

   • _____

5. Choosing the right career is harder than I thought it would be.

   • _____

   • _____

   • _____

PRACTICE

3-7 The two paragraphs that follow do not include enough support-ing evidence. Suggest some examples and details that might help each writer develop his or her ideas more fully. *Answers will vary.*

1. Anyone in a supermarket checkout line can get the latest news on celebrities' misbehavior, which is typically given a lot more attention than their good deeds. Cheating, drug addiction, and crime among the rich and famous are all on display. Supermarket tabloids report rumors as if they were confirmed facts. Celebrities' bad deeds get the most press because they sell the most papers.

2. The Latina cartoon character Dora the Explorer has been a favorite of preschoolers and their parents since 1999. She has many traits that make her appealing. Even though she was already incredibly popular, Dora's creators decided to change her appearance in 2009. Image make-overs such as this are not always successful. Time will tell if the creators made the right choice in changing Dora's looks.

3c TESTing for a Summary Statement

Teaching Tip
Remind students that a summary statement should sum up the topic sentence in different words, not just repeat it.

The third thing you do when you TEST a paragraph is to make sure it ends with a **summary statement (S)**—a sentence that reinforces your para-graph's main idea. By reminding readers what your paragraph is about, a summary statement helps to further **unify** your paragraph.

The following paragraph has no summary statement.

Overpopulation is one of the biggest concerns for scientists. In 1900, there were 1.6 billion people on Earth, a quarter of today's population. At that time, life expectancy was also much shorter than it is now. By 2000, the world's population had grown to over 6 bil-lion, and today, the average life expectancy worldwide is almost sixty-five years. The low death rate, combined with a high birth rate, is adding the equivalent of one new Germany to the world's popula-tion each year. According to a United Nations study, if present trends continue, by 2050 the world's population will be between 7.3 and 10.5 billion—so large that much of the world may be either malnour-ished or starving.

The summary statement in the following revised paragraph reinforces the paragraph's main idea and brings the paragraph to a close.

Overpopulation is one of the biggest concerns for scientists. In 1900, there were 1.6 billion people on Earth, a quarter of today's popu-lation. At that time, life expectancy was also much shorter than it is now. By 2000, the world's population had grown to over 6 billion, and today, the average life expectancy worldwide is almost sixty-five years.

The low death rate, combined with a high birth rate, is adding the equivalent of one new Germany to the world's population each year. According to a United Nations study, if present trends continue, by 2050 the world's population will be between 7.3 and 10.5 billion—so large that much of the world may be either malnourished or starving. Given these increases, it is no wonder that scientists who study population are worried.

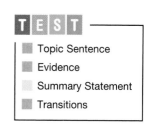

T·E·S·T

- Topic Sentence
- Evidence
- Summary Statement
- Transitions

PRACTICE 3-8 Read the following two paragraphs, which do not include summary statements. Then, on the lines below each paragraph, write a summary statement that adds unity to the paragraph by reinforcing the main idea stated in the topic sentence. Be careful not to use the same wording as the topic sentence.

1. Founded more than fifty years ago, NASCAR has become one of the most successful spectator sports in the world. In December 1947, Bill France formed the National Association for Stock Car Auto Racing (NASCAR). The first NASCAR race was held at Daytona Beach's auto race-course in 1948. From this modest start, France turned NASCAR into a highly successful business. Attendance grew 8.2 percent during 1997, and 2,102,000 fans attended the thirty-one NASCAR events in 1998. This was the first time that NASCAR attendance topped the two million mark. Then, in 2007, NASCAR negotiated a new multimillion-dollar television deal with Fox Sports/Speed, TNT, and ABC/ESPN. As a result, these networks now televise NASCAR's most popular events.

Answers will vary.

_____

_____

2. The best way to deal with scrap tires that are worn out is to recycle them. Since the early 1990s, there has been an enormous growth in the demand for recycled tire rubber—"crumb rubber"—particularly in North America. The new products made from this material are often better than similar products made of conventional materials. For example, recycled tires are used to make mulch that serves as ground cover in playgrounds. This material is safer because it cushions falls, and it is cheaper than gravel or wood chips. Material from recycled tires can also be mixed with asphalt to pave roads. The new surface is less expensive and more durable than surfaces made from conventional asphalt. Finally, recycled tires can be used to produce high-volume, low-tech products, such as livestock mats, railroad crossings, removable speed bumps, and athletic mats.

Answers will vary.

_____

_____

3d TESTing for Transitions

The final thing you do when you **TEST** a paragraph is make sure the paragraph includes **transitions (T)** that connect ideas in a clear, logical order.

Transitional words and phrases create **coherence** by indicating how ideas are connected in a paragraph—for example, in *time order*, *spatial order*, or *logical order*. By signaling the order of ideas in a paragraph, these words and phrases make it easier for readers to follow your discussion.

- You use **time** signals to show readers the order in which events occurred.

  In 1883, my great-grandfather came to this country from Russia.

- You use **spatial** signals to show readers how people, places, and things stand in relation to one another. For example, you can move from top to bottom, from near to far, from right to left, and so on.

  Next to my bed is a bookcase that also serves as a room divider.

- You use **logical** signals to show readers how your ideas are connected. For example, you can move from the least important idea to the most important idea or from the least familiar idea to the most familiar idea.

  Certain strategies can help you do well in college. First, you should learn to manage your time effectively.

Because transitional words and phrases create coherence, a paragraph without them can be difficult to understand. You can avoid this problem by checking to make sure you have included all the words and phrases that you need to link the ideas in your paragraph.

Frequently Used Transitional Words and Phrases

SOME WORDS AND PHRASES THAT SIGNAL TIME ORDER

after	finally	phrases that
afterward	later	include dates
at first	next	(for example,
before	now	"In June,"
during	soon	"In 1904")
earlier	then	
eventually	today	

SOME WORDS AND PHRASES THAT SIGNAL SPATIAL ORDER

above	in front	on the left
behind	inside	on the right
below	in the center	on top
beside	near	over
in back	next to	under
in between	on the bottom	

SOME WORDS AND PHRASES THAT SIGNAL LOGICAL ORDER

also	in fact
although	last
as a result	moreover
consequently	next
even though	not only . . . but also
first . . . second . . . third	one . . . another
for example	similarly
for instance	the least important
furthermore	the most important
however	therefore
in addition	

The following paragraph has no transitional words and phrases to link ideas.

During his lifetime, Jim Thorpe faced many obstacles. Thorpe was born in 1888, the son of an Irish father and a Native American mother. He was sent to the Carlisle Indian School in Pennsylvania. "Pop" Warner, the legendary coach at Carlisle, discovered Thorpe. Thorpe left Carlisle to play baseball for two seasons in the newly formed East Carolina minor league. He returned to Carlisle, played football, and was named to the All-American team. Thorpe went to the Olympic games in Stockholm, where he won two gold medals. Thorpe's career took a dramatic turn for the worse when a sportswriter who had seen him play baseball in North Carolina exposed him as a professional. The Amateur Athletic Union stripped him of his records and medals. Thorpe died in 1953. The International Olympic Committee returned Thorpe's Olympic medals to his family in 1982. Ironically, only in death was Thorpe able to overcome the difficulties that had frustrated him while he was alive.

The following revised paragraph is coherent because it includes transitional words and phrases that connect its ideas.

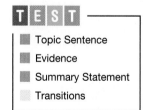

During his lifetime, Jim Thorpe faced many obstacles. Thorpe was born in 1888, the son of an Irish father and a Native American mother. In 1904, he was sent to the Carlisle Indian School in Pennsylvania. The next year, "Pop" Warner, the legendary coach at Carlisle, discovered Thorpe. Thorpe left Carlisle in 1909 to play baseball for two seasons in the newly formed East Carolina minor league. In 1912, he returned to Carlisle, played football, and was named to the All-American team. Thorpe then went to the Olympic games in Stockholm, where he won two gold medals. The next year, however, Thorpe's career took a dramatic turn for the worse when a sportswriter who had seen him play baseball in North Carolina exposed him as a professional. As a result, the Amateur Athletic Union stripped him of his records and medals. Thorpe died in 1953. After years of appeals, the International Olympic Committee returned Thorpe's Olympic medals to his family in 1982. Ironically, only in death was Thorpe able to overcome the difficulties that had frustrated him while he was alive.

PRACTICE

3-9 Read the following paragraph carefully. Then, select transitional words and phrases from the alphabetized list below, and write them in the appropriate blanks. When you have finished, reread your paragraph to make sure that it is coherent.

TRANSITIONS

afterward	last month
before	soon
in front	then
inside	

Spelling bees can be stressful, but they can also be fun. _Last month_, my sister Elizabeth competed in a televised regional spelling bee. _Before_ the competition, she and I tried to think of ways to make her less nervous. We decided to arrive early to relax and play games. On the grass _in front_ of the auditorium, we played leapfrog and read to each other from her favorite book of jokes. _Inside_, I squeezed her hand and reminded her that I would be just a wink or a smile away. She _then_ took her place on the stage. _Soon_, she was talking and laughing with the kids around her. As the competition began, she grinned at me across the rows of seats. On each of her turns, she sounded confident as she spelled the words *triumvirate*, *caboose*, and *stethoscope*. _Afterward_, she gave me a hug, chattered about the new friends she had met, and said she couldn't wait to do the spelling bee again next year.

PRACTICE

3-10 The following paragraph includes no transitions. Read the paragraph carefully. Then, after consulting the list of transitional words and phrases on pages 56–57, add appropriate transitional words and phrases to connect the paragraph's ideas in **time order**. *Answers will vary.*

In 1856, my great-great-great-grandparents, Anne and Charles McGinley, faced many hardships to come to the United States. _____ they left Ireland, their landlords, who lived in England, had raised the rent on their land so much that my ancestors could not afford to pay it. _____ it took them three years to save the money for passage. _____ they had saved the money, they had to look for a ship that was willing to take them. _____, my great-great-great-grandparents were able to leave. They and their ten children spent four long months on a small ship. Storms, strong tides, and damaged sails made the trip longer than it should have been. _____, in November 1856, they saw land, and two days later they sailed into New York Harbor. _____ they took a train to Baltimore, Maryland, where their cousins lived and where we live today. At that time, they couldn't have known how thankful their descendants would be for their courage and sacrifice.

PRACTICE

3-11   The following paragraph includes no transitions. Read the paragraph carefully. Then, after consulting the list of transitional words and phrases on pages 56–57, add appropriate transitional words and phrases to connect the paragraph's ideas in **spatial order**. *Answers will vary.*

The casinos in Atlantic City are designed to make sure you don't pay attention to anything except gambling. As soon as you walk in the door, you are steered toward the gaming room. _____ of you are the slot machines, blinking and making lots of noise. _____ of the slot machines are the table games—blackjack, roulette, and craps. _____ the gambling area, the ceiling is painted a dull, neutral color. _____ the floor is a carpet that has a complicated pattern that is hard to look at. Both the ceiling and the carpet are designed to make sure that gamblers look just at the games they are playing. _____ of the casino are the bathrooms, and you have to walk through the entire slot machine area if you want to use one. The casino designers are betting that you will not be able to resist stopping to play. As you can see, the design of the casinos makes it difficult for the average person to resist the lure of gambling.

PRACTICE

3-12 The following paragraph includes no transitions. Read the paragraph carefully. Then, after consulting the list of transitional words and phrases on pages 56–57, add appropriate transitional words and phrases to connect the paragraph's ideas in **logical order**. *Answers will vary.*

My high school had three silly rules. The _____ silly rule was that only seniors could go outside the school building for lunch. In spite of this rule, many students went outside to eat because the cafeteria was not big enough to hold everyone. Understanding the problem, the teachers just looked the other way as long as we came back to school on time. The _____ silly rule was that we had to attend 95 percent of all the classes for each course. If we did not, we were supposed to fail. Of course, that rule was never enforced, because if it were, almost every student in the school would have failed everything. The _____ silly rule was that students were not supposed to throw their hats into the air at graduation. At one point in the past, a parent—no one can remember who—complained that a falling hat could poke someone in the eye. _____, graduating classes were told that under no circumstances could they throw their hats into the air. _____, on graduation day, we did what every graduating class has always done—ignored the silly rule and threw our hats into the air.

TEST · Revise · Edit

Review the work you did for the Write First activity on page 46. Next, **TEST** your paragraph to make sure it includes a topic sentence, evidence, a summary statement, and transitions. Then, prepare a final revised and edited draft of your paragraph.

EDITING PRACTICE

TEST each of the following paragraphs to make sure it is **unified**, **well-developed**, and **coherent**. Begin by underlining the topic sentence. Then, cross out any sentences that do not support the topic sentence. If necessary, add evidence (details and examples) to support the topic sentence. Next, decide whether you need to make any changes to the paragraph's summary statement. (If the paragraph includes no summary statement, write one.) Finally, add transitional words and phrases where they are needed. *Answers will vary.*

Teaching Tip
Assign groups of three or four students to rewrite the Editing Practice paragraphs, adding details and examples.

1. In 1979, a series of mechanical and human errors in Unit 2 of the nuclear generating plant at Three Mile Island, near Harrisburg, Pennsylvania, caused an accident that changed the nuclear power industry. A combination of stuck valves, human error, and poor decisions caused a partial meltdown of the reactor core. *As a result, large* ~~Large~~ amounts of radioactive gases were released into the atmosphere. *Consequently, the* ~~The~~ governor of Pennsylvania evacuated pregnant women from the area. Other residents *then* panicked and left their homes. The nuclear regulatory agency claimed that the situation was not really dangerous and that the released gases were not a health threat. *However, activists* ~~Activists~~ and local residents disagreed with this. ~~The reactor itself remained unusable for more than ten years.~~ Large demonstrations followed the accident, including a rally of more than 200,000 people in New York City. ~~Some people came just because the day was nice.~~ By the mid-1980s, as a result of the accident at Three Mile Island, new construction of nuclear power plants in the United States had stopped.

2. A survey of cigarette advertisements shows how tobacco companies have consistently encouraged people to smoke. One of the earliest television ads showed two boxes of cigarettes dancing to an advertising jingle. ~~Many people liked these ads.~~ *However, other* Other advertisements were more subtle. Some were aimed at specific audiences. *For example,* Marlboro commercials, with the rugged Marlboro man, targeted men. *In contrast,* Virginia Slims made

an obvious pitch to women by saying, "You've come a long way, baby!"
In addition,
Salem, a mentholated cigarette, showed rural scenes and targeted peo-
                                                        Similarly,
ple who liked the freshness of the outdoors. Kent, with its "micronite

filter," appealed to those who were health conscious by claiming that

Kent contained less tar and nicotine than any other brand. ~~This claim~~
                                                                Later,
~~was not entirely true. Other brands had less tar and nicotine.~~ Merit and

other high-tar and high-nicotine cigarettes began to use advertise-
                                        Eventually, cigarette
ments that were aimed at minorities. Cigarette companies responded

to the national decline in smoking by directing advertising at young
                For instance,
people. Camel introduced the cartoon character Joe Camel, which was
                                        As these examples show, cigarette
aimed at teenagers and young adults. *companies have done whatever they could to keep people smoking despite the health risks.*

3.   Cities created police forces for a number of reasons. The first rea-

son was status: after the Civil War, it became a status symbol for cities
                                    Second, a
to have a uniformed police force. A police force provided jobs. This

meant that politicians were able to reward people who had worked to
                Third, police   *For example, police*
support them. Police forces made people feel safe. Police officers
                                In addition, they
helped visitors find their way. They took in lost children and some-
                            also
times fed the homeless. They directed traffic, enforced health regula-
                                Finally, police
tions, and provided other services. Police officers kept order. Without

a police force, criminals would have made life in nineteenth-century

cities unbearable.

COLLABORATIVE ACTIVITIES

1. Working in a group, list the reasons why you think students decide to
attend your school. After working together to arrange these reasons
in logical order—for example, from least to most important—write a
topic sentence that states the main idea these reasons suggest. Finally,
on your own, draft a paragraph in which you discuss why students
attend your school.

2. In a newspaper or magazine, find an illustration or photograph that
includes a lot of details. Then, write a paragraph describing what you
see. (Include enough supporting examples so that readers will be able
to "see" it almost as clearly as you can.) Decide on a specific spatial
order—from top to bottom or from left to right, for example—that

makes sense to you, and follow this order as you organize the details in your paragraph. Finally, trade paragraphs with another student, and offer suggestions that could improve his or her paragraph.

3. Bring to class a paragraph from a newspaper or magazine article or from one of your textbooks. Working in a group, TEST each paragraph to see if it includes all the elements of an effective paragraph. If any paragraph does not follow the guidelines outlined in this chapter, work as a group to revise it.

review checklist

TESTing Your Paragraphs

☐ A topic sentence states a paragraph's main idea. (See 3a.)

☐ A paragraph should include enough evidence—facts and examples—to support its main idea. (See 3b.)

☐ A paragraph should end with a summary statement that reinforces its main idea and helps to unify the paragraph. (See 3c.)

☐ A paragraph should include transitional words and phrases that indicate how ideas are connected. (See 3d.)

unit

2 Patterns of Paragraph Development

4 Exemplification

preview

In this chapter, you will learn to write an exemplification paragraph.

write first

Most colleges have a student services center, where you can get information and advice on making the most of the programs and support the school provides. Write a paragraph discussing the programs and services your school offers (or should offer) to help students adjust to college.

In Chapters 2 and 3, you learned how to write effective paragraphs. In Chapters 4 through 12, you will learn different ways of organizing your ideas within paragraphs. Understanding these patterns of paragraph development can help you organize ideas and become a more effective, more confident writer.

reflect

Look at the paragraph you wrote for the Write First activity on page 67, and then do the following:

1. **Reread**
   - Does your paragraph focus on the programs and services your school offers to help students adjust to college?
   - Does your paragraph begin with a topic sentence that clearly states the main idea—the point you want to make about the programs and services your school offers?
   - Do you include examples of specific programs and services?
   - Do you include details about these programs and services?
   - Do you need more examples and details?

2. **Discuss**
   Work with another student to consider the strengths and weaknesses of your exemplification paragraphs. Do you think one paragraph works better than the other? If so, why?

3. **Sum up**
   Based on your reactions to the paragraphs you and your classmate wrote, what do you think an effective exemplification paragraph should do?

4a Exemplification Paragraphs

What do we mean when we tell a friend that an instructor is *good* or that a football team is *bad*? What do we mean when we say that a movie is *boring* or that a particular war was *wrong*? To clarify general statements like these, we use **exemplification**—that is, we give **examples** to illustrate a general idea. In daily conversation and in school, you use specific examples to help explain your ideas.

GENERAL STATEMENT	SPECIFIC EXAMPLES
Today is going to be a hard day.	Today is going to be a hard day because I have a math test in the morning, a lab quiz in the afternoon, and work in the evening.

GENERAL STATEMENT	SPECIFIC EXAMPLES
My car is giving me problems.	My car is burning oil and won't start on cold mornings. In addition, I need a new set of tires.

An **exemplification paragraph** uses specific examples to explain or clarify a general idea. Personal experiences, class discussions, observations, conversations, and readings can all be good sources of examples.

When you TEST an exemplification paragraph, make sure it follows these guidelines:

T ■ An exemplification paragraph should begin with a **topic sentence** that states the paragraph's main idea.

E ■ An exemplification paragraph should present **evidence**—in the form of examples—that support and clarify the general statement made in the topic sentence. Examples should be arranged in **logical order**—for example, from least important to most important or from general to specific. The number of examples you need depends on your topic sentence. A complicated statement will probably require more examples than a relatively straightforward one.

S ■ An exemplification paragraph should end with a **summary statement** that reinforces the paragraph's main idea.

T ■ An exemplification paragraph should include **transitions** that introduce the examples and connect them to one another and to the topic sentence.

Paragraph Map: Exemplification

Topic Sentence

Example #1

Example #2

Example #3

Summary Statement

Model Paragraph: Exemplification

The following paragraph uses several examples to support the idea that some countries change their names for political reasons.

New Government, New Name

Often, when countries change their names, it is for political reasons. Sometimes a new government decides to change the country's name to separate itself from an earlier government. For example, Burma became Myanmar when a military government took over in 1989. Cambodia has had several name

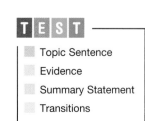

T E S T

░ Topic Sentence
░ Evidence
░ Summary Statement
░ Transitions

Examples presented in logical order

changes as well. After a coup in 1970, it was called the Khmer Republic. Then, in 1975, under communist rule, it became Kampuchea. Gaining independence from another nation is another reason for a country to change its name. For instance, in 1957, after gaining independence from Great Britain, the Gold Coast became Ghana. Another name change occurred when the French Sudan became Mali. After gaining independence from France in 1960, it decided to reject its colonial past. Finally, Zimbabwe gave up its former British name, Rhodesia, several years after winning independence. These name changes can be confusing, but they reveal the changing political climate of the countries in which they occur.

—Kim Seng (student)

Transitions in Exemplification Paragraphs

When you write an exemplification paragraph, be sure to include appropriate transitional words and phrases. These transitions help readers follow your discussion by indicating how your examples are related and how each example supports the topic sentence.

Some Transitional Words and Phrases for Exemplification

also	furthermore	the most important
finally	in addition	example
first . . . second . . .	moreover	the next example
(and so on)	one example . . .	then
for example	another example	
for instance	specifically	

grammar in context

Exemplification

When you write an exemplification paragraph, always use a comma after the introductory transitional word or phrase that introduces an example.

For example, Burma became Myanmar in 1989.

For instance, the Gold Coast changed its name to Ghana in 1957.

Finally, Zimbabwe gave up its British name after winning independence.

For information on using commas with introductory transitional words and phrases, see 34b.

Analyzing an Exemplification Paragraph

Read the exemplification paragraph below; then, follow the instructions in Practice 4-1.

Jobs of the Future

<u>College students should take courses that prepare them for the careers that will be in demand over the next ten years.</u> (For example,) the health-care field will have tremendous growth. Hundreds of thousands of medical workers—such as home-care aides, dental hygienists, and registered nurses—will be needed. (Also,) there will be an ongoing demand for workers who can operate and repair the specialized machines used in hospitals, labs, and other medical settings. (In addition,) a wide range of "green" jobs will become available as many industries work to improve their environmental practices. (For example,) construction workers, architects, and landscapers will be needed to create eco-friendly living and working spaces. (Finally,) education will be an attractive area for job seekers in the coming years. Many new teachers, especially ones who are experienced with computers, will be needed to replace the teachers who retire during the next ten years. <u>Students who know what jobs will be available can prepare themselves for the future.</u>

—Bill Broderick (student)

> **PRACTICE**
> **4-1**

1. Underline the topic sentence of the paragraph above.

2. List the specific examples the writer uses to support his topic sentence. The first example has been listed for you.

health-care jobs
_____

"green" jobs
_____

education jobs
_____

3. Circle the transitional words and phrases that the writer uses to connect ideas in the paragraph.

4. Underline the paragraph's summary statement.

> **PRACTICE**
> **4-2**

Following are four possible topic sentences for exemplification paragraphs. Copy the topic sentences on a separate sheet of paper. Then, list three or four examples you could use to support each topic sentence. For example, if you were writing a paragraph about how difficult the first week of your new job was, you could mention waking up early, getting to know your coworkers, and learning new routines. *Answers will vary.*

Teaching Tip
Before your students write exemplification paragraphs, explain the use of commas to set off introductory transitional elements (34b) and have them do Practice 34-2.

Teaching Tip
Give students a few minutes to work on Practice 4-2. Before they finish, ask some of them to share what they have written so far.

1. Getting a student loan can be challenging.

2. Internships give students valuable opportunities to develop job skills.

3. Good advice is sometimes difficult to get.

4. Some reality television shows insult the intelligence of their viewers.

4b Case Study: A Student Writes an Exemplification Paragraph

When Sarah Herman was asked to write a paragraph about work, she had little difficulty deciding on a topic. She had just finished a summer job waiting on tables in Sea Isle City, a beach community in New Jersey. She knew, without a doubt, that this was the worst job she had ever had.

Once she had decided on her topic, Sarah brainstormed to find ideas to write about. After reviewing her brainstorming notes, she listed several examples that could support her topic sentence.

Restaurant too big

Boss disrespectful

No experience

Kitchen chaotic

Customers rude

Tips bad

After reading her list, Sarah wrote the following topic sentence to express the main idea of her paragraph.

TOPIC SENTENCE Waiting on tables was the worst job I ever had.

After Sarah identified her main idea, she eliminated examples that she thought did not support her topic sentence. Then, she arranged the remaining examples in an order in which she could discuss them most effectively—in this case, from least important to most important.

TOPIC SENTENCE Waiting on tables was the worst job I ever had.
1. No experience
2. Customers rude
3. Tips bad
4. Boss disrespectful

Using her list of points as a guide, Sarah wrote the following draft of her paragraph.

Waiting on tables was the worst job I ever had. I had little experience as a food server. The first day of work was so bad that I almost quit. The customers were rude. All they wanted was to get their food as fast as possible so they could get back to the beach or the boardwalk. They were often impolite and demanding. The tips were bad. It was hard to be pleasant when you knew that the people you were waiting on were probably going to leave you a bad tip. Finally, the owner of the restaurant did not show us any respect. He often yelled at us, saying that if we didn't work harder, he would fire us. He never did, but his constant threats didn't do much to help our morale.

When she finished her draft, Sarah scheduled a conference with her instructor, who suggested that her paragraph would be stronger if she made some of her examples more specific. For example, what experience did she have that made her want to quit? Exactly how were customers rude? Her instructor also reminded her that she needed to TEST her paragraph. As she TESTed her paragraph, Sarah assessed her draft.

- She checked her **topic sentence** and decided that it was effective.
- She evaluated her **evidence**. Then, she decided to add more examples and details and deleted irrelevant details.
- She noticed that she did not have a **summary statement**, so she planned to add one at the end of her paragraph.
- She decided to add more **transitions** to make it easier for readers to follow her discussion.

After TESTing her paragraph, Sarah went on to revise and edit her draft. The final draft below includes all the elements that she looked for when she applied the TEST strategy.

My Worst Job

Waiting on tables was the worst job I ever had. First, I had never worked in a restaurant before, so I made a lot of mistakes. Once, I forgot to bring salads to a table I waited on. A person at the table complained so loudly that the owner had to calm him down. I was so frustrated and upset that I almost quit. Second, the customers at the restaurant were often rude. All they wanted was to get their food as fast as possible so they could get back to the beach or the boardwalk. They were on vacation, and they wanted to be treated well. As a result, they were frequently very demanding. No one ever said, "excuse me," "please," or "thank you," no matter what I did for them. Third, the tips were usually bad. It was hard to be pleasant when you knew that the people you were waiting on were probably going to leave you a bad tip. Finally, the owner of the restaurant never showed his workers any respect. He would yell at us, saying that if we didn't work harder, he would fire us. He never did, but his constant threats didn't do much to help our morale. Even though I survived the summer, I promised myself that I would never wait on tables again.

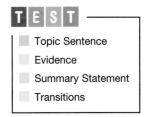

T E S T
- Topic Sentence
- Evidence
- Summary Statement
- Transitions

TEST · Revise · Edit

Look back at your response to the Write First activity on page 67. Using the TEST checklist on page 75, evaluate your exemplification paragraph to make sure it includes a topic sentence, evidence, a summary statement, and transitions. Then, prepare a revised and edited draft of your paragraph.

4c   Step-by-Step Guide: Writing an Exemplification Paragraph

Choose one of the topics below (or choose your own topic) for an exemplification paragraph. Then, use one or more of the strategies described in 2c to help you think of as many examples as you can for the topic you have chosen.

Effective (or ineffective) teachers	Things you can't do without
Qualities that make a great athlete	Terrible dates
Successful movies	Extreme sports
Challenges that older students face	Role models
Traditions your family follows	Rude behavior
Unattractive clothing styles	The advantages of recycling
Peer pressure	Acts of courage
The benefits of a vegan diet	Credit-card debt

Teaching Tip
Walk around the room, checking topic sentences. Ask students to read particularly effective ones aloud.

PRACTICE
4-3   Review your notes on the topic you chose, and list the examples that can best help you develop an exemplification paragraph on that topic.

Answers will vary.

_____

_____

_____

PRACTICE
4-4   Reread your list of examples from Practice 4-3. Then, draft a topic sentence that introduces your topic and communicates the main idea your paragraph will discuss.

Answers will vary.

_____

_____

_____

_____

PRACTICE
4-5   Arrange the examples you listed in Practice 4-3 in a logical order—for example, from least important to most important.

1. _Answers will vary._ _____

2. _____

3. _____

4. _____

Teaching Tip
Look at this exercise closely. Sometimes what students call logical order is not logical order at all.

PRACTICE
4-6   Draft your exemplification paragraph. Then, using the TEST checklist below, check your paragraph for unity, support, and coherence.

ESL Tip
In addition to this exercise, give students a proofreading exercise focusing on verb forms, verb endings, prepositions, and articles. Prepare this exercise ahead of time by keeping track of frequent errors in students' writing.

PRACTICE
4-7   Revise your exemplification paragraph.

PRACTICE
4-8   Prepare a final edited draft of your exemplification paragraph.

TESTing an exemplification paragraph

T opic Sentence Unifies Your Paragraph

☐ Do you have a clearly worded **topic sentence** that states your paragraph's main idea?

☐ Does your topic sentence state an idea that can be supported by examples?

E vidence Supports Your Paragraph's Topic Sentence

☐ Does all your **evidence** support your paragraph's main idea?

☐ Do you need to add more examples?

S ummary Statement Reinforces Your Paragraph's Unity

☐ Does your paragraph end with a **summary statement** that reinforces your main idea?

T ransitions Add Coherence to Your Paragraph

☐ Do you use **transitions** to introduce each example your paragraph discusses?

☐ Do you need to add transitions to make your paragraph clearer and to help readers follow your ideas?

4d Writing about Visuals

Look at the public service advertisement below, and think about the following questions.

- What are the key elements of the ad? How do the image and the text work together?
- What do you think the ad's primary purpose is?
- What audience do you think the ad hopes to reach?
- Do you think the ad is effective—that is, does it achieve its purpose? Does it speak in a convincing way to the audience it wants to reach?

Following the process outlined in the Step-by-Step Guide on pages 74–75, write a paragraph in which you explain why you find the ad effective or ineffective. In your paragraph, be sure to support your topic sentence with specific examples of what the ad does (or doesn't) do.

5 Narration

preview

In this chapter, you will learn to write a narrative paragraph.

write first

These four panels are part of a graphic story from Lynda Barry's book *One! Hundred! Demons!* Look at the four panels, and then write a paragraph in which you tell the story of a difficult period in your childhood. Make sure your topic sentence states the main idea of your paragraph.

"DO YOU BELIEVE IN MAGIC?" IT WAS A SONG ON THE RADIO THAT PLAYED THE SUMMER I DECIDED TO MOVE MY BED-ROOM INTO THE BASEMENT.

I'LL MEETCHA TOMORROW SORTA LATE AT NIGHT

reflect

Look at the paragraph you wrote for the Write First activity on page 77, and then do the following:

1. **Reread**
   - Does your paragraph focus on a story about a difficult period in your childhood?
   - Does your paragraph begin with a topic sentence that tells why the period you describe was difficult?
   - Do you include events and details that tell the story?

2. **Discuss**
   Work with another student to consider the strengths and weaknesses of your narrative paragraphs. Do you think one works better than the other? If so, why?

3. **Sum up**
   Based on your reactions to the paragraphs you and your classmate wrote, what do you think an effective narrative paragraph should do?

5a   Narrative Paragraphs

Teaching Tip
To help students understand the concept of narration, read aloud a tall tale or a fairy tale—or a plot summary from *Soap Opera Digest*.

ESL Tip
Remind ESL students that narration may involve writing about themselves. They might need to use personal pronouns such as *I, me, you, we,* and *us*. Refer them to the sample student paragraph on page 79.

Narration is writing that tells a story. For example, a narrative paragraph could tell how an experience you had as a child changed you, how the life of Martin Luther King, Jr. is inspiring, or how the Battle of Gettysburg was the turning point in the Civil War.

When you TEST a **narrative paragraph**, make sure it follows these guidelines:

T ▪ A narrative paragraph should begin with a **topic sentence** that states its main idea, letting readers know why you are telling a particular story.

E ▪ A narrative paragraph should present **evidence**—events and details—in **time order**, usually in the order in which they actually occurred. Effective narrative paragraphs include only those events that tell the story and avoid irrelevant information that could distract or confuse readers.

S ▪ A narrative paragraph should end with a **summary statement** that reinforces the paragraph's main idea.

T ▪ A narrative paragraph should include **transitions** that connect events to one another and to the topic sentence.

Paragraph Map: Narration

Topic Sentence

Event #1

Event #2

Event #3

Summary Statement

Teaching Tip
Refer students to 16b for information on writing a narrative essay.

Model Paragraph: Narration

The writer of the following paragraph presents a series of events to support the point that getting a tattoo is a lot easier than having one removed.

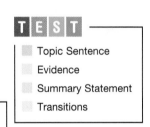

KBR Forever

It only takes a few minutes to get a tattoo, but having one removed takes a lot more time and effort. Until I met Kevin, I had never wanted a tattoo. By the time we had been together for three months, I was sure he was my soul mate. Even after a year, we could not go a day without seeing or talking to each other. When he suggested we get our initials tattooed on each other's wrists, I did not hesitate. Then, we broke up. Now, when I see that "KBR," I feel sick to my stomach. Next week, I am going to have my first laser treatment to remove the tattoo. The whole process will cost ten times what the tattoo cost, but it will be worth it. After five painful sessions, the tattoo should be gone. Breaking up with Kevin was easy, but getting rid of his initials will be a lot more trouble.

—Gillian Kavsan (student)

Events presented in time order

Transitions in Narrative Paragraphs

As you arrange your ideas in a narrative paragraph, be sure to use clear transitional words and phrases. These signals help readers follow your narrative by indicating the order of the events you discuss.

Some Transitional Words and Phrases for Narration

after	first . . . second . . . third	suddenly
as	immediately	then
as soon as	later	two hours (days, months,
before	later on	years) later
by the time	meanwhile	until
earlier	next	when
eventually	now	specific dates
finally	soon	(for example, "In 2006")

grammar in context

Narration

When you write a narrative paragraph, you tell a story. As you become involved in your story, you might forget all about sentence boundaries and begin to string events together without proper punctuation. If you do, you will create a **run-on**.

INCORRECT (RUN-ON)	We had been together for three months I was sure he was my soul mate.
CORRECT	We had been together for three months. I was sure he was my soul mate.
CORRECT	By the time we had been together for three months, I was sure he was my soul mate.

For information on run-ons, see Chapter 24.

Analyzing a Narrative Paragraph

Read this narrative paragraph; then, follow the instructions in Practice 5-1.

Two men who risked their lives in the 1904 Harwick mine disaster were the inspiration for the Hero Fund, a charity that awards money to heroes and their families. The Harwick mine disaster began with a small explosion near the entry to the Harwick mine in Pennsylvania. Within seconds, this small explosion caused a chain reaction in which more and more explosive coal dust was stirred up and ignited. Then, a strong blast sent materials and even a mule flying out of the mine shaft. Ten hours later, a rescue party led by Selwyn Taylor went down into the mine. The rescue party found only one survivor, but Taylor believed more men might still be alive deep within the mine. As he advanced, however, Taylor was himself overcome by fumes. The following day, another rescue worker, Daniel Lyle, was also overcome by fumes while searching for survivors. Neither Taylor nor Lyle found any survivors, and both men died as a result of their efforts. Three months after the mine disaster, Pittsburgh steelmaker Andrew Carnegie founded the Hero Fund to give financial assistance to the families of those injured or killed while performing heroic acts. The Hero Fund continues to honor people like Selwyn Taylor and Daniel Lyle, ordinary people who take extraordinary risks to save others' lives.

—Kevin Smiley (student)

PRACTICE

5-1

1. Underline the topic sentence of the paragraph on page 80.

2. List the major events discussed in the paragraph. The first event has been listed for you.

A small explosion occurred near the entry to the mine. _____

_____

_____

_____

_____

_____

3. Circle the transitional words and phrases that the writer uses to link events in time.

4. Underline the paragraph's summary statement.

PRACTICE

5-2

Following are four possible topic sentences for narrative paragraphs. List three or four events that could support each topic sentence. For example, if you were recalling a barbecue that turned into a disaster, you could tell about burning the hamburgers, spilling the soda, and forgetting to buy paper plates. *Answers will vary.*

1. One experience made me realize that I was no longer as young as I

   thought. _____

   _____

   _____

2. The first time I _____, I got more than I bargained for.

   _____

3. I didn't think I had the courage to _____, but when I did, I felt

   proud of myself. _____

   _____

   _____

4. I remember my reactions to one particular event very clearly.

   _____

   _____

   _____

5b   Case Study: A Student Writes a Narrative Paragraph

When Todd Kinzer's instructor asked the class to write a paragraph about an experience that had a great impact on them, Todd tried to narrow this assignment to a topic for his paragraph. He began by listing some experiences that he could write about.

> Accident at camp—Realized I wasn't as strong as I thought I was
>
> Breaking up with Lindsay—That was painful
>
> Shooting the winning basket in my last high school game—Sweet
>
> The last Thanksgiving at my grandparents' house—Happy and sad

As Todd looked over the experiences on his list, he realized that he could write about all of them. He decided, however, to focus on the last Thanksgiving he spent at his grandparents' house. This occasion was especially meaningful to him because his grandfather had died right after the holiday.

Todd began his writing process by freewriting on his topic. He typed whatever came into his mind about the dinner, without worrying about spelling, punctuation, or grammar. Here is Todd's freewriting paragraph.

> Thanksgiving. Who knew? I remember the smells when I woke up. I can see Granddad at the stove. We were all happy. He told us stories about when he was a kid. I'd heard some of them before, but so what? I loved to hear them. We ate so much I could hardly move. They say turkey has something in it that puts you to sleep. We watched football all afternoon and evening. I still can't believe Granddad is dead. I guess I have the topic for my paragraph.

When he looked over his freewriting, Todd thought he had enough ideas for a first draft of his paragraph. His draft appears below.

> Last Thanksgiving, my grandparents were up early. My grandfather stuffed the turkey, and my grandmother started cooking the other dishes. When I got up, I could smell the turkey in the oven. The table was already set for dinner, so we ate breakfast in the kitchen. My grandfather told us about the Thanksgivings he remembered from when he was a boy. When we sat down for dinner, a fire was burning in the fireplace. My grandmother said grace. My grandfather carved the turkey, and we all passed around dishes of food. For dessert, we had pecan pie and ice cream. After dinner, we watched football on TV. When I went to bed, I felt happy. This was my grandfather's last Thanksgiving.

Todd knew his first draft needed a lot of work. Before he wrote the next draft, he tried to remember what other things had happened that Thanksgiving. He also tried to decide which idea was the most important and what additional supporting information could make his paragraph stronger. Todd sent his draft to his instructor as an email attachment, and his instructor returned the draft along with his comments. After considering his instructor's suggestions and TESTing his paragraph, Todd decided to make the following changes.

- He decided to add a **topic sentence** that stated his paragraph's main idea.
- He decided to add some more details and examples and crossed out sentences that did not belong in his paragraph; now, all his **evidence** would support his main idea.
- He decided to write a stronger **summary statement**.
- He decided to add **transitions** to indicate the time order of the events in his paragraph.

After TESTing his paragraph, Todd made some additional revisions; then, he edited his paragraph, checking grammar, punctuation, mechanics, and spelling and looking carefully for typos. The final draft below includes all the elements Todd looked for when he TESTed his paragraph.

Thanksgiving Memories

This past Thanksgiving was happy and sad because it was the last one I would spend with both my grandparents. The holiday began early. At 5 o'clock in the morning, my grandfather woke up and began to stuff the turkey. About an hour later, my grandmother began cooking corn pie and pineapple casserole. At 8 o'clock, when I got up, I could smell the turkey cooking. While we ate breakfast, my grandfather told us about Thanksgivings he remembered when he was a boy. Later, my grandfather made a fire in the fireplace, and we sat down for dinner. After my grandmother said grace, my grandfather carved and served the turkey. The rest of us passed around dishes of sweet potatoes, mashed potatoes, green beans, asparagus, cucumber salad, relish, cranberry sauce, apple butter, cabbage salad, stuffing, and, of course, corn pie and pineapple casserole. For dessert, my grandmother served pecan pie with scoops of ice cream. After dinner, we turned on the TV and the whole family watched football all evening. That night, I remember thinking that life couldn't get much better. Four months later, my grandfather died in his sleep. For my family and me, Thanksgiving would never be the same.

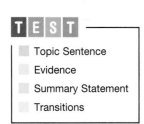

T E S T
- Topic Sentence
- Evidence
- Summary Statement
- Transitions

Teaching Tip
Refer students to 2i and 2j for information on revising and editing their paragraphs.

TEST · Revise · Edit

Look back at your response to the Write First activity on page 77. Using the TEST checklist on page 85, evaluate your narrative paragraph to make sure it includes a topic sentence, evidence, a summary statement, and transitions. Then, prepare a revised and edited draft of your paragraph.

5c Step-by-Step Guide: Writing a Narrative Paragraph

Choose one of the topics below (or choose your own topic). Then, use one or more of the strategies described in 2c to help you recall events and details to develop the topic you have chosen.

ESL Tip
Encourage ESL students to write about events that happened in their native countries.

A difficult choice	An embarrassing situation
A historic event	A disastrous note
A time of self-doubt	A sudden understanding or insight
A success	Something funny a friend did
A dangerous experience	Unexpected good luck
A lesson you learned	A conflict with authority
A happy moment	An event that changed your life
An instance of injustice	A misunderstanding

PRACTICE
5-3 Review your notes on the topic you chose, and list the events you recalled that can best help you develop a narrative paragraph on that topic.

Answers will vary.

_____

_____

_____

_____

_____

_____

Teaching Tip
You might want to stop here and have students share their ideas with the class.

PRACTICE
5-4 Reread your list of events from Practice 5-3. Then, draft a topic sentence that introduces your topic and states the main idea your paragraph will discuss.

Answers will vary.

_____

_____

PRACTICE
5-5 Arrange the events you listed in Practice 5-3 in the order in which they occurred.

1. *Answers will vary.* _____

2. _____

3. _____

4. _____

5. _____

Teaching Tip
For a quiz on dialogue, photocopy a comic strip and have students rewrite the conversation in dialogue format.

PRACTICE
5-6   Draft your narrative paragraph. Then, using the TEST checklist below, check your paragraph for unity, support, and coherence.

PRACTICE
5-7   Revise your narrative paragraph.

PRACTICE
5-8   Prepare a final edited draft of your narrative paragraph.

ESL Tip
Remind students to copy the conversation exactly as it appears in the comic. Check to make sure they do not include double subjects or extra connecting words (_Since_ it was late, _so_ he didn't take the test).

TESTing a narrative paragraph

T opic Sentence Unifies Your Paragraph

☐ Do you have a clearly worded **topic sentence** that states your paragraph's main idea?

☐ Does your topic sentence give readers an idea of why you are telling the story?

E vidence Supports Your Paragraph's Topic Sentence

☐ Do you include enough information about the events you discuss?

☐ Does all your **evidence** support your paragraph's main idea?

☐ Do you need to include more specific details to add interest to your narrative?

S ummary Statement Reinforces Your Paragraph's Unity

☐ Does your paragraph end with a **summary statement** that reinforces your main idea?

T ransitions Add Coherence to Your Paragraph

☐ Do your **transitions** indicate the time order of events in your paragraph?

☐ Do you need to add transitions to make your paragraph clearer and to help readers follow your ideas?

5d   Writing about Visuals

The picture below shows a bride and groom at a Las Vegas wedding chapel. Study the picture carefully, and then write a narrative paragraph that tells the story behind it. (If you prefer, you can write a paragraph about a wedding that you attended.) Follow the process outlined in the Step-by-Step Guide on pages 84–85.

6 Description

preview

In this chapter, you will learn to write a descriptive paragraph.

write first

Write a paragraph in which you describe a person you encounter every day—for example, a bus driver, a street vendor, or a worker in your school cafeteria. Before you begin writing, decide what general impression you want to convey about the person you are describing.

reflect

Look at the paragraph you wrote for the Write First activity on page 87, and then do the following:

1. **Reread**
   - Does your paragraph focus on a person you encounter every day?
   - Does your paragraph begin with a topic sentence that conveys a general impression of the person you describe?
   - Do you include descriptive details that help readers see the person and understand why he or she is important to you?

2. **Discuss**
   Work with another student to consider the strengths and weaknesses of your descriptive paragraphs. Do you think one works better than the other? If so, why?

3. **Sum up**
   Based on your reactions to the paragraphs you and your classmate wrote, what do you think an effective descriptive paragraph should do?

6a Descriptive Paragraphs

In a personal email, you may describe a new boyfriend or girlfriend. In a biology lab manual, you may describe the structure of a cell. In a report for a nursing class, you may describe a patient you treated.

When you write a **description**, you use words to paint a picture for your readers. With description, you use language that creates a vivid impression of what you have seen, heard, smelled, tasted, or touched. The more details you include, the better your description will be.

The following description is flat because it includes very few details.

FLAT   Today, I saw a beautiful sunrise.

In contrast, the description below is full of details that convey the writer's impression of the scene.

RICH   Early this morning as I walked along the soft sandy beach, I saw the sun rise slowly out of the ocean. At first, the ocean glowed red. Then, it turned slowly to pink, to aqua, and finally to blue. As I stood watching the sun, I heard the waves hit the shore, and I felt the cold water swirl around my toes. For a moment, even the small grey and white birds that hurried along the shore seemed to stop and watch the dazzling sight.

The revised description relies on sight (*glowed red; turned slowly to pink, to aqua, and finally to blue*), touch (*the soft sandy beach; felt the cold water*), and sound (*heard the waves hit the shore*).

When you TEST a **descriptive paragraph**, make sure it follows these guidelines:

T ▪ A descriptive paragraph should begin with a **topic sentence** that conveys the main idea or general impression you want to communicate in your paragraph—for example, "The woods behind my house may seem ordinary, but to me, they are beautiful" or "The old wooden roller coaster is a work of art."

E ▪ A descriptive paragraph should present **evidence**—specific details—that supports the topic sentence. Details should be presented in a clear **spatial order**, the order in which you observed the person, place, or thing you are describing. For example, you can move from near to far or from top to bottom.

S ▪ A descriptive paragraph should end with a **summary statement** that reinforces the paragraph's main idea.

T ▪ A descriptive paragraph should include **transitions** that connect details to one another and to the topic sentence.

Teaching Tip
Refer students to 16c for information on writing a descriptive essay.

Paragraph Map: Description

Topic Sentence

Detail #1

Detail #2

Detail #3

Summary Statement

Model Paragraph: Description

The writer of the following paragraph uses descriptive details to explain why skateboarders of all levels love the Palm Springs Skate Park.

Topic Sentence
Evidence
Summary Statement
Transitions

Palm Springs Skate Park

With its three increasingly challenging "bowls," or skate areas, Palm Springs Skate Park appeals to skateboarders of all levels. At the entrance to the park is the "flow bowl," which is perfect for skill building. The flow bowl area includes a shallow, snakelike indentation (the bowl), as well as structures meant to copy street features, such as curbs, rails, and steps. Further inside the park is the "combi bowl," which is shaped like a deep boomerang. Perfect for intermediate skateboarders doing tricks, the combi bowl has two levels that flow into each other, ultimately reaching a depth of

Details arranged in spatial order

seven and a half feet. At the far edge of the park is the "nude bowl," inspired by the classic kidney-shaped pools of Southern California, where skateboarding began. With its steep walls and its depth of nine and a half feet, the nude bowl is the most challenging part of the park. Because it offers something for every skateboarder, the Palm Springs Skate Park has become one of the most popular skate parks in Southern California.

—Heidi Decker (student)

Transitions in Descriptive Paragraphs

As you arrange your ideas in a descriptive paragraph, be sure to use appropriate transitional words and phrases to lead readers from one detail to another.

Some Transitional Words and Phrases for Description

above	in	outside
at the edge	in back of	over
at the entrance	in front of	spreading out
behind	inside	the first . . . the second
below	nearby	the least important . . .
between	next to	the most important
beyond	on	the next
down	on one side . . . on the	under
farther	other side	

grammar in context

Description

When writing a descriptive paragraph, you sometimes use **modifiers**—words and phrases that describe another word in the sentence. If a modifier cannot logically describe any word in the sentence, it is called a **dangling modifier**.

CONFUSING (DANGLING MODIFIER)   Having steep walls and a depth of nine feet, the skaters think it is the most challenging part of the park. (Do the skaters have steep walls?)

CLEAR   Having steep walls and a depth of nine feet, the nude bowl is the most challenging part of the park.

For information on how to identify and correct dangling modifiers, see Chapter 28.

Analyzing a Descriptive Paragraph

Read this descriptive paragraph; then, follow the instructions in Practice 6-1.

Gen's Lunches

My friend Gen's lunches are as original as they are delicious. Nearly every day, Gen prepares a bento box, or traditional Japanese lunch. Today, she has brought an oval baby blue bento box. In the center of the box are three flattened rice balls that Gen calls onigiri. Using strips and dots of nori seaweed, she has given her onigiri adorable eyes and smiles. Using molded deli meat, she has even added pink circles to the cheeks. Surrounding the rice balls are small portions of tasty foods. For example, above the rice to the left are three breaded and fried zucchini strips that shine with golden oil. Directly above the rice sit two peeled hardboiled eggs; I can just imagine their yummy crumbly yellow yolks. A deli-meat flower perches on each egg, and a cherry tomato snuggles nearby. Above the rice to the right nestle three wedges of sweet winter squash. The contrast between their bright orange flesh and their striped green rinds is very pleasing. Gen's bento boxes always make me hungry, but it's hard to watch her eat her lovely creations—especially the sweet onigiri with their smiling faces.

> **ESL Tip**
> Have students copy the passage several times to help them strengthen their sentence structure before they work on their own descriptions.

PRACTICE 6-1

1. Underline the topic sentence of the paragraph above.

2. In a few words, summarize the main idea of the paragraph.

   Gen's lunches are original as well as delicious.

3. What are some of the details the writer uses to describe Gen's bento box lunch? The first detail has been listed for you.

   oval baby blue box

   three flattened rice balls

   strips and dots of nori seaweed

   breaded, fried zucchini strips shining with golden oil

   two peeled hardboiled eggs with deli-meat flowers

   three wedges of bright orange winter squash with green rinds

4. Circle the transitional words and phrases that the writer uses to lead readers from one detail to another.

5. Underline the paragraph's summary statement.

PRACTICE

6-2   Each of the five topic sentences below states a possible main idea for a descriptive paragraph. List three details that could help convey this main idea. For example, to support the idea that sitting in front of a fireplace is relaxing, you could describe the crackling of the fire, the pine scent of the smoke, and the changing colors of the flames.

1. One look at the stern face of the traffic-court judge told me that my appeal would be denied.

   Answers will vary.

   _____

   _____

2. The dog was at least ten years old and had been living on the streets for a long time.

   Answers will vary.

   _____

   _____

3. The woman behind the department store makeup counter was a walking advertisement for every product she sold.

   Answers will vary.

   _____

   _____

4. One of the most interesting stores I know sells clothing from the 1970s.

   Answers will vary.

   _____

   _____

5. My ride on the Scream Machine was so exciting that I got back in line.

   Answers will vary.

   _____

   _____

6b   Case Study: A Student Writes a Descriptive Paragraph

When Jared Lopez was asked to write a descriptive paragraph about someone he admired, he decided to write about his uncle Manuel, who had been a father figure to him.

Because he was familiar with his topic, Jared did not have to brainstorm or freewrite to find ideas. He decided to begin his paragraph by giving a general description of his uncle and then concentrating on his uncle's most noticeable feature: his hands. Here is the first draft of Jared's paragraph.

> My uncle's name is Manuel, but his friends call him Manny. He is over six feet tall. Uncle Manny's eyes are dark brown, almost black. They make him look very serious. When he laughs, however, he looks friendly. His nose is long and straight, and it makes Uncle Manny look very distinguished. Most interesting to me are Uncle Manny's hands. Even though he hasn't worked as a stonemason since he opened his own construction company ten years ago, his hands are still rough and scarred. They are large and strong, but they can be gentle too.

After a conference with his instructor, Jared **TEST**ed his paragraph.

- He decided to add a **topic sentence** that stated the main idea of his description.
- He decided to add more details in his description to give readers more **evidence** of his uncle's strength and gentleness.
- He decided to add a stronger **summary statement** to unify his paragraph.
- He planned to include more **transitions** to move readers from one part of his description to the next.

After **TEST**ing his paragraph, Jared revised and edited his draft. The final draft below includes all the elements Jared looked for when he **TEST**ed it.

My Uncle Manny

> My uncle Manuel is a strong but gentle person who took care of my mother and me when my father died. Manuel, or "Manny" as his friends and family call him, is over six feet tall. This is unusual for a Mexican of his generation. The first thing most people notice about my uncle Manny is his eyes. They are large and dark brown, almost black. They make him look very serious. When he laughs, however, the sides of his eyes crinkle up and he looks warm and friendly. Another thing that stands out is his nose, which is long and straight. My mother says it makes Uncle Manny look strong and distinguished. The most striking thing about Uncle Manny is his hands. Even though he hasn't worked as a stonemason since he opened his own construction company ten years ago, his hands are still rough and scarred from carrying stones. No matter how much he tries, he can't get rid of the dirt under the skin of his fingers. Uncle Manny's hands are big and rough, but they are also gentle and comforting. To me, they show what he really is: a strong and gentle man.

T E S T
- [ ] Topic Sentence
- [ ] Evidence
- [ ] Summary Statement
- [ ] Transitions

TEST · **Revise · Edit**

Look back at your response to the Write First activity on page 87. Using the **TEST** checklist on page 95, evaluate your descriptive paragraph to make sure it includes a topic sentence, evidence, a summary statement, and transitions. Then, prepare a revised and edited draft of your paragraph.

6c Step-by-Step Guide: Writing a Descriptive Paragraph

Choose one of the topics below (or choose your own topic). Then, use one or more of the strategies described in 2c to help you come up with specific details about the topic you have chosen. If you can, observe your subject directly and write down your observations.

A favorite place	A favorite article of clothing
A place you felt trapped in	A useful object
A comfortable spot on campus	A pet
An unusual person	A building you think is ugly
Your dream house	Your car or truck
A family member or friend	The car you would like to have
A work of art	A statue or monument
A valued possession	Someone you admire
Your workplace	A cooking disaster

**PRACTICE
6-3**   Review your notes on the topic you chose, and list the details that can best help you develop a descriptive paragraph on that topic.

Answers will vary.

_____

_____

_____

_____

_____

**PRACTICE
6-4**   Reread your list of details from Practice 6-3. Then, draft a topic sentence that summarizes the idea you want to convey in your paragraph.

Answers will vary.

_____

_____

**PRACTICE
6-5**   Arrange the details you listed in Practice 6-3. You might arrange them in the order in which you have observed them—for example, from left to right, near to far, or top to bottom.

1. *Answers will vary.*_____

2. _____

3. _____

Teaching Tip
Put a section of a descriptive piece of writing on an overhead transparency. Have students model their descriptions and sentence patterns on the sample.

4. _____

5. _____

6. _____

7. _____

PRACTICE

6-6 Draft your descriptive paragraph. Then, using the TEST checklist below, check your paragraph for unity, support, and coherence.

PRACTICE

6-7 Revise your descriptive paragraph.

PRACTICE

6-8 Prepare a final edited draft of your descriptive paragraph.

TESTing a descriptive paragraph

T opic Sentence Unifies Your Paragraph

☐ Do you have a clearly worded **topic sentence** that states your paragraph's main idea?

☐ Does your topic sentence identify the person, place, or thing you will describe in your paragraph?

E vidence Supports Your Paragraph's Topic Sentence

☐ Does all your **evidence**—descriptive details—support your paragraph's main idea?

☐ Do you have enough descriptive details, or do you need to include more?

S ummary Statement Reinforces Your Paragraph's Unity

☐ Does your paragraph end with a **summary statement** that reinforces your main idea?

T ransitions Add Coherence to Your Paragraph

☐ Do your **transitions** lead readers from one detail to the next?

☐ Do you need to add transitions to make your paragraph clearer and to help readers follow your ideas?

6d Writing about Visuals

The picture below shows a house surrounded by lush landscaping. Write a paragraph describing the house for a real estate brochure. Use your imagination to invent details that describe its setting, exterior, and interior. Your goal in this descriptive paragraph is to persuade a prospective buyer to purchase the house. Follow the process outlined in the Step-by-Step Guide on pages 94–95.

7 Process

preview

In this chapter, you will learn to write a process paragraph.

write first

The picture on this page shows the board game mancala, which archeologists believe has been around in one form or another for at least 1,300 years. Write a paragraph in which you explain how to play a game you know well. Assume that your readers know nothing about the game you're describing.

reflect

Look at the paragraph you wrote for the Write First activity on page 97, and then do the following:

1. **Reread**
   - Does your paragraph focus on your favorite indoor game?
   - Does your paragraph begin with a topic sentence that identifies the game?
   - Does your paragraph tell readers how to play the game?
   - Do you include all the steps involved in playing the game?

2. **Discuss**
   Work with another student to consider the strengths and weaknesses of your process paragraphs. Do you think one works better than the other? If so, why?

3. **Sum up**
   Based on your reactions to the paragraphs you and your classmate wrote, what do you think an effective process paragraph should do?

7a   Process Paragraphs

Teaching Tip
To help students understand the concept of process, photocopy or print out the operating instructions for an appliance or electronic device. (You could also ask students to bring instruction booklets or operating manuals to class.) Have students take turns reading steps aloud, and ask the class to supply any missing transitions.

Teaching Tip
Refer students to 16d for information on writing a process essay.

When you describe a **process**, you tell readers how something works or how to do something. For example, you could explain how the optical scanner at the checkout counter of a food store works, how to hem a pair of pants, or how to send a text message. A **process paragraph** tells readers how to complete a process by listing steps in time order.

When you **TEST** a process paragraph, make sure it follows these guidelines:

T ■ A process paragraph should begin with a **topic sentence** that identifies the process you are explaining and the point you want to make about it (for example, "Parallel parking is easy once you know the secret" or "By following a few simple steps, you can design a résumé that will get noticed").

E ■ A process paragraph should discuss all the steps in the process, one at a time. These steps should be presented in strict **time order**—the order in which they occur. A process paragraph should present enough **evidence**—details and examples—to make the process clear to readers.

S ■ A process paragraph should end with a **summary statement** that reinforces the paragraph's main idea.

T ■ A process paragraph should include **transitions** that connect the steps in the process to one another and to the topic sentence.

Paragraph Map: Process

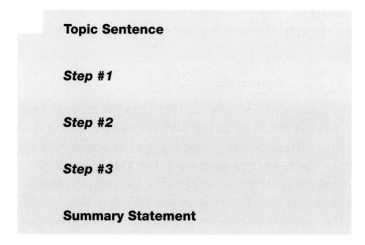

Topic Sentence

Step #1

Step #2

Step #3

Summary Statement

There are two types of process paragraphs: *process explanations* and *instructions*.

Model Paragraph: Process Explanations

In a **process explanation**, your purpose is to help readers understand how something works or how something happens—for example, how a cell phone operates or how a computer works. With a process explanation, you do not actually expect readers to perform the process.

In the following process explanation paragraph from a psychology exam, the writer explains the four stages children go through when they acquire language.

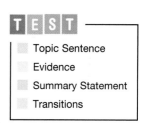

T E S T
- Topic Sentence
- Evidence
- Summary Statement
- Transitions

> Children go through four distinct stages when they learn language. The first stage begins as soon as infants are born. By crying, they let people know when they need something or if they are in pain. The second stage begins when children are about a year old and are able to communicate with single words. For example, a child will use the word *food* to mean anything from "I'm hungry" to "feed the dog." The third stage begins at about twenty months. During this stage, children begin to use two-word sentences, such as "dada car" (for "This is dada's car"). Finally, at about thirty months, children begin to learn the rules that govern language. They learn how to form simple sentences, plurals, and the past tense of verbs. No matter what language they speak, all children follow the same process when they learn language.
>
> —Jennifer Gulla (student)

— Steps presented in time order

Teaching Tip
Remind students that they should generally avoid the vague and informal pronoun *you* (as in, "You need to do well in college") in their writing. When they are giving instructions, however, the use of *you* is appropriate.

Model Paragraph: Instructions

When you write **instructions**, your purpose is to give readers the information they need to actually perform a task or activity—for example, to fill out an application, to operate a piece of machinery, or to help someone who is choking. Because you expect readers to follow your instructions, you address them directly, using **commands** to tell them what to do (*check the gauge . . . pull the valve*).

In the following paragraph, the writer gives instructions on how to break up with someone.

TEST

- Topic Sentence
- Evidence
- Summary Statement
- Transitions

Steps presented in time order

Breaking Up

If you follow a few simple steps, breaking up with someone does not have to be stressful. First, give the person an idea of what is coming so that it is not a total surprise. Make excuses for not getting together, or occasionally say that it might be better if the two of you spent more time apart. Second, go to a public place to break the news. The other person is less likely to make a scene if you are in a restaurant than if the two of you are alone. Next, gently but directly tell the other person that you want to break up. Be firm. Remember that this discussion should not turn into a debate. During this process, be sensitive to the other person's feelings. If the person gets emotional, be understanding. Finally, once the break-up is complete, go out with your friends and have some fun. That is the best way to take your mind off the situation and to meet new people. By following these simple steps, you can make a difficult situation a little bit easier.

—Nicole Riddle (student)

Transitions in Process Paragraphs

Transitions are very important in process paragraphs like the two you have just read. They enable readers to clearly identify each step—for example, *first, second, third,* and so on. In addition, they establish a sequence that lets readers move easily through the process you are describing.

Teaching Tip
Tell students that the transitional words *firstly, secondly,* and so on are commonly used in Great Britain but not in the United States. Tell them to use *first, second,* and so on instead.

Some Transitional Words and Phrases for Process

after that, after this	first	subsequently
as	immediately	the first (second, third) step
as soon as	later	the next step
at the same time	meanwhile	the last step
at this point	next	then
during	now	when
finally	once	while
	soon	

grammar in context

Process

When you write a process paragraph, you may find yourself making **illogical shifts** in tense, person, and voice. If you shift from one tense, person, number, or voice to another without good reason, you may confuse your reader.

CONFUSING First, give people an idea of what is coming so that it is not a total surprise. Excuses should be made for not getting together. (illogical shift from active to passive voice)

CLEAR First, give people an idea of what is coming so that it is not a total surprise. Make excuses for not getting together. (consistent use of active voice)

For information on how to avoid illogical shifts in tense, person, and voice, see Chapter 27.

Teaching Tip
Before your students write process paragraphs, you might want to explain how to identify and avoid illogical shifts (Chapter 27) and have them do Practices 27-1 and 27-3.

Analyzing a Process Paragraph

Read this process paragraph; then, follow the instructions in Practice 7-1.

An Order of Fries

I never realized how much work goes into making French fries until I worked at a potato processing plant in Hermiston, Oregon. The process begins with freshly dug potatoes being shoveled from trucks onto conveyor belts leading into the plant. During this stage, workers must pick out any rocks that may have been dug up with the potatoes because these could damage the automated peelers. After the potatoes have gone through the peelers, they travel on a conveyor belt through the "trim line." Here, workers cut out any bad spots, being careful not to waste potatoes by trimming too much. Next, the potatoes are sliced in automated cutters and then deep-fried for about a minute. After this, they continue along a conveyor belt to the "wet line." Here, workers

ESL Tip
Have students write a process paragraph using one of the sample paragraphs in this chapter as a model for sentence structure and style. Then, have them write a process paragraph (directed at an American audience) about a practice unique to their culture.

again look for bad spots, and they throw away any rotten pieces. (At this point,) the potatoes go to a second set of fryers for three minutes before being moved to subzero freezers for ten minutes. (Then,) it's on to the "frozen line" for a final inspection. The inspected fries are weighed by machines and (then) sealed into five-pound plastic packages, which are weighed again by workers who also check that the packages are properly sealed. (Finally,) the bags are packed into boxes and made ready for shipment to various restaurants across the western United States. <u>This complicated process goes on twenty-four hours a day to bring consumers the French fries they enjoy so much.</u>

—Cheri Rodriguez (student)

PRACTICE

1. Underline the topic sentence of the paragraph above.

2. Is this a process explanation or instructions? *process explanation*
   How do you know? *Verbs are not commands.*

3. List the steps in the process. The first step has been listed for you.

   The potatoes are unloaded, and the rocks are sorted out.

   They are peeled and carried to the "trim line."

   They are sliced and deep-fried for a minute.

   They are carried to the "wet line."

   They are fried again and then frozen.

   They get a final inspection on the "frozen line."

   They are weighed, packaged, and boxed for shipment.

4. Circle the transitional words and phrases that the writer uses to move readers from one step to the next.

5. Underline the paragraph's summary statement.

PRACTICE
7-2   On the following page are four possible topic sentences for process paragraphs. List three or four steps that explain the process each topic sentence identifies. For example, if you were explaining the process of getting a job, you could list preparing a résumé, looking at ads in newspapers or online, writing a job application letter, and going on an interview. Make sure each step follows logically from the one that precedes it.

1. Getting the lowest prices when you shop is not a simple process.

   Answers will vary.

2. Getting the most out of a student-teacher conference can take some preparation.

   Answers will vary.

3. Cage-training a puppy can be a tricky process.

   Answers will vary.

4. Choosing the perfect outfit for a job interview can be time-consuming.

   Answers will vary.

7b Case Study: A Student Writes a Process Paragraph

When Manasvi Bari was assigned to write a paragraph in which she explained a process she performed every day, she decided to write about how to get a seat on a crowded subway car. To make sure she had enough to write about, she made the following list of possible steps she could include.

Don't pay attention to heat

Get into the train

Get the first seat

Look as if you need help

Get to a pole

Don't travel during rush hour

Choose your time

Be alert

Squeeze in

After looking over her list, Manasvi crossed out steps that she didn't think were essential to the process she wanted to describe.

~~Don't pay attention to heat~~

Get into the train

Get the first seat

Look as if you need help

~~Get to a pole~~

~~Don't travel during rush hour~~

~~Choose your time~~

Be alert

Squeeze in

Once she had decided on her list of steps, she rearranged them in the order in which they should be performed.

Get into the train

Be alert

Get the first seat

Squeeze in

Look as if you need help

At this point, Manasvi thought that she was ready to begin writing her paragraph. Here is her first draft.

When the train arrives, get into the car as fast as possible. Be alert. If you see an empty seat, grab it and sit down immediately. If there is no seat, ask people to move down, or squeeze into a space that seems too small. If none of this works, you'll have to use some imagination. Look helpless. Drop your books, and look as if the day can't get any worse. Sometimes a person will get up and give you a seat. If this strategy doesn't work, stand near someone who looks as if he or she is going to get up. When the person gets up, jump into the seat as fast as you can. Don't let the people who are getting on the train get the seat before you do.

Manasvi showed the draft of her paragraph to a writing center tutor. Together, they TESTed her paragraph and made the following decisions.

- They decided that she needed to add a **topic sentence** that identified the process and stated the point she wanted to make about it.
- They decided that her **evidence**—the details and examples that described the steps in her process—was clear and complete.
- They decided that she needed to add a **summary statement** that reinforced the point of the process.
- They decided that she needed to add **transitions** that helped readers follow the steps in the process.

At this point, Manasvi revised and edited her paragraph. The final draft below includes all the elements Manasvi looked for when she TESTed her paragraph.

Surviving Rush Hour

Anyone who takes the subway to school in the morning knows how hard it is to find a seat, but by following a few simple steps, you should be able to get a seat almost every day. First, when the train arrives, get into the car as fast as possible. Be alert. As soon as you see an empty seat, grab it and sit down immediately. Meanwhile, if there is no seat, ask people to move down, or try to squeeze into a space that seems too small. If none of this works, the next step is to use some imagination. Look helpless. Drop your books, and look as if the day can't get any worse. Sometimes a person will get up and give you a seat. Don't be shy. Take it, and remember to say thank you. Finally, if this strategy doesn't work, stand near someone who looks as if he or she is going to get up. When the person gets up, jump into the seat as fast as you can. By following these steps, you should be able to get a seat on the subway and arrive at school rested and relaxed.

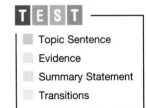

T E S T
- Topic Sentence
- Evidence
- Summary Statement
- Transitions

TEST · Revise · Edit

Look back at your response to the Write First activity on page 97. Using the TEST checklist on page 107, evaluate your process paragraph to make sure it includes a topic sentence, evidence, a summary statement, and transitions. Then, prepare a revised and edited draft of your paragraph.

7c Step-by-Step Guide: Writing a Process Paragraph

Choose one of the topics below (or choose your own topic). Use one or more of the strategies described in 2c to help you come up with as many steps as you can for the topic you have chosen.

Studying for exams
Strategies for winning
  arguments
How to arrange a tailgate party
How to be a good friend
How to discourage
  telemarketers
Your morning routine
How to deep-fry a turkey
How to perform a particular
  household repair

How to quit smoking
How to save money
How to drive in the snow
How to apply for financial aid
A process involved in a hobby
  of yours
How to build something
How to make your favorite dish
How to prepare for a storm
How to operate a piece of
  machinery

PRACTICE

7-3   Review your notes on the topic you chose, and decide whether to write a process explanation or a set of instructions. Then, on the lines below, list the steps that can best help you develop a process paragraph on that topic.

Answers will vary.
_____

_____

_____

_____

PRACTICE

7-4   Reread your list of steps from Practice 7-3. Then, draft a topic sentence that identifies the process you will discuss and communicates the point you will make about it.

Answers will vary.
_____

_____

PRACTICE

7-5   Review the steps you listed in Practice 7-3. Then, arrange them in time order, moving from the first step to the last.

1. *Answers will vary.* _____   4. _____

2. _____   5. _____

3. _____   6. _____

PRACTICE
7-6   Draft your process paragraph. Then, using the TEST checklist below, check your paragraph for unity, support, and coherence.

PRACTICE
7-7   Revise your process paragraph.

PRACTICE
7-8   Prepare a final edited draft of your process paragraph.

TESTing a process paragraph

T opic Sentence Unifies Your Paragraph

☐ Do you have a clearly worded **topic sentence** that states your paragraph's main idea?

☐ Does your topic sentence identify the process you will discuss?

☐ Does your topic sentence indicate whether you will be explaining a process or giving instructions?

E vidence Supports Your Paragraph's Topic Sentence

☐ Have you included all the steps in the process?

☐ Have you included enough **evidence**—details and examples—to make the process clear to readers?

☐ If your paragraph is a set of instructions, have you included all the information readers need to perform the process?

S ummary Statement Reinforces Your Paragraph's Unity

☐ Does your paragraph end with a **summary statement** that reinforces your main idea?

T ransitions Add Coherence to Your Paragraph

☐ Do your **transitions** move readers from one step in the process to the next?

☐ Do you need to add transitions to make your paragraph clearer and to help readers follow your ideas?

7d   Writing about Visuals

The picture below shows John Belushi as John "Bluto" Blutarski in the infamous toga scene from the 1978 film *Animal House.* Study the picture carefully, and then list the steps that would be involved in planning a party like this one. Use this list to help you write a process paragraph that presents step-by-step instructions in the order in which they need to be done. Be sure to include any necessary cautions and reminders—for example, "Don't forget to invite your neighbors"—to help your readers avoid potential problems. Follow the process outlined in the Step-by-Step Guide on pages 106–7.

8 Cause and Effect

preview

In this chapter, you will learn to write a cause-and-effect paragraph.

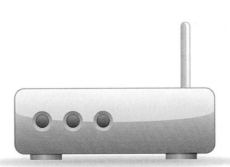

write first

This picture shows a variety of electronic devices. Write a paragraph in which you describe the impact of a particular electronic device— for example, a video game console, a smartphone, or an e-reader—on your life or the life of your family.

reflect

Look at the paragraph you wrote for the Write First activity on page 109, and then do the following:

1. **Reread**
   - Does your paragraph focus on an electronic device that has had an impact on your life or your family's life?
   - Does your paragraph begin with a topic sentence that identifies the device you are discussing and tells how it affects you (or your family)?
   - Do you include examples and details that explain the device's impact?

2. **Discuss**
   Work with another student to consider the strengths and weaknesses of your cause-and-effect paragraphs. Do you think one works better than the other? If so, why?

3. **Sum up**
   Based on your reactions to the paragraphs you and your classmate wrote, what do you think an effective cause-and-effect paragraph should do?

8a   Cause-and-Effect Paragraphs

Why is the cost of college so high in the United States? How does smoking affect a person's health? What would happen if the city increased its sales tax? How dangerous is the avian flu? All these questions have one thing in common: they try to determine the causes or effects of an action, event, or situation.

A **cause** is something or someone that makes something happen. An **effect** is something brought about by a particular cause.

Teaching Tip
You may want to point out to students that they should consider all possible causes, not just the obvious ones.

Teaching Tip
Refer students to 16e for information on writing a cause-and-effect essay.

CAUSE		EFFECT
Increased airport security	⟶	Long lines at airports
Weight gain	⟶	Health problems
Seat belt laws passed	⟶	Traffic deaths reduced

A **cause-and-effect paragraph** examines or analyzes reasons and results. It helps readers understand why something happened or is happening or shows how one thing affects another.

When you TEST a cause-and-effect paragraph, make sure it follows these guidelines:

T ▪ A cause-and-effect paragraph should begin with a **topic sentence** that tells readers whether the paragraph is focusing on causes or on effects—for example, "There are several reasons why the cost of gas is so high" (causes) or "Going to the writing center has given me confidence as well as skill as a writer" (effects).

E ▪ A cause-and-effect paragraph should present **evidence**—details and examples—to support the topic sentence. Causes or effects should be arranged in **logical order**—for example, from least to most important.

S ▪ A cause-and-effect paragraph should end with a **summary statement** that reinforces the paragraph's main idea.

T ▪ A cause-and-effect paragraph should include **transitions** that connect causes or effects to one another and to the topic sentence.

Paragraph Map: Cause and Effect

Topic Sentence

Cause (or effect) #1

Cause (or effect) #2

Cause (or effect) #3

Summary Statement

Model Paragraph: Causes

The following paragraph focuses on **causes**.

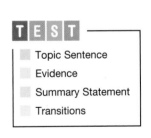

T E S T

☐ Topic Sentence
☐ Evidence
☐ Summary Statement
☐ Transitions

Why Young People Don't Vote

There are several reasons why young adults do not often vote in national elections. The first reason is that many young people are just not interested in politics. They are busy getting an education or working, and they do not take the time to think about politics or which candidate to vote for. Another reason is that they do not think that their vote is important. They think that because millions of people are voting, their vote will not have an effect on the outcome of an election. A third reason is that many young people do not think that the candidates are speaking to them. They do not think that national issues such as capital gains taxes, Social Security, and Medicare have much to do with them. Finally, many young people are turned off by politics and politicians. As far as they are concerned, politicians just want to get elected and will say anything to get votes. Until these issues are addressed, many young people will continue to stay away from the polls.

Causes arranged in logical order

—Moniquetta Hall (student)

T E S T

Topic Sentence
Evidence
Summary Statement
Transitions

Model Paragraph: Effects

The following paragraph focuses on **effects**.

The Negative Effects of Climate Change

Effects arranged in logical order

Climate change caused by global warming would have several negative effects. One effect would be an increase in the number of intense storms. Large hurricanes and other types of storms would damage property and kill many people. Another effect would be a rise in sea level. As the earth warms, the polar ice would melt and raise the level of the earth's oceans. Coastal cities and low-lying areas would probably be flooded. Still another effect would be the spread of certain kinds of diseases. Many diseases, now found only in warm areas, would spread to areas that were once cool but then became warm. Malaria and yellow fever, for example, could become as common in the United States as they are in Africa and Southeast Asia. Finally, climate change associated with global warming would affect agriculture. Farming areas, such as the Midwest, where American farmers grow corn and wheat, would become dry. As a result, there would be food shortages, and many people could go hungry. No one knows for certain what will happen, but if global warming continues, our lives will certainly be affected.

—Jackie Hue (student)

Transitions in Cause-and-Effect Paragraphs

Transitions in cause-and-effect paragraphs, as illustrated in the two paragraphs above, introduce individual causes or effects. They may also show the connections between a cause and its effects or between an effect and its causes. In addition, they may indicate which cause or effect is more important than another.

> **Some Transitional Words and Phrases for Cause and Effect**
>
> | | | |
> |---|---|---|
> | accordingly | moreover | the first (second, third) reason |
> | another cause | since | |
> | another effect | so | the most important cause |
> | as a result | the first (second, third, final) cause | the most important effect |
> | because | | therefore |
> | consequently | the first (second, third, final) effect | |
> | for | | |
> | for this reason | | |

grammar in context

Cause and Effect

When you write a cause-and-effect paragraph, you should be careful not to confuse the words *affect* and *effect*. *Affect* is a verb meaning "to influence." *Effect* is a noun meaning "result."

> One ~~affect~~ *effect* would be an increase in the number of storms. (*effect* is a noun)

> No one knows for certain what will happen, but if global warming continues, our lives will certainly be ~~effected~~ *affected*. (*affect* is a verb)

For more information on effect *and* affect, *see Chapter 37.*

Teaching Tip
Before students write cause-and-effect paragraphs, you might want to review the use of *affect* and *effect*, pointing them to the examples in 37e and to the relevant items in Practice 37–6.

Analyzing a Cause-and-Effect Paragraph

Read this cause-and-effect paragraph; then, follow the instructions in Practice 8-1.

The Decline of Orphanages in the United States

There are several reasons for the decline of U.S. orphanages after World War II. First, people discovered that children who are not hugged and snuggled become sickly. As a result, "child rescue" groups were formed to bring children back to the warmth of families. Second, although the U.S. government supported many orphanages, religious groups ran many others. Some politicians distrusted this relationship between religious groups and orphans; after all, America's founders had said church and state should be separate. Finally, the government saw that it was less expensive to give financial assistance to poor parents than to maintain large orphanages. Consequently, a program called Aid to Dependent Children, which was part of the 1935 Social Security Act, was established to support children in their own homes. In 1960, the program was expanded to include children in foster care. For these reasons, orphanages are seldom seen in the United States today.

PRACTICE

8-1

1. Underline the topic sentence of the paragraph on page 113.

2. List the words that tell you the writer is moving from one cause to another in the paragraph. The first answer has been listed for you.

First _____

Second _____

Finally _____

3. List the causes the writer describes. The first cause has been listed for you.

"Child rescue" movements were formed to bring children back to the warmth of families.

Politicians distrusted the relationship between religious groups and orphanages.

It was less expensive for the government to give financial assistance to parents than to

maintain orphanages.

4. Circle the transitional words and phrases that the writer uses to identify causes.

5. Underline the paragraph's summary statement.

PRACTICE

8-2

Following are four possible topic sentences for cause-and-effect paragraphs. After each topic sentence, list the effects that could result from the cause identified in the topic sentence. For example, if you were writing a paragraph about the effects of excessive drinking on campus, you could list low grades, health problems, and vandalism.

1. Having a baby can change your life.

Answers will vary.

_____

_____

2. Being bilingual has many advantages.

Answers will vary.

_____

_____

3. College has made me a different person.

Answers will vary.

_____

_____

4. Impulse buying can have negative effects on a person's finances.

Answers will vary.

List three causes that could support each of the following topic sentences.

1. The causes of teenage obesity are easy to identify.

Answers will vary.

---

2. Chronic unemployment can have many causes.

Answers will vary.

---

3. The high cost of college tuition is not easy to explain.

Answers will vary.

---

4. There are several reasons why professional athletes' salaries are so high.

Answers will vary.

8b   Case Study: A Student Writes a Cause-and-Effect Paragraph

When Sean Jin was asked to write a cause-and-effect essay for his composition class, he had no trouble thinking of a topic because of a debate that was going on in his hometown about building a Walmart Superstore there. He decided to write a paragraph that discussed the effects that such a store would have on the local economy.

His instructor told the class the main problem they could have in planning a cause-and-effect essay is making sure that a **causal relationship** exists—that one event actually causes another. In other words, just because one event follows another closely in time, students should not assume that the second event was caused by the first.

With this advice in mind, Sean listed the effects a Walmart would have on his small town. Here is Sean's list of effects.

Provide new jobs

Offer low-cost items

Pay low wages

Push out small businesses

After reviewing his list of effects, Sean wrote the following first draft of his paragraph.

> Walmart can have good and bad effects on a small town. It provides jobs. A large store needs a lot of employees. So, many people from the area will be able to find work. Walmart's prices are low. Families that don't have much money may be able to buy things they can't afford to buy at other stores. Not all of Walmart's effects are positive. Walmart pays employees less than other stores. Walmart provides jobs, but those jobs don't pay very much. When Walmart comes into an area, many small businesses are forced to close. They just can't match Walmart's prices or stock as much merchandise as Walmart can.

When he finished his draft, Sean went to the writing center and met with a tutor. After going over his draft with the tutor and **TEST**ing his paragraph, Sean made the following decisions.

- He decided that he needed to sharpen his **topic sentence** to tie his discussion of Walmart to the small town in which he lived.
- He decided to provide more **evidence** to support his topic sentence—for example, what exactly does Walmart pay its salespeople?
- He decided to add a **summary statement** to reinforce his main idea.
- He decided to add **transitions** to identify positive and negative effects.

After **TEST**ing his paragraph, Sean revised and edited it. The final draft below includes all the elements Sean looked for when he **TEST**ed his paragraph.

Walmart Comes to Town

When Walmart comes to a small town like mine, it can have good and bad effects. The first and most positive effect is that it provides jobs. A large Walmart Superstore needs a lot of employees, so many people will be able to find work. In my rural town, over 15 percent of the people are out of work. Walmart could give these people a chance to improve their lives. Another positive effect that Walmart can have is to keep prices low so families on tight budgets will be able to buy things they cannot afford to buy at other stores. My own observations show that many items at a local Walmart are

T E S **T**

- Topic Sentence
- Evidence
- Summary Statement
- Transitions

cheaper than those at other stores. Not all of Walmart's effects are positive, however. One negative effect Walmart can have is that it can actually lower wages in an area. My aunt, a longtime employee, says that Walmart pays beginning workers between $8 and $10 an hour. This is less than they would get in stores that pay union wages. Another negative effect Walmart can have is to drive other, smaller businesses out. When Walmart comes into an area, many small businesses are forced to close. They just cannot match Walmart's prices or selection of merchandise. It is clear that although Walmart can have a number of positive effects, it can also have some negative ones.

TEST · Revise · Edit

Look back at your response to the Write First activity on page 109. Using the TEST checklist on page 119, evaluate your cause-and-effect paragraph to make sure it includes a topic sentence, evidence, a summary statement, and transitions. Then, prepare a revised and edited draft of your paragraph.

8c Step-by-Step Guide: Writing a Cause-and-Effect Paragraph

Choose one of the topics below (or choose your own topic) for a paragraph that examines causes or effects. Then, use one or more of the strategies described in 2c to help you think of as many causes or effects as you can for the topic you have chosen.

Why a current television show or movie is so popular
Some causes (or effects) of stress
The negative health effects of junk food
Why some college students engage in binge drinking
The reasons you decided to attend college
The effects of a particular government policy
How becoming a vegetarian might change (or has changed) your life
The benefits of home cooking
Why a particular sport is popular
How an important event in your life influenced you
The possible effects of violent song lyrics on teenagers
The problems of social networking sites
Why some people find writing difficult
The major reasons that high school or college students drop out of school
How managers can get the best (or the worst) from their employees

PRACTICE 8-4 Review your notes on the topic you chose, and create a cluster diagram. Write your topic in the center of the page, and draw arrows branching out to specific causes or effects.

PRACTICE 8-5 Choose a few of the most important causes or effects from the cluster diagram you made in Practice 8-4, and list them on the lines below.

Answers will vary.

_____

_____

_____

_____

_____

PRACTICE 8-6 Reread your list of causes or effects from Practice 8-5. Then, draft a topic sentence that introduces your topic and communicates the point you will make about it.

Answers will vary.

_____

_____

_____

PRACTICE 8-7 List the causes or effects you will discuss in your paragraph, arranging them in an effective order—for example, from least to most important.

1. *Answers will vary.* _____

2. _____

3. _____

4. _____

PRACTICE 8-8 Draft your cause-and-effect paragraph. Then, using the **TEST** checklist on page 119, check your paragraph for unity, support, and coherence.

PRACTICE
8-9 Revise your cause-and-effect paragraph.

PRACTICE
8-10 Prepare a final edited draft of your cause-and-effect paragraph.

TESTing a cause-and-effect paragraph

Topic Sentence Unifies Your Paragraph

☐ Do you have a clearly worded **topic sentence** that states your paragraph's main idea?

☐ Does your topic sentence identify the cause or effect on which your paragraph will focus?

Evidence Supports Your Paragraph's Topic Sentence

☐ Do you need to add any important causes or effects?

☐ Do you need to explain your causes or effects in more detail?

☐ Does all your **evidence**—details and examples—support your paragraph's main idea?

Summary Statement Reinforces Your Paragraph's Unity

☐ Does your paragraph end with a **summary statement** that reinforces your main idea?

Transitions Add Coherence to Your Paragraph

☐ Do your **transitions** show how your ideas are related?

☐ Do your transitions clearly introduce each cause or effect?

☐ Do you need to add transitions to make your paragraph clearer and to help readers follow your ideas?

8d   Writing about Visuals

The picture below shows a homeless man with a winning lottery ticket. Write a cause-and-effect paragraph in which you discuss the ways in which this man's life might change now that he has won the lottery. Try to consider negative as well as positive effects. Follow the process outlined in the Step-by-Step Guide on pages 117–19.

9 Comparison and Contrast

preview

In this chapter, you will learn to write a comparison-and-contrast paragraph.

write first

These two pictures are from *Red Carpet Fashion Awards*, a Web site that tracks the latest in celebrity fashion trends. Look at the two pictures, and then write a paragraph in which *you* decide "who wore it better," Liv Tyler (left) or Chloë Sevigny (right).

reflect

Look at the paragraph you wrote for the Write First activity on page 121, and then do the following:

1. **Reread**
   - Does your paragraph focus on how the two pictured outfits are different?
   - Does your paragraph begin with a topic sentence that clearly states its main idea—which woman wore the outfit better, and why?
   - Do you include examples and details to explain why one woman's outfit looks better than the other's?

2. **Discuss**
   Work with another student to consider the strengths and weaknesses of your comparison-and-contrast paragraphs. Do you think one works better than the other? If so, why?

3. **Sum up**
   Based on your reactions to the paragraphs you and your classmate wrote, what do you think an effective comparison-and-contrast paragraph should do?

9a Comparison-and-Contrast Paragraphs

When you buy something—for example, a hair dryer, a smartphone, a computer, or a car—you often comparison-shop, looking at various models to determine how they are alike and how they are different. In other words, you *compare and contrast*. When you **compare**, you consider how things are similar. When you **contrast**, you consider how they are different. A **comparison-and-contrast paragraph** can examine just similarities, just differences, or both similarities and differences.

When you **TEST** a comparison-and-contrast paragraph, make sure it follows these guidelines:

T ▪ A comparison-and-contrast paragraph should begin with a **topic sentence** that tells readers whether the paragraph is going to discuss similarities, differences, or both. The topic sentence should also make clear the main point of the comparison—why you are comparing or contrasting the two subjects (for example, "The writers Toni Morrison and Maya Angelou have similar ideas about race and society" or "My parents and I have different ideas about success").

E ▪ A comparison-and-contrast paragraph should include points that support the topic sentence. These points must be supported by enough **evidence**—examples and details—to make them clear and convincing to readers. A comparison-and-contrast paragraph should discuss the same or similar points for both subjects, one by one. Points should be arranged in **logical order**—for example, from least important to most important.

S ▪ A comparison-and-contrast paragraph should end with a **summary statement** that reinforces the paragraph's main idea.

T ▪ A comparison-and-contrast paragraph should include **transitions** that connect the two subjects being compared and link the points you make about each subject.

Teaching Tip
Refer students to 16f for information on writing a comparison-and-contrast essay.

There are two kinds of comparison-and-contrast paragraphs: *subject-by-subject comparisons* and *point-by-point comparisons*.

Subject-by-Subject Comparisons

In a **subject-by-subject comparison**, you divide your comparison into two parts and discuss one subject at a time. In the first part of the paragraph, you discuss all your points about one subject. Then, in the second part, you discuss the same (or similar) points about the other subject. (In each part of the paragraph, you discuss the points in the same order.)

A subject-by-subject comparison is best for paragraphs in which you do not discuss too many points. In this situation, readers will have little difficulty remembering the points you discuss for the first subject when you move on to discuss the second subject.

Paragraph Map: Subject-by-Subject Comparison

Topic Sentence

Subject A
Point #1

Point #2

Point #3

Subject B
Point #1

Point #2

Point #3

Summary Statement

T E S T

- Topic Sentence
- Evidence
- Summary Statement
- Transitions

Model Paragraph: Subject-by-Subject Comparison

The writer of the following paragraph uses a subject-by-subject comparison to compare two places to eat on campus.

Eating on Campus

Subject A: Eating in the school cafeteria

Subject B: Eating at the food trucks

Food trucks are a good alternative to the campus cafeteria. Eating in the cafeteria takes a lot of time. Students have to go into a building, wait in line, walk down some stairs, and find a table. In addition, the cafeteria usually has a limited variety of food, with only two or three different hot meals and some prepackaged sandwiches. The food is cooked in advance, and after sitting on a steam tray for a few hours, it is dry and lukewarm. Finally, food in the cafeteria costs a lot. Students who are not on a food plan can easily spend seven or eight dollars for dinner. In contrast, the food trucks are much quicker than the cafeteria. Most food trucks serve a meal in less than five minutes. If the weather is nice, students can sit anywhere on campus and eat. In addition, the food trucks offer a lot of choice. Some of the trucks, such as the ones that sell Chinese food, even sell platters. In addition, the food from the trucks is fresh and hot most of the time. Finally, meals from a food truck usually cost less than five dollars. This is a big savings, especially if a student is on a tight budget. For this reason, the food trucks are often a better choice than the cafeteria.

—Dan Lindt (student)

Point-by-Point Comparisons

When you write a **point-by-point comparison**, you discuss a point about one subject and then discuss the same point for the second subject. You use this alternating pattern throughout the paragraph.

A point-by-point comparison is a better strategy for long paragraphs in which you discuss many points. It is also a better choice if the points you are discussing are technical or complicated. Because you compare the two subjects one point at a time, readers will be able to see one point of comparison before moving on to the next point.

Paragraph Map: Point-by-Point Comparison

Topic Sentence

Point #1

    Subject A

    Subject B

> **Point #2**
>> Subject A
>>
>> Subject B
>
> **Point #3**
>> Subject A
>>
>> Subject B
>
> **Summary Statement**

Model Paragraph: Point-by-Point Comparison

In the following paragraph, the writer uses a point-by-point-comparison to compare baseball and football.

Baseball versus Football

After being a fan for years, I understand how different baseball and football are. First, football is violent, and baseball is not. In football, the object is to tackle a person on the other team. The harder the hit, the better the tackle. In baseball, however, violence is not the object of the game. If a player gets hurt, it is usually an accident, such as when two players run into each other. Next, the words used to describe each game are different. The language of football is the language of war: linemen "blitz," quarterbacks throw "bombs," tacklers "crush" receivers, and games end in "sudden death" overtimes. The language of baseball, however, is peaceful: hitters "sacrifice," runners "slide," and pitchers throw "curves" or "sliders." Finally, the pace of each game is different. Football is played against the clock. When the clock runs out, the game is over. Unlike a football game, a baseball game does not end until nine innings are played or a tie is broken. Theoretically, a game could go on forever. Therefore, even though football and baseball are so different, I like them both.

— Deniz Bilgutay (student)

Point 1: Level of violence

Point 2: Language used to describe games

Point 3: Pace of games

Transitions in Comparison-and-Contrast Paragraphs

Transitions are important in a comparison-and-contrast paragraph. Transitions tell readers when you are changing from one point (or one subject) to another. Transitions also make your paragraph more coherent by showing readers whether you are focusing on similarities (for example, *likewise* or *similarly*) or differences (for example, *although* or *in contrast*).

Some Transitional Words and Phrases for Comparison and Contrast

although	one difference . . . another difference
but	one similarity . . . another similarity
even though	on the contrary
however	on the one hand . . . on the other hand
in comparison	similarly
in contrast	though
like	unlike
likewise	whereas
nevertheless	

---

grammar in context

Comparison and Contrast

When you write a comparison-and-contrast paragraph, you should state the points you are comparing in **parallel** terms to highlight their similarities or differences.

NOT PARALLEL First, football is violent, and violence isn't seen very often in baseball.

PARALLEL First, football is violent, and baseball is not.

For more information on revising to make ideas parallel, see Chapter 22.

Teaching Tip
Before your students write comparison-and-contrast paragraphs, you might want to explain the concept of parallelism (Chapter 22) and have them do Practices 22-1 and 22-2.

Analyzing a Comparison-and-Contrast Paragraph

Read this comparison-and-contrast paragraph; then, follow the instructions in Practice 9-1.

Virtual and Traditional Classrooms

Taking a course online is very different from taking a course in a traditional classroom. One difference is that students in an online course have more flexibility than students in a traditional course. They can do their schoolwork at any time, scheduling it around other commitments, such as jobs and childcare. Students in a traditional course, however, must go to class at a specific time and place. (Another difference is) that students in an online course can feel isolated from the teacher and other students because they never actually come into physical contact with them. Students in a traditional classroom, however, are able to connect with the teacher and their classmates because they interact with them in person. (A final difference is) that in an online course, students use email or a discussion board to discuss course material. A student who is a slow typist or whose Internet connection is unreliable is clearly at a disadvantage. In a traditional course, most of the discussion takes place in the classroom, so technology is not an issue. <u>Because online and traditional courses are so different, students must think carefully about which type of course best fits their needs.</u>

—William Hernandez (student)

PRACTICE 9-1

1. Underline the topic sentence of the paragraph above.

2. Does this paragraph deal mainly with similarities or differences?

   <u>differences</u>   How do you know? <u>The author uses transitions that show differences,</u>
   <u>such as "one difference" and "however."</u>

3. Is this paragraph a subject-by-subject or point-by-point comparison?

   <u>point-by-point</u> How do you know? <u>The author alternates between subjects,</u>
   <u>discussing one point at a time.</u>

4. List some of the contrasts the writer describes. The first contrast has been listed for you.

   <u>When it comes to their schedules, students in an online course have more flexibility</u>
   <u>than students in a traditional course do.</u>

   <u>Students in an online course may feel isolated, whereas students in a traditional</u>
   <u>classroom are able to connect with the teacher and other students because they</u>
   <u>meet with them in person.</u>

   <u>In an online course, students may have to deal with technology, whereas students</u>
   <u>in a traditional course do not.</u>

5. Circle the transitional words and phrases the writer uses to move from one point of comparison to the next.

6. Underline the paragraph's summary statement.

PRACTICE 9-2 Following are three topic sentences. Copy the topic sentences on a separate sheet of paper. Then, list three or four similarities or differences between the two subjects in each topic sentence. For example, if you were writing a paragraph comparing health care provided by a local clinic with health care provided by a private doctor, you could discuss the cost, the length of waiting time, the quality of care, and the frequency of follow-up visits. *Answers will vary.*

1. My mother (or father) and I are very different (or alike).

2. My friends and I have different views on _____.

3. Two of my college instructors have very different teaching styles.

9b Case Study: A Student Writes a Comparison-and-Contrast Paragraph

When Jermond Love was asked to write a comparison-and-contrast paragraph for his composition class, he began by brainstorming to find a topic that he could write about. When he reviewed his brainstorming notes, he came up with the following topics.

Football and soccer

Fast food and home cooking

The difference between my brother and me

Life in Saint Croix versus life in the United States

Jermond decided that he would write about the differences between life in New York City and life in Saint Croix, the Caribbean island where he was raised. He listed a few subjects that he thought he could compare and contrast. Then, he crossed out the ones he didn't want to write about.

Size

Population

~~Economy~~

Friendliness

~~Businesses~~

Lifestyle

Teaching Tip
Tell students that before two things can be compared, they need to have a **basis for comparison**: the items need to have enough in common so that a comparison is logical. For example, you could not compare people and apples (they have nothing in common). You could, however, compare people and chimpanzees—both are mammals, both live in complex social groups, and both are capable of communication.

After brainstorming some more, Jermond listed the points he could discuss for each of his four subjects. He began with basic information and then moved on to the idea he wanted to emphasize: the different lifestyles.

Size

    Saint Croix

        Small size

        Small population

        Christiansted and Frederiksted

    New York

        Large size

        Large population

        Five boroughs

Lifestyle

    Saint Croix

        Laid-back

        Friendly

    New York

        In a hurry

        Not always friendly

Jermond thought that a point-by-point organization would be easier for his readers to follow than a subject-by-subject organization. With this organization, readers would be able to keep track of his comparison as he discussed each of his points, one at a time.

Here is the first draft of Jermond's paragraph.

> Life in Saint Croix is very different from life in New York City. Saint Croix is much smaller than New York City. Saint Croix has a total population of about 60,000 people. The two main towns are Christiansted and Frederiksted. New York City is very large. Its residents are crowded into five boroughs. The lifestyle in Saint Croix is different from the lifestyle of New York City. In Saint Croix, almost everyone operates on "island time." Everyone is friendly. People don't see any point in getting anyone upset. In New York City, most people are always in a hurry. They don't take the time to slow down and enjoy life. As a result, people can seem unfriendly. They don't take the time to get to know anyone. I hope when I graduate I can stay in New York City but visit my home in Saint Croix whenever I can.

Jermond put his paragraph aside for a day and then reread it. Although he was generally satisfied with what he had written, he thought that it could be better. To help students revise their paragraphs, his instructor divided students into peer-review groups and asked them to read and discuss each other's paragraphs. After working with a classmate on his draft and **TEST**ing his paragraph, Jermond made the following decisions.

Teaching Tip
Refer students to 2i and 13i for more information on peer review.

■ He decided that his **topic sentence** was clear and specific.

■ He saw that he needed more **evidence**—details to help his readers understand the differences between his two subjects. Would readers know the location of Saint Croix? Would they know the population of Christiansted and Frederiksted? Would they know what he meant by "island time"?

■ He decided to change his **summary statement** because it didn't really reinforce the idea in his topic sentence.

■ Finally, he decided that he needed to add **transitional words and phrases** that would show when he was moving from one subject to another.

Teaching Tip
Refer students to 2i and 2j for information on revising and editing their paragraphs.

After TESTing his paragraph, Jermond revised and edited it, adding background about Saint Croix. (The classmate who read his draft had pointed out that many people in the class would not know anything about it.)

The final draft below includes all the elements Jermond looked for when he TESTed his paragraph.

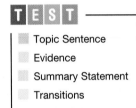

Topic Sentence
Evidence
Summary Statement
Transitions

Saint Croix versus the United States

Life in Saint Croix is very different from life in New York City. One difference between Saint Croix and New York is that Saint Croix is much smaller than New York. Saint Croix, the largest of the United States Virgin Islands, has a population of about 60,000. The two main towns on the island are Christiansted, with a population of about 3,000, and Frederiksted, with a population of only about 830. Unlike Saint Croix, New York City is large. It has a population of over 8 million crowded into the five boroughs of Manhattan, Brooklyn, the Bronx, Queens, and Staten Island. My neighborhood in Brooklyn is more than twice the size of Christiansted and Frederiksted combined. Another difference between Saint Croix and New York City is their lifestyles. Life in Saint Croix is slower than life in New York. In Saint Croix, almost everyone operates on "island time." Things get done, but people don't rush to do them. When workers say "later," they can mean "this afternoon," "tomorrow," or even "next week." No one seems to mind, as long as the job gets done. People don't see any point in getting anyone upset. In New York, however, most people are always in a hurry. They don't take the time to slow down and enjoy life. Everything is fast—fast food, fast cars, fast Internet access. As a result, people can seem unfriendly. Although Saint Croix and New York City are so different, life is interesting in both places.

TEST · **Revise · Edit**

Look back at your response to the Write First activity on page 121. Using the TEST checklist on page 133, evaluate your comparison-and-contrast paragraph to make sure it includes a topic sentence, evidence, a summary statement, and transitions. Then, prepare a revised and edited draft of your paragraph.

9c Step-by-Step Guide: Writing a Comparison-and-Contrast Paragraph

Choose one of the topics below (or choose your own topic) for a paragraph exploring similarities or differences between two subjects. Then, use one or more of the strategies described in 2c to help you think of as many similarities and differences as you can for the two subjects you have chosen. (If you decide to use clustering, create a separate cluster diagram for each of the two subjects you are comparing.)

Teaching Tip
Refer students to 2c for more on clustering as well as information on other strategies for finding ideas.

Two popular television personalities or radio talk-show hosts
Two books or graphic novels that you have read
Two cars you could consider buying
How you act in two different situations (at home and at work, for example) or with two different sets of people (such as your family and your professors)
Living in the city versus living in the country (or in a small town)
Two Web sites
Men's and women's attitudes toward dating, shopping, or conversation
A movie compared to its sequel
Public school education versus home schooling
Two competing consumer items, such as two different smartphones, two computer systems, or two video game systems
Two cultures' attitudes toward dating and marriage
Two different kinds of vacations
Two generations' attitudes toward a particular issue or subject (for example, how people in their forties and people in their teens view religion, technology, or politics)

PRACTICE
9-3

Review your notes on the topic you chose, and decide whether to focus on similarities or differences. On the following lines, list the similarities or differences that can best help you develop a comparison-and-contrast paragraph on the topic you have selected.

Answers will vary.

_____

_____

_____

_____

_____

PRACTICE
9-4

Reread your list of similarities or differences from Practice 9-3. Then, draft a topic sentence that introduces your two subjects and indicates whether your paragraph will focus on similarities or on differences.

Answers will vary.

_____

_____

_____

PRACTICE

9-5   Decide whether you will write a subject-by-subject or a point-by-point comparison. Then, use the appropriate outline below to help you plan your paragraph. Before you begin, decide on the order in which you will present your points—for example, from least important to most important. (For a subject-by-subject comparison, begin by deciding which subject you will discuss first.)

Subject-by-Subject Comparison

Subject A _Answers will vary._____

    Point 1 _____

    Point 2 _____

    Point 3 _____

    Point 4 _____

Subject B _Answers will vary._____

    Point 1 _____

    Point 2 _____

    Point 3 _____

    Point 4 _____

Point-by-Point Comparison

Point 1 _Answers will vary._____

    Subject A _____

    Subject B _____

Point 2 _Answers will vary._____

    Subject A _____

    Subject B _____

Point 3 _Answers will vary._____

    Subject A _____

    Subject B _____

Point 4 _Answers will vary._____

    Subject A _____

    Subject B _____

PRACTICE
9-6 Draft your comparison-and-contrast paragraph. Then, using the **TEST** checklist below, check your paragraph for unity, support, and coherence.

PRACTICE
9-7 Revise your comparison-and-contrast paragraph.

PRACTICE
9-8 Prepare a final edited draft of your comparison-and-contrast paragraph.

ESL Tip
Pay special attention to students' sentence structure and to their use of articles and prepositions. You may also want to spot-check verb forms and offer specific explanations or solutions. These areas often cause difficulties for nonnative speakers.

TESTing a comparison-and-contrast paragraph

Topic Sentence Unifies Your Paragraph

☐ Do you have a clearly worded **topic sentence** that states your paragraph's main idea?

☐ Does your topic sentence indicate whether you are focusing on similarities or on differences?

Evidence Supports Your Paragraph's Topic Sentence

☐ Does all your **evidence**—examples and details—support your paragraph's main idea?

☐ Do your examples and details show how your two subjects are alike or different?

☐ Do you need to discuss additional similarities or differences?

Summary Statement Reinforces Your Paragraph's Unity

☐ Does your paragraph end with a **summary statement** that reinforces your main idea?

Transitions Add Coherence to Your Paragraph

☐ Do your **transitions** indicate whether you are focusing on similarities or on differences?

☐ Do transitional words and phrases lead readers from one subject or point to the next?

☐ Do you need to add transitions to make your paragraph clearer and to help readers follow your ideas?

9d Writing about Visuals

The pictures below show two famous war memorials. Study the two photographs carefully, and then write a paragraph in which you compare them, considering both what the monuments look like and their emotional impact on you. Follow the process outlined in the Step-by-Step Guide on pages 131–33.

Iwo Jima memorial statue near Arlington National Cemetery

Vietnam Veterans Memorial in Washington, D.C.

10 Classification

preview

In this chapter, you will learn to write a classification paragraph.

write first

This picture shows fans at a baseball game. Look at the picture, and then discuss the various types of fans you might see at a particular sporting event—for example, those who concentrate on the game, those who wave signs and banners, and those who wear costumes or team gear.

reflect

Look at the paragraph you wrote for the Write First activity on page 135, and then do the following:

1. **Reread**
   - Does your paragraph focus on the different types of fans you see at a particular sporting event?
   - Does your paragraph begin with a topic sentence that identifies the sporting event you will discuss and clearly states the main idea—the point you make about the fans you are describing?
   - Do you include examples of the types of fans you are discussing?
   - Do you include enough detail to show how each category of fan is different from the others?

2. **Discuss**
   Work with another student to consider the strengths and weaknesses of your classification paragraphs. Do you think one works better than the other? If so, why?

3. **Sum up**
   Based on your reactions to the paragraphs you and your classmate wrote, what do you think an effective classification paragraph should do?

10a Classification Paragraphs

Teaching Tip
To help students understand classification, give them lists of different musical groups, foods, sports figures, and so on. Ask them to classify the items on each list. (Each list should contain at least twenty items.)

Teaching Tip
Refer students to 16g for information on writing a classi-fication essay.

When you **classify**, you sort items (people, things, ideas) into categories or groups. You classify when you organize bills into those you have to pay now and those you can pay later, or when you sort the clothes in a dresser drawer into piles of socks, T-shirts, and underwear.

In a **classification paragraph**, you tell readers how items can be sorted into categories or groups. Each category must be **distinct**. In other words, none of the items in one category should also fit into another category. For example, you would not classify novels into mysteries, romances, and e-books, because both mystery novels and romance novels could also be e-books.

When you **TEST** a classification paragraph, make sure it follows these guidelines:

T ■ A classification paragraph should begin with a **topic sentence** that introduces the subject of the paragraph. It may also identify the categories you will discuss (for example, "Before you go camping, you should sort the items you are thinking of packing into three categories: absolutely necessary, potentially helpful, and not really necessary").

E ■ A classification paragraph should discuss one category at a time. Your discussion of each category should include enough **evidence**—details and examples—to show how it is distinct from the other categories.

The categories should be arranged in **logical order**—for example, from least important to most important or from smallest to largest.

[S] ■ A classification paragraph should end with a **summary statement** that reinforces the paragraph's main idea.

[T] ■ A classification paragraph should include **transitions** to introduce the categories you discuss and connect them to one another and to the topic sentence.

Paragraph Map: Classification

Topic Sentence

Category #1

Category #2

Category #3

Summary Statement

> **Teaching Tip**
> If you think students are ready, tell them that before they classify information, they must decide on a **principle of classification**. For example, cars can be classified according to their degree of safety, and people can be classified according to their political beliefs.

> **ESL Tip**
> Have students copy this student paragraph. Tell them to read aloud as they write each sentence.

Model Paragraph: Classification

The writer of the following paragraph classifies his friends into three groups.

T E S T
- Topic Sentence
- Evidence
- Summary Statement
- Transitions

Categories of Friends

My friends can be classified into three groups: those who know what they want out of life, those who don't have a clue, and those who are still searching for goals. Friends in the first category, those who know what they want, are the most mature. They know exactly what they want to do for the rest of their lives. For this reason, they are the most predictable and the most reliable. — *First category of friend*

They are also the most boring. Friends in the second category, those who don't have a clue, are the most immature. If there is a party the night before a test, they will go to the party and try to study when they get back. Although these friends can be a bad influence, they are the most fun. — *Second category of friend*

Friends in the last category, those who are searching for goals, are somewhere between the other two types when it comes to maturity. They do not know exactly what they want to do with their lives, but they are trying to find a goal. These friends can be unpredictable, but their willingness to try new things makes them the most interesting. Even though my three groups of friends are completely different, I like all of them. — *Third category of friend*

—Daniel Corey (student)

Transitions in Classification Paragraphs

Transitions are important in a classification paragraph. They tell readers when you are moving from one category to another (for example, *the first type, the second type*). They can also indicate which categories you think are more important than others (for example, *the most important, the least important*).

Some Transitional Words and Phrases for Classification

one kind . . . another kind	the first group . . . the last group
one way . . . another way	the first type . . . the second type
the first (second, third) category	the most (or least) important group
	the next part

grammar in context

Classification

When you write a classification paragraph, you may list the categories you are going to discuss. If you use a **colon** to introduce your list, make sure that a complete sentence comes before the colon.

INCORRECT My friends can be divided into: those who know what they want out of life, those who don't have a clue, and those who are still searching for goals.

CORRECT My friends can be divided into three groups: those who know what they want out of life, those who don't have a clue, and those who are still searching for goals.

For more information on how to use a colon to introduce a list, see 36g.

Analyzing a Classification Paragraph

Read this classification paragraph; then, follow the instructions in Practice 10-1.

Three Kinds of Shoppers

Shoppers can be put into three categories: practical, recreational, and professional. The first category is made up of practical shoppers, those who shop because they need something. Practical shoppers go right to the item they are looking for in the store and then leave. They do not waste time browsing or walking aimlessly from store to store. The next category is made up of recreational shoppers, those who shop for entertainment. For them, shopping is like going to the movies or out to dinner. They do it because it is fun. They will spend hours walking through stores looking at merchandise. More often than not, they will not buy anything. For recreational shoppers, it is the activity of shopping that counts, not the purchase itself. The third category is made up of professional shoppers, those who shop because they have to. For them, shopping is a serious business. You can see them in the mall, carrying four, five, or even six bags. Whenever you walk through a mall, you will see all three types of shoppers.

—Kimberley Toomer (student)

PRACTICE
10-1

1. Underline the topic sentence of the paragraph above.

2. What is the subject of the paragraph? *kinds of shoppers*

3. What three categories does the writer describe?

   practical shoppers

   recreational shoppers

   professional shoppers

4. Circle the transitional words and phrases the writer uses to introduce the three categories.

5. Underline the paragraph's summary statement.

PRACTICE
10-2

List items in each of the following groups, then sort the items into three or four categories.

1. All the items on your desk

   Answers will vary.

   Categories: _____

2. Buildings on your college campus

   Answers will vary.

   Categories: _____

3. Web sites you visit

Answers will vary.

_____

_____

_____

Categories: _____

4. The various parts of a piece of equipment you use for a course or on the job

Answers will vary.

_____

_____

_____

Categories: _____

10b Case Study: A Student Writes a Classification Paragraph

For a college composition course, Corey Levin participated in a service-learning project at a local Ronald McDonald House, a charity that houses families of seriously ill children receiving treatment at nearby hospitals. He met several professional athletes there and was surprised to learn that many of them regularly donate time and money to charity.

When Corey was asked by his composition instructor to write a paragraph about what he had learned from his experience, he decided to write a paragraph that classified the ways in which professional athletes give back to their communities. To find ideas to write about, he jotted down the following list of categories.

Starting charitable foundations

Guidance

Responding to emergencies

Corey then listed examples under each of the three categories.

Foundations
    Michael Jordan
    Troy Aikman

Guidance
    Shaquille O'Neal
    The Philadelphia 76ers

Responding to emergencies
    Ike Reese
    Vince Carter

After completing this informal outline, Corey drafted a topic sentence for his paragraph: "High-profile athletes find many ways to give back to their communities." Then, using his informal outline as a guide, Corey wrote the following draft of his paragraph.

High-profile athletes find many ways to give back to their communities. Many athletes as well as teams do a lot to help people. I met some of them when I volunteered at the Ronald McDonald House. For example, Michael Jordan and the Chicago Bulls built a Boys' and Girls' Club on Chicago's West Side. Troy Aikman set up a foundation that builds playgrounds for children's hospitals. Shaquille O'Neal's Shaq's Paq provides guidance for inner-city children. The Philadelphia 76ers visit schools and have donated over five thousand books to local libraries. Ike Reese, formerly with the Atlanta Falcons, collects clothing and food for families that need help. Vince Carter of the Orlando Magic founded the Embassy of Hope Foundation. It distributes food to needy families at Thanksgiving and hosts a Christmas party for disadvantaged families.

Following his instructor's suggestion, Corey emailed his draft to a classmate for feedback. In her email reply to Corey, she made the following suggestions based on the TEST strategy.

- Keep the **topic sentence** the way it is. "Many ways" shows you're writing a classification paragraph.
- Add more specific **evidence**. Give examples of each category of "giving back" to support the topic sentence. You also need to explain the athletes' contributions in more detail.
- Add a **summary statement** to sum up the paragraph's main idea.
- Add **transitions** to introduce the three specific categories you're discussing.

With these comments in mind, Corey revised and edited his paragraph. The final draft below includes all the elements Corey looked for when he TESTed his paragraph.

Giving Back

High-profile athletes find many ways to give back to their communities. One way to give back is to start a charitable foundation to help young fans. For example, Michael Jordan and the Chicago Bulls built a Boys' & Girls' Club on Chicago's West Side. In addition, Troy Aikman set up a foundation that builds playgrounds for children's hospitals. Another way athletes give back to their communities is by mentoring, or giving guidance to young people. Many athletes work to encourage young people to stay in school. Shaquille O'Neal's Shaq's Paq, for example, provides guidance for inner-city children. The Philadelphia 76ers visit schools and have donated over five thousand books to local libraries. One more way athletes can contribute to their communities is to respond to emergencies. Football player Ike Reese, formerly with the Atlanta Falcons, collects clothing and food for families that need help. Basketball player Vince Carter founded the Embassy of Hope Foundation. It distributes food to needy families at Thanksgiving and hosts a Christmas party for disadvantaged families. These are just some of the ways that high-profile athletes give back to their communities.

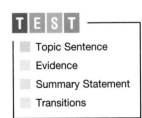

TEST

- Topic Sentence
- Evidence
- Summary Statement
- Transitions

TEST · Revise · Edit

Look back at your response to the Write First activity on page 135. Using the TEST checklist on page 143, evaluate your classification paragraph to make sure it includes a topic sentence, evidence, a summary statement, and transitions. Then, prepare a revised and edited draft of your paragraph.

10c Step-by-Step Guide: Writing a Classification Paragraph

Choose one of the topics below (or choose your own topic). Use one or more of the strategies described in 2c to help you divide the topic you have chosen into categories or classes.

Your friends
Drivers
Commuters on public transportation
Television shows
Employees or bosses
Parents or children
Types of success
Radio stations

Popular music
Fitness routines
Roommates
Part-time jobs
Teachers
Student housing
T-shirt slogans

PRACTICE
10-3 Review the information you came up with for the topic you chose. On the following lines, list three or four categories you can develop in your classification paragraph.

Category 1: _Answers will vary._ _____

Category 2: _____

Category 3: _____

Category 4: _____

PRACTICE
10-4 Reread the list of categories you made in Practice 10-3. Then, draft a topic sentence that introduces your subject and the categories you will discuss.

Answers will vary. _____

_____

_____

PRACTICE
10-5 Arrange the categories you will discuss in your classification paragraph in the order in which you will discuss them.

1. _Answers will vary._ _____

2. _____

3. _____

4. _____

PRACTICE
10-6 Draft your classification paragraph. Then, using the TEST checklist below, check your paragraph for unity, support, and coherence.

PRACTICE
10-7 Revise your classification paragraph.

PRACTICE
10-8 Prepare a final edited draft of your classification paragraph.

ESL Tip
You may want to pair non-native and native speakers to review their work in Practice 10-7. Have them use the TEST checklist as a guide.

Teaching Tip
Refer students to 2i and 2j for information on revising and editing their paragraphs.

TESTing a classification paragraph

T opic Sentence Unifies Your Paragraph

☐ Do you have a clearly worded **topic sentence** that states your paragraph's main idea?

☐ Does your topic sentence identify the categories you will discuss?

E vidence Supports Your Paragraph's Topic Sentence

☐ Does all your **evidence**—examples and details—support your paragraph's main idea?

☐ Do your examples and details indicate how each category is distinct from the others?

☐ Do you need to include more examples or details?

S ummary Statement Reinforces Your Paragraph's Unity

☐ Does your paragraph end with a **summary statement** that reinforces your main idea?

T ransitions Add Coherence to Your Paragraph

☐ Do your **transitions** clearly indicate which categories are more important than others?

☐ Do you need to add transitions to make your paragraph clearer and to help readers follow your ideas?

10d   Writing about Visuals

The picture below shows one way of classifying food: according to the kinds (and amounts) of food we need to eat for optimal nutrition. Look at the photo, and think about all the kinds of food you eat in a typical week. Then, write a paragraph in which you classify the foods you eat. The categories you create can classify the food according to such things as convenience, country of origin, ease of preparation, healthfulness, or where it is consumed. Follow the process outlined in the Step-by-Step Guide on pages 142–43.

11 Definition

preview

In this chapter, you will learn to write a definition paragraph.

Vegan (vē′gən) n.

A vegan is someone who tries to live without exploiting animals, for the benefit of animals, people and the planet.

Vegans eat a plant-based diet, with nothing coming from animals; no meat, fish, milk, eggs or honey.

Vegan lifestyle avoids leather, wool, silk & other animal products for clothing or any other purpose as much as possible.

write first

Read the definition of the word *vegan* printed on this shopping bag, and consider how it could be developed further. Then, write a one-paragraph definition of a word you learned in one of your college courses. Assume that your readers are not familiar with the term you are defining.

reflect

Look at the paragraph you wrote for the Write First activity on page 145, and then do the following:

1. **Reread**
   - Does your paragraph focus on the word you are going to define?
   - Does your paragraph begin with a topic sentence that identifies the word you define and clearly states your main idea—the central point you are going to make about the word?
   - Do you include examples and details to develop your definition?

2. **Discuss**
   Work with another student to consider the strengths and weaknesses of your definition paragraphs. Do you think one works better than the other? If so, why?

3. **Sum up**
   Based on your reactions to the paragraphs you and your classmate wrote, what do you think an effective definition paragraph should do?

11a Definition Paragraphs

During a conversation, you might say that a friend is stubborn, that a stream is polluted, or that a neighborhood is dangerous. In order to make yourself clear, you have to define what you mean by *stubborn*, *polluted*, or *dangerous*. Like conversations, academic assignments also may involve definition. In a history paper, for example, you might have to define *imperialism*; on a biology exam, you might be asked to define *mitosis*.

A **definition** tells what a word means. When you want your readers to know exactly how you are using a specific term, you define it.

When most people think of definitions, they think of the **formal definitions** they see in a dictionary. Formal definitions have a three-part structure.

- The term to be defined
- The general class to which the term belongs
- The things that make the term different from all other items in the general class to which the term belongs

TERM	CLASS	DIFFERENTIATION
Ice hockey	is a game	played on ice by two teams on skates who use curved sticks to try to hit a puck into the opponent's goal.
Spaghetti	is a pasta	made in the shape of long, thin strands.

A single-sentence formal definition is often not enough to define a specialized term (*point of view* or *premeditation*, for example), an abstract concept (*happiness* or *success*, for example), or a complicated subject (*stem-cell research*, for example). In these cases, you may need to expand the basic formal definition by writing a definition paragraph. In fact, a **definition paragraph** is an expanded formal definition.

When you TEST a definition paragraph, make sure it follows these guidelines:

T ▪ A definition paragraph should begin with a formal definition and then state the main idea in the **topic sentence**.

E ▪ A definition paragraph does not follow any one pattern of development; in fact, it may define a term by using any of the patterns discussed in this text. For example, a definition paragraph may explain a concept by *comparing* it to something else or by giving *examples*. For this reason, your discussion of each category should include **evidence**—details and examples—that is appropriate for the pattern of development that you use.

S ▪ A definition paragraph should end with a **summary statement** that reinforces the paragraph's main idea.

T ▪ A definition paragraph should include **transitions** that are appropriate for the pattern or patterns of organization you use.

Here is one possible structure for a definition paragraph. Notice that this paragraph uses a combination of **narration** and **exemplification**.

Paragraph Map: Definition

Topic Sentence

Point #1
　　Narrative

Point #2
　　Example

　　Example

Point #3
　　Example

　　Example

Summary Statement

Model Paragraph: Definition

The writer of the following paragraph uses narration and exemplification to define the term *business casual*.

Business Casual

Narrative ⎡
⎣

Examples of men's ⎡
business casual ⎣

Examples of women's ⎡
business casual ⎣

> Business casual means dressing comfortably but looking professional. Until recently, men and women dressed formally for work. For example, men wore dark suits and plain ties while women wore dark jackets and skirts. In the 1990s, however, the rise of technology companies in Silicon Valley made popular a new style of work attire, called *business casual*. Today, business casual is the accepted form of dress in most businesses. For men, this usually means wearing a collared shirt with no tie and khaki pants, sometimes with a sports jacket and loafers. For women, it means wearing a skirt or pants with a blouse or collared shirt. Women can wear low heels or flats. High-tech companies can be even more informal. They may even allow employees to wear jeans and T-shirts to work. While business casual may be the new norm, every company has its own standards for what is acceptable.

—Chase Durbin (student)

T E S T

░ Topic Sentence
░ Evidence
░ Summary Statement
░ Transitions

Transitions in Definition Paragraphs

Transitions are important for definition paragraphs. In the paragraph above, the transitional words and phrases *until recently, in the 1990s*, and *today* tell readers when they are moving from one narrative event to another. The transitional phrases *for men* and *for women* introduce examples.

The following box lists some of the transitional words and phrases that are frequently used in definition paragraphs. You can also use the transitional words and phrases associated with the specific pattern (or patterns) that you use to develop your paragraph.

Some Transitional Words and Phrases for Definition

also	often
for example	one characteristic . . . another
for men (for women)	characteristic
however	one way . . . another way
in addition	sometimes
in particular	specifically
in the 1990s (or another time)	the first kind . . . the second kind
like	until recently

grammar in context

Definition

A definition paragraph often includes a formal definition of the term or concept you are going to discuss. When you write your formal definition, be careful not to use the phrases *is where* or *is when*.

                    dressing   *looking*

Business casual is ~~when you dress~~ comfortably but ~~look~~

professional.

Analyzing a Definition Paragraph

Read this definition paragraph; then, follow the instructions in Practice 11-1.

Loans That Change Lives

Microloans are small loans given to people who live in extreme poverty. The idea for such loans originated in 1974, when a Bangladeshi economist loaned $27 to a group of local women. The women used the loan to purchase bamboo to make furniture. After they sold the furniture, they repaid the loan and kept a small profit for themselves. As a result of this experience, the economist was motivated to create a bank for microloans. Similar microcredit banks now exist throughout the world. For example, microcredit banks can be found in Bosnia, Peru, Ethiopia, and Russia. Microloans are different from ordinary loans because they are not awarded on the basis of credit history or financial means; instead, they are based on trust. A microcredit bank trusts a borrower to make money even if he or she has no or little income at the time of the loan. Some people see microloans as a wonderful opportunity for poor businesspeople; others criticize microloans because they can encourage governments to reduce their support for the poor. Even so, microloans have helped countless people all over the world to lift themselves out of poverty.

PRACTICE

1. Underline the topic sentence of the paragraph above.

2. What is the subject of this definition? *microloans*

3. What is the writer's one-sentence definition of the subject?

   Microloans are small loans given to people who live in extreme poverty.

4. List some of the specific information the writer uses to define his subject. The first piece of information has been listed for you.

   Microloans originated in Bangladesh in 1974.

   Microcredit banks now exist throughout the world—for example, in Bosnia, Peru,

   Ethiopia, and Russia.

   Microloans are based on trust, not credit history or financial means.

5. Circle the transitional words and phrases the writer uses.

6. What patterns of development does the writer use in his definition?
   List them here.

   narration

   exemplification

   comparison and contrast

7. Underline the paragraph's summary statement.

PRACTICE
11-2   Following are four possible topic sentences for definition paragraphs. Each topic sentence includes an underlined word. In
the space provided, list two possible patterns of development that you
could use to develop a definition of the underlined word. For example, you
could define the word *discrimination* by giving examples (exemplification)
and by telling a story (narration).

1. During the interview, the job candidate made a <u>sexist</u> comment.

   Possible strategy: *Answers will vary.*

   Possible strategy: *Answers will vary.*

2. <u>Loyalty</u> is one of the chief characteristics of golden retrievers.

   Possible strategy: *Answers will vary.*

   Possible strategy: *Answers will vary.*

3. More than forty years after President Johnson's Great Society initiative,
   we have yet to eliminate <u>poverty</u> in the United States.

   Possible strategy: *Answers will vary.*

   Possible strategy: *Answers will vary.*

4. The problem with movies today is that they are just too <u>violent</u>.

   Possible strategy: *Answers will vary.*

   Possible strategy: *Answers will vary.*

11b   Case Study: A Student Writes a Definition Paragraph

On a history exam, Lorraine Scipio was asked to write a one-paragraph
definition of the term *imperialism*. Lorraine had studied for the exam, so
she knew what imperialism was. Because she wanted to make sure that
she did not leave anything out of her definition (and because she had a
time limit), she quickly listed her points on the inside front cover of her
exam book. Then, she crossed out two items that did not seem relevant.

A policy of control

Military

~~Lenin~~

Establish empires

Cultural superiority

Raw materials and cheap labor

Africa, etc.

~~Cultural imperialism~~

Nineteenth-century term

Next, Lorraine reorganized her points in the order in which she planned to write about them.

Establish empires

Nineteenth-century term

Cultural superiority

Africa, etc.

Raw materials and cheap labor

A policy of control

Military

Referring to the points on her list, Lorraine wrote the following draft of her definition paragraph. Notice that she uses several different patterns to develop her definition.

> The goal of imperialism is to establish an empire. The imperialist country thinks that it is superior to the country it takes over. It justifies its actions by saying that it is helping the other country. But it isn't. Countries such as Germany, Belgium, Spain, and England have been imperialist in the past. The point of imperialism is to take as much out of the occupied countries as possible. Often, imperialist countries sent troops to occupy other countries and to keep order. As a result, imperialism kept the people in occupied countries in poverty and often broke down local governments and local traditions.

After she finished writing her paragraph, Lorraine reread it quickly, TESTing her paragraph to help her to make sure it answered the exam question. Then, she made the following decisions.

- Because the question asked for a definition, she planned to add a **topic sentence** that included a formal definition.
- She decided to strengthen her **evidence**, explaining her supporting details more fully. She also planned to delete some vague statements that did not support her topic sentence.
- She decided to add **transitional words and phrases** to make the connections between her ideas clearer.
- She decided to add a **summary statement** to reinforce the negative effects of imperialism.

Lorraine made her changes directly on the draft she had written, crossing out unnecessary information and adding missing information. She also edited her paragraph for grammar, punctuation, and mechanical errors. Then, because she had some extra time, she neatly copied over her revised and edited draft.

The final draft of Lorraine's exam answer appears below. (Because this is an exam answer, she does not include a title.) Notice that the final draft includes all the elements Lorraine looked for when she **TEST**ed her paragraph.

T E S T
- Topic Sentence
- Evidence
- Summary Statement
- Transitions

> Imperialism was a nineteenth-century term that referred to the policy by which one country took over the land or the government of another country. The object of imperialism was to establish an empire. The imperialist country thought that it was superior to the country it took over. It justified its actions by saying that it was helping the other country. For instance, countries such as Germany, Belgium, Spain, and England followed their imperialist ambitions in Africa when they claimed large areas of land. The point of imperialism was to take as much out of the occupied countries as possible. For example, in South America and Mexico, Spain removed tons of gold from the areas it occupied. It made the natives slaves and forced them to work in mines. In order to protect their interests, imperialist countries sent troops to occupy the country and to keep order. As a result, imperialism kept the people in occupied countries in poverty and often broke down local governments and local traditions. Although European imperialism occasionally had benefits, at its worst it brought slavery, disease, and death.

FYI

Writing Paragraph Answers on Exams

When you write paragraph answers on exams, you do not have much time to work, so you need to be well prepared. Know your subject well, and memorize important definitions. You may have time to write an outline, a rough draft, and a final draft, but you will have to work quickly. Your final draft should include all the elements of a good paragraph: a topic sentence, supporting details, transitions, and a summary statement.

ESL Tip
During in-class written exams, ESL students need more time than their native-speaking classmates. You may want to encourage ESL students to ask their instructors for more time.

TEST · Revise · Edit

Look back at your response to the Write First activity on page 145. Using the **TEST** checklist on page 154, evaluate your definition paragraph to make sure it includes a topic sentence, evidence, a summary statement, and transitions. Then, prepare a revised and edited draft of your paragraph.

11c Step-by-Step Guide: Writing a Definition Paragraph

Choose one of the topics below (or choose your own topic). Then, use one or more of the strategies described in 2c to help you define the term you have chosen to discuss. Name the term, and then describe it, give examples of it, tell how it works, explain its purpose, consider its history or future, or compare it with other similar things. In short, do whatever works best for defining your subject.

Teaching Tip
Encourage students to choose a topic from one of their other courses. By doing so, they can see how strategies they learn in this course can be applied to other disciplines.

A negative quality, such as envy, dishonesty, or jealousy
An ideal, such as the ideal friend or neighborhood
A type of person, such as a worrier or a show-off
A social concept, such as equality, opportunity, or discrimination
An important play or strategy in a particular sport or game
A hobby you pursue or an activity associated with that hobby
A technical term or specific piece of equipment that you use in your job
An object (such as an article of clothing) that is important to your culture or religion
A basic term in a course you are taking
A particular style of music or dancing
A controversial subject whose definition not all people agree on, such as affirmative action, right to life, or gun control
A goal in life, such as success or happiness

Teaching Tip
If you think your students are ready, point out that you can clarify a definition by negation, by telling what a term is not: Business casual *does not mean being sloppy or dressing inappropriately.*

PRACTICE 11-3 Review your notes for the topic you chose. On the lines below, list the details that can best help you to develop a definition paragraph on that topic.

Answers will vary.

_____

_____

_____

_____

Teaching Tip
Before your students write a definition paragraph, you might want to review the structure for a formal definition, pointing them to page 146.

PRACTICE 11-4 Review the details on the list you made for Practice 11-3. Then, draft a topic sentence that states the main point you want to make about the term you are going to define.

Answers will vary.

_____

_____

PRACTICE 11-5 Arrange the ideas you will discuss in your paragraph in an effective order.

1. _Answers will vary._ _____

2. _____

3. _____

4. _____

5. _____

PRACTICE 11-6 Draft your definition paragraph. Then, using the TEST checklist below, check your paragraph for unity, support, and coherence.

PRACTICE 11-7 Revise your definition paragraph.

PRACTICE 11-8 Prepare a final edited draft of your definition paragraph.

TESTing a definition paragraph

T opic Sentence Unifies Your Paragraph

☐ Do you have a clearly worded **topic sentence** that states your paragraph's main idea?

☐ Does your topic sentence identify the term you are defining?

E vidence Supports Your Paragraph's Topic Sentence

☐ Does all your **evidence**—examples and details—support your paragraph's main idea?

☐ Do you need to add more examples or details to help you define your term?

S ummary Statement Reinforces Your Paragraph's Unity

☐ Does your paragraph end with a **summary statement** that reinforces your main idea?

T ransitions Add Coherence to Your Paragraph

☐ Are your **transitions** appropriate for the pattern (or patterns) of development you use?

☐ Do you need to add transitions to make your paragraph clearer and to help readers follow your ideas?

11d   Writing about Visuals

The pictures below show various kinds of family. Look at the pictures, and then write a paragraph in which you define *family*. How do the groups below fit (or not fit) your definition? Follow the process outlined in the Step-by-Step Guide on pages 153–54.

An empty-nest couple

A mixed-race family

A two-father family

A single-parent family

preview

In this chapter, you will learn to write an argument paragraph.

12 Argument

Politics has been [too] concerned

with

right or left

instead of right or wrong.

Richard Armour

write first

Many people expressed their points of view at the Rally to Restore Sanity and/or Fear, which took place in Washington, D.C., in October 2010. Write a paragraph in which you express *your* view on a pressing political issue. Include examples from your experience or from your reading to support your position.

reflect

Look at the paragraph you wrote for the Write First activity on page 156, and then do the following:

1. **Reread**

   - Does your paragraph focus on the policy you are going to argue for or against?

   - Does your paragraph begin with a topic sentence that identifies the policy you discuss and clearly states your position on the issue?

   - Do you include specific evidence to support your topic sentence?

   - Do you include any points that support the opposing position? If so, do you argue against these points?

2. **Discuss**

   Work with another student to consider the strengths and weaknesses of your argument paragraphs. Do you think one works better than the other? If so, why?

3. **Sum up**

   Based on your reactions to the paragraphs you and your classmate wrote, what do you think an effective argument paragraph should do?

12a   Argument Paragraphs

When most people hear the word *argument*, they think of the heated exchanges on television interview programs. These discussions, however, are more like shouting matches than arguments. True **argument** involves taking a well-thought-out position on a **debatable topic**—a topic about which reasonable people may disagree (for example, "Should teenagers who commit felonies be tried as adults?").

In an **argument paragraph**, you take a position on an issue, and your purpose is to persuade readers that your position has merit. You attempt to convince people of the strength of your ideas not by shouting but by presenting **evidence**—in this case, facts and examples. In the process, you address opposing ideas, and if they are strong, you acknowledge their strengths. If your evidence is solid and your logic is sound, you will present a convincing argument.

Teaching Tip
To help students understand the concept of argument, photocopy a newspaper editorial or letter to the editor and review it in class.

Teaching Tip
Refer students to 16i for information on writing an argument essay.

FYI

Evidence

There are two kinds of **evidence**—*facts* and *examples*.

1. A **fact** is a piece of information (such as "Alaska officially became a state in 1959") that can be verified. If you make a statement, you should be prepared to support it with facts—using, for example, statistics, observations, or statements that are generally accepted as true.

2. An **example** is a specific illustration of a general statement. To be convincing, an example should clearly relate to the point you are making.

Teaching Tip
Remind students that at this point, their evidence will consist mainly of information from their own experience. Later, when they become more experienced writers, they will support their points with expert opinions that they get from research. Refer them to Unit 4.

When you **TEST** an argument paragraph, make sure it follows these guidelines:

Teaching Tip
Point out to students that many of the self-professed "experts" who post their ideas on the Internet are not authorities.

T ■ An argument paragraph should begin with a **topic sentence** that states your position. Using words like *should, should not,* or *ought to* in your topic sentence will make your position clear to your readers.

> The federal government <u>should</u> lower taxes on gasoline.

> The city <u>ought to</u> spend 20 percent of its budget on helping businesses convert to sustainable energy sources.

E ■ An argument paragraph should present points that support the topic sentence in **logical order**. For example, if your purpose is to argue in favor of placing warning labels on unhealthy snack foods, you should give reasons—arranging them from least important to most important—why this policy should be instituted. Each of these points should then be supported with **evidence**—facts and examples.

An argument paragraph should also address and **refute** (argue against) opposing arguments. By showing that an opponent's arguments are weak, inaccurate, or misguided, you strengthen your own position. If an opposing argument is particularly strong, you may want to **concede** (accept) its strengths and then point out its weaknesses or shortcomings.

Teaching Tip
Emphasize the importance of refuting opposing arguments.

S ■ An argument paragraph should end with a **summary statement** that reinforces the paragraph's main idea—the position you take on the issue.

T ■ An argument paragraph should include **transitions** to connect the points you are making to one another and to the topic sentence.

Paragraph Map: Argument

Topic Sentence

Point #1

Point #2

Point #3

Opposing Argument #1
(plus refutation)

Opposing Argument #2
(plus refutation)

Summary Statement

Model Paragraph: Argument

The following paragraph argues in favor of an emergency notification system for college students.

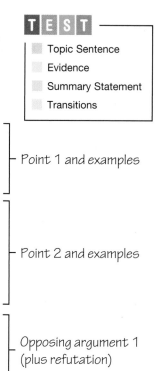

T|**E**|**S**|**T**
- Topic Sentence
- Evidence
- Summary Statement
- Transitions

Why Our School Should Set Up an Emergency Notification System

Our school should set up an emergency notification system that would deliver an instant message to students' cell phones in a campus crisis. The first reason why we should set up an emergency notification system is that it is needed. Currently, it takes an hour or two to inform the whole campus of something—for example, that school is closing because of bad weather or that a school event has been cancelled. ⎤ Point 1 and examples

Another reason why we should set up an emergency notification system is that it will make our campus safer by warning students if a crime takes place on campus. For example, when a shooting took place in 2007 on the campus of Virginia Tech, the school was unable to warn students to evacuate the campus. The result was that more than thirty people were killed. An emergency notification system might have saved the lives of many of these people. ⎤ Point 2 and examples

One objection to an instant-messaging emergency notification system is that email notification works just as well. However, although many students check their email just once or twice a day, most students carry cell phones and read instant messages whenever they get them. Another objection is that some students do not ⎤ Opposing argument 1 (plus refutation)

Opposing argument 2
(plus refutation)

have cell phones. The same system that delivers instant messages to students, however, could also deliver messages to digital message boards around campus. Because communicating with students in a crisis situation can save lives, our school should set up an emergency notification system.

—Ashley Phillips (student)

Transitions in Argument Paragraphs

Transitions are important in argument paragraphs. In the paragraph above, the transitional words and phrases *the first reason* and *another reason* tell readers they are moving from one point to another. In addition, the transitional phrases *one objection* and *another objection* indicate that the writer is addressing two opposing arguments.

Some Transitional Words and Phrases for Argument

accordingly	finally	nonetheless
admittedly	first . . . second . . .	of course
after all	for this reason	one . . . another
although	however	on the one hand . . .
because	in addition	on the other hand
but	in conclusion	since
certainly	in fact	the first reason
consequently	in summary	therefore
despite	meanwhile	thus
even so	moreover	to be sure
even though	nevertheless	truly

grammar in context

Argument

When you write an argument paragraph, you should use both compound sentences and complex sentences. By doing this, you not only show the relationship between ideas but also eliminate choppy sentences.

COMPOUND
SENTENCE
An emergency notification system will help all of us
, and it
communicate better. ~~It~~ will ensure our school's safety.

COMPLEX
SENTENCE
Because communicating
~~Communicating~~ with students in a crisis situation
, our
can save lives. ~~Our~~ school should set up an emergency

notification system.

For more information on how to create compound sentences, see Chapter 19. For more information on how to create complex sentences, see Chapter 20.

Analyzing an Argument Paragraph

Read this argument paragraph; then, follow the instructions in Practice 12-1.

Why We Need Full-Body Scanners

Because of their advantages, airport full-body scanners are a necessary tool in the fight against terrorism. One reason why airport scanners are necessary is that the federal government needs a quick and effective way of screening passengers. Because of their ease of operation, whole-body scanners accomplish this goal. Well over a million people fly throughout the United States each day. A single airport scanner is capable of screening thousands of people a day and is much faster than other methods of screening. Another reason why airport scanners are necessary is that they provide an additional layer of security. For example, scanners are able to detect both metallic and nonmetallic items that are taped to the body. In other words, scanners will detect both weapons and bomb materials that metal detectors might miss. People who oppose scanners say that they are unsafe. However, the literature that the government distributes at airports makes it clear that airport scanners expose passengers to less radiation than they experience when they fly at high altitudes. Opponents also point out that scanners violate the Constitution's guarantee of privacy because they show a three-dimensional image of a person's naked body. To deal with this objection, the Transportation Security Administration has made sure that the TSA officer who operates a scanner never sees the images of the person being scanned. He or she sees only a screen that indicates whether the person has successfully cleared the screening. In addition, the images themselves are deleted immediately after a person has left the screening area. Given the recent attempts that terrorists have made to attack the United States, airport scanners are a useful and effective way of keeping people safe when they fly.

—Carl Manni (student)

PRACTICE

12-1

1. Underline the topic sentence of the paragraph on page 161.

2. What issue is the subject of the paragraph?

   Airport full-body scanners

3. What is the writer's position?

   Full-body airport scanners are necessary.

4. What specific points does the writer use to support his topic sentence?

   The federal government needs a quick and easy way to screen passengers.

   Full-body scanners provide an extra level of security.

5. List some evidence (facts and examples) that the writer uses to support his points. The first piece of evidence has been listed for you.

   A single full-body scanner is capable of screening thousands of people a day.

   It is faster than other methods of screening.

   Scanners can detect both metallic and nonmetallic objects.

   They can detect things that metal detectors miss.

6. What other evidence could the writer have used?

   He could have used his own experience at the airport to illustrate how easy it

   is to go through scanners. He also could have done some research and found

   some additional factual material in the form of statistics.

7. What opposing arguments does he mention?

   Scanners are unsafe.

   Scanners violate the Constitution's guarantee of privacy.

8. How does he refute these arguments?

   He points out that full-body scanners expose people to very low levels of radiation.

   He gives examples of the steps the TSA has taken to ensure people's privacy.

9. Circle the transitional words and phrases the writer uses to move readers through his argument.

10. Underline the paragraph's summary statement.

PRACTICE

12-2 Following are four topic sentences for argument paragraphs. List two or three points that could support each topic sentence. For example, if you were arguing in support of laws requiring motorcycle riders to wear safety helmets, you could say helmets cut down on medical costs and save lives. *Answers will vary.*

1. High school graduates should be required to perform a year of public service before going to college.

   _____

   _____

   _____

2. All student athletes should be paid a salary by their college or university.

   _____

   _____

   _____

3. College students caught cheating should be expelled.

   _____

   _____

4. The U.S. government should provide free college tuition.

   _____

   _____

   _____

PRACTICE

12-3 Choose one of the topic sentences from Practice 12-2. Then, list two types of evidence that could support each point you listed. For example, if you said that wearing safety helmets saves lives, you could list "accident statistics" and "statements by emergency room physicians."

Answers will vary.

_____

_____

PRACTICE

12-4 List opposing arguments for the topic sentences you selected for Practice 12-3. Then, list the weaknesses of each of these arguments.

Opposing argument #1: _____

Weaknesses: _____

Opposing argument #2: _____

Weaknesses: _____

12b Case Study: A Student Writes an Argument Paragraph

Phillip Zhu, a computer science major, was asked to write an argument paragraph on a topic that interested him. Because he was taking a course in computer ethics, he decided to write about an issue that had been discussed in class: the way employers have recently begun searching social networking sites, such as MySpace, to find information about job applicants.

Phillip had already formed an opinion about this issue, and he knew something about the topic. For this reason, he was able to write a topic sentence right away.

> Employers should not use social networking sites to find information about job applicants.

Phillip then listed the following ideas that he could use to support his topic sentence.

Social networking sites should be private

People exaggerate on social networking sites

Stuff meant to be funny

No one warns applicant

Need email address to register

Expect limited audience

Employers can misinterpret what they find

Employers going where they don't belong

Not an accurate picture

Not fair

Not meant to be seen by job recruiters

Phillip then arranged his ideas into an informal outline.

> Social networking sites should be private
> > Need email address to register
> > Expect limited audience
> > Employers going where they don't belong
>
> People exaggerate on social networking sites
> > Stuff meant to be funny
> > Not meant to be seen by job recruiters
> > No one warns applicant
>
> Employers can misinterpret what they find
> > Not an accurate picture
> > Not fair

Once Phillip finished his informal outline, he tried to think of possible arguments against his position because he knew he would have to consider and refute these opposing arguments in his paragraph. He came up with two possible arguments against his position.

1. Employers should be able to find out as much as they can.

2. Applicants have only themselves to blame.

Phillip then wrote the following draft of his paragraph.

> Employers should not use social networking sites to find information about job applicants. For one thing, social networking sites should be private. By visiting these sites, employers are going where they do not belong. People also exaggerate on social networking sites. They say things that are not true, and they put things on the sites they would not want job recruiters to see. No one ever tells applicants that recruiters search these sites, so they feel safe posting all kinds of material. Employers can misinterpret what they read. Employers and recruiters need to get as much information as they can. They should not use unfair ways to get this information. Applicants have only themselves to blame for their problems. They need to be more careful about what they put up online. This is true, but most applicants don't know that employers will search social networking sites.

After finishing his draft, Phillip scheduled a conference with his instructor. Together, they went over his paragraph and TESTed his paragraph. They agreed that Phillip needed to make the following changes.

- They decided he needed to make his **topic sentence** more specific and more forceful.
- They decided he should add more **evidence** (details and examples) to his discussion. For example, what social networking sites is he talking about? Which are restricted? How do employers gain access to these sites?

- They decided he needed to delete irrelevant discussion blaming job applicants for their problems.
- They decided he should add **transitional words and phrases** to clearly identify the points he is making in support of his argument and also to identify the two opposing arguments he discusses.
- They decided he needed to add a strong **summary statement** to reinforce his position.

After **TEST**ing his paragraph, Phillip revised and edited it. The final draft below includes all the elements Phillip looked for when he **TEST**ed his paragraph.

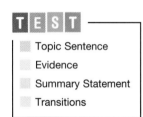

T E S T

- Topic Sentence
- Evidence
- Summary Statement
- Transitions

Unfair Searching

Employers should not use social networking sites, such as MySpace and Facebook, to find information about job applicants. First, social networking sites should be private. People who use these sites do not expect employers to access them. However, some employers routinely search social networking sites to find information about job applicants. Doing this is not right, and it is not fair. By visiting these sites, employers are going where they do not belong. Another reason employers should not use information from social networking sites is that people frequently exaggerate on them or say things that are not true. They may also put statements and pictures on the sites that they would not want job recruiters to see. Because no one ever tells applicants that recruiters search these sites, they feel safe posting embarrassing pictures or making exaggerated claims about drinking or sex. Finally, employers can misinterpret the material they see. As a result, they may reject a good applicant because they take seriously what is meant to be a joke. Of course, employers need to get as much information about a candidate as they can. They should not, however, use unfair tactics to get this information. In addition, prospective employers should realize that the profile they see on a social networking site does not accurately represent the job applicant. For these reasons, employers should not use social networking sites to do background checks.

TEST · Revise · Edit

Look back at your response to the Write First activity on page 156. Using the **TEST** checklist on page 169, evaluate your argument paragraph to make sure it includes a topic sentence, evidence, a summary statement, and transitions. Then, prepare a revised and edited draft of your paragraph.

12c Step-by-Step Guide: Writing an Argument Paragraph

Choose one of the topics below (or choose your own topic). Then, on a separate sheet of paper, use one or more of the strategies described in 2c to help you focus on a specific issue to discuss in an argument paragraph.

AN ISSUE RELATED TO YOUR SCHOOL

Grading policies	Financial aid
Required courses	All-male or all-female classes
Attendance policies	Childcare facilities
Campus security	Sexual harassment policies
Cell phones in class	The physical condition of classrooms

AN ISSUE RELATED TO YOUR COMMUNITY

The need for a traffic signal, a youth center, or something else you think would benefit your community

An action you think local officials should take, such as changing school hours, cleaning up a public space, or improving services for the elderly

A new law you would like to see enacted

A current law you would like to see changed

A controversy you have been following in the news

PRACTICE 12-5

Once you have chosen a topic from the lists above, write a journal entry about your position on the issue. Consider the following questions: Why do you feel the way you do? Do you think many people share your views, or do you think you are in the minority? What specific actions do you think should be taken? What objections are likely to be raised against your position? How might you respond to these objections?

PRACTICE 12-6

Review your journal entry on the topic you chose, and list below as many points as you can in support of your position.

Answers will vary.

Supporting points:

1. _____

2. _____

3. _____

4. _____

5. _____

> **Teaching Tip**
> Before students write argument paragraphs, you might want to explain how to use dependent words like subordinating conjunctions and relative pronouns to form complex sentences (Chapter 20) and have students do Practices 20-3 through 20-6.

> **ESL Tip**
> ESL students may be uncomfortable choosing controversial topics. You may want to encourage them to discuss topic possibilities with you.

> **Teaching Tip**
> Divide students into pairs, and let each student take a turn arguing against the other's position on a particular topic (preferably the one the other student is writing about). Have students jot down their opponent's objections and later refute them in their own paragraphs.

ESL Tip
When students are paired, remind ESL writers that they do not need to agree or arrive at a consensus on the topic.

PRACTICE

12-7 Draft a topic sentence that clearly expresses the position you will take in your paragraph.

Answers will vary.

_____

_____

Teaching Tip
Because argument paragraphs can be hard to organize, you might want to require students to write outlines before they begin.

PRACTICE

12-8 On the lines below, arrange the points that support your position in an order that you think will be convincing to your audience.

1. *Answers will vary.* _____

2. _____

3. _____

4. _____

5. _____

PRACTICE

12-9 In the space provided, list the evidence (facts and examples) that you could use to support each of your points. *Answers will vary.*

Evidence for point 1: _____

_____

Evidence for point 2: _____

_____

Evidence for point 3: _____

_____

PRACTICE

12-10 Look again at your journal entry, and list the opposing arguments you plan to refute.

1. *Answers will vary.* _____

2. _____

PRACTICE

12-11 Draft your argument paragraph. Then, using the **TEST** checklist on page 169, check your paragraph for unity, support, and coherence.

PRACTICE

12-12   Now, revise your argument paragraph.

PRACTICE

12-13   Prepare a final edited draft of your argument paragraph.

Teaching Tip
Refer students to 2i and 2j for information on revising and editing their paragraphs.

TESTing an argument paragraph

T opic Sentence Unifies Your Paragraph

☐ Do you have a clearly worded **topic sentence** that states your paragraph's main idea?

☐ Does your topic sentence state your position on a debatable issue?

E vidence Supports Your Paragraph's Topic Sentence

☐ Does all your **evidence** support your paragraph's main idea?

☐ Have you included enough evidence to support your points, or do you need to add more?

☐ Do you summarize and refute opposing arguments?

S ummary Statement Reinforces Your Paragraph's Unity

☐ Does your paragraph end with a strong **summary statement** that reinforces your main idea?

T ransitions Add Coherence to Your Paragraph

☐ Do you use **transitions** to let readers know when you are moving from one point to another?

☐ Do you use transitional words and phrases to indicate when you are addressing opposing arguments?

☐ Do you need to add transitions to make your paragraph clearer and to help readers follow your ideas?

12d Writing about Visuals

Reprinted below is a public service advertisement about the dangers of texting while driving. Many states are considering (and some have already enacted) laws that ban cell phone use by drivers in moving vehicles. Look at the ad, and then write a paragraph in which you argue either that such a ban is a good idea or that people's concerns are exaggerated and that texting is no more dangerous than other activities that drivers routinely engage in. Follow the process outlined in the Step-by-Step Guide on pages 167–69.

unit
3 Writing Essays

13 Writing an Essay

write first

Most people would agree that window washers like this one have challenging jobs. What was the hardest job you ever had? This is the topic you will be writing about as you go through this chapter. (If you have never had a job, you may write about a specific task that you disliked or about a hard job that a friend or relative has had.)

Much of the writing you do in school will be more than just one paragraph. Often, you will be asked to write an **essay**—a group of paragraphs on a single subject. When you write an essay, you follow the same process you follow when you write a paragraph: you begin by planning and then move on to organizing your ideas, drafting, TESTing, and revising and editing.

In this chapter, you will see how the strategies you learned for writing paragraphs can help you write essays.

Step 1: Planning

13a Understanding Essay Structure

Teaching Tip
Remind students that most writing situations outside of school require more than a single paragraph. The skills they learn in Unit 3 can also be helpful for these writing tasks.

An **essay** is a group of paragraphs on a single subject.

Understanding the structure of a paragraph can help you understand the structure of an essay. In a paragraph, the main idea is stated in a **topic sentence**, and the rest of the paragraph supports this main idea with **evidence** (details and examples). **Transitional words and phrases** help readers follow the discussion. The paragraph ends with a **summary statement** that reinforces the main idea.

Paragraph

Teaching Tip
Refer students to Chapter 2 for more on writing a paragraph.

The **topic sentence** states the main idea of the paragraph.

Evidence (details and examples) supports the main idea.

Transitional words and phrases show the connections between ideas.

A **summary statement** ends the paragraph.

Teaching Tip
Explain to students that an essay includes more ideas, more discussion, and more support than a paragraph does. Even so, because of their structural similarities, the skills students developed for writing paragraphs will also help them to write essays.

The structure of an essay is similar to the structure of a paragraph:

Teaching Tip
Discuss how the TEST elements work in an essay. Ask students to compare a paragraph with the sample essay on pages 176–77.

- The essay's first paragraph—the *introduction*—begins with opening remarks that create interest and closes with a **thesis statement**. This thesis statement, like a paragraph's topic sentence, presents the main idea. (For more on introductions, see 15a.)

- The *body* of the essay contains several paragraphs that support the thesis statement. Each body paragraph begins with a topic sentence that states the main idea of the paragraph. The other sentences in the paragraph support the topic sentence with **evidence** (details and examples).

- **Transitional words and phrases** lead readers from sentence to sentence and from paragraph to paragraph.

■ The last paragraph—the *conclusion*—ends the essay. The conclusion includes a **summary statement** that sums up the essay's main idea and reinforces the thesis. It ends with concluding remarks. (For more on conclusions, see 15b.)

The first letters of these four key elements—**t**hesis statement, **e**vidence, **s**ummary statement, and **t**ransitions—spell TEST. Just as you did with paragraphs, you can TEST your essays to see whether they include all the elements of an effective essay.

Many of the essays you will write in college will have a **thesis-and-support** structure.

Essay

> **Opening remarks** introduce the subject being discussed in the essay.
> The **thesis statement** presents the essay's main idea.

⌐ Introduction

> The **topic sentence** states the essay's first point.
> **Evidence** (details and examples) supports the topic sentence.
> **Transitional words and phrases** connect the examples and details and show how they are related.

⌐ First body paragraph

> The **topic sentence** states the essay's second point.
> **Evidence** (details and examples) supports the topic sentence.
> **Transitional words and phrases** connect the examples and details and show how they are related.

⌐ Second body paragraph

> The **topic sentence** states the essay's third point.
> **Evidence** (details and examples) supports the topic sentence.
> **Transitional words and phrases** connect the examples and details and show how they are related.

⌐ Third body paragraph

> The **summary statement** reinforces the thesis, summarizing the essay's main idea.
> **Concluding remarks** present the writer's final thoughts on the subject.

⌐ Conclusion

> **Teaching Tip**
> Take this opportunity to explain thesis-and-support structure to students.

> **Teaching Tip**
> You might want to tell students that although the model essays in this book show the summary statement as the first sentence of the conclusion, it can also appear elsewhere in the conclusion.

The following essay by Jennifer Chu illustrates the structure of an essay. (Note that transitional words and phrases are shaded.)

Becoming Chinese American

Introduction

Although I was born in Hong Kong, I have spent most of my life in the United States. However, my parents have always made sure that I did not forget my roots. They always tell stories of what it was like to live in Hong Kong. To make sure my brothers and sisters and I know what is happening in China, my parents subscribe to Chinese cable TV. When we were growing up, we would watch the celebration of the Chinese New Year, the news from Asia, and Chinese movies

Thesis statement

and music videos. As a result, even though I am an American, I value many parts of traditional Chinese culture.

First body paragraph

(*Topic sentence* states essay's first main point.)

The Chinese language is an important part of my life as a Chinese American. Unlike some of my Chinese friends, I do not think the Chinese language is unimportant or embarrassing. First, I feel that it is my duty as a Chinese American to learn Chinese so that I can pass it on to my children. In addition, knowing Chinese enables me to communicate with my relatives. Because my

Evidence
(details and examples)

parents and grandparents do not speak English well, Chinese is our main form of communication. Finally, Chinese helps me identify with my culture. When I speak Chinese, I feel connected to a culture that is over five thousand years old. Without the Chinese language, I would not be who I am.

Second body paragraph

(*Topic sentence* states essay's second main point.)

Chinese food is another important part of my life as a Chinese American. One reason for this is that everything we Chinese people eat has a history and a meaning. At a birthday meal, for example, we serve long noodles and buns in the shape of peaches. This is because we believe that long noodles represent long life and that peaches are served in heaven. Another reason is

Evidence
(details and examples)

that to Chinese people, food is a way of reinforcing ties between family and friends. For instance, during a traditional Chinese wedding ceremony, the bride and the groom eat nine of everything. This is because the number nine stands for the Chinese words "together forever." By taking part in this ritual, the bride and groom start their marriage by making Chinese customs a part of their life together.

<u>Religion is the most important part of my life as a Chinese American.</u>   **Third body paragraph**

At various times during the year, Chinese religious festivals bring together the   (*Topic sentence* states essay's third main point.)

people I care about the most. During Chinese New Year, my whole family goes

to the temple, where we say prayers and welcome others with traditional New

Year's greetings. After leaving the temple, we all go to Chinatown and eat dim   Evidence (details and examples)

sum until the lion dance starts. As the colorful lion dances its way down the

street, people beat drums and throw firecrackers to drive off any evil spirits

that may be around. Later that night, parents give children gifts of money in

red envelopes that symbolize joy and happiness in the coming year.

<u>My family has taught me how important it is to hold on to my Chinese</u>   (*Summary statement* reinforces essay's main idea.)

<u>culture.</u> When I was six, my parents sent me to a Chinese-American grade

school. My teachers thrilled me with stories of Fa Mulan, the Shang Dynasty,   **Conclusion**

and the Moon God. I will never forget how happy I was when I realized how

special it is to be Chinese. This is how I want my own children to feel. I want

them to be proud of who they are and to pass their language, history, and

culture on to the next generation.

PRACTICE

13-1   The following essay is organized according to the diagram on page 175. Read the essay, and then follow the instructions after it.

Finding a Doctor

Maybe you have moved to a new city, and you need to find a new doctor for yourself and your family. Maybe your doctor has retired. Or maybe
you need a specialist to help you deal with a difficult medical problem. In — Introduction
any case, your goal is clear: to find a doctor. <u>There are several strategies
you can use to help you find a good doctor.</u>

<u>First, look for a well-qualified doctor.</u> (One way) to begin is to identify
the best hospital in the area and find a doctor on the staff there. Good
doctors are attracted to good hospitals, so this is a good place to start — First body paragraph
your search. (In addition,) recommendations from friends and neighbors
can also be useful. Once you have some names, find out whether the doctors are board certified in their specific fields. Board certification means

First body paragraph

that doctors have had extensive training in their specialties. You can find out whether a doctor is board certified by going to the American Board of Medical Specialties Web site.

Second body paragraph

(Second,) decide what things are important to you. (For example,) how far are you willing to travel to see the doctor? Also, consider when the doctor is available. Many doctors do not have office hours on weekends. Is this acceptable, or will you need evening or Saturday appointments? Will you be able to see the doctor at any time, or will you have to go to a hospital emergency room? (Finally,) find out how you will pay for the medical care you receive. If you have medical insurance, find out if the doctor accepts your plan. If you do not have medical insurance, find out what payment options the doctor offers. Will you have to pay the entire bill at once, or will you be able to arrange a payment plan?

Third body paragraph

(Next,) make an appointment to visit the office and meet the doctor. If the office seems crowded and disorganized, be on your guard. The doctor may be overscheduled, overworked, understaffed, or simply disorganized. (Also,) see how long it takes to see the doctor. Unless the doctor is called away to an emergency, you should not have to sit in the waiting room for more than an hour. (Finally,) see if you feel comfortable talking to the doctor. If the doctor seems rushed or uninterested, take this as an indication of the type of medical care you will get. Finally, both the doctor and the office staff should treat you with respect. They should take the time to ask about your general health and to update your medical records.

Conclusion

Finding a good doctor requires careful planning and a lot of work. You may even have to take the time to see several doctors and assess each one. Remember, though, there are no shortcuts. If the result of all your hard work is a qualified doctor who really cares about your well-being, then your time will have been well spent.

1. Underline the essay's thesis. Then, copy it on the lines below.

   _____

   _____

2. Underline the topic sentence of each body paragraph.

3. What point does the first body paragraph make?

   You should find out whether the doctor is well qualified. _____

   _____

4. What point does the second body paragraph make?

   You need to decide what things are most important to you. _____

   _____

5. What point does the third body paragraph make?

   You should make an appointment to visit the office and meet the doctor. _____

   _____

6. Circle the transitions used in the essay. How do they connect the essay's ideas?

   The transitions clearly introduce sequential steps in the process of finding

   a good doctor. _____

7. What sentence in the conclusion reinforces the essay's main idea? Underline this summary statement.

13b Moving from Assignment to Topic

Many essays you write in college begin as **assignments** given to you by your instructors. Before you focus on any assignment, however, you should take time to think about your **purpose** and your **audience**. In other words, you should think about what you want to accomplish by writing your essay—and about who will read it. Once you have considered these issues, you are ready to move on to thinking about the specifics of your assignment.

The following assignments are typical of those you might be given in your composition class.

Teaching Tip
Refer students to 2b for more on audience and purpose.

- Discuss some things you would change about your school.
- What can college students do to improve the environment?
- Discuss an important decision you made during the past three years.

Because these assignments are so general, you need to narrow them before you can start to write. What specific things would you change? Exactly what could you do to improve the environment? Answering these questions will help you narrow these assignments into **topics** that you can write about.

ASSIGNMENT	TOPIC
Discuss some things you would change about your school.	Three things I would change to improve the quality of life at Jackson County Community College
What can college students do to improve the environment?	The campus recycling project

Jared White, a student in a first-year composition course, was given the following assignment.

ASSIGNMENT

Discuss an important decision you made during the past few years.

Jared narrowed this assignment to the following topic:

TOPIC

Deciding to go back to school

For the rest of this chapter, you will be following Jared's writing process.

PRACTICE

13-2 Decide whether the following topics are narrow enough for an essay of four or five paragraphs. If a topic is suitable, write *OK* in the blank. If it is not, write in the blank a revised version of the same topic that is narrow enough for a brief essay.

Examples

Successful strategies for quitting smoking _OK_____

Horror movies ___1950s Japanese monster movies_____

1. Violence in American public schools ___Answers will vary._____

   Example: the need for metal detectors in a local high school

2. Ways to improve your study skills _OK_____

   _____

3. Using pets as therapy for nursing-home patients _OK_____

   _____

4. Teachers ___Answers will vary._____

   Example: qualities of an effective teacher

5. Safe ways to lose weight _OK_____

   _____

decide on a topic

Look back at the Write First activity on page 173. To narrow this assignment to a topic you can write about, you need to decide which hard job to focus on. On the lines below, list several jobs you could discuss.

Answers will vary.

FYI

Visit the Study Guides and Strategies Web site (studygs.net/writing/prewriting.htm) to learn how to use one of the graphic organizers or to find other information about the writing process.

13c   Finding Ideas to Write About

Before you start writing about a topic, you need to find out what you have to say about it. Sometimes ideas may come to you easily. More often, you will have to use specific strategies, such as *freewriting* or *brainstorming*, to help you come up with ideas.

Teaching Tip
Refer students to 2c for a full discussion of ways of finding material to write about.

Freewriting

When you **freewrite**, you write for a fixed period of time without stopping. When you do **focused freewriting**, you write with a topic in mind. Then, you read what you have written and choose ideas you think you can use.

The following focused freewriting was written by Jared White on the topic "Deciding to go back to school."

> Deciding to go back to school. When I graduated high school, I swore I'd never go back to school. Hated it. Couldn't wait to get out. What was I thinking? How was I supposed to support myself? My dad's friend needed help. He taught me how to paint houses. I made good money, but it was boring. I couldn't picture myself doing it forever. Even though I knew I was going to have to go back to school, I kept putting off the decision. Maybe I was lazy. Maybe I was scared—probably both. I had this fear of being turned down.

How could someone who had bad grades all through high school go to college?
Also, I'd been out of school for six years. And even if I did get in
(a miracle!), how would I pay for it? How would I live? Well, here I am—
the first one in my family to go to college.

Jared's freewriting

PRACTICE
13-3   Reread Jared White's freewriting. If you were advising Jared, which ideas would you tell him to explore further? Why?

freewrite

Choose two of the jobs you listed for the Write First activity on page 181. Freewrite about each of them. Then, choose one of the jobs to write about. Circle the ideas that you would like to explore further in an essay.

Brainstorming

When you **brainstorm** (either individually or with others in a group), you write down (or type) all the ideas you can think of about a particular topic. After you have recorded as much material as you can, you look over your notes and decide which ideas are useful and which ones are not.

Here are Jared White's brainstorming notes about his decision to go back to school.

<u>Deciding to Go Back to School</u>
Money a problem
No confidence
Other students a lot younger
Paying tuition—how?
No one in family went to college
Friends not in college
Couldn't see myself in college
Relationship with Beth
Considered going to trade school
Computer programmer?

Grades bad in high school
Time for me to grow up
Wondered if I would get in
Found out about community college
Admission requirements not bad
Afraid—too old, failing out, looking silly
Took time to get used to routine
Found other students like me
Liked studying

Jared's brainstorming

PRACTICE

13-4 Reread Jared White's brainstorming notes. Which ideas would you advise him to explore further? Why?

brainstorm

Review the freewriting you did in the Write First activity on page 182. Brainstorm about the job for which you have found the most interesting ideas. What ideas about the job did you get from brainstorming that you did not get from freewriting? Write these ideas on the lines below.

Answers will vary.

Keeping a Journal

When you keep a **journal**, you keep an informal record of your thoughts and ideas. As you learned in Chapter 2, your journal can be a notebook (or section of a notebook) or a file on your computer. In your journal, you record your thoughts about your assignments, identify ideas that you want to explore further, and keep notes about things you read or see. After rereading your journal entries, you can decide to explore an idea further in another journal entry or to use material from a specific entry in an essay.

Following is an entry in Jared White's journal that he eventually used in his essay about returning to school.

> When I was working as a house painter, I had a conversation that helped convince me to go to college. One day, I started talking to the guy whose house I was painting. I told him that I was painting houses until I figured out what I was going to do with the rest of my life. He asked me if I had considered going to college. I told him that I hadn't done well in high school, so I didn't think college was for me. He told me that I could probably get into the local community college. That night I looked at the community college's Web site to see if going to college might be a good idea.

Jared's journal entry

write journal entries

Write some journal entries for the topic you have been exploring for this chapter: the hardest job you ever had. Which of your entries do you want to explore further? Which could you use in your essay?

13d Stating Your Thesis

After you have gathered information about your topic, you need to decide on a thesis for your essay. You do this by reviewing the ideas from your brainstorming, freewriting, and journal entries and then asking, "What is the main point I want to make about my topic?" The answer to this question is the **thesis** of your essay. You express this point in a **thesis statement**: a single sentence that clearly expresses the main idea that you will discuss in the rest of your essay.

Keep in mind that each essay has just one thesis statement. The details and examples in the body of the essay all support (add to, discuss, or explain) this thesis statement.

TOPIC	THESIS STATEMENT
Three things I would change about Jackson County Community College	If I could change three things to improve Jackson County Community College, I would expand the food choices, decrease class size in first-year courses, and ship some of my classmates to the North Pole.
The campus recycling project	The recycling project recently begun on our campus should be promoted more actively.

The difficulty of going back to school	Though I realized it would be difficult in some ways, I decided that if I really wanted to attend college full time, I could.

Like a topic sentence in a paragraph, a thesis statement in an essay tells readers what to expect. An effective thesis statement has two important characteristics.

Teaching Tip
You may want to remind students not to state the thesis in their essay's first sentence.

1. *An effective thesis statement makes a point about a topic, expressing the writer's opinion or unique view of the topic. For this reason, it must do more than state a fact or announce what you plan to write about.*

STATEMENT OF FACT	Many older students are returning to school.
ANNOUNCEMENT	In this essay, I would like to discuss the difficulties many older students have going back to school.
EFFECTIVE THESIS STATEMENT	Though I realized it would be difficult in some ways, I decided that if I really wanted to attend college full time, I could.

A statement of fact is not an effective thesis statement because it gives you nothing to develop in your essay. After all, how much can you say about the *fact* that many older students are returning to school? Likewise, an announcement of what you plan to discuss gives readers no indication of the position you will take on your topic. Remember, an effective thesis statement makes a point.

2. *An effective thesis statement is clearly worded and specific.*

VAGUE THESIS STATEMENT	Television commercials are not like real life.
EFFECTIVE THESIS STATEMENT	Television commercials do not accurately portray women or minorities.

The vague thesis statement above gives readers no sense of the ideas the essay will discuss. It does not say, for example, *why* television commercials are not realistic. The effective thesis statement is more focused. It signals that the essay will discuss television commercials that present unrealistic portrayals of women and minorities.

Teaching Tip
Tell students that at this stage of the process, their thesis statements are not definite but tentative. They will probably change this tentative thesis statement as they write and revise their essays.

FYI

Evaluating Your Thesis Statement

Once you have a thesis statement, you need to evaluate it to determine if it is effective. Asking the following questions will help you decide:

- Is your thesis statement a complete sentence?.
- Does your thesis statement clearly express the main idea you will discuss in your essay?

(continued on next page)

(continued from previous page)

■ Is your thesis statement specific and focused? Does it make a point that you can cover within your time and page limits?

■ Does your thesis statement make a point about your topic—not just state a fact or announce what you plan to write about?

■ Does your thesis statement avoid vague language?

■ Does your thesis statement avoid statements like "I think" or "In my opinion"?

After freewriting, brainstorming, and reviewing his journal entries, Jared White decided on the following topic and thesis statement for his essay:

Though I realized it would be difficult in some ways, I decided that if I really wanted to attend college full time, I could.

Jared knew that his thesis statement had to be a complete sentence. He also knew that it had to make a point about his topic. Finally, he knew that it had to be both clearly worded and specific. When Jared reviewed his thesis statement, he felt sure that it did these things and that it expressed an idea he could develop in his essay.

PRACTICE

13-5 In the space provided, indicate whether each of the following items is a statement of fact (*F*), an announcement (*A*), a vague statement (*VS*), or an effective thesis (*ET*).

Examples

My drive to school takes more than an hour. ____*F*____

I hate my commute between home and school. ____*VS*____

1. Students who must commute a long distance to school are at a disadvantage compared to students who live close by. ____*ET*____

2. In this paper, I will discuss cheating. ____*A*____

3. Schools should establish specific policies to discourage students from cheating. ____*ET*____

4. Cheating is a problem. ____*VS*____

5. Television commercials are designed to sell products. ____*F*____

6. I would like to explain why some television commercials are funny. ____*A*____

7. Single parents have a rough time. ____*VS*____

8. Young people are starting to abuse alcohol and drugs at earlier ages than in the past. ____*F*____

9. Alcohol and drug abuse are both major problems in our society.

_____ *VS*

10. Families can do several things to help children avoid alcohol and

drugs. ___*ET*___

PRACTICE

13-6   Label each of the following thesis statements *VS* if it is too vague, *F* if it is factual, *A* if it is an announcement, or *ET* if it is an effective thesis. On a separate sheet of paper, rewrite those that are not effective thesis statements.

1. Different types of amusement parks appeal to different types of people.

_____ *VS*

2. There are three reasons why Election Day should be a national holi-

day. ___*ET*___

3. Every four years, voters in the United States elect a new president.

_____ *F*

4. My paper will prove that DVDs are better than videotapes. ___*A*___

5. The largest fish is the whale shark. ___*F*___

6. Scientists once thought that the dinosaurs were killed off by climate

change. ___*F*___

7. NASCAR drivers could do several things to make their sport safer.

_____ *ET*

8. This paper will discuss the increase in the number of women in the

military since the 1970s. ___*A*___

9. Movies provide great entertainment. ___*VS*___

10. Computers have enabled teachers to create new classroom techniques.

_____ *ET*

PRACTICE

13-7   Rewrite the following vague thesis statements to make them effective.

Example

My relatives are funny.

Rewrite: ___*My relatives think they are funny, but sometimes their humor*___

___*can be offensive.*___

Answers will vary.

1. Online courses have advantages.

2. Airport security is more trouble than it is worth.

3. Athletes are paid too much.

4. Many people get their identities from their cars.

5. Cheating in college is out of control.

PRACTICE

13-8   A list of broad topics for essays follows. Select five of these topics, narrow them, and generate a thesis statement for each.
Answers will vary.

1. Terrorism

2. Reality television

3. U.S. immigration policies

4. Music

5. Texting in class

6. Required courses

7. Computer games

8. Disciplining children

9. Street sense

10. The cost of gasoline

PRACTICE

13-9   Read the following groups of statements. Then, write a thesis statement that could express the main point of each group.

1. Thesis statement _____ *Answers will vary.* _____

_____

- *Gap year* is a term that refers to a year that students take off before they go to college.
- Many college students spend most of their time studying and socializing with their peers.
- Studies show that high school students who take a year off before they go to college get better grades.
- Many students take community service jobs in order to broaden their interests and to increase their social awareness.

2. Thesis statement _____ *Answers will vary.* _____

_____

- Some people post too much personal information on social networking sites such as Facebook.
- Child predators frequently use social networking sites to find their victims.
- Some experts believe that people can become addicted to social networking sites.
- Employers have fired employees because of information they have seen on their social networking sites.

3. Thesis statement _*Answers will vary.*_ _____

_____

- A student at the Indiana University at Bloomington was able to create her own major in environmental ethics.
- Drexel University has begun recruiting students who would design their own majors.
- Some students get bored with traditional majors that force them to choose from a rigid list of courses.
- Many employers are impressed with students who design their own majors.

4. Thesis statement _*Answers will vary.*_ _____

_____

- One way to pay for college is to get a job.
- The majority of students supplement their college tuition with loans or grants.
- According to the College Board, only 22 percent of all federal aid for college tuition goes to scholarships.
- Some students enlist in the armed forces and become eligible for tuition assistance programs.

5. Thesis statement _*Answers will vary.*_ _____

_____

- You can save time in the kitchen by washing and putting away items as you cook.
- Keep your kitchen well stocked so that you will not have to run to the store to get an ingredient.
- Keep your countertops free of clutter so you don't have to put things away before you cook.
- Shred things like cheese in advance and store them in plastic bags.

state your thesis

Review your freewriting, brainstorming, and journal entries from the Write First activities on pages 182–84. Then, write a thesis statement for your essay on the lines below.

Thesis statement: _*Answers will vary.*_ _____

_____

_____

Step 2: Organizing

13e Choosing Supporting Points

Once you have decided on a thesis statement, look over your freewriting, brainstorming, and journal entries again. Identify the **evidence** (details and examples) that best supports your thesis, and cross out any evidence that does not.

Jared White made the following list of supporting points about his decision to go back to school. When he reviewed his list, he crossed out several points that he thought would not support his thesis.

Deciding to Go Back to School: Pros and Cons

Money a problem

~~No confidence~~

Other students a lot younger

Paying tuition—how?

No one in family went to college

Friends not in college

Couldn't see myself in college

~~Relationship with Beth~~

~~Considered going to trade school~~

~~Computer programmer?~~

Grades bad in high school

Wondered if I would get in

Found out about community college

Admission requirements not bad

Afraid—too old, failing out, looking dumb

~~Took time to get used to routine~~

Found other students like me

Liked studying

Jared's list of supporting points

PRACTICE

13-10   Look at Jared's list of supporting points on page 190. Are there any points he crossed out that you think he should keep? Are there any other points he should cross out?

13f   Making an Outline

After you have selected the points you think will best support your thesis, make an informal outline. Begin by arranging your supporting points into groups. Then, arrange them in the order in which you will discuss them (for example, from general to specific, or from least important to most important). Arrange the supporting points for each group in the same way. This informal outline can guide you as you write.

When Jared White looked over his list of supporting points, he saw that they fell into three groups of excuses for not going back to school: not being able to pay tuition, not being a good student in high school, and not being able to picture himself in college. He arranged his points under these three headings to create the following informal outline.

Excuse 1: Not being able to pay tuition

   Needed to work to live

   Didn't have much saved

   Found out about community college (low tuition)

   Found out about grants, loans

Excuse 2: Not being a good student in high school

   Got bad grades in high school: wasn't motivated and didn't work

   Looked into admission requirements at community college—doable!

   Made a commitment to improve study habits

Excuse 3: Not being able to picture myself in college

   No college graduates in family

   No friends in college

   Afraid of being too old, looking dumb

   Found other students like me

   Found out I liked studying

Jared's informal outline

PRACTICE
13-11   Look over Jared's informal outline on page 191. Do you think his arrangement is effective? Can you suggest any other ways he might have arranged his points?

FYI

Preparing a Formal Outline

An informal outline like the one that appears above is usually all you need to plan a short essay. However, some writers—especially when they are planning a longer, more detailed essay—prefer to use formal outlines.

Formal outlines use a combination of numbered and lettered headings to show the relationships among ideas. For example, the most important (and most general) ideas are assigned a Roman numeral; the next most important ideas are assigned capital letters. Each level develops the idea above it, and each new level is indented.

Here is a formal outline of the points that Jared planned to discuss in his essay.

Thesis statement: Though I realized it would be difficult in some ways, I decided that if I really wanted to attend college full time, I could.

  I. Difficulty: Money
    A. Needed to work to live
    B. Didn't have much money saved
    C. Found out about community college (low tuition)
    D. Found out about grants/loans
  II. Difficulty: Academic record
    A. Got bad grades in high school
      1. Didn't care
      2. Didn't work
    B. Found out about reasonable admissions requirements at community college
    C. Committed to improving study habits
  III. Difficulty: Imagining myself as a student
    A. Had no college graduates in family
    B. Had no friends in school
    C. Felt anxious
      1. Too old
      2. Out of practice at school
    D. Found other students like me
    E. Discovered I like studying

make an outline

On the lines below, recopy the thesis statement you wrote in the Write First box on page 189.

_____

_____

Now, review the freewriting, brainstorming, and journal entries you wrote in response to the Write First activities on pages 182–84. List below the points you plan to use to support your thesis statement. Cross out any points that do not support your thesis statement.

_Answers will vary._____

_____

_____

_____

_____

Finally, group your supporting points to create an informal outline that will guide you as you write.

Step 3: Drafting

13g   Drafting Your Essay

After you have decided on a thesis for your essay and have arranged your supporting points in the order in which you will discuss them, you are ready to draft your essay.

At this stage of the writing process, you should not worry about spelling or grammar or about composing a perfect introduction or conclusion. Your main goal is to get your ideas down so you can react to them. Remember that the draft you are writing will be revised, so leave extra space between lines as you type. (If you are writing your draft by hand, write on every other line.) Follow your outline, but don't hesitate to depart from it if you think of new points.

As you draft your essay, be sure that it has a **thesis-and-support** structure—that it states a thesis and supports it with evidence (details and examples). Include a **working title**, a temporary title that you will revise later so that it accurately reflects the content of your completed essay. This working title will help you focus your ideas.

Following is the first draft of Jared White's essay.

Teaching Tip
Refer students to Chapter 15 for a discussion of introductions and conclusions.

Teaching Tip
Refer students to 15a for a discussion of titles.

Going Back to School

I was out of school for six years after I graduated from high school. The decision to return to school was one I had a lot of difficulty making. I had been around enough to know that without more education, I'd never get anywhere in life, but I always found reasons for not taking the plunge. However, after a lot of thinking, I realized that my reasons for not going to college were just excuses. Though I realized it would be difficult in some ways, I decided that if I really wanted to attend college full time, I could.

My first excuse for not going to college was that I couldn't afford to go to school full time. I had worked since I finished high school, but I hadn't put much money away. I kept wondering how I would pay for books and tuition. I needed to support myself and pay for rent, food, and car expenses. I was working as a house painter, and a house I was painting belonged to a college instructor. Painting wasn't hard work, but it was boring. I'd start in the morning and work without a break until lunch. We began talking. When I told him about my situation, he told me I should look at our local community college. He also told me about some loans and grants I'd probably be able to apply for. I went online and looked at the college's Web site. I found out that tuition was forty dollars a credit, much less than I thought it would be. If I got just one of the grants he mentioned, I might be able to make it.

Now that I had taken care of my first excuse, I had to deal with my second—that I hadn't been a good student in high school. When I was a teenager, I didn't care much about school. School bored me to death. Probably as a result, I got bad grades. Now that I was considering going back to school, though, I wondered what price I would have to pay for my laziness and immaturity. The answer to this question was not as bad as I thought it would be. According to the community college's Web site, all I needed to be admitted was a high school diploma and county residence. I would have to take some placement tests, but I would be judged on my ability, not my high school grades. I knew I could do better if I made a real effort to study harder and smarter. The Web site was easy to navigate, and I had no problem finding information.

I had a hard time picturing myself in college. No one in my family had ever gone to college. My friends were just like me; they all went to work right after high school. I had no role model or mentor who could give me advice. I thought I was just too old for college. After all, I was probably at least six years older than most of the students. How would I be able to keep up with the younger students in the class? I hadn't opened a textbook for years, and I'd never really learned how to study. Most of my fears disappeared during my first few weeks of classes. I saw a lot of students who were as old as I was, and some were even older. Studying didn't seem to be a problem either. I actually enjoyed learning. History, which had put me to sleep in high school, suddenly became interesting. So did math and English. It soon became clear to me that I was going to like being in college.

Going to college as a full-time student has changed my life, both personally and financially. I am no longer the same person I was in high school. I allowed laziness and insecurity to hold me back. Now, I have options that I didn't have before. When I graduate from community college, I plan to transfer to the state university and get a four-year degree.

Jared's first draft

PRACTICE

13-12 Reread Jared White's first draft. What changes would you suggest he make? What might he add? What might he delete? Which of his supporting details and examples are most effective?

draft your essay

Draft an essay about the job you chose in the Write First activity on page 173. Be sure to include the thesis statement you developed in the Write First activity on page 189 as well as the points you listed in the Write First activity on page 193. (Be sure to include a working title.)

Step 4: TESTing

13h TESTing Your Essay

Before you begin to revise the first draft of your essay, you should TEST it to make sure it contains the four elements that make it clear and effective.

Teaching Tip
Refer students to Chapter 3 for information on TESTing their paragraphs.

T ■ **Thesis Statement**—Does your essay include a thesis statement that states your main idea?

E ■ **Evidence**—Does your essay include evidence—examples and details—that supports your thesis statement?

S ■ **Summary Statement**—Does your essay's conclusion include a summary statement that reinforces your thesis and sums up your main idea?

T ■ **Transitions**—Does your essay include transitional words and phrases that show readers how your ideas are related?

As you reread your essay, use the TEST strategy to identify the four elements of an effective essay. If your essay includes them, you can move on to revise and edit it. If not, you should supply whatever is missing.

When Jared reread the draft of his essay, he used the **TEST** strategy to help him quickly survey his essay.

- He decided that his **thesis statement** clearly stated his main idea.
- He thought he could add some more **evidence** in his body paragraphs and delete some irrelevant details.
- He thought his **summary statement** summed up the idea expressed in his thesis statement.
- He realized he needed to add more **transitions** to connect ideas.

TEST your essay

TEST the essay you drafted for the Write First activity on page 195.

Step 5: Revising and Editing

13i Revising Your Essay

When you **revise** your essay, you do not simply correct errors; instead, you resee, rethink, reevaluate, and rewrite your work. Some of the changes you make—such as adding, deleting, or rearranging sentences or even whole paragraphs—will be major. Others will be small—for example, adding or deleting words or phrases.

It is a good idea to revise on hard copy and not on the computer screen. On hard copy, you are able to see a full page—or even two pages next to each other—as you revise. When you have finished, you can type your changes into your document. (Do not delete sentences or paragraphs until you are certain you do not need them; instead, move unwanted material to the end of your draft.)

Before you begin revising, put your essay aside for a while. This "cooling-off" period allows you to see your draft more objectively when you return to it. (Keep in mind that revision is usually not a neat process. When you revise, you write directly on your draft: draw arrows, underline, cross out, and write above lines and in the margins.)

There are a number of strategies you can use to help you revise: you can schedule a conference with your instructor, make an appointment at the writing center, participate in a peer-review session with your

Teaching Tip
Suggest that students revise and edit on hard copy before they type the changes into their documents.

Teaching Tip
Refer students to Chapter 3 for more on how to TEST their paragraphs.

classmates, communicate with your instructor electronically, or use a revision checklist, such as the one on page 198. Sometimes, you may decide to use just one of these strategies (for example, when you are writing a short paper), but at other times, you may employ several of them (for example, when you are writing a research paper). The following chart shows you the advantages of each revision strategy.

REVISING YOUR ESSAY	
STRATEGY	**ADVANTAGES**
FACE-TO-FACE CONFERENCE WITH INSTRUCTOR	▪ Provides one-to-one feedback that can't be obtained in the classroom ▪ Builds a student-teacher relationship ▪ Enables students to collaborate with their instructors ▪ Allows students to ask questions that they might not ask in a classroom setting
WRITING CENTER	▪ Offers students a less formal, less stressful environment than an instructor conference ▪ Enables students to get help from trained tutors (both students and professionals) ▪ Provides a perspective other than the instructor's ▪ Offers specialized help to students whose first language is not English
PEER REVIEW	▪ Enables students working on the same assignment to share insights with one another ▪ Gives students the experience of writing for a real audience ▪ Gives students several different readers' reactions to their work ▪ Enables students to benefit from the ideas of their classmates

Teaching Tip
You can find more information about teaching students how to give a useful peer response at learner.org/workshops/middlewriting/images/pdf/W7ReadPeer.pdf and gwu.edu/~uwp/docs/Peer_Review_WID_WORKSHOP_MATERIAL-2008.pdf.

(continued)

ELECTRONIC COMMUNICATION WITH INSTRUCTOR	▪ Enables students to submit email questions before a draft is due
	▪ Gives students quick answers to their questions
	▪ Enables instructors to give feedback by annotating drafts electronically
	▪ Enables students to react to their instructor's responses when they have time
	▪ Eliminates time spent traveling to instructor's office
REVISION CHECKLIST	▪ Gives students a tool that enables them to revise in an orderly way
	▪ Enables students to learn to revise independently
	▪ Enables students to focus on specific aspects of their writing

FYI

You can find suggestions online for giving useful peer responses by searching "peer response" on the Web sites for the Alamo Colleges (alamo.edu) and Harvard University (harvard.edu).

self-assessment checklist

Revising Your Essay

☐ Does your essay have an introduction, a body, and a conclusion?

☐ Does your introduction include a clearly worded thesis statement that states your essay's main idea?

☐ Does each body paragraph have a topic sentence?

☐ Does each topic sentence introduce a point that supports the thesis?

☐ Does each body paragraph include enough details and examples to support the topic sentence?

☐ Are the body paragraphs unified, well developed, and coherent?

☐ Does your conclusion include a concluding statement that restates your thesis or sums up your main idea?

13j   Editing Your Essay

When you **edit** your essay, you check grammar and sentence structure. Then, you look at punctuation, mechanics, and spelling. As you edit, think carefully about the questions in the Self-Assessment Checklist below.

Teaching Tip
You might create a class wiki at wikispaces.com and encourage or require students to use that space for group work in writing and editing an essay online.

self-assessment checklist

Editing Your Essay

EDITING FOR COMMON SENTENCE PROBLEMS

☐ Have you avoided run-ons? (See Chapter 24.)

☐ Have you avoided sentence fragments? (See Chapter 25.)

☐ Do your subjects and verbs agree? (See Chapter 26.)

☐ Have you avoided illogical shifts? (See Chapter 27.)

☐ Have you avoided dangling and misplaced modifiers? (See Chapter 28.)

EDITING FOR GRAMMAR

☐ Are your verb forms and verb tenses correct? (See Chapters 29 and 30.)

☐ Have you used nouns and pronouns correctly? (See Chapter 31.)

☐ Have you used adjectives and adverbs correctly? (See Chapter 32.)

EDITING FOR PUNCTUATION, MECHANICS, AND SPELLING

☐ Have you used commas correctly? (See Chapter 34.)

☐ Have you used apostrophes correctly? (See Chapter 35.)

☐ Have you used capital letters where they are required? (See 36a.)

☐ Have you used quotation marks correctly where they are needed? (See 36b.)

☐ Have you spelled every word correctly? (See Chapter 37.)

When Jared White typed the first draft of his essay about deciding to return to college, he left extra space so he could write more easily between the lines. Before revising this draft, he met with his instructor to discuss it. Then, he used the Self-Assessment Checklist on page 198 to help him revise his essay.

Jared's draft, with his handwritten revisions and edits along with the transitions he added after he finished TESTing his essay, appears on the following page.

~~Going Back to School~~ Starting Over
⋀

The other day, my sociology instructor mentioned that half the students enrolled in college programs across the country are twenty-five or older. His remarks caught my attention because I am one of those students.

I was out of school for six years after I graduated from high school.
⋀
The decision to return to school was one I had a lot of difficulty making. I had been around enough to know that without more education, I'd never get anywhere in life, but I always found reasons for not taking the plunge. However, after a lot of thinking, I realized that my reasons for not going to college were just excuses. Though I realized it would be difficult in some ways, I decided that if I really wanted to attend college full time, I could.

My first excuse for not going to college was that I couldn't afford to go to school full time. I had worked since I finished high school, but I hadn't put much money away. I kept wondering how I would pay for books and tuition. I also needed to support myself and pay for rent, food, and car
⋀
The solution to my problem came unexpectedly.
expenses. I was working as a house painter, and a house I was painting
⋀
belonged to a college instructor. ~~Painting wasn't hard work, but it was boring.~~
During my lunch break, we
~~I'd start in the morning and work without a break until lunch.~~ We began
⋀
talking. When I told him about my situation, he told me I should look at our local community college. He also told me about some loans and grants
Later,
I'd probably be able to apply for. I went online and looked at the college's
⋀
Web site. I found out that tuition was forty dollars a credit, much less than I thought it would be. If I got just one of the grants he mentioned, I

The money I'd saved, along with what I could make painting houses on the weekends, could get me through.

might be able to make it.
⋀

Now that I had taken care of my first excuse, I had to deal with my second—that I hadn't been a good student in high school. When I was a

In class, I would stare out the window or watch the second hand on the clock move slowly around. I never bothered with homework. School just didn't interest me.

teenager, I didn't care much about school.
In fact, school
~~School~~ bored me ~~to death~~. Probably
⋀   ⋀
as a result, I got bad grades. Now that I was considering going back to school, though, I wondered what price I would have to pay for my laziness and immaturity. The answer to this question was not as bad as I thought it would be. According to the community college's Web site, all I needed to be admitted was a high school diploma and county residence. I would have to take some placement tests, but I would be judged on my ability, not my high school grades. I knew I could do better if I made a real effort to study harder

and smarter. ~~The Web site was easy to navigate, and I had no problem~~

~~finding information.~~

     My biggest problem still bothered me:
     ∧ I had a hard time picturing myself in college. No one in my family

had ever gone to college. My friends were just like me; they all went to

work right after high school. I had no role model or mentor who could give

          Besides,
me advice. ∧ I thought I was just too old for college. After all, I was probably at

least six years older than most of the students. How would I be able to keep

up with the younger students in the class? I hadn't opened a textbook for

                              However, most
years, and I'd never really learned how to study. ∧ ~~Most~~ of my fears disappeared

during my first few weeks of classes. I saw a lot of students who were as old

as I was, and some were even older. Studying didn't seem to be a problem

either. I actually enjoyed learning. History, which had put me to sleep in high

school, suddenly became interesting. So did math and English. It soon became

clear to me that I was going to like being in college.

     Going to college as a full-time student has changed my life, both

personally and financially. I am no longer the same person I was in high

          In the past,
school. ∧ I allowed laziness and insecurity to hold me back. Now, I have options

that I didn't have before. When I graduate from community college, I plan to

transfer to the state university and get a four-year degree.   The other day,
one of my instructors asked me if I had ever considered becoming a teacher. The truth
is, I never had, but now I might. I'd like to be able to give kids like me the tough,
realistic advice I wish someone had given me.

PRACTICE
13-13   Working in a group of three or four students, answer the following questions:

- What kind of material did Jared White add to his draft?
- What did he delete?
- Why do you think he made these changes?
- Do you agree with Jared's changes?

Be prepared to discuss your reactions to these changes with the class.

     When his revisions and edits were complete, Jared proofread his essay
to make sure he had not missed any errors. The final revised and edited
version of his essay appears on pages 202–3. (Marginal annotations have
been added to highlight key features of his paper; transitional words and
phrases are shaded.) Notice that the final draft includes all the elements
Jared looked for when he TESTed his essay.

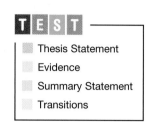

Jared White
Professor Wilkinson
English 120
7 Oct. 2011

Starting Over

Introduction

The other day, my sociology instructor mentioned that half the students enrolled in college programs across the country are twenty-five or older. His remarks caught my attention because I am one of those students. I was out of school for six years after I graduated from high school. The decision to return to school was one I had a lot of difficulty making. I had been around enough to know that without more education, I would never get anywhere in life, but I always found reasons for not taking the plunge. However, after a lot of thinking, I realized that my reasons for not going to college were just

Thesis statement

excuses. Though I realized it would be difficult in some ways, I decided that if I really wanted to attend college full time, I could.

Topic sentence (first main point)

My first excuse for not going to college was that I couldn't afford to go to school full time. I had worked since I finished high school, but I hadn't

Evidence (details and examples)

put much money away. I kept wondering how I would pay for books and tuition. I also needed to support myself and pay for rent, food, and car expenses. The solution to my problem came unexpectedly. I was working as a house painter, and a house I was painting belonged to a college instructor. During my lunch break, we began talking. When I told him about my situation, he told me I should look at our local community college. He also told me about some loans and grants I'd probably be able to apply for. Later, I went online and looked at the college's Web site. I found out that tuition was forty dollars a credit, much less than I thought it would be. If

Body paragraphs

I got just one of the grants he mentioned, I might be able to make it. The money I'd saved, along with what I could make painting houses on the weekends, could get me through.

Topic sentence (second main point)

Now that I had taken care of my first excuse, I had to deal with my second—that I hadn't been a good student in high school. When I was a

Evidence (details and examples)

teenager, I didn't care much about school. In fact, school bored me. In class, I would stare out the window or watch the second hand on the clock move slowly around. I never bothered with homework. School just didn't interest me. Probably as a result, I got bad grades. Now that I was considering going back to school, though, I wondered what price I would have to pay for my laziness and immaturity. The answer to this question was not as bad as I thought it would be. According to the community college's Web site, all I needed to be admitted was a high school diploma and county residence. I would have to take some placement tests, but I would be judged on my ability, not my high school grades. I knew I could do better if I made a real effort to study harder and smarter.

Topic sentence (third main point)

My biggest problem still bothered me: I had a hard time picturing myself in college. No one in my family had ever gone to college. My friends were just like me; they all went to work right after high school. I had no role model or mentor who could give me advice. Besides, I thought I was just too old for college. After all, I was probably at least six years older than most of the students. How would I be able to keep up with the younger students in the class? I hadn't opened a textbook for years, and I'd never really learned how to study. However, most of my fears disappeared during my first few weeks of classes. I saw a lot of students who were as old as I was, and some were even older. Studying didn't seem to be a problem either. I actually enjoyed learning. For example, history, which had put me to sleep in high school, suddenly became interesting. So did math and English. It soon became clear to me that I was going to like being in college.

Going to college as a full-time student has changed my life, both personally and financially. I am no longer the same person I was in high school. In the past, I allowed laziness and insecurity to hold me back. Now, I have options that I didn't have before. When I graduate from community college, I plan to transfer to the state university and get a four-year degree. The other day, one of my instructors asked me if I had ever considered becoming a teacher. The truth is, I never had, but now I might. I'd like to be able to give kids like me the tough, realistic advice I wish someone had given me.

Evidence (details and examples)

Body paragraphs

Summary statement

Conclusion

PRACTICE

13-14 Reread the final draft of Jared White's essay. Working in a group of three or four students, answer these questions:

■ Do you think this draft is better than his first draft (shown on pages 200–201)?

■ What other changes could Jared have made?

Be prepared to discuss your group's answers with the class.

13k Checking Your Essay's Format

The **format** of an essay is the way it looks on a page—for example, the size of the margins, the placement of page numbers, and the amount of space between lines. Most instructors expect you to follow a certain format when you type an essay. The model essay format illustrated on the following page is commonly used in composition classes. Before you hand in an essay, you should make sure that it follows this model (or the guidelines your instructor gives you).

Essay Format: Sample First Page

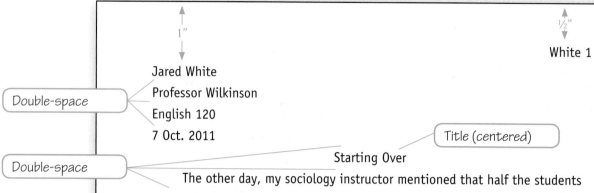

1"

½"

White 1

Jared White
Professor Wilkinson
English 120
7 Oct. 2011

Double-space

Title (centered)

Starting Over

Double-space

The other day, my sociology instructor mentioned that half the students enrolled in college programs across the country are twenty-five or older. His remarks caught my attention because I am one of those students. I was out of school for six years after I graduated from high school. The decision to return to school was one I had a lot of difficulty making. I had been around enough to know that without more education, I would never get anywhere in life, but I always found reasons for not taking the plunge. However, after a lot of thinking, I realized that my reasons for not going to college were just excuses. Though I realized it would be difficult in some ways, I decided that if I really wanted to attend college full time, I could.

Indent ½ inch

My first excuse for not going to college was that I couldn't afford to go to school full time. I had worked since I finished high school, but I hadn't put much money away. I kept wondering how I would pay for books and tuition. I also needed to support myself and pay for rent, food, and car expenses. The solution to my problem came unexpectedly. I was working as a house painter, and a house I was painting belonged to a college instructor. During my lunch break, we began talking. When I told him about my situation, he told me I should look at our local community college. He also told me . . .

← 1" →   ← 1" →

Teaching Tip
Using your school's course management system, you can have students post their essays to an online class discussion board and respond to one another, or you can have pairs of students exchange essay drafts by email.

Note: The bottom margin of each page should be one inch.

revise and edit

Revise your draft, using the Self-Assessment Checklist on page 198 to guide you. (If your instructor gives you permission, you may use one of the other revision strategies listed in the chart on pages 197–98.) When you have finished revising, edit your draft, using the Self-Assessment Checklist on page 199 as a guide. Then, prepare a final revised and edited draft of your essay. Finally, make sure that your essay's format follows your instructor's guidelines.

EDITING PRACTICE

1. The following student essay is missing its thesis statement and topic sentences and has no summary statement. First, write an appropriate thesis statement on the lines provided. (Make sure your thesis statement clearly communicates the essay's main idea.) Then, fill in the topic sentences for the second, third, and fourth paragraphs. Finally, add a summary statement in the conclusion.

Preparing for a Job Interview

I have looked at a lot of books and many Web sites that give advice on how to do well on a job interview. Some recommend practicing your handshake, and others suggest making eye contact. This advice is useful, but not many books tell how to get mentally prepared for an interview.

[Thesis statement:] _Answers will vary._

_____

_____

Woman at job interview

    [Topic sentence for the second paragraph:] _Answers will vary._

_____

_____

Feeling good about how I look is important, so I usually wear a jacket and tie to an interview. Even if you will not be dressing this formally on the job, try to make a good first impression. For this reason, you should never come to an interview dressed in jeans or shorts. Still, you should be careful not to overdress. For example, wearing a suit or a dressy dress to an interview at a fast-food restaurant might make you feel good, but it could also make you look as if you do not really want to work there.

    [Topic sentence for the third paragraph:] _Answers will vary._

_____

_____

Going on an interview is a little like getting ready to compete in a sporting event. You have to go in with the right attitude. If you think you are not going to be successful, chances are that you will not be. So, before I go on any interview,

I spend some time building my confidence. I tell myself that I can do the job and that I will do well in the interview. By the time I get to the interview, I have convinced myself that I am the right person for the job.

[Topic sentence for the fourth paragraph:] *Answers will vary.*

_____

_____

Most people go to an interview knowing little or nothing about the job. They expect the interviewer to tell them what they will have to do. Once, an interviewer told me that he likes a person who has taken the time to do his or her homework. Since that time, I have always done some research before I go on an interview— even for a part-time job. Most of the time, my research is nothing more than a quick look at the company Web site, but this kind of research really pays off. At my last interview, for example, I was able to talk in detail about the job I would do. The interviewer must have been impressed because she offered me the job on the spot.

Man arriving at job interview

[Summary statement:] *Answers will vary.*

_____

_____

Of course, following my suggestions will not guarantee that you get a job. You still have to do well at the interview itself. Even so, getting mentally prepared for the interview will give you an advantage over people who do almost nothing before they walk in the door.

2. Now, using the topic sentence below, write another body paragraph that you could add to the essay above. (This new paragraph will go right before the essay's conclusion.)

Another way to prepare yourself mentally is to anticipate and answer some typical questions interviewers ask. [New body paragraph:]

Answers will vary.

_____

_____

_____

COLLABORATIVE ACTIVITIES

1. On your own, find a paragraph in a magazine or a newspaper about an issue that interests you. Then, working in a group of three students, select one of the paragraphs. Choose three supporting points that you could develop in a short essay, and then brainstorm about these points. Finally, write a sentence that could serve as the thesis statement for an essay.

2. Working in a group, come up with thesis statements suitable for essays on three of the following topics.

   Living on a budget   Gun safety
   Social-networking sites   Drawbacks of online dating
   Safe driving   Patriotism
   Sustainable energy   Community service
   Honesty   Preparing for a test

3. Exchange your group's three thesis statements with those of another group. Choose the best one of the other group's thesis statements. A member of each group can then read the thesis statement to the class and explain why the group chose the thesis statement it did.

> **Teaching Tip**
> Refer students to 13d for information on stating a thesis.

review checklist

Writing an Essay

- [ ] Most essays have a thesis-and-support structure. The thesis statement presents the main idea, and the body paragraphs support the thesis. (See 13a.)

- [ ] Begin by focusing on your assignment, audience, and purpose to help you find a topic. (See 13b.)

- [ ] Find ideas to write about. (See 13c.)

- [ ] Identify your main idea, and develop an effective thesis statement. (See 13d.)

- [ ] List the points that best support your thesis, and arrange them in the order in which you plan to discuss them, creating an informal outline of your essay. (See 13e and 13f.)

- [ ] Write your first draft, making sure your essay has a thesis-and-support structure. (See 13g.)

- [ ] TEST your essay. (See 13h.)

- [ ] Revise your essay. (See 13i.)

- [ ] Edit your essay. (See 13j.)

- [ ] Make sure your essay's format is correct. (See 13k.)

14 TESTing Your Essays

okcupid

37,696 online now

Already a member?

Username

Password

Sign In

Forgot your password?

" The Google of online dating "
— *The Boston Globe*

" The best free dating site "
— *About.com*

Join Us!

Join the best dating site on Earth

OkCupid – Free Dating

Welcome to OkCupid!
We just need a few things to get starte

Gender   I'm female

Orientation I'm straight

Status   I'm single

Next

write first

Thousands of people have used sites like OkCupid to meet people. Assume that you are writing an article about online dating for your school newspaper. What tips would you give students who were thinking about using an online dating site? What are the advantages and disadvantages of meeting people this way? Make sure your article is written in the form of a thesis-and-support essay.

Just as you **TEST** your paragraphs, you should also **TEST** your essays. **TEST**ing will tell you whether your essay includes the basic elements it needs to be effective. Once you finish **TEST**ing your essay, you will go on to revise and edit it.

Thesis Statement
Evidence
Summary Statement
Transitions

14a   TESTing for a Thesis

The first thing you do when you **TEST** your essay is to make sure it has a clear **thesis statement (T)** that identifies the essay's main idea. By stating the main idea, your thesis statement helps to unify your essay.

The following introduction is from an essay written by a student, Amber Ransom, on the dangers of social networking. Notice that Amber states her thesis in the last sentence of her introduction, where readers expect to see it.

INTRODUCTION

Social-networking sites have many advantages. These sites, such as Facebook and MySpace, enable people to create profiles and to personalize them with pictures. "Friends" can browse these profiles and post comments that can then be viewed by anyone who has access to the profile. Many people meet online and then go on to form close friendships in real life. Some schools even set up social-networking sites for students so they can keep in touch, get advice, ask questions about schoolwork, and get feedback on assignments. Despite their many benefits, however, social-networking sites can create serious problems that people should be aware of.

TEST
- Thesis Statement
- Evidence
- Summary Statement
- Transitions

14b   TESTing for Evidence

The next thing you do when you **TEST** your essay is to check your **evidence (E)**. Make sure that the body of your essay includes enough details and examples to support your thesis. Remember that without evidence, your essay is really only a series of unsupported general statements. A well-developed essay includes enough evidence to explain, illustrate, and clarify the points you are making.

At this stage, most of your evidence will come from your personal experience and observations or from class lectures or discussions. (Later, when you do research, you will be able to support your thesis with information from print or electronic sources.)

The following body paragraphs are from Amber Ransom's essay on the dangers of social networking. Notice that each of Amber's body paragraphs includes a topic sentence that connects the paragraph to her thesis. In addition, the body paragraphs include the evidence Amber needs to develop and support the points she makes in her essay.

BODY PARAGRAPHS

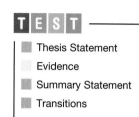

Thesis Statement
Evidence
Summary Statement
Transitions

One problem with social-networking sites is the amount of time people devote to them. Some users spend hours every day just checking in with their "friends." This can be an especially serious problem for some students, who can become more interested in socializing online than in learning. Because they can access social-networking sites with their smartphones and laptops, they often spend more time in class communicating with their friends than listening to their instructors. These problems are not limited to students. In fact, some people have been fired from their jobs because of their excessive involvement with social-networking sites. For example, a waitress was fired because she couldn't resist posting pictures of herself at the beach on a day when she was supposed to be at home sick, and a medical technician was fired because of negative comments he made online about his supervisor.

Another problem with social-networking sites is that they can reveal a lot of personal information. Some people include so much personal information in their profiles that they risk identity theft, identity fraud, or even worse. Even though sites like Facebook have privacy settings, users often ignore them and post personal information such as birthdays, schools they attended, dates of graduation, email addresses, job titles, pets' names, and even phone numbers. Dishonest people can access this information, allowing them to establish false identities, get credit cards, and gain access to checking accounts. An even more serious problem occurs with sexual predators, who routinely surf social-networking sites to search for victims. Children are especially vulnerable to these predators because they are often unaware of the danger.

One of the most serious problems with social-networking sites is that they make cyberbullying—the use of computers (as well as cell phones and other devices) to embarrass, annoy, or even threaten others—easier. Cyberbullies spread vicious rumors by posting false stories on bulletin boards. Sometimes they set up false profiles on networking sites, using people's real names, pictures, and email addresses. As a result, victims are flooded with anonymous email messages that harass and threaten them. In one famous case, Megan Meier, a fourteen-year-old girl, committed suicide after being cyberbullied by the jealous mother of a former friend. The mother set up a false MySpace account and pretended to be a boy, taunting Megan so much that she eventually committed suicide.

14c   TESTing for a Summary Statement

The third thing you do when you **TEST** your essay is to look at your conclusion and make sure that it includes a **summary statement (S)**. Most often, your conclusion will begin with this statement, which reinforces your essay's thesis. By reinforcing your thesis, this summary statement helps to unify your essay.

The following conclusion is from Amber Ransom's essay on the dangers of social networking. Notice that it begins with a summary statement and ends with some general concluding remarks.

CONCLUSION

Despite their benefits, social-networking sites have created many problems. The amount of time that people spend on these sites, the lack of privacy, and the use of sites by cyberbullies are a concern for everyone. Unfortunately, many people underestimate the potential danger of social-networking sites. As a result, they post personal information and make it easy for someone to target them. Once users know the risks, however, they can take steps to keep themselves and their families safe. The basic rule for everyone who uses these sites is not to post information about yourself that you do not want everyone to know.

Teaching Tip
Tell students that the summary statement should not simply restate the thesis. It should emphasize the main idea of the essay.

T E S T
- Thesis Statement
- Evidence
- Summary Statement
- Transitions

14d   TESTing for Transitions

The last thing you do when you **TEST** your essay is to make sure that it includes **transitions (T)**—words and phrases that connect your ideas. Make sure you have included all the transitions you need to tell readers how one sentence (or paragraph) is connected to another. Including transitions makes your essay coherent, with its sentences arranged in a clear, logical sequence that helps readers understand your ideas.

By linking sentences and paragraphs, transitions emphasize the relationship between ideas and help readers understand your essay's logic. By reminding readers of what has come before, transitions prepare readers for new information and help them understand how it fits into the discussion.

Transitions are categorized according to their function. For example, they may indicate **time order** (*first, second, now, next, finally,* and so on), **spatial order** (*above, behind, near, next to, over,* and so on), or **logical order** (*also, although, therefore, in fact,* and so on). (For a full list of transitions, see 3d.)

Here are the thesis statement and the body paragraphs from Amber Ransom's essay on the dangers of social networking. Notice how the highlighted transitions link the sentences and the paragraphs of the essay.

Teaching Tip
You may want to point out to students how Amber's topic sentences help to unify her essay by referring to the thesis statement.

TEST

- Thesis Statement
- Evidence
- Summary Statement
- Transitions

THESIS + BODY PARAGRAPHS

Despite their many benefits, social-networking sites can create serious problems that people should be aware of.

One problem with social-networking sites is the amount of time people devote to them. Some users spend hours every day just checking in with their "friends." This can be an especially serious problem for some students, who can become more interested in socializing online than in learning. Because they can access social-networking sites with their smartphones and laptops, they often spend more time in class communicating with their friends than listening to their instructors. These problems are not limited to students. In fact, some people have been fired from their jobs because of their excessive involvement with social-networking sites. For example, a waitress was fired because she couldn't resist posting pictures of herself at the beach on a day when she was supposed to be at home sick, and a medical technician was fired because of negative comments he made online about his supervisor.

Another problem with social-networking sites is that they can reveal a lot of personal information. Some people include so much personal information in their profiles that they risk identity theft, identity fraud, or even worse. Even though sites like Facebook have privacy settings, users often ignore them and post personal information such as birthdays, schools they attended, dates of graduation, email addresses, job titles, pets' names, and even phone numbers. Dishonest people can access this information, allowing them to establish false identities, get credit cards, and gain access to checking accounts. An even more serious problem occurs with sexual predators, who routinely surf social-networking sites to search for victims. Children are especially vulnerable to these predators because they are often unaware of the danger.

One of the most serious problems with social-networking sites is that they make cyberbullying—the use of computers (as well as cell phones and other devices) to embarrass, annoy, and even threaten others—easier. Cyberbullies spread vicious rumors by posting false stories on bulletin boards. Sometimes they set up false profiles on networking sites, using people's real names, pictures, and email addresses. As a result, victims are flooded with anonymous email messages that harass and threaten them. In one famous case, Megan Meier, a fourteen-year-old girl, committed suicide after being cyberbullied by the jealous mother of a former friend. The mother set up a false MySpace account and pretended to be a boy, taunting Megan so much that she eventually committed suicide.

14e Putting It Together

Here is Amber Ransom's completed essay, which includes a title and the heading required by her instructor.

Amber Ransom
Professor Fallows
Composition 101
5 Nov. 2011

T **E** **S** **T**
Thesis Statement
Evidence
Summary Statement
Transitions

The Dangers of Social Networking

Social-networking sites have many advantages. These sites, such as Facebook and MySpace, enable people to create profiles and to personalize them with pictures. "Friends" can browse these profiles and post comments that can then be viewed by anyone who has access to the profile. Many people meet online and then go on to form close friendships in real life. Some schools even set up social-networking sites for students so they can keep in touch, get advice, ask questions about schoolwork, and get feedback on assignments. Despite their many benefits, however, social-networking sites can create serious problems that people should be aware of.

One problem with social-networking sites is the amount of time people devote to them. Some users spend hours every day just checking in with their "friends." This can be an especially serious problem for some students, who can become more interested in socializing online than in learning. Because they can access social-networking sites with their smartphones and laptops, they often spend more time in class communicating with their friends than listening to their instructors. These problems are not limited to students. In fact, some people have been fired from their jobs because of their excessive involvement with social-networking sites. For example, a waitress was fired because she couldn't resist posting pictures of herself at the beach on a day when she was supposed to be at home sick, and a medical technician was fired because of negative comments he made online about his supervisor.

Another problem with social-networking sites is that they can reveal a lot of personal information. Some people include so much personal information in their profiles that they risk identity theft, identity fraud, or even worse. Even though sites like Facebook have privacy settings, users often ignore them and post personal information such as birthdays, schools they attended, dates of graduation, email addresses, job titles, pets' names, and even phone numbers. Dishonest people can access this information, allowing them to establish false identities, get credit cards, and gain access to checking accounts. An even more serious problem occurs with sexual predators, who routinely surf social-networking sites to search for victims. Children are especially vulnerable to these predators because they are often unaware of the danger.

One of the most serious problems with social-networking sites is that they make cyberbullying—the use of computers (as well as cell phones and other devices) to embarrass, annoy, or even threaten others—easier. Cyberbullies spread vicious rumors by posting false stories on bulletin boards. Sometimes they set up false profiles on networking sites, using people's real names, pictures, and email addresses. As a result, victims are flooded with anonymous email messages that harass and threaten them. In one famous case, Megan

Introduction

Thesis statement

Topic sentence
(first main point)

Evidence
(details and examples)

Topic sentence
(second main point)

Body paragraphs

Evidence
(details and examples)

Topic sentence
(third main point)

Evidence
(details and examples)

Meier, a fourteen-year-old girl, committed suicide after being cyberbullied by the jealous mother of a former friend. The mother set up a false MySpace account and pretended to be a boy, taunting Megan so much that she eventually committed suicide.

Summary statement

Despite their benefits, social-networking sites have created many problems. The amount of time that people spend on these sites, the lack of privacy, and the use of sites by cyberbullies are concerns for everyone. Unfortunately, many people underestimate the potential danger of social-networking sites. As a result, they post personal information and make it easy for someone to target them. Once users know the risks, however, they can take steps to keep themselves and their families safe. The basic rule for everyone who uses these sites is not to post information about yourself that you do not want everyone to know.

Conclusion

PRACTICE

14-1   Read the final draft of Amber's essay. What changes would you make to her essay? For example, do you think her thesis is appropriate? What additional evidence could she have included? Does her summary statement help to unify her essay? Does she include enough transitions?

TEST · Revise · Edit

Look back at your response to the Write First activity on page 208. Then, TEST your essay to make sure that it includes a thesis statement, evidence, a summary statement, and transitions. Finally, prepare a revised and edited draft of your essay.

EDITING PRACTICE

A first-year student wrote the following essay for his composition class. Read the essay, TEST it, and then answer the questions on pages 216–17.

The Case Against Enhanced Water

Flavored (or "enhanced") water has grown in popularity since it was introduced in the late 1960s. Soft-drink companies such as Coca-Cola and Pepsi own most enhanced water brands. These companies have spent millions of dollars trying to convince consumers that enhanced water is better than ordinary water. However, that is not necessarily true.

There is no question that our bodies need fluid to stay hydrated. In fact, most experts say that people should drink about 64 ounces (eight cups) of water a day. Only athletes and people who are involved in strenuous activities, such as hiking and distance running, need to drink significantly more water. These individuals may benefit from the salt and carbohydrates found in sports drinks like Gatorade, but they are the exception. People who exercise at a normal rate, for about an hour a day, usually need only a few additional cups of plain water to restore lost fluids.

Despite marketing claims to the contrary, it is not clear that enhanced water is more healthful than tap water. The labels on most enhanced water drinks, such as vitaminwater and SoBe Lifewater, make health claims that have not been scientifically proven. For instance, the label on vitaminwater's drink Defense implies that its vitamins and minerals will prevent a person from getting sick. Most scientists agree, however, that there is no magic formula for preventing illness. Another example of a misleading claim appears on the label of SoBe's strawberry-kiwi-flavored Calm-o-mile drink, which lists herbs that are supposed to relieve stress. However, there are not enough herbs in this drink to provide any health benefits. Moreover, many enhanced water drinks actually contain ingredients that the body does not need—for example, caffeine, artificial flavors and colors, and sugar or artificial sweeteners.

In addition to making questionable marketing claims, manufacturers of enhanced water often present nutritional information in a confusing way. For example, a quick glance at the label on a SoBe Lifewater drink would lead someone to believe that a single serving has 40 calories, 16 grams of carbohydrates, and 10 grams of sugar. These amounts may seem reasonable, but a closer look at the label reveals that each 20-ounce bottle actually contains two-and-a-half servings. In other words, a person who drinks the whole bottle actually consumes 100 calories, 40 grams of carbohydrates, and 25 grams of sugar—more carbohydrates and sugar than in a glazed doughnut.

In most cases, regular tap water is all people need to stay healthy and hydrated. The drink manufacturers ignore this fact, instead emphasizing the point that enhanced water is lower in calories and sugar than nondiet soft drinks. They also say that although the herbs and vitamins in their drinks may not have proven health benefits, at least they are not harmful. Finally, the drink manufacturers claim that their products actually encourage people to drink more fluids. Although some of these claims may be true, consumers do not need the extra ingredients in enhanced water or the extra cost.

PRACTICE

14-2

1. Underline the essay's thesis statement. Does the thesis statement clearly and accurately express the essay's main idea? If necessary, revise the thesis on the lines below.

Answers will vary.

_____

2. What evidence does the writer provide to support the ideas in the first body paragraph? What additional evidence could the writer have provided?

3. What evidence does the writer provide to support the ideas in the second body paragraph? What additional evidence could the writer have provided?

4. What evidence does the writer provide to support the ideas in the third body paragraph? What additional evidence could the writer have provided?

5. Does the essay's conclusion include a summary statement? If not, write one on the lines below.

Answers will vary.

_____

_____

6. Does the writer provide enough transitions? If necessary, add transitions to the essay.

COLLABORATIVE ACTIVITIES

1. Bring to class an essay that you have written. Exchange papers with another student, and TEST his or her essay to see if it includes all the required elements.

2. Bring in an op-ed column that appears in a newspaper (either print or online). Working in a group of three or four students, TEST the op-ed article, and decide what changes you would make to improve it.

review checklist

TESTing Your Essays

☐ An essay should include a thesis statement that identifies its main idea. (See 14a.)

☐ An essay should include evidence—details and examples—to support its thesis. (See 14b.)

☐ An essay's conclusion should include a summary statement that reinforces the thesis and helps unify the essay. (See 14c.)

☐ An essay should include transitions that indicate how ideas are connected. (See 14d.)

preview

In this chapter, you will learn to
- write an introduction (15a)
- choose a title (15a)
- write a conclusion (15b)

15 Introductions and Conclusions

write first

This picture shows Charlie Chaplin caught in a factory machine in the film *Modern Times* (1936). Think about the title of the film and what the scene here seems to convey, and then print out a copy of the essay about your hardest job that you wrote for Chapter 13. At the end of this chapter, you will work on the introduction and conclusion of this essay.

When you draft an essay, you usually focus on the **body** because it is the section in which you develop your ideas. A well-constructed essay, however, is more than a series of body paragraphs. It also includes an **introduction** and a **conclusion**, both of which contribute to the essay's overall effectiveness.

15a   Introductions

An **introduction** is the first thing people see when they read your essay. If your introduction is interesting, it will make readers want to read further. If it is not, readers may get bored and stop reading.

Your introduction should be a full paragraph that moves from general to specific ideas. It should begin with some general **opening remarks** that will draw readers into your essay. The **thesis statement**, a specific sentence that presents the main idea of your essay, usually comes at the end of the introduction. The following diagram illustrates the shape of an introduction.

Here are some options you can experiment with when you write your introductions. (In each of the sample introductory paragraphs that follow, the thesis statement is underlined and labeled.)

Beginning with a Narrative

You can begin an essay with a narrative drawn from your own experience or from a current news event.

> On September 11, 2001, terrorists crashed two airplanes into the twin towers at the World Trade Center. Almost immediately, hundreds of firefighters rushed inside the buildings to try to save as many lives as possible. Their actions saved many people, but half the firefighters—over three hundred—died when the twin towers collapsed. <u>The sad fact is that until a tragedy occurs, most people never think about how dangerous a firefighter's job really is.</u>
>
> —Richard Pogue (student)   Thesis statement

Teaching Tip
Remind students that the introduction should be a full paragraph.

Teaching Tip
Explain to students that the inverted triangle refers to the movement of ideas from general to specific in the introductory paragraph.

Teaching Tip
Find two introductory paragraphs (one that is catchy and one that is dull), and read each one to the class. After you read each introduction, ask students whether they would like to hear the rest of the essay—and why or why not.

Beginning with a Question (or a Series of Questions)

Asking one or more questions at the beginning of your essay is an effective strategy. Because readers expect you to answer the questions, they will want to read further.

Teaching Tip
Remind students that general questions should be used only in an essay's introductory paragraph. Overusing questions in an essay may show that the writer does not know what he or she wants to say.

> What's wrong with this picture? A teenage girl sits under a Christmas tree, opening her presents. She is excited when she gets a new sweater and the running shoes she has been wanting. On the surface, everything seems fine. However, the girl's parents are uncomfortable because they know that children from developing countries probably worked long hours in sweatshops to make the American teenager's Christmas presents. <u>Instead of feeling guilty, people like this girl's parents should take steps to end child labor and help poor children live better lives.</u>
>
> —Megan Davia (student)

Thesis statement

Beginning with a Definition

A definition at the beginning of your essay can give readers important information. As the following introduction shows, a definition can help explain a complicated idea or a confusing concept.

Teaching Tip
Students love to begin their introductions with definitions. Encourage them to avoid introducing a definition with a tired opening phrase such as "According to *Webster's* . . ." or "*The American Heritage Dictionary* defines . . ."

> I admit it: I suffer from the bad habit of procrastination—putting things off until the last minute. Recently, I learned that procrastination, like any habit, is a behavior that can be controlled. To control a habit, a person has to remember to resist the behavior. For example, someone who bites her nails simply needs to notice what she is doing and to take her hands away from her mouth—again and again, if necessary. Some habits, like nail biting, are harmless. Others, like procrastination, can cause stress, guilt, and, in my case, frenzied work hours, missed classes, and low test grades. <u>Given my situation, I have decided that if I am going to succeed, I must resist the temptation to procrastinate.</u>
>
> —Deborah Keller (student)

Thesis statement

Teaching Tip
Send students to an online source such as bartleby.com to find appropriate quotations for both introductions and conclusions.

Beginning with a Quotation

An appropriate saying or some interesting dialogue can draw readers into your essay.

Teaching Tip
Remind students that when they quote or paraphrase, they must document their sources. Refer them to 17d and 17h.

> According to the comedian Jerry Seinfeld, "When you're single, you are the dictator of your own life. . . . When you're married, you are part of a vast decision-making body." In other words, before you can do anything when you are married, you have to talk it over with someone else. These words kept going through my mind as I thought about asking my girlfriend to marry me. The more I thought about Seinfeld's words, the more I put off asking. <u>I never thought about the huge price that I would pay for this delay.</u>
>
> —Dan Brody (student)

Thesis statement

Beginning with a Surprising Statement

You can begin your essay with a surprising or unexpected statement. Because your statement takes readers by surprise, it catches their attention.

> Some of the smartest people I know never went to college. In fact, some of them never finished high school. They still know how to save 20 percent on the price of a dinner, fix their own faucets when they leak, get discounted prescriptions, get free rides on a bus to Atlantic City, use public transportation to get anywhere in the city, and live on about twenty-two dollars a day. These are my grandparents' friends. Some people would call them old and poor. <u>I would call them survivors who have learned to make it through life on nothing but a Social Security check.</u>
>
> —Sean Ragas (student)

Thesis statement

FYI

What to Avoid in Introductions

When writing an introduction, avoid the following:

- Beginning your essay by announcing what you plan to write about.

  PHRASES TO AVOID

  This essay is about . . .
  In my essay, I will discuss . . .

- Apologizing for your ideas.

  PHRASES TO AVOID

  Although I don't know much about this subject . . .
  I might not be an expert, but . . .

FYI

Choosing a Title

Every essay should have a **title** that suggests the subject of the essay and makes people want to read it.

- Capitalize all words except for articles (*a, an, the*), prepositions (*at, to, of, around,* and so on), and coordinating conjunctions (*and, but,* and so on), unless they are the first or last word of the title.

- Do not underline or italicize your title or enclose it in quotation marks. Do not type your title in all capital letters.

(continued on next page)

(continued from previous page)

■ Center the title at the top of the first page. Double-space between the title and the first line of your essay.

As you consider a title for your paper, think about the following options.

■ *A title can highlight a key word or term that appears in the essay.*
In Praise of the F Word
Rice

■ *A title can be a straightforward announcement.*
Dnt Txt N Drv
How Your Body Works

■ *A title can establish a personal connection with readers.*
The Men We Carry in Our Minds
How Facebook Is Making Friending Obsolete

■ *A title can be a familiar saying or a quotation from your essay itself.*
Men Are from Mars, Women Are from Venus
I Want a Wife

PRACTICE
15-1   Look through the student essays in Chapter 16, and find one introduction you think is particularly effective. Be prepared to explain the strengths of the introduction you chose.

PRACTICE
15-2   Using the different options for creating titles discussed in the FYI box above, write two titles for each of the essays described below. *Answers will vary.*

1. A student writes an essay about three people who disappeared mysteriously: Amelia Earhart, aviator; Ambrose Bierce, writer; and Jimmy Hoffa, union leader. In the body paragraphs, the student describes the circumstances surrounding their disappearances.

_____

_____

2. A student writes an essay arguing against doctors' letting people select the gender of their babies. In the body paragraphs, she presents reasons why she thinks it is unethical.

_____

_____

3. A student writes an essay explaining why America should elect a woman president. In the body paragraphs, he gives his reasons.

_____

_____

4. A student writes an essay describing the harmful effects of steroids on student athletes. In the body paragraphs, he shows the effects on the heart, brain, and other organs.

_____

_____

5. A student writes an essay explaining why she joined the Navy Reserve. In the body paragraphs, she discusses her need to earn money for college tuition, her wish to learn a trade, and her desire to see the world.

_____

_____

15b Conclusions

Because your conclusion is the last thing readers see, they often judge your entire essay by its effectiveness. For this reason, conclusions should be planned, drafted, and revised carefully.

Like an introduction, a **conclusion** should be a full paragraph. It should begin with a **summary statement** that reinforces the essay's main idea, and it should end with some general **concluding remarks**. The following diagram illustrates the general shape of a conclusion.

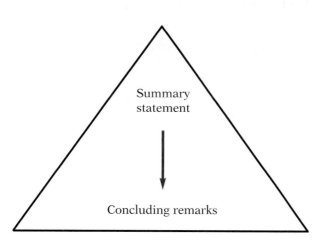

Here are some options you can experiment with when you write your conclusions. (In each of the sample concluding paragraphs that follow, the summary statement is underlined and labeled.)

Teaching Tip
Tell students not to use the exact words of their thesis when they restate their essay's main idea.

Teaching Tip
Advise students to draft their body paragraphs before they spend much time writing introductions or conclusions. After they have developed the body of their essay, they can revise their introduction and conclusion so those paragraphs are consistent with the direction that their essay has taken.

Teaching Tip
Explain to students that the triangle refers to the movement of ideas from specific to general in the concluding paragraph.

Concluding with a Narrative

A narrative conclusion can bring an event discussed in the essay to a logical, satisfying close.

Summary statement

Being a firefighter is often a very dangerous job. The firefighters who died on September 11, 2001, show how true this fact is. They rushed into the two burning World Trade towers without thinking about what could happen to them. Even as the buildings were collapsing, they continued to help people escape. At the end of the day, they did the job they had been trained to do, and they did it well. These brave people are role models for me and for other volunteer firefighters around the country. They remind all of us of how important the job we do really is.

—Richard Pogue (student)

> **Teaching Tip**
> Point out that the conclusions in 15b correspond to the introductions in 15a. Make sure students know that they can use any of the strategies in 15b when they write their own conclusions—not just the ones that match the corresponding introductions shown here.

Concluding with a Recommendation

Once you think you have convinced readers that a problem exists, you can make recommendations in your conclusion about how the problem should be solved.

Summary statement

Several steps can be taken to deal with the problem of child labor. First, people should educate themselves about the problem. They can begin by going to Web sites that give information about child labor. Then, they can join an organization such as Human Rights Watch or the Global Fund for Children. These groups sponsor programs that help child laborers in their own countries. Finally, people can stop supporting businesses that benefit either directly or indirectly from child labor. If all of us are committed to change, we can do a lot to reduce this problem worldwide.

—Megan Davia (student)

> **Teaching Tip**
> Read aloud several different types of conclusions, and have the class categorize them.

Concluding with a Quotation

A well-chosen quotation—even a brief one—can be an effective concluding strategy. In the following paragraph, the quotation reinforces the main idea of the essay.

Summary statement

With more time and hard work, I am sure I will overcome the habit that has caused me so much trouble over the years. Still, learning how to stop procrastinating has not been easy. According to the poet Edward Young, "Procrastination is the thief of time," and in my case, this statement couldn't be more true. My habit of procrastinating has caused me to miss classes, get low grades on tests, and develop low self-esteem. Now that I have decided to take control of my behavior, I feel a lot better about myself. By focusing on my poor time-management skills, forcing myself to complete assignments days or weeks before they are due, and realizing that not everything I do has to be perfect, I have begun to turn my situation around. Of course, progress has been slow, and occasionally I still put off studying for a quiz or delay beginning a big project. For the most part, however, I am dealing with my problem.

—Deborah Keller (student)

Concluding with a Prediction

This type of conclusion not only sums up the thesis but also looks to the future.

My hesitation cost me more than I ever could have dreamed. When Jen thought that I didn't want to marry her, she broke up with me. For the past three months, I have been trying to get back together with her. We have gone out a few times, and I am trying to convince her to trust me again. I hope that sometime soon we will look back at this situation and laugh. Meanwhile, all I can do is tell Jen that I am sorry and keep hoping.

Summary statement

—Dan Brody (student)

FYI

What to Avoid in Conclusions

When writing a conclusion, avoid the following:

- Introducing new ideas. Your conclusion should sum up the ideas you discuss in your essay, not open up new lines of thought.

- Apologizing for your opinions, ideas, or conclusions. Apologies will undercut your readers' confidence in you.

  PHRASES TO AVOID

  At least that is my opinion . . .
  I could be wrong, but . . .

- Using unnecessary phrases to announce your essay is coming to a close.

  PHRASES TO AVOID

  In summary, . . .
  In conclusion, . . .

> **Teaching Tip**
> Explain that in essay exams, when time is limited, a one-sentence restatement of the thesis is often enough for a conclusion. Likewise, an essay exam may require just a one- or two-sentence introduction.

PRACTICE

15-3 Look at the student essays in Chapter 16, locating one conclusion you think is particularly effective. Be prepared to explain the strengths of the conclusion you chose.

TEST · Revise · Edit

Look back at the essay you wrote in response to the Write First activity on page 173 (Chapter 13). **TEST** what you have written one more time. Then, revise and edit your introduction and conclusion. Make sure your introduction creates interest, prepares readers for the essay to follow, and includes a clear thesis statement. Then, make sure your conclusion contains a summary statement and includes general concluding remarks. Finally, make sure your essay has an appropriate title.

EDITING PRACTICE

The following student essay has an undeveloped introduction and conclusion. Decide what introductory and concluding strategies would be best for the essay. Then, rewrite both the introduction and the conclusion. Finally, suggest an interesting title for the essay.

Answers will vary.

The Most Dangerous Jobs

This essay is about three of the most dangerous jobs. They are piloting small planes, logging, and fishing.

Flying a small plane can be dangerous. For example, pilots who fly tiny planes that spray pesticides on farmers' fields do not have to comply with the safety rules for large airplanes. They also have to fly very low in order to spray the right fields. This leaves little room for error. Also, pilots of air-taxis and small commuter planes die in much greater numbers than airline pilots do. In some places, like parts of Alaska, there are long distances and few roads, so many small planes are needed. Their pilots are four times more likely to die than other pilots because of bad weather and poor visibility. In general, flying a small plane can be very risky.

Another dangerous job is logging. Loggers always are at risk of having parts of trees or heavy machinery fall on them. Tree trunks often have odd shapes, so they are hard to control while they are being transported. As a result, they often break loose from equipment that is supposed to move them. In addition, weather conditions, like snow or rain, can cause dangers. Icy or wet conditions increase the risk to loggers, who can fall from trees or slip when they are sawing a tree. Because loggers often work in remote places, it is very hard to get prompt medical aid. For this reason, a wound that could easily be treated in a hospital may be fatal to a logger.

Perhaps the most dangerous occupation is working in the fishing industry. Like loggers, professional fishermen work in unsafe conditions. They use heavy machinery to pull up nets and to move large amounts of fish. The combination of icy or slippery boat decks and large nets and cages makes the job unsafe. The weather is often very bad, so fishermen are at risk of falling overboard during a storm and drowning. In fact, drowning is the most common cause of death in this industry. Also, like logging, fishing is done far from medical help, so even minor injuries can be very serious.

In conclusion, piloting, logging, and fishing are three of the most dangerous occupations.

COLLABORATIVE ACTIVITIES

1. Bring to class several copies of an essay you wrote for another class. Have each person in your group comment on your essay's introduction and conclusion. Revise the introduction and conclusion in response to your classmates' suggestions.

2. Find a magazine or newspaper article that interests you. Cut off the introduction and conclusion, and bring the body of the article to class. Ask your group to decide on the best strategies for introducing and concluding the article. Then, collaborate on writing new opening and closing paragraphs and an interesting title.

3. Working in a group, think of interesting and appropriate titles for essays on each of the topics listed below. Try to use as many of the different options outlined in the FYI box on pages 221–22 as you can.

The difficulty of living with a roommate
The dangers of gambling
The need for regular exercise
The joys of living in the city (or in the country)
The responsibilities of having a pet
Things that make life easier
The stress of job interviews
The obligation to vote
The advantages and disadvantages of bicycle lanes
The problems of being a parent
The need for religious tolerance

review checklist

Introductions and Conclusions

☐ The introduction of your essay should include opening remarks and a thesis statement. (See 15a.) You can begin an essay with any of the following options.

A narrative	A quotation
A question	A surprising statement
A definition	

☐ Your title should suggest the subject of your essay and make people want to read further. (See 15a.)

☐ The conclusion of your essay should include a summary statement and some general concluding remarks. (See 15b.) You can conclude an essay with any of the following options.

A narrative	A quotation
A recommendation	A prediction

16 Patterns of Essay Development

Teaching Tip
You might want to tell students that many essays combine two or more patterns. Refer them to the Chapter Review on page 295.

As you learned in Chapters 4 through 12, writers have a variety of options for developing ideas within a paragraph. These options include *exemplification, narration, description, process, cause and effect, comparison and contrast, classification, definition,* and *argument.* When you write an essay, you can use these same patterns of development to help you organize your material.

In your college courses, different assignments and writing situations call for different patterns of essay development.

■ If an essay exam question asked you to compare two systems of government, you would use *comparison and contrast.*

■ If an English composition assignment asked you to tell about a childhood experience, you would use *narration.*

■ If a section of a research paper on environmental pollution called for examples of dangerous waste-disposal practices, you would use *exemplification.*

The skills you learned when you wrote paragraphs can also be applied to writing essays.

16a   Exemplification Essays

Teaching Tip
Refer students to Chapter 4 for information on writing an exemplification paragraph.

Exemplification illustrates a general statement with one or more specific examples. An **exemplification essay** uses specific examples to support a thesis.

When you TEST an **exemplification** essay, make sure it includes all these elements:

T ■ **Thesis Statement**—The introduction of an exemplification essay should include a clear **thesis statement** that identifies the essay's main idea—the idea the examples will support.

E ■ **Evidence**—The body paragraphs should present examples that support the thesis. Each body paragraph should be introduced by a topic sentence that identifies the example or group of related examples that the paragraph will discuss.

S ■ **Summary Statement**—The conclusion of an exemplification essay should include a **summary statement** that reinforces the essay's thesis.

T ■ **Transitions**—An exemplification essay should use appropriate **transitional words and phrases** to connect examples within paragraphs and between one paragraph and another.

Moving from Assignment to Thesis

ESL Tip
Some ESL students might have questions about how to choose a topic. Tell them that sometimes instructors assign the topic for the essay, while other times students choose the topics themselves.

The wording of your assignment may suggest that you write an exemplification essay. For example, you may be asked to *illustrate* or to *give examples.* Once you decide that your assignment calls for exemplification, you need to develop a thesis that reflects this purpose.

ASSIGNMENT

Education   Should children be taught only in their native languages or in English as well? Support your answer with examples of specific students' experiences.

Literature   Does William Shakespeare's *Othello* have to end tragically? Illustrate your position with references to specific characters.

Composition   Discuss the worst job you ever had, including plenty of specific examples to support your thesis.

THESIS STATEMENT

The success of students in a bilingual third-grade class suggests the value of teaching elementary-school students in English as well as in their native languages.

Each of the three major characters in *Othello* contributes to the play's tragic ending.

My summer job at a fast-food restaurant was my worst job because of the endless stream of rude customers, the many boring tasks I had to perform, and my manager's insensitivity.

> **Teaching Tip**
> For examples of exemplification essays by professional writers, see 39a.

> **Teaching Tip**
> Tell students that many everyday writing tasks call for exemplification. For example, a parent committee's report for a day-care center might present examples of possible environmental hazards in the school building.

Organizing an Exemplification Essay

In an exemplification essay, each body paragraph can develop a single example or discuss several related examples. The topic sentence should introduce the example (or group of related examples) that the paragraph will discuss. Each example you select should clearly support your thesis.

> **Teaching Tip**
> Make sure students know that ¶ is the symbol for a paragraph.

Essay Map: *One Example per Paragraph*

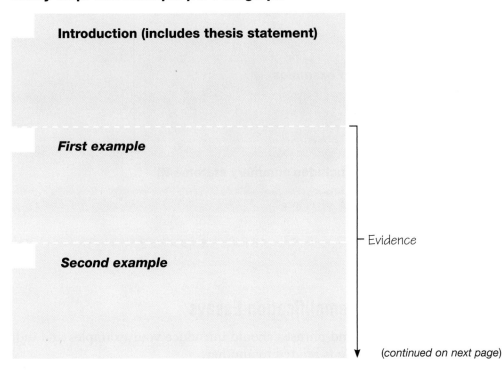

Introduction (includes thesis statement)

First example

Second example

Evidence

(continued on next page)

(continued from previous page)

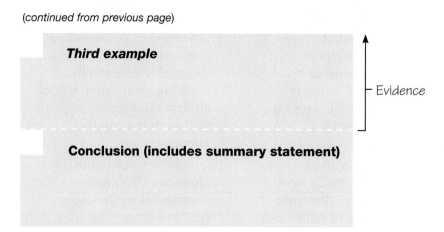

Essay Map: *Several Related Examples per Paragraph*

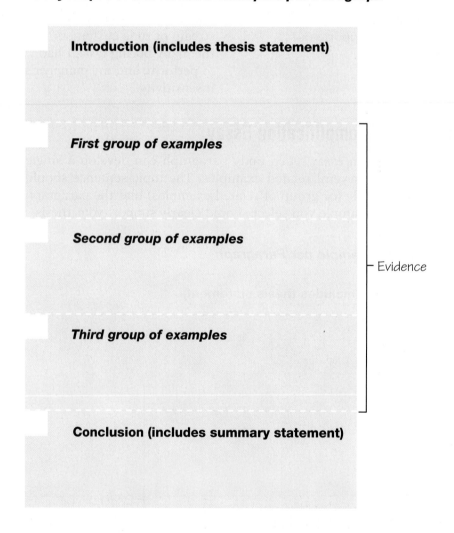

Transitions in Exemplification Essays

Transitional words and phrases should introduce your examples and indicate how one example is related to another.

> ## Some Transitional Words and Phrases for Exemplification.
>
> | | | |
> |---|---|---|
> | also | furthermore | the most important |
> | besides | in addition | example |
> | finally | moreover | the next example |
> | first | one example . . . | |
> | for example | another example | |
> | for instance | specifically | |

Case Study: A Student Writes an Exemplification Essay

When Kyle Sims, a student in a first-year writing course, was asked to write an essay about a popular hobby or interest, he didn't know how to narrow this broad topic. His instructor encouraged students to use their own experience as a source of ideas. Kyle imagined that most of his classmates would write about topics like video games or sports. He did know a lot about sports, but his knowledge came from being a spectator, not a participant. He decided to use this knowledge by writing about extreme sports, a topic he thought would be different from (and therefore more interesting than) the topics his classmates might choose.

Once he had settled on a topic, Kyle did some freewriting on his laptop. When he read over his freewriting, he saw that he had come up with three kinds of information: ideas about the dangers of extreme sports, about the challenges they present, and about the equipment they require. His thesis statement—"Extreme sports are different from more familiar sports because they are dangerous, they are physically challenging, and they require specialized equipment"—identified these three kinds of information. After brainstorming about each of these ideas, he had enough material for a first draft.

As he wrote his first draft, Kyle devoted one paragraph to each kind of information, using examples to develop his body paragraphs. When he finished his draft, he TESTed it to make sure it included a thesis statement, supporting evidence, a summary statement, and transitional words and phrases. He was satisfied with his thesis, which told readers what points he was going to make about extreme sports and also conveyed the idea that they were not like ordinary sports. His summary statement seemed logical and appropriate. In reading over his examples to support his thesis, he realized that his readers might not know much about extreme sports. Kyle then added more examples to illustrate a range of different kinds of extreme sports and more transitions to lead readers from one example to the next.

After checking his draft against the TEST checklist for exemplification (see page 236), Kyle revised his draft, rewriting his topic sentences so they clearly identified the three points he wanted to make about extreme sports. When he finished his revision, he edited and proofread carefully and made sure his essay met his instructor's format requirements.

The following final draft includes all the elements Kyle looked for when he TESTed his essay.

Model Exemplification Essay

Read Kyle Sims's finished essay, and answer the question in Practice 16-1.

Going to Extremes

Introduction

Thesis statement

Topic sentence (first point)

Evidence (details and examples)

Topic sentence (second point)

Evidence (details and examples)

Body paragraphs

Topic sentence (third point)

Evidence (details and examples)

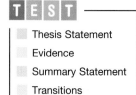

T E S T

☐ Thesis Statement
☐ Evidence
☐ Summary Statement
☐ Transitions

Conclusion

Summary statement

For years, sports like football, baseball, and basketball have been popular in cities, suburbs, and small rural towns. For some young people, however, these sports no longer seem exciting, especially when compared to "extreme sports," such as snowboarding and BMX racing. Extreme sports are different from more familiar sports because they are dangerous, they are physically challenging, and they require specialized equipment.   1

First, extreme sports are dangerous. For example, snowboarders take chances with snowy hills and unpredictable bumps. They zoom down mountains at high speeds, which is typical of extreme sports. In addition, snowboarders and skateboarders risk painful falls as they do their tricks. Also, many extreme sports, like rock climbing, bungee jumping, and sky diving, are performed at very high altitudes. Moreover, the bungee jumper has to jump from a very high place, and there is always a danger of getting tangled with the bungee cord. People who participate in extreme sports accept—and even enjoy—these dangers.   2

In addition, extreme sports are very difficult. For instance, surfers have to learn to balance surfboards while dealing with wind and waves. Bungee jumpers may have to learn how to do difficult stunts while jumping off a high bridge or a dam. Another example of the physical challenge of extreme sports can be found in BMX racing. BMX racers have to learn to steer a lightweight bike on a dirt track that has jumps and banked corners. These extreme sports require skills that most people do not naturally have. These special skills have to be learned, and participants in extreme sports enjoy this challenge.   3

Finally, almost all extreme sports require specialized equipment. For example, surfers need surfboards that are light but strong. They can choose epoxy boards, which are stronger, or fiberglass boards, which are lighter. They can choose shortboards, which are shorter than seven feet and are easier to maneuver. Or, they can use longboards, which are harder and slower to turn in the water but are easier to learn on. Also, surfers have to get special wax for their boards to keep from slipping as they are paddling out into the water. For surfing in cold water, they need wetsuits that trap their own body heat. Other extreme sports require different kinds of specialized equipment, but those who participate in them are willing to buy whatever they need.   4

Clearly, extreme sports are very different from other sports. Maybe it is because they are so different that they have become so popular in recent years. Already, snowboarding and other extreme sports are featured in the Winter Olympics. In the future, the Olympics will include skateboarding and BMX racing. The Summer and Winter X Games are televised on ESPN and ABC, and sports like BMX racing, snowboarding, surfing, and snowmobiling get national attention on these programs. With all this publicity, extreme sports are likely to become even more popular—despite their challenges.   5

PRACTICE
16-1

1. Restate Kyle's thesis in your own words.

2. What three points about extreme sports does Kyle make in the topic sentences of his body paragraphs?

3. What examples of extreme sports does Kyle give in paragraph 1? What examples of dangers does he give in paragraph 2? In paragraph 4, Kyle discusses surfing, giving examples of the equipment surfers need. List this equipment.

4. Is Kyle's introduction effective? How else might he have opened his essay?

5. Paraphrase Kyle's summary statement.

6. What is this essay's greatest strength? What is its greatest weakness?

grammar in context

Exemplification

When you write an exemplification essay, you may introduce your examples with transitional words and phrases like *First* or *In addition*. If you do, be sure to use a comma.

First, extreme sports are dangerous.

In addition, extreme sports are very difficult.

Finally, almost all extreme sports require specialized equipment.

For information on using commas with introductory transitional words and phrases, see 34b.

Teaching Tip
Before your students write exemplification essays, you might want to explain the use of commas to set off introductory elements (34b) and have them do Practice 34-2.

Step-by-Step Guide: Writing an Exemplification Essay

Now, you are ready to write an exemplification essay on one of the topics listed below (or a topic of your choice).

TOPICS

Reasons to start (or not to start) college right after high school
The three best products ever invented
What kinds of people or images should appear on U.S. postage stamps? Why?
Advantages (or disadvantages) of being a young parent
Athletes who really are role models
Four items students need to survive in college
What messages do rap or hip-hop artists send to listeners?
Study strategies that work
Traits of a good employee
Three or four recent national or world news events that gave you hope

As you plan, draft, and revise your essay, follow these steps:

- Make sure your topic calls for exemplification.
- Find ideas to write about.
- Identify your main idea, and write a thesis statement.

Teaching Tip
Refer students to Chapter 13 for detailed information on the process of writing an essay.

- Choose examples and details to support your thesis.
- Arrange your supporting examples in a logical order, making an outline if necessary.
- Draft your essay.
- TEST your essay, referring to the TESTing an Exemplification Essay checklist below.
- Revise and edit your essay, referring to the two Self-Assessment checklists in Chapter 13.

TESTing an exemplification essay

Thesis Statement Unifies Your Essay

☐ Does your introduction include a **thesis statement** that clearly states your essay's main idea?

Evidence Supports Your Essay's Thesis Statement

☐ Does all of your **evidence**—examples and details—support your thesis, or should some evidence be deleted?

☐ Do you have *enough* evidence to support your thesis?

Summary Statement Reinforces Your Essay's Main Idea

☐ Does your conclusion include a **summary statement** that reinforces your essay's thesis?

Transitions

☐ Do you include **transitions** that move readers from one example to the next?

16b Narrative Essays

Teaching Tip
Refer students to Chapter 5 for information on writing a narrative paragraph.

Narration tells a story, usually presenting a series of events in chronological (time) order, moving from beginning to end. A **narrative essay** can tell a personal story, or it can recount a recent or historical event or a fictional story.

When you TEST a **narrative** essay, make sure it includes all these elements:

T ■ **Thesis Statement**—The introduction of a narrative essay should include a **thesis statement** that communicates your main idea—the point you are making in the story you will tell.

E ■ **Evidence**—The body paragraphs should tell the story, one event at a time, with each event providing **evidence** to support your thesis. Events are usually presented in chronological (time) order.

S ■ **Summary Statement**—The conclusion of a narrative essay should include a **summary statement** that reinforces the essay's main idea.

T ■ **Transitions**—Throughout your narrative essay, **transitional words and phrases** should connect events in time, showing how one event leads to the next.

Moving from Assignment to Thesis

The wording of your assignment may suggest that you write a narrative essay. For example, you may be asked to *tell*, *trace*, *summarize events*, or *recount*. Once you decide that your assignment calls for narration, you need to develop a thesis statement that reflects this purpose.

ASSIGNMENT	THESIS STATEMENT
Composition Tell about a time when you had to show courage even though you were afraid.	In extraordinary circumstances, a person can exhibit great courage and overcome fear.
American history Summarize the events that occurred during President Franklin Delano Roosevelt's first one hundred days in office.	Although many thought they were extreme, the measures enacted by Roosevelt during his first one hundred days in office were necessary to fight the economic depression.
Political science Trace the development of the Mississippi Freedom Democratic Party.	As the Mississippi Freedom Democratic Party developed, it found a voice that spoke for equality and justice.

> **Teaching Tip**
> For examples of narrative essays by professional writers, see 39b.

> **Teaching Tip**
> Tell students that many everyday writing tasks call for narration. For example, a job application letter might summarize previous work experience.

Organizing a Narrative Essay

When you write a narrative essay, you can discuss one event or several in each paragraph of your essay.

Essay Map: *One Event per Paragraph*

Introduction (includes thesis statement)

First event

Evidence

(continued on next page)

(continued from previous page)

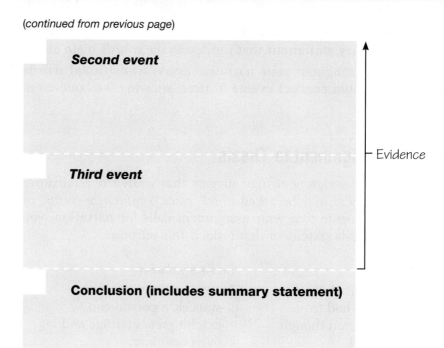

Second event

Third event

— Evidence

Conclusion (includes summary statement)

Essay Map: *Several Events per Paragraph*

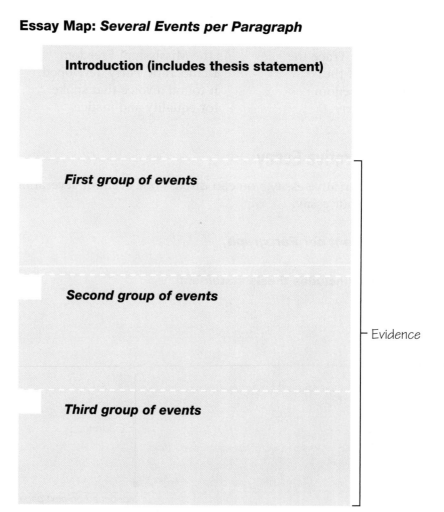

Introduction (includes thesis statement)

First group of events

Second group of events

— Evidence

Third group of events

Conclusion (includes summary statement)

Transitions in Narrative Essays

Sometimes, to add interest to your narrative, you may decide not to use exact chronological order. For example, you might begin with the end of your story and then move back to the beginning to trace the events that led to this outcome. However you arrange the events, carefully worded topic sentences and clear transitional words and phrases will help readers follow your narrative.

Some Transitional Words and Phrases for Narration

after	eventually	next
as	finally	now
as soon as	first . . . second . . .	soon
at first	third	then
at the same time	immediately	two hours (days,
before	later	months, years)
by this time	later on	later
earlier	meanwhile	when

Case Study: A Student Writes a Narrative Essay

Elaina Corrato, a returning student who was older than most of her classmates, wasn't sure how to proceed when her writing instructor gave the class an assignment to write about a milestone in their lives. The first topic that came to mind was her recent thirtieth birthday, but she was reluctant to reveal her age to her classmates. However, when she learned that no one except her instructor would read her essay, she decided to write about this topic. After all, her birthday was a very recent experience—and one that she had strong emotions about—so she knew she would have plenty to say.

Elaina began by rereading entries she had made in her writing journal in the days before and after her birthday as well as on the day itself. These entries gave her all the material she needed for her first draft, which she decided would focus on the "big day" itself. Even before she began to write, she saw that her essay would be a narrative that traced her reactions to the events she experienced on that day.

As she drafted her essay, Elaina was careful to discuss events in the order in which they occurred and to include transitional words and phrases to move her discussion from one event to the next. Because she knew what she wanted to say, she found it easy to write a well-developed first draft that included plenty of information. When she TESTed her essay, however, she saw at once that she had not stated a thesis or included a summary statement to reinforce the main idea of her essay. She knew she needed to include a thesis statement, but she wasn't sure what that thesis should be.

WORD POWER

milestone an important event; a turning point

At this point, Elaina emailed her draft to her instructor and asked him for suggestions. (Her instructor offered this option to students whose off-campus work commitments made it difficult for them to schedule face-to-face conferences.) He explained that her thesis should not be just a general overview of the day's events ("My thirtieth birthday was an event-filled day"); instead, it should make a point about how those events affected her. With this advice, Elaina found it was not difficult to write a thesis that expressed how she felt about turning thirty. Once she had a thesis statement, she was able to add a summary statement that reinforced her main idea, ending her essay on an optimistic note. With all the required elements in place, she went on to revise, edit, and proofread her essay.

The final draft that follows includes all the elements Elaina looked for when she **TEST**ed her essay.

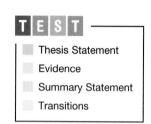

T E S T
- Thesis Statement
- Evidence
- Summary Statement
- Transitions

Model Narrative Essay

Read Elaina Corrato's finished essay, and answer the questions in Practice 16-2.

Reflections

Introduction

Turning thirty did not bother me at all. My list of "Things to Do before I Die" was far from complete, but I knew I had plenty of time to do them. In fact, turning thirty seemed like no big deal to me. If anything, it was a milestone I was happy to be approaching. <u>Unfortunately, other people had different ideas about this milestone, and eventually their ideas made me rethink my own.</u>

Thesis statement

Topic sentence (first point)

<u>As the big day approached, my family kept teasing me about it.</u> My sister kept asking me if I felt any different. She couldn't believe I wasn't upset, but I didn't pay any attention to her. I was looking forward to a new chapter in my life. I liked my job, I was making good progress toward my college degree, and I was healthy and happy. Why should turning thirty be a problem? So, I made no special plans for my birthday, and I decided to treat it as just another day.

Evidence (details and examples)

Body paragraphs

Topic sentence (second point)

<u>My birthday fell on a Saturday, and I enjoyed the chance to sleep in.</u> After I got up and had breakfast, I did my laundry and then set out for the supermarket. I rarely put on makeup or fixed my hair on Saturdays. After all, I didn't have to go to work or to school. I was only running errands in the neighborhood. Later on, though, as I waited in line at the deli counter, I caught sight of my reflection in the mirrored meat case. At first, I thought it wasn't really me. The woman staring back at me looked so old! She had bags under her eyes, and she even had a few gray hairs. I was so upset by my reflection that on my way home I stopped and bought a mud mask—guaranteed to make me look younger.

Evidence (details and examples)

Topic sentence (third point)

<u>As I walked up the street toward my house, I saw something attached to the front railing.</u> When I got closer, I realized that it was a bunch of balloons, and they were black balloons. There was also a big sign that said "Over the Hill" in big black letters. I'd been trying to think about my birthday in positive terms, but my family seemed to have other ideas. Obviously, it was time for the mud mask.

Evidence (details and examples)

1

2

3

4

5   <u>After quickly unloading my groceries, I ran upstairs to apply the mask.</u> The box promised a "rejuvenating look," and that was exactly what I wanted. I spread the sticky brown mixture on my face, and it hardened instantly. As I sat on my bed, waiting for the mask to work its magic, I heard the doorbell ring. Then, I heard familiar voices and my husband calling me to come down, saying that I had company. I couldn't answer him. I couldn't talk (or even smile) without cracking the mask. At this point, I retreated to the bathroom to make myself presentable for my friends and family. This task was not easy.

6   <u>When I managed to scrub off the mud mask, my face was covered with little red pimples.</u> Apparently, my sensitive skin couldn't take the harsh chemicals. At first, I didn't think the promise of "rejuvenated" skin was what I got. I had to admit, though, that my skin did look a lot younger. In fact, when I finally went downstairs to celebrate my birthday, I looked as young as a teenager—a teenager with acne.

7   <u>Despite other people's grim warnings, I discovered that although turning thirty was a milestone, it wasn't a game-changer.</u> I learned a lot that day, and I learned even more in the days that followed. What I finally realized was that I couldn't ignore turning thirty, but having a thirtieth birthday didn't have to mean that my life was over.

Topic sentence (fourth point)

Evidence (details and examples)

Body paragraphs

Topic sentence (fifth point)

Evidence (details and examples)

Summary statement

Conclusion

PRACTICE
16-2

1. Restate the thesis statement of "Reflections" in your own words.

2. What specific events and details support Elaina's thesis? List as many as you can.

3. Do you think paragraph 2 is necessary? How would Elaina's essay be different without it?

4. Paraphrase Elaina's summary statement. Do you think her summary statement effectively reinforces her essay's main idea?

5. What is this essay's greatest strength? What is its greatest weakness?

grammar in context

Narration

When you write a narrative essay, you tell a story. When you get caught up in your story, you might sometimes find yourself stringing a list of incidents together without proper punctuation, creating a **run-on**.

INCORRECT   As the big day approached, my family kept teasing me about it, my sister kept asking me if I felt any different.

CORRECT   As the big day approached, my family kept teasing me about it. My sister kept asking me if I felt any different.

For information on how to identify and correct run-ons, see Chapter 24.

Teaching Tip
Before your students write narrative essays, you might want to explain how to identify and correct run-ons (Chapter 24) and have them do Practices 24-1 and 24-7.

ESL Tip
Your ESL students may need to review verb tenses before writing a narrative essay.

Step-by-Step Guide: Writing a Narrative Essay

Now, you are ready to write a narrative essay on one of the topics listed below (or a topic of your choice).

TOPICS

The story of your education
Your idea of a perfect day
The plot summary of a terrible book or movie
A time when you had to make a split-second decision
Your first confrontation with authority
An important historical event
A day on which everything went wrong
A story from your family's history
Your employment history, from first to most recent job
A biography of your pet

As you plan, draft, and revise your essay, follow these steps:

- Make sure your topic calls for narration.

- Find ideas to write about.

- Identify your main idea, and write a thesis statement.

- Choose events and details to support your thesis.

- Arrange events in chronological order, making an outline if necessary.

- Draft your essay.

- **TEST** your essay, referring to the **TEST**ing a Narrative Essay checklist below.

- Revise and edit your essay, referring to the two Self-Assessment checklists in Chapter 13.

TESTing a narrative essay

Thesis Statement Unifies Your Essay

☐ Does your introduction include a **thesis statement** that clearly states your essay's main idea?

Evidence Supports Your Essay's Thesis Statement

☐ Does all of your **evidence**—examples and details—support your thesis, or should some evidence be deleted?

☐ Do you include *enough* evidence—examples and details—to make your narrative interesting?

☐ Are the events you discuss arranged in clear chronological (time) order?

S ummary Statement Reinforces Your Essay's Main Idea

☐ Does your conclusion include a **summary statement** that reinforces your essay's thesis?

T ransitions

☐ Do you include enough **transitions** to make the sequence of events clear to your reader?

☐ Do you need to add any transitional words or phrases to make the sequence of events clearer and help readers follow your ideas?

16c   Descriptive Essays

Description tells what something looks, sounds, smells, tastes, or feels like. A **descriptive essay** uses details to give readers a clear, vivid picture of a person, place, or object.

When you describe a person, place, object, or scene, you can use **objective description**, reporting only what your senses of sight, sound, smell, taste, and touch tell you ("The columns were two feet tall and made of white marble"). You can also use **subjective description**, conveying your attitude or your feelings about what you observe ("The columns were tall and powerful looking, and their marble surface seemed as smooth as ice"). Many essays combine these two kinds of description.

> **Teaching Tip**
> Refer students to Chapter 6 for information on writing a descriptive paragraph.

FYI

Figures of Speech

Descriptive writing, particularly subjective description, is frequently enriched by **figures of speech**—language that creates special or unusual effects.

■ A **simile** uses *like* or *as* to compare two unlike things.

Her smile was like sunshine.

■ A **metaphor** compares two unlike things without using *like* or *as*.

Her smile was a light that lit up the room.

■ **Personification** suggests a comparison between a nonliving thing and a person by giving the nonliving thing human traits.

The sun smiled down on the crowd.

When you TEST a **descriptive** essay, make sure it includes all these elements:

- **T** ■ **Thesis Statement**—A descriptive essay should include a **thesis statement** that expresses the essay's main idea.
- **E** ■ **Evidence**—The body paragraphs should include **evidence**—examples and descriptive details—that supports the thesis. Details should be arranged in a logical order—for example, from far to near or from top to bottom.
- **S** ■ **Summary Statement**—The conclusion of a descriptive essay should include a **summary statement** that reinforces the essay's thesis.
- **T** ■ **Transitions**—A descriptive essay should include **transitional words and phrases** that connect details and show how they are related.

Moving from Assignment to Thesis

The wording of your assignment may suggest that you write a descriptive essay. For example, it may ask you to *describe* or to *tell what an object looks like*. Once you decide that your assignment calls for description, you need to develop a thesis statement that reflects this purpose.

<aside>
Teaching Tip
For examples of descriptive essays by professional writers, see 39c.
</aside>

<aside>
Teaching Tip
Tell students that many everyday writing tasks call for description. For example, a statement to an insurance company after an automobile accident might describe damage to the car.
</aside>

ASSIGNMENT	THESIS STATEMENT
Composition Describe a room that was important to you when you were a child.	Pink-and-white striped wallpaper, tall shelves of cuddly stuffed animals, and the smell of Oreos dominated the bedroom I shared with my sister.
Scientific writing Describe a piece of scientific equipment.	The mass spectrometer is a complex instrument, but every part is ideally suited to its function.
Art history Choose one modern painting and describe its visual elements.	The disturbing images crowded together in Pablo Picasso's *Guernica* suggest the brutality of war.

Organizing a Descriptive Essay

When you plan a descriptive essay, you focus on selecting details that help your readers see what you see, feel what you feel, and experience what you experience. Your goal is to create a single **dominant impression**, a central theme or idea to which all the details relate—for example, the liveliness of a street scene or the quiet of a summer night. This dominant impression unifies the description and gives readers an overall sense of what the person, place, object, or scene looks like (and perhaps what it sounds, smells, tastes, or feels like).

You can arrange details in a descriptive essay in many different ways. For example, you can move from least to most important details, from top to bottom (or from bottom to top or side to side), or from far to near (or near to far). Each of your essay's body paragraphs may focus on one key characteristic of the subject you are describing or on several related descriptive details.

Essay Map: *Least to Most Important*

Introduction (includes thesis statement)

Least important details

More important details ⎤
                        ⎬ Evidence
Most important details ⎦

Conclusion (includes summary statement)

Essay Map: *Top to Bottom*

Introduction (includes thesis statement)

Details at top

Evidence ↓

(continued on next page)

(continued from previous page)

Details in middle

Details on bottom

⎤
⎢ Evidence
⎦

Conclusion (includes summary statement)

Essay Map: *Far to Near*

Introduction (includes thesis statement)

Distant details

⎤
⎢
⎢
⎢ Evidence
⎢
⎢
⎦

Closer details

Closest details

Conclusion (includes summary statement)

Transitions in Descriptive Essays

As you write, use transitional words and expressions to connect details and show how they work together to create a full picture for readers. (Many of these useful transitions indicate location or distance.)

Some Transitional Words and Phrases for Description		
above	in front of	outside
behind	inside	over
below	nearby	the least important
between	next to	the most important
beyond	on	under
in	on one side . . . on	
in back of	the other side	

Case Study: A Student Writes a Descriptive Essay

James Greggs, a student in a first-year composition course, was asked to write an objective description, recording details as he observed them, without including his own opinions or feelings about his observations.

All the students in James's class were also enrolled in sociology, psychology, or education courses with service-learning requirements that reinforced course content. For this reason, James's instructor asked that their descriptive essays focus on a person, setting, or item related to their service-learning experiences.

Although James was enjoying his service-learning project—building a deck for elderly residents of a trailer home—he had trouble deciding which aspect of this project to write about. At first, he thought he might describe his team supervisor or on one of the other students he worked with, but when he brainstormed to find details to include in his essay, he found he had a hard time being objective about his coworkers. Although he was required to keep a journal for the service-learning component of his sociology class, he realized that these entries focused on his own reactions and included few objective details. He finally settled on writing a description of the deck his team built for the trailer home. This didn't strike him as a particularly interesting subject, but he was confident that he could describe the trailer and the deck in objective terms.

Consulting photos he had taken of the building site and diagrams he had prepared of the trailer, James wrote a first draft, arranging his material from far (the field in which the trailer sat) to near (the trailer itself and the deck he helped build).

When James finished his draft and **TEST**ed it, he saw that his essay had no thesis statement—no sentence that tied all the details together to show the main idea he wanted his description to convey. At this point, he emailed his instructor for help, but she reminded him that he had missed her deadline for scheduling appointments. She recommended that he make an appointment with a tutor in the writing center.

James's writing center tutor suggested that his essay would be more interesting and convincing if his thesis tied the objective details of the project to his conclusions about its value. What did his class contribute? What did they learn? Was the project worth the trouble? She also reviewed his draft with him, suggesting places where he could expand or clarify his description. Because his assignment called for a descriptive essay, not a process essay, she recommended that he delete material that summarized the steps his group took as they built the deck. Finally, she reminded him that he would need to write a summary statement to reinforce his thesis.

When James revised his draft, he incorporated his tutor's suggestions and added both a thesis statement and a summary statement. He also added transitional words and phrases to move readers through his description, added more detail, and deleted irrelevant material. Then, he edited and proofread his essay.

The following final draft includes all the elements James looked for when he **TEST**ed his essay.

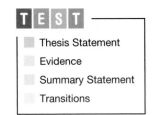

T|**E**|**S**|**T**
- Thesis Statement
- Evidence
- Summary Statement
- Transitions

Model Descriptive Essay

Read James Greggs's finished essay, and answer the questions in Practice 16-3.

Building and Learning

Introduction

Throughout the United States, houses reflect not only the lives of the people who live in them but also the diversity of the American population. Some are large and elaborate, others are modest but well maintained, and still others are in need of repair. Unfortunately, most college students know little about homes other than those in their own neighborhood. I too was fairly sheltered until I participated in a service-learning project for my sociology class. For this project, I, along with some classmates, added a deck to a trailer that was the home of three elderly sisters living on Social Security and disability.

Thesis statement
It was hard work, but my experience convinced me that all college students should be required to do some kind of service-learning project.

Topic sentence (first point)
The trailer we worked on was located at the end of a small dirt road about thirty minutes from campus.

Evidence (details and examples)

Body paragraphs
Patches of green and brown grass dotted the land around the trailer, and in the far right-hand corner of the property stood three tall poplar trees. Although the bushes in the front of the trailer were trimmed, the woods behind the trailer were beginning to overrun the property. (We were told that members of a local church came once a month to trim the hedges and cut back the trees.) Dominating the right front corner of the lawn, a circular concrete basin looked like a large birdbath. The basin housed a white well pipe with a rusted blue cap. About thirty feet to the left of the concrete basin stood a telephone pole and a bright red metal mailbox.

3   <u>Like the property on which it stood, the trailer was well maintained.</u> It was approximately thirty-five feet long and seven feet high; it rested on cinderblocks, which raised it about three feet off the ground. Under the trailer was an overturned white plastic chair. The trailer itself was covered with sheets of white vinyl siding that ran horizontally, except for the bottom panels on the right side, which ran vertically. The vinyl panels closest to the roof were slightly discolored by dirt and green moss.

Topic sentence (second point)

Evidence (details and examples)

4   <u>At the left end of the trailer was a small window—about two feet wide and one foot high.</u> Next to the window was a dark red aluminum door that was outlined in green trim. It had one window at eye level divided by metal strips into four small sections. The number "24" in white plastic letters was glued to the door below this window. To the right of the door was a lightbulb in a black ceramic socket. Next to the light was a large window that was actually two vertical rows of three windows—each the same size as the small window on the left. Further to the right were two smaller windows. Each of these small windows tilted upward and was framed with silver metal strips. On either side of each of these windows was a pair of green metal shutters.

Topic sentence (third point)

Evidence (details and examples)

Body paragraphs

5   <u>The deck we built replaced three wooden steps that had led up to the trailer.</u> A white metal handrail stood on the right side of these steps. It had been newly painted and was connected to the body of the trailer by a heart-shaped piece of metal. In front of the steps, two worn gray wooden boards led to the road.

Topic sentence (fourth point)

Evidence (details and examples)

6   <u>Building the deck was hard work, but the finished deck provided a much better entranceway than the steps did and also gave the trailer a new look.</u> The deck was not very large—ten feet by eight feet—but it extended from the doorway to the area underneath the windows immediately to the right of the door. We built the deck out of pressure-treated lumber so that it wouldn't rot or need painting. We also built three steps that led from the deck to the lawn, and we surrounded the deck with a wooden railing that ran down the right side of the steps. After we finished, we bought two white plastic chairs at a local thrift store and put them on the deck.

Topic sentence (fifth point)

Evidence (details and examples)

7   <u>Now that I look back at the project, I believe that activities like this should be part of every student's college education.</u> Both the residents of the trailer and our class benefited from the service-learning project. The residents of the trailer were happy with the deck because it gave them a place to sit when the weather was nice. They also liked their trailer's new look. Those of us who worked on the project learned that a few days' work could make a real difference in other people's lives.

Summary statement

Conclusion

PRACTICE

16-3

1. Paraphrase James's thesis statement.

2. What determines the order in which James arranges the elements of his description?

3. What details does James provide to describe the property, the trailer, and the deck?

4. What kind of signals do James's transitions give readers? Do you think he includes enough transitions? Where could he add more?

5. This essay is primarily an objective description. Does it include any subjective details?

6. What is this essay's greatest strength? What is its greatest weakness?

grammar in context

Description

When you write a descriptive essay, you may use **modifiers**—words and phrases that describe other words in the sentence—to create a picture of your subject. If you place a modifying word or phrase too far from the word it is supposed to describe, you create a potentially confusing **misplaced modifier**.

CONFUSING   Next to the window outlined in green trim was a dark red aluminum door. (Was the window outlined in green trim?)

CLEAR   Next to the window was a dark red aluminum door outlined in green trim.

For information on how to identify and correct misplaced modifiers, see Chapter 28.

Teaching Tip
Before your students write descriptive essays, you might want to explain how to identify modifiers (28a and 28b) and have them do Practice 28-1.

Step-by-Step Guide: Writing a Descriptive Essay

Now, you are ready to write a descriptive essay on one of the topics listed below (or a topic of your choice).

TOPICS

An abandoned building

A person or fictional character who makes you laugh (or frightens you)

Your room (or your closet or desk)

A family photograph

A historical site or monument

An advertisement

An object you cherish

Someone whom everyone notices

Someone whom no one notices

The home page of a Web site you visit often

As you plan, draft, and revise your essay, follow these steps:

- Make sure your topic calls for description.
- Find ideas to write about.
- Decide what dominant impression you want to convey.
- Choose details that help to convey your dominant impression.
- Write a thesis statement that identifies your main ideas.
- Arrange your details in an effective order, making an outline if necessary.
- Draft your essay.
- TEST your essay, referring to the TESTing a Descriptive Essay checklist on page 251.

Teaching Tip
Refer students to Chapter 13 for detailed information on the process of writing an essay.

■ Revise and edit your essay, referring to the two Self-Assessment checklists in Chapter 13.

TESTing a descriptive essay

▌T hesis Statement Unifies Your Essay

☐ Does your introduction include a **thesis statement** that communicates your essay's main idea?

☐ Does your introduction identify the subject of your description?

▌E vidence Supports Your Essay's Thesis Statement

☐ Does all of your **evidence**—examples and details—support the dominant impression conveyed by your thesis, or should some be deleted?

☐ Do you describe your subject in enough detail, or do you need to add more details to create a more vivid picture?

☐ Are your examples arranged in an effective order within your essay and within paragraphs?

▌S ummary Statement Reinforces Your Essay's Main Idea

☐ Does your conclusion include a **summary statement** that reinforces your essay's thesis?

▌T ransitions

☐ Do you include **transitions** that introduce your examples and details and move readers smoothly from one aspect of your subject to another?

16d Process Essays

A **process** is a series of chronological steps that produces a particular result. **Process essays** explain the steps in a procedure, telling how something is (or was) done. A process essay can be organized as either a *process explanation* or a set of *instructions*.

When you TEST a **process** essay, make sure it includes all these elements:

T ■ **Thesis Statement**—A process essay should include a **thesis statement** that expresses the essay's main idea, identifying the process you will explain and telling why it is important or why you are explaining it.

E ■ **Evidence**—To support your thesis statement, the body paragraphs should identify and explain all the steps in the process. Each paragraph's topic sentence should identify the step (or group of related steps) that the paragraph will explain. Steps should be presented in strict chronological (time) order.

<aside>
Teaching Tip
Refer students to Chapter 7 for information on writing a process paragraph.
</aside>

S　■ **Summary Statement**—The conclusion of a process essay should include a **summary statement** that reinforces the essay's thesis.

T　■ **Transitions**—A process essay should include **transitional words and phrases** that link the steps in the process and show how they are related.

Moving from Assignment to Thesis

The wording of your assignment may suggest that you write a process essay. For example, you may be asked to *explain a process, give instructions, give directions,* or *give a step-by-step account.* Once you decide that your assignment calls for process, you need to develop a thesis statement that reflects this purpose.

ASSIGNMENT	THESIS STATEMENT
American government　Explain the process by which a bill becomes a law.	The process by which a bill becomes a law is long and complex, involving numerous revisions and a great deal of compromise.
Pharmacy practice　Summarize the procedure for conducting a clinical trial of a new drug.	To ensure that drugs are safe and effective, scientists follow strict procedural guidelines for testing and evaluating them.
Technical writing　Write a set of instructions for applying for a student internship in a government agency.	If you want to apply for a government internship, you need to follow several important steps.

If your purpose is simply to help readers understand a process, not actually perform it, you will write a process explanation. **Process explanations**, like the first two examples above, often use present tense verbs ("Once a bill *is* introduced in Congress" or "A scientist first *submits* a funding application") to explain how a procedure is generally carried out. However, when a process explanation describes a specific procedure that was completed in the past, it uses past tense verbs ("The next thing I *did*").

If your purpose is to enable readers to actually perform the steps in a process, you will write instructions. **Instructions**, like the technical writing example above, always use present-tense verbs in the form of commands to tell readers what to do ("First, *meet* with your adviser").

Organizing a Process Essay

Whether your essay is a process explanation or a set of instructions, you can either devote a full paragraph to each step of the process or group a series of minor steps together in a single paragraph.

Essay Map: *One Step per Paragraph*

Introduction (includes thesis statement)

First step in process

Second step in process

⎤ Evidence

Third step in process

Conclusion (includes summary statement)

Essay Map: *Several Steps per Paragraph*

Introduction (includes thesis statement)

First group of steps

Evidence

(continued on next page)

(continued from previous page)

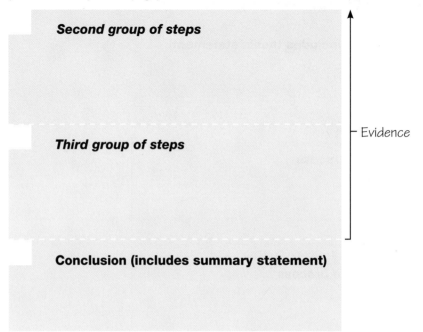

As you write your process essay, discuss each step in the order in which it is performed, making sure your topic sentences clearly identify the function of each step or group of steps. (If you are writing instructions, you may also include reminders or warnings that readers might need to know when performing the process.)

Transitions in Process Essays

Transitions are extremely important in process essays because they enable readers to follow the sequence of steps in the process and, in the case of instructions, to perform the process themselves.

Some Transitional Words and Phrases for Process

after that	immediately	the final step
as	later	the first (second,
as soon as	meanwhile	third) step
at the end	next	then
at the same time	now	the next step
before	once	when
finally	soon	while
first	subsequently	

Case Study: A Student Writes a Process Essay

Jen Rossi, a student in a first-year writing course, was given this assignment:

Explain the steps in a process that you are very familiar with but that your classmates probably do not know much about. Be sure your essay is structured as a process explanation, not as a set of instructions.

When she considered what she might want to write about, Jen rejected familiar process topics like following a recipe or performing a repair because she thought those seemed better suited to instructions. Instead, she decided to explain how she goes about selling items at flea markets.

Jen knew a lot about this topic, but she still needed to brainstorm to get all the steps down on paper. After she listed all the steps she could think of, she arranged them in chronological order and checked to make sure that no step was missing. When she drafted her essay, she made sure she identified each step with transitional words and phrases like "The first step," "The next step," and "Finally."

Jen's biggest challenge was developing a thesis statement. Before she wrote her draft, she came up with a tentative thesis—"Selling at a flea market is a process that requires a number of steps"—but she knew this sentence was only a placeholder. Her thesis statement told readers what she planned to write about, but it didn't tell them why she was explaining this process or how she felt about it.

When she TESTed her draft, she saw that while she had a tentative thesis and plenty of support, she had not included a summary statement. She quickly jotted down a sentence—"These are the steps in selling at a flea market"—that she could revise when she revised her thesis statement.

With the help of classmates in her peer-review group, Jen revised her thesis statement and summary statement so they both communicated her essay's main idea: that following a process established a routine that made her flea market selling easier. She also added a few more examples (for instance, examples of heavy and small items in paragraph 5 and examples of small and large items in paragraph 7) in response to suggestions from her classmates. Once she made these revisions, she went on to edit and proofread her essay.

The final draft that follows includes all the elements Jen looked for when she TESTed her essay.

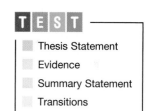

T E S T
- Thesis Statement
- Evidence
- Summary Statement
- Transitions

Model Process Essay

Read Jen Rossi's finished essay, and answer the questions in Practice 16-4.

For Fun and Profit

1   My first experience selling items at a flea market was both fun and profitable. In fact, it led to a hobby that is also a continuing source of extra money. That first time took a lot of work, but the routine I established then has made each flea market easier.

2   The first step in the process is to call to reserve a spot at the flea market. If possible, I like to get a spot near the entrance, where there is a lot of foot traffic. Then, I recruit a helper—usually my brother or one of my roommates—and we get to work.

3   The next step is sorting through all the items I managed to accumulate since the last flea market. My helper comes in handy here, encouraging me to sell ugly or useless things I may want to hold on to. We make three piles—keep, sell, and trash—and one by one, we place every item in a pile. (Before we decide to sell or throw out an item, I check with all my roommates to make sure I'm not accidentally throwing out one of their prized possessions.)

Introduction

Thesis statement

Topic sentence
(first point)

Body paragraphs

Topic sentence
(second point)

Evidence
(details and examples)

Topic sentence
(third point)

Evidence
(details and examples)

<u>Next comes pricing the items for sale, which is actually the hardest step for me.</u> It's always difficult to accept the fact that I might have to set a low price for something that has sentimental value for me (a giant stuffed animal, for example). It's just as hard to set a high price on the ugly lamp or old record album that might turn out to be someone's treasure. At my first flea market, I returned with a lot of unsold items, and I later realized I had sold other items too cheaply. I never made these mistakes again.

4

Topic sentence
(fourth point)

Evidence
(details and examples)

Topic sentence
(fifth point)

<u>The next step is my least favorite: packing up items to be sold.</u> I usually borrow my friend's van for the heavy items (boxes of books or dishes, for example). The small items (knickknacks, silk flowers, stray teaspoons) can be transported in my brother's car.

5

<u>The final steps in my preparation take place on the day before the event.</u> I borrow a couple of card tables from friends of my parents. Then, I go to the bank and get lots of dollar bills and quarters, and I collect piles of newspaper and plastic supermarket bags. Now, my planning is complete.

6

Topic sentence
(sixth point)

Body paragraphs

<u>On the day of the flea market, I get up early, and my helper and I load the two vehicles.</u> When we arrive at the site where the event is to be held, one of us unloads the cars. The other person sets things up, placing small items (such as dishes and DVDs) on the card tables and large items (such as my parents' old lawnmower) on the ground near the tables.

7

Topic sentence
(seventh point)

Evidence
(details and examples)

<u>Then, the actual selling begins.</u> Before I can even set up our tables, people start picking through my things, offering me cash for picture frames, pots and pans, and video games. We develop a system as the day goes on: one of us persuades buyers that that old meat grinder or vase is just what they've been looking for, and the other person negotiates the price with prospective buyers. Then, while one of us wraps small items in the newspapers or bags we brought (and helps carry large items to people's cars), the other person takes the money and makes change.

8

Conclusion

Summary statement

Finally, at the end of the day, the routine comes to an end. I count my money and give a share to my helper. We then load all the unsold items into the car and van and bring them back to my apartment. <u>The process ends when we store the unsold items in the back of my closet so it will be easy to pack them up again and follow the same routine for the next flea market.</u>

9

PRACTICE
16-4

1. Restate Jen's thesis statement in your own words.

2. What identifies Jen's essay as a process explanation rather than a set of instructions?

3. Review the transitional words and phrases that link the steps in the process. Are any other transitions needed? If so, where?

4. List the major steps in the process of selling at a flea market. Does Jen present these steps in strict chronological order?

5. Paraphrase Jen's summary statement. Do you think she needs to revise this sentence so it more clearly reinforces her thesis statement?

6. What is the essay's greatest strength? What is its greatest weakness?

grammar in context

Process

When you write a process essay, you may have problems keeping tense, person, and voice consistent throughout. If you shift from one tense, person, or voice to another without good reason, you will confuse your readers.

CONFUSING   We make three piles—keep, sell, and trash—and one by one, every item was placed in a pile. (shift from active to passive voice and from present to past tense)

CLEAR   We make three piles—keep, sell, and trash—and one by one, we place every item in a pile. (consistent voice and tense)

For information on how to avoid illogical shifts in tense, person, and voice, see Chapter 27.

Teaching Tip
Before your students write pro-cess essays, you might want to explain how to avoid illogical shifts (Chapter 27) and have them do Practices 27-1 through 27-4.

Step-by-Step Guide: Writing a Process Essay

Now, you are ready to write a process essay on one of the topics listed below (or a topic of your choice).

TOPICS

An unusual recipe
Finding an apartment
Applying for a job
Getting dressed for a typical Saturday night
A religious ritual or cultural ceremony
A task you often do at work
A do-it-yourself project that didn't get done
Your own writing process
A self-improvement program (past, present, or future)
Applying for financial aid

As you plan, draft, and revise your essay, follow these steps:

- Make sure your topic calls for process.
- Decide whether you want to explain a process or write instructions.
- Find ideas to write about.
- Identify your main idea, and write a thesis statement.
- Identify the most important steps in the process.
- List the steps in chronological order, making an outline if necessary.
- Draft your essay.
- TEST your essay, referring to the TESTing a Process Essay checklist on page 258.
- Revise and edit your essay, referring to the two Self-Assessment checklists in Chapter 13.

Teaching Tip
Refer students to Chapter 13 for detailed information on the process of writing an essay.

TESTing a process essay

Thesis Statement Unifies Your Essay

☐ Does your introduction include a **thesis statement** that expresses your essay's main idea, identifying the process you will explain and indicating why you are writing about it?

Evidence Supports Your Essay's Thesis Statement

☐ Does all of your **evidence** support your thesis, or should some evidence be deleted?

☐ Do you identify and explain every step that readers will need to understand (or perform) the process?

☐ Are the steps in the process given in strict chronological order?

☐ If you are writing instructions, have you included all necessary warnings or reminders?

Summary Statement Reinforces Your Essay's Main Idea

☐ Does your conclusion include a **summary statement** that reinforces your essay's thesis?

Transitions

☐ Do you include **transitions** that introduce your steps and clearly show how the steps in the process are related?

16e   Cause-and-Effect Essays

Teaching Tip
Refer students to Chapter 8 for information on writing a cause-and-effect paragraph.

A **cause** makes something happen; an **effect** is a result of a particular cause or event. **Cause-and-effect essays** identify causes or predict effects; sometimes, they do both.

When you TEST a **cause-and-effect** essay, make sure it includes all these elements:

T ▪ **Thesis Statement**—The introduction of a cause-and-effect essay should include a **thesis statement** that communicates the essay's main idea and indicates whether it will focus on causes or on effects.

E ▪ **Evidence**—The body paragraphs should include **evidence**—details and examples—to illustrate the causes or effects you examine. The topic sentence of each paragraph should identify the causes or effects the paragraph will discuss.

S ▪ **Summary Statement**—The conclusion of a cause-and-effect essay should include a **summary statement** that reinforces the essay's thesis.

T ▪ **Transitions**—A cause-and-effect essay should include **transitional words and phrases** that make clear which causes led to which effects.

Moving from Assignment to Thesis

The wording of your assignment may suggest that you write a cause-and-effect essay. For example, the assignment may ask you to *explain why, predict the outcome, list contributing factors, discuss the consequences*, or tell what *caused* something else or how something is *affected* by something else. Once you decide that your assignment calls for cause and effect, you need to develop a thesis statement that reflects this purpose.

Teaching Tip
Tell students that many everyday writing tasks involve discussing causes and effects. For example, a letter to a community's zoning board might discuss possible consequences of building a road, mall, or multiplex.

ASSIGNMENT	THESIS STATEMENT
Women's studies What factors contributed to the rise of the women's movement in the 1970s?	The women's movement of the 1970s had its origins in the peace and civil rights movements of the 1960s.
Public health Discuss the possible long-term effects of smoking.	In addition to its well-known negative effects on smokers themselves, smoking also causes significant problems for those exposed to secondhand smoke.
Media and society How has the Internet affected the lives of those who have grown up with it?	The Internet has created a generation of people who learn differently from those in previous generations.

A cause-and-effect essay can focus on causes or on effects. When you write about causes, be sure to examine *all* relevant causes. You should emphasize the cause you consider the most important, but do not forget to consider other causes that may be significant. Similarly, when you write about effects, consider *all* significant effects of a particular cause, not just the first few that you think of.

If your focus is on finding causes, as it is in the first assignment above, your introductory paragraph should identify the effect (the women's movement). If your focus is on predicting effects, as it is in the second and third assignments listed above, you should begin by identifying the cause (smoking, the Internet).

Teaching Tip
For examples of cause-and-effect essays by professional writers, see 39e.

Organizing a Cause-and-Effect Essay

In the body of your essay, you will probably devote a full paragraph to each cause (or effect). You can also group several related causes (or effects) together in each paragraph.

Essay Map: *Identifying Causes*

> **Introduction (includes thesis statement that identifies effect)**

(continued on next page)

(continued from previous page)

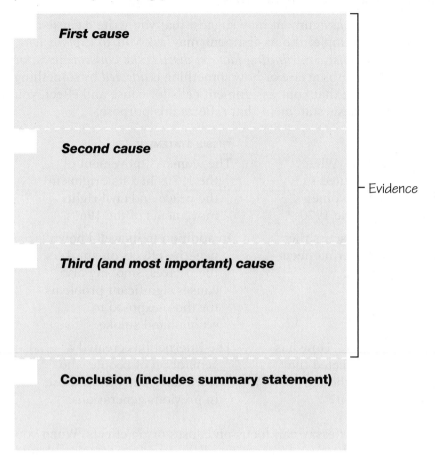

First cause

Second cause

Third (and most important) cause

Evidence

Conclusion (includes summary statement)

Essay Map: *Predicting Effects*

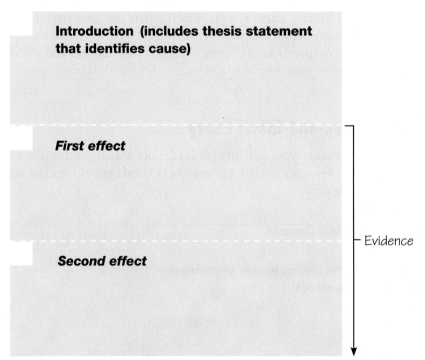

Introduction (includes thesis statement that identifies cause)

First effect

Evidence

Second effect

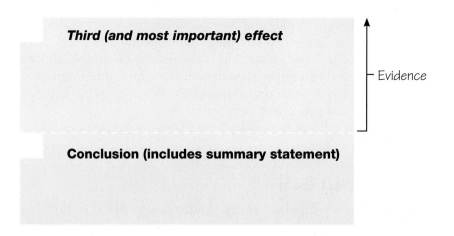

Third (and most important) effect

— Evidence

Conclusion (includes summary statement)

Transitions in Cause-and-Effect Essays

Transitions are important in cause-and-effect essays because they establish causal connections, telling readers that A caused B and not the other way around. They also make it clear that events have a *causal* relationship (A *caused* B) and not just a *sequential* relationship (A *came before* B). Remember, when one event follows another, the second is not necessarily the result of the first. For example, an earthquake may occur the day before you fail an exam, but that doesn't mean the earthquake caused you to fail.

> ### Some Transitional Words and Phrases for Cause and Effect
>
> | | | |
> |---|---|---|
> | accordingly | for this reason | the most important |
> | another cause | since | cause |
> | another effect | so | the most important |
> | as a result | the first (second, | effect |
> | because | third) cause | therefore |
> | consequently | the first (second, | |
> | for | third) effect | |

Case Study: A Student Writes a Cause-and-Effect Essay

In an orientation course for first-year education majors, Andrea DeMarco was asked to write a personal essay about an event that changed her life. She decided immediately to write about her parents' brief separation, an event that occurred when she was eight years old but that still affects her today.

Before she wrote her first draft, Andrea talked to her older sister and brother to see what they remembered about the separation. Armed with this basic information and her own memories, Andrea drafted her essay.

The wording of her assignment—to write about an event that changed her life—told Andrea that her essay would have a cause-and-effect structure. In her draft, she included a thesis statement—"My parents' separation made everything different"—that echoed the wording of the assignment. As she wrote, she was careful to include words and phrases like *because* and *as a result* to make the cause-and-effect emphasis clear and to distinguish

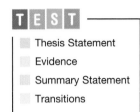

Thesis Statement
Evidence
Summary Statement
Transitions

between the cause (the separation) and its effects. Her summary statement also reinforced the cause-and-effect emphasis of her essay.

When Andrea TESTed her draft, she saw that it included all the required elements—thesis statement, evidence, summary statement, and transitions—so she moved on to revise her draft. When she finished her revisions, she edited and proofread her essay.

The final draft that follows includes all the elements Andrea looked for when she TESTed her essay.

Model Cause-and-Effect Essay

Read Andrea DeMarco's finished essay, and answer the questions in Practice 16-5.

How My Parents' Separation Changed My Life

Introduction

Until I was eight, I lived the perfect all-American life with my perfect all-American family. I lived in a suburb of Albany, New York, with my parents, my sister and brother, and our dog, Daisy. We had a ping-pong table in the basement, a barbecue in the backyard, and two cars in the garage. My dad and mom were high school teachers, and every summer we took a family vacation. Then, it all changed. My parents' separation made everything different.

Thesis statement

Topic sentence (first point)

One day, just before Halloween, when my sister was twelve and my brother was fourteen (Daisy was seven), our parents called us into the kitchen for a family conference. We didn't think anything was wrong at first; they were always calling these annoying meetings. We figured it was time for us to plan a vacation, talk about household chores, or be nagged to clean our rooms. As soon as we sat down, though, we knew this was different. We could tell Mom had been crying, and Dad's voice cracked when he told us the news. They were separating—they called it a "trial separation"—and Dad was moving out of our house.

Evidence (details and examples)

Topic sentence (second point)

After that day, everything seemed to change. Every Halloween we always had a big jack-o'-lantern on our front porch. Dad used to spend hours at the kitchen table cutting out the eyes, nose, and mouth and hollowing out the insides. That Halloween, because he didn't live with us, things were different. Mom bought a pumpkin, and I guess she was planning to carve it up. But she never did, and we never mentioned it. It sat on the kitchen counter for a couple of weeks, getting soft and wrinkled, and then it just disappeared.

Evidence (details and examples)

Body paragraphs

Topic sentence (third point)

Other holidays were also different because Mom and Dad were not living together. Our first Thanksgiving without Dad was pathetic. I don't even want to talk about it. Christmas was different, too. We spent Christmas Eve with Dad and our relatives on his side and Christmas Day with Mom and her family. Of course, we got twice as many presents as usual. I realize now that both our parents were trying to make up for the pain of the separation. The worst part came when I opened my big present from Mom: Barbie's Dream House. This was something I had always wanted. Even at eight, I knew how hard it must

Evidence (details and examples)

1

2

3

4

have been for Mom to afford it. The trouble was, I had gotten the same thing from Dad the night before.

5   <u>The separation affected each of us in different ways.</u> The worst effect of my parents' separation was not the big events but the disruption in our everyday lives. Dinner used to be a family time, a chance to talk about our day and make plans. But after Dad left, Mom seemed to stop eating. Sometimes she would just have coffee while we ate, and sometimes she wouldn't eat at all. She would microwave some frozen thing for us or heat up soup or cook some hot dogs. We didn't care—after all, now she let us watch TV while we ate—but we did notice.

6   <u>Other parts of our routine changed, too.</u> Because Dad didn't live with us anymore, we had to spend every Saturday and every Wednesday night at his apartment, no matter what else we had planned. Usually, he would take us to dinner at McDonald's on Wednesdays, and then we would go back to his place and do our homework or watch TV. That wasn't too bad. Saturdays were a lot worse. We really wanted to be home, hanging out with our friends in our own rooms in our own house. Instead, we had to do some planned activity with Dad, like go to a movie or a hockey game.

7   <u>As a result of what happened in my own family, it is hard for me to believe any relationship is forever.</u> By the end of the school year, my parents had somehow worked things out, and Dad was back home again. That June, at a family conference around the kitchen table, we made our summer vacation plans. We decided on Williamsburg, Virginia, the all-American vacation destination. So, things were back to normal, but I wasn't, and I'm still not. Now, ten years later, my mother and father are all right, but I still worry they'll split up again. And I worry about my own future husband and how I will ever be sure he's the one I'll stay married to.

Topic sentence (fourth point)

Evidence (details and examples)

Body paragraphs

Topic sentence (fifth point)

Evidence (details and examples)

Summary statement

Conclusion

PRACTICE

16-5   1. Restate Andrea's thesis statement in your own words.

2. List the specific effects of her parents' separation that Andrea identifies.

3. Review the transitional words and phrases Andrea uses to make causal connections clear to her readers. Do you think she needs more of these transitions? If so, where?

4. Is Andrea's relatively long concluding paragraph effective? Why or why not? Do you think it should be shortened or divided into two paragraphs?

5. Is Andrea's straightforward title effective, or should she have used a more creative or eye-catching title? Can you suggest an alternative?

6. What is this essay's greatest strength? What is its greatest weakness?

grammar in context

Cause and Effect

When you write a cause-and-effect essay, you may have trouble remembering the difference between *affect* and *effect*.

The worst ~~affect~~ *effect* of my parents' separation was not the big events but the disruption in our everyday lives. (*effect* is a noun)

The separation ~~effected~~ *affected* each of us in different ways. (*affect* is a verb)

For information on affect *and* effect, *see Chapter 37.*

Step-by-Step Guide: Writing a Cause-and-Effect Essay

Now, you are ready to write a cause-and-effect essay on one of the topics listed below (or a topic of your choice).

TOPICS

A teacher's positive (or negative) effect on you
Why you voted a certain way in a recent election (or why you did not vote)
How your life would be different if you dropped out of school (or quit your job)
How a particular invention has changed your life
Why texting is so popular
A movie or book that changed the way you look at life
How a particular season (or day of the week) affects your mood
How having a child would change (or has changed) your life
How a particular event made you grow up

As you plan, draft, and revise your essay, follow these steps:

- Make sure your topic calls for cause and effect.
- Decide whether your essay will focus on causes, effects, or both.
- Find ideas to write about.
- Identify your main idea, and write a thesis statement.
- Choose causes or effects to support your thesis.
- Arrange causes and effects in an effective order, making an outline if necessary.
- Draft your essay.
- **TEST** your essay, referring to the **TEST**ing a Cause-and-Effect Essay checklist on page 265.
- Revise and edit your essay, referring to the two Self-Assessment checklists in Chapter 13.

TESTing a cause-and-effect essay

T hesis Statement Unifies Your Essay

☐ Does your introduction include a **thesis statement** that indicates your main idea and makes clear whether your essay will focus on causes or effects?

E vidence Supports Your Essay's Thesis Statement

☐ Does all of your **evidence**—examples and details—support your thesis, or should some evidence be deleted?

☐ Do you identify all causes or effects relevant to your topic, or do you need to add any?

☐ Have you arranged causes and effects to indicate which are more important than others?

☐ Does each body paragraph identify and explain one particular cause or effect (or several closely related causes or effects)?

S ummary Statement Reinforces Your Essay's Main Idea

☐ Does your conclusion include a **summary statement** that reinforces your essay's thesis?

T ransitions

☐ Do you include **transitions** that introduce each of your causes or effects and make your essay's cause-and-effect connections clear?

16f Comparison-and-Contrast Essays

Comparison identifies similarities, and **contrast** identifies differences. **Comparison-and-contrast essays** explain how two things are alike or how they are different; sometimes, they discuss both similarities and differences.

When you TEST a **comparison-and-contrast** essay, make sure it includes all these elements:

T ▪ **Thesis Statement**—The introduction of a comparison-and-contrast essay should include a **thesis statement** that communicates the essay's main idea, telling readers what two items you are going to compare or contrast and whether you are going to emphasize similarities or differences.

Teaching Tip
Refer students to Chapter 9 for information on writing a comparison-and-contrast paragraph.

E ▪ **Evidence**—The body paragraphs should include **evidence**—details and examples—that supports the thesis statement. The topic sentence of each paragraph should identify the similarity or difference the paragraph will examine.

S ▪ **Summary Statement**—The conclusion of a comparison-and-contrast essay should include a **summary statement** that reinforces the essay's thesis.

T ▪ **Transitions**—A comparison-and-contrast essay should include **transitional words and phrases** to help readers move from point to point and from subject to subject.

Moving from Assignment to Thesis

The wording of your assignment may suggest that you write a comparison-and-contrast essay—for example, by asking you to *compare, contrast, discuss similarities,* or *identify differences.* Once you decide that your assignment calls for comparison and contrast, you need to develop a thesis statement that reflects this purpose.

Teaching Tip
Tell students that many everyday writing tasks call for comparison and contrast. For example, a report to a supervisor at work might compare the merits of two procedures or two suppliers.

ASSIGNMENT	THESIS STATEMENT
Philosophy What basic similarities do you find in the beliefs of Henry David Thoreau and Martin Luther King, Jr.?	Although King was more politically active, both he and Thoreau strongly supported the idea of civil disobedience.
Nutrition How do the diets of native Japanese and Japanese Americans differ?	As they become more and more assimilated, Japanese Americans consume more fats than native Japanese do.
Literature Contrast the two sisters in Alice Walker's short story "Everyday Use."	Unlike Maggie, Dee—her more successful, better-educated sister—has rejected her family's heritage.

Teaching Tip
For examples of comparison-and-contrast essays by professional writers, see 39f.

Organizing a Comparison-and-Contrast Essay

Teaching Tip
Tell students that in a comparison, their points must match up. If an essay discusses the appearance and behavior of one breed of dog, it also needs to discuss the same two points for the other breeds being discussed.

When you organize a comparison-and-contrast essay, you can choose either a *point-by-point* or a *subject-by-subject* arrangement. A **point-by-point** comparison alternates between the two subjects you are comparing or contrasting, moving back and forth from one subject to the other. A **subject-by-subject** comparison treats its two subjects separately, first fully discussing one subject and then moving on to consider the other subject. In both kinds of comparison-and-contrast essays, the same points are discussed in the same order for both subjects.

Essay Map: *Point-by-Point Comparison*

Introduction (thesis statement identifies subjects to be compared or contrasted)

First point discussed for both subjects

Second point discussed for both subjects

Evidence

Third point discussed for both subjects

Conclusion (includes summary statement)

Essay Map: *Subject-by-Subject Comparison*

Introduction (thesis statement identifies subjects to be compared or contrasted)

(continued on next page)

(continued from previous page)

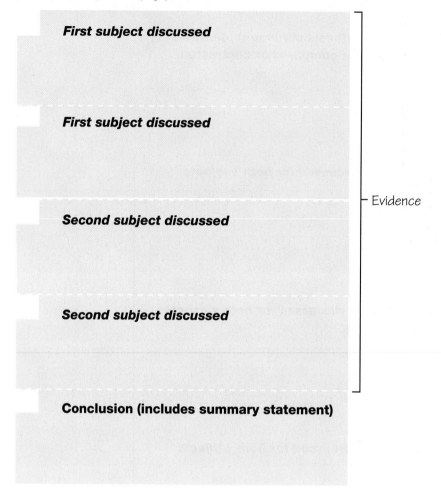

First subject discussed

First subject discussed

Second subject discussed

Second subject discussed

Evidence

Conclusion (includes summary statement)

Transitions in Comparison-and-Contrast Essays

The transitional words and phrases you use in a comparison-and-contrast essay tell readers whether you are focusing on similarities or on differences. Transitions also help move readers through your essay from one subject to the other and from one point of comparison or contrast to the next.

> ### Some Transitional Words and Phrases for Comparison and Contrast
>
> | | |
> |---|---|
> | although | likewise |
> | but | nevertheless |
> | even though | on the contrary |
> | however | on the one hand . . . on the other hand |
> | in comparison | similarly |
> | in contrast | unlike |
> | instead | whereas |
> | like | |

Case Study: A Student Writes a Comparison-and-Contrast Essay

Nisha Jani, a student in a first-year writing course, was given the following assignment:

> Some people claim that males and females are so different that at times they seem to belong to two different species. Do you agree, or do you think males and females are more alike than different? Write an essay that supports your position.

When Nisha read this assignment, the key words *different* and *alike* told her that the assignment called for a comparison-and-contrast essay. After brainstorming, she decided to write about the differences between boys and girls—specifically, middle-school boys and girls. She didn't want to write a serious essay, and she thought she could use humor if she wrote about the habits of two typical seventh-graders. Based on her own experiences and those of her younger brother and sister, Nisha thought that the differences between seventh-grade boys and girls would be more interesting (and more obvious) than the similarities. So, when she drafted a thesis statement for her essay, she made sure that it focused on differences: "The typical boy and girl lead very different lives."

Once she had a thesis statement, she listed some of the most obvious differences between male and female seventh graders, including the way girls and boys get ready for school, how they behave in class and during lunch, and what they do after school. When she reviewed the ideas on her list, she decided to follow her two subjects (Johnny and Jane) through a typical school day, and this decision led her to structure her essay as a point-by-point comparison that would contrast boys' and girls' behavior at different points of their day.

When Nisha thought she had enough material to write about, she wrote a draft of her essay. Then, she TESTed her draft to see if it included a thesis statement, supporting evidence, a summary statement, and transitional words and phrases. Although her TEST showed her that she had included all the required elements, she thought she still needed to revise to strengthen her draft. After a conference with her instructor, she revised her thesis statement to make it a bit more specific, added more examples and details, sharpened her summary statement so it reinforced her essay's main idea, and added more transitions to make the contrast between her two subjects clearer. After she finished these revisions, she edited her essay.

The final draft that follows includes all the elements Nisha looked for when she TESTed her essay.

Model Comparison-and-Contrast Essay

Read Nisha Jani's finished essay, and answer the questions in Practice 16-6.

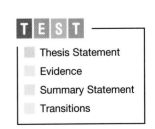

TE**S**T	
☐ Thesis Statement	
☐ Evidence	
☐ Summary Statement	
☐ Transitions	

Another Ordinary Day

1   "Boys are from Jupiter and get stupider / Girls are from Mars and become movie stars / Boys take a bath and smell like trash / Girls take a shower and smell like a flower." As simple playground songs like this one suggest, the two

Introduction

sexes are very different. As adults, men and women have similar goals, values, and occupations, but as children and teenagers, boys and girls often seem to belong to two different species. In fact, from the first moment of the day to the last, the typical boy and girl live very different lives.

The sun rises, and the alarm clock signals the beginning of another day for Johnny and Jane, two seventh-grade classmates. Johnny, an average thirteen-year-old boy, wakes up late and has to hurry. He throws on his favorite jeans, a baggy T-shirt, and a baseball cap. Then, he has a hearty high-cholesterol breakfast and runs out of the house to school, usually forgetting some vital book or homework assignment. Jane, unlike Johnny, wakes up early and takes her time. She takes a long shower and then blow-dries her hair. For Jane, getting dressed can be a very difficult process, one that often includes taking everything out of her closet and calling friends for advice. After she makes her decision, she helps herself to some food (probably low- or no-fat) and goes off to school, making sure she has with her everything she needs.

School is a totally different experience for Johnny and Jane. Johnny will probably sit in the back of the classroom with a couple of other guys, throwing paper airplanes and spitballs. These will be directed at the males they do not like and the females they think are kind of cute. (However, if their male friends ever ask the boys about these girls, they will say girls are just losers and deny that they like any of them.) On the opposite side of the classroom, however, Jane is focused on a very different kind of activity. At first, it looks as if she is carefully copying the algebra notes that the teacher is putting on the board, but her notes have absolutely nothing to do with algebra. Instead, she is writing about boys, clothes, and other topics that are much more important to her than the square root of one hundred twenty-one. She proceeds to fold the note into a box or other creative shape, which can often put origami to shame. As soon as the teacher turns her back, the note is passed and the process begins all over again.

Lunch, a vital part of the school day, is also very different for Johnny and Jane. On the one hand, for Johnny and his friends, it is a time to compare baseball cards, exchange sports facts, and of course tell jokes about every bodily function imaginable. In front of them on the table, their trays are filled with pizza, soda, fries, and chips, and this food is their main focus. For Jane, on the other hand, lunch is not about eating; it is a chance to exchange the latest gossip about who is going out with whom. The girls look around to see what people are wearing, what they should do with their hair, and so on. Jane's meal is quite a bit smaller than Johnny's: it consists of a small low-fat yogurt and half a bagel (if she feels like splurging, she will spread some cream cheese on the bagel).

After school, Johnny and Jane head in different directions. Johnny rushes home to get his bike and meets up with his friends to run around and play typical "guy games," like pick-up basketball or touch football. Johnny and his friends play with every boy who shows up, whether they know him or not. They may get into physical fights and arguments, but they always plan to meet up again the next day. In contrast to the boys, Jane and her friends are very selective. Their circle is a small one, and they do everything together.

Thesis statement

Topic sentence (first point)

Evidence (details and examples)

Topic sentence (second point)

Evidence (details and examples)

Body paragraphs

WORD POWER
origami the Japanese art of folding paper into shapes representing flowers or animals

Topic sentence (third point)

Evidence (details and examples)

Topic sentence (fourth point)

Evidence (details and examples)

2

3

4

5

Some days, they go to the mall (they will not necessarily buy anything there, but they will consider the outing productive anyway because they will have spent time together). Most days, though, they just talk, with the discussion ranging from school to guys to lipstick colors. When Jane gets home, she will most likely run to the phone and talk for hours to the same three or four girls.

Body paragraphs

6   <u>At the age of twelve or thirteen, boys and girls do not seem to have very much in common.</u> Given this situation, it is amazing that boys and girls grow up to become men and women who interact as neighbors, friends, and coworkers. What is even more amazing is that so many grow up to share lives and raise families together, treating each other with love and respect.

Summary statement

Conclusion

**PRACTICE
16-6**

1. Restate Nisha's thesis statement in your own words.

2. Does Nisha's opening paragraph identify the subjects she will discuss? Does it tell whether she will focus on similarities or on differences?

3. Nisha's essay is a point-by-point comparison. What four points does she discuss for each of her two subjects?

4. Review the topic sentences in Nisha's body paragraphs. What part of the day does each topic sentence identify?

5. Review the transitional words and phrases Nisha uses to move readers from one subject (Johnny) to the other (Jane). Do you think these transitions are effective, or should they be revised to make the contrast clearer?

6. What is this essay's greatest strength? What is its greatest weakness?

grammar in context

Comparison and Contrast

When you write a comparison-and-contrast essay, you need to present the points you are comparing or contrasting in **parallel** terms to highlight their similarities or differences.

┌─PARALLEL─┐
Johnny, an average thirteen-year-old boy, wakes up late and has

to hurry.
┌─PARALLEL─┐
Jane, unlike Johnny, wakes up early and takes her time.

For information on revising to make ideas parallel, see Chapter 22.

> **Teaching Tip**
> Before your students write comparison-and-contrast essays, you might want to explain the concept of parallelism (Chapter 22) and have them do Practices 22-1 and 22-2.

Step-by-Step Guide: Writing a Comparison-and-Contrast Essay

Now, you are ready to write a comparison-and-contrast essay on one of the topics listed below (or a topic of your choice).

TOPICS

Two coworkers

Two movie heroes

How you expect your life to be different from the lives of your parents

Men's and women's ideas about their body images

Two ways of studying for an exam

Risk-takers and people who play it safe

Country and city living (or, compare suburban living with either)

Two popular magazines (features, ads, target audiences, pictures)

Leaders and followers

Designer products and counterfeit products

Optimists and pessimists

Teaching Tip
Refer students to Chapter 13 for detailed information on the process of writing an essay.

As you plan, draft, and revise your essay, follow these steps:

- Make sure your topic calls for comparison and contrast.
- Find ideas to write about.
- Decide whether you want to discuss similarities, differences, or both.
- Identify your main idea and write a thesis statement.
- Identify specific points of comparison or contrast to support your thesis.
- Decide whether to structure your essay as a point-by-point or subject-by-subject comparison.
- Arrange your points in a logical order, making an outline if necessary.
- Draft your essay.
- TEST your essay, referring to the TESTing a Comparison-and-Contrast Essay checklist below.
- Revise and edit your essay, referring to the two Self-Assessment checklists in Chapter 13.

TESTing a comparison-and-contrast essay

Thesis Statement Unifies Your Essay

☐ Does your introduction include a **thesis statement** that expresses your main idea, identifying the two subjects you will compare and indicating whether your essay will examine similarities or differences?

Evidence Supports Your Essay's Thesis Statement

☐ Have you discussed all significant points of comparison or contrast that apply to your two subjects, supporting each with specific examples and details?

☐ Does all of your **evidence**—examples and details—support your thesis, or should some evidence be deleted?

☐ Have you treated similar points for both of your subjects?

☐ Is your essay's organization consistent with either a point-by-point comparison or a subject-by-subject comparison?

Summary Statement Reinforces Your Essay's Main Idea

☐ Does your conclusion include a **summary statement** that reinforces your essay's thesis, reminding readers what your two subjects are and how they are alike or different?

Transitions

☐ Do you include **transitions** that introduce each of your points of comparison or contrast and move readers from one subject or point to another?

16g Classification Essays

Classification is the act of sorting items into appropriate categories. **Classification essays** divide a whole (your subject) into parts and sort various items into categories.

When you TEST a **classification** essay, make sure it includes all these elements:

T ▪ **Thesis Statement**—The introduction of a classification essay should include a **thesis statement** that communicates the essay's main idea and indicates what the essay will classify.

E ▪ **Evidence**—The body paragraphs should provide **evidence**—examples and details—to support the thesis statement. The topic sentence of each paragraph should identify the category it will discuss.

S ▪ **Summary Statement**—The conclusion of a classification essay should include a **summary statement** that reinforces the essay's thesis.

T ▪ **Transitions**—A classification essay should include **transitional words and phrases** to show how categories are related to one another and to the thesis.

Moving from Assignment to Thesis

The wording of your assignment may suggest that you write a classification essay. For example, you may be asked to consider *kinds, types, categories, components, segments,* or *parts of a whole.* Once you decide that your assignment calls for classification, you need to develop a thesis statement that reflects this purpose.

Teaching Tip
Refer students to Chapter 10 for information on writing a classification paragraph.

Teaching Tip
Tell students that many everyday writing tasks call for classification. For example, the coach of a youth sports team might write a recruitment flyer classifying player requirements by age, grade, and level of experience.

Teaching Tip
For examples of classification essays by professional writers, see 39g.

ASSIGNMENT	THESIS STATEMENT
Business What kinds of courses are most useful for students planning to run their own businesses?	Courses dealing with accounting, management, and computer science offer the most useful skills for future business owners.
Biology List the components of blood and explain the function of each.	Red blood cells, white blood cells, platelets, and plasma have distinct functions.
Education Classify elementary school children according to their academic needs.	The elementary school population includes special-needs students, students with reading and math skills at or near grade level, and academically gifted students.

Organizing a Classification Essay

As a rule, each paragraph of a classification essay examines a separate category—a different part of the whole. For example, a paragraph could focus on one kind of course in the college curriculum, one component of the blood, or one type of child. Within each paragraph, you discuss the individual items that you have put into a particular category—for example, accounting courses, red blood cells, or gifted students. If you consider some categories less important than others, you may decide to discuss those minor categories together in a single paragraph, devoting full paragraphs only to the most significant categories.

Essay Map: *One Category in Each Paragraph*

Introduction (thesis statement identifies whole and its major categories)

First category

Second category

Evidence

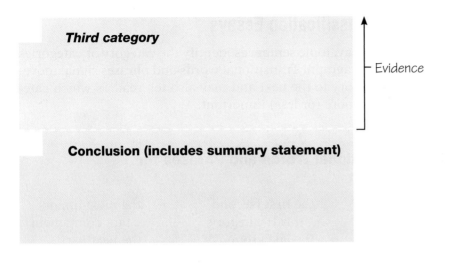

> **Third category**
>
> ⎤ Evidence
>
> **Conclusion (includes summary statement)**

Essay Map: *Major Categories in Separate Paragraphs;*
Minor Categories Grouped Together

> **Introduction (thesis statement identifies whole and its major categories)**
>
> *Minor categories*
>
> *First major category*   ⎤ Evidence
>
> **Second (and more important) major category**
>
> **Conclusion (includes summary statement)**

Transitions in Classification Essays

In a classification essay, topic sentences identify the category or categories discussed in each paragraph. Transitional words and phrases signal movement from one category to the next and may also tell readers which categories you consider more (or less) important.

Some Transitional Words and Phrases for Classification

one kind . . . another kind	the first (second, third) category	the most important component
the final type	the last group	the next part

Case Study: A Student Writes a Classification Essay

Rob O'Neal was given the following assignment in his writing course:

> Write a classification essay focusing on a type of consumer product—for example, cell phones, jeans, mountain bikes, or hair gels. Discuss three or four categories of the product you select, examining the same features for each category.

At first, Rob was overwhelmed by the possibilities; after all, he was a consumer, and there were many products to choose from. Stuck in traffic on his way home from school, he started noticing the names of the different cars around him and thinking about all the different models he had learned to identify when he was younger and fascinated by everything related to cars. At this point, he realized that he could write his essay about cars, classifying them on the basis of the kinds of names they had.

When Rob got home, he brainstormed, listing all the car names he could think of. Then, he made a cluster diagram to help him sort all the names into categories. When he looked over his diagram, he saw that he could arrange the car names he had listed into three categories—those that suggest exciting destinations, those that suggest toughness, and those that suggest exploration and discovery. Identifying these three categories led him to a thesis for his essay: "The names auto manufacturers choose for their cars appeal to Americans' deepest desires."

When he drafted his essay, Rob developed each branch of his cluster diagram into one of his body paragraphs and wrote topic sentences that clearly identified and defined each category. When he TESTed his essay, he saw that it included all the required elements, but he still wasn't completely satisfied with his draft. To help him plan his revision, he made a writing center appointment and went over his draft with a tutor. She advised him to add more examples of each kind of car name as well as more transitional words and phrases—such as *for example* and *also*—to help readers move smoothly through his essay. When he finished making the revisions suggested by his writing center tutor (as well as some he decided on himself), he went on to edit and proofread his essay.

The final draft that follows includes all the elements Rob looked for when he **TEST**ed his essay.

Model Classification Essay

Read Rob O'Neal's finished essay, and answer the questions in Practice 16-7.

Selling a Dream

1   The earliest automobiles were often named after the men who manufactured them—Ford, Studebaker, Nash, Olds, Chrysler, Dodge, Chevrolet, and so on. Over the years, however, American car makers began competing to see what kinds of names will sell the most cars. Many car names seem to be chosen simply for how they sound: Alero, Corvette, Neon, Probe, Caprice. Many others, however, are designed to sell specific dreams to consumers. Americans always seem to want to be, do, and become something different. They want to be tough and brave, to explore new places, to take risks. The names auto manufacturers choose for their cars appeal to Americans' deepest desires.

2   Some American cars are named for places people dream of traveling to. Park Avenue, Malibu, Riviera, Seville, Tahoe, Yukon, Aspen, and Durango are some names that suggest escape—to New York City, California, Europe, the West. Other place names—Sebring, Daytona, and Bonneville, for example—are associated with the danger and excitement of car racing. And then there is the El Dorado, a car named for a fictional paradise: a city of gold.

3   Other car names convey rough and tough, even dangerous, images. Animal names fall into this category, with models like Ram, Bronco, and Mustang suggesting powerful, untamed beasts. The "rough and tough" category also includes car names that suggest the wildness of the Old West: Wrangler and Rodeo, for example. Because the American auto industry was originally centered near Detroit, Michigan, where many cities have Indian names, cars named for the cities where they are manufactured inherited these names. Thus, cars called Cadillac, Pontiac, and Cherokee recall the history of Indian nations, and these too might suggest the excitement of the untamed West.

4   The most interesting car names in terms of the dream they sell, however, were selected to suggest exploration and discovery. Years ago, some car names honored real explorers, like DeSoto and LaSalle. Now, model names only sell an abstract idea. Still, American car names like Blazer, Explorer, Navigator, Mountaineer, Expedition, Caravan, and Voyager (as well as the names of foreign cars driven by many Americans, such as Nissan's Pathfinder and Quest and Honda's Passport, Pilot, and Odyssey) have the power to make drivers feel they are blazing new trails and discovering new worlds—when in fact they may simply be carpooling their children to a soccer game or commuting to work.

5   Most people take cars for granted, but manufacturers still try to make consumers believe they are buying more than just transportation. Today, however, the car is just an ordinary piece of machinery, a necessity for many people. Sadly, the automobile is no longer seen as the amazing invention it once was.

T E S T
- Thesis Statement
- Evidence
- Summary Statement
- Transitions

Introduction

Thesis statement

Topic sentence (first point)

Evidence (details and examples)

Topic sentence (second point)

Evidence (details and examples)

Body paragraphs

Topic sentence (third point)

Evidence (details and examples)

Summary statement

Conclusion

PRACTICE
16-7

1. Restate Rob's thesis statement in your own words.

2. What three categories of car names does Rob discuss in his essay?

3. Is Rob's treatment of the three categories similar? Does he present the same kind of information for each kind of car name?

4. How do Rob's topic sentences move readers from one category to the next? How do they link the three categories?

5. Do you think Rob should have included additional examples in each category? Should he have included any additional categories?

6. What is this essay's greatest strength? What is its greatest weakness?

grammar in context

Classification

When you write a classification essay, you may want to list the categories you are going to discuss or the examples in each category. If you do, use a **colon** to introduce your list, and make sure that a complete sentence comes before the colon.

> Many car names seem to be chosen simply for how they sound: Alero, Corvette, Neon, Probe, Caprice.

For information on how to use a colon to introduce a list, see 36g.

Teaching Tip
Before your students write classification essays, you might want to explain the use of the colon to introduce a list (36g) and have students do the relevant items in Practice 36-8.

Step-by-Step Guide: Writing a Classification Essay

Now, you are ready to write a classification essay on one of the topics below (or a topic of your own).

TOPICS

Types of teachers (or bosses)	Traits of oldest children, middle children, and youngest children
Ways to lose (or gain) weight	
Items hanging on your walls	Kinds of desserts
Kinds of moods	Kinds of workers you encounter in a typical day
Kinds of stores in a local shopping mall	College students' clothing choices
Kinds of learning styles	Kinds of tattoos

As you plan, draft, and revise your essay, follow these steps:

■ Make sure your topic calls for classification.

■ Find ideas to write about.

■ Identify your main idea, and write a thesis statement.

Teaching Tip
Refer students to Chapter 13 for detailed information on the process of writing an essay.

- Decide what categories you will discuss.
- Sort examples and details into categories.
- Arrange your categories in an effective order, making an outline if necessary.
- Draft your essay.
- TEST your essay, referring to the TESTing a Classification Essay checklist below.
- Revise and edit your essay, referring to the two Self-Assessment checklists in Chapter 13.

TESTing a classification essay

Thesis Statement Unifies Your Essay

☐ Does your introduction include a **thesis statement** that clearly identifies the subject of your classification and the categories you will discuss?

Evidence Supports Your Essay's Thesis Statement

☐ Does all of your **evidence**—details and examples—support your thesis, or should some evidence be deleted?

☐ Have you treated each major category similarly and with equal thoroughness?

Summary Statement Reinforces Your Essay's Main Idea

☐ Does your conclusion include a **summary statement** that reinforces your essay's thesis?

Transitions

☐ Do you include **transitions** that introduce your categories and lead readers from one category to the next?

16h   Definition Essays

Definition explains the meaning of a term or concept. A **definition essay** presents an *extended definition*, using various patterns of development to move beyond a simple dictionary definition.

> **Teaching Tip**
> Refer students to Chapter 11 for information on writing a definition paragraph.

When you **TEST** a **definition** essay, make sure it includes all the following elements:

T ■ **Thesis Statement**—The introduction of a definition essay should include a **thesis statement** that communicates the essay's main idea and identifies the term you are going to define.

E ■ **Evidence**—The body paragraphs should include **evidence**—examples and details—that supports the thesis statement and defines your term. Body paragraphs may use different patterns of development.

S ■ **Summary Statement**—The conclusion of a definition essay should include a **summary statement** that reinforces the essay's thesis.

T ■ **Transitions**—A definition essay should include **transitional words and phrases** to move readers from one section of the definition to the next.

Moving from Assignment to Thesis

The wording of your assignment may suggest that you write a definition essay. For example, you may be asked to *define* or *explain* or to answer the question *What is x?* or *What does x mean?* Once you decide that your assignment calls for definition, you need to develop a thesis statement that reflects this purpose.

> **Teaching Tip**
> For examples of definition essays by professional writers, see 39h.

> **Teaching Tip**
> Tell students that many everyday writing tasks call for definition. For example, a letter of complaint to a neighborhood business might define terms like *excessive noise* and *rude behavior*.

> **Teaching Tip**
> Tell students that when they write a definition, the term being defined should be italicized.

ASSIGNMENT	THESIS STATEMENT
Art Explain the meaning of the term *performance art*.	Unlike more conventional forms of art, *performance art* extends beyond the canvas.
Biology What did Darwin mean by the term *natural selection*?	*Natural selection*, popularly known as "survival of the fittest," is a good deal more complicated than most people think.
Psychology What is *attention deficit disorder*?	*Attention deficit disorder* (ADD), once narrowly defined as a childhood problem, is now known to affect adults as well as children.

Organizing a Definition Essay

As the thesis statements above suggest, definition essays can be developed in various ways. For example, you can define something by telling how it occurred (narration), by describing its appearance (description), by giving a series of examples (exemplification), by telling how it operates (process), by telling how it is similar to or different from something else (comparison and contrast), or by discussing its parts (classification).

Some definition essays use a single pattern of development; others combine several patterns of development, perhaps using a different one in each paragraph.

Essay Map: *Single Pattern of Development*

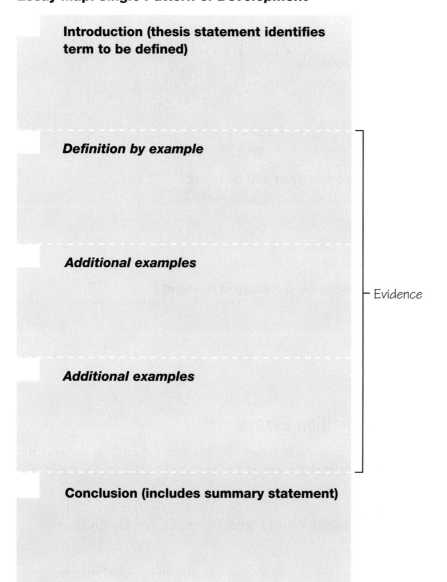

Introduction (thesis statement identifies term to be defined)

Definition by example

Additional examples

Additional examples

Evidence

Conclusion (includes summary statement)

Essay Map: *Combination of Several Different Patterns of Development*

Introduction (thesis statement identifies term to be defined)

(continued on next page)

(continued from previous page)

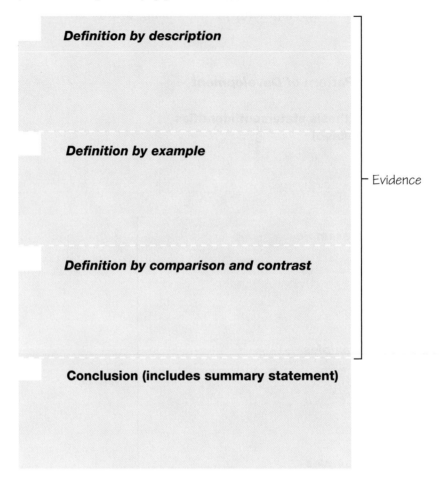

Definition by description

Definition by example

Evidence

Definition by comparison and contrast

Conclusion (includes summary statement)

Transitions in Definition Essays

The kinds of transitions used in a definition essay depend on the specific pattern or patterns of development in the essay.

Some Transitional Words and Phrases for Definition

also	like
for example	one characteristic . . . another characteristic
in addition	one way . . . another way
in particular	specifically

Case Study: A Student Writes a Definition Essay

Kristin Whitehead, a student in a first-year writing course, was given the following assignment:

> From the attached list, choose a slang term, an abbreviation or shorthand used in text messages, or a technical term used in one of your classes. Write an essay in which you define this term, developing your definition with any patterns that seem appropriate.

Because her instructor gave the class a list of topics to choose from, Kristin was able to decide on a topic quickly. She chose to define *street smart*, a term with which she was very familiar. She was particularly interested in defining this term because she felt it was something few college students she knew seemed to understand. She thought of herself as a street-smart person and was impatient with some of her fellow first-year students, who she felt lacked this important quality.

Kristin had learned from experience how important it was to be street smart, and she brainstormed about her experiences to find information to guide her as she drafted her essay. In her thesis statement, she indicated why she was defining this term (because she saw it as a "vital survival skill"), and in her body paragraphs she defined her term by giving examples of behavior that she considered to be (and *not* to be) street smart.

When she TESTed her draft, she was satisfied with the wording of her thesis statement and her supporting evidence, but she knew that she still needed to add a summary statement that did more than just repeat the wording of her thesis statement; she also needed to add clearer topic sentences. Since she knew she was going to meet with her peer-review group, she decided to ask her classmates for advice about these two issues. With their help, she revised her summary statement and tied her body paragraphs together by adding the same introductory phrase to the topic sentences of paragraphs 2, 3, and 4. When she finished revising her essay, Kristin went on to edit and proofread it.

The final draft that follows includes all the elements Kristin looked for when she TESTed her essay.

Model Definition Essay

Read Kristin Whitehead's finished essay, and answer the questions in Practice 16-8.

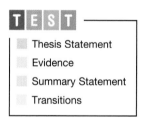

T E S T

- Thesis Statement
- Evidence
- Summary Statement
- Transitions

Street Smart

Introduction

1   I grew up in a big city, so I was practically born street smart. I learned the hard way how to act and what to do, and so did my friends. To us, being *street smart* meant having common sense. We wanted to be cool, but we needed to be safe, too. Now I go to college in a big city, and I realize that not everyone here grew up the way I did. Many students are from suburbs or rural areas, and they are either terrified of the city or totally ignorant of city life. The few suburban or rural students who are willing to venture downtown are not street smart—but they should be. Being street smart is a vital survival skill, one that everyone should learn.

Thesis statement

2   For me, being street smart means knowing how to protect my possessions. Friends of mine who are not used to city life insist on wearing all their jewelry when they go downtown. I think this is asking for trouble, and I know better. I always tuck my chain under my shirt and leave my gold earrings home. Another thing that surprises me is how some of my friends wave their money around. They always seem to be standing on the street, trying to count their change or stuff dollars into their wallets. Street-smart people make sure to put their money safely away in their pockets or purses before they leave a store. A street-smart person will also carry a backpack, a purse strapped across the chest, or no purse at all. A person who is not street smart carries a purse

Topic sentence (first point)

Evidence (details and examples)

Body paragraphs

loosely over one shoulder or dangles it by its handle. Again, these people are asking for trouble.

Topic sentence (second point)

Evidence (details and examples)

Body paragraphs

Topic sentence (third point)

Evidence (details and examples)

Summary statement

Conclusion

<u>Being street smart also means protecting myself.</u> It means being aware of my surroundings at all times and looking alert. A lot of times, I have been downtown with people who kept stopping on the street to talk about where they should go next or walking up and down the same street over and over again. A street-smart person would never do this. It is important that I look as if I know where I am going at all times, even if I don't. Whenever possible, I decide on a destination in advance, and I make sure I know how to get there. Even if I am not completely sure where I am headed, I make sure my body language conveys my confidence in my ability to reach my destination.

<u>Finally, being street smart means protecting my life.</u> A street-smart person does not walk alone, especially after dark, in an unfamiliar neighborhood. A street-smart person does not ask random strangers for directions; when lost, he or she asks a shopkeeper for help. A street-smart person takes main streets instead of side streets. When faced with danger or the threat of danger, a street-smart person knows when to run, when to scream, and when to give up money or possessions to avoid violence.

<u>Being street smart is vitally important—sometimes even a matter of life and death.</u> Some people think it is a gift, but I think it is something almost anyone can learn. Probably the best way to learn how to be street smart is to hang out with people who know where they are going.

3

4

5

PRACTICE

16-8

1. Restate Kristin's thesis statement in your own words.

2. In your own words, define the term *street smart*. Why does this term require more than a one-sentence definition?

3. Where does Kristin use examples to develop her definition? Where does she use comparison and contrast?

4. What phrase does Kristin repeat in her topic sentences to tie her essay's three body paragraphs together?

5. Kristin's conclusion is quite a bit shorter than her other paragraphs. Do you think she should expand this paragraph? If so, what should she add?

6. What is this essay's greatest strength? What is its greatest weakness?

Teaching Tip
Before your students write definition essays, you might want to review the correct structure for a definition sentence, pointing them to the box on page 148. Depending on the particular patterns students use to develop their definitions, you can also refer them to the specific exercises noted in the Grammar in Context boxes in other sections of this chapter.

grammar in context

Definition

When you write a definition essay, you may begin with a one-sentence definition that you expand in the rest of your essay. When you write your definition sentence, do not use the phrases *is when* or *is where*.

means knowing

For me, being street smart ~~is when I know~~ how to protect my

possessions.

> *means protecting*
> Being street smart is also ~~where I protect~~ myself.
>   ^
>
> *For information on how to structure a definition sentence, see the Grammar in Context box in 11a.*

Step-by-Step Guide: Writing a Definition Essay

Now, you are ready to write a definition essay on one of the topics listed below (or a topic of your choice).

TOPICS

Upward mobility	Responsibility	Courage
Peer pressure	Procrastination	Happiness
Success	Security	Home
Loyalty	Ambition	Family

As you plan, draft, and revise your essay, follow these steps:

- Make sure your topic calls for definition.
- Find ideas to write about.
- Identify your main idea, and write a thesis statement.
- Decide what patterns of development to use to support your thesis.
- Arrange supporting examples and details in an effective order, making an outline if necessary.
- Draft your essay.
- **TEST** your essay, referring to the **TEST**ing a Definition Essay checklist below.
- Revise and edit your essay, referring to the two Self-Assessment checklists in Chapter 13.

> **Teaching Tip**
> Refer students to Chapter 13 for detailed information on the process of writing an essay.

TESTing a definition essay

Thesis Statement Unifies Your Essay

☐ Does your introduction include a **thesis statement** that identifies the term your essay will define and provides a brief definition?

Evidence Supports Your Essay's Thesis Statement

☐ Is all of your **evidence**—examples and details—clearly related to the term you are defining, or should some items be deleted?

(continued on next page)

(continued from previous page)

☐ Do you use appropriate patterns of development to support your definition, or should you explore other options?

Summary Statement Reinforces Your Essay's Main Idea

☐ Does your conclusion include a **summary statement** that reinforces your essay's thesis?

Transitions

☐ Do you include **transitions** that introduce your points and link your ideas?

16i   Argument Essays

Argument takes a stand on a debatable issue—that is, an issue that has two sides (and can therefore be debated). An **argument essay** uses different kinds of *evidence*—facts, examples, and expert opinion—to persuade readers to accept a position.

When you **TEST** an **argument** essay, make sure it includes all these elements:

T ▪ **Thesis Statement**—The introduction of an argument essay should include a **thesis statement** that expresses the essay's main idea: the position you will take on the issue.

E ▪ **Evidence**—The body paragraphs should include **evidence**—facts, examples, and expert opinion—to support the thesis statement convincingly. Evidence can be arranged *inductively* or *deductively*. The topic sentence of each body paragraph should identify one point of support for your thesis.

S ▪ **Summary Statement**—The conclusion of an argument essay should include a strong **summary statement** that reinforces the essay's thesis.

T ▪ **Transitions**—An argument essay should include logical **transitional words and phrases** that show how your points are related and move readers through your argument.

Moving from Assignment to Thesis

The wording of your assignment may suggest that you write an argument essay. For example, you may be asked to *debate, argue, consider, give your opinion, take a position,* or *take a stand.* Once you decide that your assignment calls for argument, you need to develop a thesis statement that reflects this purpose.

Teaching Tip
Refer students to Chapter 12 for information on writing an argument paragraph.

ASSIGNMENT	THESIS STATEMENT
Composition Explain your position on a current social issue.	People should be able to invest some of their Social Security contributions in the stock market.
American history Do you believe that General Lee was responsible for the South's defeat at the Battle of Gettysburg? Why or why not?	Because Lee refused to listen to the advice given to him by General Longstreet, he is largely responsible for the South's defeat at the Battle of Gettysburg.
Ethics Should physician-assisted suicide be legalized?	Although many people think physician-assisted suicide should remain illegal, it should be legal in certain situations.

Teaching Tip
Tell students that many everyday writing tasks call for argument. For example, a letter to the editor of a newspaper might take a stand on a political, social, economic, religious, or environmental issue affecting the writer's family or community.

Teaching Tip
For examples of argument essays by professional writers, see 39i.

Organizing an Argument Essay

An argument essay can be organized *inductively* or *deductively*. An **inductive argument** moves from the specific to the general—that is, from a group of specific observations to a general conclusion based on these observations. An essay on the first topic in the list above, for example, could be an inductive argument. It could begin by presenting facts, examples, and expert opinion about the benefits of investing in the stock market and end with the conclusion that people should be able to invest part of their Social Security contributions in the stock market.

A **deductive argument** moves from the general to the specific. A deductive argument begins with a **major premise** (a general statement that the writer believes his or her audience will accept) and then moves to a **minor premise** (a specific instance of the belief stated in the major premise). It ends with a **conclusion** that follows from the two premises. For example, an essay on the last topic in the list above could be a deductive argument. It could begin with the major premise that all terminally ill patients who are in great pain should be given access to physician-assisted suicide. It could then go on to state and explain the minor premise that a particular patient is both terminally ill and in great pain, offering facts, examples, and the opinions of experts to support this premise. The essay could conclude that this patient should, therefore, be allowed the option of physician-assisted suicide. The deductive argument presented in the essay would have three parts.

MAJOR PREMISE   All terminally ill patients who are in great pain should be allowed to choose physician-assisted suicide.

MINOR PREMISE   John Lacca is a terminally ill patient who is in great pain.

CONCLUSION   Therefore, John Lacca should be allowed to choose physician-assisted suicide.

Before you present your argument, think about whether your readers are likely to be hostile toward, neutral toward, or in agreement with your position. Once you understand your audience, you can decide which points to make in support of your argument.

Begin each paragraph of your argument essay with a topic sentence that clearly states a point in support of your thesis. Throughout your essay, try to include specific examples that will make your arguments persuasive. Keep in mind that arguments that rely just on generalizations are not as convincing as those that include vivid details and specific examples. Finally, strive for a balanced, moderate tone, and avoid name-calling or personal attacks.

In addition to presenting your case, your essay should also briefly summarize arguments *against* your position and **refute** them (that is, argue against them) by identifying factual errors or errors in logic. If an opposing argument is particularly strong, concede its strength—but try to point out some weaknesses as well. If you deal with opposing arguments in this way, your audience will see you as a fair and reasonable person.

Essay Map: *Inductive Argument*

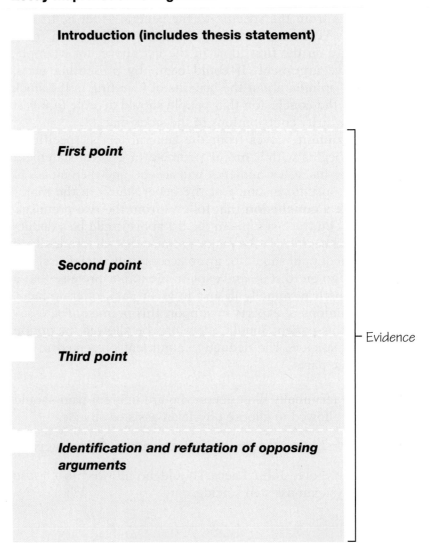

Introduction (includes thesis statement)

First point

Second point   — Evidence

Third point

Identification and refutation of opposing arguments

Conclusion (includes summary statement)

Essay Map: *Deductive Argument*

Introduction (includes thesis statement)

Major premise stated and explained

Minor premise stated and explained

Minor premise further explained   ⎤ Evidence

Opposing arguments identified and refuted

Conclusion (includes summary statement)

Transitions in Argument Essays

Transitions are extremely important in argument essays because they not only signal the movement from one part of the argument to another but also relate specific points to one another and to the thesis statement.

Some Transitional Words and Phrases for Argument

accordingly	granted	of course
admittedly	however	on the one
although	in addition	hand . . . on the
because	in conclusion	other hand
but	indeed	since
certainly	in fact	so
consequently	in summary	therefore
despite	meanwhile	thus
even so	moreover	to be sure
even though	nevertheless	truly
finally	nonetheless	
first, second . . .	now	

Case Study: A Student Writes an Argument Essay

Peter Charron, a student in a first-year writing course, was assigned to write an argument essay on a controversial issue of his choice. His instructor suggested that students find a topic by reading their campus and local newspapers, going online to read national news stories and political blogs, and watching public affairs programs on television. Peter took her advice and also talked about his assignment with friends and family members. One issue that caught his interest was the question of whether to grant amnesty to undocumented immigrants. Although Peter felt sympathy for this group, he also knew that they were breaking the law. Because this issue clearly had at least two sides, and because he wasn't sure at the outset what position he could best support, Peter thought it would be a good topic to explore further.

Peter began by brainstorming, recording all his ideas on this complex issue. In addition to ideas he had thought of as he read, he also included ideas he developed as he listened to his parents and to his boss at the restaurant where he worked on weekends. When he read over his brainstorming notes, he saw that he had reasonable arguments both for and against granting amnesty for undocumented immigrants. At this point, he wasn't sure what position to take in his essay, so he made an appointment for a conference with his instructor.

Peter's instructor pointed out that he could make a good case either for or against granting amnesty; like many controversial issues, this one had no easy answers. She encouraged him to support the position that seemed right to him and to use the information on the other side when he went on to introduce (and refute) opposing arguments. She also recommended

WORD POWER

amnesty the overlooking or pardoning of offenses

that he email his first draft to her so she could see how her suggestion worked out.

Following his instructor's advice, Peter decided to argue in favor of permitting undocumented immigrants to remain in the United States and work toward citizenship. Before he began to draft his essay, he drafted a thesis that stated his position on the issue; then, he arranged supporting points from his brainstorming list into an outline he could follow as he wrote. As he put his ideas down on paper, he focused on providing specific evidence to support his thesis and on explaining his position as clearly and thoroughly as possible. He paid special attention to choosing transitional words and phrases that would indicate how his points were logically connected to one another.

When Peter finished his draft, he **TEST**ed it, taking a quick inventory to make sure he had included all four necessary components of an essay. Then, he emailed his draft to his instructor. Following her suggestions, he revised his draft, this time focusing on his topic sentences, his presentation (and refutation) of opposing arguments, and his introductory and concluding paragraphs. When he was satisfied with his revisions, he edited and proofread his paper.

The final draft that follows includes all the elements Peter looked for when he **TEST**ed his essay.

Model Argument Essay

Read Peter Charron's finished essay below, and answer the questions in Practice 16-9.

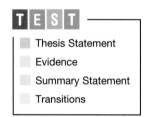

T E S T
- Thesis Statement
- Evidence
- Summary Statement
- Transitions

Amnesty for Undocumented Immigrants

1   More than twelve million undocumented immigrants now live in the United States. Is it practical to send them all back home? Should they be allowed to stay? Despite their illegal entry, if they have worked and raised their families in the United States for years, these people should be allowed to stay in this country and, eventually, to become American citizens.

2   Many people object to the idea of amnesty, an official pardon for past illegal acts. Certainly, in this case, amnesty would forgive immigrants for entering the country illegally. However, this amnesty would not come without penalty. First, they would be heavily fined. In addition, they would have to show that they have jobs and can speak English. Moreover, to become American citizens, they would have to wait at least thirteen years. So, even though they would be granted amnesty, they still would be punished for entering the United States illegally.

3   Undocumented immigrants come to this country to work, and they often take low-wage jobs that businesses would otherwise find difficult or impossible to fill. For example, undocumented immigrants often work as migrant laborers—planting, cultivating, and picking crops like lettuce and tomatoes. In the Southwest, where there are many Mexican immigrants, laborers often work in the construction industry. The meat packing, landscaping, and hotel industries also use immigrant workers, not all of whom are in this country legally. Finally, the health care industry needs more and more people every year who will work for low pay as caregivers, providing personal care to the

Introduction

Thesis statement

Topic sentence
(first point)

Evidence
(details and examples)

Body paragraphs

Topic sentence
(second point)

Evidence
(details and examples)

elderly and disabled. It would be very hard to fill all these jobs without illegal immigrants.

Topic sentence (third point)

Giving amnesty to undocumented immigrants is not a perfect solution, but it would solve many problems. Now, these immigrants feel they have to hide from authorities because they are afraid they will be deported. Therefore, they may delay seeking needed medical care. As a result, they may wind up in a hospital emergency room when they are seriously ill. This is expensive for everyone. In addition, children of undocumented immigrants often cannot attend college because college scholarships require documents—and, even if students can afford the tuition, they must be legal in order to get even a part-time job. Consequently, it is very hard for undocumented immigrants to improve their lives or the lives of their children.

Evidence (details and examples)

Body paragraphs

Topic sentence (fourth point)

People who oppose immigration amnesty say that it would encourage disrespect for the law. This may be so. Nevertheless, in this case, there is no good alternative. It would be impossible to track down and deport the more than twelve million immigrants now in the United States illegally. Moreover, even if it were possible, a huge labor shortage would result. Another objection to the idea of amnesty is the claim that undocumented immigrants take jobs away from American citizens. However, according to the Department of Labor, this is not true. In fact, undocumented immigrants tend to work at jobs that citizens are unwilling to take. Finally, some say that the American way of life is being weakened by illegal immigrants. However, just the opposite is true: the United States has always been enriched by immigrants, whether legal or not. In fact, immigration is the lifeblood of the nation.

Evidence (details and examples)

Summary statement

Granted, undocumented immigrants broke the law when they entered the country but many of them have earned the right to remain in the United States. Besides, even if it were possible to send them all back, the results would be disastrous for them and for the nation. Therefore, the best solution is to find a way to allow them to stay. By coming to America, they have shown that they want to work. They should be allowed to do so. Thus, America can remain a nation that welcomes immigrants from all over the world.

Conclusion

PRACTICE

16-9   1. In your own words, explain the position Peter takes in his essay.

2. List the facts and examples Peter uses to support his thesis. Where does he include expert opinion?

3. Can you think of any supporting evidence that Peter does not include?

4. Review the transitional words and phrases Peter uses. How do they move his argument along? Should he add any transitions?

5. Throughout his essay, Peter acknowledges that some immigrants have broken the law. Do you think this strategy is a good idea? Why or why not?

6. Where does Peter address opposing arguments? Can you think of other arguments he should have addressed?

7. What is this essay's greatest strength? What is its greatest weakness?

grammar in context

Argument

When you write an argument essay, you need to show the relationships between your ideas by combining sentences to create **compound sentences** and **complex sentences**.

> Undocumented immigrants come to this country to work. ~~They~~ *, and they* often take low-wage jobs that businesses would otherwise find difficult or impossible to fill. (compound sentence)
>
> Now, these immigrants feel they have to hide from authorities. *because they* ~~They~~ are afraid they will be deported. (complex sentence)

For information on how to create compound sentences, see Chapter 19. For information on how to create complex sentences, see Chapter 20.

Teaching Tip
Before your students write argument essays, you might want to explain the use of subordinating conjunctions and relative pronouns to form complex sentences and have students do Practices 20-3 through 20-6.

Step-by-Step Guide: Writing an Argument Essay

Now, you are ready to write an argument essay on one of the topics listed below (or a topic of your choice).

TOPICS

Teenagers who commit serious crimes should (or should not) be tried as adults.

Citizens without criminal records should (or should not) be permitted to carry concealed weapons.

Human beings should (or should not) be used in medical research experiments.

Parents should (or should not) be permitted to use government vouchers to pay private school tuition.

College financial aid should (or should not) be based solely on merit.

Government funds should (or should not) be used to support the arts.

Public high schools should (or should not) be permitted to distribute condoms to students.

The minimum wage should (or should not) be raised.

College athletes should (or should not) be paid to play.

Convicted felons should (or should not) lose the right to vote.

ESL Tip
Before drafting, group native and nonnative speakers together to discuss essay topics.

As you plan, draft, and revise your essay, follow these steps:

- Make sure your topic calls for argument.
- Find ideas to write about.
- Decide on the position you will support, and write a thesis statement that clearly expresses this position.
- List the key points in support of your thesis.
- Arrange your key supporting points in an effective order.

Teaching Tip
Refer students to Chapter 13 for detailed information on the process of writing an essay.

- List evidence (facts, examples, and expert opinion) in support of each point.
- List arguments against your position.
- Make an outline that includes key supporting and opposing points.
- Draft your essay.
- TEST your essay, referring to the TESTing an Argument Essay checklist below.
- Revise and edit your essay, referring to the two Self-Assessment checklists in Chapter 13.

TESTing an argument essay

Thesis Statement Unifies Your Essay

☐ Does your introduction include a **thesis statement** that clearly expresses the stand you take on the issue you will discuss? Is this issue debatable—that is, does it really have two sides?

Evidence Supports Your Essay's Thesis Statement

☐ Does all of your **evidence**—examples and details—support your thesis, or should some evidence be deleted?

☐ Do you have *enough* evidence to support your points?

☐ Have you considered whether readers are likely to be hostile toward, neutral toward, or in agreement with your position— and have you chosen your points accordingly?

☐ Is your evidence presented in a clear inductive or deductive order?

Summary Statement Reinforces Your Essay's Main Idea

☐ Does your conclusion include a **summary statement** that reinforces your essay's thesis?

Transitions

☐ Do you include **transitions** that introduce your points?

☐ Do you include enough transitional words and phrases to help readers follow the logic of your argument?

Although this chapter presents student essays that are structured primarily around a single pattern of development—exemplification, narration, description, process, cause and effect, comparison and contrast, classification, definition, or argument—professional writers often combine several patterns in a single essay.

The following short newspaper commentary, "Is It 'Natural' to Do Things the Hard Way?" by Betsy Hart, combines several of the patterns of development that are explained and illustrated in this chapter. Read the essay carefully, and then answer the Questions for Discussion on page 296.

Is It "Natural" to Do Things the Hard Way?

Betsy Hart

What is so great about nature? Since the beginning of time, mankind's quest has been one of overcoming the ravages of nature. To find heat where there was cold, food where there was hunger, shelter where there was only exposure to the elements.

Later, man looked to medicine to cure or alleviate the ravages of injury and disease, and education to overcome our natural ignorance. The Industrial Age led to mechanization, so the natural limits of man's labor and his ability to travel great distances increased exponentially, and the Technological Age has done the same for the mind.

Man's eternal striving to conquer or at least tame nature means that today people are living twice as long as they did just one hundred years ago, and except in the darkest recesses of the world, those lives aren't just longer, but healthier, better-fed, and more prosperous.

So why is "natural" back?

There is the notion, which has actually gone in and out of fashion for at least the last thirty years or so, that "natural" is somehow superior to its alternatives. Today that idea is "in" with a vengeance.

For example, the market for organic foods continues to grow by leaps and bounds. I'm supposed to buy the expensive "organic" baby food for my eleven-month-old, and feed her brother and sisters "natural" Tyson chicken (because "I can" the ad says), and I should certainly pick up some organic breads and vegetables on my way to the checkout counter. Such foodstuffs carry the cachet of being nutritionally superior.

But I wouldn't touch any of it with a ten-foot pole. For one thing, "organic" has a pretty imprecise definition, so who even knows what's in that stuff? For another, one favored "natural" fertilizer for the organic crowd is cow manure, which can be loaded with the deadly E. coli bacteria. And I never again want to come home from the grocery store having mistakenly bought organic lettuce (meaning no chemical pesticides) only to find it crawling with bugs.

I don't worry about theoretical, minute amounts of pesticide residue on food, which has never been shown to cause illness but which does allow food to be produced abundantly and cheaply so that folks can consume varied, more healthful diets. I do worry about the food that's—gulp—natural.

Of course, the ultimate in natural may be the growing "home-birth" movement—no doctors, certainly no medication, and lots of friends standing by, even watching. The Associated Press recently reported that for a small but expanding contingent, "unattended" births are the rage, meaning that no midwife is even present.

Sure, some folks may not cotton to calm, protected births in hospitals where the mother can relax and enjoy herself because a safe medication relieves her pain and doctors are standing by to attend to life-threatening emergencies. But those who feel they are somehow superior because they tortured themselves with a "natural" home birth would do well to remember such births were the way of nature in the past, which is why mothers and their newborns so often didn't survive them.

It seems that some people just get excited about doing things the hard way.

Where I absolutely positively draw the line is in organic makeup and skin treatments. I mean, if there was ever a time and place for chemicals, this is it! But *Health* magazine reports this month that the "green movement" has hit the cosmetics counter big-time. According to a poll conducted by the magazine, 83 percent of women prefer "all-natural" products. (Though perhaps it goes without saying that these women couldn't define what that meant.) *Health* magazine reports that "natural" cosmetic stores such as the Body Shop are booming.

Fortunately, even the magazine admits that the organics might not look as good or as "natural" as their synthetic counterparts, and that the lack of preservatives in organic makeup can mean it harbors all kinds of dangerous—though natural—bacteria and fungi.

"Natural" is everywhere. From the kind of energy we use, to the kind of homes we build, even to the material used in today's breast implants, natural is "in"—no matter if it doesn't work nearly as well, is more scarce, makes things much more tedious or even dangerous, and/or is a lot more expensive.

Yep, since man first walked the Earth, he's been trying to get away from nature in things large and small. Which only makes this generation's strange attachment to "natural" so obviously . . . unnatural.

QUESTIONS FOR DISCUSSION

1. What patterns of development are used in this essay? Work with another student to decide where each pattern is used. Then, label the section of the essay where each pattern appears.

2. What is the thesis of this essay? Restate it in your own words. If you were to add this thesis statement to the essay, where would you put it?

3. How does each pattern of development that you identified in Question 1 support the essay's thesis?

4. Look again at the thesis statement you supplied in your answer to Question 2. What pattern of development does it suggest?

5. What do you think is this essay's primary pattern of development? Explain.

review checklist

Patterns of Essay Development

☐ Exemplification essays use specific examples to support a thesis. (See 16a.)

☐ Narrative essays tell a story by presenting a series of events in chronological order. (See 16b.)

☐ Descriptive essays use details to give readers a clear, vivid picture of a person, place, or object. (See 16c.)

☐ Process essays explain the steps in a procedure, telling how something is (or was) done or how to do something. (See 16d.)

☐ Cause-and-effect essays identify causes or predict effects. (See 16e.)

☐ Comparison-and-contrast essays explain how two things are alike or how they are different. (See 16f.)

☐ Classification essays divide a whole into parts and sort various items into categories. (See 16g.)

☐ Definition essays use various patterns of development to develop an extended definition. (See 16h.)

☐ Argument essays take a stand on a debatable issue, using evidence to persuade readers to accept a position. (See 16i.)

unit
4 Research

17 Writing a Research Paper

Google
directory

Web   Images   Groups   News   Shopping   Maps   Scholar   more »

[Google Search]   Preferences
Directory Help

The web organized by topic into categories.

Arts
Music, Movies, Performing Arts, …

Business
Industrial Goods and Services, Finance, …

Computers
Software, Internet, Programming, …

Games
Video Games, Roleplaying, Board Games, …

Health
Conditions and Diseases, Medicine, Animal, …

World
Deutsch, Español, Fr

Home
Cooking, Family, Gardening, …

Kids and Teens
International, School Time, Games, …

News
Newspapers, Media, Colleges and Universities, …

Recreation
Pets, Outdoors, Food, …

Reference
Education, Biography, Museums, …

Regional
North America, Europe, Oceania, …

Science
Biology, Social Sciences, Technology, …

Shopping
Home and Garden, Crafts, Sports, …

Society
Religion and Spirituality, Law, Issues, …

Sports
Soccer, Equestrian, Football, …

write first

Google directory enables users to search for information by clicking on increasingly specific categories and subcategories. Some students use this tool when they begin their research.

Suppose that you are going to write a short research paper on a topic of your own choosing. Brainstorm about possible topics, and then list some topics that you could research and write about.

In some essays, you use your own ideas to support your thesis. In other essays—such as argument essays—your own knowledge about a subject might not be enough to support your thesis. In these situations, you will have to supplement your ideas with **research**—a careful examination of the ideas and opinions of others. Doing research gives you a number of advantages:

- It exposes you to a cross-section of opinion.
- It helps you find supporting material for your essay. For example, an expert's opinion, a memorable quotation, or a useful fact or statistic can make your essay more interesting, more authoritative, and more convincing.
- It tells readers that you are someone who has gained a fuller understanding of your topic—and for this reason are worth listening to.

When you write an essay that calls for research, you find material on the Internet, in the library, and in other places. This information may be in print or electronic form, and it may be drawn from a variety of sources—for example, journals, magazines, newspapers, pamphlets, blogs, encyclopedias, DVDs, and books.

When you write an essay that requires research, you will have an easier time if you follow this process:

1. Choose a topic.
2. Do research.
3. Take notes.
4. Watch out for plagiarism.
5. Develop a thesis.
6. Make an outline.
7. Write your paper.
8. Document your sources.

17a Choosing a Topic

The first step in writing an essay that calls for research is finding a topic to write about. Before you choose a topic, ask the following questions.

- What is your page limit?
- When is your paper due?
- How many sources are you expected to use?
- What kind of sources are you expected to use?

The answers to these questions will help you tell if your topic is too broad or too narrow.

When May Compton, a student in a composition course, was asked to write a three- to four-page essay that was due in five weeks, she decided that she wanted to write about the counterfeit designer goods that seemed to be for sale everywhere. She knew, however, that the general topic "counterfeit designer goods" would be too broad for her essay.

May was used to seeing sidewalk vendors selling brand-name sunglasses and jewelry. Recently, she and her friends had been invited to a "purse party," where they were able to buy expensive handbags at extremely low prices. Even though these handbags were not identified as fakes, she was sure that they were. Because May was a marketing major, she wondered how these copies were marketed and sold. She also wondered if these counterfeits had any negative effects on consumers.

May decided to explore the problem of counterfeit designer merchandise in her paper because she could discuss it in the required number of pages and would be able to finish her paper within the five-week time limit.

choose a topic

Look at the brainstorming list that you compiled for the Write First activity on page 301. Then, choose a topic that you could research and write about. Keep in mind that the topic you choose should be one that you are interested in as well as one that you know something about.

17b Doing Research

Finding Information in the Library

The best place to start your research is with the resources of your college library: print and electronic resources that you cannot find anywhere else—including on the Internet. For the best results, you should do your library research systematically. Begin by searching the library's online catalog and electronic databases; then, look for any additional facts or statistics that you need to support your ideas.

FYI

The Resources of the Library

The Online Catalog
Once you get a general sense of your topic, you can consult the library's catalog. Libraries have **online catalogs**—information systems that enable you to search all the resources held by the library. By typing in words or phrases related to your topic, you can find books, periodicals, and other materials that you can use in your paper.

(continued on next page)

(continued from previous page)

Electronic Databases

After consulting the online catalog, you should look at the **electronic databases**—such as InfoTrac and ProQuest—that your library subscribes to. These databases enable you to obtain information from newspapers, magazines, and journals that you cannot freely access on the Internet. Most enable you to retrieve the full text of articles. (You can usually search your library's databases remotely, from home or from anywhere on campus.)

Sources for Facts and Statistics

As you write your paper, you may find that you need certain facts or statistics to support particular points. Works like *Facts on File*, the *Information Please Almanac*, and the *Statistical Abstract of the United States* can help you find this information. These and similar publications are available online; your reference librarian can recommend appropriate sources.

Remember that once you find information in the library, you still have to **evaluate** it—that is, determine its usefulness and reliability. For example, an article in a respected periodical such as the *New York Times* or the *Wall Street Journal* is more trustworthy and believable than one in a tabloid such as the *National Enquirer* or the *Sun*. You should also look at the date of publication to decide if the book or article is up to date. Finally, consider the author. Is he or she an expert? Does the author have a particular point of view to advance? Your instructor or college librarian can help you select sources that are both appropriate and reliable.

Finding Information on the Internet

The Internet can give you access to a great deal of information that can help you support your points and develop your essay. Once you are online, you need to connect to a **search engine**, a program that helps you find information by sorting through the millions of documents that are available on the Internet. Among the most popular search engines are Google, Yahoo!, and Bing.

There are three ways to use a search engine to access information:

1. *You can enter a Web site's URL.* All search engines have a box in which you can enter a Web site's electronic address, or **uniform resource locator (URL)**. When you click on the URL or hit your computer's Enter or Return key, the search engine connects you to the Web site.

2. *You can do a keyword search.* All search engines let you do a **keyword search**. You type a term into a box, and the search engine looks for documents that contain the term, listing all the **hits** that it found.

3. *You can do a subject search.* Some search engines, such as Google, let you do a **subject search**. First, you choose a broad subject from a list of subjects: *The Humanities, The Arts, Entertainment, Business,* and so on. Each of these general subjects leads you to more specific subjects, until eventually you get to the subtopic that you want.

FYI

Accessing Web Sites: Troubleshooting

Sometimes, your computer will tell you that a site is unavailable or does not exist. When this occurs, consider the following strategies before moving on to another site:

- *Check to make sure the URL is correct.* To reach a site, you have to type its URL accurately. Do not add spaces between items in the address or put a period at the end. Any error will send you to the wrong site—or to no site at all.

- *Try using just part of the URL.* If the URL is very long, use just the part that ends in the **extension** (for example, .edu, .org, .com, .net, .gov, etc.). If this part of the URL doesn't take you where you want to go, you have an incorrect address.

- *Try revisiting the site later.* Sometimes, Web sites experience technical problems that prevent them from being accessed. Your computer will tell you if a site is temporarily unreachable.

Teaching Tip
Point out that a Web site's URL can give information about the site's purpose. For example, the abbreviation *.edu* indicates that the site is sponsored by an educational institution, *.gov* indicates a government agency, *.org* indicates a nonprofit organization, and *.com* indicates a business.

Not every site you access is a valuable source of information. Just as you would with a print source, you should determine whether information you find on the Internet is believable and useful.

With the Internet, however, you have problems that you generally don't have with the print sources in your college library. Because anyone can publish on the Internet, it is often difficult—if not impossible—to judge the credentials of an author or the accuracy of his or her claims. To make matters worse, sometimes sources are anonymous and have no listed author at all. Dates can also be missing, and so it may be difficult to tell when information was originally posted and when it was updated. Finally, it is often hard to determine if a site has a purpose other than providing information. For example, is the site trying to sell something or put forward a political agenda? If it is, it may contain information that is biased or incorrect.

You can judge the reliability of Internet sources by asking some basic questions.

- *Who is the author of the site?* Avoid information written by unnamed authors or by authors with questionable credentials.

- *Who is the sponsoring organization?* Be especially careful of using information from Web sites that are sponsored by companies trying to sell something or organizations that have a particular bias.

- *Can you verify information contained in the site?* Make sure you are able to check the source of the information. For example, you should see if an article on a site includes a bibliography. Also, cross-check information you find there. Does the same information appear in other sources that appear to be reliable?

- *Does the Web site contain errors?* In addition to factual errors, look out for mistakes in grammar or spelling. Errors such as these should raise a red flag about the accuracy of the information on the site you are visiting.

■ *Do the links on the site work?* Make sure that the links on the site you are visiting are "live." The presence of "dead" links is a good indication that a site is not being properly maintained.

■ *Is the information up to date?* Make sure the site's information is current. Avoid sites that contain information that seems old or outdated. A reliable site will usually include the date information was posted and the date it was revised.

When in doubt, the surest strategy for determining whether a site is reliable is to check with a reference librarian or with your instructor. Unless you can be absolutely certain that a site is reliable, do not use it as a source.

FYI

Using Wikipedia as a Source

Most college students regularly consult Wikipedia, the open-source online encyclopedia. The rationale behind Wikipedia is that if a large number of people review information, errors will eventually be discovered and corrected. Because there are no full-time editors, however, Wikipedia articles can (and do) contain inaccurate as well as biased information. In addition, anyone—not just experts—can write and edit entries. Understandably, some instructors distrust—or at least question—the accuracy of Wikipedia entries. Before you use Wikipedia as a source, get your instructor's permission. (Keep in mind that many instructors do not consider articles from *any* encyclopedia—print or electronic—acceptable for college research.) Even if you have permission to use Wikipedia, be sure to check the accuracy of the information you find there by comparing it to the information in other sources you are using.

May began her research by doing a subject search of her library's online catalog to see what books it listed on her topic. Under the general subject of *counterfeits*, she found the headings *counterfeit coins* and *counterfeit money*. She did not, however, find any books on counterfeit designer goods. She thought that her topic might be too recent for any books to have been published on the subject, so she turned to her library's databases.

A quick look at the InfoTrac database showed May that many recent articles had been written about counterfeit designer merchandise. Although some articles just reported police raids on local counterfeiting operations, a few discussed the reasons for counterfeiting and the negative effects of counterfeit goods.

Because May's topic was so current, she found that the Internet was her best source of information. Using the keywords *counterfeit designer goods* and *designer handbags knockoffs*, she located several recent newspaper and magazine articles about her topic. For example, using Google to search for the term *counterfeit designer goods*, she found a site maintained by the Resource for Security Executives that gave recent statistics of counterfeit seizures by the Department of Homeland Security. Using the same search terms on Yahoo!, May found an article in the *Arizona Republic* that discussed the purse parties that are often used to sell counterfeit designer handbags.

FYI

Avoiding Plagiarism

When you transfer information from Web sites into your notes, you may carelessly cut and paste text without recording where the material came from. If you then copy this material into your paper, you are committing **plagiarism**—stealing someone else's ideas. Also keep in mind that you must document *all* material that you get from the Internet, just as you document material that you get from print sources. For information on documentation, see 17h. For information on plagiarism, see 17d.

find information

Look back at the topic you chose for the Write First activity on page 303. Then, do research in the library and on the Internet to help you find information on this topic. Remember, you will be using this information to support the points you make in your research paper.

17c   Taking Notes

Once you have gathered the source material you will need, read it carefully, recording any information you think you can use in your essay. Record your notes either in computer files that you have created for this purpose or on index cards.

Remember that taking notes involves more than just copying down or downloading information. As you record information, you should put it into a form that you can use when you write your paper. For this reason, you should always *paraphrase, summarize,* and *quote* relevant information from your sources.

Paraphrasing

When you **paraphrase**, you use your own words to convey a source's key ideas. You paraphrase when you want to include detailed information from the source but not the author's exact words. Paraphrase is useful when you want to make a difficult discussion easier to understand while still presenting a comprehensive overview of the original.

Writing a Paraphrase

1. Read the passage until you understand it.

2. Note the main idea of the passage, and list key supporting points.

3. Draft your paraphrase, beginning with the source's main idea and then presenting the source's most important supporting points.

4. When you revise, make sure you have used your own words and phrasing, and not the words or sentence structure of the original. Use quotation marks to identify any unique or memorable phrases that you have borrowed from the source.

5. Document your source.

Here is a passage from the article "Hot Fakes," by Joanie Cox, followed by May's paraphrase.

ORIGINAL

Always pay close attention to the stitching. On a Kate Spade bag, the logo is stitched perfectly straight; it's not a sticker. Most designers stitch a simple label to the inside of their purses. On Chanel bags, however, the interior label is usually stamped and tends to match the color of the exterior. Study the material the bag is made from. A real Chanel Ligne Cambon multipocket bag, for example, is constructed from buttery lambskin leather, not vinyl.

PARAPHRASE

It is often possible to tell a fake designer handbag from a genuine one by looking at the details. For example, items such as logos should not be crooked. You should also look for the distinctive features of a particular brand of handbag. Counterfeiters will not take the time to match colors, and they may use vinyl instead of expensive leather (Cox).

Summarizing

Unlike a paraphrase, which presents the key points of a source in detail, a **summary** is a general restatement, in your own words, of just the main idea of a passage. For this reason, a summary is always much shorter than the original.

Writing a Summary

1. Read the passage until you understand it.

2. Jot down the main idea of the passage.

3. As you write, make sure you use your own words, not those of your source.

4. When you revise, make sure your summary contains only the ideas of the source.

5. Document your source.

Teaching Tip
Remind students that they should read a passage several times and then put it aside before trying to paraphrase it. Looking at the material as they write is likely to lead to plagiarism.

Teaching Tip
Explain that Internet sources often do not contain page numbers. For this reason, parenthetical documentation of Internet sources may consist of just the author's last name (or, if no author is given, the shortened title of the article).

Teaching Tip
Remind students that in a paraphrase or summary, they present only the source's ideas, not their own ideas or opinions about the source.

Here is May's summary of the original passage on page 308.

SUMMARY

Buyers who want to identify fake handbags should check details such as the way the label is sewn and the material the item is made from (Cox).

Quoting

When you **quote**, you use the author's exact words as they appear in the source, including all punctuation and capitalization. Enclose all words from your source in quotation marks—*followed by appropriate documentation.* Because quotations can distract readers, use them only when you think that the author's exact words will add something to your discussion.

Teaching Tip
Make sure that you reinforce to students the importance of documenting not just quoted material but also any ideas that they borrow from their sources.

When to Quote

1. Quote when the words of a source are so memorable that to put them into your own words would lessen their impact.
2. Quote when the words of a source are so distinctive that a paraphrase or summary would change the meaning of the original.
3. Quote when the words of a source add authority to your discussion. The words of a recognized expert can help you make your point convincingly.

Here is how May incorporated a quotation from the original passage on page 308 into her notes.

QUOTATION

Someone who wants to buy an authentic designer handbag should look carefully at the material the purse is made from. For example, there is a big difference between vinyl and Chanel's "buttery lambskin leather" (Cox).

Working Sources into Your Writing

To show readers why you are using a source and to help you blend source material smoothly into your essay, try to introduce paraphrases, summaries, and quotations with a phrase that identifies the source or its author. You can position this identifying phrase at various places in a sentence.

As one marketing expert points out, "A real Chanel Ligne Cambon multipocket bag, for example, is constructed from buttery lambskin leather, not vinyl" (Cox).

"A real Chanel Ligne Cambon multipocket bag, for example," says one marketing expert, "is constructed from buttery lambskin leather, not vinyl" (Cox).

"A real Chanel Ligne Cambon multipocket bag, for example, is constructed from buttery lambskin leather, not vinyl," observes one marketing expert (Cox).

FYI

Integrating Sources

Instead of repeating the word *says,* use some of the words below when you introduce quotations.

admits	concludes	points out
believes	explains	remarks
claims	notes	states
comments	observes	suggests

take notes

Review the information you gathered for the Write First activity on page 307. Then, take notes, making sure that you paraphrase, summarize, and quote your sources. Keep your notes either in computer files or on index cards. (Don't forget to include full source information, including page numbers with these notes.)

17d   Watching Out for Plagiarism

As a rule, you must **document** (give source information for) all words, ideas, or statistics from an outside source. You must also document all visuals—tables, graphs, photographs, and so on—that you do not create yourself. (It is not necessary, however, to document **common knowledge**, factual information widely available in various reference works.)

When you present information from another source as if it is your own (whether you do it intentionally or unintentionally), you commit **plagiarism**—and plagiarism is theft. Although most plagiarism is accidental, the penalties can still be severe. You can avoid plagiarism by understanding what you must document and what you do not have to document.

FYI

What to Document

You should document

- All word-for-word quotations from a source
- All summaries and paraphrases of material from a print or electronic source
- All ideas—opinions, judgments, and insights—of others
- All tables, graphs, charts, and statistics that you get from a source

You do not need to document

- Your own ideas
- Common knowledge
- Familiar quotations

Read the following paragraph from "The Facts on Fakes!" (an unsigned article on the National Association of Resale & Thrift Shops Web site) and the four rules that follow. This material will help you understand the most common causes of plagiarism and show you how to avoid it.

ORIGINAL

Is imitation really the sincerest form of flattery? Counterfeiting deceives the consumer and tarnishes the reputation of the genuine manufacturer. Brand value can be destroyed when a trademark is imposed on counterfeit products of inferior quality—hardly a form of flattery! Therefore, prestigious companies who are the targets of counterfeiters have begun to battle an industry that copies and sells their merchandise. They have filed lawsuits and in some cases have employed private investigators across the nation to combat the counterfeit trade. A quick search of the Internet brings up dozens of press releases from newspapers throughout the country, all reporting instances of law enforcement cracking down on sellers of counterfeit goods by confiscating bogus merchandise and imposing fines.

Rule 1. Document Ideas from Your Sources

PLAGIARISM

When counterfeits are sold, the original manufacturer does not take it as a compliment.

Even though the student writer does not quote her source directly, she must still identify the article as the source of this material because it expresses the article's ideas, not her own.

CORRECT

When counterfeits are sold, the original manufacturer does not take it as a compliment ("Facts").

Rule 2. Place Borrowed Words in Quotation Marks

PLAGIARISM

It is possible to ruin the worth of a brand by selling counterfeit products of inferior quality—hardly a form of flattery ("Facts").

Although the student writer cites the source, the passage incorrectly uses the source's exact words without quoting them. She must quote the borrowed words.

CORRECT (BORROWED WORDS IN QUOTATION MARKS)

CORRECT (BORROWED WORDS IN QUOTATION MARKS)

It is possible to ruin the worth of a brand by selling "counterfeit products of inferior quality—hardly a form of flattery" ("Facts").

Rule 3. Use Your Own Phrasing

PLAGIARISM

Is copying a design a compliment? Not at all. The fake design not only tries to fool the buyer but also harms the original company. It can ruin the worth of a brand. Because counterfeits are usually of poor quality, they pay the original no compliment. As a result, companies whose products are often copied have started to fight back. They have sued the counterfeiters and have even used private detectives to identify phony goods. Throughout the United States, police have fined people who sell counterfeits and have seized their products ("Facts").

Even though the student writer acknowledges "The Facts on Fakes!" as her source, and even though she does not use the source's exact words, her passage closely follows the order, emphasis, sentence structure, and phrasing of the original.

In the following passage, the writer uses her own wording, quoting one distinctive phrase from the source.

CORRECT

According to "The Facts on Fakes!" it is not a compliment when an original design is copied by a counterfeiter. The poor quality of most fakes is "hardly a form of flattery." The harm to the image of the original manufacturers has caused them to fight back against the counterfeiters, sometimes using their own detectives. As a result, lawsuits and criminal charges have led to fines and confiscated merchandise ("Facts").

Note: Even though the paragraph ends with parenthetical documentation, the quotation requires its own citation.

Rule 4. Distinguish Your Ideas from the Source's Ideas

PLAGIARISM

Counterfeit goods are not harmless. Counterfeiting not only fools the consumer, but it also destroys confidence in the quality of the real thing. Manufacturers know this and have begun to fight back. A number have begun to sue "and in some cases have employed private investigators across the nation to combat the counterfeit trade" ("Facts").

In the passage above, only the quotation in the last sentence seems to be borrowed from the article "The Facts on Fakes!" In fact, however, the ideas in the second sentence also come from this article.

Teaching Tip
Point out that the quotation does not require separate documentation because it is clear that all the borrowed material in the passage is from the same source.

In the following passage, the writer uses an identifying phrase to acknowledge the borrowed material in the second sentence.

Teaching Tip
Reinforce that each quotation requires its own separate parenthetical documentation.

CORRECT

Counterfeit goods are not harmless. According to the article "The Facts on Fakes!" counterfeiting not only fools the consumer, but it also destroys confidence in the quality of the real thing. Manufacturers know this and have begun to fight back. A number have begun to sue "and in some cases have employed private investigators across the nation to combat the counterfeit trade" ("Facts").

watch out for plagiarism

Look back at the notes you took in response to the Write First activity on page 310. First, make sure that you have included documentation for all information that came from a source. Then, check your notes against the examples in 17d to make sure that you have avoided the most common types of accidental plagiarism.

17e   Developing a Thesis

After you have taken notes, review the information you have gathered, and develop a thesis statement. Your **thesis statement** is a single sentence that states the main idea of your paper and tells readers what to expect.

After reviewing her notes, May Compton came up with the following thesis statement for her paper on counterfeit designer goods.

Teaching Tip
Remind students that at this stage, a thesis statement is tentative. For more information on thesis statements, see 13d.

THESIS STATEMENT

People should not buy counterfeit designer merchandise, no matter how tempted they are to do so.

develop a thesis

Review the notes you took in response to the Write First activity on page 310. Then, review this information, and draft a thesis statement that you can use in your essay.

17f Making an Outline

Once you have a thesis statement, you are ready to make an outline. Your outline, which covers just the body paragraphs of your paper, can be either a **topic outline** (in which each idea is expressed in a word or a short phrase) or a **sentence outline** (in which each idea is expressed in a complete sentence).

After reviewing her notes, May Compton wrote the following sentence outline for her paper:

Teaching Tip
Point out that May's outline uses Roman numerals for first-level headings, capital letters for second-level headings, and numbers for third-level headings. All the outline's points are stated in parallel terms. Refer students to the box on outlining in 13f.

I. Many people consider real designer goods too expensive.
   A. Genuine designer merchandise costs ten times more than it costs to make it.
   B. Even people who can afford it buy fakes.
II. Buying designer knockoffs is a form of stealing.
   A. The buyer is stealing the work of the original designer.
   B. Counterfeiting operations take jobs away from legitimate workers.
   C. The buyer is stealing the sales taxes that would be paid by the original designer.
III. Buying designer knockoffs supports organized crime.
   A. The production of designer knockoffs requires money and organization, which often comes from organized crime.
   B. Buying knockoffs supports other illegal activities.
      1. The profits of selling knockoffs support murder, prostitution, and drug rings.
      2. Knockoffs are made in shops that violate labor and other laws.
IV. There is evidence that designer knockoffs support terrorism.
   A. The 1993 World Trade Center bombing has been connected to a counterfeit operation.
   B. The 2001 World Trade Center bombing has been connected to counterfeiting.
   C. The 2004 Madrid train bombing has been connected to counterfeiting.

make an outline

Review the notes you took in response to the Write First activity on page 310 as well as the thesis you drafted in response to the Write First activity on page 313. Then, make an outline of the body paragraphs of your paper.

Begin by copying down your thesis statement. Then, arrange your information into categories and subcategories. Remember, each category of your outline must have at least two divisions—two Roman numerals, two capital letters, and so on. (For more on outlining, see 13f.)

17g   Writing Your Paper

Once you have decided on a thesis and written an outline, you are ready to write a draft of your essay. When you are finished, you will TEST, revise, and edit your paper.

- Begin with an **introduction** that includes your thesis statement. Usually, your introduction will be a single paragraph, but sometimes it will be longer.

- In the **body** of your essay, support your thesis statement with specific evidence. Each body paragraph should develop a single point, and these paragraphs should have clear topic sentences so that your readers will know exactly what points you are making. Use transitional words and phrases to help readers follow your ideas.

- Finally, write a **conclusion** that gives readers a sense of completion. Like your introduction, your conclusion will usually be a single paragraph, but it can be longer. It should include a summary statement that reinforces your thesis statement.

Remember, you will probably write several drafts of your essay before you hand it in. As you draft your essay, be sure to include parenthetical citations so that you do not lose track of your sources and accidentally commit plagiarism. After you revise and edit, you can check to make sure your documentation formats are correct. (See 17h for information on documentation.)

May Compton's completed essay on counterfeit designer goods begins on page 322.

write your paper

Using your thesis statement and your outline to guide you, write a draft of your research paper.

TEST · Revise · Edit

TEST the draft of your paper by referring to the TEST checklist on page 217. Then, use the Self-Assessment checklists in 13i and 13j to help you revise and edit your paper.

17h Documenting Your Sources

When you **document** your sources, you tell readers where you found the information you used in your essay. The Modern Language Association (MLA) recommends the following documentation style for essays that use sources. This format consists of *parenthetical references* in the body of the paper that refer to a *works-cited list* at the end of the paper.

Parenthetical References in the Text

A parenthetical reference should include enough information to lead readers to a specific entry in your works-cited list. A typical parenthetical reference consists of the author's last name and the page number (Brown 2).

If you use more than one work by the same author, include a shortened form of the title in the parenthetical reference (Brown, "Demand" 2). Notice that there is no comma and no *p* or *p*. before the page number.

Whenever possible, introduce information from a source with a phrase that includes the author's name. (If you do this, include only the page number in parentheses.) Place documentation so that it does not interrupt the flow of your ideas, preferably at the end of a sentence.

> As Jonathan Brown observes in "Demand for Fake Designer Goods Is Soaring," as many as 70 percent of buyers of luxury goods are willing to wear designer brands alongside of fakes (2).

In the four special situations listed below, the format for parenthetical references departs from these guidelines.

1. WHEN YOU ARE CITING A WORK BY TWO AUTHORS

   > Instead of buying nonbranded items of similar quality, many customers are willing to pay extra for the counterfeit designer label (Grossman and Shapiro 79).

2. WHEN YOU ARE CITING A WORK WITHOUT PAGE NUMBERS

   > A seller of counterfeited goods in California "now faces 10 years in prison and $20,000 in fines" (Cox).

3. WHEN YOU ARE CITING A WORK WITHOUT A LISTED AUTHOR OR PAGE NUMBERS

   > More counterfeit goods come from China than from any other country ("Counterfeit Goods").

Note: Material from the Internet or from a library's electronic databases frequently lacks some publication information—for example, page or paragraph numbers. For this reason, the parenthetical references that cite it may contain just the author's name (as in example 2 above) or just a shortened title (as in example 3) if the article appears without an author.

4. WHEN YOU ARE CITING A STATEMENT BY ONE AUTHOR THAT IS QUOTED IN A WORK BY ANOTHER AUTHOR

   > Speaking of consumers' buying habits, designer Miuccia Prada says, "There is a kind of an obsession with bags" (qtd. in Thomas 23).

FYI

Formatting Quotations

1. **Short quotations**   Quotations of no more than four typed lines share the same margins as the rest of your paper. End punctuation comes after the parenthetical reference (which follows the quotation marks).

   According to Dana Thomas, customers often "pick up knockoffs for one-tenth the legitimate bag's retail cost, then pass them off as real" ("Terror's Purse Strings").

2. **Long quotations**   Quotations of more than four lines are set off from the text of your paper. Begin a long quotation one inch from the left-hand margin, and do not enclose it in quotation marks. Do not indent the first line of a single paragraph. If a quoted passage has more than one paragraph, indent the first line of each paragraph (including the first) an extra one-quarter inch. Introduce a long quotation with a complete sentence followed by a colon, and place the parenthetical reference one space *after* the end punctuation.

   In her article, Dana Thomas describes a surprise visit to a factory that makes counterfeit purses:

   > On a warm winter afternoon in Guangzhao, I accompanied Chinese police officers on a raid in a decrepit tenement. We found two dozen children, ages 8 to 13, gluing and sewing together fake luxury-brand handbags. The police confiscated everything, arrested the owner and sent the children out. Some punched their timecards, hoping to still get paid. ("Terror's Purse Strings")

The Works-Cited List

The works-cited list includes all the works you **cite** (refer to) in your essay. Use the guidelines in the box on page 321 to help you prepare your list.

The following sample works-cited entries cover the situations you will encounter most often.

Periodicals

JOURNALS

A **journal** is a periodical aimed at readers who know a lot about a particular subject—literature or history, for example.

When citing an article from a journal, include the volume number of the journal, followed by a period and the issue number. Leave no space after the period. Include page numbers, if there are any, and the medium of publication, such as *Print* or *Web*. Add the name of the online database (such as Academic Search Premier) if you used one to find the source. For all Web sources, add the date you accessed the source.

Article in a Print Journal

> Kessler-Harris, Alice. "Why Biography?" *American Historical Review* 114.3
> (2009): 625-30. Print.

Article in a Journal Accessed through an Online Database

> Favret, Mary A. "Jane Austen at 25: A Life in Numbers." *English Language
> Notes* 46.1 (2008): 9-20. *Expanded Academic ASAP*. Web. 9 Mar. 2011.

MAGAZINES

A **magazine** is a periodical aimed at general readers, rather than people
who already know a lot about a subject. Frequently, an article in a magazine is not printed on consecutive pages. For example, it may begin on
page 40, skip to page 47, and continue on page 49. If this is the case, your
citation should include only the first page, followed by a plus sign. Include
the medium of publication.

Article in a Monthly or Bimonthly Magazine

> McLean, Bethany. "Fannie Mae's Last Stand." *Vanity Fair* Feb. 2009: 118+. Print.

Article in a Weekly or Biweekly Magazine

> Weisberg, Jacob. "All Lobbyists Are Not Created Equal." *Newsweek* 27 Apr.
> 2009: 35. Print.

Article in a Magazine Accessed through an Online Database

> Larmer, Brook. "The Real Price of Gold." *National Geographic* Jan. 2009: 34-61.
> *Academic Search Premier*. Web. 23 Feb. 2011.

NEWSPAPERS

List page numbers, section numbers, and any special edition information
(such as "late ed.") as provided by the source. If the article falls into a special category, such as an editorial, letter to the editor, or review, add this
label to your entry.

Article in a Newspaper

> Campoy, Ana. "'Water Hog' Label Haunts Dallas." *Wall Street Journal*
> 15 July 2009, late ed.: A4. Print.

Article from a Newspaper Accessed through an Online Database

> Marklein, Mary Beth. "Virtually Eliminating Snow Days." *USA Today* 8 Feb.
> 2011, sec. A: 01. *National Newspaper Index*. Web. 9 Mar. 2011.

Editorial

> "Waiting Game." Editorial. *New York Times* 15 July 2009: A24. Print.

Books

Books by One Author

List the author with last name first. Italicize the title. Include the city of
publication and a shortened form of the publisher's name—for example,

Teaching Tip
Remind students that an entry
with no listed author begins
with the title. The remaining
parts of the entry follow in
normal order.

Bedford for *Bedford/St. Martin's*. Use the abbreviation *UP* for *University Press*, as in *Princeton UP* and *U of Chicago P*. Include the date of publication. End with the medium of publication.

> Russo, Richard. *Bridge of Sighs*. New York: Knopf, 2007. Print.

Books by Two or Three Authors

List second and subsequent authors with first name first, in the order in which they are listed on the book's title page.

> Mooney, Chris, and Sheril Kirshenbaum. *Unscientific America: How
>   Scientific Illiteracy Threatens Our Future*. New York: Basic, 2009. Print.

Books by More Than Three Authors

List only the first author, followed by the abbreviation *et al.* ("and others").

> Beer, Andrew, et al. *Consuming Housing? Transitions through the Housing
>   Market in the 21st Century*. Bristol: Policy Press, 2010. Print.

Two or More Books by the Same Author

List two or more books by the same author in alphabetical order according to title. In each entry after the first, use three unspaced hyphens (followed by a period) instead of the author's name.

> Alda, Alan. *Never Have Your Dog Stuffed*. New York: Arrow, 2007. Print.
> ---. *Things I Overheard While Talking to Myself*. New York: Random, 2007. Print.

Edited Book

> Thompson, Hunter S. *Gonzo*. Ed. Steve Crist. Los Angeles: AMMO Books, 2007.
>   Print.

Translation

> Garcia Marquez, Gabriel. *Living to Tell the Tale*. Trans. Edith Grossman.
>   New York: Knopf, 2004. Print.

Revised Edition

> Roberts, Cokie. *We Are Our Mothers' Daughters*. Rev. ed. New York:
>   HarperCollins, 2010. Print.

Anthology

> Adler, Frances P., Debra Busman, and Diana Garcia, eds. *Fire and Ink:
>   An Anthology of Social Action Writing*. Tucson: U of Arizona P, 2009. Print.

Essay in an Anthology

> Welty, Eudora. "Writing and Analyzing a Story." *Signet Book of American Essays*.
>   Ed. M. Terry Weiss and Helen Weiss. New York: Signet, 2006. 21-30. Print.

Section or Chapter of a Book

> Mueenuddin, Daniyal. "Lily." In *Other Rooms, Other Wonders*. New York: Norton,
>   2010. Print.

> **Teaching Tip**
> Tell students that when the abbreviation *ed.* comes *after* a name, it means "editor" (*eds.* means "editors"). When the abbreviation *Ed.* comes *before* one or more names, it means "edited by."

Internet Sources

Full source information is not always available for Internet sources. When citing Internet sources, include whatever information you can find—ideally, the name of the author (or authors), the title of the article or other document (in quotation marks), the title of the site (italicized), the sponsor or publisher, the date of publication or last update, and the date on which you accessed the source. Include the medium of publication (Web) between the publication date and the access date.

It is not necessary to include a Web address (URL) when citing an electronic source. Readers can usually find the source merely by typing the author, title, and other identifying information into a search engine or database. However, you should include a URL if your instructor requires that you do so or if you think readers might not be able to locate the source without it. In these cases, enclose the URL in angle brackets at the end of your citation (as illustrated in the "Personal Site" entry below).

Document within a Web Site

> Baker, Fred W. "Army Lab Works to Improve Soldier Health, Performance." *DefenseLINK*. U.S. Department of Defense, 25 June 2009. Web. 15 Aug. 2011.

Personal Site

> Bricklin, Dan. Home page. Dan Bricklin, 7 July 2011. Web. 15 July 2011. <www.bricklin.com>.

Article in an Online Reference Book or Encyclopedia

> "Sudan." *Infoplease World Atlas and Map Library*. Pearson Education, 2009. Web. 29 Apr. 2011.

Article in an Online Newspaper

> Wilbon, Michael. "The 'One and Done' Song and Dance." *Washington Post*. The Washington Post Company, 25 June 2009. Web. 1 Sept. 2010.

Teaching Tip
Refer students to a handbook for additional models.

Online Editorial

> "Innovation and the LAUSD." Editorial. *Los Angeles Times*. Los Angeles Times, 14 July 2009. Web. 31 July 2011.

Article in an Online Magazine

> Chen, Brian X. "Microsoft to Open Retail Stores Next to Apple's." *Wired*. CondéNet, 15 July 2009. Web. 15 July 2010.

FYI

Preparing the Works-Cited List

▪ Begin the works-cited list on a new page after the last page of your paper.

▪ Number the works-cited page as the next page of your paper.

▪ Center the heading Works Cited one inch from the top of the page; do not italicize the heading or place it in quotation marks.

▪ Double-space the list.

▪ List entries alphabetically according to the author's last name.

▪ Alphabetize unsigned articles according to the first major word of the title.

▪ Begin typing each entry at the left-hand margin.

▪ Indent second and subsequent lines of each entry one-half inch.

▪ Separate major divisions of each entry—author, title, and publication information—by a period and one space.

document your sources

Check to make sure that you have included correct parenthetical citations in the body of your paper for all information that requires documentation. Then, consult the guidelines above, and prepare your works-cited list.

Sample MLA-Style Paper

On the pages that follow is May Compton's completed essay on the topic of counterfeit designer goods. The paper uses MLA documentation style and includes a works-cited page.

Compton 1

May Compton

Professor DiSalvo

English 100

29 April 2011

The True Price of Counterfeit Goods

At purse parties in city apartments and suburban homes, customers can buy "designer" handbags at impossibly low prices. On street corners, sidewalk vendors sell name-brand perfumes and sunglasses for much less than their list prices. On the Internet, buyers can buy fine watches for a fraction of the prices charged by manufacturers. Is this too good to be true? Of course it is. All of these "bargains" are knockoffs—counterfeit copies of the real thing. What the people who buy these items do not know (or prefer not to think about) is that the money they are spending supports organized crime—and, sometimes, terrorism. For this reason, people should not buy counterfeit designer merchandise, no matter how tempted they are to do so.

People who buy counterfeit designer merchandise defend their actions by saying that designer products are very expensive. This is certainly true. According to Dana Thomas, the manufacturers of genuine designer merchandise charge more than ten times what it costs to make it. A visitor from Britain, who bought an imitation Gucci purse in New York City for fifty dollars, said, "The real thing is so overpriced. To buy a genuine Gucci purse, I would have to pay over a thousand dollars" (qtd. in "Counterfeit Goods"). Even people who can easily afford to pay the full amount buy fakes. For example, movie stars like Jennifer Lopez openly wear counterfeit goods, and many customers think that if it is all right for celebrities like Lopez to buy fakes, it must also be all right for them too (Malone). However, as the well-known designer Giorgio Armani points out, counterfeiters create a number of problems for legitimate companies because they use the brand name but do not maintain quality control ("10 Questions").

What most people choose to ignore is that buying counterfeit items is really stealing. The FBI estimates that in the United States alone, companies lose about $250 billion as a result of counterfeits (Wallace). In addition, buyers of counterfeit items avoid the state and local sales taxes that legitimate companies pay. Thus, New York City alone loses about a billion dollars every year as a result of the sale of counterfeit merchandise ("Counterfeit Goods"). When this happens, everyone loses. After all, a billion dollars would pay for a lot of police officers and teachers, would fill a lot of potholes, and would pave a lot of streets. Buyers of counterfeit designer goods do not think of themselves as thieves, but that is exactly what they really are.

Include your last name and the page number on the upper-right-hand corner of every page.

Include your name, instructor's name, course title, and date on first page.

Introduction

Center your title; do not italicize or underline.

Thesis statement

Paragraph combines paraphrase, quotation, and May's own ideas.

Paragraph contains May's own ideas combined with paraphrases of material from two articles.

Compton 2

Buyers of counterfeit merchandise also do not realize that the sale of knockoffs supports organized crime. Most of the profits go to the criminal organization that either makes or imports the counterfeit goods—not to the person who sells the items. In fact, the biggest manufacturer and distributor of counterfeit items is organized crime (Nellis). Michael Kessler, who heads a company that investigates corporate crime, makes this connection clear when he describes the complicated organization that is needed to make counterfeit perfume:

> They need a place that makes bottles, a factory with pumps to fill the bottles, a printer to make the labels, and a box manufacturer to fake the packaging. Then, they need a sophisticated distribution network, as well as all the cash to set everything up. (qtd. in Malone)

Kessler concludes that only an organized crime syndicate—not any individual— has the money to support this illegal activity. For this reason, anyone who buys counterfeits may also be supporting activities such as prostitution, drug distribution, smuggling of illegal immigrants, gang warfare, extortion, and murder (Nellis). In addition, the people who make counterfeits often work in sweatshops where labor and environmental laws are ignored. The illegal factories are often located in countries where children usually work long hours for very low pay (Malone). In fact, as Dana Thomas points out, a worker in China who makes counterfeits earns only a fraction of the salary of a worker who makes the real thing.

Finally, and perhaps most shocking, is the fact that some of the money earned from the sale of counterfeit designer goods also supports international terrorism. For example, Kim Wallace reports that during Al-Qaeda training, terrorists are advised to sell fakes to get money for their operations. According to Interpol, an international police organization, the bombing of the World Trade Center in 1993 was paid for in part by the sale of counterfeit T-shirts. Also, evidence suggests that associates of the 2001 World Trade Center terrorists may have been involved with the production of imitation designer goods (Malone). Finally, the 2004 bombing of commuter trains in Madrid was financed in part by the sale of counterfeits. In fact, an intelligence source states, "It would be more shocking if Al-Qaeda *wasn't* involved in counterfeiting. The sums involved are staggering—it would be inconceivable if money were not being raised for their terrorist activities" (qtd. in Malone). Most people would never consciously support terrorism, but customers who buy counterfeit purses or fake perfume may be doing just that.

Consumers should realize that when they buy counterfeits, they are actually breaking the law. By doing so, they are making it possible for organized crime syndicates and terrorists to earn money for their illegal activities. Although buyers of

Long quotation is set off one inch from the left-hand margin. No quotation marks are used.

Paragraph contains May's own ideas as well as a paraphrase and a quotation.

Compton 3

counterfeit merchandise justify their actions by saying that the low prices are impossible to resist, they might reconsider if they knew the uses to which their money was going. The truth of the matter is that counterfeit designer products, such as handbags, sunglasses, jewelry, and T-shirts, are luxuries, not necessities. By resisting the temptation to buy knockoffs, consumers could help to eliminate the companies that hurt legitimate manufacturers, exploit workers, and even finance international terrorism.

Conclusion contains May's original ideas, so no documentation is necessary.

Compton 4

Works Cited

Armani, Giorgio. "10 Questions for Giorgio Armani." *Time*. Time, 12 Feb. 2009.
    Web. 24 Mar. 2011.

"Counterfeit Goods Are Linked to Terror Groups." *International Herald Tribune*.
    International Herald Tribune, 12 Feb. 2007. Web. 24 Mar. 2011.

Malone, Andrew. "Revealed: The True Cost of Buying Cheap Fake Goods." *Mail Online*.
    Daily Mail, 29 July 2007. Web. 25 Mar. 2011.

Nellis, Cynthia. "Faking It: Counterfeit Fashion." *About.com: Women's Fashion*.
    About.com, 2009. Web. 24 Mar. 2011.

Thomas, Dana. "Terror's Purse Strings." Editorial. *New York Times* 30 Aug. 2007,
    late ed.: A23. Print.

Wallace, Kim. "A Counter-Productive Trade." *TimesDaily.com*. Times Daily, 29
    July 2007. Web. 31 Mar. 2011.

> Works-cited list starts a new page.

> This Internet source has no listed author.

> First lines of entries are set flush left; subsequent lines are indented one-half inch.

ACTIVITY: AVOIDING PLAGIARISM

Read the paragraph below, from the article "The New Math on Campus," by Alex Williams. Then, read the three student paragraphs that use this article as a source. In each of these paragraphs, student writers have accidentally committed plagiarism. On the line below each student paragraph, explain the problem. Then, edit the paragraph so that it correctly documents the source and avoids plagiarism.

> North Carolina, with a student body that is nearly 60 percent female, is just one of many large universities that at times feel eerily like women's colleges. Women have represented about 57 percent of enrollments at American colleges since at least 2000, according to a recent report by the American Council on Education. Researchers there cite several reasons: women tend to have higher grades; men tend to drop out in disproportionate numbers; and female enrollment skews higher among older students, low-income students, and black and Hispanic students.

Answers will vary.

About 60% female, the University of North Carolina is an example of large

universities with many more women than men. According to a report from the

American Council on Education, one reason is that "female enrollment skews

higher among older students, low-income students, and black and Hispanic

students" (Williams). If this is true, what will this mean for the black and

Hispanic communities?

The ideas in the first sentence are taken from the source, but the writer makes it

sound as if only the quotation in the second sentence is from the source.

In recent years, colleges and universities have taken on a very different

atmosphere. The reason is clear to anyone who takes a casual look around at just

about any college campus. Women now outnumber men, so much so that some

colleges at times feel eerily like women's colleges (Williams). This situation seems

likely to continue in the years to come.

The writer uses the source's exact words without quoting them.

Why do women outnumber men in today's colleges? Researchers at the

American Council on Education mention a few reasons: women often have higher grades, men tend to drop out in larger numbers, and female enrollment

is especially high for some groups such as older students, low-income students,

and black and Hispanic students (Williams). These reasons may all be true at our

school, which certainly has more women than men.

The writer's paraphrase is too close to the words of the source.

ACTIVITY: CREATING A WORKS-CITED LIST

Write a works-cited list for a paper that uses the sources below. Then, alphabetize your list. Make sure that you use the correct format for each type of source.

Article in a Journal Accessed through an Online Database

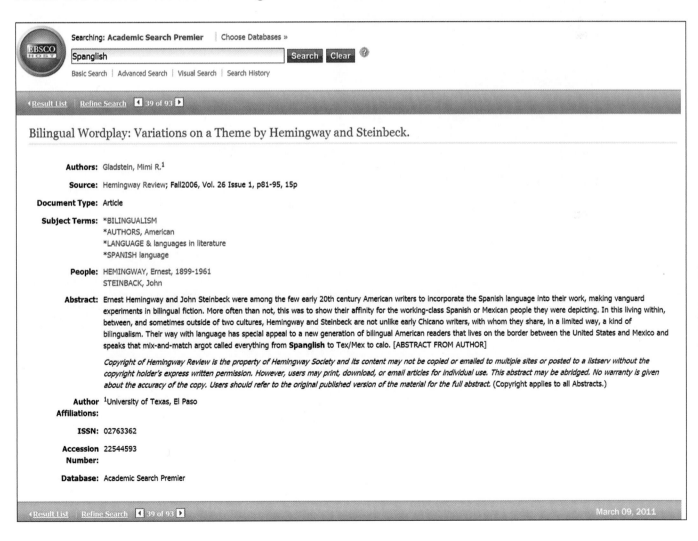

Book (Print)

Library of Congress Cataloging-in-Publication Data

Spanglish / edited by Ilan Stavans.
  p. cm. — (The Ilan Stavans library of Latino civilization, ISSN 1938–615X)
 Includes bibliographical references and index.
 ISBN 978–0–313–34804–4 (alk. paper)
 1. Spanish language—Foreign elements—English. 2. English language—
Influence on Spanish. 3. Languages in contact—America. I. Stavans,
Ilan.
 PC4582.E6S63   2008
  460'.4221—dc22   2008014855

British Library Cataloguing in Publication Data is available.

Library of Congress Catalog Card Number: 2008014855
ISBN: 978–0–313–34804–4
ISSN: 1938–615X

First published in 2008

Greenwood Press, 88 Post Road West, Westport, CT 06881
An imprint of Greenwood Publishing Group, Inc.
www.greenwood.com

Printed in the United States of America

 ™

The paper used in this book complies with the
Permanent Paper Standard issued by the National
Information Standards Organization (Z39.48–1984).

10 9 8 7 6 5 4 3 2 1

iv

Document within a Web Site

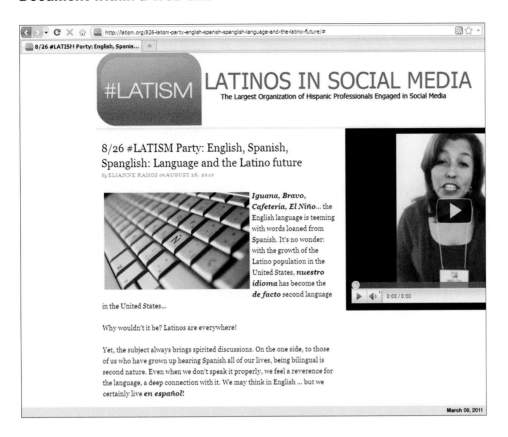

Works Cited

Gladstein, Mimi R. "Bilingual Wordplay: Variations on a Theme by Hemingway

and Steinbeck." *Hemingway Review* 26.1 (2006): 81-95. *Academic*

Search Premier. Web. 9 Mar. 2011.

Ramos, Elianne. "#LATISM Party: English, Spanish, Spanglish: Language

and the Latino Future." *#LATISM.* Latinos in Social Media, 26 Aug.

2010. Web. 9 Mar. 2011.

Stavans, Ilan, ed. *Spanglish.* Westport: Greenwood Press, 2008. Print.

COLLABORATIVE ACTIVITY: RESEARCHING AND OUTLINING A PAPER

1. Read the following list of topics. Then, working in a group of three or four students, choose a topic that interests members of the group. Work together to do some initial research on your topic, using an Internet search engine, an electronic database, and another library resource. Find five to seven sources of information on your topic.

   TOPICS

   - *The enrollment of more women than men in college*—What are some causes? What are some consequences?
   - *Spanglish*—What is it? Is it a problem? Is it an advantage?
   - *Facebook and other social media*—What are the dangers of posting information online?
   - *Online learning*—How does it compare to classroom learning?
   - *Careers of the future*—What are the fastest-growing careers?
   - *Disciplining children*—Is spanking an appropriate method of discipline? Is there a better method?
   - *Obesity rates in the United States*—Are they increasing and, if so, why? What can be done?
   - *Zoos*—Are they cruel? Are some better for animals than others?
   - *Newspapers*—Are they disappearing? If so, should something be done to save them? What will take their place?
   - *Volunteering*—Is this a good way to get job experience?
   - *Video games*—Do they do some good? Do they promote violence?
   - *Texting*—Are teenagers spending too much of their time texting? What are the advantages and disadvantages of texting?
   - *Happiness*—What things make people the happiest?

2. Now, work together to evaluate your sources. Are all of your sources reliable? Which sources seem likely to be the most useful for a paper?

3. Review your sources, and then choose a topic that these sources could help you develop. As a group, draft a possible thesis statement for a short paper. On your own, read and take notes on the sources. Then, again working as a group, make an outline for a paper that could support your thesis.

unit

5 Writing Effective Sentences

18 Writing Simple Sentences

preview

In this chapter, you will learn to

- identify a sentence's subject (18a)
- identify prepositions and prepositional phrases (18b)
- distinguish a prepositional phrase from a subject (18b)
- identify a sentence's verb (18c)

write first

Many baseball fans wish they could trade places with someone like Chase Utley, a second baseman for the Philadelphia Phillies with a storybook career. Think for a bit about someone with whom you would like to trade places, and then write a paragraph about why you'd like to trade. What appeals to you about this person's life?

A **sentence** is a group of words that expresses a complete thought. Every sentence includes both a subject and a verb. A **simple sentence** consists of a single **independent clause**: one <u>subject</u> and one <u>verb</u>.

Chase Utley <u>plays</u> baseball.

18a Subjects

Every sentence includes a subject. The **subject** of a sentence tells who or what is being talked about in the sentence. Without a subject, a sentence is not complete. In the following three sentences, the subject is underlined.

<u>Derek Walcott</u> won the Nobel Prize in Literature.

<u>He</u> was born in St. Lucia.

<u>St. Lucia</u> is an island in the Caribbean.

The subject of a sentence can be a noun or a pronoun. A **noun** names a person, place, or thing—*Derek Walcott, St. Lucia*. A **pronoun** takes the place of a noun—*I, you, he, she, it, we, they,* and so on.

The subject of a sentence can be *singular* or *plural*. A **singular subject** is one person, place, or thing (*Derek Walcott, St. Lucia, he*).

A **plural subject** is more than one person, place, or thing (*poems, people, they*).

<u>Readers</u> admire Walcott's poems.

A plural subject that joins two subjects with *and* is called a **compound subject**.

<u>St. Lucia and Trinidad</u> are Caribbean islands.

PRACTICE

18-1 In the paragraph below, underline the subject of each sentence.

Example: The poet's <u>parents</u> were both teachers.

(1) <u>Derek Walcott</u> has had an interesting career. (2) His <u>ancestors</u> came from Africa, the Netherlands, and England. (3) Born in 1930, <u>Walcott</u> spent his early years on the Caribbean island of St. Lucia. (4) <u>Writing</u> occupied much of his time. (5) His early <u>poems</u> were published in Trinidad. (6) <u>He</u> later studied in Jamaica and in New York. (7) <u>Walcott</u> eventually became a respected poet. (8) <u>He</u> was a visiting lecturer at Harvard in 1981. (9) In 1990, <u>he</u> published *Omeros*. (10) This

long <u>poem</u> about classical Greek heroes is set in the West Indies. (11) In 1992, the <u>poet</u> won a Nobel Prize. (12) <u>Walcott</u> later collaborated with songwriter Paul Simon on *The Capeman*, a Broadway musical.

PRACTICE
18-2 Underline the subject in each sentence. Then, write *S* above singular subjects and *P* above plural subjects. Remember, compound subjects are plural.

    Example: <u>Agritainment</u> introduces tourists to agriculture and entertainment at the same time.

1. Today, <u>tourists</u> can have fun on working farms.
2. In the past, <u>visitors</u> came to farms just to pick fruits and vegetables.
3. Now, some <u>farms</u> have mazes and petting zoos.
4. One <u>farm</u> has a corn maze every year.
5. Sometimes the <u>maze</u> is in the shape of a train.
6. <u>Visitors</u> can also enjoy giant hay-chute slides, pedal go-carts, and hayrides.
7. Working <u>farms</u> start agritainment businesses to make money.
8. However, <u>insurance companies and lawyers</u> worry about the dangers of agritainment.
9. <u>Tourists</u> have gotten animal bites, fallen from rides and machinery, and gotten food poisoning.
10. <u>Agritainment</u>, like other businesses, has advantages and disadvantages.

18b Prepositional Phrases

A **prepositional phrase** consists of a **preposition** (a word such as *on, to, in,* or *with*) and its **object** (the noun or pronoun it introduces).

PREPOSITION	+	OBJECT	=	PREPOSITIONAL PHRASE
on		the stage		on the stage
to		Nia's house		to Nia's house
in		my new car		in my new car
with		them		with them

Teaching Tip
Refer students to 33m and 33n for more on prepositions.

Teaching Tip
Tell students that a phrase is a group of words that lacks a subject or a verb or both. For this reason, a phrase cannot stand alone as a sentence. Refer them to 25b.

Because the object of a preposition is a noun or a pronoun, it may seem to be the subject of a sentence. However, the object of a preposition can never be the subject of a sentence. To identify a sentence's true subject, cross out each prepositional phrase. (Remember, every prepositional phrase is introduced by a preposition.)

SUBJECT   PREP PHRASE
The cost ~~of the repairs~~ was astronomical.

PREP PHRASE   PREP PHRASE   SUBJECT
~~At the end of the novel~~, ~~after an exciting chase~~, the lovers flee
PREP PHRASE
~~to Mexico~~.

Frequently Used Prepositions

about	before	except	on	underneath
above	behind	for	onto	until
across	below	from	out	up
after	beneath	in	outside	upon
against	beside	inside	over	with
along	between	into	through	within
among	beyond	like	throughout	without
around	by	near	to	
as	despite	of	toward	
at	during	off	under	

PRACTICE
18-3   Each of the following sentences includes at least one prepositional phrase. To identify each sentence's subject, begin by crossing out each prepositional phrase. Then, underline the subject of the sentence.

Example: ~~In 1968~~, George C. Wallace ~~of the American Independent Party~~ won 13 percent ~~of the vote~~.

(1) ~~In presidential elections~~, third-party candidates have attracted many voters. (2) ~~With more than 27 percent of the vote~~, Theodore Roosevelt was the strongest third-party presidential candidate ~~in history~~. (3) ~~In the 1912 race with Democrat Woodrow Wilson and Republican William H. Taft~~, Roosevelt ran second ~~to Wilson~~. (4) ~~Before Roosevelt~~, no third-party candidate had won a significant number ~~of votes~~. (5) ~~In recent years~~, however, some candidates ~~of other parties~~ made strong showings. (6) ~~In 1980~~, John B. Anderson, an Independent, got almost 7 percent ~~of the vote~~. (7) ~~With nearly 19 percent of the~~

popular vote, Independent <u>Ross Perot</u> ran a strong race against Democrat Bill Clinton and Republican George Bush in 1992. (8) In 2000, with the support of many environmentalists, <u>Ralph Nader</u> challenged Al Gore and George W. Bush for the presidency. (9) In 2004, <u>Nader</u> was also on the ballot in many states. (10) The two-party <u>system</u> of the United States has survived despite many challenges by third-party candidates.

18c   Verbs

In addition to its subject, every sentence also includes a verb. This **verb** (also called a **predicate**) tells what the subject does or connects the subject to words that describe or rename it. Without a verb, a sentence is not complete.

Teaching Tip
Refer students to Chapter 25 for information on how to recognize and correct fragments.

Action Verbs

An **action verb** tells what the subject does, did, or will do.

> David Beckham <u>plays</u> soccer.
> Amelia Earhart <u>flew</u> across the Atlantic.
> Renee <u>will drive</u> to Tampa on Friday.

Action verbs can also show mental and emotional actions.

> Travis always <u>worries</u> about his job.

Sometimes the subject of a sentence performs more than one action. In this case, the sentence includes two or more action verbs that form a **compound predicate**.

> He <u>hit</u> the ball, <u>threw</u> down his bat, and <u>ran</u> toward first base.

PRACTICE
18-4   In the following sentences, underline each action verb twice. Some sentences contain more than one action verb.

Example: Some young women <u>read</u> romance novels.

1. Many critics <u>see</u> one romance novel as just like another.

2. The plot usually <u>involves</u> a beautiful young woman, the heroine, in some kind of danger.

3. A handsome stranger <u>offers</u> his help.

4. At first, the heroine <u>distrusts</u> him.

ESL Tip
Consider adding ESL-specific correction symbols to your standard list. Common ESL errors include problems with noun endings, verbs, articles, word choice, and sentence structure.

5. Then, another man <u>enters</u> the story and <u>wins</u> the heroine's trust.

6. Readers, however, <u>see</u> this man as an evil villain.

7. Almost too late, the heroine too <u>realizes</u> the truth.

8. Luckily, the handsome hero <u>returns</u> and <u>saves</u> her from a nasty fate.

9. Many readers <u>enjoy</u> the predictable plots of romance novels.

10. However, most literary critics <u>dislike</u> these books.

Linking Verbs

A **linking verb** does not show action. Instead, it connects the subject to a word or words that describe or rename it. The linking verb tells what the subject is (or what it was, will be, or seems to be).

A googolplex <u>is</u> an extremely large number.

Many linking verbs, like *is*, are forms of the verb *be*. Other linking verbs refer to the senses (*look, feel,* and so on).

The photocopy <u>looks</u> blurry.

Some students <u>feel</u> anxious about the future.

Teaching Tip
Tell students that some linking verbs, such as *look, smell, turn,* and *taste,* can also function as action verbs: *I will <u>look</u> for a clearer photocopy.*

Teaching Tip
Have students memorize these linking verbs.

Frequently Used Linking Verbs

act	feel	seem
appear	get	smell
be (am, is, are,	grow	sound
was, were)	look	taste
become	remain	turn

PRACTICE
18-5 In the following sentences, underline each linking verb twice.

Example: Many urban legends <u>seem</u> true.

1. Urban legends <u>are</u> folktales created to teach a lesson.

2. One familiar urban legend <u>is</u> the story of Hookman.

3. According to this story, a young man and woman <u>are</u> alone in Lovers' Lane.

4. They <u>are</u> in a car, listening to a radio announcement.

5. An escaped murderer <u>is</u> nearby.

6. The murderer's left hand <u>is</u> a hook.

7. The young woman <u>becomes</u> hysterical.

8. Suddenly, Lovers' Lane <u>seems</u> very dangerous.

9. Later, they <u>are</u> shocked to see a hook hanging from the passenger-door handle.

10. The purpose of this legend <u>is</u> to convince young people to avoid dangerous places.

PRACTICE

18-6 Underline every verb in each of the following sentences twice. Remember that a verb can be an action verb or a linking verb.

Example: Airplane pilots and investment bankers <u>use</u> checklists.

(1) In *The Checklist Manifesto*, surgeon Atul Gawande <u>argues</u> for using checklists in operating rooms. (2) Gawande <u>reminds</u> readers of the complexity of modern medicine. (3) Currently, there <u>are</u> 6,000 drugs and 4,000 medical and surgical procedures. (4) Each year, the number of drugs and procedures <u>increases</u>. (5) As a result, even knowledgeable and highly trained surgeons <u>make</u> mistakes. (6) For some types of patients, the error rate <u>is</u> very high. (7) For example, doctors <u>deliver</u> inappropriate care to 40 percent of patients with coronary artery disease. (8) Luckily, checklists <u>make</u> a big difference for these and other patients. (9) In fact, checklists <u>reduce</u> complications by more than one-third. (10) It <u>is</u> hard to imagine an argument against such a simple and effective tool.

Helping Verbs

Many verbs consist of more than one word. For example, the verb in the following sentence consists of two words.

Minh <u>must make</u> a decision about his future.

In this sentence, *make* is the **main verb**, and *must* is a **helping verb**.

Frequently Used Helping Verbs			
does	will	must	should
did	was	can	would
do	were	could	
is	have	may	
are	has	might	
am	had		

A sentence's **complete verb** is made up of a main verb plus any helping verbs that accompany it. In the following sentences, the complete verb is underlined twice, and the helping verbs are checkmarked.

Minh should have gone earlier.

Did Minh ask the right questions?

Minh will work hard.

Minh can really succeed.

FYI

Helping Verbs with Participles

Participles, such as *going* and *gone*, cannot stand alone as main verbs in a sentence. They need a helping verb to make them complete.

INCORRECT   Minh going to the library.

CORRECT   Minh is going to the library.

INCORRECT   Minh gone to the library.

CORRECT   Minh has gone to the library.

PRACTICE

18-7   The verbs in the sentences that follow consist of a main verb and one or more helping verbs. In each sentence, underline the complete verb twice, and put a check mark above each helping verb.

Example: In 1954, the Salk polio vaccine was given to more than a million schoolchildren.

(1) By the 1950s, polio had become a serious problem throughout the United States. (2) For years, it had puzzled doctors and researchers. (3) Thousands had become ill each year in the United States alone. (4) Children should have been playing happily. (5) Instead, they would get very sick. (6) Polio was sometimes called infantile paralysis. (7) In fact, it did cause paralysis in children and in adults as well. (8) Some patients could

breathe only with the help of machines called iron lungs. (9) Others
would remain in wheelchairs for life. (10) By 1960, Jonas Salk's vaccine
had reduced the incidence of polio in the United States by more than
90 percent.

TEST · Revise · Edit

Look back at your response to the Write First activity on page 333.
Circle every subject and verb. Then, try to replace some of them with
more descriptive subjects (like *linebacker* instead of *athlete*) and action
verbs (for example, *shouted* or *whispered* instead of *said*). When you have
finished, TEST the entire paragraph. Then, revise and edit your work.

EDITING PRACTICE

Read the following student essay. Underline the subject of each sentence once, and underline the complete verb of each sentence twice. Begin by crossing out the prepositional phrases. The first sentence has been done for you. *Answers will vary.*

Russell Simmons at the NAACP Image Awards, 2007

The Beastie Boys at the MTV Video Music Awards, 2004

Hip-Hop Pioneer

For years, hip-hop has been extremely popular among young people. Russell Simmons is one of the most important people in hip-hop. He started the record label Def Jam. Simmons is responsible for getting hip-hop music accepted by mainstream audiences. Simmons also showed the world a successful black-owned business.

Simmons was born in Queens, New York, in 1957. He began to promote hip-hop in 1978. Simmons started to represent rap artists with his production company, Rush Productions. One of his clients was his own brother, Joseph. Simmons called Joseph's group Run-D.M.C. With producer Rick Rubin, Simmons started the Def Jam record label. Def Jam's artists had a rebellious quality. Many listeners loved them.

Def Jam, part of Simmons's corporation Rush Communications, was soon known as a creative company. It introduced the work of many black artists (as well as some white groups) to a multicultural audience. Def Jam released recordings of Public Enemy, the Beastie Boys, and other hip-hop artists. The movie *Krush Groove* dramatized the founding of the company. It was a big success with fans of hip-hop. In 1991, Simmons began the HBO series *Def Comedy Jam*. This series featured the uncensored comedy of many African Americans, including Martin Lawrence, Chris Rock, and Jamie Foxx. In 2002, Simmons brought the show to Broadway as the Russell Simmons *Def Poetry Jam*.

Russell Simmons became a very successful businessman. In addition to Def Jam, Rush Communications includes several other businesses. One of them is Phat Farm, a line of clothing for men. Another is Baby Phat. This is a line of women's clothing. Simmons also started *One World*. This magazine focused on the hip-hop lifestyle. In 1999, Simmons sold his share of Def Jam for $100 million. By then, he was respected as both a music promoter and a businessman.

In the past, hip-hop was criticized as a fad. Now, however, hip-hop has entered the broader American culture. More than anyone, Russell Simmons has been responsible for hip-hop's success.

COLLABORATIVE ACTIVITIES

1. Fold a sheet of paper in half vertically. Working in a group of three or four students, spend two minutes listing as many nouns as you can in the column to the left of the fold. When your time is up, exchange papers with another group of students. Limiting yourselves to five minutes, write an appropriate action verb beside each noun. Each noun will now be the subject of a short sentence.

2. Choose five short sentences from those you wrote for Collaborative Activity 1. Working in the same group, collaborate to create more fully developed sentences. First, expand each subject by adding words or prepositional phrases that give more information about the subject. (For example, you could expand *boat* to *the small, leaky boat with the red sail.*) Then, expand each sentence further, adding ideas after the verb. (For example the sentence *The boat bounced* could become *The small, leaky boat with the red sail bounced helplessly on the water.*)

3. Work in a group of three or four students to write one original sentence for each of the linking verbs listed on page 338. When you have finished, exchange papers with another group. Now, try to add words and phrases to the other group's sentences to make them more interesting.

> **ESL Tip**
> Arrange groups so that nonnative speakers are not isolated from native speakers.

> **Teaching Tip**
> Make sure your students are working only with simple sentences.

review checklist

Writing Simple Sentences

☐ A sentence expresses a complete thought. The subject tells who or what is being talked about in the sentence. (See 18a.)

☐ A prepositional phrase consists of a preposition and its object (the noun or pronoun it introduces). (See 18b.)

☐ The object of a preposition cannot be the subject of a sentence. (See 18b.)

☐ An action verb tells what the subject does, did, or will do. (See 18c.)

☐ A linking verb connects the subject to a word or words that describe or rename it. (See 18c.)

☐ Many verbs are made up of more than one word. The complete verb in a sentence includes the main verb plus any helping verbs. (See 18c.)

preview

In this chapter, you will learn to

- form compound sentences with coordinating conjunctions (19a)
- form compound sentences with semicolons (19b)
- form compound sentences with transitional words and phrases (19c)

19 Writing Compound Sentences

write first

As you are no doubt aware, some teenage students attend their high school graduations holding their children. Think for a bit about how these responsibilities might affect their future studies; then, write a letter to the president of your college explaining why your campus needs a day-care center. (If your school already has a day-care center, explain why it deserves continued—or increased—funding.)

The most basic kind of sentence, a **simple sentence**, consists of a single **independent clause**: one <u>subject</u> and one <u>verb</u>.

European <u>immigrants</u> <u>arrived</u> at Ellis Island.

A **compound sentence** is made up of two or more simple sentences (independent clauses).

19a   Using Coordinating Conjunctions

One way to form a compound sentence is by joining two independent clauses with a **coordinating conjunction** preceded by a comma.

Many European immigrants arrived at Ellis Island, <u>but</u> many Asian immigrants arrived at Angel Island.

WORD POWER

coordinate (verb) to link two or more things that are equal in importance, rank, or degree

Coordinating Conjunctions			
and	for	or	yet
but	nor	so	

Coordinating conjunctions join two ideas of equal importance. They describe the relationship between two ideas, showing how and why the ideas are related. Different coordinating conjunctions have different meanings.

- To indicate addition, use *and*.

    He acts like a child, <u>and</u> people think he is cute.

- To indicate contrast or contradiction, use *but* or *yet*.

    He acts like a child, <u>but</u> he is an adult.
    He acts like a child, <u>yet</u> he longs to be taken seriously.

- To indicate a cause-and-effect relationship, use *so* or *for*.

    He acts like a child, <u>so</u> we treat him like one.
    He acts like a child, <u>for</u> he craves attention.

- To present alternatives, use *or*.

    He acts like a child, <u>or</u> he is ignored.

- To eliminate alternatives, use *nor*.

    He does not act like a child, <u>nor</u> does he look like one.

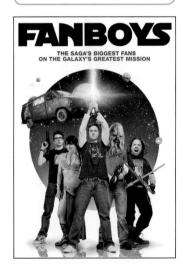

Use the letters that spell FANBOYS to help you remember the coordinating conjunctions.

F	for
A	and
N	nor
B	but
O	or
Y	yet
S	so

Teaching Tip
Remind students that in a compound sentence, there is a complete sentence on each side of the coordinating conjunction.

Teaching Tip
Remind students *not* to use a comma before a coordinating conjunction if it does not join two independent clauses.

FYI

Commas with Coordinating Conjunctions

When you use a coordinating conjunction to join two independent clauses into a single compound sentence, always put a comma before the coordinating conjunction.

We can stand in line all night, or we can go home now.

PRACTICE

19-1 Fill in the coordinating conjunction—*and, but, for, nor, or, so,* or *yet*—that most logically links the two parts of each compound sentence. Remember to insert a comma before each coordinating conjunction.

Example: Fairy tales have been told by many people around the world, *but* the stories by two German brothers may be the most famous. *Answers will vary.*

(1) Jakob and Wilhelm Grimm lived in the nineteenth century, *and* they wrote many well-known fairy tales. (2) Most people think fondly of fairy tales, *but/yet* the Brothers Grimm wrote many unpleasant and violent stories. (3) In their best-known works, children are abused, *and* endings are not always happy. (4) Either innocent children are brutally punished for no reason, *or* they are neglected. (5) For example, in "Hansel and Gretel," the stepmother mistreats the children, *and* their father abandons them in the woods. (6) In this story, the events are horrifying, *but/yet* the ending is still happy. (7) The children outwit the evil adults, *so/and* they escape unharmed. (8) Apparently, they are not injured physically, *nor* are they harmed emotionally. (9) Nevertheless, their story can hardly be called pleasant, *for* it remains a story of child abuse and neglect.

PRACTICE

19-2 Join each of the following pairs of independent clauses with a coordinating conjunction. Be sure to place a comma before the coordinating conjunction.

Example: A computer makes drafting essays easier*, and it* ~~It~~ also makes revision easier. *Answers will vary.*

1. Training a dog to heel is difficult*, for dogs* ~~Dogs~~ naturally resist strict control from their owners.

2. A bodhran is an Irish drum*, and it* ~~It~~ is played with a wooden stick.

3. Students should spend two hours of study time for each hour of class time*, or they* ~~They~~ may not do well in the course.

4. Years ago, students wrote their lessons on slates*, so the* ~~The~~ teacher was able to correct each student's work individually.

5. Each state in the United States has two senators*, but the* ~~The~~ number of representatives depends on a state's population.

6. In 1973, only 2.5 percent of those in the U.S. military were women*, but today,* ~~Today,~~ that percentage has increased to about 20 percent.

7. A small craft advisory warns boaters of bad weather conditions*, for these* ~~These~~ conditions can be dangerous to small boats.

8. A DVD looks like a CD*, but it* ~~It~~ can hold fifteen times as much information.

9. Hip-hop fashions include sneakers and baggy pants*, and these* ~~These~~ styles are very popular among young men.

10. Multiple births have become more and more common*, and even* ~~Even~~ some septuplets can now survive.

PRACTICE

19-3 Add coordinating conjunctions to combine some of the simple sentences in the following paragraph. Remember to put a comma before each coordinating conjunction you add.

Example: Years ago, few Americans lived to be one hundred*, but today,* ~~Today,~~ there are over 70,000 centenarians. *Answers will vary.*

(1) Diet, exercise, and family history may explain centenarians' long lives*, but this* ~~(2) This~~ is not the whole story. (3) A recent study showed surprising similarities among centenarians. (4) They did not all avoid tobacco and alcohol*, nor* ~~(5) They~~ did not *they* have low-fat diets. (6) In fact, they ate relatively

Teaching Tip
If your students are ready, have them revise this paragraph by varying the sentence openings. Teach or review options for sentence openings, referring students to 21b.

large amounts of fat, cholesterol, and sugar. _, so diet_ (7) ~~Diet~~ could not explain their long lives. (8) They did, however, share four key traits. (9) First, all the centenarians were optimistic about life. _, and all_ (10) ~~All~~ were positive thinkers. (11) They also had deep religious faith. (12) In addition, they had all continued to lead physically active lives. _, and they_ (13) ~~They~~ remained mobile even as elderly people. (14) Finally, all were able to adapt to loss. (15) They had all lost friends, spouses, or children. _, but they_ (16) ~~They~~ were able to get on with their lives.

PRACTICE

19-4 Write another simple sentence to follow each of the sentences below. Then, connect the sentences with a coordinating conjunction and the correct punctuation.

Example: Many patients need organ transplants. _, but there is a serious shortage of organ donors._

Answers will vary.

1. Smoking in bed is dangerous. _____

_____

2. Many cars are now equipped with GPS systems. _____

_____

3. Diamonds are very expensive. _____

_____

4. Kangaroos carry their young in pouches. _____

_____

5. Dancing is good exercise. _____

_____

6. Motorcycle helmet laws have been dropped in some states. _____

_____

7. Some businesses sponsor bowling leagues for their employees. ___

_____

8. Pretzels are a healthier snack than potato chips. _____

_____

9. Many so-called juices actually contain very little real fruit juice. ___

_____

Teaching Tip
Have students write some of their sentences on the board.

10. People tend to resist change. _____

_____

19b Using Semicolons

Another way to create a compound sentence is by joining two simple sentences (independent clauses) with a **semicolon**. A semicolon connects clauses whose ideas are closely related.

> The AIDS Memorial Quilt contains thousands of panels; each panel represents a life lost to AIDS.

Also use a semicolon to show a strong contrast between two ideas.

> With new drugs, people can live with AIDS for years; many people, however, cannot get these drugs.

FYI

Avoiding Fragments

A semicolon can only join two complete sentences (independent clauses). A semicolon cannot join a sentence and a fragment.

INCORRECT	———————— FRAGMENT ———————— Because millions worldwide are still dying of AIDS; more research is needed.
CORRECT	———————— SENTENCE ———————— Millions worldwide are still dying of AIDS; more research is needed.

PRACTICE

19-5 Each of the following items consists of one simple sentence. Create a compound sentence for each item by changing the period to a semicolon and then adding another simple sentence.

Example: My brother is addicted to fast food*; he eats it every day.* _____
Answers will vary

1. Fast-food restaurants are an American institution. _____

_____

2. Families often eat at these restaurants. _____

_____

3. Many teenagers work there. _____

_____

4. McDonald's is known for its hamburgers. _____

_____

5. KFC is famous for its fried chicken. _____

_____

6. Taco Bell serves Mexican-style food. _____

_____

7. Pizza Hut specializes in pizza. _____

_____

8. Many fast-food restaurants offer some low-fat menu items. _____

_____

9. Some offer recyclable packaging. _____

_____

10. Some even have playgrounds. _____

_____

19c Using Transitional Words and Phrases

Teaching Tip
Remind students to place a semicolon before every transitional word or phrase that joins two independent clauses. (If they leave out the semicolon, they will create a run-on.) Refer them to 24b.

Another way to create a compound sentence is by combining two simple sentences (independent clauses) with a **transitional word or phrase**. When you use a transitional word or phrase to join two sentences, always place a semicolon *before* the transitional word or phrase and a comma *after* it.

Some college students receive grants; <u>however</u>, others must take out loans.

He had a miserable time at the party; <u>in addition</u>, he lost his wallet.

Teaching Tip
Have students memorize this list and the one on the following page.

Frequently Used Transitional Words

also	instead	still
besides	later	subsequently
consequently	meanwhile	then
eventually	moreover	therefore
finally	nevertheless	thus
furthermore	now	
however	otherwise	

◢ **Frequently Used Transitional Phrases**

after all	in comparison
as a result	in contrast
at the same time	in fact
for example	in other words
for instance	of course
in addition	on the contrary

Adding a transitional word or phrase makes the connection between ideas in a sentence clearer and more precise than it would be if the ideas were linked with just a semicolon. Different transitional words and phrases convey different meanings.

- Some signal addition (*also, besides, furthermore, in addition, moreover,* and so on).

    I have a lot on my mind; <u>also</u>, I have a lot of things to do.

- Some make causal connections (*therefore, as a result, consequently, thus,* and so on).

    I have a lot on my mind; <u>therefore</u>, it is hard to concentrate.

- Some indicate contradiction or contrast (*nevertheless, however, in contrast, still,* and so on).

    I have a lot on my mind; <u>still</u>, I must try to relax.

- Some present alternatives (*instead, on the contrary, otherwise,* and so on).

    I have a lot on my mind; <u>otherwise</u>, I could relax.
    I will try not to think; <u>instead</u>, I will relax.

- Some indicate time sequence (*eventually, finally, at the same time, later, meanwhile, now, subsequently, then,* and so on).

    I have a lot on my mind; <u>meanwhile</u>, I still have work to do.

PRACTICE

19-6 Add semicolons and commas where required to set off transitional words and phrases that join two independent clauses.

Example: Ketchup is a popular condiment; therefore, it is available in almost every restaurant.

(1) Andrew F. Smith, a food historian, wrote a book about the tomato; later, he wrote a book about ketchup. (2) This book, *Pure Ketchup,* was

WORD POWER

condiment a prepared sauce or pickle used to add flavor to food

a big project in fact Smith worked on it for five years. (3) The word *ketchup* may have come from a Chinese word however Smith is not certain of the word's origins. (4) Ketchup has existed since ancient times in other words it is a very old product. (5) Ketchup has changed a lot over the years for example special dyes were developed in the nineteenth century to make it red. (6) Smith discusses many other changes for instance preservative-free ketchup was invented in 1907. (7) Ketchup is now used by people in many cultures still salsa is more popular than ketchup in the United States. (8) Today, designer ketchups are being developed meanwhile Heinz has introduced green and purple ketchup in squeeze bottles. (9) Some of today's ketchups are chunky in addition some ketchups are spicy. (10) Ketchup continues to evolve meanwhile Smith has written a book about hamburgers.

PRACTICE
19-7   Consulting the lists of transitional words and phrases on pages 350–51, choose a word or phrase that logically connects each pair of simple sentences below into one compound sentence. Be sure to punctuate appropriately.

> **Example:**   *Time*'s Man of the Year is often a prominent politician; *however, sometimes*
> ~~Sometimes~~ it is not.   *Answers will vary.*

(1) Every year since 1927, *Time* has designated a Man of the Year. *; however, the* The Man of the Year has almost never been an average man—or even a "man" at all. (2) In the 1920s and 1930s, world leaders were often chosen. *; for example,* Franklin Delano Roosevelt was chosen twice. (3) During World War II, Hitler, Stalin, Churchill, and Roosevelt were all chosen. *; in fact,* Stalin was featured twice. (4) Occasionally, the Man of the Year was not an individual. *; for instance, in* In 1950, it was The American Fighting Man. (5) In 1956, The Hungarian Freedom Fighter was Man of the Year. *; then, in* In 1966, *Time* editors chose The Young Generation. (6) A few women have been selected. *; for example,* Queen Elizabeth II of England was featured in 1952. (7) In 1975, American Women were honored as a group. *; nevertheless, the* The Man of the Year has nearly always

been male. (8) Very few people of color have been designated Man of the

Year, *; still,* Martin Luther King Jr. was honored in 1963. (9) The Man of the

Year has almost always been one or more human beings, *; however, the* The Computer

was selected in 1982 and Endangered Earth in 1988. (10) In 2003, *Time*

did not choose a politician, *; instead, it* It honored The American Soldier. (11) In

2005, *Time* wanted to honor the contributions of philanthropists, *; thus, the* The

magazine named Bill Gates, Melinda Gates, and Bono its Persons of

the Year. (12) For 2010, *Time* instead chose an entrepreneur, *; then, its* Its pick was

Facebook founder Mark Zuckerberg.

> **WORD POWER**
> **philanthropist** someone who tries to improve human lives through charitable aid

PRACTICE
19-8

Add the suggested transitional word or phrase to each of the simple sentences below. Then, add a new independent clause to follow it. Be sure to punctuate correctly.

Example: Commuting students do not really experience campus life. (however)

Commuting students do not really experience campus life; however, there are some

benefits to being a commuter.

Answers will vary.

1. Campus residents may have a better college experience. (still)

   Campus residents may have a better college experience; still, being a commuter has

   its advantages.

2. Living at home gives students access to home-cooked meals. (in contrast)

   Living at home gives students access to home-cooked meals; in contrast, dorm

   residents have to eat dining hall food or takeout.

3. Commuters have a wide choice of jobs in the community. (on the other hand)

   Commuters have a wide choice of jobs in the community; on the other hand, students

   living on campus may have to take on-campus jobs.

4. Commuters get to see their families every day. (however)

   Commuters get to see their families every day; however, dorm students may live

   far from home.

> **Teaching Tip**
> Students may find it challenging to generate original material for Practices 19-8 and 19-9. For this reason, you might have them work in pairs or small groups.

5. There are also some disadvantages to being a commuter. (for example)

   There are also some disadvantages to being a commuter; for example, commuters may

   have trouble scheduling meetings with study groups.

6. Unlike dorm students, many commuters have family responsibilities. (in fact)

   Unlike dorm students, many commuters have family responsibilities; in fact, they may

   have children of their own.

7. Commuters might have to help take care of their parents or grandparents. (in addition)

   Commuters might have to help take care of their parents or grandparents; in addition,

   they might have to babysit for younger siblings.

8. Commuters might need a car to get to school. (consequently)

   Commuters might need a car to get to school; consequently, they might have higher

   expenses than dorm residents.

9. Younger commuters may have to follow their parents' rules. (of course)

   Younger commuters may have to follow their parents' rules; of course, dorms also

   have rules.

10. Commuting to college has pros and cons. (therefore)

    Commuting to college has pros and cons; therefore, commuters are not necessarily at

    a disadvantage.

PRACTICE

19-9 Using both the specified topics and transitional words and phrases, create five compound sentences. Be sure to punctuate appropriately.

Example
Topic: fad diets
Transitional phrase: for example

People are always falling for fad diets; for example, some people eat only

pineapple to lose weight.

Answers will vary.

1. *Topic:* laws to protect people with disabilities
   Transitional phrase: in addition

   _____

   _____

Teaching Tip
Have students work in pairs in this exercise, and then write their sentences on the board. Get at least two versions of each sentence.

2. *Topic:* single men and women as adoptive parents
   Transitional word: however

   _____

   _____

3. *Topic:* prayer in public schools
   Transitional word: therefore

   _____

   _____

4. *Topic:* high school proms
   Transitional word: also

   _____

   _____

5. *Topic:* course requirements at your school
   Transitional word: instead

   _____

   _____

TEST · Revise · Edit

Look back at your response to the Write First activity on page 344.
TEST what you have written. Then, revise and edit your work, checking
each compound sentence to make sure you have used the coordinating
conjunction or transitional word or phrase that best conveys your
meaning and that you have punctuated these sentences correctly.

EDITING PRACTICE

Read the following student essay. Then, create compound sentences by linking pairs of simple sentences where appropriate, joining them with a coordinating conjunction, a semicolon, or a transitional word or phrase. Remember to put commas before coordinating conjunctions and to use semicolons and commas correctly with transitional words and phrases. The first two sentences have been combined for you. *Answers may vary.*

Map of Ukraine

My Grandfather's Life

My great-grandparents were born in Ukraine*, but they* They raised my grandfather in western Pennsylvania. The ninth of their ten children, he had a life I cannot begin to imagine. To me, he was my big, strong, powerful grandfather*; however, he* He was also a child of poverty.

My great-grandfather worked for the American Car Foundry. The family lived in a company house*, and they* They shopped at the company store. In 1934, my great-grandfather was laid off*, so he* He went to work digging sewer lines for the government. At that time, the family was on welfare. Every week, they were entitled to get food rations*, and my* My grandfather would go to pick up the food. The family desperately needed the prunes, beans, flour, margarine, and other things.

For years, my grandfather wore his brothers' hand-me-down clothes*; in addition, he* He wore thrift-shop shoes with cardboard over the holes in the soles. He was often hungry*, so he* He would sometimes sit by the side of the railroad tracks, waiting for the engineer to throw him an orange. My grandfather would do any job to earn a quarter*; for example, once,* Once, he weeded a mile-long row of tomato plants. For this work, he was paid twenty-five cents and a pack of NECCO wafers.

My grandfather saved his pennies*; eventually,* Eventually, he was able to buy a used bicycle for two dollars. He dropped out of school at fourteen and got a job*, for the* The family badly needed his income. He woke up every day at 4 a.m.*, and he* He rode his bike to his job at a meatpacking plant. He worked for fifty cents a day.

In 1943, at the age of seventeen, my grandfather joined the U.S. Navy*; thus, he* He discovered a new world. For the first time in his life, he had enough to eat.

He was always first in line at the mess hall,*; in fact, he* He went back for seconds and thirds before anyone else. After the war ended in 1945, he was discharged from the Navy. He went to work in a meat market in New York City,*; the* The only trade he knew was the meat business. Three years later, when he had saved enough to open his own store, Pete's Quality Meats, he knew his life of poverty was finally over.

World War II sailor

COLLABORATIVE ACTIVITIES

1. Working in a small group, pair each of the simple sentences in the left-hand column below with a sentence in the right-hand column to create ten compound sentences. Use as many different coordinating conjunctions as you can to connect the independent clauses. Be sure each coordinating conjunction you choose conveys a logical relationship between ideas, and remember to put a comma before each one. You may use some of the listed sentences more than once. *Note:* Many different combinations—some serious and factually accurate, some humorous—are possible.

Some dogs wear little sweaters.	Many are named Hamlet.
Pit bulls are raised to fight.	They live in groups.
Bonobos are pygmy chimpanzees.	One even sings Christmas carols.
Many people fear Dobermans.	They can wear bandanas.
Leopards have spots.	They can play Frisbee.
Dalmatians can live in firehouses.	Many live in equatorial Zaire.
Horses can wear blankets.	Some people think they are gentle.
All mules are sterile.	They don't get cold in winter.
Great Danes are huge dogs.	They are half horse and half donkey.
Parrots can often speak.	They can be unpredictable.

2. Work in a group of three or four students to create a cast of five characters for a movie, a television pilot, or a music video. Working individually, write five descriptive simple sentences—one about each character. Then, exchange papers with another student. Add a semicolon and a transitional word or phrase to each sentence on the list to create five new compound sentences.

Example

ORIGINAL SENTENCE   Mark is a handsome heartthrob.

NEW SENTENCE   Mark is a handsome heartthrob; unfortunately, he has green teeth.

review checklist

Writing Compound Sentences

☐ A compound sentence is made up of two simple sentences (independent clauses).

☐ A coordinating conjunction—*and, but, for, nor, or, so,* or *yet*—can join two independent clauses into one compound sentence. A comma always comes before the coordinating conjunction. (See 19a.)

☐ A semicolon can join two independent clauses into one compound sentence. (See 19b.)

☐ A transitional word or phrase can also join two independent clauses into one compound sentence. When it joins two independent clauses, a transitional word or phrase is always preceded by a semicolon and followed by a comma. (See 19c.)

20 Writing Complex Sentences

preview

In this chapter, you will learn to
- identify complex sentences (20a)
- use subordinating conjunctions to form complex sentences (20b)
- use relative pronouns to form complex sentences (20c)

write first

In 1963, the U.S. government began requiring that all cigarette packages include a warning label, two versions of which appear on this page. Think about why this law might have passed. Then, write a paragraph about a different law that you think should be passed, and explain why you think this law is necessary.

20a Identifying Complex Sentences

As you learned in Chapter 19, an **independent clause** can stand alone as a sentence.

INDEPENDENT   The <u>exhibit</u> <u>was</u> controversial.
CLAUSE

However, a **dependent clause** cannot stand alone as a sentence.

DEPENDENT   Because the exhibit was controversial
CLAUSE

What happened because the exhibit was controversial? To answer this question, you need to add an independent clause that completes the idea begun in the dependent clause. The result is a **complex sentence**—a sentence that consists of one independent clause and one or more dependent clauses.

┌─────────────DEPENDENT CLAUSE─────────────┐ ┌─INDEPENDENT CLAUSE─┐
COMPLEX   Because the exhibit was controversial, many people
SENTENCE   └──────────────────────┘
           came to see it.

Teaching Tip
Review the concept of subordination. Discuss how adding a subordinating conjunction can make one idea depend on another for completion.

PRACTICE

20-1   In the blank following each of the items below, indicate whether the group of words is an independent clause (*IC*) or a dependent clause (*DC*).

Example: The American diner began as a horse-drawn lunch wagon.

_____*IC*_____

1. When lunch wagons added stools and counters in the late 1800s.

_____*DC*_____

2. Some expanded lunch wagons had fancy woodwork and glass.

_____*IC*_____

3. Because of laws that restricted operating hours. _____*DC*_____

4. Lunch wagon operators turned their wagons into diners. _____*IC*_____

5. The name *diner* came from railroad dining cars. _____*IC*_____

6. Because some diners were converted railroad cars. _____*DC*_____

7. Diners added bathrooms, booths, and landscaping in the 1920s to attract female customers. _____*IC*_____

8. Even though many diners moved from cities to suburbs after World War II. _____DC_____

9. Diners later began competing with fast-food restaurants by adding fancy interiors and shingled roofs. _____IC_____

10. Today, food trucks compete with both fast-food restaurants and diners. _____IC_____

PRACTICE
20-2   In the blank following each of the items below, indicate whether the group of words is an independent clause (*IC*) or a dependent clause (*DC*).

Example: When novelist Toni Morrison was born in Ohio in 1931. _____DC_____

1. As a young reader, Toni Morrison liked the classic Russian novelists. _____IC_____

2. After she graduated from Howard University with a bachelor's degree in English. _____DC_____

3. Morrison based her novel *The Bluest Eye* on a childhood friend's prayers to God for blue eyes. _____IC_____

4. While she raised two sons as a single mother and worked as an editor at Random House. _____DC_____

5. As her reputation as a novelist grew with the publication of *Song of Solomon* and *Tar Baby*. _____DC_____

6. Her picture appeared on the cover of *Newsweek* in 1981. _____IC_____

7. Before her novel *Beloved* won the 1988 Pulitzer Prize for fiction. _____DC_____

8. *Beloved* was made into a film starring Oprah Winfrey. _____IC_____

9. In 1993, Morrison became the first African-American woman to win the Nobel Prize in Literature. _____IC_____

10. Who published the novel *A Mercy* in 2008 to favorable reviews. _____DC_____

20b Using Subordinating Conjunctions

One way to form a complex sentence is to use a **subordinating conjunction**—a word such as *although* or *because*—to join two simple sentences (independent clauses).

TWO SIMPLE SENTENCES Muhammad Ali was stripped of his heavyweight title for refusing to go into the army. Many people admired his antiwar position.

COMPLEX SENTENCE
————— DEPENDENT CLAUSE —————
Although Muhammad Ali was stripped of his heavyweight title for refusing to go into the army,

many people admired his antiwar position.

Frequently Used Subordinating Conjunctions

after	even though	since	whenever
although	if	so that	where
as	if only	than	whereas
as if	in order that	that	wherever
as though	now that	though	whether
because	once	unless	while
before	provided that	until	
even if	rather than	when	

As the chart below shows, different subordinating conjunctions express different relationships between dependent and independent clauses.

Relationship between Clauses	Subordinating Conjunction	Example
Time	after, before, since, until, when, whenever, while	When the whale surfaced, Ahab threw his harpoon.
Reason or cause	as, because	Scientists scaled back the project because the government cut funds.
Result or effect	in order that, so that	So that students' math scores will improve, many schools have begun special programs.

Condition	even if, if, unless	The rain forest may disappear <u>unless steps are taken immediately</u>.
Contrast	although, even though, though	<u>Although Thomas Edison had almost no formal education</u>, he was a successful inventor.
Location	where, wherever	Pittsburgh was built <u>where the Allegheny and Monongahela Rivers meet</u>.

FYI

Punctuating with Subordinating Conjunctions

In a complex sentence, use a comma after the dependent clause.

————DEPENDENT CLAUSE———— ——INDEPENDENT CLAUSE——
Although she wore the scarlet letter, Hester carried herself proudly.

Do not use a comma after the independent clause.

——INDEPENDENT CLAUSE—— ——DEPENDENT CLAUSE——
Hester carried herself proudly although she wore the scarlet letter.

PRACTICE

20-3 In the blank in each of the sentences below, write an appropriate subordinating conjunction. Look at the list of subordinating conjunctions on page 362 to help you choose a conjunction that expresses the logical relationship between the two clauses it links. (The required punctuation has been provided.)

Example: Movie cowboys are usually portrayed as white _although_ many were African American. *Answers may vary.*

(1) Few people today know about black cowboys _even though_ they were once common. (2) _After_ the transcontinental railroad was built, cowboys were in high demand. (3) The ranchers hired cowboys to drive their cattle to the Midwest, _where_ the cows were loaded on trains headed to eastern cities. (4) Many former slaves became cowboys _because_ they wanted a new start. (5) Many African Americans also became cowboys _because_ they had experience working with horses and

cattle on Southern plantations or farms. (6) However, black cowboys faced difficulties _____*when*_____ they arrived in the West. (7) African-American cowboys often had to work much harder than whites _____*in order to*_____ earn the same pay and respect. (8) _____*Although*_____ almost one-fourth of cowboys were black, few writers wrote about them. (9) The myth of the white-only cowboy was spread in novels, films, and television shows _____*as if*_____ black cowboys never existed. (10) Black cowboys did appear in some films of the 1970s _____*although*_____ by this time Westerns were no longer popular. (11) Things started to change in the 1970s _____*when*_____ several museums honored black, Indian, and Mexican cowboys. (12) _____*Because*_____ African-American cowboys have finally received some recognition, their history can now be more fully understood.

PRACTICE

20-4   Combine each of the following pairs of sentences to create one complex sentence. Use a subordinating conjunction from the list on page 362 to indicate the relationship between the dependent and independent clauses in each sentence. Make sure you include a comma where one is required.

> **Example:**   Orville and Wilbur Wright built the first powered plane/
> *although they*
> ^They had no formal training as engineers. *Answers may vary.*

Although professional   *, in*
1. ^Professional midwives are used widely in Europe/ ^In the United States,
   they usually practice only in areas with few doctors.

When   *, a*
2. ^John Deere constructed his first steel plow in 1837/ ^A new era began in
   farming.

                                     even though he
3. Stephen Crane describes battles in *The Red Badge of Courage*/ ^He never
   saw a war.

When   *, thousands*
4. ^Elvis Presley died in 1977/ ^Thousands of his fans gathered in front of
   his mansion.

After   *, the*
5. ^Jonas Salk developed the first polio vaccine in the 1950s/ ^The number
   of polio cases in the United States declined.

As the   *, some*
6. ^The salaries of baseball players rose in the 1980s/ ^Some sportswriters
   predicted a drop in attendance at games.

7. The Du Ponts arrived from France in 1800, American gunpowder was

   not as good as French gunpowder.

   Before the

8. Margaret Sanger opened her first birth-control clinic in America in

   1916, She was arrested and put in jail.

   After , *she*

9. Thaddeus Stevens thought plantation land should be given to freed

   slaves, He disagreed with Lincoln's peace terms for the South.

   Because , *he*

10. Steven Spielberg directed some very popular movies, He did not win

    an Academy Award until *Schindler's List* in 1993.

    Even though , *he*

20c Using Relative Pronouns

Another way to form a complex sentence is to use **relative pronouns** (*who, that, which,* and so on) to join two simple sentences (independent clauses).

TWO SIMPLE SENTENCES Harry Potter is an adolescent wizard. He attends Hogwarts School of Witchcraft and Wizardry.

DEPENDENT CLAUSE

COMPLEX SENTENCE Harry Potter, who attends Hogwarts School of Witchcraft and Wizardry, is an adolescent wizard.

Note: The relative pronoun always refers to a word or words in the independent clause. (In the complex sentence above, *who* refers to *Harry Potter*.)

Teaching Tip
Reinforce that a dependent clause introduced by a relative pronoun does not express a complete thought. It is therefore a fragment. Refer students to 25d.

Relative Pronouns

that	which	whoever	whomever
what	who	whom	whose

Relative pronouns indicate the relationships between the ideas in the independent and dependent clauses they link.

TWO SIMPLE SENTENCES Nadine Gordimer comes from South Africa. She won the Nobel Prize in Literature in 1991.

COMPLEX SENTENCE Nadine Gordimer, who won the Nobel Prize in Literature in 1991, comes from South Africa.

TWO SIMPLE SENTENCES Last week I had a job interview. It went very well.

COMPLEX SENTENCE Last week I had a job interview that went very well.

Teaching Tip
Tell students that when they create a complex sentence, the relative pronoun substitutes for a noun or another pronoun in one of the original simple sentences.

TWO SIMPLE SENTENCES	Transistors have replaced vacuum tubes in radios and televisions. They were invented in 1948.
COMPLEX SENTENCE	Transistors, which were invented in 1948, have replaced vacuum tubes in radios and televisions.

PRACTICE

20-5 In each of the following complex sentences, underline the dependent clause once, and underline the relative pronoun twice. Then, draw an arrow from the relative pronoun to the word or words to which it refers.

Example: MTV, which was the first television network devoted to popular music videos, began in 1981.

1. MTV's very first music video, which was performed by a group called the Buggles, contained the lyric "Video killed the radio star."

2. The earliest videos on MTV were simple productions that recorded live studio performances.

3. Recording executives, who had been doubtful of MTV at first, soon realized the marketing potential of music videos.

4. Music videos eventually became complicated productions that featured special effects and large casts of dancers.

5. Music video directors gained recognition at MTV's Video Music Awards presentation, which first aired in September 1984.

6. *The Real World*, a reality series that featured a group of young people living together in New York City, was introduced by MTV in 1992.

7. MTV's later reality shows featured celebrities such as Jessica Simpson, who starred in *Newlyweds: Nick and Jessica* in 2003.

8. Today, MTV, which devotes less and less time to music videos, produces many hours of original programming.

9. One of MTV's newest reality shows, which features cast members at the beach, is *Jersey Shore*.

10. Critics of MTV's format have included musicians such as Justin Timberlake, who challenged MTV to play more videos.

PRACTICE
20-6 Combine each of the following pairs of simple sentences into one complex sentence. Use the relative pronoun that follows each pair.

Example: Elias Howe invented an early type of zipper. He was too busy with his other invention—the sewing machine—to work on it. (who)

Elias Howe, who invented an early type of zipper, was too busy with his other

invention—the sewing machine—to work on it.

Answers will vary.

1. Early zippers were just hooks and eyes. These hooks and eyes were fastened to a cloth tape. (that)

   Early zippers were just hooks and eyes that were fastened to a cloth tape.

   _____

2. Gideon Sundback invented the first useful zipper. He worked endless hours to help him stop grieving for his wife. (who)

   Gideon Sundback, who worked endless hours to help him stop grieving for his wife,

   invented the first useful zipper.

3. Their "high" price kept early zippers from becoming popular. It was about eighteen cents. (which)

   Their "high" price, which was about eighteen cents, kept early zippers from becoming popular.

   _____

4. The word *zipper* began as a brand name. It was coined by a company executive. (which)

   The word zipper, which began as a brand name, was coined by a company executive.

   _____

5. At first, zipper manufacturers could not convince people to use zippers in clothing. They sold many zippers for boots. (who)

   At first, zipper manufacturers, who sold many zippers for boots, could not convince

   people to use zippers in clothing.

TEST · Revise · Edit

Look back at your response to the Write First activity on page 359. TEST what you have written. Then, revise and edit your work, checking carefully to make sure that you have used subordinating conjunctions and relative pronouns correctly and that your complex sentences are punctuated correctly.

EDITING PRACTICE

Read the following student essay. Then, revise it by combining pairs of simple sentences with subordinating conjunctions or relative pronouns that indicate the relationship between them. Be sure to punctuate correctly. The first two sentences have been combined for you. *Answers will vary.*

Graffiti on a city building

Community Art

When a
A city has a crime problem, ~~The~~ *,the* police and the courts try to solve it. Some cities have come up with creative ways to help young people stay out of trouble. One example is the Philadelphia Mural Arts Program. *,which* ~~It~~ offers free art education for high school students.

In the 1960s, Philadelphia had a serious problem. *,which* ~~The problem~~ was graffiti. Graffiti artists had painted their designs on buildings all over the city. A solution to the problem was the Philadelphia Anti-Graffiti Network. *,which* ~~This~~ offered graffiti artists an alternative. *If the* The artists would give up graffiti. *,they* ~~They~~ would not be prosecuted. The artists *,who* enjoyed painting. ~~They~~ could paint murals on public buildings instead. They could create beautiful landscapes, portraits of local heroes, and abstract designs. The graffiti artists *,who* had once been lawbreakers. ~~They~~ could now help beautify the city.

The Mural Arts Program began in 1984 as a part of the Philadelphia Anti-Graffiti Network. By 1996, the Philadelphia Anti-Graffiti Network was focusing on eliminating graffiti, and its Mural Arts Program was working to improve the community. *Although it* It now no longer worked with graffiti offenders. *,it* ~~It~~ started after-school and summer programs for students. The Mural Arts Program got national recognition in 1997. ~~That is~~ when President Bill Clinton helped paint a mural. So far, the Mural Arts Program has completed more than 2,800 murals. *,which* ~~This~~ is more than any other public art program in the country.

, who come from all parts of the city,
Over 20,000 students have taken part in the Mural Arts Program. ~~The students come from all parts of the city.~~ In one part of the program, students work alongside

professional artists. The students get to paint parts of the artists' murals themselves.

The artwork *, which* is on public buildings. ~~The~~ artwork can be seen by everyone.

The Mural Arts Program *, which is now over a quarter of a century old,* continues to build a brighter future for students and

their communities. ~~It is now over a quarter of a century old.~~ *When students* Students help bring

people together to create a mural, *they* ~~They~~ feel a stronger connection to their

community and more confidence in themselves. *After they* ~~They~~ leave the program, *they* ~~They~~ are

equipped to make a positive difference in their communities and in their own lives.

COLLABORATIVE ACTIVITIES

1. Working in a group of four students, make a list of three or four of your favorite television shows. Then, divide into pairs, and with your partner, write two simple sentences describing each show. Next, use subordinating conjunctions or relative pronouns to combine each pair of sentences into one complex sentence. With your group, discuss how the ideas in each complex sentence are related, and make sure you have used the subordinating conjunction or relative pronoun that best conveys this relationship.

   Example: *The Brady Bunch* portrays a 1970s family. It still appeals to many viewers.

   Although *The Brady Bunch* portrays a 1970s family, it still appeals to many viewers.

2. Imagine that you and the members of your group live in a neighborhood where workers are repairing underground power lines. As they work, the workers talk loudly and use foul language. Write a short letter of complaint to the power company in which you explain that the workers' behavior is offensive to you and to your children. Tell the company that you want the offensive behavior to end. Write the first draft of your letter in simple sentences. After you have written this draft, work as a group to combine as many sentences as you can with subordinating conjunctions and relative pronouns.

3. Assume you are in a competition to determine which student group in your class is best at writing complex sentences. Working in a group, prepare a letter to your instructor in which you present the strengths of your group. Be sure to use a subordinating conjunction or relative pronoun in each of the sentences in your letter. Finally, as a class, evaluate the letters, and choose the letter that is most convincing.

review checklist

Writing Complex Sentences

- [ ] A complex sentence consists of one independent clause (simple sentence) combined with one or more dependent clauses. (See 20a.)

- [ ] Subordinating conjunctions—dependent words such as *although, after, when, while,* and *because*—can join two independent clauses into one complex sentence. (See 20b.)

- [ ] Relative pronouns—dependent words such as *who, which,* and *that*—can also join two independent clauses into one complex sentence. The relative pronoun shows the relationship between the ideas in the two independent clauses that it links. (See 20c.)

21 Writing Varied Sentences

preview

In this chapter, you will learn to

- vary sentence types (21a)
- vary sentence openings (21b)
- combine sentences (21c)
- mix long and short sentences (21d)

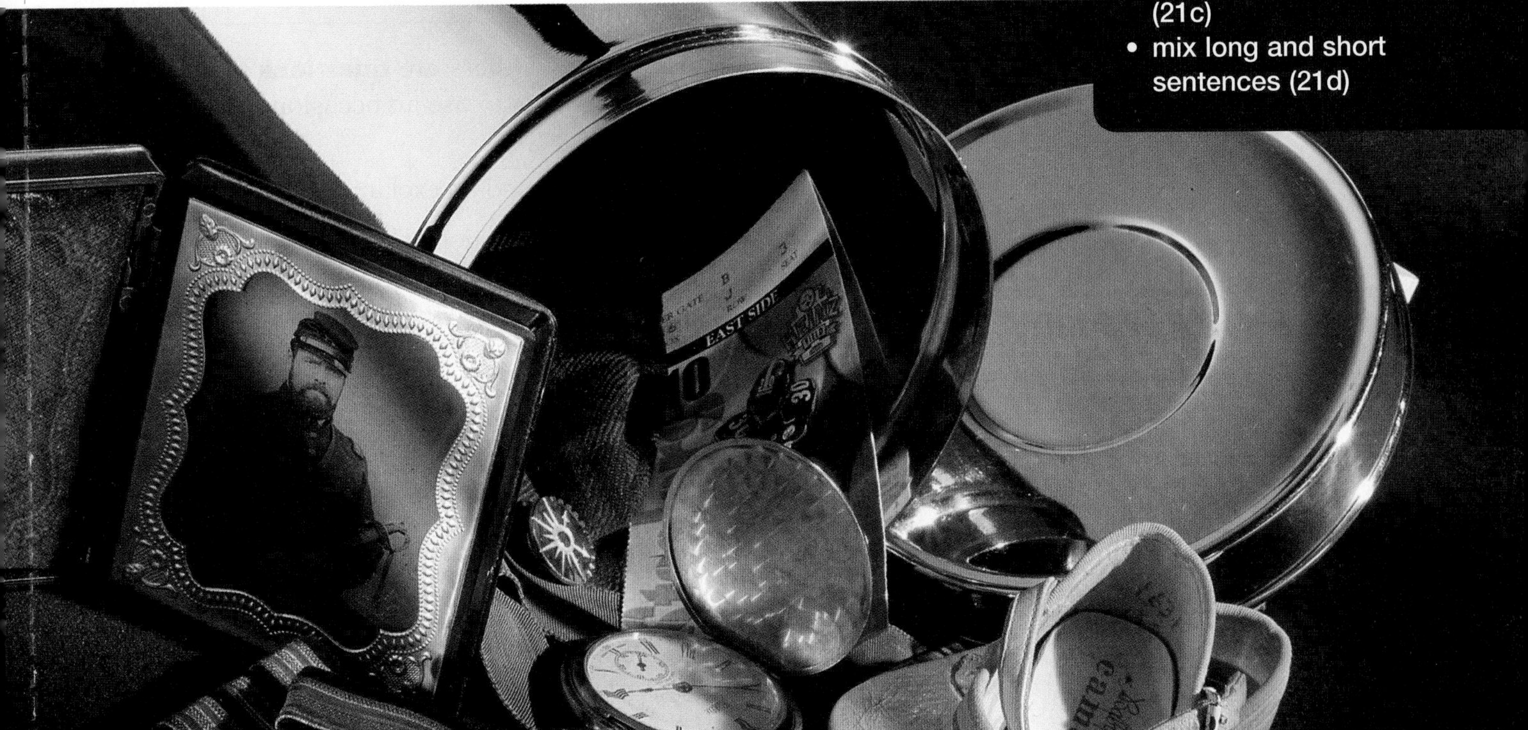

write first

This picture shows items about to be preserved in a time capsule at the History Center in Pittsburgh. Write a paragraph (or an essay) about a time capsule you might construct for your children to open when they are adults. What items would you include? How would you expect each item to communicate to your children what you and your world were like? Be sure to include explanations for your decisions.

Sentence variety is important because a paragraph of varied sentences flows more smoothly, is easier to read and understand, and is more interesting than one in which all the sentences are structured in the same way.

21a Varying Sentence Types

Most English sentences are **statements**. Others are **questions** or **exclamations**. One way to vary your sentences is to use an occasional question or exclamation where it is appropriate.

In the following paragraph, a question and an exclamation add variety.

Question

Exclamation

Jacqueline Cochran, the first woman pilot to break the sound barrier, was one of the most important figures in aviation history. In 1996, the United States Postal Service issued a stamp honoring Cochran; the words "Pioneer Pilot" appear under her name. <u>What did she do to earn this title and this tribute?</u> Cochran broke more flight records than anyone else in her lifetime and won many awards, including the United States Distinguished Service Medal in 1945 and the United States Air Force Distinguished Flying Cross in 1969. During World War II, she helped form the WASPs, the Women's Air Force Service Pilots program, so that women could fly military planes to their bases (even though they were not allowed to go into combat). Remarkably, she accomplished all this with only three weeks of flying instruction. She only got her pilot's license in the first place because she wanted to start her own cosmetics business and flying would enable her to travel quickly around the country. Although she never planned to be a pilot, once she discovered flying she quickly became the best. <u>Not surprisingly, when the Postal Service honored Jacqueline Cochran, it was with an airmail stamp!</u>

PRACTICE
21-1   Revise the following paragraph by changing one of the statements into a question and one of the statements into an exclamation.

Example: The cell phone may be making the wristwatch obsolete. (statement)

Is the cell phone making the wristwatch obsolete? (question)

Answers will vary.

(1) As cell phones and other small electronic devices become more common, fewer people are wearing watches. (2) Most cell phones, BlackBerries, iPads, and MP3 players display the time. (3) Moreover, cell phone clocks give very accurate time. (4) This is because they set

themselves with satellite signals. (5) They also adjust automatically to
time-zone changes. (6) *How can typical*   Typical wristwatches cannot compete with these
convenient features. (7) After all, unlike the newer devices, watches are
not computers. (8) However, watches do remain appealing for other
reasons. (9) For many people, they are fashion accessories or status
symbols. (10) For other, more old-fashioned people, the watch is essential
for telling time.

21b Varying Sentence Openings

When all the sentences in a paragraph begin the same way, your writing is
likely to seem dull and repetitive. In the following paragraph, for example,
every sentence begins with the subject.

> Scientists have been observing a disturbing phenomenon. The
> population of frogs, toads, and salamanders has been declining. This
> decline was first noticed in the mid-1980s. Some reports blamed chem-
> ical pollution. Some biologists began to suspect that a fungal disease
> was killing these amphibians. The most reasonable explanation seems
> to be that the amphibians' eggs are threatened by solar radiation. This
> radiation penetrates the thinned ozone layer, which used to shield
> them from the sun's rays.

Beginning with Adverbs

Instead of opening every sentence in a paragraph with the subject, you can
try beginning some sentences with one or more **adverbs**.

> Scientists have been observing a disturbing phenomenon.
> <u>Gradually but steadily</u>, the population of frogs, toads, and sala-
> manders has been declining. This decline was first noticed in the
> mid-1980s. Some reports blamed chemical pollution. Some biolo-
> gists began to suspect that a fungal disease was killing these
> amphibians. <u>However</u>, the most reasonable explanation seems to
> be that the amphibians' eggs are threatened by solar radiation.
> This radiation penetrates the thinned ozone layer, which used to
> shield them from the sun's rays.

PRACTICE
21-2   Underline the adverb in each of the following sentences, and then rewrite the sentence so that the adverb appears at the beginning. Be sure to punctuate correctly.

Example: The artist Tupac Amaru Shakur was <u>occasionally</u> known by the names 2Pac, Makaveli, or Pac.

Occasionally, the artist Tupac Amaru Shakur was known by the names 2Pac,

Makaveli, or Pac.

1. Tupac was <u>initially</u> a roadie and backup dancer for the rap group Digital Underground.

   Initially, Tupac was a roadie and backup dancer for the rap group Digital Underground.

2. He <u>then</u> released the album *2Pocalypse Now*, praised and criticized because of its frank lyrics.

   Then, he released the album 2Pocalypse Now, praised and criticized because of its

   frank lyrics.

3. Tupac <u>next</u> faced conflicts with rival rap artists, leading to his being shot and spending time in prison.

   Next, Tupac faced conflicts with rival rap artists, leading to his being shot and spending

   time in prison.

4. Tupac was <u>generally</u> known for his top-selling albums, but he also was a movie actor, a poet, and a social activist.

   Generally, Tupac was known for his top-selling albums, but he also was a movie

   actor, a poet, and a social activist.

5. His influence continued, <u>however</u>, after his 1996 murder, and some fans even believe that he is still alive.

   However, his influence continued after his 1996 murder, and some fans even believe

   that he is still alive.

PRACTICE
21-3   Underline the adverb in each of the following sentences, and then rewrite the sentence so that the adverb appears at the beginning. Be sure to punctuate correctly.

Example: An internship is <u>usually</u> a one-time work or service experience related to a student's career plans.

Usually, an internship is a one-time work or service experience related to a student's

career plans.

1. Internships are <u>sometimes</u> paid or counted for academic credit.

   Sometimes, internships are paid or counted for academic credit.

2. The student should <u>first</u> talk to an academic advisor.

First, the student should talk to an academic advisor.

3. The student should <u>next</u> write a résumé listing job experience, education, and interests.

Next, the student should write a résumé listing job experience, education, and interests.

4. The student can <u>then</u> send the résumé to organizations that are looking for interns.

Then, the student can send the résumé to organizations that are looking for interns.

5. Going to job fairs and networking are <u>often</u> good ways to find internships.

Often, going to job fairs and networking are good ways to find internships.

PRACTICE
21-4
In each of the following sentences, fill in the blank with an appropriate adverb. Be sure to punctuate correctly.

Example: ___*Slowly,*___ the sun crept over the horizon.
Answers will vary.

1. _____ the speeding car appeared from out of nowhere.

2. _____ it crashed into the guardrail.

3. _____ the car jackknifed across the highway.

4. _____ drivers behind the car slammed on their brakes.

5. _____ someone called 911.

6. _____ a wailing siren could be heard.

7. _____ the ambulance arrived.

8. _____ emergency medical technicians went to work.

9. _____ a police officer was on hand to direct traffic.

10. _____ no one was badly hurt in the accident.

Beginning with Prepositional Phrases

Another way to create sentence variety is to begin some sentences with prepositional phrases. A **prepositional phrase** (such as *along the river* or *near the diner*) is made up of a preposition and its object.

Teaching Tip
Refer students to the list of frequently used prepositions in 18b.

<u>In recent years</u>, scientists have observed a disturbing phenomenon. Gradually but steadily, the population of frogs, toads, and salamanders has been declining. This was first noticed in the mid-1980s. <u>At first</u>, some reports blamed chemical pollution. <u>After a while</u>, some biologists began to suspect that a fungal disease was killing them. However, the most reasonable explanation seems to be that the amphibians' eggs are threatened by solar radiation. This radiation penetrates the thinned ozone layer, which used to shield them from the sun's rays.

Teaching Tip
Refer students to 18b for more on prepositions.

PRACTICE
21-5 Underline the prepositional phrase in each of the following sentences, and then rewrite the sentence so that the prepositional phrase appears at the beginning. Be sure to punctuate correctly.

Example: Very few American women did factory work <u>before the 1940s</u>.

Before the 1940s, very few American women did factory work.

Teaching Tip
Refer students to Chapters 18 and 31 for more on prepositional phrases.

1. Many male factory workers became soldiers <u>during World War II</u>.

   During World War II, many male factory workers became soldiers.

2. The U.S. government encouraged women to take factory jobs <u>in the war's early years</u>.

   In the war's early years, the U.S. government encouraged women to take factory jobs.

Teaching Tip
You may want to remind students that *to* can act as a preposition (*to the store*) or as part of an infinitive (*to help*).

3. Over six million women took factory jobs <u>between 1942 and 1945</u>.

   Between 1942 and 1945, over six million women took factory jobs.

4. A new female image emerged <u>with this greater responsibility and independence</u>.

   With this greater responsibility and independence, a new female image emerged.

5. Many women wore pants <u>for the first time</u>.

   For the first time, many women wore pants.

6. Most women lost their factory jobs <u>after the war</u> and returned to "women's work."

   After the war, most women lost their factory jobs and returned to "women's work."

PRACTICE
21-6 In each of the following sentences, fill in the blank with an appropriate prepositional phrase. Be sure to punctuate correctly.

Example: <u>*At the start of the New York marathon,*</u> Justin felt as if he could run forever.

Answers will vary.

1. _____ he warmed up by stretching and bending.

2. _____ all the runners were crowded together.

3. _____ they crossed a bridge over the Hudson River.

4. _____ the route became more and more challenging.

5. _____ Justin grabbed some water from a helpful onlooker.

6. _____ he staggered across the finish line.

Teaching Tip
Refer students to the list of frequently used prepositions in 18b.

PRACTICE

21-7 Every sentence in the following paragraph begins with the subject, but several contain prepositional phrases or adverbs that could be moved to the beginning. To vary the sentence openings, move prepositional phrases to the beginnings of four sentences, and move adverbs to the beginnings of two other sentences. Be sure to place a comma after these introductory phrases.

By the end of the 1800s,

Example: ‸Spain ~~by the end of the 1800s~~ had lost most of its colonies.
Answers will vary.

In the Cuban-American community, people

(1) People ~~in the Cuban-American community~~ often mention José Julián

Martí as one of their heroes. (2) José Martí was born in Havana in 1853, at

By the time he was sixteen years old, he

a time when Cuba was a colony of Spain. (3) He had started a newspaper

In 1870, the

demanding Cuban freedom ~~by the time he was sixteen years old.~~ (4) The

Spanish authorities forced him to leave Cuba and go to Spain ‸ ~~in 1870.~~

Openly continuing his fight, he

(5) He published his first pamphlet calling for Cuban independence while

in Spain, ~~openly continuing his fight.~~ (6) He then lived for fourteen years

During his time in New York, he

in New York City. (7) He started the journal of the Cuban Revolutionary

Party ~~during his time in New York.~~ (8) Martí's essays and poems argued

Passionately following up his words with actions, he

for Cuba's freedom and for the individual freedom of Cubans. (9) He died

in battle against Spanish soldiers in Cuba, ~~passionately following up his~~

~~words with actions.~~

21c Combining Sentences

You can also create sentence variety by experimenting with different ways of combining sentences.

Using *-ing* Modifiers

A **modifier** identifies or describes other words in a sentence. You can use an *-ing* modifier to combine two sentences.

TWO SENTENCES	Duke Ellington composed more than a thousand songs. He worked hard to establish his reputation.
COMBINED WITH *-ING* MODIFIER	Composing more than a thousand songs, Duke Ellington worked hard to establish his reputation.

When the two sentences above are combined, the *-ing* modifier (*composing more than a thousand songs*) describes the new sentence's subject (*Duke Ellington*).

Teaching Tip
Tell students that another way to vary sentences is to combine them to create compound and complex sentences. Refer students to Chapters 19 and 20.

Teaching Tip
Remind students to place a comma after a phrase that is introduced by an *-ing* or *-ed* modifier.

Teaching Tip
You may want to introduce students to the term *present participle modifier.*

PRACTICE

21-8 Use an *-ing* modifier to combine each of the following pairs of sentences into a single sentence. Eliminate any unnecessary words, and place a comma after each *-ing* modifier.

Example: Many American colleges are setting an example for the rest of the country. They are going green.

Setting an example for the rest of the country, many American colleges are going green.

1. Special lamps in the dorms of one Ohio college change from green to red. They warn of rising energy use.

Changing from green to red, special lamps in the dorms of one Ohio college warn of

rising energy use.

2. A Vermont college captures methane from dairy cows. It now needs less energy from other sources.

Capturing methane from dairy cows, a Vermont college now needs less energy

from other sources.

3. Student gardeners at a North Carolina college tend a campus vegetable plot. They supply the cafeteria with organic produce.

Tending a campus vegetable plot, student gardeners at a North Carolina college

supply the cafeteria with organic produce.

4. A building on a California campus proves that recycled materials can be beautiful. It is built from redwood wine casks.

Proving that recycled materials can be beautiful, a building on a California campus is

built from redwood wine casks.

5. Some colleges offer courses in sustainability. They are preparing students to take the green revolution beyond campus.

Offering courses in sustainability, some colleges are preparing students to take the

green revolution beyond campus.

PRACTICE

21-9 To complete each of the following sentences, fill in the blank with an appropriate *-ing* modifier. Be sure to punctuate correctly.

Example: *Selling candy door to door,* the team raised money for new uniforms. *Answers will vary.*

1. _____ the judge called for order in the courtroom.

2. _____ the miners found silver instead.

3. _____ migrating birds often travel long distances in the early fall.

4. _____ fans waited patiently to purchase tickets for the rock concert.

5. _____ the child seemed frightened.

PRACTICE

21-10   Complete each of the following sentences by adding an appropriate independent clause after the *-ing* modifier. Be sure to punctuate correctly.

Example: Blasting its siren *, the fire truck raced through the busy* _____

streets.

Answers will vary.

1. Stepping up to home plate _____

_____

2. Traveling at high speeds _____

_____

3. Suffering in the ninety-degree weather _____

_____

4. Looking both ways _____

_____

5. Talking to a group of news reporters _____

_____

Using *-ed* Modifiers

You can also use an *-ed* modifier to combine two sentences.

TWO SENTENCES	Nogales is located on the border between Arizona and Mexico. It is a bilingual city.
COMBINED WITH -ED MODIFIER	Located on the border between Arizona and Mexico, Nogales is a bilingual city.

When the two sentences above are combined, the *-ed* modifier (*located on the border between Arizona and Mexico*) describes the new sentence's subject (*Nogales*).

> **Teaching Tip**
> You may want to introduce students to the term *past participle modifier* and to explain that some past participle modifiers (*taught, known, spent,* and so on) are irregular and do not end in *-ed* or *-d.*

Teaching Tip
Remind students that
modifying phrases should refer
clearly to the words they
describe. Refer them to 28a
and 28b.

Teaching Tip
Tell students that combining
sentences with -ed modifiers
makes their writing more
concise. Refer them to 23b.

PRACTICE

21-11   Use an -ed modifier to combine each of the following pairs of sentences into a single sentence. Eliminate any unnecessary words, and use a comma to set off each -ed modifier. When you are finished, underline the -ed modifier in each sentence.

Example: Potato chips and cornflakes were invented purely by accident. They are two of America's most popular foods.

Invented purely by accident, potato chips and cornflakes are two of America's most

popular foods.

1. George Crum was employed as a chef in a fancy restaurant. He was famous for his french fries.

Employed as a chef in a fancy restaurant, George Crum was famous for his french fries.

2. A customer was dissatisfied with the fries. He complained and asked for thinner fries.

Dissatisfied with the fries, a customer complained and asked for thinner fries.

3. The customer was served thinner fries. He was still not satisfied and complained again.

Served thinner fries, the customer was still not satisfied and complained again.

4. Crum was now very annoyed. He decided to make the fries too thin and crisp to eat with a fork.

Now very annoyed, Crum decided to make the fries too thin and crisp to eat with a fork.

5. The customer was thrilled with the extra-thin and crisp potatoes. He ate them all.

Thrilled with the extra-thin and crisp potatoes, the customer ate them all.

6. Potato chips were invented to get even with a customer. They are the most popular snack food in America today.

Invented to get even with a customer, potato chips are the most popular snack

food in America today.

7. Dr. John Kellogg was concerned about the diet of patients at his hospital. He and his brother set out to make healthy foods.

Concerned about the diet of patients at his hospital, Dr. John Kellogg and his brother

set out to make healthy foods.

8. The brothers were called away on an urgent matter. They left a pot of boiled wheat on the stove.

Called away on an urgent matter, the brothers left a pot of boiled wheat on the stove.

9. The wheat had hardened by the time they returned. It broke into flakes when they rolled it.

   Hardened by the time they returned, the wheat broke into flakes when they rolled it.

10. The brothers were delighted with the results. They came up with a new flake made of corn.

    Delighted with the results, the brothers came up with a new flake made of corn.

PRACTICE
21-12 To complete each of the following sentences, fill in the blank with an appropriate *-ed* modifier. Be sure to punctuate correctly.

Example: _____*Buried for many years,*_____ the treasure was discovered by accident. *Answers will vary.*

1. _____ the child started crying when the storm began.

2. _____ the hikers rested on the rocks at the top of the mountain.

3. _____ the small boat almost sank.

4. _____ the balloons in Macy's Thanksgiving Day parade soared above the crowds.

5. _____ family stories help families keep their traditions alive.

PRACTICE
21-13 Complete each of the following sentences by adding an appropriate independent clause after the -ed modifier. Be sure to punctuate correctly.

Example: Promoted as children's books *, the Harry Potter stories also*

appeal to adults. *Answers will vary.*

1. Annoyed by her parents _____

   _____

2. Abandoned in the woods for three days _____

   _____

3. Bored by the same old routine _____

_____

4. Confronted with the evidence _____

_____

5. Asked whether or not they supported the president _____

_____

Using Compound Subjects or Compound Predicates

A **compound subject** consists of two nouns or pronouns, usually joined by *and*. A **compound predicate** consists of two verbs, usually joined by *and*. You can use a compound subject or a compound predicate to combine two sentences.

TWO SENTENCES	Elijah McCoy was an African-American inventor. Garrett Morgan was also an African-American inventor.
COMBINED WITH COMPOUND SUBJECT	Elijah McCoy and Garrett Morgan were African-American inventors.
TWO SENTENCES	Arundhati Roy's first novel, *The God of Small Things*, appeared in 1997. It won the Pulitzer Prize.
COMBINED WITH COMPOUND PREDICATE	Arundhati Roy's first novel, *The God of Small Things*, appeared in 1997 and won the Pulitzer Prize.

ESL Tip
Offer ESL students a mini-lesson on subject-verb agreement before they begin. Spot-check their work.

PRACTICE
21-14   Combine each of the following pairs of sentences into one sentence by creating a compound subject.

Example: Tattooing has been practiced across times and cultures. Other forms of body art have also been practiced across times and cultures.

Tattooing and other forms of body art have been practiced across times and cultures.

Teaching Tip
Remind students that a compound subject joined by *and* takes a plural verb. Refer them to 26b.

1. In ancient times, "Ötzi the Iceman" had tattoos. Egyptian mummies also had tattoos.

In ancient times, "Ötzi the Iceman" and Egyptian mummies had tattoos.

2. Modern electric machines are a method of tattooing. Sharpened sticks with ink are another method of tattooing.

Modern electric machines and sharpened sticks with ink are methods of tattooing.

3. In recent years, increased interest in tattooing has led to higher-quality tattoos. Improved equipment has also led to much higher-quality tattoos.

In recent years, increased interest in tattooing and improved equipment have led to

higher-quality tattoos.

4. According to surveys, over 30 percent of American adults under thirty have tattoos. About 15 percent of all American adults have tattoos.

According to surveys, over 30 percent of American adults under thirty and about

15 percent of all American adults have tattoos.

5. Tom Leppard, an Englishman in his seventies, is entirely covered by tattoos. Lucky Diamond Rich, a New Zealander in his forties, is also entirely covered by tattoos.

Tom Leppard, an Englishman in his seventies, and Lucky Diamond Rich, a New Zealander

in his forties, are entirely covered by tattoos.

PRACTICE
 Combine each of the following pairs of sentences into a single sentence by creating a compound predicate.

Example: Over the years, many college sports teams have had American Indian nicknames. These teams have used American Indian mascots.

Over the years, many college sports teams have had American Indian nicknames

and have used American Indian mascots.

1. Beginning in the 1960s, American Indian groups objected. They asked teams to change their names and mascots.

Beginning in the 1960s, American Indian groups objected and asked teams to change

their names and mascots.

2. According to some studies, use of these names and mascots creates a negative learning environment for American Indian college students. It can affect their self-esteem.

According to some studies, use of these names and mascots creates a negative learning

environment for American Indian college students and can affect their self-esteem.

3. In 1972, Stanford University changed all its teams' names from the Indians to the Cardinal. It dropped its mascot.

In 1972, Stanford University changed all its teams' names from the Indians to the

Cardinal and dropped its mascot.

4. Many other colleges took similar actions. They found new names and symbols for their teams.

Many other colleges took similar actions and found new names and symbols for

their teams.

5. In 2005, the NCAA listed college teams with potentially offensive mascots and symbols. It banned these mascots and symbols from post-season games.

In 2005, the NCAA listed college teams with potentially offensive mascots and

symbols and banned these mascots and symbols from postseason games.

6. Some people disagree with these actions. They see the teams' use of American Indian names as a sign of admiration rather than negative stereotyping.

Some people disagree with these actions and see the teams' use of American Indian

names as a sign of admiration rather than negative stereotyping.

Teaching Tip
Remind students not to put a comma between the two parts of a compound subject or between the two parts of a compound predicate. Refer them to 34a.

PRACTICE
21-16 Combine each of the following pairs of sentences into one sentence by creating a compound subject or a compound predicate. Remember that a compound subject joined by *and* takes a plural verb.

Example: Valentino Achak Deng overcame an incredibly hard childhood in Marial Bai, Sudan. He is now helping other people in Sudan
              , and
as well as Sudanese Americans. (compound predicate)

(1) During Sudan's civil war, Valentino Achak Deng became separated
        and
from his parents. He wound up in a refugee camp after avoiding soldiers,
land mines, and even lions. (2) He came to the United States as a refugee.
                                        and
He took many jobs to work his way through college. (3) In Atlanta, he met
                                 and
the young novelist Dave Eggers. He asked Eggers to help him write a book
                                            and Eggers
about his life. (4) While working on *What Is the What*, Valentino went
                             and the resulting poverty
to Sudan. ~~Eggers also went to Sudan.~~ (5) War had deprived the children
of Marial Bai of schooling. ~~The resulting poverty, too, had deprived the~~
~~children of schooling.~~ (6) The money from the book goes to a foundation
                   and
started by Valentino. It has already made possible Marial Bai's first high
school—for girls as well as boys. (7) Girls in Sudan usually cannot go to
      but
school. They now have a school that welcomes them.

Teaching Tip
Show students that using a compound subject or a compound predicate to combine two sentences also results in a more concise sentence. Refer them to 23b.

Using Appositives

An **appositive** is a word or word group that identifies, renames, or describes a noun or pronoun. Creating an appositive is often a good way to combine two sentences about the same subject.

TWO SENTENCES   C. J. Walker was the first American woman to become a self-made millionaire. She marketed a line of hair-care products for black women.

COMBINED WITH APPOSITIVE   C. J. Walker, the first American woman to become a self-made millionaire, marketed a line of hair-care products for black women.

In the example above, the appositive appears in the middle of a sentence. However, an appositive can also come at the beginning or at the end of a sentence.

The first American woman to become a self-made millionaire, C. J. Walker marketed a line of hair-care products for black women. (appositive at the beginning)

Several books have been written about C. J. Walker, the first American woman to become a self-made millionaire. (appositive at the end)

PRACTICE

21-17   Combine each of the following pairs of sentences into one sentence by creating an appositive. Note that the appositive may appear at the beginning, in the middle, or at the end of the sentence. Be sure to use commas appropriately.

Example: On Friday, I will take my car to Joe's Garage, Joe's is a shop that replaces mufflers.

Answers may vary.

1. The iPhone is a product released by Apple in 2007, It is not only a phone but also a camera, a multimedia player, and a Web browser.

2. Canada's Edmonton Corn Maze, is one of the largest mazes in North America, It covers fifteen acres of ground and usually takes visitors an hour to complete.

3. After retiring from British soccer, David Beckham joined a U.S. team, That team is the LA Galaxy.

4. *A native of Benin,* Angélique Kidjo sings in several different languages, including French, English, Yoruba, and Fon. She is a native of Benin.

5. Stepping outside for a cigarette is an activity that used to be acceptable at most workplaces, It is now being banned by many companies.

PRACTICE

21-18 Combine each of the following pairs of sentences into one sentence by creating an appositive. Note that the appositive may appear at the beginning, in the middle, or at the end of the sentence. Be sure to use commas appropriately.

Example: *Wikipedia* is a popular online information source, It is

available in more than two hundred languages.
Answers may vary.

(1) *Wikipedia* is one of the largest reference sites on the Web, It is
A
different from other encyclopedias in many ways. (2) This site is a constant
, this site
work-in-progress, It allows anyone to add, change, or correct informa-

tion in its articles. (3) For this reason, researchers have to be careful when

using information from *Wikipedia*, *Wikipedia* is a source that may contain

factual errors. (4) The older articles are the ones that have been edited and

corrected the most, These often contain the most trustworthy informa-

tion. (5) Despite some drawbacks, *Wikipedia* has many notable advantages,
, including
These advantages include free and easy access, up-to-date information,

and protection from author bias.

Teaching Tip
Remind students that most instructors will not permit them to use *Wikipedia* as a research source.

Teaching Tip
Explain to students that an appositive can be introduced by a word or phrase like *including* or *such as*.

21d Mixing Long and Short Sentences

Teaching Tip
For information on creating compound and complex sentences, refer students to Chapters 19 and 20.

A paragraph of short, choppy sentences—or a paragraph of long, rambling sentences—can be monotonous. By mixing long and short sentences, perhaps combining some simple sentences to create **compound** and **complex** sentences, you can create a more interesting paragraph.

In the following paragraph, the sentences are all short, and the result is boring and hard to follow.

> The world's first drive-in movie theater opened on June 6, 1933. This drive-in was in Camden, New Jersey. Automobiles became more popular. Drive-ins did too. By the 1950s, there were more than four thousand drive-ins in the United States. Over the years, the high cost of land led to a decline in the number of drive-ins. So did the rising popularity of television. Soon, the drive-in movie theater had almost disappeared. It was replaced by the multiplex. In 1967, there were forty-six drive-ins in New Jersey. Today, only one is still open. That one is the Delsea Drive-in in Vineland, New Jersey.

The revised paragraph that follows is more interesting and easier to read. (Note that the final short sentence is retained for emphasis.)

The world's first drive-in movie theater opened on June 6, 1933, in Camden, New Jersey. As automobiles became more popular, drive-ins did too, and by the 1950s, there were more than four thousand drive-ins in the United States. Over the years, the high cost of land and the rising popularity of television led to a decline in the number of drive-ins. Soon, the drive-in movie theater had almost disappeared, replaced by the multiplex. In 1967, there were forty-six drive-ins in New Jersey, but today, only one is still open. That one is the Delsea Drive-in in Vineland, New Jersey.

PRACTICE

21-19 The following paragraph contains a series of short, choppy sentences that can be combined. Revise the paragraph so that it mixes long and short sentences. Be sure to use commas and other punctuation appropriately.

Example: Kente cloth has special significance for many African
    , but some
Americans. ~~Some~~ other people do not understand this significance.
    Answers will vary.

                                                    and
(1) Kente cloth is made in western Africa. ~~(2) It is~~ produced primarily
    , *who*
by the Ashanti people. (3) It has been worn for hundreds of years by African
royalty. ~~(4) They~~ consider it a sign of power and status. (5) Many African
                                        because they
Americans wear kente cloth. ~~(6) They~~ see it as a link to their heritage.
                                            , *and each*
(7) Each pattern on the cloth has a name. ~~(8) Each~~ color has a special
significance. (9) For example, red and yellow suggest a long and healthy
    while green   *Although*
life. ~~(10) Green~~ and white suggest a good harvest. (11) African women may
wear kente cloth as a dress or head wrap. ~~(12)~~ African-American women,
like men, usually wear strips of cloth around their shoulders. (13) Men and
                                                            ; *in fact, it*
women of African descent wear kente cloth as a sign of racial pride. ~~(14) It~~
often decorates college students' gowns at graduation.

TEST · Revise · Edit

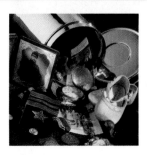

Look back at your response to the Write First activity on page 371. TEST what you have written. Then, using the strategies discussed in this chapter that seem appropriate, revise your writing so that your sentences are varied, interesting, and smoothly connected. Finally, edit your work.

EDITING PRACTICE

The following student essay lacks sentence variety. All of its sentences begin with the subject, and the essay includes a number of short, choppy sentences. Using the strategies discussed in this chapter, revise the essay to achieve greater sentence variety. The first sentence has been edited for you. *Answers will vary.*

Toys by Accident

Many popular toys and games are the result of accidents. *when people* ~~People~~ try to invent one thing but discover something else instead. Sometimes they are not trying to invent anything at all. *and* ~~They~~ are completely surprised to find a new product.

Play-Doh is one example of an accidental discovery. *, a popular preschool toy,* Play-Doh ~~is a popular preschool toy~~. Play-Doh first appeared in Cincinnati. *where a* ~~A~~ company made a compound to clean wallpaper. *and* ~~They~~ sold it as a cleaning product. The company then realized that this compound could be a toy. *Molding* ~~Children could mold~~ it like clay. *, children* ~~They~~ could use it again and again. The new toy was an immediate hit. Play-Doh was first sold in 1956. *Since* ~~Since~~ then, more than two billion cans of ~~Play-Doh~~ have been sold.

Play-Doh

The Slinky was discovered by Richard James. *He* was an engineer. At the time, he was trying to invent a spring to keep ships' instruments steady at sea. *Although he* ~~He~~ tested hundreds of springs of varying sizes, metals, and tensions. *, none* ~~None~~ of them worked. One spring fell off the desk and "walked" down a pile of books. *, and* ~~It~~ went end over end onto the floor. *Thinking* ~~He thought~~ his children might enjoy playing with it. *James* took the spring home. They loved it. Every child in the neighborhood wanted one. *When the* ~~The~~ first Slinky was demonstrated at Gimbel's Department Store in Philadelphia in 1945. *, all* ~~All~~ four hundred Slinkys were sold within ninety minutes. *Simple* ~~The Slinky is simple~~ and inexpensive. *, the* ~~The~~ Slinky is still popular with children today.

Slinky

The Frisbee was also discovered by accident. According to one story, a group of Yale University students were eating pies from a local bakery. *Frisbies,* ~~The bakery was called Frisbies~~. *After they* ~~They~~ finished eating the pies. *, they* ~~They~~ started throwing the empty pie tins around. A carpenter in California made a plastic version, *and* He called it the Pluto Platter. The Wham-O company bought the patent on the product, *and* Wham-o renamed it the Frisbee after the bakery. This is how the Frisbee came to be.

Some new toys are not developed by toy companies. Play-Doh, the Frisbee, and the Slinky are examples of very popular toys that were discovered by accident. Play-Doh started as a cleaning product, *, the* The Slinky was discovered by an engineer who was trying to invent something else, *, and the* The Frisbee was invented by students having fun. *Discovered* The toys were discovered unexpectedly, *, all* All three toys have become classics.

Frisbee

COLLABORATIVE ACTIVITIES

1. Read the following list of sentences. Working in a small group, change one sentence to a question and one to an exclamation. Then, add adverbs or prepositional phrases at the beginning of several of the sentences in the list.

   Many well-known African-American writers left the United States in the years following World War II.
   Many went to Paris.
   Richard Wright was a novelist.
   He wrote *Native Son* and *Black Boy.*
   He wrote *Uncle Tom's Children.*
   He left the United States for Paris in 1947.
   James Baldwin wrote *Another Country, The Fire Next Time,* and *Giovanni's Room.*
   He also wrote essays.
   He came to Paris in 1948.
   Chester Himes was a detective story writer.
   He arrived in Paris in 1953.
   William Gardner Smith was a novelist and journalist.
   He also left the United States for Paris.
   These expatriates found Paris more hospitable than America.
   They also found it less racist.

2. Continuing to work in your group, use the strategies discussed and illustrated in 21c and 21d to help you combine the sentences on the list above into a varied and interesting paragraph. (You may keep the sentences in the order in which they appear.)

3. When your group's revisions are complete, trade paragraphs with another group and further edit the other group's paragraph to improve sentence variety and coherence.

review checklist

Writing Varied Sentences

☐ Vary sentence types. (See 21a.)

☐ Vary sentence openings. (See 21b.)

☐ Combine sentences. (See 21c.)

☐ Mix long and short sentences. (See 21d.)

22 Using Parallelism

preview

In this chapter, you will learn to
- recognize parallel structure (22a)
- use parallel structure (22b)

write first

This picture shows a green market in an urban neighborhood, part of a growing trend that many people think is making U.S. cities more livable. Write a paragraph or essay discussing three positive things about your own neighborhood, school, or workplace. Support your statements with specific examples.

22a Recognizing Parallel Structure

Parallelism is the use of matching words, phrases, clauses, and sentence structure to highlight similar ideas in a sentence. When you use parallelism, you are telling readers that certain ideas are related. By repeating similar grammatical patterns to express similar ideas, you create sentences that are clearer, more concise, and easier to read.

In the following examples, the parallel sentences highlight similar ideas; the other sentences do not.

PARALLEL	NOT PARALLEL
Please leave <u>your name</u>, <u>your number</u>, and <u>your message</u>.	Please leave <u>your name</u>, <u>your number</u>, and <u>you should also leave a message</u>.
I plan to <u>graduate</u> from high school and <u>become</u> a nurse.	I plan to <u>graduate</u> from high school, and then <u>becoming</u> a nurse would be a good idea.
The grass was <u>soft</u>, <u>green</u>, and <u>sweet smelling</u>.	The grass was <u>soft</u>, <u>green</u>, and <u>the smell was sweet</u>.
<u>Making the team</u> was one thing; <u>staying on it</u> was another.	<u>Making the team</u> was one thing, but it was very difficult <u>to stay on it</u>.
<u>We can register</u> for classes in person, or <u>we can register</u> by email.	<u>We can register</u> for classes in person, or <u>registering</u> by email is another option.

PRACTICE

22-1 In the following sentences, decide whether the underlined words and phrases are parallel. If so, write *P* in the blank. If not, rewrite the sentences so that the underlined ideas are presented in parallel terms.

Examples: The missing dog had <u>brown fur</u>, <u>a red collar</u>, and <u>a long tail</u>. ____*P*____

Signs of drug abuse in teenagers include <u>falling grades</u>, <u>mood swings</u>, and ~~<u>they lose</u>~~ weight ^*loss.* /_____

1. The food in the cafeteria is <u>varied</u>, <u>tasty</u>, and <u>it is healthy</u>. _____

2. Do you want the job done <u>quickly</u>, or do you want it done <u>well</u>? ____*P*____

3. Last summer <u>I worked at the library</u>, <u>babysat for my neighbor's daughter</u>, *volunteered at a soup kitchen.* and ^~~<u>there was a soup kitchen where I volunteered</u>~~. _____

4. Pandas eat bamboo leaves, and ~~eucalyptus leaves are eaten by koalas~~. *(koalas eat)* _____

5. Skydiving is frightening but fun. ___P___

6. A number of interesting people work at the co-op with me, including an elderly German man, ~~there is~~ a middle-aged Chinese woman, and a teenaged Mexican boy. _____

7. The bell rang, and the students stood up. ___P___

8. To conserve energy while I was away, I unplugged the television, closed the curtains, and ~~the thermostat was set~~ at 65 degrees. *(set)* _____

9. I put away the dishes; will you put away the laundry? ___P___

10. For several weeks after the storm, the supermarkets had no eggs, ~~they were out of milk~~, and ~~they did not have any~~ bread. *(or)* _____

22b Using Parallel Structure

Parallel structure is especially important in *paired items, items in a series,* and *items in a list or outline.*

Teaching Tip
Remind students that many everyday writing tasks require parallelism. For example, items listed on a résumé should be in parallel form.

Paired Items

Use parallel structure when you connect ideas with a **coordinating conjunction**—*and, but, for, nor, or, so,* and *yet.*

> George believes in doing a good job and minding his own business.

> You can pay me now or pay me later.

You should also use parallel structure for paired items joined by *both . . . and, not only . . . but also, either . . . or, neither . . . nor,* and *rather . . . than.*

> Jan is both skilled in writing and fluent in French.

> The group's new recording not only has a dance beat but also has thought-provoking lyrics.

> I'd rather eat one worm by itself than eat five worms with ice cream.

Items in a Series

Use parallel structure for items in a series—words, phrases, or clauses. (Be sure to use commas to separate three or more items in a series. Never put a comma after the final item.)

Teaching Tip
Refer students to 34a for more on punctuating items in a series.

> Every Wednesday I have English, math, and psychology. (three words)

Increased demand, <u>high factory output</u>, and <u>a strong dollar</u> will help the economy. (three phrases)

She is a champion because she <u>stays in excellent physical condition</u>, <u>puts in long hours of practice</u>, and <u>has an intense desire to win</u>. (three clauses)

Items in a List or in an Outline

Use parallel structure for items in a numbered or bulleted list.

There are three reasons to open an Individual Retirement Account (IRA):
1. To save money
2. To reduce taxes
3. To be able to retire

Use parallel structure for the elements in an outline.

A. Types of rocks
 1. Igneous
 2. Sedimentary
 3. Metamorphic

Teaching Tip
Practice 22-2 works well as a test and is quick and easy to grade. You may want to save this exercise for the end of the chapter.

PRACTICE

22-2 Fill in the blanks in the following sentences with parallel words, phrases, or clauses of your own that make sense in context.

Example: At the lake, we can _____*go for a swim*_____, _____*paddle a canoe*_____, and _____*play volleyball*_____.
Answers will vary.

1. When I get too little sleep, I am _____, _____, and _____.

2. I am good at _____ but not at _____.

3. My ideal mate is _____ and _____.

4. I personally define success not only as _____ but also as _____.

5. I use my computer for both _____ and _____.

6. I like _____ and _____.

7. You need three qualities to succeed in college: _____, _____, and _____.

8. I enjoy not only _____ but also _____.

9. I would rather _____ than _____.

10. Football _____, but baseball _____.

Teaching Tip
Remind students to use commas to separate three or more items in a series.

**PRACTICE
22-3** Rewrite the following sentences so that matching ideas are presented in parallel terms. Add punctuation as needed.

Example: Some experts believe homework is harmful to learning, and also it is harmful to children's health and to family life.

Some experts believe homework is harmful to learning, to children's health,

and to family life.

Answers may vary.

1. Experts who object to homework include Dorothy Rich and Harris Cooper, and another expert, Alfie Kohn, also objects to homework.

   Experts who object to homework include Dorothy Rich, Harris Cooper, and

   Alfie Kohn.

2. Harris Cooper of Duke University says that middle school students do not benefit from more than one and a half hours of homework, and more than two hours of homework does not benefit high school students.

   Harris Cooper of Duke University says that middle school students do not

   benefit from more than one and a half hours of homework and that high school

   students do not benefit from more than two hours of homework.

3. In his book *The Homework Myth*, Alfie Kohn says that homework creates family conflict, and stress is also created in children.

   In his book The Homework Myth, Alfie Kohn says that homework creates both family

   conflict and stress in children.

4. Kohn suggests that children could do other things after school to develop their bodies and minds, and they could also do some things to develop their family relationships.

   Kohn suggests that children could do other things after school to develop their

   bodies, minds, and family relationships.

5. Kohn believes that instead of doing homework, children could interview parents about family history and also chemistry could be learned through cooking.

   Kohn believes that instead of doing homework, children could interview parents

   about family history and learn about chemistry through cooking.

6. Harris Cooper advises that homework should take a short amount of time and should advance learning and also reading skills should be promoted.

Harris Cooper advises that homework should take a short amount of time,

advance learning, and promote reading skills.

_____

7. There seems to be no relationship between the amount of homework assigned and students are getting lower test scores.

There seems to be no relationship between the amount of homework assigned

and students' lower test scores.

8. For example, students in countries that assign less homework, such as Japan and Denmark, score higher on achievement tests than American students, and the Czech Republic does too.

For example, students in countries that assign less homework, such as Japan,

Denmark, and the Czech Republic, score higher on achievement tests than

American students.

9. Students in countries that assign more homework, such as Greece and Thailand, score lower on achievement tests than American students; in Iran, they also assign more homework.

Students in countries that assign more homework, such as Greece, Thailand, and

Iran, score lower on achievement tests than American students.

_____

10. All critics of homework agree that elementary school students receive too much homework, middle school students receive too much homework, and too much homework is done by high school students.

All critics of homework agree that elementary school, middle school, and high school

students receive too much homework.

_____

ESL Tip
Spot-check the writing of individual ESL students for parallel sentence constructions.

TEST · Revise · Edit

Look back at your response to the Write First activity on page 391. TEST what you have written. Then, revise and edit your work, checking carefully to make sure you used parallel structure to highlight similar ideas or items in your sentences. If you used parallel structure to present three or more items in a series, make sure you used commas to separate the items.

EDITING PRACTICE

Read the following student essay, which contains examples of faulty parallelism. Identify the sentences you think need to be corrected, and make the changes required to achieve parallelism. Be sure to supply all words necessary for clarity, grammar, and sense. Add punctuation as needed. The first error has been edited for you. *Answers will vary.*

Self-Made Men and Women Helping Others

Many self-made people go from poverty to ~~achieving~~ success. Quite a few of them not only achieve such success but also ~~they~~ help others. Three of these people are Oprah Winfrey, Alfredo Quiñones-Hinojosa, and Geoffrey Canada. Their lives are very different, but all possess great strength, *determination,* ~~being determined,~~ and concern for others.

Oprah is one of the most influential people in the world*,* and ~~she has more money than almost anyone in the world.~~ *one of the wealthiest.* She came from a very poor family. First, she lived with her grandmother on a Mississippi farm, and then *she lived with* her mother in Milwaukee. During this time she was abused by several relatives. When she was thirteen, she was sent to Nashville to live with her father. He used strict discipline, and *he* ~~she~~ was taught *her* ~~by him~~ to value education. Through her own determination and *ambition,* ~~because she was ambitious,~~ Winfrey got a job at a local broadcasting company. This started her career. However, Oprah was not satisfied with being successful. Through Oprah's Angel Network and the Oprah Winfrey Leadership Academy, she helps others and *makes* ~~making~~ the world a better place.

Today, Alfredo Quiñones-Hinojosa is a top brain surgeon and *conducts* ~~conducting~~ research on new ways to treat brain cancer. At age nineteen, he was an illegal immigrant from Mexico, worked in the fields, and *did not know* ~~without~~ any English. When he told his cousin he wanted to learn English and get a better job, his cousin told him he was crazy. Then, while a welder on a railroad crew, he fell into an empty petroleum tank and was almost *died* ~~dying~~ from the fumes. However, Alfredo overcame these hardships. He enrolled in a community college, and with determination and by

Oprah Winfrey

Alfredo Quiñones-Hinojosa

397

work
working hard, he began to change his life. He won a scholarship to Berkeley, went
wound
on to medical school at Harvard, and eventually winding up as director of the
brain tumor program at Johns Hopkins University. In 1997, he became a citizen of
the United States. At each step of the way, he has made a special effort to reach
out to students from low-income backgrounds and to inspire others.

Geoffrey Canada grew up in a New York City neighborhood that was poor,
violent.
dangerous, and where violence was not uncommon. His mother was a single parent
who struggled to support Geoffrey and his three brothers. Geoffrey learned to
survive on the streets, but he also studied a lot in school. Thanks to this hard work,
he won a scholarship to college in Maine and went on to a career in education.
deciding
Deciding to leave his neighborhood in New York wasn't hard, but to decide to come
back wasn't hard either. He wanted to help children in poor families to succeed in
to
school and so they could have better lives. With this in mind, he started the Harlem
Children's Zone (HCZ). HCZ includes (1) workshops for parents, (2) a preschool and
three charter schools, and (3) running health programs for children and families.
President Obama has said he would like to see more programs like HCZ.

Oprah Winfrey, Alfredo Quiñones-Hinojosa, and Geoffrey Canada have very
in education.
different careers—in entertainment, in medicine, and educating children.
However, all three overcame great adversity, all three have achieved enormous
success, and they have helped others. They have helped their communities, their
country, and have contributed to the world.

COLLABORATIVE ACTIVITIES

1. Working in a group, list three or four qualities that you associate with
   each word in the following pairs.

   Brothers/sisters
   Teachers/students
   Parents/children
   City/country
   Fast food/organic food
   Movies/TV shows
   Work/play

2. Write a compound sentence comparing each of the preceding pairs of words. Use a coordinating conjunction to join the clauses, and make sure each sentence uses clear parallel structure, mentions both words, and includes the qualities you listed for the words in Collaborative Activity 1.

Answers will vary.

3. Choose the three best sentences your group has written for Collaborative Activity 2. Assign one student from each group to write these sentences on the board so the entire class can read them. The class can then decide which sentences use parallelism most effectively.

review checklist

Using Parallelism

- [ ] Use matching words, phrases, clauses, and sentence structure to highlight similar items or ideas. (See 22a.)

- [ ] Use parallel structure with paired items. (See 22b.)

- [ ] Use parallel structure for items in a series. (See 22b.)

- [ ] Use parallel structure for items in a list or outline. (See 22b.)

23 Using Words Effectively

write first

This picture shows a house on the island of Bermuda. Look the house over carefully, and then describe *your* dream house. Would it resemble the house in the picture, or would it be different? How? What would be inside the house? Be as specific as possible.

23a   Using Specific Words

Specific words refer to particular people, places, things, ideas, or qualities. **General words** refer to entire classes or groups. Sentences that contain specific words are more precise and vivid than those that contain only general words.

SENTENCES WITH GENERAL WORDS	SENTENCES WITH SPECIFIC WORDS
While walking in the woods, I saw an <u>animal</u>.	While walking in the woods, I saw a <u>baby skunk</u>.
<u>Someone</u> decided to run for Congress.	<u>Rebecca</u> decided to run for Congress.
<u>Weapons</u> are responsible for many murders.	<u>Unregistered handguns</u> are responsible for many murders.
Denise bought new <u>clothes</u>.	Denise bought a new <u>blue dress</u>.
I really enjoyed my <u>meal</u>.	I really enjoyed my <u>pepperoni pizza with extra cheese</u>.
Darrell had always wanted a <u>classic car</u>.	Darrell had always wanted a <u>black 1969 Chevrolet Camaro</u>.

Teaching Tip
Put a sentence on the board (for example, *The man was injured in an accident involving a shark.*), and have students work as a team to make the sentence more specific and concrete. Asking students to write a news story about the sentence usually results in excellent paragraphs.

FYI

Using Specific Words

One way to strengthen your writing is to avoid general words like *good, nice,* or *great.* Take the time to think of more specific words. For example, when you say the ocean looked *pretty,* do you really mean that it *sparkled, glistened, rippled, foamed, surged,* or *billowed*?

Teaching Tip
Warn students that the synonyms they see listed in a thesaurus almost never have precisely the same meanings. For example, ask students to discuss the differences in meaning of the words in this FYI box.

PRACTICE

23-1   In the following passage, underline the specific words that help you imagine the scene the writer describes. The first sentence has been done for you.

Last summer, I spent three weeks backpacking through <u>the remote rural province of Yunnan in China</u>. One day, I came across four farm women playing a <u>game of mahjong</u> on a <u>patch of muddy ground</u>. Squatting on <u>rough wooden stools</u> around a <u>faded green folding table</u>, the women picked up and discarded <u>the smooth ivory</u> mahjong tiles as if they were playing cards. In the <u>grassy field</u> around them, their <u>chestnut-colored horses</u> grazed with <u>heavy red and black market bags</u> tied to their backs. <u>A veil of shimmering white fog</u> hung over a nearby hill, and one woman sat under a <u>black umbrella</u> to shelter herself from the sun. A fifth woman watched, with her <u>wrinkled hands</u> on her hips and a <u>frown</u> on her face. The only sound was <u>the sharp click</u> of the tiles and <u>the soft musical talk</u> of the women as they played.

ESL Tip
Nonnative speakers often have trouble with adjective order. Explain why they should write *The <u>tall</u>, <u>slender</u> man drove away in a <u>shiny</u> <u>new</u> car.* Refer them to 33k.

PRACTICE

23-2 In the blank beside each of the five general words below, write a more specific word. Then, use the more specific word in an original sentence.

Example: child _____six-year-old_____

All through dinner, my six-year-old chattered excitedly about his first

day of school.

Answers will vary.

1. emotion _____

_____

_____

2. building _____

_____

_____

3. said _____

_____

_____

4. animal _____

_____

_____

5. went _____

_____

_____

PRACTICE

23-3 The following one-paragraph job-application letter uses many general words. Rewrite the paragraph, substituting specific words and adding details where necessary. Start by making the first sentence, which identifies the job, more specific: for example, "I would like to apply for the <u>dental technician</u> position you advertised on <u>March 15 in the *Post*</u>." Then, add information about your background and qualifications. Expand the original paragraph into a three-paragraph letter.

I would like to apply for the position you advertised in today's paper. I graduated from high school and am currently attending college. I have taken several courses that have prepared me for the duties the position requires. I also have several personal qualities that I think you would find useful in a person holding this position. In addition, I have had certain experiences that qualify me for such a job. I would appreciate the opportunity to meet with you to discuss your needs as an employer. Thank you.

23b Using Concise Language

Concise language says what it has to say in as few words as possible. Too often, writers use words and phrases that add nothing to a sentence's meaning. A good way to test a sentence for these words is to see if crossing them out changes the sentence's meaning. If the sentence's meaning does not change, you can assume that the words you crossed out are unnecessary.

~~It is clear that the~~ *The* United States was not ready to fight World War II.

~~In order to~~ *To* follow the plot, you must make an outline.

Sometimes you can replace several unnecessary words with a single word.

~~Due to the fact that~~ *Because* I was tired, I missed my first class.

FYI

Using Concise Language

The following wordy phrases add nothing to a sentence. You can usually delete or condense them with no loss of meaning.

WORDY	CONCISE
It is clear that	(delete)
It is a fact that	(delete)
The reason is because	Because
The reason is that	Because
It is my opinion that	I think/I believe
Due to the fact that	Because
Despite the fact that	Although
At the present time	Today/Now
At that time	Then
In most cases	Usually
In order to	To
In the final analysis	Finally
Subsequent to	After

Unnecessary repetition—saying the same thing twice for no reason—can also make your writing wordy. When you revise, delete repeated words and phrases that add nothing to your sentences.

My instructor told me the book was ~~old-fashioned and~~ outdated. (An old-fashioned book *is* outdated.)

The ~~terrible~~ tragedy of the fire could have been avoided. (A tragedy is *always* terrible.)

Teaching Tip Point out that a short sentence is not necessarily a concise sentence. A sentence is concise when it contains only the words needed to convey its ideas.

Teaching Tip Encourage students to avoid flowery language and complicated sentences. Good writing is clear and concise.

PRACTICE

23-4   To make the following sentences more concise, eliminate any unnecessary repetition, and delete or condense wordy expressions.

Example: ~~It is a fact that each individual~~ ^Each^ production of *Sesame*

Street around the world is geared toward the local children ~~in that~~

~~region.~~ *Answers will vary.*

(1) ~~In order to~~ ^To^ meet the needs of international children ~~all over the~~

~~world,~~ Sesame Workshop helps produce versions of its popular show

Sesame Street in other countries ~~outside the United States.~~ (2) ~~Due to the~~

~~fact that~~ ^Because^ each country has different issues ~~and concerns,~~ the content of

these shows varies. (3) ~~In most cases,~~ ^Usually,^ the producers focus on ~~and con-~~

~~centrate on~~ the cultural diversity in their country. (4) ~~In order to~~ ^To^ develop

the most appropriate material for their shows, producers also consult

with ~~and talk to~~ local educators and child development experts, ~~people who~~

~~are experts in the field.~~ (5) ~~At the present time,~~ ^Today,^ versions of *Sesame Street*

exist in a wide variety of ~~places and~~ countries. They include Mexico, Russia,

South Africa, Bangladesh, and Egypt. (6) Created in 1972, Mexico's *Plaza*

Sésamo is one of the oldest international versions, ~~having been around~~

~~longer than versions in other countries.~~ (7) This Spanish-language show

includes ~~and brings in familiar and~~ well-known characters like Elmo and

Cookie Monster as well as ~~unique and~~ original characters like Abelardo

and Pancho. (8) Like all versions of *Sesame Street*, *Plaza Sésamo*'s main

~~and most important~~ focus is on ~~educating and~~ teaching children about

letters, numbers, and the diverse world around them.

Teaching Tip
Discuss the importance of
knowing the intended audience. In college, the audience
for student writing is usually a
professor. Slang, texting, and
IM languages are not suitable
for such an audience.

23c   Avoiding Slang

Slang is nonstandard language that calls attention to itself. It is usually
associated with a particular social group—computer users or teenagers,
for example. Often, it is used for emphasis or to produce a surprising or
original effect. Because it is very informal, slang is not acceptable in your
college writing.

My psychology exam was really ~~sweet.~~ _easy._

On the weekends, I like to ~~chill~~ _relax_ and watch movies on my laptop.

If you have any question about whether a term is slang or not, look it up in a dictionary. If the term is identified as _slang_ or _informal_, find a more suitable term.

FYI

Avoiding Abbreviations and Shorthand

While abbreviations and shorthand such as _LOL, BTW, IMO,_ and _2day_ are acceptable in informal electronic communication, they are not acceptable in your college writing, in emails to your instructors, or in online class discussions.

In my opinion,
~~IMO~~ your essay needs a strong thesis statement.

you   _today._
I would like to meet with ~~u~~ for a conference ~~2day.~~

PRACTICE
23-5 Edit the following sentences, replacing the slang expressions with clearer, more precise words and phrases.

yelled at me
Example: My father ~~lost it~~ when I told him I crashed the car.

Answers will vary.
                    upset,
1. Whenever I get ~~bummed,~~ I go outside and jog.

                                        exhausted.
2. Tonight I'll have to leave by 11 because I'm ~~wiped out.~~

   I don't like
3. ~~I'm not into~~ movies or television.

                                        get me angry.
4. Whenever we argue, my boyfriend knows how to ~~push my buttons.~~

   was   lucky
5. I really ~~lucked out~~ when I got this job.

23d Avoiding Clichés

Clichés are expressions—such as "easier said than done" and "last but not least"—that have been used so often that they have lost their meaning. These worn-out expressions get in the way of clear communication.

When you identify a cliché in your writing, replace it with a direct statement—or, if possible, with a fresher expression.

CLICHÉ   When school was over, she felt ~~free as a bird~~.

                              seriously ill
CLICHÉ   These days, you have to be ~~sick as a dog~~ before you are

admitted to a hospital.

ESL Tip
Every culture uses clichés. You may ask your ESL students to translate some native expressions for the class.

Teaching Tip
Ask students for other examples of overused expressions. Write these ideas on the board, and have students think of more original or more direct ways of expressing them.

FYI

Avoiding Clichés

Here are examples of some clichés you should avoid in your writing.

back in the day	play God
better late than never	pushing the envelope
beyond a shadow of a doubt	raining cats and dogs
break the ice	selling like hotcakes
cutting edge	the bottom line
face the music	think outside the box
give 110 percent	touched base
hard as a rock	tried and true
it goes without saying	water under the bridge
keep your eye on the ball	what goes around comes around

PRACTICE

23-6 Cross out any clichés in the following sentences. Then, either substitute a fresher expression or restate the idea more directly.

                                                                free of financial worries
Example: Lottery winners often think they will be ~~on easy street~~ for
                                                              ^

the rest of their lives. *Answers will vary.*

(1) Many people think that a million-dollar lottery jackpot allows the
                                    long hours   *a comfortable life.*
winner to stop working ~~like a dog~~ and start living ~~high on the hog.~~ (2) ~~All~~
                              ^   *In fact,*   ^
~~things considered,~~ however, the reality for lottery winners is quite differ-
                ^   *win big prizes*
ent. (3) For one thing, lottery winners who ~~hit the jackpot~~ do not always
                                              ^
receive their winnings all at once; instead, yearly payments—for example,

$50,000—can be paid out over twenty years. (4) Of that $50,000 a year,
                                                            winner
close to $20,000 goes to taxes and anything else the ~~lucky stiff~~ already owes
                                                        ^
the government, such as student loans. (5) Next come relatives and friends
who ask for money,   *with difficult choices to make.*
~~with their hands out,~~ leaving winners ~~between a rock and a hard place.~~
^   *give*   ^   *lose the friendship of*
(6) They can either ~~cough up~~ gifts and loans or ~~wave bye-bye~~ to many
                      ^   *Even worse,*   ^
of their loved ones. (7) ~~Adding insult to injury,~~ many lottery winners lose
                                    ^
their jobs because employers think that, now that they are "millionaires,"

they no longer need to draw a salary. (8) Many lottery winners wind up
                      seriously   *Faced with financial difficulties,*
~~way over their heads~~ in debt within a few years. (9) ~~In their hour of need,~~
^   ^

many might like to sell their future payments to companies that offer

lump-sum payments of forty to forty-five cents on the dollar. (10) This is

usually impossible,
~~easier said than done,~~ however, because most state lotteries do not allow
   ^

winners to sell their winnings.

23e   Using Similes and Metaphors

A **simile** is a comparison of two unlike things that uses *like* or *as*.

> His arm hung at his side <u>like</u> a broken branch.
> He was <u>as</u> content <u>as</u> a cat napping on a windowsill.

A **metaphor** is a comparison of two unlike things that does not use *like* or *as*.

> Invaders from another world, the dandelions conquered my garden.
> He was a beast of burden, hauling cement from the mixer to the building site.

The force of similes and metaphors comes from the surprise of seeing two seemingly unlike things being compared. Used in moderation, similes and metaphors can make your writing more lively and more interesting.

PRACTICE

23-7   Use your imagination to complete each of the following items by creating three original similes.

Example: A boring class is like _____*toast without jam.*_____

_____*a four-hour movie.*_____

_____*a bedtime story.*_____

Answers will vary.

1. A good friend is like _____

_____

_____

2. A thunderstorm is like _____

_____

_____

3. A workout at the gym is like _____

_____

_____

PRACTICE

23-8   Think of a person you know well. Using that person as your subject, fill in each of the following blanks to create metaphors. Try to complete each metaphor with more than a single word, as in the example.

    Example: If ____*my baby sister*____ were an animal, ___*she*___ would be

____*a curious little kitten.*____

Answers will vary.

1. If _____ were a musical instrument, _____ would be _____

_____

2. If _____ were a food, _____ would be _____

_____

3. If _____ were a means of transportation, _____ would be _____

_____

4. If _____ were a natural phenomenon, _____ would be _____

_____

5. If _____ were a toy, _____ would be _____

_____

23f Avoiding Sexist Language

Sexist language refers to men and women in insulting terms. Sexist language is not just words like *stud* or *babe,* which many people find objectionable. It can also be words or phrases that unnecessarily call attention to gender or that suggest a job or profession is held only by a man (or only by a woman) when it actually is not.

You can avoid sexist language by being sensitive and using a little common sense. There is always an acceptable nonsexist alternative for a sexist term.

SEXIST	NONSEXIST
man, mankind	humanity, humankind, the human race
businessman	executive, businessperson
fireman, policeman, mailman	firefighter, police officer, letter carrier
male nurse, woman engineer	nurse, engineer
congressman	member of Congress, representative
stewardess, steward	flight attendant
man and wife	man and woman, husband and wife
manmade	synthetic
chairman	chair, chairperson
anchorwoman, anchorman	anchor
actor, actress	actor

Teaching Tip
Point out that, in addition to avoiding sexist language, students should avoid potentially offensive references to a person's age, physical condition, or sexual orientation.

Teaching Tip
Refer students to 31e for more on subjects like *everyone* (indefinite pronoun antecedents).

FYI

Avoiding Sexist Language

Do not use *he* when your subject could be either male or female.

SEXIST Everyone should complete his assignment by next week.

You can correct this problem in three ways.

- *Use* he or she *or* his or her.

  Everyone should complete his or her assignment by next week.

- *Use plural forms.*

  Students should complete their assignments by next week.

- *Eliminate the pronoun.*

  Everyone should complete the assignment by next week.

**PRACTICE
23-9** Edit the following sentences to eliminate sexist language.

or her (or omit "his")

Example: A doctor should be honest with his patients.

Answers will vary.

police officers

1. Many people today would like to see more policemen patrolling the streets.

2. The attorneys representing the plaintiff are Geraldo Diaz and ~~Mrs.~~ Barbara Wilkerson.

3. ~~Every~~ *All the* soldier picked up *their* ~~his~~ weapons.

4. Christine Fox is the ~~female~~ mayor of Port London, Maine.

5. Travel to other planets will be a significant step for ~~man.~~ *humanity.*

TEST · Revise · Edit

Look back at your response to the Write First activity on page 400. TEST what you have written. Then, revise and edit your work, making sure that your language is specific as well as concise and that you have avoided slang, clichés, and sexist language. Finally, add a simile or metaphor to add interest to your writing.

EDITING PRACTICE

Read the following student essay carefully, and then revise it. Make sure that your revision is concise, uses specific words, and includes no slang, sexist language, or clichés. Add an occasional simile or metaphor if you like. The first sentence has been edited for you. *Answers will vary.*

Unexpected Discoveries

When we hear the word "accident," we think of bad things. *, like dented fenders and broken glass.* But accidents can be good, *lucky,* too. Modern science has made advances as a result of accidents. ~~It is a~~ fact that *A* a scientist sometimes works ~~like a dog~~ *hard* for years in ~~his~~ *the* laboratory, only to make ~~a weird~~ *an unexpected* discovery ~~because of a mistake.~~ *.*

The most famous example of a ~~good,~~ beneficial accident is the discovery of penicillin. A scientist, Alexander Fleming, had seen many soldiers die of infections after they were wounded in World War I. ~~All things considered,~~ *In fact,* many more soldiers died ~~due to the fact that~~ *from* infections occurred than from wounds. Fleming wanted to find a drug that could ~~put an end to~~ *cure* these ~~terrible,~~ fatal infections. One day in 1928, Fleming went on vacation, leaving a pile of dishes in the lab sink. ~~As luck would have it,~~ *Luckily,* he had been growing bacteria in those dishes. When he came back, he noticed that one of the dishes looked moldy. ~~What was strange was that~~ *Strangely,* near the mold, the bacteria were dead ~~as a doornail.~~ ~~It was crystal clear to~~ Fleming *realized* that the mold had killed the bacteria. He had discovered penicillin, the first antibiotic.

Alexander Fleming

Everyone has heard the name "Goodyear." ~~It was~~ Charles Goodyear ~~who~~ made a discovery that ~~changed and~~ revolutionized the rubber industry. In the early nineteenth century, rubber products ~~became thin and runny~~ *melted* in hot weather and cracked in cold weather. One day in 1839, Goodyear accidentally dropped some rubber mixed with sulfur on a hot stove. It ~~changed color and~~ turned black. After being cooled, it could be stretched, *, like a rubber band,* and it would return to its original size and shape. This kind of rubber is now used in tires and in many other products.

Another ~~thing~~ *product* was also discovered because of a lab accident involving rubber. In 1953, Patsy Sherman, a ~~female~~ chemist for the 3M company, was trying to find

Charles Goodyear

Patsy Sherman

a new type of rubber. She created a batch of ~~man-made,~~ synthetic liquid rubber.

Some of the liquid accidentally spilled onto a lab assistant's new white canvas

sneaker. Her assistant used everything ~~but the kitchen sink~~ *available* to clean the shoe, but

nothing worked. ~~Over time,~~ *After a few weeks,* the rest of the shoe became dirty, but the part where

the spill had hit was still clean ~~as a whistle.~~ Sherman realized that she had found

a chemical something that could actually keep fabrics clean by ~~doing a number on~~ *blocking* dirt. The

3M Corporation named this brand new product Scotchgard.

Scientists ~~A scientist~~ can be clumsy and ~~careless,~~ but sometimes ~~his~~ *their* mistakes lead

to ~~great and~~ important discoveries. Penicillin, better tires, and Scotchgard are

examples of products that were the result of scientific accidents.

COLLABORATIVE ACTIVITIES

1. Photocopy two or three paragraphs of description from a romance novel, a western novel, or a mystery novel. Bring your paragraphs to class. Working in a group, choose one paragraph that seems to need clearer, more specific language.

2. As a group, revise the paragraph you chose for Collaborative Activity 1, making it as specific as possible and eliminating any clichés or sexist language.

3. Exchange your revised paragraph from Collaborative Activity 2 with the paragraph revised by another group, and check the other group's work. Make any additional changes you think the paragraph needs.

review checklist

Using Words Effectively

☐ Use specific words that convey your ideas clearly and precisely. (See 23a.)

☐ Use concise language that says what it has to say in the fewest possible words. (See 23b.)

☐ Avoid slang. (See 23c.)

☐ Avoid clichés. (See 23d.)

☐ When appropriate, use similes and metaphors to make your writing more lively and more interesting. (See 23e.)

☐ Avoid sexist language. (See 23f.)

Read the following student essay. Then, edit it by creating more effective sentences. Combine simple sentences into compound or complex sentences, use parallelism, create varied sentences, and use words that are concise, specific, and original. The first editing change has been made for you.

Answers will vary.

Eating Street Food

Street food, food cooked and served at a portable stand, is extremely popular in the United States. ~~Street~~ *Usually, street* food customers ~~usually~~ get their food quickly*, and* ~~They~~ do not pay much. Some regional or ethnic foods are sold as street food*. After some* ~~Then, they~~ become popular ~~There~~ *. Although there* are concerns about the cleanliness and freshness of street food*, these* ~~These~~ problems can be avoided. ~~It is a fact that~~ *Street* food has many advantages.

Because street ~~Street~~ food is the original fast food*, it* ~~Street food~~ is both fast and cheap. Customers usually do not have much time to wait for it to be cooked*, so vendors* ~~Vendors~~ have to offer food that can be made beforehand or prepared quickly. The original U.S. street food is the hot dog*. ~~It~~ can be steamed ahead of time and quickly be put into a bun. *If some* Some customers want ~~things like~~ relish, onions, and chili*, they* ~~They~~ can be added. Street food does not cost as much as restaurant food. *Although vendors* ~~Vendors~~ usually have to buy a license ~~in order~~ to sell food at a particular location*, they* ~~They~~ do not have to rent a store, pay ~~waiters and waitresses~~ *servers,* and supply tablecloths and dishes *. Therefore,* ~~therefore~~ they can charge much less than a restaurant. Street food customers don't have to make *spend the* ~~the commitment of~~ time and money required at a sit-down restaurant*, and they* ~~They~~ don't have to tip the server. Customers cannot sit at tables, however*, because there* ~~There~~ are no tables. *Instead, they* ~~They~~ have to eat while standing or walking. Customers often don't have much time*, so this* ~~This~~ situation suits them. Students need fast and cheap food, *especially on college campuses, students* ~~especially on college campuses. Food carts~~ *are popular.* ~~make them happy as a clam.~~

Street food is often regional or ethnic. Vendors sell cheese steaks and soft pretzels in Philadelphia. They sell reindeer sausages in Alaska*. ~~They sell~~ tacos and tamales in Mexican neighborhoods*, and* ~~In Chicago, customers can buy~~ kielbasa sandwiches and pierogies *in Chicago.* ~~Often,~~ food carts offer ethnic foods to customers

Hot dog vendor

Mexican snacks

who are tasting them for the first time. ~~A person~~ can see if ~~he likes~~ Indian *(People)* *(they like)* curry, Israeli falafel, Italian panini, or a gyro ~~from Greece~~. Because of the success *(Greek)* of street vendors, many ethnic foods ~~have gone mainstream~~ and are now widely offered in sit-down restaurants.

~~There is some concern~~ about the safety of street food. ~~Refrigeration~~ may be *(Some people worry)* *(In food carts, refrigeration)* limited or nonexistent~~.~~ ~~Cleanliness~~ sometimes can be a problem. ~~Food~~ from a *(, and cleanliness)* *(However, food)* street-corner cart may be safer than food cooked in a restaurant kitchen~~.~~ ~~In the~~ *(, where)* ~~restaurant,~~ it may sit for a long time. Also, ~~due to the fact that~~ food carts may *(because)* lack refrigeration, ~~very fresh ingredients~~ ~~are often used~~. Still, customers should *(the food often contains)* follow some tips for buying street food. The food should be kept covered until it is cooked~~.~~ ~~The money~~ ~~and~~ food should not be touched by the ~~same individual~~. Local *(, and the)* *(person preparing the food.)* customers are a good guide to the best street food~~.~~ ~~They~~ know where the food is *(because they)* freshest. A long line usually indicates a good and safe source of street food.

In the United States, street food is especially varied. ~~In the United States,~~ *(where there are many immigrants,)* ~~there are many immigrants~~. ~~Food~~ is an important part of culture~~.~~ ~~The~~ popularity of *(Because food)* *(, the)* ethnic street food can be a sign that the immigrants' culture has been accepted.

Falafel cart

unit
6 Solving Common Sentence Problems

24 Run-Ons

preview

In this chapter, you will learn to
- recognize run-ons (24a)
- correct run-ons in five different ways (24b)

write first

Why do you think so many American children are physically out of shape? What do you think can be done about this problem? Write a paragraph or an essay in which you suggest answers to these questions.

WORD POWER

fused joined together

WORD POWER

splice (verb) to join together at the ends

24a Recognizing Run-Ons

A **sentence** consists of at least one independent clause—one subject and one verb.

College costs are rising.

A **run-on** is an error that occurs when two sentences are joined incorrectly. There are two kinds of run-ons: *fused sentences* and *comma splices*.

■ A **fused sentence** occurs when two sentences are joined without any punctuation.

FUSED SENTENCE [College costs are rising] [many students are worried.]

■ A **comma splice** occurs when two sentences are joined with just a comma.

COMMA SPLICE [College costs are rising], [many students are worried.]

PRACTICE

24-1 Some of the sentences in the following paragraph are correct, but others are run-ons. In the answer space after each sentence, write *C* if the sentence is correct, *FS* if it is a fused sentence, and *CS* if it is a comma splice.

Example: Using a screen reader is one way for blind people to access the Web, two popular programs are JAWS for Windows and Window-Eyes. _____CS_____

(1) The Internet should be accessible to everyone, this is not always the case. _____CS_____ (2) Many blind computer users have trouble finding information on the Web. _____C_____ (3) Often, this is the result of poor Web design it is the designer's job to make the site accessible. _____FS_____ (4) Most blind people use special software called screen readers, this technology translates text into speech or Braille. _____CS_____ (5) However, screen readers do not always work well the information is sometimes hard to access. _____FS_____ (6) Web sites need to be understandable to all Internet users. _____C_____ (7) The rights of blind Internet users may be protected by the Americans with Disabilities Act (ADA). _____C_____ (8) We will have to wait for more cases to come to trial then we will know more. _____FS_____

(9) Meanwhile, we have to rely on software companies to make the necessary changes, this will take some time. ___*CS*___ (10) However, there are incentives for these companies, the 1.5 million blind computer users are all potential customers. ___*CS*___

24b Correcting Run-Ons

FYI

Correcting Run-Ons

You can correct run-ons in five ways:

1. *Use a period to create two separate sentences.*
   College costs are rising. Many students are worried.

2. *Use a coordinating conjunction (**and, but, or, nor, for, so,** or **yet**) to connect ideas.*
   College costs are rising, and many students are worried.

3. *Use a semicolon to connect ideas.*
   College costs are rising; many students are worried.

4. *Use a semicolon followed by a transitional word or phrase to connect ideas.*
   College costs are rising; as a result, many students are worried.

5. *Use a dependent word (**although, because, when,** and so on) to connect ideas.*
   Because college costs are rising, many students are worried.

Teaching Tip
Remind students that computer grammar checkers sometimes identify a sentence as a run-on simply because it is long. However, a long sentence can be perfectly correct. Before they make changes, students should be sure they actually have an error (two independent clauses joined without punctuation or with just a comma).

The pages that follow explain and illustrate the five different ways to correct run-ons.

1. **Use a period to create two separate sentences.** Be sure each sentence begins with a capital letter and ends with a period.

INCORRECT (FUSED SENTENCE)	Gas prices are very high some people are buying hybrid cars.
INCORRECT (COMMA SPLICE)	Gas prices are very high, some people are buying hybrid cars.
CORRECT	Gas prices are very high. Some people are buying hybrid cars. (two separate sentences)

PRACTICE

24-2   Correct each of the following run-ons by using a period to create two separate sentences. Be sure both of your new sentences begin with a capital letter and end with a period.

Example: Stephen Colbert used to appear on *The Daily Show with Jon Stewart*. *Now,* ~~now,~~ he has his own show called *The Colbert Report*.

1. In 2010, David Cameron became prime minister of the United Kingdom. *He* ~~he~~ replaced Gordon Brown.

2. New York–style pizza usually has a thin crust. Chicago-style "deep-dish pizza" has a thick crust.

3. Last week, Soraya won a text-messaging contest. *The* ~~the~~ prize for being the fastest was five hundred dollars.

4. In some parts of Canada's Northwest Territory, the only way to transport supplies is over frozen lakes. *Being* ~~being~~ an ice road trucker is one of the most dangerous jobs in the world.

5. In 1961, the first Six Flags opened in Arlington, Texas. *The* ~~the~~ six flags represent the six governments that have ruled the area that is now Texas.

Teaching Tip
Refer students to 19a for more on connecting ideas with a coordinating conjunction and information on choosing the most appropriate coordinating conjunction.

2. **Use a coordinating conjunction to connect ideas.** If you want to indicate a particular relationship between ideas—for example, cause and effect or contrast—you can connect two independent clauses with a coordinating conjunction that makes this relationship clear. Always place a comma before the coordinating conjunction.

Coordinating Conjunctions

and	or	for	yet
but	nor	so	

INCORRECT (FUSED SENTENCE)	Some schools require students to wear uniforms other schools do not.
INCORRECT (COMMA SPLICE)	Some schools require students to wear uniforms, other schools do not.
CORRECT	Some schools require students to wear uniforms, but other schools do not. (clauses connected with the coordinating conjunction *but*, preceded by a comma)

PRACTICE

24-3 Correct each of the following run-ons by using a coordinating conjunction (*and, but, or, nor, for, so,* or *yet*) to connect ideas. Be sure to put a comma before each coordinating conjunction.

Example: Many college students use Facebook to keep up with old

friends _∧*, and* they also use the site to find new friends.

Answers will vary.

1. A car with soft tires gets poor gas mileage _∧*so* keeping tires inflated is a

good way to save money on gas.

2. It used to be difficult for football fans to see the first-down line on

television _∧*but* the computer-generated yellow line makes it much easier.

3. Indonesia has more volcanoes than any other country in the world _∧*, but* the

United States has the biggest volcano in the world, Hawaii's Mauna Loa.

4. Chefs can become famous for cooking at popular restaurants _∧*, or* they can

gain fame by hosting television shows.

5. Overcrowded schools often have to purchase portable classrooms or

trailers _∧*, yet* this is only a temporary solution.

3. **Use a semicolon to connect ideas.** If you want to indicate a particularly close connection—or a strong contrast—between two ideas, use a semicolon.

INCORRECT (FUSED SENTENCE)	Most professional basketball players go to college most professional baseball players do not.
INCORRECT (COMMA SPLICE)	Most professional basketball players go to college, most professional baseball players do not.
CORRECT	Most professional basketball players go to college; most professional baseball players do not. (clauses connected with a semicolon)

> **Teaching Tip**
> Tell students that if a period will not work where the semicolon is, then the semicolon is probably incorrect. Refer students to 19b for more on connecting ideas with a semicolon.

PRACTICE

24-4 Correct each of the following run-ons by using a semicolon to connect ideas. Do not use a capital letter after the semicolon unless the word that follows it is a proper noun.

Example: From 1930 until 2006, Pluto was known as a planet _∧*;* it is

now known as a "dwarf planet."

1. Of all the states, Alaska has the highest percentage of Native American

residents _∧*;* 16 percent of Alaskans are of Native American descent.

2. Satellites and global positioning systems (GPS) can help farmers to better understand the needs of their crops; these new tools are part of a trend called "precision agriculture."

3. Enforcing traffic laws can be difficult; some cities use cameras to photograph cars that run red lights.

4. Old landfills can sometimes be made into parks; Cesar Chavez Park in Berkeley, California, is one example.

5. Freestyle motocross riders compete by doing jumps and stunts; some famous FMX riders are Carey Hart, Nate Adams, and Travis Pastrana.

4. **Use a semicolon followed by a transitional word or phrase to connect ideas.** To show how two closely linked ideas are related, add a transitional word or phrase after the semicolon. The transition will indicate the specific relationship between the two clauses.

> **INCORRECT (FUSED SENTENCE)** Finding a part-time job can be challenging some-times it is even hard to find an unpaid internship.
>
> **INCORRECT (COMMA SPLICE)** Finding a part-time job can be challenging, some-times it is even hard to find an unpaid internship.
>
> **CORRECT** Finding a part-time job can be challenging; in fact, sometimes it is even hard to find an unpaid internship. (clauses connected with a semicolon followed by the transitional phrase *in fact*)

Some Frequently Used Transitional Words and Phrases

after all	for this reason	now
also	however	still
as a result	in addition	then
eventually	in fact	therefore
finally	instead	thus
for example	moreover	unfortunately
for instance	nevertheless	

For more complete lists of transitional words and phrases, see 19c.

PRACTICE
24-5 Correct each of the following run-ons by using a semicolon, followed by the transitional word or phrase in parentheses, to connect ideas. Be sure to put a comma after the transitional word or phrase.

Example: When babies are first born, they can only see black and
; still,
white most baby clothes and blankets are made in pastel colors. (still)

1. Restaurant goers can expect to see different condiments in different
   ; for example,
   regions of the country, few tables in the Southwest are without a bottle
   of hot sauce. (for example)

2. Every April, millions of people participate in TV-Turnoff Week by not
   ; instead,
   watching television they read, spend time with family and friends, and
   generally enjoy their free time. (instead)

3. Today, few people can count on company pension plans, thirty years
   ; however,
   ago, most people could. (however)

4. Many people see bottled water as a waste of money tap water is free.
   ; after all,
   (after all)

5. Dog breeders who run "puppy mills" are only concerned with making
   ; unfortunately,
   money they are not particularly concerned with their dogs' well-being.
   (unfortunately)

PRACTICE

24-6 In each of the following sentences, circle the transitional word or phrase whose meaning best links the two independent clauses, and then punctuate the sentence correctly.

Example: I have a lot of homework to do tonight therefore/however I can't go to the movies with you.

1. This chapter is very convincing for example/in fact it may be the most convincing part of the book.

2. The principal misused school funds for this reason/nevertheless he was fired.

3. Yoga can improve balance and coordination therefore/in addition it can increase strength and flexibility.

4. Many scientists are concerned about climate change thus/however some are skeptical about its dangers.

5. Credit card debt can have a negative impact on a person's credit rating also/still it can be a terrible emotional burden.

Teaching Tip
Students may need help in choosing the right transition. You may want to define the words in the box on page 422 and give examples of their use before you assign Practice 24-6.

FYI

Connecting Ideas with Semicolons

Run-ons often occur when you use a transitional word or phrase to join two independent clauses *without also using a semicolon*.

INCORRECT (FUSED SENTENCE)	It is easy to download information from the Internet however it is not always easy to evaluate the information.
INCORRECT (COMMA SPLICE)	It is easy to download information from the Internet, however it is not always easy to evaluate the information.

To avoid this kind of run-on, always put a semicolon before the transitional word or phrase and a comma after it.

CORRECT	It is easy to download information from the Internet; however, it is not always easy to evaluate the information.

5. **Use a dependent word to connect ideas.** When one idea is dependent on another, you can connect the two ideas by adding a dependent word, such as *when, who, although,* or *because.*

INCORRECT (FUSED SENTENCE)	American union membership was high in the mid-twentieth century it has declined in recent years.
INCORRECT (COMMA SPLICE)	American union membership was high in the mid-twentieth century, it has declined in recent years.
CORRECT	Although American union membership was high in the mid-twentieth century, it has declined in recent years. (clauses connected with the dependent word *although*)
CORRECT	American union membership, which was high in the mid-twentieth century, has declined in recent years. (clauses connected with the dependent word *which*)

Some Frequently Used Dependent Words

after	even though	unless
although	if	until
as	instead	when
because	since	which
before	that	who

For complete lists of dependent words, including subordinating conjunctions and relative pronouns, see 20b and 20c.

PRACTICE

24-7   Correct each run-on in the following paragraph by adding a dependent word. Consult the list on page 424 to help you choose a logical dependent word. Be sure to add correct punctuation where necessary.

Consult the list on page 424

Teaching Tip
Refer students to Chapter 20 for information on how to punctuate complex sentences.

Example: Harlem was a rural area until the nineteenth century*,*
when improved transportation linked it to lower Manhattan. *Answers will vary.*

Even though contemporary
(1) ~~Contemporary~~ historians have written about the Harlem Renais-
Although
sance, its influence is still not widely known. (2) Harlem was populated

mostly by European immigrants at the turn of the last century, it saw an
As this
influx of African Americans beginning in 1910. (3) ~~This~~ migration from the

South continued Harlem became one of the largest African-American com-
After many
munities in the United States. (4) ~~Many~~ black artists and writers settled in

Harlem during the 1920s, African-American art flowered. (5) This "Harlem
, although
Renaissance" was an important era in American literary history it is not
When scholars
even mentioned in some textbooks. (6) ~~Scholars~~ recognize the great works

of the Harlem Renaissance, they point to the writers Langston Hughes

and Countee Cullen and the artists Henry Tanner and Sargent Johnson.
After
(7) ~~Zora~~ Neale Hurston moved to Harlem from her native Florida in 1925,
Because
she began a book of African-American folklore. (8) ~~Harlem~~ was an exciting

place in the 1920s people from all over the city went there to listen to jazz
After the
and to dance. (9) ~~The~~ white playwright Eugene O'Neill went to Harlem to

audition actors for his play *The Emperor Jones*, he made an international
When the
star of the great Paul Robeson. (10) ~~The~~ Great Depression occurred in the

1930s it led to the end of the Harlem Renaissance.

PRACTICE

24-8   Correct each of the following run-ons in one of these four ways: by creating two separate sentences, by using a coordinating conjunction, by using a semicolon, or by using a semicolon followed by a transitional word or phrase. Remember to put a semicolon before, and a comma after, each transitional word or phrase.

Example: Some fish-and-chip shops in Scotland sell deep-fried
. Children
MARS bars ~~children~~ are the biggest consumers of these calorie-rich

bars. *Answers will vary.*

1. Twenty-five percent of Americans under the age of fifty have one or more tattoos ⌃*, and* 50 percent of Americans under the age of twenty-five have one or more tattoos.

2. The ancient Greeks built their homes facing south ⌃ *;* this practice took advantage of light and heat from the winter sun.

3. In 1985, a team of musical artists recorded "We Are the World" in support of African famine relief ⌃ *;* in 2010, artists recorded the same song in support of Haitian earthquake relief.

4. The comic-strip cat Garfield is not cuddly ⌃*, and* Garzooka, a superhero cat who spits up radiated hairballs, is even less cuddly.

5. Horse-racing fans love jockey Calvin Borel for his enthusiasm during postrace interviews ⌃*, and* fellow jockeys respect him for his work ethic.

6. The average Swiss eats twenty-three pounds of chocolate each year ⌃ *; however,* the average American eats less than half that amount.

7. Flamenco—a Spanish style of dancing, singing, and clapping—was traditionally informal and unplanned ⌃ *; for this reason,* it has been compared to improvisational American jazz.

8. Seattle is considered to have the most-educated population of any major city ⌃*, but* the medium-sized city of Arlington, Virginia, has a higher percentage of college graduates.

9. In Acadia National Park in Maine, large stones line the edges of steep trails ⌃ *. The* stones are called "Rockefeller's teeth" in honor of the trails' patron.

10. Allen Ginsberg was charged with obscenity for his book of poems, *Howl* ⌃ *; eventually,* the charges were dismissed at trial.

**PRACTICE
24-9** Correct each run-on in the following paragraph in the way that best indicates the relationship between ideas. Be sure to use appropriate punctuation.

Example: E. L. Doctorow's *Homer and Langley* tells the story of two

eccentric brothers ⌃*, and* it shows that truth can be stranger than fiction.

Answers will vary.

(1) The Collyer brothers were wealthy and educated ⌃*; nevertheless,* they lived and

died alone in a filthy apartment. (2) Langley and Homer Collyer were the

sons of a doctor and an opera singer ⌃*, and* the brothers seemed to be as talented

and motivated as their parents. (3) Langley played piano and studied

engineering ⌃*;* Homer had a law degree. (4) However, in their twenties

and thirties, the brothers did not have jobs ⌃*; instead,* they lived with their parents

in a Manhattan apartment. (5) *When their* ⌃Their parents died ⌃*;* Langley and Homer

inherited the apartment. (6) Gradually, they became frightened of outsiders

⌃*; as a result,* they boarded up the windows and set traps for burglars. (7) *After they* ⌃They stopped

paying their bills ⌃*;* their heat, water, and electricity were shut off. (8) They

also became compulsive hoarders ⌃*;* they could not throw anything away.

(9) They accumulated thousands and thousands of books, numerous

bundles of old newspapers, and fourteen pianos ⌃*; also,* they saved tons of garbage.

(10) They got their water from a public park ⌃*, and* they collected discarded food

from grocery stores and butcher shops. (11) Eventually, Langley was

caught in one of his own burglar traps, the ~~trap~~ *which* sent three bundles of

newspapers and a suitcase tumbling on top of him. (12) Langley died of

his injuries ⌃*, and* Homer died by his side, surrounded by mountains of trash.

TEST · Revise · Edit

Look back at your responses to the Write First activity on page 417.
TEST what you have written. Then, revise and edit your work, making
sure you identify and correct any run-ons.

EDITING PRACTICE: PARAGRAPH

Read the following student paragraph, and revise it to eliminate run-ons. Correct each run-on in the way that best indicates the relationship between ideas. Be sure to use appropriate punctuation. The first error has been corrected for you. *Answers may vary.*

Cold Cases

Cold cases are criminal investigations that have not been solved, *so* they are not officially closed. *When new* New evidence is found, cold cases may be reexamined. DNA tests might provide new clues, *or* a witness may come forward with new testimony. The new evidence might lead to new suspects , *or* it might change the nature of the crime. In some cases, an accident might be reclassified a homicide , in other cases a murder might be ruled a suicide. Sometimes a person who was convicted of a crime is found to be innocent. Cold cases usually involve violent crimes , rape and murder are two examples. *Although investigators* Investigators sometimes reopen very old cold cases, they usually focus on more recent cases with living suspects. For serious crimes, there is no limit on how much time may pass before a suspect is brought to justice, *and* a criminal may be convicted many years after the crime was committed. When cold cases are solved, the crime is not undone , nevertheless victims' families finally feel that justice has been served.

EDITING PRACTICE: ESSAY

Read the following student essay, and revise it to eliminate run-ons. Correct each run-on in the way that best indicates the relationship between ideas, and be sure to punctuate correctly. The first error has been corrected for you. *Answers may vary.*

Comic-Book Heroes

Comic-book heroes have a long history , *. They* they originated in comic strips and radio shows. In the "Golden Age" of comic books, individual superheroes were the most popular characters , *. Then,* then teams and groups of superheroes were introduced. Today, some of these superheroes can be found in movies and in longer works of graphic fiction. Over the years, superheroes have remained very popular.

One of the first comic-book heroes was Popeye. Popeye had no supernatural *Although*
powers, he battled his enemy, Bluto, with strength supplied by spinach. Another
early comic-book hero was The Shadow *who* he fought crime while wearing a cape and
mask. The Shadow first appeared in comic books in 1930 *and* later the character had
his own radio show.

The late 1930s and 1940s are considered the Golden Age of comic books *;*
many famous comic-book heroes were introduced at that time. The first Superman
comic appeared in 1939. *When* Superman came out from behind his secret identity as
Clark Kent, he could fly "faster than a speeding bullet." Superman was the first
comic-book hero who clearly had a superhuman ability to fight evil. Batman was
different from Superman *;* he had no real superpowers. Also, Superman was decent
but
and moral, Batman was willing to break the rules. Wonder Woman appeared in
. She
1941, she truly had superhuman qualities. For example, she could catch a bullet in
one hand. She could also regrow a limb, *and* she could tell when someone was not
telling the truth.

Superheroes sometimes had help. Batman had Robin, *and* Wonder Woman had her
sister, Wonder Girl. Sometimes there were superhero teams *;* these were groups
of superheroes who helped each other fight evil. The first team was the Justice
, which
League of America it included Superman, Batman, and Wonder Woman. Eventually,
the Justice League fought against threats to the existence of the earth *;* these
, who
threats even included alien invasions. Another superhero team was the X-Men they
were mutants with supernatural abilities.

Now, comic books are not as popular as they used to be *;* however, superheroes
can still be found in popular movies. Superman has been the main character in
. There
many movies there have also been several successful Batman, Spiderman, Iron
Man, and Fantastic Four movies. In longer works of graphic fiction, Superman,
; in addition,
Batman, and the Fantastic Four are still heroes *;* recent works of graphic fiction
feature Captain America and the Runaways. Apparently, people still want to see
superheroes fight evil and win.

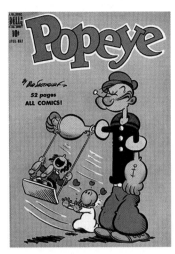

Popeye *comic book*

Spiderman **2** *movie poster*

COLLABORATIVE ACTIVITIES

1. Find an interesting paragraph in a newspaper or magazine article or on the Web. Working in a small group, recopy it onto a separate sheet of paper, creating run-ons. Exchange exercises with another group.

2. Work in a small group to correct each fused sentence and comma splice in an exercise prepared by another group of students. When you have finished, return the exercise to the group that created it.

3. Continuing to work with members of your group, evaluate the other group's work on your exercise, comparing it to the original newspaper or magazine paragraph. Pay particular attention to punctuation. Where the students' version differs from the original, decide whether their version is incorrect or whether it represents an acceptable (or even superior) alternative to the original.

review checklist

Run-Ons

☐ A run-on is an error that occurs when two sentences are joined incorrectly. There are two kinds of run-ons: fused sentences and comma splices. (See 24a.)

☐ A fused sentence occurs when two sentences are incorrectly joined without any punctuation. (See 24a.)

☐ A comma splice occurs when two sentences are joined with just a comma. (See 24a.)

☐ Correct a run-on in one of the following ways:

1. by creating two separate sentences

   _____. _____.

2. by using a coordinating conjunction

   _____, [coordinating conjunction] _____.

3. by using a semicolon

   _____; _____.

4. by using a semicolon followed by a transitional word or phrase

   _____; [transitional word or phrase], _____.

5. by using a dependent word

   [Dependent word] _____, _____.

   _____ [dependent word] _____. (See 24b.)

25 Fragments

preview

In this chapter, you will learn to

- recognize fragments (25a)
- correct missing-subject fragments (25b)
- correct phrase fragments (25c)
- correct -ing fragments (25d)
- correct dependent clause fragments (25e)

write first

Imagine you are writing a magazine ad for your favorite beverage, footwear, or health or beauty product. In a short paragraph or two, describe the product you chose as compellingly as possible. Include a few possible advertising slogans.

25a Recognizing Fragments

A **fragment** is an incomplete sentence. Every sentence must include at least one subject and one verb, and every sentence must express a complete thought. If a group of words does not do *both* these things, it is a fragment and not a sentence—even if it begins with a capital letter and ends with a period.

The following is a complete sentence.

SENTENCE	The <u>actors</u> in the play <u>were</u> very talented. (The sentence includes both a subject and a verb and expresses a complete thought.)

Because a sentence must have both a subject and a verb and express a complete thought, the following groups of words are not complete sentences; they are fragments.

FRAGMENT (NO VERB)	The actors in the play. (What point is being made about the actors?)
FRAGMENT (NO SUBJECT)	Were very talented. (Who were very talented?)
FRAGMENT (NO SUBJECT OR VERB)	Very talented. (Who was very talented?)
FRAGMENT (DOES NOT EXPRESS COMPLETE THOUGHT)	Because the actors in the play were very talented. (What happened because they were very talented?)

FYI

Spotting Fragments

Fragments almost always appear next to complete sentences.

┌─ **COMPLETE SENTENCE** ─┐ ┌──── **FRAGMENT** ────┐
Celia took two electives. Physics 320 and Spanish 101.

The fragment above does not have a subject or a verb. The complete sentence that comes before it, however, has both a subject (*Celia*) and a verb (*took*).

Often, you can correct a fragment by attaching it to an adjacent sentence that supplies the missing words. (This sentence will usually appear right before the fragment.)

Celia took two electives, Physics 320 and Spanish 101.

WORD POWER

adjacent next to

PRACTICE

25-1 Some of the following items are fragments, and others are complete sentences. On the line following each item, write *F* if it is a fragment and *S* if it is a complete sentence.

Example: Star formations in the night sky. ___*F*___

1. To save as much as possible for college. ___*F*___

2. The judge gave her a two-year sentence. ___*S*___

3. A birthday on Christmas Day. ___*F*___

4. Because he lost ten pounds on his new diet. ___*F*___

5. Working in the garden and fixing the roof. ___*F*___

6. Sonya flew to Mexico. ___*S*___

7. Starts in August in many parts of the country. ___*F*___

8. And slept in his own bed last night. ___*F*___

9. Famous for her movie roles. ___*F*___

10. A phone that also plays music and takes photos. ___*F*___

PRACTICE

25-2 In the following passage, some of the numbered groups of words are missing a subject, a verb, or both. Identify each fragment by labeling it *F*. Then, decide how each fragment could be attached to another word group to create a complete new sentence. Finally, rewrite the entire passage, using complete sentences, on the lines provided.

> **ESL Tip**
> Nonnative speakers may not have any more trouble with fragments than other students.

Example: Martha Grimes, Ruth Rendell, and Deborah Crombie

write detective novels. _____ Set in England. ___*F*___

Rewrite: *Martha Grimes, Ruth Rendell, and Deborah Crombie write*

detective novels set in England.

(1) Sara Paretsky writes detective novels. _____ (2) Such as *Burn Marks* and *Guardian Angel*. ___*F*___ (3) These novels are about V. I. Warshawski. _____ (4) A private detective. ___*F*___ (5) V. I. lives and works in Chicago. _____ (6) The Windy City. ___*F*___ (7) Every day as a detective. ___*F*___ (8) V. I. takes risks. _____ (9) V. I. is tough. _____ (10) She is also a woman. _____

Rewrite:

Sara Paretsky writes detective novels, such as Burn Marks and Guardian Angel.

These novels are about V. I. Warshawski, a private detective. V. I. lives and works

in Chicago, the Windy City. Every day as a detective, V. I. takes risks. V. I. is tough.

She is also a woman.

PRACTICE
25-3   In the following paragraph, some of the numbered groups of words are missing a subject, a verb, or both. First, underline each fragment. Then, decide how each fragment could be attached to a nearby word group to create a complete new sentence. Finally, rewrite the entire paragraph, using complete sentences, on the lines provided.

   Example: Gatorade was invented at the University of Florida. To help the Florida Gators fight dehydration.

   Rewrite: *Gatorade was invented at the University of Florida to help the*

   Florida Gators fight dehydration.

   (1) Doctors discovered that football players were losing electrolytes and carbohydrates. (2) Through their sweat. (3) They invented a drink. (4) That replaced these important elements. (5) Gatorade tasted terrible. (6) But did its job. (7) The Florida Gators survived a very hot season. (8) And won most of their games. (9) Now, Gatorade is used by many college and professional football teams. (10) As well as baseball, basketball, tennis, and soccer teams.

Rewrite:

Doctors discovered that football players were losing electrolytes and carbohydrates

through their sweat. They invented a drink that replaced these important elements.

Gatorade tasted terrible but did its job. The Florida Gators survived a very hot season and

won most of their games. Now, Gatorade is used by many college and professional football

teams as well as baseball, basketball, tennis, and soccer teams.

25b Missing-Subject Fragments

Every sentence must include both a subject and a verb. If the subject is left out, the sentence is incomplete. In the following example, the first word group is a sentence. It includes both a subject (*He*) and a verb (*packed*). However, the second word group is a fragment. It includes a verb (*took*), but it does not include a subject.

┌─────────── SENTENCE ───────────┐ ┌─────── FRAGMENT ───────┐
He packed his books and papers. And also took an umbrella.

The best way to correct this kind of fragment is to attach it to the sentence that comes right before it. This sentence will usually contain the missing subject.

CORRECT He packed his books and papers and also took an umbrella.

Another way to correct this kind of fragment is to add the missing subject.

CORRECT He packed his books and papers. He also took an umbrella.

PRACTICE

25-4 Each of the following items includes a missing-subject fragment. Using one of the two methods explained above, correct each fragment.

Example: Back-to-school sales are popular with students. And with their parents.

Back-to-school sales are popular with students and with their parents.   or

Back-to-school sales are popular with students. The sales are also popular

with their parents.
Answers may vary.

1. Quitting smoking is very hard. But is worth the effort.

   Quitting smoking is very hard but is worth the effort.

2. Some retailers give a lot of money to charity. And even donate part of their profits.

   Some retailers give a lot of money to charity and even donate part of their

   profits.

3. Geography bees resemble spelling bees. But instead test the contestants' knowledge of countries around the world.

   Geography bees resemble spelling bees but instead test the contestants' knowledge of

   countries around the world.

4. School uniforms are often preferred by parents. And also favored by many school principals.

School uniforms are often preferred by parents and also favored by many school principals.

5. During the Cold War, the Soviet Union and the United States were rivals. But never actually fought a war with each other.

During the Cold War, the Soviet Union and the United States were rivals but never actually fought a war with each other.

6. Scooters have been around for many years. And have recently become popular again.

Scooters have been around for many years and have recently become popular again.

7. After cosmetic surgery, one can look younger. And feel younger, too.

After cosmetic surgery, one can look younger and feel younger, too.

8. Online shopping sites sometimes offer free shipping. Or have lower prices than local stores.

Online shopping sites sometimes offer free shipping or have lower prices than local stores.

9. Pro football linemen can weigh more than 300 pounds. But are still able to run fast.

Pro football linemen can weigh more than 300 pounds but are still able to run fast.

10. Using an electric toothbrush can be good for one's teeth. And promote healthy gums.

Using an electric toothbrush can be good for one's teeth and promote healthy gums.

25c   Phrase Fragments

Every sentence must include a subject and a verb. A **phrase** is a group of words that is missing a subject or a verb or both. When you punctuate a phrase as if it is a sentence, you create a fragment.

If you spot a phrase fragment in your writing, you can often correct it by attaching it to the sentence that comes directly before it.

Appositive Fragments

An **appositive** identifies, renames, or describes a noun or a pronoun. An appositive cannot stand alone as a sentence.

To correct an appositive fragment, attach it to the sentence that comes right before it. (This sentence will contain the noun or pronoun that the appositive describes.)

⌐ FRAGMENT ¬

INCORRECT   He decorated the room in his favorite colors. Brown and black.

CORRECT   He decorated the room in his favorite colors, brown and black.

Sometimes a word or expression like *including, such as, for example,* or *for instance* introduces an appositive. Even if an appositive is introduced by one of these expressions, it is still a fragment.

⌐ FRAGMENT ¬

INCORRECT   A balanced diet should include high-fiber foods. Such as leafy vegetables, fruits, beans, and whole-grain bread.

CORRECT   A balanced diet should include high-fiber foods, such as leafy vegetables, fruits, beans, and whole-grain bread.

Teaching Tip
Refer students to 21c for more on appositives. For information on punctuating appositives, refer them to 34c.

Prepositional Phrase Fragments

A **prepositional phrase** consists of a preposition and its object. A prepositional phrase cannot stand alone as a sentence. To correct a prepositional phrase fragment, attach it to the sentence that comes immediately before it.

⌐ FRAGMENT ¬

INCORRECT   She promised to stand by him. In sickness and in health.

CORRECT   She promised to stand by him in sickness and in health.

Teaching Tip
Refer students to 18b for more on prepositional phrases.

Infinitive Fragments

An **infinitive** consists of *to* plus the base form of the verb (*to be, to go, to write*). An infinitive phrase (*to be free, to go home, to write a novel*) cannot stand alone as a sentence. You can usually correct an infinitive fragment by attaching it to the sentence that comes directly before it.

FRAGMENT

INCORRECT   Eric considered dropping out of school. To start his own business.

CORRECT   Eric considered dropping out of school to start his own business.

You can also add the words needed to complete the sentence.

CORRECT   Eric considered dropping out of school. He wanted to start his own business.

PRACTICE
25-5   In the following paragraph, some of the numbered groups of words are phrase fragments. First, identify each fragment by labeling it *F*. Then, decide how each fragment could be attached to an adjacent sentence to create a complete new sentence. Finally, rewrite the entire paragraph, using complete sentences, on the lines provided.

Example: Mazes have been popular among puzzle solvers. _____ For years. _____*F*_____

Rewrite: _Mazes have been popular among puzzle solvers for years._

(1) Mazes challenge people to find their way. _____ (2) Through a complicated route. ___*F*___ (3) Mazes have been constructed out of paving stones, cornfields, and rooms. _____ (4) Connected by doors. ___*F*___ (5) Printed mazes can be solved with a pen or pencil. _____ (6) During the 1970s, many books and magazines published printed mazes. _____ (7) For children and adults. ___*F*___ (8) There is no foolproof way to escape. _____ (9) From a maze. ___*F*___ (10) One strategy is to keep turning to either the right or the left. _____ (11) To keep from getting lost. ___*F*___ (12) Mazes can be fun to explore. _____ (13) On foot or on paper. ___*F*___

Rewrite:

Mazes challenge people to find their way through a complicated route. Mazes have been

constructed out of paving stones, cornfields, and rooms connected by doors.

Printed mazes can be solved with a pen or pencil. During the 1970s, many books

and magazines published printed mazes for children and adults. There is no

foolproof way to escape from a maze. One strategy is to keep turning to either the

right or the left to keep from getting lost. Mazes can be fun to explore on foot or

on paper.

PRACTICE

25-6   In the following paragraph, some of the numbered groups of words are phrase fragments. First, underline each fragment. Then, decide how each fragment could be attached to an adjacent sentence to create a complete new sentence. Finally, rewrite the entire paragraph, using complete sentences, on the lines provided.

Example: Florence Nightingale worked as a nurse. During the Crimean War.

Rewrite: *Florence Nightingale worked as a nurse during the Crimean War.*

(1) Nurses' uniforms have changed a lot. (2) Over the years. (3) Originally, nurses' uniforms looked like nuns' habits because nuns used to take care. (4) Of sick people. (5) In the late 1800s, a student of Florence Nightingale created a brown uniform. (6) With a white apron and cap. (7) This uniform was worn by student nurses at her school. (8) The Florence Nightingale School of Nursing and Midwifery. (9) Eventually, nurses began to wear white uniforms, white stockings, white shoes, and starched white caps. (10) To stress the importance of cleanliness. (11) Many older people remember these uniforms. (12) With affection. (13) Today, most nurses wear bright, comfortable scrubs. (14) To help patients (especially children) feel more at ease.

Rewrite:

Nurses' uniforms have changed a lot over the years. Originally, nurses' uniforms looked

like nuns' habits because nuns used to take care of sick people. In the late 1800s, a student

of Florence Nightingale created a brown uniform with a white apron and cap. This uniform was

worn by student nurses at her school, the Florence Nightingale School of Nursing and

Midwifery. Eventually, nurses began to wear white uniforms, white stockings, white shoes,

and starched white caps to stress the importance of cleanliness. Many older people

remember these uniforms with affection. Today, most nurses wear bright, comfortable

scrubs to help patients (especially children) feel more at ease.

PRACTICE

25-7 Each of the following items is a phrase fragment, not a sentence. Correct each fragment by adding any words needed to turn the fragment into a complete sentence. (You may add words before or after the fragment.)

Example: During World War I. *A flu epidemic killed millions of people during*

World War I. or *During World War I, a flu epidemic killed millions of people.*

Answers will vary.

1. To be the best player on the team. _____

   _____

2. From a developing nation in Africa. _____

   _____

3. Such as tulips or roses. _____

   _____

4. Behind door number 3. _____

   _____

5. Including my parents and grandparents. _____

   _____

6. With a new car in the driveway. _____

   _____

7. To make a difficult career decision. _____

   _____

8. For a long time. _____

   _____

9. Turkey, stuffing, mashed potatoes, and cranberry sauce. _____

   _____

10. In less than a year. _____

_____

25d   *-ing* Fragments

Every sentence must include a subject and a verb. If the verb is incomplete, a word group is a fragment, not a sentence.

An *-ing* verb cannot be a complete verb. It needs a **helping verb** to complete it. An *-ing* verb, such as *looking*, cannot stand alone in a sentence without a helping verb (*is looking*, *was looking*, *were looking*, and so on). When you use an *-ing* verb without a helping verb, you create a fragment.

┌──────── FRAGMENT ────────┐

INCORRECT   The twins are full of mischief. Always looking for trouble.

The best way to correct an *-ing* fragment is to attach it to the sentence that comes right before it.

CORRECT   The twins are full of mischief, always looking for trouble.

Another way to correct an *-ing* fragment is to add a subject and a helping verb.

CORRECT   The twins are full of mischief. They are always looking for trouble.

Teaching Tip
Tell students that helping verbs include forms of *be*, *have*, and *do*. Refer them to 18c for a list of frequently used helping verbs.

Teaching Tip
Remind students to be careful not to create dangling modifiers with participles. Refer them to 28b.

FYI

Being

As you write, be careful not to use the *-ing* verb *being* as if it were a complete verb.

INCORRECT   I decided to take a nap. The outcome being that I slept through calculus class.

To correct this kind of fragment, substitute a form of the verb *be* that can serve as the main verb in a sentence—for example, *is*, *was*, *are*, or *were*.

CORRECT   I decided to take a nap. The outcome was that I slept through calculus class.

Teaching Tip
You may want to refer students to 34d for information on punctuating restrictive and nonrestrictive clauses.

PRACTICE

25-8 Each of the following items includes an *-ing* fragment. In each case, correct the fragment by attaching it to the sentence before it.

Example: Certain tips can help grocery shoppers. Saving them a lot of money.

Certain tips can help grocery shoppers, saving them a lot of money.

1. Always try to find a store brand. Costing less than the well-known and widely advertised brands.

   Always try to find a store brand costing less than the well-known and widely

   advertised brands.

2. Look for a product's cost per pound. Comparing it to the cost per pound of similar products.

   Look for a product's cost per pound, comparing it to the cost per pound of

   similar products.

3. Examine sale-priced fruits and vegetables. Checking carefully for damage or spoilage.

   Examine sale-priced fruits and vegetables, checking carefully for damage

   or spoilage.

4. Buy different brands of the same product. Trying each one to see which brand you like best.

   Buy different brands of the same product, trying each one to see which brand

   you like best.

5. Use coupons whenever possible. Keeping them handy for future shopping trips.

   Use coupons whenever possible, keeping them handy for future shopping trips.

PRACTICE

25-9 Each of the following items includes an *-ing* fragment. Turn each fragment into a complete sentence by adding a subject and a helping verb. Write your revised sentence on the line below each fragment.

Teaching Tip
If you like, you can give students the option of correcting these fragments by adding the missing words—for example, *Running up and down the stairs, Jane slipped and fell.*

Example: Running up and down the stairs.

Revised: *Jane and her dog are always running up and down the stairs.*

Answers may vary.

1. Trying to decide where to live.

Revised: _____

_____

2. Sleeping whenever he could.

Revised: _____

_____

3. Learning to be a good neighbor.

Revised: _____

_____

4. Turning off all the lights in the house.

Revised: _____

_____

5. Volunteering to help.

Revised: _____

_____

6. Really feeling optimistic about the future.

Revised: _____

_____

7. Always complaining about the lab manual.

Revised: _____

_____

8. Deciding whether or not to get a new cell phone.

Revised: _____

_____

9. Minding their own business.

Revised: _____

_____

10. Finally handing me the car keys.

Revised: _____

_____

Teaching Tip
Refer students to 20a for more on identifying independent and dependent clauses.

25e Dependent Clause Fragments

Every sentence must include a subject and a verb. A sentence must also express a complete thought.

A **dependent clause** is a group of words that is introduced by a dependent word, such as *although, because, that,* or *after.* A dependent clause includes a subject and a verb, but it does not express a complete thought. Therefore, it cannot stand alone as a sentence. To correct a dependent clause fragment, you must complete the thought.

The following dependent clause is incorrectly punctuated as if it were a sentence.

> **FRAGMENT**   After Simon won the lottery.

This fragment includes both a subject (*Simon*) and a complete verb (*won*), but it does not express a complete thought. What happened after Simon won the lottery? To turn this fragment into a sentence, you need to complete the thought.

> **SENTENCE**   After Simon won the lottery, <u>he quit his night job.</u>

Some dependent clauses are introduced by dependent words called **subordinating conjunctions**.

> **FRAGMENT**   Although Marisol had always dreamed of visiting America.

This fragment includes a subject (*Marisol*) and a complete verb (*had dreamed*), but it is not a sentence; it is a dependent clause introduced by the subordinating conjunction *although.*

To correct this kind of fragment, attach it to an **independent clause** (a simple sentence) to complete the idea. (You can often find the independent clause you need right before or right after the fragment.)

> **SENTENCE**   Although Marisol had always dreamed of visiting America, <u>she did not have enough money for the trip until 1985.</u>

Subordinating Conjunctions

after	even though	since	whenever
although	if	so that	where
as	if only	than	whereas
as if	in order that	that	wherever
as though	now that	though	whether
because	once	unless	while
before	provided that	until	
even if	rather than	when	

For information on how to use subordinating conjunctions, see 20b.

FYI

Correcting Dependent Clause Fragments

The simplest way to correct a dependent clause fragment is to cross out the dependent word that makes the idea incomplete.

~~Although~~ Marisol had always dreamed of visiting America.

However, when you delete the dependent word, readers may have trouble seeing the connection between the new sentence and the one before or after it. A better way to revise is to attach the dependent clause fragment to an adjacent independent clause, as illustrated on page 444.

Other dependent clauses are introduced by dependent words called **relative pronouns**.

> **FRAGMENT**   Novelist Richard Wright, <u>who</u> came to Paris in 1947.

> **FRAGMENT**   A quinceañera, <u>which</u> celebrates a Latina's fifteenth birthday.

> **FRAGMENT**   A key World War II battle <u>that</u> was fought on the Pacific island of Guadalcanal.

Each of the above sentence fragments includes a subject (*Richard Wright, quinceañera, battle*) and a complete verb (*came, celebrates, was fought*). However, they are not sentences because they do not express complete thoughts. In each case, a relative pronoun creates a dependent clause.

To correct each of these fragments, add the words needed to complete the thought.

> **SENTENCE**   Novelist Richard Wright, who came to Paris in 1947, <u>spent the rest of his life there</u>.

> **SENTENCE**   A quinceañera, which celebrates a Latina's fifteenth birthday, <u>signifies her entrance into womanhood</u>.

> **SENTENCE**   A key World War II battle that was fought on the Pacific island of Guadalcanal <u>took place in 1943</u>.

Teaching Tip
You may want to refer students to 34d for information on punctuating restrictive and nonrestrictive clauses.

Relative Pronouns

that	who	whomever
what	whoever	whose
which	whom	

For information on how to use relative pronouns, see 20c.

PRACTICE

25-10 Correct each of the following dependent clause fragments by attaching it to the sentence before or after it. If the dependent clause comes at the beginning of a sentence, place a comma after it.

Example: Before it became a state. West Virginia was part of Virginia.

Before it became a state, West Virginia was part of Virginia.

1. Because many homeless people are mentally ill. It is hard to find places

   for them to live. *Because many homeless people are mentally ill, it is hard*

   to find places for them to live.

2. People do not realize how dangerous raccoons can be. Even though

   they can be found in many parts of the United States. *People do not*

   realize how dangerous racoons can be, even though they can be found in many

   parts of the United States.

3. I make plans to be a better student. Whenever a new semester begins.

   I make plans to be a better student whenever a new semester begins.

4. Until something changes. We will just have to accept the situation.

   Until something changes, we will just have to accept the situation.

5. Because it is a very controversial issue. My parents and I have agreed

   not to discuss it. *Because it is a very controversial issue, my parents and I have*

   agreed not to discuss it.

Teaching Tip
Review punctuation with complex sentences. Refer students to 20b.

PRACTICE

25-11 Correct each of these dependent clause fragments by adding the words needed to complete the idea.

Example: Many minor species of animals, which are rapidly disappearing.

Many minor species of animals, which are rapidly disappearing, need to be

protected.

Answers will vary.

1. The film that frightened me. _____

   _____

2. People who drink and drive. _____

   _____

3. Some parents who are very strict with their children. ＿＿＿＿＿＿

＿＿＿＿＿＿＿＿＿＿＿＿＿＿＿＿＿＿＿＿＿＿＿＿＿

4. The Vietnam War, which many Americans did not support. ＿＿＿＿

＿＿＿＿＿＿＿＿＿＿＿＿＿＿＿＿＿＿＿＿＿＿＿＿＿

5. Animals that are used in medical research. ＿＿＿＿＿＿＿＿＿

＿＿＿＿＿＿＿＿＿＿＿＿＿＿＿＿＿＿＿＿＿＿＿＿＿

PRACTICE
25-12   Each of the following is a fragment. Some are missing a subject, some are phrases incorrectly punctuated as sentences, others do not have a complete verb, and still others are dependent clauses punctuated as sentences. Turn each fragment into a complete sentence, writing the revised sentence on the line below the fragment. Whenever possible, try creating two different revisions.

    Example: Waiting in the dugout.

    Revised: *Waiting in the dugout, the players chewed tobacco.*

    Revised: *The players were waiting in the dugout.*
    Answers will vary.

1. Although three-year-olds are still very attached to their parents.

Revised: ＿＿＿＿＿＿＿＿＿＿＿＿＿＿＿＿＿＿＿＿＿＿

＿＿＿＿＿＿＿＿＿＿＿＿＿＿＿＿＿＿＿＿＿＿＿＿＿

Revised: ＿＿＿＿＿＿＿＿＿＿＿＿＿＿＿＿＿＿＿＿＿＿

＿＿＿＿＿＿＿＿＿＿＿＿＿＿＿＿＿＿＿＿＿＿＿＿＿

2. Going around in circles.

Revised: ＿＿＿＿＿＿＿＿＿＿＿＿＿＿＿＿＿＿＿＿＿＿

＿＿＿＿＿＿＿＿＿＿＿＿＿＿＿＿＿＿＿＿＿＿＿＿＿

Revised: ＿＿＿＿＿＿＿＿＿＿＿＿＿＿＿＿＿＿＿＿＿＿

＿＿＿＿＿＿＿＿＿＿＿＿＿＿＿＿＿＿＿＿＿＿＿＿＿

3. To win the prize for the most unusual costume.

Revised: ＿＿＿＿＿＿＿＿＿＿＿＿＿＿＿＿＿＿＿＿＿＿

＿＿＿＿＿＿＿＿＿＿＿＿＿＿＿＿＿＿＿＿＿＿＿＿＿

Revised: ＿＿＿＿＿＿＿＿＿＿＿＿＿＿＿＿＿＿＿＿＿＿

＿＿＿＿＿＿＿＿＿＿＿＿＿＿＿＿＿＿＿＿＿＿＿＿＿

4. Students who thought they could not afford to go to college.

Revised: _____

_____

Revised: _____

_____

5. On an important secret mission.

Revised: _____

_____

Revised: _____

_____

6. Because many instructors see cheating as a serious problem.

Revised: _____

_____

Revised: _____

_____

7. Hoping to get another helping of chocolate fudge cake.

Revised: _____

_____

Revised: _____

_____

8. The rule that I always felt was the most unfair.

Revised: _____

_____

Revised: _____

_____

9. A really exceptional worker.

Revised: _____

_____

Revised: _____

_____

10. Finished in record time.

Revised: _____

_____

Revised: _____

_____

TEST · Revise · Edit

Look back at your response to the Write First activity on page 431. Reread each word group you have punctuated as a sentence, starting with the last one and working your way back; make sure that each one contains a subject and a verb. Then, underline any words ending in *-ing*, any subordinating conjunctions, and the words *which, that,* and *who*, and make sure that the word groups they appear in are complete sentences. When you have finished, TEST the entire paragraph. Then, revise and edit your work.

EDITING PRACTICE: PARAGRAPH

Read the following student paragraph, which includes incomplete sentences. Underline each fragment. Then, correct the fragment by attaching it to an adjacent sentence that completes the idea. Be sure to punctuate correctly. The first fragment has been underlined and corrected for you.

Answers will vary.

The Hidden Costs of Knockoffs

Fake designer clothing and bags seem inexpensive, *, but they* ~~But~~ come with hidden costs. The first cost is to the workers, *, who* ~~Who~~ are often children earning only pennies for each item they make. The second cost is to the buyer, *of* ~~Of~~ the bargain purse or shirt. Counterfeit goods fall apart easily, *because* ~~Because~~ they are made quickly from cheap materials. The third cost is to society. Profits from knockoffs are not taxed, *and* ~~And~~ in some cases even support terrorism. The good news is that it is illegal, *to* ~~To~~ sell a product with a fake designer label. Unfortunately, however, it is not illegal to buy counterfeit goods. Therefore, it is up to shoppers to consider the hidden costs of knockoffs, *before* ~~Before~~ giving in to that "designer" deal.

EDITING PRACTICE: ESSAY

Read the following student essay, which includes incomplete sentences. Underline each fragment. Then, correct the fragment by attaching it to an adjacent sentence that completes the idea. Be sure to punctuate correctly. The first fragment has been underlined and corrected for you.

Answers will vary.

Bad Behavior at the Movies

Some people have completely stopped, *going* ~~Going~~ to the movies. They have not stopped because they dislike the movies but because they dislike the rude moviegoers, *who* ~~Who~~ ruin their experience. One big problem is irritating cell phone use. There are also problems with noise, *and* ~~And~~ with sharing the theater space with strangers. All these issues can make going to the movies seem like more trouble than it is worth.

Cell phones cause all sorts of problems, *in* ~~In~~ movie theaters. People are told to turn off their phones, *but* ~~But~~ do not always do so. Loud cell phone conversations can be infuriating. ⌃*to* To people who want to hear the movie. When a phone rings during an important scene in the movie. ⌃*, it* It is especially annoying. Some moviegoers even complain that bright text message screens distract them. ⌃*from* From the movie. Of course, theaters could use jammers. ⌃*to* To block all cell phone signals. Unfortunately, they would also block incoming emergency calls.

Noise in the movies also comes from other sources. ⌃*, such* Such as crying babies. People pay money to watch a movie. ⌃*, not* Not to listen to a baby screaming. Crinkling candy wrappers are also annoying. In addition, some moviegoers insist on talking to each other. ⌃*during* During the movie. In fact, they may make watching a movie an interactive event. ⌃*, talking* Talking to the actors and telling them what they should do next. If they have seen the movie before, they may recite lines of dialogue before the actors do. ⌃*, spoiling* Spoiling the suspense for everyone else. Sometimes people even talk loudly about subjects. ⌃*that* That have nothing to do with the movie. In all these cases, the noise is a problem. ⌃*for* For anyone who wants to watch the movie and hear the actors on the screen.

Mother and baby at the movies

Finally, going to the movies requires sharing the theater with other people. ⌃*who* Who are neither relatives nor friends. Unfortunately, many people behave in movie theaters the same way they behave at home. ⌃*when* When they are watching television. They may put their feet up on the seats in front of them. ⌃*, making* Making it impossible for others to sit there. Moviegoers become very annoyed if someone sits right in front of them. ⌃*and* And blocks their view of the screen. Of course, these issues do not come up at home. ⌃*, where* Where friends and relatives can easily work out any problems.

Couple kissing in a movie theater

Irritating movie behavior has driven many people to stop going to movie theaters. To end this rude behavior, moviegoers need to become aware of the needs of others. ⌃*and* And make a real effort to change their behavior. Selfishness is the problem; thinking about other people is the solution.

COLLABORATIVE ACTIVITIES

1. Exchange workbooks with another student, and read each other's responses to the Write First activity on page 431. On a separate sheet of paper, list five fragments that describe the product your partner has

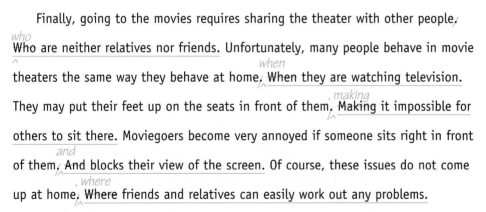

written about. When your own workbook is returned to you, revise each fragment written by your partner, creating a complete sentence for each one. Finally, add one of these new sentences to your own Write First activity.

2. Working in a group of three or four students, add different subordinating conjunctions to sentences *a* through *d* below to create several different fragments. (See 20b for a list of subordinating conjunctions.) Then, turn each of the resulting fragments into a complete sentence by adding a word group that completes the idea.

Example

SENTENCE	FRAGMENT	NEW SENTENCE
I left the party.	As I left the party	As I left the party, I fell.
	After I left the party	After I left the party, the fun stopped.
	Until I left the party	Until I left the party, I had no idea it was so late.

SENTENCES

a. My mind wanders.
b. She caught the ball.
c. He made a wish.
d. Disaster struck.

3. Working in a group of three or four students, build as many sentences as you can from the fragments listed below. Use your imagination to create as many creative sentences as you can.

Example

FRAGMENT Knowing he has an incredible memory

SENTENCES Zack, knowing he has an incredible memory, wonders how he managed to forget everything he learned about chemistry.

Knowing he has an incredible memory, Monty the Magnificent is confident that he can amaze his audience.

FRAGMENTS

a. wandering in the desert
b. never worrying about anything
c. looking for his ideal mate
d. always using as much ketchup as possible
e. starting a new job

review checklist

Fragments

☐ A fragment is an incomplete sentence. Every sentence must include a subject and a verb and express a complete thought. (See 25a.)

☐ Every sentence must include a subject. (See 25b.)

☐ Phrases cannot stand alone as sentences. (See 25c.)

☐ Every sentence must include a complete verb. (See 25d.)

☐ Dependent clauses cannot stand alone as sentences. (See 25e.)

Teaching Tip
As a review, read some sentences (and some fragments) to the class, and ask students to explain why each item is or is not a complete sentence.

26 Subject-Verb Agreement

write first

This painting by Ralph Fasanella is called *Baseball Panorama*. In a paragraph, describe what is happening on the field and in the stands. (Use present tense verbs.)

26a Understanding Subject-Verb Agreement

A sentence's subject (a noun or a pronoun) and its verb must **agree**: singular subjects take singular verbs, and plural subjects take plural verbs.

The <u>museum</u> <u>opens</u> at ten o'clock. (singular noun subject *museum* takes singular verb *opens*)

Both <u>museums</u> <u>open</u> at ten o'clock. (plural noun subject *museums* takes plural verb *open*)

<u>She</u> always <u>watches</u> the eleven o'clock news. (singular pronoun subject *she* takes singular verb *watches*)

<u>They</u> always <u>watch</u> the eleven o'clock news. (plural pronoun subject *they* takes plural verb *watch*)

Teaching Tip
Refer students to 31b and 31c for more on identifying plural noun and pronoun subjects.

Teaching Tip
Point out that subject-verb agreement presents special problems with the irregular verb *be*. Refer students to 26c.

Subject-Verb Agreement with Regular Verbs

	SINGULAR	PLURAL
First person	I play	Molly and I/we play
Second person	you play	you play
Third person	he/she/it plays	they play
	the man plays	the men play
	Molly plays	Molly and Sam play

Teaching Tip
On the board, write a sentence with a subject-verb agreement error—for example, *The boss want to hear from you.* Point out that usually an *-s* follows either the subject or the verb but not both. (Consider giving an example of an exception to this rule—for example, *Charles wants to hear from you.*)

PRACTICE
26-1
Underline the correct form of the verb in each of the following sentences. Make sure the verb agrees with its subject.

Example: Radio stations (<u>broadcast</u>/broadcasts) many kinds of music.

(1) Most music fans (<u>know</u>/knows) about salsa, a popular style of Latin music. (2) However, they (<u>need</u>/needs) a little education when it comes to ranchera, a blend of several traditional forms of Mexican music. (3) These forms (<u>include</u>/includes) mariachi music as well as ballads and waltz-like tunes. (4) Ranchera (appeal/<u>appeals</u>) to a wide audience of Americans of Mexican descent. (5) Its performers (<u>sell</u>/sells) millions of records a year, and often they (<u>top</u>/tops) *Billboard*'s Latin charts.

ESL Tip
Remember that ESL writers will not "hear" the correct form as native speakers instinctively do. ESL students will require more emphasis on formal rules.

(6) In fact, Mexican recordings (outsell/outsells) any other form of Latin music in the United States. (7) This popularity (surprise/surprises) many people. (8) Older ranchera lovers (tend/tends) to be first-generation, working-class immigrants, but more and more young listeners (seem/seems) drawn to ranchera. (9) Whenever one Los Angeles nightclub (host/hosts) a ranchera night, it (draw/draws) a large number of English-speaking fans in their twenties. (10) Clearly, ranchera musicians (deserve/deserves) more attention from the music industry.

PRACTICE
26-2 Fill in the blank with the correct present tense form of the verb.

Example: Americans _commute_ an average of 25 minutes to work each day. (commute)

(1) "Extreme commuters" _spend_ at least 90 minutes getting to work. (spend) (2) Their commutes _take_ much longer than the average American's trip to work. (take) (3) Sometimes, an extreme commuter even _crosses_ state lines to get to work. (cross) (4) Often, a person _chooses_ an extra-long commute for housing reasons. (choose) (5) Far outside the city, the "exurbs" _offer_ more affordable houses. (offer) (6) A more rural area usually _provides_ more peaceful surroundings as well. (provide) (7) Many extreme commuters _hate_ the time they spend commuting. (hate) (8) Others _enjoy_ the time they get to think, talk to other commuters, or listen to music. (enjoy) (9) In any case, extreme commuters usually _travel_ a long way to work because they have to. (travel) (10) For better or worse, more and more people _become_ extreme commuters every year. (become)

26b Compound Subjects

Teaching Tip
Tell students that the rules that govern compound subjects joined by *and* or *or* also govern compound subjects joined by *neither . . . nor.*

The subject of a sentence is not always a single word. It can also be a **compound subject**, made up of two or more subjects joined by *and* or *or*. To avoid subject-verb agreement problems with compound subjects, follow these rules.

1. When the parts of a compound subject are connected by *and,* the compound subject takes a plural verb.

   <u>John and Marsha</u> <u>share</u> an office.

2. When the parts of a compound subject are connected by *or,* the verb agrees with the part of the subject that is closer to it.

   <u>The mayor or the council members</u> <u>meet</u> with community groups.

   <u>The council members or the mayor</u> <u>meets</u> with community groups.

Teaching Tip
Tell students that an *-s* following a verb usually means the subject is singular. For example, in the sentence *He plays golf,* because *he* refers to just one person, the verb needs an *-s.* (Point out the exception that occurs with *I* and *you.*)

PRACTICE

26-3   Underline the correct form of the verb in each of the following sentences. Make sure that the verb agrees with its compound subject.

> **Example:**   Every summer, wind and rain (<u>pound</u>/pounds) the small shack on the beach.

1. Trophies and medals (<u>fill</u>/fills) my sister's bedroom.

2. Mashed potatoes and gravy (<u>come</u>/comes) with all our chicken dinners.

3. The instructor or his graduate students (<u>grade</u>/grades) the final exams.

4. A voice coach and a piano instructor (<u>teach</u>/teaches) each of the gifted students.

5. Pollen or cat hair (trigger/<u>triggers</u>) allergies in many people.

6. Psychologists or social workers (<u>provide</u>/provides) crisis counseling.

7. Exercise and healthy eating habits (<u>lead</u>/leads) to longer lives.

8. Both parents or only the father (walk/<u>walks</u>) the bride down the aisle at a wedding.

9. The restaurant owner and his daughters (<u>greet</u>/greets) customers as they enter.

10. Flowers or a get-well balloon (cheer/<u>cheers</u>) people up when they are ill.

26c   *Be, Have,* and *Do*

Teaching Tip
You may need to remind students that standard written English does not use *be* as a helping verb. For example, *He be trying to get my attention* is incorrect.

The verbs *be, have,* and *do* are irregular in the present tense. For this reason, they can present problems with subject-verb agreement. Memorizing their forms is the only sure way to avoid such problems.

Subject-Verb Agreement with *Be*

	SINGULAR	PLURAL
First person	I am	we are
Second person	you are	you are
Third person	he/she/it is	they are
	Tran is	Tran and Ryan are
	the boy is	the boys are

Subject-Verb Agreement with *Have*

	SINGULAR	PLURAL
First person	I have	we have
Second person	you have	you have
Third person	he/she/it has	they have
	Shana has	Shana and Robert have
	the student has	the students have

Subject-Verb Agreement with *Do*

	SINGULAR	PLURAL
First person	I do	we do
Second person	you do	you do
Third person	he/she/it does	they do
	Ken does	Ken and Mia do
	the book does	the books do

PRACTICE

26-4   Fill in the blank with the correct present tense form of the verb *be*, *have*, or *do*.

Example: Sometimes, people ___*do*___ damage without really meaning to. (do)

(1) Biologists ___*have*___ serious worries about the damage that invading species of animals can cause. (have) (2) The English sparrow ___*is*___ one example. (be) (3) It ___*has*___ a role in the decline in the number of bluebirds. (have) (4) On the Galapagos Islands, cats ___*are*___ another example. (be) (5) Introduced by early explorers, they currently ___*do*___ much damage to the eggs of the giant tortoises that live on the islands. (do) (6) Scientists today ___*are*___ worried now about a new problem. (be)

(7) This _____*is*_____ a situation caused by wildlife agencies that put exotic fish into lakes and streams. (be) (8) They _____*do*_____ this to please those who enjoy fishing. (do) (9) Although popular with people who fish, this policy _____*has*_____ major drawbacks. (have) (10) It _____*has*_____ one drawback in particular: many native species of fish have been pushed close to extinction. (have)

26d   Words between Subject and Verb

Keep in mind that a verb must always agree with its subject. Don't be confused when a group of words (for example, a prepositional phrase) comes between the subject and the verb. These words do not affect subject-verb agreement.

Teaching Tip
Refer students to 18b for more on prepositional phrases and for a list of prepositions.

CORRECT	High <u>levels</u> of mercury <u>occur</u> in some fish.
CORRECT	<u>Water</u> in the fuel lines <u>causes</u> an engine to stall.
CORRECT	<u>Food</u> between the teeth <u>leads</u> to decay.

An easy way to identify the subject of the sentence is to cross out the words that come between the subject and the verb.

High levels ~~of mercury~~ occur in some fish.

Water ~~in the fuel lines~~ causes an engine to stall.

Food ~~between the teeth~~ leads to decay.

FYI

Words between Subject and Verb

Look out for words such as *in addition to, along with, together with, as well as, except,* and *including.* Phrases introduced by these words do not affect subject-verb agreement.

<u>St. Thomas</u>, ~~along with St. Croix and St. John~~, <u>is</u> part of the United States Virgin Islands.

PRACTICE

26-5 In each of the following sentences, cross out the words that separate the subject and the verb. Then, underline the subject of the sentence once and the verb that agrees with the subject twice.

Example: The messages ~~on the phone~~ (say/<u>says</u>) that Carol is out of town.

1. Each summer, <u>fires</u> ~~from lightning~~ (cause/<u>causes</u>) great damage.

2. <u>Books</u> downloaded ~~onto an eReader~~ usually (<u>cost</u>/costs) less than print books.

3. <u>One</u> ~~out of ten men~~ (<u>gets</u>/get) prostate cancer.

4. The <u>woodstove</u> ~~in the living room~~ (heat/<u>heats</u>) the entire house.

5. <u>Trans fat</u> ~~in a variety of foods~~ (lead/<u>leads</u>) to increased rates of heart disease.

6. A good <u>set</u> ~~of mechanic's tools~~ (<u>costs</u>/cost) a lot of money.

7. <u>New Orleans</u>, ~~along with other Gulf Coast cities,~~ (<u>suffers</u>/suffer) from severe flooding.

8. The <u>United States</u> ~~as well as Germany and Japan~~ (<u>produces</u>/produce) the world's best cars.

9. <u>Fans</u> ~~at a concert~~ (gets/<u>get</u>) angry if the band is late.

10. The <u>book</u> ~~on the table~~ (look/<u>looks</u>) interesting.

26e Collective Noun Subjects

Collective nouns are words (such as *family* and *audience*) that name a group of people or things but are singular. Because they are singular, they always take singular verbs.

$\overset{\text{s}}{\text{The \underline{team}}}\ \overset{\text{v}}{\underline{\text{practices}}}$ five days a week in the gym.

Frequently Used Collective Nouns

army	club	family	jury
association	committee	gang	mob
band	company	government	team
class	corporation	group	union

PRACTICE

26-6   Fill in the blank with the correct present tense form of the verb.

Example: Our government ____is____ democratically elected by the people. (be)

1. The Caribbean Culture Club ____meets____ on the first Thursday of every month. (meet)

2. The company no longer ____provides____ health insurance for part-time employees. (provide)

3. The basketball team ____is____ competing in the division finals next week. (be)

4. After two days, the jury ____has____ been unable to reach a verdict. (have)

5. The union ____wants____ guaranteed raises for its members. (want)

26f   Indefinite Pronoun Subjects

Indefinite pronouns—*anybody, everyone,* and so on—do not refer to a particular person, place, or idea.

Most indefinite pronouns are singular and take singular verbs.

        s   v
No one likes getting up early.

    s   v
Everyone likes to sleep late.

     s   v
Somebody likes beets.

> **Teaching Tip**
> Remind students that many indefinite pronouns end in *-one, -body,* or *-thing.* These words are almost always singular.

Singular Indefinite Pronouns

another	either	neither	somebody
anybody	everybody	nobody	someone
anyone	everyone	no one	something
anything	everything	nothing	
each	much	one	

> **Teaching Tip**
> Refer students to 31e for more on pronoun-antecedent agreement with indefinite pronouns.

A few indefinite pronouns (*both, many, several, few, others*) are plural and take plural verbs.

     s   v
Many were left homeless by the flood.

FYI

Indefinite Pronouns as Subjects

If a prepositional phrase comes between the indefinite pronoun and the verb, cross out the prepositional phrase to help you identify the sentence's subject.

<u>Each</u> ~~of the boys~~ <u>has</u> a bike.

<u>Many</u> ~~of the boys~~ <u>have</u> bikes.

PRACTICE
26-7 Underline the correct verb in each sentence.

Example: As my friends and I know, anything (helps/help) when it comes to paying for college.

1. One of my friends (has/have) an academic scholarship.

2. Another (relies/rely) entirely on loans.

3. Several of us (works/work) on weekends.

4. Everybody (says/say) that work-study jobs are best.

5. Many of the most interesting work-study jobs (is/are) located on campus.

6. Others (places/place) students off campus with nonprofits or government agencies.

7. Some of the work-study jobs (tends/tend) to be better than a regular job.

8. Not everyone (understands/understand) the demands of school, but work-study employers do.

9. Nobody (says/say) juggling work and school is simple, but work-study makes it easier.

10. Each of my work-study friends (is/are) glad to have this option.

Teaching Tip
Explain to students that the indefinite pronoun *some* can be singular or plural depending on what it refers to.

26g Verbs before Subjects

A verb always agrees with its subject—even if the verb comes *before* the subject. In questions, for example, word order is reversed, with the verb coming before the subject or with the subject coming between two parts of the verb.

Where **is** the **bank**?
(v above "is", s above "bank")

Are **you** **going** to the party?
(v above "Are", s above "you", v above "going")

If you have trouble identifying the subject of a question, answer the question with a statement. (In the statement, the subject will come before the verb.)

Where **is** the **bank**? The **bank** **is** on Walnut Street.
(v above "is", s above "bank"; s above "bank", v above "is")

ESL Tip
Point out that questions depart from conventional English word order. Write a series of statements on the board, and have students change them into questions.

FYI

There Is and *There Are*

When a sentence begins with *there is* or *there are*, the word *there* is not the subject of the sentence. The subject comes after the form of the verb *be*.

There **is** one **chief justice** on the Supreme Court.
(v above "is", s above "chief justice")

There **are** nine **justices** on the Supreme Court.
(v above "are", s above "justices")

PRACTICE
26-8

Underline the subject of each sentence, and circle the correct form of the verb.

Example: Who (is/are) the baseball player who broke Hank Aaron's home-run record?

1. Where (do/does) snakes go in the winter?

2. Why (do/does) people who cannot afford them buy lottery tickets?

3. (Is/Are) there any states that do not follow Daylight Savings Time?

4. How (do/does) an immigrant become a citizen?

5. There (is/are) three branches of government in the United States.

6. There (is/are) one way to improve vocabulary—read often.

7. There (is/are) some money available for financial aid.

8. There (is/are) four steps involved in changing the oil in a car.

9. What (is/are) the country with the highest literacy rate?

10. Where (do/does) the football team practice in the off-season?

TEST · Revise · Edit

Look back at your response to the Write First activity on page 454. TEST what you have written. Then, revise and edit your work, making sure that all your verbs agree with their subjects. Pay particular attention to agreement problems when sentences contain the following elements:

- Compound subjects
- The verbs *be, have,* and *do*
- Words between the subject and the verb
- Collective noun subjects
- Indefinite pronoun subjects
- Verbs before subjects

EDITING PRACTICE: PARAGRAPH

Read the following student paragraph, which includes errors in subject-verb agreement. Decide whether each of the underlined verbs agrees with its subject. If it does not, cross out the verb, and write in the correct form. If it does, write *C* above the verb. The first sentence has been done for you.

Conflict Diamonds

Today, many people <u>know</u> [*C*] about conflict diamonds, and most <u>wants</u> [*want*] this violent trade to end. These illegal diamonds <u>comes</u> [*come*] from countries where there <u>are</u> [*is*] civil war. Most often, the origin of these stones <u>is</u> [*C*] an unstable central or west African nation. Rebel groups in these countries <u>mines</u> [*mine*] the diamonds and <u>sells</u> [*sell*] them to raise money for weapons. In the process, local people, who <u>does</u> [*do*] not benefit from the sale of the diamonds, often <u>gets</u> [*get*] hurt or killed. How <u>does</u> [*C*] a person who wants to buy a diamond avoid buying a conflict diamond? Once a diamond <u>reach</u> [*reaches*] the store, neither a customer nor a gem expert <u>have</u> [*has*] the ability to see its history just by looking at it. However, a consumer can ask for proof that the diamond <u>is</u> [*C*] "conflict-free." Each of the diamonds in a store <u>are</u> [*is*] supposed to have an official certificate to prove that it <u>is</u> [*C*] legal.

Couple choosing an engagement ring

EDITING PRACTICE: ESSAY

Read the following student essay, which includes errors in subject-verb agreement. Decide whether each of the underlined verbs agrees with its subject. If it does not, cross out the verb, and write in the correct form. If it does, write *C* above the verb. The first sentence has been done for you.

Party in the Parking Lot

Fun at football games <u>are</u> [*is*] not limited to cheering for the home team. Many people <u>arrives</u> [*arrive*] four or five hours early, <u>sets</u> [*set*] up grills in the parking lot, and <u>start</u> [*C*] cooking. Typically, fans <u>drives</u> [*drive*] to the stadium in a pickup truck, a station wagon, or an SUV. They <u>open</u> [*C*] up the tailgate, <u>puts</u> [*put*] out the food, and <u>enjoys</u> [*enjoy*] the atmosphere with their friends. In fact, tailgating <u>is</u> [*C*] so popular that, for some fans, it is more important than the game itself.

Tailgaters deep-frying a turkey

Tailgating in a stadium parking lot

Eagles and Patriots fans at Superbowl XXXIX (2005)

What *do* [does] it take to tailgate? First, most tailgaters *plan* [C] their menus in advance. To avoid forgetting anything, they *makes* [make] lists of what to bring. Disposable paper plates, along with a set of plastic cups, *make* [C] it unnecessary to bring home dirty dishes. Jugs of water *is* [are] essential, and damp towels *helps* [help] clean up hands and faces. Also, lightweight chairs or another type of seating *is* [C] important.

At the game, parking near a grassy area or at the end of a parking row *are* [is] best. This location *give* [gives] tailgaters more space to cook and eat. If the food *are* [is] ready two hours before the game *start,* [starts,] there *is* [C] plenty of time to eat and to clean up.

Some tailgaters *buys* [buy] expensive equipment. The simple charcoal grill *have* [has] turned into a combination grill, cooler, and fold-out table with a portable awning. There *is* [are] grills with their own storage space. Other grills *swings* [swing] out from the tailgate to provide easy access to the vehicle's storage area. Some deluxe grills even *has* [have] their own beer taps, stereo systems, and sinks.

Whatever equipment tailgaters *brings* [bring] to the game, the most important factors *is* [are] food and companionship. There *is* [C] a tradition of sharing food and swapping recipes with other tailgaters. Most tailgaters *loves* [love] to meet and compare notes on recipes. For many, the tailgating experience *is* [C] more fun than the game itself.

COLLABORATIVE ACTIVITIES

1. Working in a group of four students, list ten nouns (five singular and five plural)—people, places, or things—on the left-hand side of a sheet of paper. Beside each noun, write the present tense form of a verb that could logically be used with the noun. Exchange papers with another group, and check to see that singular nouns are used with singular verbs and plural nouns are used with plural verbs.

2. Working with your group, expand each noun-and-verb combination you listed in Collaborative Activity 1 into a complete sentence. Next, write a sentence that could logically follow each of these sentences, using a pronoun as the subject of the new sentence. Make sure the pronoun you choose refers to the noun in the previous sentence, as in this example: *Alan watches three movies a week. He is addicted to films.* Check to be certain the subjects in your sentences agree with the verbs.

3. Exchange the final version of your edited Write First activity with another student in your group. Answer the following questions about each sentence in your partner's work.

■ Does the sentence contain a compound subject?

■ Does the sentence contain words that come between the subject and the verb?

■ Does the sentence contain an indefinite pronoun used as a subject?

■ Does the sentence contain a verb that comes before the subject?

As you answer these questions, check to make sure all the verbs agree with their subjects. When your own work is returned to you, make any necessary corrections.

review checklist

Subject-Verb Agreement

☐ Singular subjects (nouns and pronouns) take singular verbs, and plural subjects take plural verbs. (See 26a.)

☐ Special rules govern subject-verb agreement with compound subjects. (See 26b.)

☐ The irregular verbs *be, have,* and *do* often present problems with subject-verb agreement in the present tense. (See 26c.)

☐ Words that come between the subject and the verb do not affect subject-verb agreement. (See 26d.)

☐ Collective nouns are singular and take singular verbs. (See 26e.)

☐ Most indefinite pronouns, such as *no one* and *everyone*, are singular and take a singular verb when they serve as the subject of a sentence. A few are plural and take plural verbs. (See 26f.)

☐ A sentence's subject and verb must always agree, even if the verb comes before the subject. (See 26g.)

27 Illogical Shifts

write first

This picture shows a mother and daughter on Take Your Daughters and Sons to Work Day. Do you think programs like this help children succeed? Think for a bit about how parents can motivate their children to set appropriate goals and work to achieve them. Then, write a short paragraph expressing your ideas.

A **shift** occurs whenever a writer changes **tense**, **person**, or **voice**. As you write and revise, be sure that any shifts you make are **logical**—that is, that they occur for a reason.

27a Shifts in Tense

Tense is the form a verb takes to show when an action takes place or when a situation occurs. Some shifts in tense are necessary—for example, to indicate a change from past time to present time.

LOGICAL SHIFT When they first came out, cell phones were large and bulky, but now they are small and compact.

An **illogical shift in tense** occurs when a writer shifts from one tense to another for no apparent reason.

ILLOGICAL SHIFT IN TENSE The dog walked to the fireplace. Then, he circles twice and lies down in front of the fire. (shift from past tense to present tense)

REVISED The dog walked to the fireplace. Then, he circled twice and lay down in front of the fire. (consistent use of past tense)

REVISED The dog walks to the fireplace. Then, he circles twice and lies down in front of the fire. (consistent use of present tense)

Teaching Tip
Refer students to Chapters 29 and 30 for more on tense.

PRACTICE 27-1

Edit the following sentences to correct illogical shifts in tense. If a sentence is correct, write *C* in the blank.

Example: The 100th Battalion of the 442nd Infantry is the only remaining United States Army Reserve ground combat unit that fought in World War II. _____*c*_____

(1) During World War II, the 100th Battalion of the 442nd Combat Infantry Regiment was made up of young Japanese Americans who *were* are eager to serve in the U.S. Army. _____ (2) At the start of World War II, 120,000 Japanese Americans *were* are sent to relocation camps because the government feared that they might be disloyal to the United States. _____ (3) However, in 1943, the United States needed more soldiers, so it *sent* sends recruiters to the camps to ask for volunteers. _____ (4) The

Teaching Tip
Have students assign a year to each verb. For instance, in the first exercise sentence, both actions occur in the past, so both should use the past tense. In the example sentence, the first action occurs in the present, so it requires the present tense; the second action occurs in the past, so it requires the past tense. Students enjoy this activity, and it helps them remember to watch for unwarranted tense shifts.

Japanese-American volunteers are *were* organized into the 442nd Combat Infantry Regiment. _____ (5) The soldiers of the 442nd Infantry fought in some of the bloodiest battles of the war, including the invasion of Italy at Anzio and a battle in Bruyeres, France, where they capture *captured* over two hundred enemy soldiers. _____ (6) When other U.S. troops are *were* cut off by the enemy, the 442nd Infantry soldiers were sent to rescue them. _____ (7) The Japanese-American soldiers suffered the highest casualty rate of any U.S. unit and receive *received* over eighteen thousand individual decorations. _____ (8) Former senator Daniel Inouye of Hawaii, a Japanese American, was awarded the Distinguished Service Cross for his bravery in Italy and has *had* to have his arm amputated. _____ (9) The 442nd Infantry was awarded more decorations than any other combat unit of its size and earns *earned* eight Presidential Unit citations. _____ (10) Today, the dedication and sacrifice of the 442nd Infantry was *is* seen as evidence that Japanese Americans were patriotic and committed to freedom and democracy. _____

27b Shifts in Person

Person is the form a pronoun takes to show who is speaking, spoken about, or spoken to.

Person

	SINGULAR	PLURAL
First person	I	we
Second person	you	you
Third person	he, she, it	they

An **illogical shift in person** occurs when a writer shifts from one person to another for no apparent reason.

ILLOGICAL SHIFT IN PERSON	The hikers were told that you had to stay on the trail. (shift from third person to second person)
REVISED	The hikers were told that they had to stay on the trail. (consistent use of third person)

ILLOGICAL SHIFT IN PERSON	Anyone can learn to cook if you practice. (shift from third person to second person)
REVISED	You can learn to cook if you practice. (consistent use of second person)
REVISED	Anyone can learn to cook if he or she practices. (consistent use of third person)

PRACTICE

27-2 The following sentences contain illogical shifts in person. Edit each sentence so that it uses pronouns consistently. Be sure to change any verbs that do not agree with the new subjects.

Example: Before a person finds a job in the fashion industry, ~~you have~~ to have some experience. *[he or she has]*

(1) Young people who want careers in the fashion industry do not always realize how hard ~~you~~ *[they]* will have to work. (2) They think that working in the world of fashion will be glamorous and that ~~you~~ *[they]* will make a lot of money. (3) In reality, no matter how talented ~~you are~~ *[he or she is,]* a recent college graduate entering the industry is paid only about $22,000 a year. (4) The manufacturers who employ new graduates expect ~~you~~ *[them]* to work at least three years at this salary before ~~you~~ *[they]* are promoted. (5) A young designer may get a big raise if ~~you are~~ *[he or she is]* very talented, but this is unusual. (6) New employees have to pay their dues, and ~~you~~ *[they]* soon realize that most of ~~your~~ *[their]* duties are boring. (7) An employee may land a job as an assistant designer but then find that ~~you have~~ *[he or she has]* to color in designs that have already been drawn. (8) Other beginners discover that ~~you~~ *[they]* spend most of ~~your~~ *[their]* time typing up orders. (9) If a person is serious about working in the fashion industry, ~~you have~~ *[he or she has]* to be realistic. (10) For most newcomers to the industry, the ability to do what ~~you~~ *[they]* are told to do is more important than ~~your~~ *[their]* talent.

27c   Shifts in Voice

Voice is the form a verb takes to indicate whether the subject is acting or is acted upon. When the subject is acting, the sentence is in the **active voice**. When the subject is acted upon, the sentence is in the **passive voice**.

ACTIVE VOICE	Nat Turner organized a slave rebellion in August 1831. (Subject *Nat Turner* is acting.)
PASSIVE VOICE	A slave rebellion was organized by Nat Turner in 1831. (Subject *rebellion* is acted upon.)

An **illogical shift in voice** occurs when a writer shifts from active to passive voice or from passive to active voice for no apparent reason.

ILLOGICAL SHIFT IN VOICE	J. D. Salinger wrote *The Catcher in the Rye,* and *Franny and Zooey* was also written by him. (active to passive)
REVISED	J. D. Salinger wrote *The Catcher in the Rye,* and he also wrote *Franny and Zooey.* (consistent use of active voice)
ILLOGICAL SHIFT IN VOICE	Radium was discovered by Marie Curie in 1910, and she won a Nobel Prize in chemistry in 1911. (passive to active)
REVISED	Marie Curie discovered radium in 1910, and she won a Nobel Prize in chemistry in 1911. (consistent use of active voice)

FYI

Correcting Illogical Shifts in Voice

You should usually use the active voice in your college writing because it is stronger and more direct than the passive voice.

To change a sentence from the passive to the active voice, determine who or what is acting, and make this noun the subject of a new active voice sentence.

PASSIVE VOICE	The campus escort service is used by my friends. (*My friends* are acting.)
ACTIVE VOICE	My friends use the campus escort service.

PRACTICE

27-3 The following sentences contain illogical shifts in voice. Revise each sentence by changing the underlined passive voice verb to the active voice.

Example

Two teachers believed they could help struggling students in New York

City schools, so "Chess in the Schools" was founded by them.

Two teachers believed they could help struggling students in New York

City schools, so they founded "Chess in the Schools."

ESL Tip
Have students label passive and active verbs before they make their corrections.

1. Chess develops critical-thinking skills, and self-discipline and self-esteem <u>are developed</u> by players, too.

   Chess develops critical-thinking skills, and players develop self-discipline and

   self-esteem, too.

2. Because players face complicated chess problems, good problem-solving skills <u>are developed</u> by them.

   Because players face complicated chess problems, they develop good problem-solving

   skills.

3. Student chess players improve their concentration, and reading and math skills <u>can be improved</u> through this better concentration.

   Student chess players improve their concentration, and this better concentration

   can improve reading and math skills.

4. Chess teaches students how to lose as well as win, and that ability <u>will be needed</u> by students throughout their lives.

   Chess teaches students how to lose as well as win, and students will need that

   ability throughout their lives.

5. "Chess in the Schools" also helps keep students out of trouble because of the conflict-resolution skills <u>developed</u> by them.

   "Chess in the Schools" also helps keep students out of trouble because of the conflict-

   resolution skills they develop.

TEST · **Revise · Edit**

Look back at your response to the Write First activity on page 468. TEST what you have written. Then, revise and edit your work, paying particular attention to illogical shifts in tense, person, or voice.

EDITING PRACTICE: PARAGRAPH

Read the following student paragraph, which includes illogical shifts in tense, person, and voice. Edit the passage to eliminate the unnecessary shifts, making sure subjects and verbs agree. The first error has been corrected for you.

The Origin of Baseball Cards

The first baseball cards appeared in the late 1800s. These cardboard pictures *were* are inserted in packs of cigarettes. Some people collected the cards, and the *used* cigarette companies use the cards to encourage people to buy their products. By *found they* the early twentieth century, it was found by candy makers that one could use baseball cards to sell candy to children, so they developed new marketing plans. *contained* For example, each Cracker Jack box contains a baseball card. In 1933, gum manufacturers packaged bubble gum with baseball cards to make "bubble gum cards." Children could trade these cards. Sometimes, children would put cards in *turned.* the spokes of their bike wheels. The cards made noise when the wheels turns. *was* Eventually, the bubble gum is dropped by the card manufacturers, and people just bought the cards. Still, collecting baseball cards was seen as just a hobby for children until the 1970s, when dealers began to sell their rarest cards at high *are* prices. Today, baseball-card collectors were mainly adults who are interested in investment, not baseball. For example, in 2007, a rare Honus Wagner baseball *sold* card sells for a record 2.8 million dollars.

1909 Honus Wagner baseball card, which sold for over two million dollars in 2007

EDITING PRACTICE: ESSAY

Read the following essay, which includes illogical shifts in tense, person, and voice. Edit the passage to eliminate the illogical shifts, making sure subjects and verbs agree. The first sentence has been edited for you.

A Different Kind of Vacation

During our upcoming winter break, my sister and I *are* were going to Belize to help build a school. Like many people, we want to travel and see new places, *do* but we did not want to be tourists who only see what is in a guidebook. We also want to help people who are less fortunate than we ~~were~~ *are.* Volunteering gives us

the opportunity to combine travel with community service and to get to know a

different culture at the same time.

These days, many people are using ~~his or her~~ *their* vacation time to do volunteer

work. Lots of charitable organizations offer short-term projects during

school or holiday breaks. For most projects, no experience ~~was~~ *is* necessary. All

people need is ~~his or her~~ *their* interest in other people and a desire to help.

For example, last year my aunt ~~goes~~ *went* to Tanzania to work in a health clinic.

She loved her experience volunteering in a poor rural community where ~~you help~~ *she helped*

local doctors. She also loved the host family who shared ~~their~~ *its* modest house

with her. Before she left Tanzania, she and some of the other volunteers ~~climb~~ *climbed*

Mount Kilimanjaro. She said it was the best vacation she had ever had.

Although many volunteer vacations focus on improving schools or health

care, a wide range of projects ~~was~~ *is* available. Everyone can find work that

suits ~~their~~ *his or her* interests. For instance, people can volunteer to help preserve the

environment, or ~~you~~ *they* can work to protect women's rights. Countries all over the

world welcome volunteers because ~~help is needed by a lot of people.~~ *a lot of people need help.*

My sister and I decided to help with the school in Belize because we believe

a clean and safe place to learn ~~is deserved by everyone.~~ *everyone deserves.* We are also eager to do

some construction, get to know the local people, and enjoy the warm weather.

If we have enough time, we ~~hoped~~ *hope* to visit some Mayan ruins as well. All in all,

we are looking forward to a rewarding and unforgettable experience.

Teaching Tip
Remind students that a collective noun such as *family* is usually singular and is used with a singular pronoun. Refer them to 31e.

COLLABORATIVE ACTIVITIES

1. Write five sentences that include shifts from present to past tense, some logical and some illogical. Exchange sentences with another student, and revise any errors you find.

2. As a group, make up a test with five sentences containing illogical shifts in tense, person, and voice. Exchange tests with another group in the class. After you have taken their test, compare your answers with theirs.

review checklist

Illogical Shifts

- [ ] An illogical shift in tense occurs when a writer shifts from one tense to another for no apparent reason. (See 27a.)

- [ ] An illogical shift in person occurs when a writer shifts from one person to another for no apparent reason. (See 27b.)

- [ ] An illogical shift in voice occurs when a writer shifts from active to passive voice or from passive to active voice for no apparent reason. (See 27c.)

28 Misplaced and Dangling Modifiers

preview

In this chapter, you will learn to recognize and correct
- misplaced modifiers (28a)
- dangling modifiers (28b)

write first

Think about your favorite food. Then—whether you've actually ever prepared it or not—try to write a recipe for it. Begin by describing the food; then, list the ingredients, and explain how to make it ready for the table.

A **modifier** is a word or word group that identifies or describes another word in a sentence. Many word groups that act as modifiers are introduced by *-ing* (present participle) or *-ed* (past participle) modifiers. To avoid confusion, a modifier should be placed as close as possible to the word it modifies—ideally, directly before or directly after it.

Working in his garage, Steve Jobs invented the personal computer.

Rejected by Hamlet, Ophelia goes mad and drowns herself.

Used correctly, *-ing* and *-ed* modifiers provide useful information. Used incorrectly, however, these types of modifiers can be very confusing.

The two most common problems with modification are *misplaced modifiers* and *dangling modifiers*.

28a   Correcting Misplaced Modifiers

A **misplaced modifier** appears to modify the wrong word because it is placed incorrectly in the sentence. To correct this problem, move the modifier so it is as close as possible to the word it is supposed to modify (usually directly before or after it).

INCORRECT   Sarah fed the dog wearing her pajamas. (Was the dog wearing Sarah's pajamas?)

CORRECT   Wearing her pajamas, Sarah fed the dog.

INCORRECT   Dressed in a raincoat and boots, I thought my son was prepared for the storm. (Who was dressed in a raincoat and boots?)

CORRECT   I thought my son, dressed in a raincoat and boots, was prepared for the storm.

**PRACTICE
28-1**   Underline the modifier in each of the following sentences. Then, draw an arrow to the word it modifies.

Example: Helping people worldwide, Doctors Without Borders is a group of volunteer medical professionals.

1. <u>Suffering from famine and other disasters</u>, some people are unable to help themselves.

2. <u>Feeding and healing them</u>, Doctors Without Borders improves their lives.

3. <u>Responding to a recent earthquake</u>, doctors arrived within three days to help with the relief effort.

4. <u>Setting up refugee camps in Thailand</u>, the group quickly helped its first survivors.

5. Some doctors, <u>chartering a ship called *The Island of Light*</u>, once provided medical aid to people escaping Vietnam by boat.

PRACTICE
28-2   Rewrite the following sentences, which contain misplaced modifiers, so that each modifier clearly refers to the word it logically modifies.

Example: Mark ate a pizza standing in front of the refrigerator.

Standing in front of the refrigerator, Mark ate a pizza.

1. The cat broke the vase frightened by a noise.

Frightened by a noise, the cat broke the vase.

_____

2. Running across my bathroom ceiling, I saw two large, hairy bugs.

I saw two large, hairy bugs running across my bathroom ceiling.

_____

3. Lori looked at the man sitting in the chair with red hair.

Lori looked at the man with red hair sitting in the chair.

_____

4. *ET* is a film about an alien directed by Steven Spielberg.

ET is a film directed by Steven Spielberg about an alien.

_____

5. Covered with chocolate sauce, Fred loves ice cream sundaes.

   Fred loves ice cream sundaes covered with chocolate sauce.

   _____

6. After reading the poem, the meaning became clear to me.

   The meaning became clear to me after reading the poem.

   _____

7. The deer was hit by a car running across the street.

   Running across the street, the deer was hit by a car.

   _____

8. Dressed in a beautiful wedding gown, the groom watched the bride walk down the aisle.

   The groom watched the bride walk down the aisle in a beautiful wedding gown.

   _____

9. The exterminator sprayed the insect wearing a mask.

   Wearing a mask, the exterminator sprayed the insect.

   _____

10. With a mysterious smile, Leonardo da Vinci painted the *Mona Lisa*.

    Leonardo da Vinci painted the Mona Lisa with a mysterious smile.

    _____

28b Correcting Dangling Modifiers

A **dangling modifier** "dangles" because the word it modifies does not appear in the sentence. Often, a dangling modifier comes at the beginning of a sentence and appears to modify the noun or pronoun that follows it.

<u>Using my computer,</u> the report was finished in two days.

In the sentence above, the modifier *Using my computer* seems to be modifying *the report*. But this makes no sense. (How can the report use a computer?) The word the modifier should logically refer to is missing. To correct this sentence, you need to supply this missing word.

<u>Using my computer,</u> I finished the report in two days.

To correct a dangling modifier, supply a word to which the modifier can logically refer.

INCORRECT Moving the microscope's mirror, the light can be directed onto the slide. (Can the light move the mirror?)

CORRECT Moving the microscope's mirror, you can direct the light onto the slide.

INCORRECT Paid in advance, the furniture was delivered. (Was the furniture paid in advance?)

CORRECT Paid in advance, the movers delivered the furniture.

PRACTICE

28-3 Each of the following sentences contains a dangling modifier. To correct each sentence, add a word to which the modifier can logically refer.

Example: Waiting inside, my bus passed by.

Waiting inside, I missed my bus.

Answers will vary.

1. Paid by the school, the books were sorted in the library.

   _____

   _____

2. Pushing on the brakes, my car would not stop for the red light.

   _____

   _____

3. Short of money, the trip was canceled.

   _____

   _____

4. Working overtime, his salary almost doubled.

   _____

   _____

5. Angered by the noise, the concert was called off.

   _____

   _____

6. Using the correct formula, the problem was easily solved.

_____

_____

7. Tired and hungry, the assignment was finished by midnight.

_____

_____

8. Sitting on a park bench, the pigeons were fed.

_____

9. Staying in bed on Sunday, the newspaper was read from beginning to end.

_____

_____

10. Driving for a long time, my leg began to hurt.

_____

PRACTICE

28-4 Complete the following sentences, making sure to include a word to which each modifier can logically refer.

Example: Dancing with the man of her dreams, *she decided it was*

time to wake up.

Answers will vary.

1. Blocked by the clouds, _____

_____

2. Applying for financial aid, _____

_____

3. Settled into his recliner chair, _____

_____

4. Fearing that they might catch a cold, _____

_____

5. Hearing strange noises through the wall, _____

_____

6. Soaked by the rain, _____

_____

7. Looking at Facebook until after midnight, _____

_____

8. Lighting the candles, _____

_____

9. Donated by disaster aid groups, _____

_____

10. Wearing their best clothes, _____

_____

TEST · Revise · Edit

Look back at your response to the Write First activity on page 477. TEST what you have written. Then, revise and edit your work, paying particular attention to *-ing* and *-ed* modifiers. Check your work to make sure that you do not have any misplaced or dangling modifiers.

EDITING PRACTICE: PARAGRAPH

Read the following student paragraph, which includes modification errors. Rewrite sentences where necessary to correct misplaced and dangling modifiers. In some cases, you may have to supply a word to which the modifier can logically refer. The first incorrect sentence has been corrected for you. *Answers will vary.*

Beyond Mickey Mouse

For more than twenty years, Pixar computer animation studios have produced movies. Sketched by hand before Pixar, ~~artists provided thousands of pictures~~ for *thousands of pictures were provided by artists* traditional animated films. Led by Steve Jobs, animation ~~was revolutionized by~~ *Pixar revolutionized* ~~Pixar.~~ Using computers, special software ~~was used by animators~~ *animators used* to create speech and movement. Invented by Pixar, animators ~~were~~ able to achieve startling life-*this software enabled* like effects. The typical Pixar plot shows characters growing as they move into the world. Encouraging this growth, the characters' friends offer advice and guidance. The first commercially successful Pixar film was *Toy Story*. Completed in 1995, *Toy Story's* *it* the use of computer animation made *Toy Story* a success. *Toy Story* was followed by *A Bug's Life*, *Finding Nemo*, and *The Incredibles*. Bringing in more than $525 *were* million, ~~audiences made~~ these movies very successful. In 2006, Disney bought Pixar for $7.4 billion. Now, the company that pioneered traditional animation eighty years ago owns Pixar.

Scene from Toy Story

EDITING PRACTICE: ESSAY

Read the following student essay, which includes modification errors. Rewrite sentences to correct dangling and misplaced modifiers. In some cases, you will have to supply a word to which the modifier can logically refer. The first sentence has been corrected for you.

Eating as a Sport

often
After eating a big meal, ~~the food often makes~~ you feel stuffed. Imagine how someone participating in competitive eating feels. To win, you have to eat more

competitive eaters eat

food faster than anyone else. Training for days, many different kinds of food

are eaten in these contests. For example, contestants eat chicken wings, pizza,

participants consider

ribs, hot dogs, and even matzo balls. Training for events, competitive eating

a competitive eater can make

is considered a sport by participants. By winning, a good living can be made by

these contests

a competitive eater. Considered dangerous by some, competitive eaters and their

fans nevertheless continue to grow.

The way it works is that each competitor eats the same weight or portion of

judges tell   to

food. Giving the signal, the competitors begin eating. Breaking the food in pieces

they can use

or just eating the food whole, any technique can be used. The competitors, soaked

by soaking it in water.

in water, can make the food softer. They can even eat hot dogs separately from

their buns. Good competitors are usually not overweight. In fact, some are quite

extra fat hurts

thin. Keeping the stomach from expanding, competitors are hurt by extra fat. By

competitors stretch

drinking large amounts of water, their stomachs stretch and increase their chances

of winning. This is one technique many competitors use when they train.

The International Federation of Competitive Eating watches over the contests

its Web site lists

to make sure they are fair and safe. Providing the dates and locations, contests

are listed on its Web site. Often, contests are held at state fairs. Also listing

the Web site invites

participants, prizes, and rankings of winners, new participants are invited. Before

new participants must indicate

entering the contests, their eating specialty and personal profile must be indicated

by new participants. Competitors must also be at least eighteen years old.

Many competitive eaters participate in lots of contests. For example, weighing

Sonya Thomas ate

only 100 pounds, 8.1 pounds of sausage was eaten in only 10 minutes by Sonya

Thomas. At another contest, she ate 46 crab cakes in 10 minutes. Held in the

competitive eating contests draw

United States, some participants come from other countries. For instance,

Takeru Kobayashi, who comes from Japan, once ate 18 pounds of cow brains in

15 minutes. Winners usually get cash prizes. The largest prize, $20,000, was

awarded in a hot dog–eating contest at Coney Island, which was televised by ESPN.

By eating 66 hot dogs and their buns in 12 minutes, the contest was won by Joey

Joey Chestnut (left) and Takeru Kobayashi at a hot dog–eating contest in Coney Island

Joey Chestnut wins the contest

Chestnut, a professional speed eater, *, won the contest.* Almost 50,000 people attended the contest in person, and millions watched on television.

There is some concern about competitive eating. By stretching the stomach, ~~a person's health may be affected.~~ *person may affect his or her health.* There is also concern about obesity and over-eating. Worried about choking, *some people argue that* events should have doctors present ~~some people argue.~~ Still, many people like to watch these contests, and they seem to be getting more popular each year.

COLLABORATIVE ACTIVITIES

1. Working in a group of five or six students, make a list of five *-ing* modifiers and five *-ed* modifiers. Exchange your list with another group, and complete one another's sentences.

   Examples

   <u>Typing</u> as fast as he could, *John could not wait to finish his screenplay.* _____

   <u>Frightened</u> by a snake, *the horse ran away.* _____

2. Working in a team of three students, compete with other teams to compose sentences that contain outrageous and confusing dangling or misplaced modifiers. As a class, correct the sentences. Then, vote on which group wrote the best sentences.

3. In a group of four or five students, find examples of confusing dangling and misplaced modifiers in magazines and newspapers. Rewrite the sentences, making sure each modifier is placed as close as possible to the word it describes.

review checklist

Misplaced and Dangling Modifiers

☐ Correct a misplaced modifier by placing the modifier as close as possible to the word it modifies. (See 28a.)

☐ Correct a dangling modifier by supplying a word to which the modifier can logically refer. (See 28b.)

Read the following student essay, which contains run-ons, sentence fragments, errors with subject-verb agreement, illogical shifts, and dangling and misplaced modifiers. Edit the essay to correct the errors. The first error has been corrected for you. *Answers will vary.*

Not In My Back Yard

NIMBY, a term that was coined in 1980, stands for "Not In My Back Yard." "NIMBYs" are people who are against certain changes in their communities, *even* Even though these changes will benefit the general population. For example, NIMBYs may oppose new public housing, "big box" stores, prisons, airports, or highways, *because they* Because may harm the community. These people also fear the presence in their neighborhoods of certain groups, *such* Such as people with certain disabilities. They *do* did not want these people, *to* To live anywhere near them. NIMBYs have raised important issues, *about* About the conflict between the rights of the individual and the rights of the population as a whole.

NIMBYs are suspicious of the government, *because* they worry that the government will ignore their community's needs. For example, the government may say new jobs will be available, however, what if the jobs pay low wages? What if the new employers force locally owned small stores out of business? Low-income housing may be badly needed, but what if one of the results *is* are a reduction in the value of nearby property? What if the strains on schools and traffic *are* is unacceptable? NIMBYs always worry about these questions.

NIMBYs understand that certain facilities must be built or improved nevertheless, they worry that each change may have *its* their own negative effects. *although their community needs* For example, needing new airport runways in order to reduce delays, NIMBYs object to the increased noise it causes. *they cause.* Although new sources of energy *are* is badly needed, NIMBYs oppose the noise pollution, *that* That windmills would bring to their community. New sites may be needed to dispose of hazardous waste, but NIMBYs are afraid of leaking waste containers, *that* That may contaminate homes and neighborhoods.

Demonstrators protest a proposed Walmart Supercenter

Wind turbines in California

487

Finally, there is always going to be fears. Of the unknown. Group homes for
are

of

people with physical disabilities and mental illness is often a problem for
are

NIMBYs. They are also opposed to having sex offenders living in their community.

Of course, no one wants a dangerous criminal living in their neighborhood.
his or her

However, if someone has completed the required prison sentence, they have to
he or she has

live somewhere. Some of these negative attitudes is a result of lack of information
are

others are based on a parent's real concerns about the safety of their children.
parents'

Parents did not quarrel with the right of sex offenders to find a place to live they
do

just do not want them to live anywhere near their children. NIMBYs feel that they

have to protect themselves and their families.

The conflicts of NIMBY involve a real moral dilemma. On the one hand, belief

in the importance of individuals mean that people should rely on themselves, not
means

on government. On the other hand, belief in social responsibility means that people

should think about the well-being of others. The conflict between these two

positions may be very difficult to resolve. Because sometimes the needs of the
because

individual is in conflict with the needs of the general community.
are

*Disabled resident and aide at a
group home for children*

Understanding Basic Grammar

29 Verbs: Past Tense

preview

In this chapter, you will learn to
- understand regular verbs in the past tense (29a)
- understand irregular verbs in the past tense (29b)
- deal with problem verbs in the past tense (29c and 29d)

write first

The obituary on the following page provides a short recap of the life of singer Michael Jackson. Read the obituary, and then write one for yourself. (Refer to yourself by name or by *he* or *she*.) As you write, assume that you have led a long life and have achieved everything you hoped you would. Be sure to include the accomplishments for which you would most like to be remembered. Remember to use transitional words and phrases that clearly show how one event in your life relates to another.

A Star Idolized and Haunted, Michael Jackson Dies at 50

June 26, 2009

Michael Jackson, whose quintessentially American tale of celebrity and excess took him from musical boy wonder to global pop superstar to sad figure haunted by lawsuits, paparazzi and failed plastic surgery, was pronounced dead on Thursday afternoon at U.C.L.A. Medical Center after arriving in a coma, a city official said. Mr. Jackson was 50, having spent 40 of those years in the public eye he loved. . . .

From his days as the youngest brother in the Jackson 5 to his solo career in the 1980s and early 1990s, Mr. Jackson was responsible for a string of hits like . . . "I'll Be There" . . .

"Billie Jean" and "Black or White" that exploited his high voice, infectious energy and ear for irresistible hooks. . . .

Mr. Jackson ushered in the age of pop as a global product—not to mention an age of spectacle and pop culture celebrity. He became more character than singer: his sequined glove, his whitened face, his moonwalk dance move became embedded in the cultural firmament.

His entertainment career hit high-water marks with the release of "Thriller," from 1982 . . . and with the "Victory" world tour that reunited him with his brothers in 1984.

Tense is the form a verb takes to show when an action or situation takes place. The **past tense** indicates that an action occurred in the past.

29a Regular Verbs

Regular verbs form the past tense by adding either -*ed* or -*d* to the **base form** of the verb (the present tense form of the verb that is used with *I*).

We register<u>ed</u> for classes yesterday.

Walt Disney produce<u>d</u> short cartoons in 1928.

Regular verbs that end in -*y* form the past tense by changing the *y* to *i* and adding -*ed*.

tr<u>y</u>	tr<u>ied</u>
appl<u>y</u>	appl<u>ied</u>

PRACTICE 29-1

Change the regular verbs below to the past tense.

Example: Every year, my mother ~~visits~~ *visited* her family in Bombay.

(1) My mother always ~~returns~~ *returned* from India with henna designs on her hands and feet. (2) In India, women called henna artists ~~create~~ *created* these patterns. (3) Henna ~~originates~~ *originated* in a plant found in the Middle East, India, Indonesia, and northern Africa. (4) Many women in these areas ~~use~~ *used* henna to color their hands, nails, and parts of their feet. (5) Men ~~dye~~ *dyed* their beards as well as the manes and hooves of their horses. (6) They also ~~color~~ *colored* animal

skins with henna. (7) In India, my mother always ~~celebrates~~ *celebrated* the end of the Ramadan religious fast by going to a "henna party." (8) A professional henna artist ~~attends~~ *attended* the party to apply new henna decorations to the women. (9) After a few weeks, the henna designs ~~wash~~ *washed* off. (10) In the United States, my mother's henna designs ~~attract~~ *attracted* the attention of many people.

29b   Irregular Verbs

Unlike regular verbs, whose past tense forms end in *-ed* or *-d*, **irregular verbs** have irregular forms in the past tense. In fact, their past tense forms may look very different from their present tense forms.

The following chart lists the base form and past tense form of many of the most commonly used irregular verbs.

Irregular Verbs in the Past Tense

BASE FORM	PAST	BASE FORM	PAST
awake	awoke	forgive	forgave
be	was, were	freeze	froze
beat	beat	get	got
become	became	give	gave
begin	began	go (goes)	went
bet	bet	grow	grew
bite	bit	have	had
blow	blew	hear	heard
break	broke	hide	hid
bring	brought	hold	held
build	built	hurt	hurt
buy	bought	keep	kept
catch	caught	know	knew
choose	chose	lay (to place)	laid
come	came	lead	led
cost	cost	leave	left
cut	cut	let	let
dive	dove (dived)	lie (to recline)	lay
do	did	light	lit
draw	drew	lose	lost
drink	drank	make	made
drive	drove	meet	met
eat	ate	pay	paid
fall	fell	quit	quit
feed	fed	read	read
feel	felt	ride	rode
fight	fought	ring	rang
find	found	rise	rose
fly	flew	run	ran

Teaching Tip
Point out that when students edit their writing, they should use the computer's Search or Find command to locate the irregular verbs that give them the most trouble.

ESL Tip
Ask students to give examples of irregular verbs in their native languages.

ESL Tip
Irregular past tense verb forms are challenging for native speakers and even more so for nonnative speakers. Have students write sentences using some of the verbs in the chart.

(continued on next page)

(continued from previous page)

BASE FORM	PAST	BASE FORM	PAST
say	said	stick	stuck
see	saw	sting	stung
sell	sold	swear	swore
send	sent	swim	swam
set	set	take	took
shake	shook	teach	taught
shine	shone (shined)	tear	tore
sing	sang	tell	told
sit	sat	think	thought
sleep	slept	throw	threw
speak	spoke	understand	understood
spend	spent	wake	woke
spring	sprang	wear	wore
stand	stood	win	won
steal	stole	write	wrote

PRACTICE

29-2 Fill in the correct past tense form of each irregular verb in parentheses, using the chart above to help you. If you cannot find a particular verb on the chart, look it up in a dictionary.

Example: In 1987, Connie and Howard Cleary ___*began*___ (begin) a movement to improve safety on college campuses.

(1) Connie and Howard Cleary's daughter, Jeanne, ___*was*___ (be) murdered on the Lehigh University campus. (2) Jeanne ___*thought*___ (think) she was safe. (3) However, her attacker ___*got*___ (get) into her dorm room through three different doors that had been left unlocked. (4) Shockingly, Jeanne's attacker actually ___*went*___ (go) to Lehigh. (5) Shattered by the loss of their daughter, her parents ___*did*___ (do) not withdraw into their pain. (6) Instead, they ___*felt*___ (feel) that the best memorial to their daughter would be the prevention of similar crimes, so they founded Security on Campus, Inc. (7) SOC ___*made*___ (make) legal information available to victims of crimes on college campuses. (8) Because of the efforts of SOC, Congress ___*wrote*___ (write) a law that forced colleges to disclose their crime statistics. (9) Colleges also ___*had*___ (have) to explain how they tried to protect their students. (10) Because of this law, the number of campus crimes ___*fell*___ (fall).

29c Problem Verbs: *Be*

The irregular verb *be* can cause problems because it has two different past tense forms—*was* for singular subjects and *were* for second-person singular subjects as well as for plural subjects. (All other English verbs have just one past tense form.)

<u>Carlo</u> <u>was</u> interested in becoming a city planner. (singular)

<u>They</u> <u>were</u> happy to help out at the school. (plural)

Past Tense Forms of the Verb *Be*

	Singular	Plural
First person	I was tired.	We were tired.
Second person	You were tired.	You were tired.
Third person	He was tired.	
	She was tired.	They were tired.
	It was tired.	
	The man was tired.	Frank and Billy were tired.

PRACTICE

29-3 Edit the following passage for errors in the use of the verb *be*. Cross out any underlined verbs that are incorrect, and write the correct forms above them. If a verb form is correct, label it *C*.

Example: Before 1990, there ~~was~~ *were* no female Hispanic astronauts in the NASA program.

(1) Although there had never before been a Hispanic woman astronaut, it <u>was</u> *C* impossible for NASA to ignore Ellen Ochoa's long career in physics and engineering. (2) When Ochoa <u>was</u> *C* young, her main interests <u>was</u> *were* music, math, and physics. (3) After getting a degree in physics at San Diego State University, she <u>were</u> *was* considering a career in music or business. (4) However, she <u>was</u> *C* convinced by her mother to continue her education. (5) In 1983, Ochoa <u>was</u> *C* studying for a doctorate in electrical engineering at Stanford University when the first female astronaut, Sally Ride, flew on the space shuttle. (6) Ochoa <u>were</u> *was* inspired by Sally Ride to become an astronaut. (7) More than 2,000 people <u>was</u> *were* also inspired to apply for the astronaut program. (8) In 1990, Ochoa <u>was</u> *C* picked to fly into space.

(9) On one of her flights, she <u>was</u>^c a mission specialist and used a remote-controlled robotic arm to catch a satellite. (10) After four space flights, Ochoa <u>were</u> *was* made Director of Flight Crew Operations.

29d Problem Verbs: *Can/Could* and *Will/Would*

The helping verbs *can/could* and *will/would* present problems because their past tense forms are sometimes confused with their present tense forms.

Can/Could

Can, a present tense verb, means "is able to" or "are able to."

First-year students <u>can</u> apply for financial aid.

Could, the past tense of *can*, means "was able to" or "were able to."

Escape artist Harry Houdini claimed that he <u>could</u> escape from any prison.

Will/Would

Will, a present tense verb, talks about the future from a point in the present.

A solar eclipse <u>will</u> occur in ten months.

Would, the past tense of *will*, talks about the future from a point in the past.

I told him yesterday that I <u>would</u> think about it.

Would is also used to express a possibility or wish.

If we stuck to our budget, we <u>would</u> be better off.
Laurie <u>would</u> like a new stuffed animal.

FYI

Will and *Would*

Note that *will* is used with *can* and that *would* is used with *could*.

I will feed the cats if I can find their food.
I would feed the cats if I could find their food.

PRACTICE 29-4

Circle the appropriate helping verb from the choices in parentheses.

Example: People who don't want to throw things away (**can**, could) rent a self-storage unit.

(1) In the past, warehouse storage (will, **would**) provide a place to store excess items. (2) However, people (will, **would**) have to hire moving vans and (can, **could**) hardly ever have access to their stored items. (3) They (will, **would**) have to sign an expensive long-term contract. (4) Now, however, they (**can**, could) take advantage of another option. (5) They (**can**, could) store possessions in a space as small as a closet or as large as a house. (6) With self-storage, people (**can**, could) easily move their belongings in and out of the storage unit. (7) When they need more space, they (**will**, would) be able to get it. (8) In fact, the managers of self-storage facilities (**can**, could) suggest how much space owners (**will**, would) need. (9) The only person who (**can**, could) get into the self-storage unit is the person who has rented it. (10) If people need a hand truck to move their belongings, they (**can**, could) usually borrow one. (11) All in all, using self-storage (**can**, could) solve a lot of problems for people with too many possessions.

TEST · Revise · Edit

Look back at your response to the Write First activity on page 491.
TEST what you have written. Then, revise and edit your work,
making sure that you have used the correct past tense form for each of
your verbs.

EDITING PRACTICE

Read the following student essay, which includes errors in past tense verb forms. Decide whether each of the underlined past tense verbs is correct. If the verb is correct, write *C* above it. If it is not, cross out the verb, and write in the correct past tense form. The first sentence has been corrected for you. (If necessary, consult the list of irregular verbs on pages 493–94.)

Mary-Kate Olsen, who has suffered from anorexia

Home page for anorexia treatment Web site

Healing

The window seat <u>were</u> [*was*] our favorite place to sit. I piled pillows on the ledge and <u>spended</u> [*spent*] several minutes rearranging them. Then, my friend and I <u>lied</u> [*lay*] on our backs and propped our feet on the wall. We <u>sat</u> [*C*] with our arms around our legs and <u>thinked</u> [*thought*] about the mysteries of life.

We stared at the people on the street below and <u>wonder</u> [*wondered*] who they <u>was</u> [*were*] and where they <u>was</u> [*were*] going. We imagined that they <u>can</u> [*could*] be millionaires, foreign spies, or drug smugglers. We believed that everyone except us <u>leaded</u> [*led*] wonderful and exciting lives.

I <u>heard</u> [*C*] a voice call my name. Reluctantly, I <u>standed</u> [*stood*] up, tearing myself away from my imaginary world. My dearest and oldest friend—my teddy bear—and I came back to the real world. I grabbed Teddy and <u>brung</u> [*brought*] him close to my chest. Together, we <u>go</u> [*went*] into the cold dining room, where twelve other girls <u>sit</u> [*sat*] around a table eating breakfast. None of them looked happy.

In the unit for eating disorders, meals <u>was</u> [*were*] always tense. Nobody <u>wants</u> [*wanted*] to eat, but the nurses watched us until we <u>eated</u> [*ate*] every crumb. I <u>set</u> [*C*] Teddy on the chair beside me and stared gloomily at the food on our plate. I closed my eyes and <u>taked</u> [*took*] the first bite. I <u>feeled</u> [*felt*] the calories adding inches of ugly fat. Each swallow <u>were</u> [*was*] like a nail being ripped from my finger. At last, it <u>was</u> [*C*] over. I had survived breakfast.

Days passed slowly. Each passing minute <u>was</u> [*C*] a victory. After a while, I learned how to eat properly. I learned about other people's problems. I also learned that people loved me. Eventually, even Teddy stopped feeling sorry for me. I <u>begun</u> [*began*] to smile—and laugh. Sometimes, I even considered myself happy. My doctors challenged me—and, surprisingly, I <u>rised</u> [*rose*] to the occasion.

COLLABORATIVE ACTIVITIES

1. Working in a group of three or four students, choose a famous living figure—an actor, a sports star, or a musician, for example—and brainstorm together to list details about this person's life. Then, working on your own, use the details to write a profile of the famous person.

2. Working in a group, list several current problems that you think could be solved within ten or fifteen years. Each member of the group should then select a problem from the list and write a paragraph or two describing how the problem could be solved. As a group, arrange the paragraphs so that they form the body of an essay. Develop a thesis statement, write an introduction and a conclusion, and then revise the body paragraphs of the essay.

3. Form a group with three other students. What national or world events do you remember most clearly? Take ten minutes to list news events that you think have defined the last five years. On your own, write a short essay in which you discuss the significance of the three or four events that the members of your group agree were the most important.

review checklist

Verbs: Past Tense

- The past tense is the form a verb takes to show that an action occurred in the past. (See 29a.)

- Regular verbs form the past tense by adding either -ed or -d to the base form of the verb. (See 29a.)

- Irregular verbs have irregular forms in the past tense. (See 29b.)

- *Be* has two different past tense forms—*was* for singular subjects and *were* for second-person singular subjects as well as for plural subjects. (See 29c.)

- *Could* is the past tense of *can*. *Would* is the past tense of *will*. (See 29d.)

preview

In this chapter, you will learn to
- identify regular past participles (30a)
- identify irregular past participles (30b)
- use the present perfect tense (30c)
- use the past perfect tense (30d)
- use past participles as adjectives (30e)

30 Verbs: Past Participles

write first

This still from the 2005 film *Mad Hot Ballroom* shows children practicing ballroom dancing. Write a paragraph about an activity—a hobby or a sport, for example—that you have been involved in for a relatively long time. Begin by identifying the activity and stating why it has been important to you. Then, describe the activity, paying particular attention to what you have gained from it over the years.

30a Regular Past Participles

Every verb has a past participle form. The **past participle** form of a regular verb is identical to its past tense form. Both are formed by adding either *-ed* or *-d* to the **base form** of the verb (the present tense form of the verb that is used with the pronoun *I*).

PAST TENSE
He earned a fortune.

PAST PARTICIPLE
He has earned a fortune.

PAST TENSE
He created a work of art.

PAST PARTICIPLE
He has created a work of art.

PRACTICE

30-1   Fill in the correct past participle form of each regular verb in parentheses.

Example: Recently, vacationers have _discovered_ (discover) some new opportunities to get away from it all and to do good at the same time.

(1) Volunteer vacationers have _visited_ (visit) remote areas to build footpaths, cabins, and shelters. (2) Groups such as Habitat for Humanity have _offered_ (offer) volunteers a chance to build homes in low-income areas. (3) Habitat's Global Village trips have _raised_ (raise) awareness about the lack of affordable housing in many countries. (4) Participants in Sierra Club programs have _donated_ (donate) thousands of work hours all over the United States. (5) Sometimes these volunteers have _joined_ (join) forest service workers to help restore wilderness areas. (6) They have _cleaned_ (clean) up trash at campsites. (7) They have also _removed_ (remove) nonnative plants. (8) Some volunteer vacationers have _traveled_ (travel) to countries such as Costa Rica, Russia, and Thailand to help with local projects. (9) Other vacationers have _served_ (serve) as English teachers. (10) Volunteering vacations have _helped_ (help) to strengthen cross-cultural understanding.

Teaching Tip
Refer students to 18c for information on helping verbs.

30b Irregular Past Participles

Irregular verbs nearly always have irregular past participles. Irregular verbs do not form the past participle by adding *-ed* or *-d* to the base form of the verb.

The following chart lists the base form, the past tense form, and the past participle of the most commonly used irregular verbs.

ESL Tip
Encourage students to keep a record of irregular verbs that give them trouble.

Teaching Tip
Although this work may seem basic, students need to practice using some of these challenging verb forms in sentences.

Irregular Past Participles

BASE FORM	PAST TENSE	PAST PARTICIPLE
awake	awoke	awoken
be (am, are)	was (were)	been
beat	beat	beaten
become	became	become
begin	began	begun
bet	bet	bet
bite	bit	bitten
blow	blew	blown
break	broke	broken
bring	brought	brought
build	built	built
buy	bought	bought
catch	caught	caught
choose	chose	chosen
come	came	come
cost	cost	cost
cut	cut	cut
dive	dove, dived	dived
do	did	done
draw	drew	drawn
drink	drank	drunk
drive	drove	driven
eat	ate	eaten
fall	fell	fallen
feed	fed	fed
feel	felt	felt
fight	fought	fought
find	found	found
fly	flew	flown
forgive	forgave	forgiven
freeze	froze	frozen
get	got	got, gotten
give	gave	given
go	went	gone
grow	grew	grown
have	had	had
hear	heard	heard
hide	hid	hidden
hold	held	held
hurt	hurt	hurt
keep	kept	kept
know	knew	known

BASE FORM	PAST TENSE	PAST PARTICIPLE
lay (to place)	laid	laid
lead	led	led
leave	left	left
let	let	let
lie (to recline)	lay	lain
light	lit	lit
lose	lost	lost
make	made	made
meet	met	met
pay	paid	paid
quit	quit	quit
read	read	read
ride	rode	ridden
ring	rang	rung
rise	rose	risen
run	ran	run
say	said	said
see	saw	seen
sell	sold	sold
send	sent	sent
set	set	set
shake	shook	shaken
shine	shone, shined	shone, shined
sing	sang	sung
sit	sat	sat
sleep	slept	slept
speak	spoke	spoken
spend	spent	spent
spring	sprang	sprung
stand	stood	stood
steal	stole	stolen
stick	stuck	stuck
sting	stung	stung
swear	swore	sworn
swim	swam	swum
take	took	taken
teach	taught	taught
tear	tore	torn
tell	told	told
think	thought	thought
throw	threw	thrown
understand	understood	understood
wake	woke, waked	woken, waked
wear	wore	worn
win	won	won
write	wrote	written

PRACTICE

30-2 Fill in the correct past participle of each irregular verb in parentheses. Refer to the chart above as needed. If you cannot find a particular verb on the chart, look it up in a dictionary.

Example: Occasionally, a wildfire has ___*caught*___ (catch) firefighters unprepared.

(1) Wildfires have always ___*been*___ (be) a part of nature. (2) In some cases, fires have ___*come*___ (come) and ___*gone*___ (go) without causing much destruction. (3) In other cases, fires have ___*cost*___ (cost) people a lot of time, money, and pain. (4) All of us have ___*had*___ (have) to accept the fact that healthy forests occasionally burn. (5) However, according to some people, wildfires have ___*become*___ (become) more dangerous and more common in recent years. (6) One reason is that more people have ___*built*___ (build) houses close to wooded areas. (7) In addition, many areas of the United States have ___*seen*___ (see) unusually hot and dry weather. (8) Occasionally, fires have ___*swept*___ (sweep) through acres of forest before firefighters could set up firebreaks. (9) However, firefighters have ___*done*___ (do) their best to stop fires that threaten people's property. (10) In all cases, firefighting agencies have ___*made*___ (make) protection of human life their first priority.

PRACTICE

30-3 Edit the following paragraph for errors in irregular past participles. Cross out any underlined past participles that are incorrect, and write in the correct form above them. If the verb form is correct, label it *C*.

Example: In recent years, some people have ~~standed~~ *stood* up against overseas sweatshops.

(1) Buying products from overseas sweatshops has ~~became~~ *become* controversial over the last few decades. (2) American manufacturers have ~~sended~~ *sent* their materials to developing countries where employees work under terrible conditions for very low wages. (3) Violations of basic U.S. labor laws—such as getting extra pay for overtime and being paid on time— have ~~lead~~ *led* to protests. (4) Low-wage workers in developing countries have

found
finded themselves facing dangerous working conditions as well as verbal

and sexual abuse. (5) Even well-known retailers—such as Walmart, Nike,

C
Reebok, Tommy Hilfiger, and Target—have gotten in trouble for sell-

been
ing items made in sweatshops. (6) Recently, colleges have be criticized

for using overseas sweatshops to make clothing featuring school names.

spoken   *C*
(7) Students have spoke out against such practices, and schools have had

lost
to respond. (8) While some manufacturers may have losed money by

understood
increasing wages for overseas workers, they have understanded that this

C
is the right thing to do. (9) They have made a promise to their customers

that they will not employ sweatshop labor. (10) Critics have argue, how-
argued

ever, that in developing countries sweatshop jobs are often an improve-

ment over other types of employment.

30c   The Present Perfect Tense

The past participle can be combined with the present tense forms of *have*
to form the **present perfect tense**.

The Present Perfect Tense

(*have* or *has* + past participle)

SINGULAR	PLURAL
I have gained.	We have gained.
You have gained.	You have gained.
He has gained.	They have gained.
She has gained.	
It has gained.	

- Use the present perfect tense to indicate an action that began in the
  past and continues into the present.

  PRESENT PERFECT   The nurse has worked at the Welsh Mountain
                     clinic for two years. (The working began in the
                     past and continues into the present.)

- Use the present perfect tense to indicate that an action has just
  occurred.

  PRESENT PERFECT   I have just eaten. (The eating has just occurred.)

Teaching Tip
Tell students that the words
just, now, already, and *recently*
show that an action has just
occurred.

PRACTICE

30-4   Circle the appropriate verb tense (past tense or present perfect) from the choices in parentheses.

Example: When I was in Montreal, I (heard, have heard) both English and French.

(1) When I (visited, have visited) Montreal, I was surprised to discover a truly bilingual city. (2) Montreal (kept, has kept) two languages as a result of its history. (3) Until 1763, Montreal (belonged, has belonged) to France. (4) Then, when France (lost, has lost) the Seven Years' War, the city (became, has become) part of England. (5) When I was there last year, most people (spoke, have spoken) both French and English. (6) Although I (knew, have known) no French, I (found, have found) that I was able to get along quite well. (7) For example, all the museums (made, have made) their guided tours available in English. (8) Most restaurants (offered, have offered) bilingual menus. (9) There (were, have been) even English radio and television stations and English newspapers. (10) In Montreal, I (felt, have felt) both at home and in a foreign country.

PRACTICE

30-5   Fill in the appropriate tense (past tense or present perfect) of the verb in parentheses.

Example: Bath towels and mattresses are just two of the many things that _have increased_ (increase) in size over the last few years.

(1) In recent years, the size of many everyday items _has changed_ (change) drastically. (2) Cell phones and computers _have undergone_ (undergo) the biggest changes. (3) There was a time, not long ago, when a single computer _filled_ (fill) an entire room. (4) Likewise, the first cell phones were more than a foot long and _weighed_ (weigh) as much as two pounds. (5) Since then, we _have developed_ (develop) sophisticated machines that fit in a pocket and weigh as little as a few ounces. (6) However, while these items have shrunk, other things _have gotten_ (get) bigger.

(7) In 1980, when 7-Eleven _____invented_____ (invent) the 32-ounce Big Gulp,
it was the largest drink on the market. (8) Now, the Big Gulp looks small
to most of us because the average size of a fountain soda _____has increased_____
(increase) significantly. (9) Television screens _____have grown_____ (grow) as
well. (10) While twenty years ago most viewers _____watched_____ (watch)
TV on a 20-inch screen, many of today's viewers are demanding screens
that are 60 inches or larger.

30d The Past Perfect Tense

The past participle can also be used to form the **past perfect tense**, which
consists of the past tense of *have* plus the past participle.

The Past Perfect Tense

(*had* + past participle)

SINGULAR	PLURAL
I had returned.	We had returned.
You had returned.	You had returned.
He had returned.	They had returned.
She had returned.	
It had returned.	

Use the past perfect tense to show that an action occurred before
another past action.

PAST PERFECT TENSE   PAST TENSE

Chief Sitting Bull <u>had fought</u> many battles before he <u>defeated</u> General
Custer. (The fighting was done before Sitting Bull defeated Custer.)

PRACTICE

30-6 Underline the appropriate verb tense (present perfect or past
perfect) from the choices in parentheses.

Example: Although he (has missed/<u>had missed</u>) his second free
throw, the crowd cheered for him anyway.

1. Meera returned to Bangladesh with the money she (has raised/<u>had raised</u>).

2. Her contributors believe that she (<u>has shown</u>/had shown) the ability to spend money wisely.

3. The planner told the commission that she (has found/<u>had found</u>) a solution to the city's traffic problem.

4. It seems clear that traffic cameras (<u>have proven</u>/had proven) successful in towns with similar congestion problems.

5. Emily says she (<u>has saved</u>/had saved) a lot of money by driving a motor scooter instead of a car.

6. She sold the car she (has bought/<u>had bought</u>) three years before.

7. Because they are huge fans, Esteban and Tina (<u>have camped</u>/had camped) out in front of the theater to buy tickets.

8. The people who (have waited/<u>had waited</u>) all night were the first to get tickets.

9. Sam and Ryan volunteer at Habitat for Humanity, where they (<u>have learned</u>/had learned) many useful skills.

10. After they (have completed/<u>had completed</u>) 500 hours of work, they were eligible to get their own house.

30e Past Participles as Adjectives

In addition to functioning as verbs, past participles can also function as adjectives modifying nouns that follow them.

> I cleaned up the <u>broken</u> glass.

> The <u>exhausted</u> runner finally crossed the finish line.

Past participles are also used as adjectives after **linking verbs**, such as *seemed* or *looked*.

> <u>Jason</u> seemed <u>surprised</u>.

> <u>He</u> looked <u>shocked</u>.

Teaching Tip
Refer students to 32a for more on the use of adjectives as modifiers.

Teaching Tip
Remind students that a linking verb—such as *seemed* or *looked*—connects a subject to the word that describes it. (See 18c.)

PRACTICE

30-7 Edit the following passage for errors in past participle forms used as adjectives. Cross out any underlined participles that are incorrect, and write the correct form above them. If the participle form is correct, label it *C*.

Teaching Tip
When they write, some students omit *-ed* endings in past participles because they do not pronounce them.

Example: College students are often <u>worried</u> ^C^ about money.

(1) College students are <u>surprise</u> ^surprised^ when they find <u>preapprove</u> ^preapproved^ applications for credit cards in their mail. (2) Credit-card companies also recruit <u>targeted</u> ^C^ students through booths that are <u>locate</u> ^located^ on or near college campuses. (3) The booths are <u>design</u> ^designed^ to attract new customers with offers of gifts. (4) Why have companies gone to all this trouble to attract <u>qualified</u> ^C^ students? (5) Most older Americans already have at least five credit cards that are <u>stuff</u> ^stuffed^ in their wallets. (6) Banks and credit-card companies see younger college students as a major <u>untapped</u> ^C^ market. (7) According to experts, students are a good credit risk because <u>concern</u> ^concerned^ parents usually bail them out when they cannot pay a bill. (8) Finally, people tend to feel emotionally <u>tie</u> ^tied^ to their first credit card. (9) Companies want to be the first card that is <u>acquire</u> ^acquired^ by a customer. (10) For this reason, credit-card companies target <u>uninform</u> ^uninformed^ college students.

TEST · Revise · Edit

Look back at your response to the Write First activity on page 500. TEST what you have written. Then, revise and edit your work, paying particular attention to present perfect and past perfect verb forms and to past participles used as adjectives.

EDITING PRACTICE

Read the following student essay, which includes errors in the use of past participles and in the use of the perfect tenses. Decide whether each of the underlined verbs or participles is correct. If it is correct, write *C* above it. If it is not, write in the correct verb form. The first error has been corrected for you.

Using Technology to Get Out the Vote

These days, the Internet <u>became</u> *[has become]* one of the most common ways for political

candidates to reach voters and to raise money for election campaigns. In addition,

social-networking sites and text-messaging <u>have allow</u> *[allowed]* candidates to connect more

easily with young people. In the past, far too many young voters <u>have</u> *[C]* not <u>took</u> *[taken]*

part in U.S. elections. Recently, however, young voters <u>had participated</u> *[have]* in greater

numbers, perhaps thanks to their familiarity with technology.

Over the last few years, political campaigns <u>have finded</u> *[found]* that they can

attract voters and election workers by using the Internet. Both Democrats and

Republicans <u>used</u> *[have used]* email and online advertising to persuade voters to support

candidates and to provide vote-by-mail ballots. At the same time, their Web sites

and blogs <u>had stimulate</u> *[have stimulated]* interest in politics and <u>have provide</u> *[provided]* ways for young

people to meet each other and work for their candidates.

In 2004, both major political parties <u>have used</u> the Internet to gain young

voters' support. Hoping to draw young people to the campaign trail, John Kerry's

campaign <u>has worked</u> with Moveon.org to organize and publicize a tour of popular

musicians. GeorgeWBush.com <u>offered</u> *[C]* young Republicans ways to use the Internet

to create a pro-Bush poster, download pro-Bush screen savers, and order

pro-Bush items. With these online promotions, both parties definitely <u>have catched</u> *[caught]*

the interest of young people. However, the use of technology <u>had played</u> an even

greater role in the 2008 presidential election.

In addition to using the Internet, 2008 candidates <u>have discover</u> *[discovered]* new ways of

reaching young voters: text-messaging, social networking, and YouTube. Candidates

<u>have keeped</u> *[kept]* supporters informed by texting them with up-to-the-minute campaign

news. They <u>have use</u> *[used]* sites like Facebook to link up and unite supporters. Candidates also had recognized the potential that YouTube have provided. This popular video-

sharing site had not existed in 2004. However, in 2008, most of the presidential

candidates have had political ads, short talks, and debate clips on YouTube. Posting

enabled
videos there had enable them to reach millions of voters without paying a cent.

After the 2008 presidential election, many experts have suggested that

given
young voters' technological competence had gave them more political strength.

C
Commentators also credited young voters, in part, for the election of Barack

Obama. Twice as many 18- to 29-year-olds have voted for Obama as voted for

acknowledged
John McCain. Many had acknowledge that the Obama campaign's use of texting,

had   *C*
emailing, and blogging has most likely helped the candidate win young people's

support. In the years to come, the use of technology will certainly influence future

U.S. elections, and young voters, even more profoundly.

COLLABORATIVE ACTIVITIES

1. Exchange Write First responses with another student. Read each other's work, making sure that past participles and perfect tenses are used correctly.

2. Assume that you are a restaurant employee who has been nominated for the Employee-of-the-Year Award. To win this award (along with a thousand-dollar prize), you have to explain in writing what you have done during the past year to deserve this honor. Write a letter to your supervisor and the awards committee. When you have finished, trade papers with another student and edit his or her letter. Read all the letters to the class, and have the class decide which is the most convincing.

Teaching Tip
Collaborative Activity 2 works well for getting students involved in a classroom discussion.

review checklist

Verbs: Past Participles

☐ The past participle of regular verbs is formed by adding *-ed* or *-d* to the base form. (See 30a.)

☐ Irregular verbs usually have irregular past participles. (See 30b.)

☐ The past participle is combined with the present tense forms of *have* to form the present perfect tense. (See 30c.)

☐ The past participle is used to form the past perfect tense, which consists of the past tense of *have* plus the past participle. (See 30d.)

☐ The past participle can function as an adjective. (See 30e.)

31 Nouns and Pronouns

MATT GROENING

write first

The TV show *The Simpsons* first aired in 1989 and continues
to entertain viewers today. Write about a particular TV show,
musical group, or movie you like and explain why you like it.
Assume your readers are not familiar with the subject you are
writing about.

31a   Identifying Nouns

A **noun** is a word that names a person (*singer, Jay-Z*), an animal (*dolphin, Flipper*), a place (*downtown, Houston*), an object (*game, Scrabble*), or an idea (*happiness, Darwinism*).

A **singular noun** names one thing. A **plural noun** names more than one thing.

FYI

When to Capitalize Nouns

Most nouns, called **common nouns**, begin with lowercase letters.

character   holiday

Some nouns, called **proper nouns**, name particular people, animals, places, objects, or events. A proper noun always begins with a capital letter.

Homer Simpson   Labor Day

Teaching Tip
Refer students to 36a for information on capitalizing proper nouns.

31b   Forming Plural Nouns

Most nouns that end in consonants add -*s* to form plurals. Other nouns add -*es* to form plurals. For example, most nouns that end in -*o* add -*es* to form plurals. Other nouns, whose singular forms end in -*s*, -*ss*, -*sh*, -*ch*, -*x*, or -*z*, also add -*es* to form plurals. (Some nouns that end in -*s* or -*z* double the *s* or *z* before adding -*es*.)

SINGULAR	PLURAL
street	streets
radio	radios
gas	gases
class	classes
bush	bushes
church	churches
fox	foxes
quiz	quizzes

ESL Tip
Briefly review subject-verb agreement. Remind students that if the subject ends in -*s*, the verb usually does not. Refer students to Chapter 26.

ESL Tip
Tell students that they can sometimes tell whether a word is singular or plural by the word that introduces it. For example, *each* always introduces a singular noun, and *many* always introduces a plural noun. Refer students to 33d.

Irregular Noun Plurals

Some nouns form plurals in unusual ways.

■ Nouns whose plural forms are the same as their singular forms

SINGULAR	PLURAL
a deer	a few deer
this species	these species
a television series	two television series

■ Nouns ending in -*f* or -*fe*

SINGULAR	PLURAL
each half	both halves
my life	our lives
a lone thief	a gang of thieves
one loaf	two loaves
the third shelf	several shelves

Exceptions: *roof* (plural *roofs*), *proof* (plural *proofs*), *belief* (plural *beliefs*)

■ Nouns ending in -*y*

SINGULAR	PLURAL
another baby	more babies
every worry	many worries

Note that when a vowel (*a, e, i, o, u*) comes before the *y*, the noun has a regular plural form: *monkey* (plural *monkeys*), *day* (plural *days*).

■ Hyphenated compound nouns

SINGULAR	PLURAL
Lucia's sister-in-law	Lucia's two favorite sisters-in-law
a mother-to-be	twin mothers-to-be
the first runner-up	all the runners-up

Note that the plural ending is attached to the compound's first word: *sister, mother, runner*.

■ Miscellaneous irregular plurals

SINGULAR	PLURAL
that child	all children
a good man	a few good men
the woman	lots of women
my left foot	both feet
a wisdom tooth	my two front teeth
this bacterium	some bacteria

Teaching Tip
Refer students to 33d for information on determiners (*that, a, the, my, this,* and so on).

PRACTICE

31-1 Next to each of the following singular nouns, write the plural form of the noun. Then, circle the irregular noun plurals.

Examples: bottle ___*bottles*___   child ___(*children*)___

1. headache ___*headaches*___

2. life ___(*lives*)___

3. foot ___(*feet*)___

4. chain ___*chains*___

5. deer ___(*deer*)___

6. honey ___*honeys*___

7. bride-to-be ___(*brides-to-be*)___

8. woman ___(*women*)___

9. loaf ___(*loaves*)___

10. kiss ___*kisses*___

11. beach ___*beaches*___

12. duty ___(*duties*)___

13. son-in-law ___(*sons-in-law*)___

14. species ___(*species*)___

15. wife ___(*wives*)___

16. city ___(*cities*)___

17. elf ___(*elves*)___

18. tooth ___(*teeth*)___

19. catalog ___*catalogs*___

20. patty ___(*patties*)___

Teaching Tip
Tell students that when a noun has an irregular plural, the dictionary lists its plural form.

PRACTICE

31-2 Proofread the underlined nouns in the following paragraph, checking to make sure singular and plural forms are correct. If a correction needs to be made, cross out the noun, and write the correct form above it. If the noun is correct, write *C* above it.

Example: Because of scans and pat downs, getting through security

lines at ~~airportes~~ *airports* has become more and more difficult.

(1) Since September 11, 2001, ~~traveler-to-bes~~ *travelers-to-be* need to think carefully about what they pack in their carry-on luggage. (2) All airlines have to protect the ~~lifes~~ *lives* of the men *C* and ~~woman~~ *women* who fly on their planes. (3) On some days *C*, long ~~delayes~~ *delays* in the security lines occur as screeners carry out their ~~dutys~~ *duties*. (4) Most people *C* understand that they should never carry weapons and explosives onto a plane. (5) Hunters have to accept the fact that all firearms *C* must be unloaded and checked in at the gate and that ~~boxs~~ *boxes* of ammunition should be packed separately. (6) Most people are aware that items *C* like nail clippers and ~~tweezerz~~ *tweezers* are now

permitted but that other sharp ~~tooles~~ *tools*, like ~~knifes~~ *knives* and razor blades, are still forbidden. (7) However, some individuals forget that most ~~shampoos~~, ~~lotiones~~ *lotions*, and ~~drinkes~~ *drinks* are only allowed in very small ~~quantitys~~ *quantities*. (8) When packing ~~liquides~~ *liquids* or ~~gels~~ in their carry-on luggage, ~~traveleres~~ *travelers* must be sure that each container holds no more than three ounces and that all contain-ers fit in a quart-size plastic bag. (9) Emptying the ~~contentes~~ *contents* of water bottles and coffee ~~cupes~~ *cups* can seem frustrating and unnecessary to many passengers. (10) However, most passengers accept these small inconve-niences and minor irritations because they want to fly safely.

31c Identifying Pronouns

A **pronoun** is a word that refers to and takes the place of a noun or another pronoun. In the following sentence, the pronouns *she* and *her* take the place of the noun *Michelle*.

> Michelle was really excited because <u>she</u> had finally found a job that made <u>her</u> happy. (*She* refers to *Michelle*; *her* refers to *she*.)

Pronouns, like nouns, can be singular or plural.

■ Singular pronouns (*I, he, she, it, him, her*, and so on) always take the place of singular nouns or pronouns.

> Geoff left his jacket at work, so <u>he</u> went back to get <u>it</u> before <u>it</u> could be stolen. (*He* refers to *Geoff*; *it* refers to *jacket*.)

■ Plural pronouns (*we, they, our, their*, and so on) always take the place of plural nouns or pronouns.

> Jessie and Dan got up early, but <u>they</u> still missed <u>their</u> train. (*They* refers to *Jessie and Dan*; *their* refers to *they*.)

■ The pronoun *you* can be either singular or plural.

> When the volunteers met the mayor, they said, "We really admire <u>you</u>." The mayor replied, "I admire <u>you</u>, too." (In the first sentence, *you* refers to *the mayor*; in the second sentence, *you* refers to *the volunteers*.)

Teaching Tip
Tell students that using too many pronouns can make a paragraph boring, especially when pronouns begin several sentences in a row. Encourage them to vary their sentence openings. Refer them to 21b.

FYI

Demonstrative Pronouns

Demonstrative pronouns—*this, that, these,* and *those*—point to one or more items.

- *This* and *that* point to one item: This is a work of fiction, and that is a nonfiction book.

- *These* and *those* point to more than one item: These are fruits, but those are vegetables.

PRACTICE

31-3   In the following sentences, fill in each blank with an appropriate pronoun.

Example: Ever since _____*I*_____ had my first scuba-diving experience, _____*I*_____ have wanted to search for sunken treasure.

(1) Three friends and _____*I*_____ decided to explore an area off the Florida coast where a shipwreck had occurred almost three hundred years ago. (2) The first step was to buy a boat; _____*we*_____ all agreed on a used rubber boat with a fifteen-horsepower engine. (3) _____*It*_____ had hardly been used and was in very good condition. (4) _____*We*_____ also needed some equipment, including an anchor and metal detectors. (5) If there was treasure on the bottom of the ocean, _____*we*_____ would find it. (6) _____*I*_____ stayed in the boat while my friends made the first dive. (7) At first, _____*they*_____ found only fish and sea worms, but _____*they*_____ didn't give up. (8) Finally, one of the metal detectors started beeping because _____*it*_____ had located a cannon and two cannonballs. (9) Then, it started beeping again; this time, _____*it*_____ had found some pieces of pottery and an old pistol. (10) Although our group didn't find any coins, _____*we*_____ all enjoyed our search for sunken treasure.

31d Pronoun-Antecedent Agreement

Teaching Tip
Try to assign both practices in 31d. Pronoun-antecedent agreement errors are very common in student writing.

The word that a pronoun refers to is called the pronoun's **antecedent**. In the following sentence, the noun *leaf* is the antecedent of the pronoun *it*.

The leaf turned yellow, but it did not fall.

A pronoun must always agree with its antecedent. If an antecedent is singular, as it is in the sentence above, the pronoun must be singular. If the antecedent is plural, as it is in the sentence below, the pronoun must also be plural.

The leaves turned yellow, but they did not fall.

If an antecedent is feminine, the pronoun that refers to it must also be feminine.

Melissa passed her driver's exam with flying colors.

If an antecedent is masculine, the pronoun that refers to it must also be masculine.

Matt wondered what courses he should take.

If an antecedent is **neuter** (neither masculine nor feminine), the pronoun that refers to it must also be neuter.

The car broke down, but they refused to fix it again.

PRACTICE

31-4   In the following sentences, circle the antecedent of each underlined pronoun. Then, draw an arrow from the pronoun to the antecedent it refers to.

Example: College students today often fear they will be the victims of crime on campus.

(1) Few campuses are as safe as they should be, experts say. (2) However, crime on most campuses is probably no worse than it is in any other community. (3) Still, students have a right to know how safe their campuses are. (4) My friend Joyce never walks on campus without her can of Mace. (5) Joyce believes she must be prepared for the worst.

(6) Her boyfriend took a self-defense course that he said was very help-ful. (7) My friends do not let fear of crime keep them from enjoying the college experience. (8) We know that our school is doing all it can to make the campus safe.

PRACTICE

31-5   Fill in each blank in the following passage with an appropriate pronoun.

Example: Americans celebrate July 4 because ____*it*____ is Independence Day.

(1) For some Germans, November 9 is a day to celebrate positive change; for others, ____*it*____ recalls the human potential for violence and destruction. (2) November 9, designated "World Freedom Day," is important because ____*it*____ is the day the Berlin Wall fell. (3) On that day in 1989, residents of East and West Germany were allowed to cross the barrier that had separated ____*them*____ since the end of World War II. (4) However, Germans have mixed feelings about this date because November 9 also reminds ____*them*____ of a dark moment in their history. (5) On the night of November 9, 1938, Nazis took sledgehammers and axes to as many Jewish businesses, synagogues, and homes as ____*they*____ could find. (6) In German, this violent event is called *Kristallnacht*; in English, ____*it*____ is known as "the Night of Broken Glass." (7) Because November 9 has been so important in German history, journalists sometimes refer to ____*it*____ as Germany's "day of fate." (8) Coincidentally, Albert Einstein, a German Jew, received the Nobel Prize on November 9, 1921; the theories ____*he*____ described have changed how scientists think. (9) Thus, November 9 in Germany is a day of opposites; like so many dates in human history, ____*it*____ marks both triumph and tragedy.

31e Special Problems with Agreement

Certain kinds of antecedents can cause problems for writers because they cannot easily be identified as singular or plural.

Compound Antecedents

A **compound antecedent** consists of two or more words connected by *and* or *or*.

Teaching Tip
Refer students to 26b for information on subject-verb agreement with compound subjects.

■ Compound antecedents connected by *and* are plural, and they are used with plural pronouns.

> During World War II, Belgium and France tried to protect their borders.

■ Compound antecedents connected by *or* may take a singular or a plural pronoun. The pronoun always agrees with the word that is closer to it.

> Is it possible that European nations or Russia may send its [not *their*] troops?

> Is it possible that Russia or European nations may send their [not *its*] troops?

PRACTICE

31-6 In each of the following sentences, underline the compound antecedent, and circle the connecting word (*and* or *or*). Then, circle the appropriate pronoun in parentheses.

Example: Marge (and) Homer Simpson love (his or her/(their)) children very much in spite of the problems they cause.

1. Either *24* (or) *Lost* had the highest ratings for any television show in ((its)/ their) final episode.

2. In *South Park*, Geek 1 (and) Geek 2 help create a time machine out of (his/(their)) friend Timmy's wheelchair.

ESL Tip
If nonnative speakers have trouble with culture-specific references, allow them to work in pairs with native speakers.

3. Both Netflix (and) Blockbuster offer (its/(their)) movie rentals online.

4. Either cable stations (or) the networks hire the most attractive anchors to host (its/(their)) prime-time shows.

5. Recent movies (and) documentaries about penguins have delighted (its/ (their)) audiences.

6. In baseball, pitchers (and) catchers communicate (his or her/(their)) plays with hand signals.

7. Either Playstation2 (or) Xbox gives ((its)/their) players many hours of gaming fun.

8. In summer, many parents (and) children enjoy spending (his or her/ (their)) time at water parks.

9. Hurricanes (or) tornadoes can be frightening to (its/(their)) victims.

Indefinite Pronoun Antecedents

Most pronouns refer to a specific person or thing. However, **indefinite pronouns** do not refer to any particular person or thing.

Most indefinite pronouns are singular.

Singular Indefinite Pronouns

another	everybody	no one
anybody	everyone	nothing
anyone	everything	one
anything	much	somebody
each	neither	someone
either	nobody	something

Teaching Tip
You might want to tell students that some indefinite pronouns (such as *all, any, more, most, none,* and *some*) can be either singular or plural. (*All* is quiet. *All* were qualified.)

When an indefinite pronoun antecedent is singular, use a singular pronoun to refer to it.

Everything was in its place. (*Everything* is singular, so it is used with the singular pronoun *its*.)

Teaching Tip
Refer students to 26f for information on subject-verb agreement with indefinite pronouns.

FYI

Indefinite Pronouns with *Of*

The singular indefinite pronouns *each, either, neither,* and *one* are often used in phrases with *of—each of, either of, neither of,* or *one of*—followed by a plural noun. Even in such phrases, these indefinite pronoun antecedents are always singular and take singular pronouns.

Each of the routes has its [not *their*] own special challenges.

ESL Tip
Remind students that singular indefinite pronouns do not have plural forms.

A few indefinite pronouns are plural.

Plural Indefinite Pronouns

both
few
many
others
several

When an indefinite pronoun antecedent is plural, use a plural pronoun to refer to it.

> They all wanted to graduate early, but few received their diplomas in January. (*Few* is plural, so it is used with the plural pronoun *their*.)

FYI

Using *His* or *Her* with Indefinite Pronouns

Even though the indefinite pronouns *anybody, anyone, everybody, everyone, somebody, someone,* and so on are singular, many people use plural pronouns to refer to them.

> Everyone must hand in their completed work before 2 p.m.

This usage is widely accepted in spoken English. Nevertheless, indefinite pronouns like *everyone* are singular, and written English requires a singular pronoun.

However, using the singular pronoun *his* to refer to *everyone* suggests that *everyone* refers to a male. Using *his or her* is more accurate because the indefinite pronoun can refer to either a male or a female.

> Everyone must hand in his or her completed work before 2 p.m.

When used over and over again, *he or she, him or her,* and *his or her* can create wordy or awkward sentences. Whenever possible, use plural forms.

> All students must hand in their completed work before 2 p.m.

PRACTICE

31-7 In the following sentences, first circle the indefinite pronoun. Then, circle the pronoun in parentheses that refers to the indefinite pronoun antecedent.

Example: (Each) of the lacrosse players will have (his or her/their)

own locker at training camp.

1. (Everyone) likes to choose (his or her/their) own class schedule.

2. (Somebody) left (his or her/their) iPod on the bus.

3. (Most) of the *American Idol* contestants did (his or her/their) best for the judges.

4. (Someone) in the audience forgot to turn off (his or her/their) cell phone before the performance.

5. (Neither) of the dogs wanted to have (its/their) coat brushed.

6. Coach Reilly personally gave (each) of the players (his or her/their) trophy.

7. (Both) of the soldiers donated (his or her/their) cars to Purple Heart, an organization that helps veterans.

8. (No one) should ever give (his or her/their) Social Security number to a telephone solicitor.

9. (Anyone) who works hard in college can usually receive (his or her/their) degree.

10. (Everyone) loves receiving presents on (his or her/their) birthday.

PRACTICE

31-8 Edit the following sentences for errors in pronoun-antecedent agreement. When you edit, you have two options: either substitute *its* or *his or her* for *their* to refer to the singular antecedent, or replace the singular antecedent with a plural word.

Examples: Everyone is responsible for ~~their~~ *his or her* own passport and money.

All
~~Each~~ of the children took their books out of their backpacks.

Answers may vary.

1. Either of the hybrid cars comes with their *its* own tax rebate.

2. Anyone who loses their *his or her* locker key must pay $5.00 for a new one.

3. Everyone loves seeing their *his or her* home team win.

4. Somebody left their *his or her* scarf and gloves on the subway.

5. ~~Almost everyone waits~~ *Most people wait* until the last minute to file their tax returns.

6. ~~Each~~ *All the students* student returned their library books on time.

7. Everything we need to build the model airplane comes in their *its* kit.

8. Anyone who wants to succeed needs to develop their *his or her* public-speaking skills.

9. One of the hockey teams just won ~~their~~ *its* first Olympic medal.

10. No one leaving the show early will get ~~their~~ *his or her* money back.

Collective Noun Antecedents

Collective nouns are words (such as *band* and *team*) that name a group of people or things but are singular. Because they are singular, collective noun antecedents are used with singular pronouns.

The **band** played on, but **it** never played our song.

Frequently Used Collective Nouns

army	club	gang	mob
association	committee	government	posse
band	company	group	team
class	family	jury	union

PRACTICE

31-9 Circle the collective noun antecedent in the following sentences. Then, circle the correct pronoun in parentheses.

Example: The (jury) returned with ((its)/their) verdict.

1. The (company) offers good benefits to ((its)/their) employees.

2. All five study (groups) must hand in (its/(their)) projects by Tuesday.

3. Any (government) should be concerned about the welfare of ((its)/their) citizens.

4. The Asian Students (Union) is sponsoring a party to celebrate ((its)/their) twentieth anniversary.

5. Every (family) has ((its)/their) share of problems.

6. To join the electricians' (union), applicants had to pass ((its)/their) test.

7. Even the best (teams) have (its/(their)) bad days.

8. The (orchestra) has just signed a contract to make ((its)/their) first recording.

9. The math (class) did very well with ((its)/their) new teacher.

10. The (club) voted to expand ((its)/their) membership.

PRACTICE

31-10 Edit the following passage for correct pronoun-antecedent agreement. First, circle the antecedent of each underlined pronoun. Then, cross out any pronoun that does not agree with its antecedent, and write the correct form above it. If the pronoun is correct, write *C* above it.

Example: Many Americans believe that the country is ready for its
first female president.

(1) The history of woman suffrage in the United States shows that
women were determined to achieve her equal rights. (2) Before 1920, most
American women were not allowed to vote for the candidates they preferred.
(3) Men ran the government, and a woman could not express their views
at the ballot box. (4) However, in the mid-1800s, women began to demand
her right to vote—or "woman suffrage." (5) Supporters of woman suffrage
believed everyone, regardless of their gender, should be able to vote. (6) At
the first woman suffrage convention, Elizabeth Cady Stanton and Lucretia
Mott gave speeches explaining his or her views. (7) Susan B. Anthony started
the National Woman Suffrage Association, which opposed the Fifteenth
Amendment to the Constitution because it gave the vote to black men but
not to women. (8) The first state to permit women to vote was Wyoming,
and soon other states became more friendly to her cause. (9) Many women
participated in marches where he or she carried banners and posters for
their cause. (10) During World War I, the U.S. government found that the
cooperation of women was essential to their military success. (11) Finally,
in 1919, the House of Representatives and the states gave its approval
to the Nineteenth Amendment, which gave American women the right
to vote.

31f Vague and Unnecessary Pronouns

Vague and unnecessary pronouns clutter up your writing and make it hard
to understand. Eliminating them will make your writing clearer and easier
for readers to follow.

Vague Pronouns

A pronoun should always refer to a specific antecedent. When a pronoun—such as *they* or *it*—has no antecedent, readers will be confused.

VAGUE PRONOUN	On the news, <u>they</u> said baseball players would strike. (Who said baseball players would strike?)
VAGUE PRONOUN	<u>It</u> says in today's paper that our schools are over-crowded. (Who says schools are overcrowded?)

If a pronoun does not refer to a specific word in the sentence, replace the pronoun with a noun.

REVISED	On the news, the <u>sportscaster</u> said baseball players would strike.
REVISED	An <u>editorial</u> in today's paper says that our schools are overcrowded.

Unnecessary Pronouns

When a pronoun comes directly after its antecedent, it is unnecessary.

UNNECESSARY PRONOUN	The librarian, <u>he</u> told me I should check the database.

In the sentence above, the pronoun *he* serves no purpose. Readers do not need to be directed back to the pronoun's antecedent (the noun *librarian*) because it appears right before the pronoun. The pronoun should therefore be deleted.

REVISED	The librarian told me I should check the database.

> **Teaching Tip**
> Remind students that only an intensive pronoun can come right after its antecedent: *I <u>myself</u> prefer to wait*. Refer them to 31i.

PRACTICE

31-11 The following sentences contain vague or unnecessary pronouns. Revise each sentence on the line below it.

Example: On their Web site, they advertised a special offer.

On its Web site, the Gap advertised a special offer.

Answers may vary.

1. In Jamaica, they love their spectacular green mountains.

   Jamaicans love their spectacular green mountains.

2. My hamster, he loves his exercise wheel.

   My hamster loves his exercise wheel.

3. On *Jeopardy!* they have to give the answers in the form of questions.

   Jeopardy! contestants have to give the answers in the form of questions.

4. On televisions all over the world, they watched the moon landing.

On televisions all over the world, viewers watched the moon landing.

5. In Sociology 320, they do not use a textbook.

In Sociology 320, students do not use a textbook.

31g   Pronoun Case

A **personal pronoun** refers to a particular person or thing. Personal pronouns change form according to their function in a sentence. Personal pronouns can be *subjective*, *objective*, or *possessive*.

Personal Pronouns

SUBJECTIVE	OBJECTIVE	POSSESSIVE
I	me	my, mine
he	him	his
she	her	her, hers
it	it	its
we	us	our, ours
you	you	your, yours
they	them	their, theirs
who	whom	whose
whoever	whomever	

Teaching Tip
Refer students to 31h for information on how to use *who* and *whom*.

Subjective Case

When a pronoun is a subject, it is in the **subjective case**.

Finally, <u>she</u> realized that dreams could come true.

Teaching Tip
You may want to tell students that the subjective case is used for the subject of a clause as well as for the subject of a sentence.

Objective Case

When a pronoun is an object, it is in the **objective case**.

If Joanna hurries, she can stop <u>him</u>. (The pronoun *him* is the object of the verb *can stop*.)

Professor Miller sent <u>us</u> information about his research. (The pronoun *us* is the object of the verb *sent*.)

Marc threw the ball to <u>them</u>. (The pronoun *them* is the object of the preposition *to*.)

Possessive Case

When a pronoun shows ownership, it is in the **possessive case**.

> Hieu took <u>his</u> lunch to the meeting. (The pronoun *his* indicates that the lunch belongs to Hieu.)

> Debbie and Kim decided to take <u>their</u> lunches, too. (The pronoun *their* indicates that the lunches belong to Debbie and Kim.)

Teaching Tip
Tell your students that they may find it helpful to consult the pronoun chart on page 527 while they do this exercise.

PRACTICE

31-12 In the following passage, fill in the blank after each pronoun to indicate whether the pronoun is subjective (*S*), objective (*O*), or possessive (*P*).

Example: Famous criminals Bonnie and Clyde committed their

___*P*___ crimes in broad daylight.

(1) Bonnie Parker and Clyde Barrow are remembered today because they ___*S*___ were the first celebrity criminals. (2) With their ___*P*___ gang, Bonnie and Clyde robbed a dozen banks as well as many stores and gas stations. (3) In small towns, they ___*S*___ terrorized the police. (4) Capturing them ___*O*___ seemed impossible. (5) To many Americans, however, their ___*P*___ crimes seemed exciting. (6) Because Bonnie was a woman, she ___*S*___ was especially fascinating to them ___*O*___. (7) During their ___*P*___ crimes, Bonnie and Clyde would often carry a camera, take photographs of themselves, and then send them ___*O*___ to the newspapers, which were happy to publish them ___*O*___. (8) By the time they ___*S*___ were killed in an ambush by Texas and Louisiana law officers, Bonnie and Clyde were famous all over the United States.

31h Special Problems with Pronoun Case

When you are trying to determine which pronoun case to use in a sentence, three kinds of pronouns can cause problems: pronouns in compounds, pronouns in comparisons, and the pronouns *who* and *whom* (or *whoever* and *whomever*).

Pronouns in Compounds

Sometimes a pronoun is linked to a noun or to another pronoun with *and* or *or* to form a **compound**.

> <u>The teacher and I</u> met for an hour.
>
> <u>He or she</u> can pick up Jenny at school.

To determine whether to use the subjective or objective case for a pronoun in the second part of a compound, follow the same rules that apply for a pronoun that is not part of a compound.

- If the compound is a subject, use the subjective case.

    > <u>Toby and I</u> [not *me*] like jazz.
    >
    > <u>He and I</u> [not *me*] went to the movies.

- If the compound is an object, use the objective case.

    > The school sent <u>my father and me</u> [not *I*] the financial-aid forms.
    >
    > This argument is between <u>Kate and me</u> [not *I*].

FYI

Choosing Pronouns in Compounds

To determine which pronoun case to use in a compound that joins a noun and a pronoun, rewrite the sentence with just the pronoun.

> Toby and [*I* or *me*?] like jazz.
>
> I like jazz. (not *Me like jazz*)
>
> Toby and I like jazz.

> **Teaching Tip**
> Remind students that the first-person pronoun always comes last in compounds like *Toby and I* and *my father and <u>me</u>*.

> **Teaching Tip**
> Explain that the objective case is used with the contraction *let's*: <u>*Let's*</u> (let us) you and <u>*me*</u> (not *I*) go swimming. Remind students that *let's* includes the objective case pronoun *us*.

PRACTICE

31-13 In the following sentences, the underlined pronouns are parts of compounds. Check them for correct subjective or objective case. If the pronoun is incorrect, cross it out, and write the correct form above it. If the pronoun is correct, write *C* above it.

   C
Example: My classmates and <u>I</u> were surprised by the results of a study on listening.

(1) According to a recent study, the average listener remembers only 50 percent of what <u>him</u>^*he* or <u>her</u>^*she* hears. (2) Two days later, <u>he</u>^*C* or <u>she</u>^*C* can correctly recall only 25 percent of the total message. (3) My friend Alyssa and <u>me</u>^*I* decided to ask our school to sponsor a presentation about listening in the classroom. (4) One point the speaker made was especially helpful to

Alyssa and _I_. (5) We now know that _us_ and the other students in our class each have four times more mental "room" than we need for listening. (6) The presenter taught the other workshop participants and _we_ how to use this extra space. (7) Now, whenever one of our professors pauses to write on the board or take a sip of water, Alyssa and _I_ remember to silently summarize the last point _he_ or _she_ made. (8) Throughout the lecture, we pay attention to the big ideas and overall structure that the professor wants the other students and _us_ to take away. (9) Also, to keep ourselves actively thinking about the topic, we try to predict where the professor will lead our peers and _us_ next. (10) Above all, we do not waste our mental energy on distractions that other students and _us_ ourselves create, such as dropped books or our own worries. (11) Comedian Lily Tomlin's advice to "listen with an intensity most people save for talking" now makes a lot of sense to Alyssa and _me_.

Pronouns in Comparisons

Sometimes a pronoun appears after the word _than_ or _as_ in the second part of a **comparison**.

> John is luckier <u>than I</u>.
> The inheritance changed Raymond as much <u>as her</u>.

- If the pronoun is a subject, use the subjective case.

  > John is luckier <u>than I</u> [am].

- If the pronoun is an object, use the objective case.

  > The inheritance changed Raymond as much <u>as</u> [it changed] <u>her</u>.

FYI

Choosing Pronouns in Comparisons

Sometimes, the pronoun you use can change your sentence's meaning. For example, if you say, "I like Cheerios more than _he_," you mean that you like Cheerios more than the other person likes them.

> I like Cheerios more than he [does].

If, however, you say, "I like Cheerios more than _him_," you mean that you like Cheerios more than you like the other person.

> I like Cheerios more than [I like] him.

PRACTICE
31-14 Each of the following sentences includes a comparison with a pronoun following the word *than* or *as*. Write in each blank the correct form (subjective or objective) of the pronoun in parentheses. In brackets, add the word or words needed to complete the comparison.

Example: Many people are better poker players than __*I [am]*__ (I/me).

1. The survey showed that most people like the candidate's wife as much as __*[they like] him*__ (he/him).

2. No one enjoys shopping more than __*she [does]*__ (she/her).

3. My brother and Aunt Cecile were very close, so her death affected him more than __*[it affected] me*__ (I/me).

4. No two people could have a closer relationship than __*they [have]*__ (they/them).

5. My neighbor drives better than __*I [do]*__ (I/me).

6. He may be as old as __*I [am]*__ (I/me), but he does not have as much work experience.

7. That jacket fits you better than __*[it fits] me*__ (I/me).

8. The other company had a lower bid than __*we [had]*__ (we/us), but we were awarded the contract.

Who and *Whom*, *Whoever* and *Whomever*

To determine whether to use *who* or *whom* (or *whoever* or *whomever*), you need to know how the pronoun functions within the clause in which it appears.

- When the pronoun is the subject of the clause, use *who* or *whoever*.

    I wonder <u>who</u> wrote that song. (*Who* is the subject of the clause *who wrote that song*.)

    I will vote for <u>whoever</u> supports the youth center. (*Whoever* is the subject of the clause *whoever supports the youth center*.)

- When the pronoun is the object, use *whom* or *whomever*.

    <u>Whom</u> do the police suspect? (*Whom* is the direct object of the verb *suspect*.)

    I wonder <u>whom</u> the song is about. (*Whom* is the object of the preposition *about* in the clause *whom the song is about*.)

    Vote for <u>whomever</u> you prefer. (*Whomever* is the object of the verb *prefer* in the clause *whomever you prefer*.)

> **Teaching Tip**
> Tell students that in conversation, people often use *who* for both subjective case (*Who wrote that song?*) and objective case (*Who are you going with?*). In writing, however, they should always use *whom* for the objective case: *With whom are you going?*

FYI

Who and *Whom*

To determine whether to use *who* or *whom*, try substituting another pronoun for *who* or *whom* in the clause. If you can substitute *he* or *she*, use *who*; if you can substitute *him* or *her*, use *whom*.

> [Who/Whom] wrote a love song? He wrote a love song.
>
> [Who/Whom] was the song about? The song was about her.

The same test will work for *whoever* and *whomever*.

PRACTICE

31-15 Circle the correct form—*who* or *whom* (or *whoever* or *whomever*)—in parentheses in each sentence.

Example: With (who/**whom**) did Rob collaborate?

1. The defense team learned (**who**/whom) was going to testify for the prosecution.

2. (Who/**Whom**) does she think she can find to be a witness?

3. The runner (**who**/whom) crosses the finish line first will be the winner.

4. They will argue their case to (**whoever**/whomever) will listen.

5. It will take time to decide (**who**/whom) is the record holder.

6. Take these forms to the clerk (**who**/whom) is at the front desk.

7. We will have to penalize (**whoever**/whomever) misses the first training session.

8. (Who/**Whom**) did Kobe take to the prom?

9. We saw the man (**who**/whom) fired the shots.

10. To (who/**whom**) am I speaking?

31i Reflexive and Intensive Pronouns

Two special kinds of pronouns, *reflexive pronouns* and *intensive pronouns*, end in *-self* (singular) or *-selves* (plural). Although the functions of the two kinds of pronouns are different, their forms are identical.

Reflexive and Intensive Pronouns

Singular Forms

ANTECEDENT	REFLEXIVE OR INTENSIVE PRONOUN
I	myself
you	yourself
he	himself
she	herself
it	itself

Plural Forms

ANTECEDENT	REFLEXIVE OR INTENSIVE PRONOUN
we	ourselves
you	yourselves
they	themselves

Reflexive Pronouns

Reflexive pronouns indicate that people or things did something to themselves or for themselves.

Rosanna lost <u>herself</u> in the novel.

You need to watch <u>yourself</u> when you mix those solutions.

Mehul and Paul made <u>themselves</u> cold drinks.

Intensive Pronouns

Intensive pronouns always appear directly after their antecedents, and they are used for emphasis.

I <u>myself</u> have had some experience in sales and marketing.

The victim <u>himself</u> collected the reward.

They <u>themselves</u> were uncertain of the significance of their findings.

> **Teaching Tip**
> Remind students not to use reflexive or intensive pronouns as subjects: *Kim and I* (not *Kim and myself*) started work on Monday.

PRACTICE
31-16
Fill in the correct reflexive or intensive pronoun in each of the following sentences.

Example: The opening act was exciting, but the main attraction

_____*itself*_____ was boring.

1. My aunt welcomed her visitors and told them to make _____*themselves*_____ at

home.

2. Migrating birds can direct ___themselves___ through clouds, storms, and moonless nights.

3. The First Lady ___herself___ gave a speech at the rally.

4. We all finished the marathon without injuring ___ourselves___.

5. Even though the government offered help to flood victims, the residents ___themselves___ did most of the rebuilding.

6. Sometimes he finds ___himself___ daydreaming in class.

7. The guide warned us to watch ___ourselves___ on the slippery path.

8. The senators were not happy about committing ___themselves___ to vote for lower taxes.

9. She gave ___herself___ a manicure.

10. Although everyone else in my family can sing or play a musical instrument, I ___myself___ am tone-deaf.

TEST · Revise · Edit

Look back at your response to the Write First activity on page 512. TEST what you have written. Then, revise and edit your work, paying special attention to your use of nouns and pronouns.

EDITING PRACTICE

Read the following student essay, which includes noun and pronoun errors. Check for errors in plural noun forms, pronoun case, and pronoun-antecedent agreement. Then, make any editing changes you think are necessary. The first sentence has been edited for you. *Answers may vary.*

Cell Phone Misbehavior

manners
Good ~~manneres~~ used to mean using the right fork and holding the door

open for others. Today, however, people may find that good manners are more
they
complicated than ~~it~~ used to be. New inventions have led to new challenges.

Cell phones, in particular, have created some problems.
people
One problem is the "cell yell," which is the tendency of ~~a person~~ to shout

while they are using their cell phones. Why do we do this? Maybe we do not realize

how loudly we are talking. Maybe we yell out of frustration. Anyone can become
he or she loses   *batteries*
angry when ~~they lose~~ a call. Dead ~~batterys~~ can be infuriating. Unfortunately,
yellers annoy
~~the yeller annoys~~ everyone around them.
themselves
Even if cell-phone users ~~theirselves~~ speak normally, other people can hear them.
I
My friends and ~~me~~ are always calling each other, and we do not always pay attention
who
to ~~whom~~ can hear us. The result is that other people are victims of "secondhand

conversations." These conversations are not as bad for people's health as secondhand
they are   *Who*
smoke, but ~~it is~~ just as annoying. ~~Whom~~ really wants to hear about the private
lives   *whoever*
~~lifes~~ of strangers? Restrooms used to be private; now, ~~whomever~~ is in the next stall
his or her
can overhear someone's private cell-phone conversation and learn ~~their~~ secrets.
users   *their*
Also, some cell-phone ~~user~~ seem to think that getting ~~his~~ calls is more

important than anything else that might be going on. Phones ring, chirp, or
concerts,   *churches,*
play silly tunes at ~~concertes,~~ in classrooms, at weddings, in ~~churchs,~~ and even
its
at funerals. Can you picture a grieving family at a cemetery having ~~their~~ service
their
interrupted by a ringing phone? People should have enough sense to turn off ~~his~~

~~or her~~ cell phones at times like these.

In the United States, there are more than 150 million cell phones. Many
them.
people hate their cell phones, but they do not think they can live without ~~it.~~

Apple iPhone

Man using a cell phone on bus

The problem is that cell phones became popular before there were any rules for *its* use. However, even if the government passed laws about cell-phone behavior, *they* would have a tough time enforcing *it*. In any case, *us* cell-phone users should not need laws to make us behave *ourself*.

their

it

them.

we

ourselves.

COLLABORATIVE ACTIVITIES

1. Working in a group, fill in the following chart, writing one noun on each line. If the noun is a proper noun, be sure to capitalize it.

CARS	TREES	FOODS	FAMOUS COUPLES	CITIES
Answers will vary.				
_____	_____	_____	_____	_____
_____	_____	_____	_____	_____
_____	_____	_____	_____	_____
_____	_____	_____	_____	_____
_____	_____	_____	_____	_____
_____	_____	_____	_____	_____

Now, using as many of the nouns listed above as you can, write a one-paragraph news article that describes an imaginary event. Exchange your work with another group, and check the other group's article to be sure the correct pronoun refers to each noun. Return the articles to their original groups for editing.

2. Working in a group, write a silly story that uses each of these nouns at least once: *Martians, eggplant, MTV, toupee, kangaroo, Iceland, bat, herd,* and *kayak*. Then, exchange stories with another group. After you have read the other group's story, edit it so that it includes all of the following pronouns: *it, its, itself, they, their, them, themselves.* Return the edited story to its authors. Finally, reread your group's story, and check to make sure pronoun-antecedent agreement is clear and correct.

review checklist

Nouns and Pronouns

- [ ] A noun is a word that names something. A singular noun names one thing; a plural noun names more than one thing. (See 31a.)

- [ ] Most nouns add -*s* or -*es* to form plurals. Some nouns have irregular plural forms. (See 31b.)

- [ ] A pronoun is a word that refers to and takes the place of a noun or another pronoun. (See 31c.)

- [ ] The word a pronoun refers to is called the pronoun's antecedent. A pronoun and its antecedent must always agree. (See 31d.)

- [ ] Compound antecedents connected by *and* are plural and are used with plural pronouns. Compound antecedents connected by *or* may take singular or plural pronouns. (See 31e.)

- [ ] Most indefinite pronoun antecedents are singular and are used with singular pronouns; some are plural and are used with plural pronouns. (See 31e.)

- [ ] Collective noun antecedents are singular and are used with singular pronouns. (See 31e.)

- [ ] A pronoun should always refer to a specific antecedent. (See 31f.)

- [ ] Personal pronouns can be in the subjective, objective, or possessive case. (See 31g.)

- [ ] Pronouns present special problems when they are used in compounds and comparisons. The pronouns *who* and *whom* and *whoever* and *whomever* can also cause problems. (See 31h.)

- [ ] Reflexive and intensive pronouns must agree with their antecedents. (See 31i.)

preview

In this chapter, you will learn to
- understand the difference between adjectives and adverbs (32a)
- identify demonstrative adjectives (32a)
- form comparatives and superlatives of adjectives and adverbs (32b)

32 Adjectives and Adverbs

write first

This picture shows children being homeschooled by their mother. Write about the advantages and disadvantages of being educated at home by parents instead of at school by professional teachers.

32a   Identifying Adjectives and Adverbs

Adjectives and adverbs are words that modify (identify or describe) other words. They help make sentences more specific and more interesting.

An **adjective** answers the question *What kind? Which one?* or *How many?* Adjectives modify nouns or pronouns.

> The Turkish city of Istanbul spans two continents. (*Turkish* modifies the noun *city*, and *two* modifies the noun *continents*.)

> It is fascinating because of its location and history. (*Fascinating* modifies the pronoun *it*.)

Teaching Tip
Explain that some adjectives, such as *Turkish*, are capitalized because they are formed from proper nouns. Refer students to 31a.

FYI

Demonstrative Adjectives

Demonstrative adjectives—*this, that, these,* and *those*—do not describe other words. They simply identify particular nouns.

This and *that* identify singular nouns and pronouns.

> This Web site is much more up-to-date than that one.

These and *those* identify plural nouns.

> These words and phrases are French, but those expressions are Creole.

Teaching Tip
You might remind students not to use demonstrative adjectives in nonstandard phrases like *this here* and *that there*.

An **adverb** answers the question *How? Why? When? Where?* or *To what extent?* Adverbs modify verbs, adjectives, or other adverbs.

> Traffic moved steadily. (*Steadily* modifies the verb *moved*.)

> Still, we were quite impatient. (*Quite* modifies the adjective *impatient*.)

> Very slowly, we moved into the center lane. (*Very* modifies the adverb *slowly*.)

FYI

Distinguishing Adjectives from Adverbs

Many adverbs are formed when *-ly* is added to an adjective form.

ADJECTIVE	ADVERB
slow	slowly
nice	nicely
quick	quickly
real	really

Teaching Tip
Point out that some adjectives—*lovely, friendly,* and *lively,* for example—end in *-ly*. Caution students not to mistake these words for adverbs.

(continued on next page)

(continued from previous page)

ADJECTIVE	Let me give you one quick reminder. (*Quick* modifies the noun *reminder*.)
ADVERB	He quickly changed the subject. (*Quickly* modifies the verb *changed*.)

PRACTICE
32-1

In the following sentences, circle the correct form (adjective or adverb) from the choices in parentheses.

Example: Beatles enthusiasts all over the world have formed tribute bands devoted to the (**famous**/famously) group's music.

(1) To show appreciation for their favorite musicians, tribute bands go to (**great**/greatly) lengths. (2) Fans who have a (real/**really**) strong affection for a particular band may decide to play its music and copy its style. (3) Sometimes they form their own groups and have successful careers (simple/**simply**) performing that band's music. (4) These groups are (usual/**usually**) called "tribute bands." (5) Most tribute bands are (passionate/**passionately**) dedicated to reproducing the original group's work. (6) They not only play the group's songs but (careful/**carefully**) imitate the group's look. (7) They study the band members' facial expressions and body movements and create (**exact**/exactly) copies of the band's costumes and instruments. (8) Some more (**inventive**/inventively) tribute bands take the original band's songs and interpret them (different/**differently**). (9) For example, by performing Beatles songs in the style of Metallica, the tribute band Beatallica has created a (**unique**/uniquely) sound. (10) Some people believe such tributes are the (**ultimate**/ultimately) compliment to the original band; others feel (**sure**/surely) that tribute groups are just copycats who (serious/**seriously**) lack imagination.

Teaching Tip
Explain that a linking verb such as *feel* is followed by an adjective, not an adverb. Refer students to 18c.

FYI

Good and *Well*

Be careful not to confuse *good* and *well*. Unlike regular adjectives, whose adverb forms add *-ly*, the adjective *good* is irregular. Its adverb form is *well*.

ADJECTIVE   Fred Astaire was a good dancer. (*Good* modifies the noun *dancer*.)

ADVERB   He danced especially well with Ginger Rogers. (*Well* modifies the verb *danced*.)

Always use *well* when you are describing a person's health.

He really didn't feel well [not *good*] after eating the entire pizza.

PRACTICE

32-2   Circle the correct form (*good* or *well*) in the sentences below.

Example: It can be hard for some people to find a (good/well) job that they really like.

(1) Some people may not do (good/well) sitting in an office. (2) Instead, they may prefer to find jobs that take advantage of their (good/well) physical condition. (3) Such people might consider becoming smoke jumpers—firefighters who are (good/well) at parachuting from small planes into remote areas to battle forest fires. (4) Smoke jumpers must be able to work (good/well) even without much sleep. (5) They must also handle danger (good/well). (6) They look forward to the (good/well) feeling of saving a forest or someone's home. (7) As they battle fires, surrounded by smoke and fumes, smoke jumpers may not feel very (good/well). (8) Sometimes, things go wrong; for example, when their parachutes fail to work (good/well), jumpers may be injured or even killed. (9) Smoke jumpers do not get paid particularly (good/well). (10) However, they are proud of their strength and endurance and feel (good/well) about their work.

32b Comparatives and Superlatives

Teaching Tip
Tell students that some adverbs—such as *very*, *somewhat*, *quite*, *extremely*, *rather*, and *moderately*—as well as the demonstrative adjectives *this*, *that*, *these*, and *those*, do not have comparative or superlative forms.

Teaching Tip
Tell students that the adjective *unique* means "the only one." For this reason, it has no comparative or superlative form (*more unique* and *most unique* are incorrect). Other absolute adjectives that do not have comparative or superlative forms are *perfect*, *impossible*, *infinite*, and *dead*.

The **comparative** form of an adjective or adverb compares two people or things. Adjectives and adverbs form the comparative with *-er* or *more*. The **superlative** form of an adjective or adverb compares more than two things. Adjectives and adverbs form the superlative with *-est* or *most*.

ADJECTIVES	This film is <u>dull</u> and <u>predictable</u>.
COMPARATIVE	The film I saw last week was even <u>duller</u> and <u>more predictable</u> than this one.
SUPERLATIVE	The film I saw last night was the <u>dullest</u> and <u>most predictable</u> one I've ever seen.
ADVERBS	For a beginner, Jane did needlepoint <u>skillfully</u>.
COMPARATIVE	After she had watched the demonstration, Jane did needlepoint <u>more skillfully</u> than Rosie.
SUPERLATIVE	Of the twelve beginners, Jane did needlepoint the <u>most skillfully</u>.

Forming Comparatives and Superlatives

Adjectives

■ One-syllable adjectives generally form the comparative with *-er* and the superlative with *-est*.

great   greater   greatest

■ Adjectives with two or more syllables form the comparative with *more* and the superlative with *most*.

wonderful   more wonderful   most wonderful

Exception: Two-syllable adjectives ending in *-y* add *-er* or *-est* after changing the *y* to an *i*.

funny   funnier   funniest

Adverbs

■ All adverbs ending in *-ly* form the comparative with *more* and the superlative with *most*.

efficiently   more efficiently   most efficiently

■ Some other adverbs form the comparative with *-er* and the superlative with *-est*.

soon   sooner   soonest

Solving Special Problems with Comparatives and Superlatives

The following rules will help you avoid errors with comparatives and superlatives.

Teaching Tip
Tell students that when they form comparatives, they should have only one ending with an *r* sound (not *more greater* or *more better*, for example).

■ Never use both *-er* and *more* to form the comparative or both *-est* and *most* to form the superlative.

> Nothing could have been <u>more awful</u>. (not *more awfuller*)

> Space Mountain is the <u>most frightening</u> (not *most frighteningest*) ride at Disney World.

■ Never use the superlative when you are comparing only two things.

> This is the <u>more serious</u> (not *most serious*) of the two problems.

■ Never use the comparative when you are comparing more than two things.

> This is the <u>worst</u> (not *worse*) day of my life.

PRACTICE

32-3 Fill in the correct comparative form of the word supplied in parentheses.

Example: Children tend to be _____*noisier*_____ (noisy) than adults.

1. Traffic always moves _____*more slowly*_____ (slow) during rush hour than late at night.

2. The weather report says temperatures will be _____*colder*_____ (cold) tomorrow.

3. Some elderly people are _____*healthier*_____ (healthy) than younger people.

4. It has been proven that pigs are _____*more intelligent*_____ (intelligent) than dogs.

5. When someone asks you to repeat yourself, you usually answer _____*more loudly*_____ (loud).

6. The _____*taller*_____ (tall) of the two buildings was damaged by the earthquake.

7. They want to teach their son to be _____*more respectful*_____ (respectful) of women than many young men are.

8. Las Vegas is _____*more famous*_____ (famous) for its casinos than for its natural resources.

9. The WaterDrop is _____*wilder*_____ (wild) than any other ride in the amusement park.

10. You must move _____*more quickly*_____ (quick) if you expect to catch the ball.

PRACTICE
32-4 Fill in the correct superlative form of the word supplied in parentheses.

Example: Today, tattoos are created _most frequently_ (frequently) by a professional using an electric tattoo machine.

(1) Getting a tattoo used to be one of the _surest_ (sure) and _most shocking_ (shocking) ways to demonstrate one's individuality. (2) Today, however, only the _most daring_ (daring) tattoos cause a stir. (3) According to the _most recent_ (recent) polls, 36 percent of 18- to 25-year-olds in the United States have at least one tattoo. (4) Tattoos are _most common_ (common) among people between 26 and 40, 40 percent of whom have one or more. (5) One might expect people in the _most competitive_ (competitive) years of their careers not to get tattoos that might limit their job opportunities. (6) However, now that so many people have tattoos, only the _most conventional_ (conventional) employers find them shocking. (7) People still tend to place their tattoos in the _safest_ (safe) and _most easily_ (easily) hidden spots, like the back or the upper arm. (8) That trend is starting to change, though; getting a hand or neck tattoo is one of the _latest_ (late) fads. (9) In the past, prisoners and gang members were the _most likely_ (likely) people to get tattoos in the _most visible_ (visible) locations. (10) Today, however, some of the _most popular_ (popular) media stars and sports heroes have tattoos.

FYI

Good/Well and Bad/Badly

Most adjectives and adverbs form the comparative with -er or more and the superlative with -est or most. The adjectives good and bad and their adverb forms well and badly are exceptions.

ADJECTIVE	COMPARATIVE FORM	SUPERLATIVE FORM
good	better	best
bad	worse	worst

ADVERB	COMPARATIVE FORM	SUPERLATIVE FORM
well	better	best
badly	worse	worst

PRACTICE

32-5   Fill in the correct comparative or superlative form of *good, well, bad,* or *badly.*

Example: She is at her ____*best*____ (good) when she is under pressure.

1. Today in track practice, Luisa performed ____*better*____ (well) than she has in weeks.

2. In fact, she ran her ____*best*____ (good) time ever in the fifty meter.

3. When things are bad, we wonder whether they will get ____*better*____ (good) or ____*worse*____ (bad).

4. I've had some bad meals before, but this is the ____*worst*____ (bad).

5. The world always looks ____*better*____ (good) when you're in love than when you're not.

6. Athletes generally play the ____*worst*____ (badly) when their concentration is poorest.

7. The Sport Shop's prices may be good, but Athletic Attic's are the ____*best*____ (good) in town.

8. There are ____*better*____ (good) ways to solve conflicts than by fighting.

9. People seem to hear ____*better*____ (well) when they agree with what you're saying than when they don't agree with you.

10. Of all the children, Manda took the ____*best*____ (good) care of her toys.

TEST · Revise · Edit

Look back at your response to the Write First activity on page 538. TEST what you have written. Then, revise and edit your work, paying special attention to your use of adjectives and adverbs.

EDITING PRACTICE

Read the following student essay, which includes errors in the use of adjectives and adverbs. Make any changes necessary to correct adjectives incorrectly used for adverbs and adverbs incorrectly used for adjectives. Also, correct any errors in the use of comparatives and superlatives and in the use of demonstrative adjectives. Finally, try to add some adjectives and adverbs that you feel would make the writer's ideas clearer or more specific. The first sentence has been edited for you. *Answers may vary.*

Starting Over

A wedding can be the *most joyful* ~~joyfullest~~ occasion in two people's lives, the beginning of a couple's ~~most~~ happiest years. For some unlucky women, however, a wedding can be the *worst* ~~worse~~ thing that ever happens; it is the beginning not of their happiness but of their battered lives. As I went through the joyful day of my wedding, I wanted *badly* ~~bad~~ to find happiness for the rest of my life, but what I hoped and wished for did not come true.

I was married in the savannah belt of the Sudan in the eastern part of Africa, where I grew up. I was barely twenty-two years old. The first two years of my marriage progressed *peacefully,* ~~peaceful,~~ but problems started as soon as our first child was born.

Many American women say, "If my husband hit me just once, that would be it. I'd leave." But *this modern* ~~those~~ attitude does not work in cultures where tradition has overshadowed women's rights and divorce is not accepted. All women can do is accept their *sad* ~~sadly~~ fate. Battered women give many reasons for staying in their *abusive* marriages, but fear is the *most common.* ~~commonest.~~ Fear immobilizes these women, ruling their decisions, their actions, and their very lives. This is how it was for me.

Of course, I was *really* ~~real~~ afraid whenever my husband hit me. I would run to my mother's house and cry, but she would always talk me into going back and being more *patient* ~~patiently~~ with my husband. Our tradition discourages divorce, and wife-beating is taken for granted. The situation is really quite ironic: the religion I practice sets harsh punishments for abusive husbands, but tradition has so overpowered religion that the laws do not really work very *well.* ~~good.~~

Map of Sudan

Sudanese wedding ceremony

One night, I asked myself whether life had treated me fair. *(fairly,)* True, I had a high

school diploma and two of the beautifullest *(most beautiful)* children in the world, but all this was

not enough. I realized that to stand up to the husband who treated me so bad, *(badly,)* I

would have to achieve a more better education than he had. That night, I decided

to get a college education in the United States. My husband opposed *(strongly)* my decision,

but with the support of my father and mother, I was able to begin to change my

life. My years as a student and single parent in the United States have been real *(really)*

difficult for me, but I know I made the right choice.

COLLABORATIVE ACTIVITIES

1. Working in a small group, write a plot summary for an imaginary film. Begin with one of the following three sentences.

   ■ Dirk and Clive were sworn enemies, but that night on Boulder Ridge they vowed to work together just this once, for the good of their country.

   ■ Genevieve entered the room in a cloud of perfume, and when she spoke, her voice was like velvet.

   ■ The desert sun beat down on her head, but Susanna was determined to protect what was hers, no matter what the cost.

2. Trade summaries with another group. Add as many adjectives and adverbs as you can to the other group's summary. Make sure each modifier is appropriate.

3. Reread your own group's plot summary, and edit it carefully, paying special attention to the way adjectives and adverbs are used.

Teaching Tip
Students tend to use the same adjectives over and over again. Encourage them to move beyond *great*, *nice*, *unique*, and so on.

ESL Tip
You may want to refer students to 33k for information on placing modifiers in order.

review checklist

Adjectives and Adverbs

☐ Adjectives modify nouns or pronouns. (See 32a.)

☐ Demonstrative adjectives—*this*, *that*, *these*, and *those*—identify particular nouns. (See 32a.)

☐ Adverbs modify verbs, adjectives, or other adverbs. (See 32a.)

☐ To compare two people or things, use the comparative form of an adjective or adverb. To compare more than two people or things, use the superlative form of an adjective or adverb. (See 32b.)

☐ The adjectives *good* and *bad* and their adverb forms *well* and *badly* have irregular comparative and superlative forms. (See 32b.)

33 Grammar and Usage for ESL Writers

write first

This painting by Frederick Childe Hassam shows American flags displayed on the Fourth of July, Independence Day. Using the present tense, write a paragraph explaining how you and your family celebrate a holiday that is important to you.

Learning English as a second language involves more than just learning grammar. In fact, if you have been studying English as a second language, you may know more about English grammar than many native speakers do. However, you will still need to learn the conventions and rules that most native speakers already know.

33a   Subjects in Sentences

English requires that every sentence state its subject. Every independent clause and every dependent clause must also have a subject.

> **INCORRECT**   Elvis Presley was only forty-two years old when died. (When who died?)
>
> **CORRECT**   Elvis Presley was only forty-two years old when he died.

When the real subject follows the verb and the normal subject position before the verb is empty, it must be filled by a "dummy" subject, such as *it* or *there*.

> **INCORRECT**   Is hot in this room.
>
> **CORRECT**   It is hot in this room.
>
> **INCORRECT**   Are many rivers in my country.
>
> **CORRECT**   There are many rivers in my country.

Standard English also does not permit a two-part subject in which the second part of the subject is a pronoun referring to the same person or thing as the first part.

> **INCORRECT**   The Caspian Sea it is the largest lake in the world.
>
> **CORRECT**   The Caspian Sea is the largest lake in the world.

PRACTICE

33-1   Each of the following sentences is missing the subject of a dependent or an independent clause. On the lines after each sentence, rewrite it, adding an appropriate subject. Then, underline the subject you have added. *Answers will vary.*

Example: Because college students often have very little money, are always looking for inexpensive meals.

Because college students often have very little money, they are always looking

for inexpensive meals.

Teaching Tip
You may want to do a diagnostic error analysis to discover the most frequent or common grammar errors of your nonnative-speaking students. If there is a large variation in the group, consider offering individualized or small-group mini lessons.

Teaching Tip
Have students keep error logs and use them consistently. Logs should be kept simple, with limited categories.

Teaching Tip
Refer students to 18a for more on subjects.

1. Ramen noodles are a popular choice for students because are cheap, tasty, and easy to prepare.

   Ramen noodles are a popular choice for students because <u>they</u> are cheap, tasty,

   and easy to prepare.

2. In minutes, a student can enjoy hot noodles flavored with chicken, shrimp, or beef, and sell vegetarian versions, too.

   In minutes, a student can enjoy hot noodles flavored with chicken, shrimp, or beef,

   and <u>stores</u> sell vegetarian versions, too.

3. Although high in carbohydrates (a good source of energy), also contain saturated and trans fats and few vitamins or minerals.

   Although high in carbohydrates (a good source of energy), <u>ramen noodles</u> also

   contain saturated and trans fats and few vitamins or minerals.

4. Cookbooks provide special recipes for preparing ramen noodles; include "Ramen Shrimp Soup" and "Ramen Beef and Broccoli."

   Cookbooks provide special recipes for preparing ramen noodles; <u>they</u> include

   "Ramen Shrimp Soup" and "Ramen Beef and Broccoli."

5. Ramen noodles are not just popular with American college students; are also popular in many other countries around the world.

   Ramen noodles are not just popular with American college students; <u>they</u> are also

   popular in many other countries around the world.

6. The noodles have even found their way to the International Space Station, where enjoy them in space.

   The noodles have even found their way to the International Space Station,

   where <u>astronauts</u> enjoy them in space.

7. The noodles originated in China many years ago, where were deep fried so that they could be stored for a long time without spoiling.

   The noodles originated in China many years ago, where <u>they</u> were deep fried so

   that they could be stored for a long time without spoiling.

8. For today's college students, however, spoilage is not a problem because are usually eaten long before their expiration date.

   For today's college students, however, spoilage is not a problem because <u>the</u>

   <u>noodles</u> are usually eaten long before their expiration date.

PRACTICE
33-2   The following sentences contain unnecessary two-part subjects. Cross out the unnecessary pronoun. Then, rewrite each sentence correctly on the lines provided.

Example: Travelers to China ~~they~~ often visit the Great Wall.

Travelers to China often visit the Great Wall.

1. The first parts of the Great Wall ~~they~~ were built around 200 A.D.

   The first parts of the Great Wall were built around 200 A.D.

2. The Great Wall ~~it~~ was built to keep out invading armies.

   The Great Wall was built to keep out invading armies.

3. The sides of the Great Wall ~~they~~ are made of stone, brick, and earth.

   The sides of the Great Wall are made of stone, brick, and earth.

4. The top of the Great Wall ~~it~~ is paved with bricks, forming a roadway for horses.

   The top of the Great Wall is paved with bricks, forming a roadway for horses.

5. The Great Wall ~~it~~ is so huge that it can be seen by astronauts in space.

   The Great Wall is so huge that it can be seen by astronauts in space.

33b   Plural Nouns

In English, most nouns add -*s* to form plurals. Every time you use a noun, ask yourself whether you are talking about one item or more than one, and choose a singular or plural form accordingly. Consider the following sentence.

CORRECT   The <u>books</u> in both <u>branches</u> of the <u>library</u> are deteriorating.

The three nouns in this sentence are underlined: one is singular (*library*), and the other two are plural (*books*, *branches*). The word *both* is not enough to indicate that *branch* is plural. Even if a sentence includes information that tells you that a noun is plural, you must always use a form of the noun that indicates that it is plural.

> **Teaching Tip**
> Tell students that many nouns—such as *child* and *man*—have irregular plural forms. Refer them to 31b.

> **Teaching Tip**
> Refer students to 31a and 31b for more on singular and plural nouns.

PRACTICE

33-3   Underline the plural nouns in the following sentences. (Not all of the sentences contain plural nouns.)

Example: Mass immigration and lack of employment created unexpected social <u>problems</u> in the United States in the nineteenth century.

1. In 1850, New York City estimated that about thirty thousand homeless <u>children</u> lived on its <u>streets</u>.

2. The <u>children</u> were considered "<u>orphans</u>" because their <u>parents</u> had died, lost <u>jobs</u>, or were ill.

3. A social service agency in New York City suggested a solution to this problem.

4. The solution was to send these <u>children</u> to America's heartland—to <u>states</u> like Iowa, Kansas, and Arkansas.

5. There, the <u>children</u> could be accepted into <u>families</u> and help with farming and other <u>chores</u>.

6. In 1854, the first "orphan train" headed to western <u>cities</u> and <u>towns</u>.

7. The <u>children</u> were lined up in a local hall, looked over, and selected by interested <u>families</u>.

8. Then, the remaining <u>children</u> got back on the train and went on to the next town to go through the process again.

9. Most of the <u>children</u> found happy <u>homes</u> and loving <u>parents</u>, but <u>others</u> were treated like <u>servants</u> by their new <u>families</u>.

10. By 1930, social service <u>agencies</u> had begun to reconsider the plan and stopped the orphan <u>trains</u>.

33c   Count and Noncount Nouns

A **count noun** names one particular thing or a group of particular things that can be counted: *a teacher, a panther, a bed, an ocean, a cloud, an ice cube; two teachers, many panthers, three beds, two oceans, several clouds, some ice cubes.* A **noncount noun** names things that cannot be counted: *gold, cream, sand, blood, smoke, water.*

Count nouns usually have a singular form and a plural form: *cube, cubes*. Noncount nouns usually have only a singular form: *water*. Note how the nouns *cube* and *water* differ in the way they are used in sentences.

CORRECT	The glass is full of ice cubes.
CORRECT	The glass is full of water.
INCORRECT	The glass is full of waters.
CORRECT	The glass contains five ice cubes.
CORRECT	The glass contains some water.
INCORRECT	The glass contains five waters.

Often, the same idea can be expressed with either a count noun or a noncount noun.

COUNT	NONCOUNT
people (plural of *person*)	humanity [*not* humanities]
tables, chairs, beds	furniture [*not* furnitures]
letters	mail [*not* mails]
supplies	equipment [*not* equipments]
facts	information [*not* informations]

Some words can be either count or noncount, depending on the meaning intended.

COUNT	He had many interesting experiences at his first job.
NONCOUNT	It is often difficult to get a job if you do not have experience.

Here are some guidelines for using count and noncount nouns:

- Use a count noun to refer to a living animal, but use a noncount noun to refer to the food that comes from that animal.

COUNT	There are three live lobsters in the tank.
NONCOUNT	This restaurant specializes in lobster.

- If you use a noncount noun for a substance or class of things that can come in different varieties, you can often make that noun plural if you want to talk about those varieties.

NONCOUNT	Cheese is a rich source of calcium.
COUNT	Many different cheeses come from Italy.

Teaching Tip

Tell students that sometimes a noncount noun, such as *water*, appears to have a plural form (*waters*). Although such forms end in *-s*, they are verbs and not plural nouns: *The water is cold. He waters the plants every Friday.*

Teaching Tip

Remind students that certain frequently used nouns are noncount nouns and therefore have no plural forms: *information, clothing, equipment, furniture, homework, luggage.* These words never have *-s* endings.

- If you want to shift attention from a concept in general to specific examples of it, you can often use a noncount noun as a count noun.

NONCOUNT   You have a great deal of talent.

COUNT   My talents do not include singing.

PRACTICE

33-4   In each of the following sentences, decide if the underlined word is being used as a count or a noncount noun. If it is being used as a noncount noun, circle the *N* following the sentence. If it is being used as a count noun, circle the *C*.

Examples: As a Peace Corps volunteer in Ecuador, Dave Schweiden-

back realized how important bicycles could be.   N   Ⓒ

Using his imagination, Dave figured out an effective way to recycle

America's unwanted bicycles.   Ⓝ   C

1. Pedals for Progress is an American nonprofit organization.   N   Ⓒ

2. Founded in 1991 by Dave Schweidenback, the group collects and repairs

old bicycles and sends them to countries where they are needed.   N   Ⓒ

3. Pedals for Progress aims to reduce the amount of bicycle waste that

ends up in American landfills.   Ⓝ   C

4. People in the United States throw away millions of bikes and bike

parts every year.   N   Ⓒ

5. At the same time, lack of transportation is a serious problem for many

people in developing countries.   Ⓝ   C

6. Without an efficient and affordable way to get to work, a person can-

not hold a job.   N   Ⓒ

7. A working bicycle provides an easy and environmentally friendly way

to get around.   N   Ⓒ

8. Bicycles from Pedals for Progress only cost the user a small amount of

money.   Ⓝ   C

9. To help maintain these recycled bikes, the organization also helps to

establish local repair shops.   N   Ⓒ

10. By making it easier for people to work, Pedals for Progress hopes to

reduce poverty.   Ⓝ   C

Determiners with Count and Noncount Nouns

Determiners are adjectives that *identify* rather than describe the nouns they modify. Determiners may also *quantify* nouns (that is, indicate an amount or a number).

Determiners include the following words.

- Articles: *a, an, the*
- Demonstrative pronouns: *this, these, that, those*
- Possessive pronouns: *my, our, your, his, her, its, their*
- Possessive nouns: *Sheila's, my friend's,* and so on
- *Whose, which, what*
- *All, both, each, every, some, any, either, no, neither, many, most, much, a few, a little, few, little, several, enough*
- All numerals: *one, two,* and so on

Teaching Tip
Use direct feedback when marking the work of nonnative speakers. Correct any incorrect usage of articles.

When a determiner is accompanied by one or more other adjectives, the determiner always comes first. For example, in the phrase *my expensive new digital watch, my* is a determiner; you cannot put *expensive, new, digital,* or any other adjective before *my*.

A singular count noun must always be accompanied by a determiner—for example, *my watch* or *the new digital watch,* not just *watch* or *new digital watch.* However, noncount nouns and plural count nouns sometimes have determiners but sometimes do not. *This honey is sweet* and *Honey is sweet* are both acceptable, as are *These berries are juicy* and *Berries are juicy.* (In each case, the meaning is different.) You cannot say, *Berry is juicy,* however; say instead, *This berry is juicy, Every berry is juicy,* or *A berry is juicy.*

FYI

Determiners

Some determiners can be used only with certain types of nouns.

- *This* and *that* can be used only with singular nouns (count or noncount): *this berry, that honey.*
- *These, those, a few, few, many, both,* and *several* can be used only with plural count nouns: *these berries, those apples, a few ideas, few people, many students, both sides, several directions.*
- *Much, little,* and *a little* can be used only with noncount nouns: *much affection, little time, little honey.*
- *Some, enough, all,* and *most* can be used only with noncount or plural count nouns: *some honey, some berries; enough trouble, enough problems; all traffic, all roads; most money, most coins.*

Teaching Tip
Students need to memorize the information in this box.

Teaching Tip
You might point out to students that *a few* and *a little* have positive connotations (*A few* seats are left), while *few* and *little* have negative connotations (*Few* seats are left).

(continued on next page)

(continued from previous page)

> ■ *A, an, every, each, either,* and *neither* can be used only with singular count nouns: *a berry, an elephant, every possibility, each citizen, either option, neither candidate.*

PRACTICE

33-5 In each of the following sentences, circle the more appropriate choice from each pair of words or phrases in parentheses.

Examples: Volcanoes are among the most destructive of (all/every) natural forces on earth.

People have always been fascinated and terrified by (this/these) force of nature.

1. Not (all/every) volcano is considered a danger.

2. In (major some/some major) volcanic eruptions, huge clouds rise over the mountain.

3. In 2010, ash from a volcano in Iceland caused (many/much) disruption for airline passengers throughout Europe.

4. (A few violent/Violent a few) eruptions are so dramatic that they blow the mountain apart.

5. (Most/Much) volcanic eruptions cannot be predicted.

6. Since the 1400s, (many/much) people—almost 200,000—have lost their lives in volcanic eruptions.

7. When a volcano erupts, (little/a little) can be done to prevent property damage.

8. By the time people realize an eruption is about to take place, there is rarely (many/enough) time to escape.

9. Volcanoes can be dangerous, but they also produce (a little/some) benefits.

10. For example, (a few/a little) countries use energy from underground steam in volcanic areas to produce electric power.

33e   Articles

The **definite article** *the* and the **indefinite articles** *a* and *an* are determiners that tell readers whether the noun that follows is one they can identify (*the book*) or one they cannot yet identify (*a book*).

The Definite Article

When the definite article *the* is used with a noun, the writer is saying to readers, "You can identify which particular thing or things I have in mind. The information you need to make that identification is available to you. Either you have it already, or I am about to give it to you."

Readers can find the necessary information in the following ways.

- By looking at other information in the sentence

  Meet me at <u>the</u> corner of Main Street and Lafayette Road.

  In this example, *the* is used with the noun *corner* because other words in the sentence tell readers which particular corner the writer has in mind: the one located at Main and Lafayette.

- By looking at information in other sentences

  Aisha ordered a slice of pie and a cup of coffee. <u>The</u> pie was delicious. She asked for a second slice.

  Here, *the* is used before the word *pie* in the second sentence to indicate that it is the same pie identified in the first sentence. Notice, however, that the noun *slice* in the third sentence is preceded by an indefinite article (*a*) because it is not the same slice referred to in the first sentence.

- By drawing on general knowledge

  <u>The</u> earth revolves around <u>the</u> sun.

  Here, *the* is used with the nouns *earth* and *sun* because readers are expected to know which particular things the writer is referring to.

FYI

The Definite Article

Always use *the* (rather than *a* or *an*) in the following situations:

- Before the word *same*: *the same day*
- Before the superlative form of an adjective: *the youngest son*
- Before a number indicating order or sequence: *the third time*

Indefinite Articles

When an indefinite article is used with a noun, the writer is saying to readers, "I don't expect you to have enough information right now to identify a particular thing that I have in mind. I do, however, expect you to recognize that I'm referring to only one item."

Consider the following sentences.

We need <u>a</u> table for our computer.

I have <u>a</u> folding table; maybe you can use that.

In the first sentence, the writer is referring to a hypothetical table, not an actual one. Because the table is indefinite to the writer, it is clearly indefinite to the reader, so *a* is used, not *the*. The second sentence refers to an actual table, but because the writer does not expect the reader to be able to identify the table specifically, it is also used with *a* rather than *the*.

> **WORD POWER**
>
> **hypothetical** assumed or supposed; not supported by evidence

FYI

Indefinite Articles

Unlike the definite article (*the*), the indefinite articles *a* and *an* occur only with singular count nouns. *A* is used when the next sound is a consonant, and *an* is used when the next sound is a vowel. In choosing *a* or *an*, pay attention to sound rather than to spelling: *a house, a year, a union,* but *an hour, an uncle.*

> **Teaching Tip**
> Refer students to the box on page 623 for a review of vowels and consonants.

No Article

Only noncount and plural count nouns can stand without articles: *butter, chocolate, cookies, strawberries* (but <u>a</u> *cookie* or <u>the</u> *strawberry*).

Nouns without articles can be used to make generalizations.

<u>Infants</u> need <u>affection</u> as well as <u>food</u>.

Here, the absence of articles before the nouns *infants, affection,* and *food* indicates that the statement is not about particular infants, affection, or food but about infants, affection, and food in general. Remember not to use *the* in such sentences; in English, a sentence like *The infants need affection as well as food* can only refer to particular, identifiable infants, not to infants in general.

> **Teaching Tip**
> Refer students to 33c for more on count and noncount nouns.

> **Teaching Tip**
> Sometimes, no article is used for particular (actual) things, usually to suggest quantity: *I can hear <u>dogs</u> barking.*

Articles with Proper Nouns

Proper nouns can be divided into two classes: names that take *the* and names that take no article.

- Names of people usually take no article unless they are used in the plural to refer to members of a family, in which case they take *the*: *Napoleon, Mahatma Gandhi* (but <u>the</u> *Parkers*).
- Names of places that are plural in form usually take *the*: *the Andes, the United States.*

> **Teaching Tip**
> Refer students to 36a for more on proper nouns.

- The names of most places on land (cities, states, provinces, and countries) take no article: *Salt Lake City, Mississippi, Alberta, Japan.* The names of most bodies of water (rivers, seas, and oceans, although not lakes or bays) take *the*: *the Mississippi, the Mediterranean, the Pacific* (but *Lake Erie, San Francisco Bay*).
- Names of streets take no article: *Main Street.* Names of unnumbered highways take *the*: *the Belt Parkway.*

PRACTICE

33-6 In the following passage, decide whether each blank needs a definite article (*the*), an indefinite article (*a* or *an*), or no article. If a definite or indefinite article is needed, write it in the space provided. If no article is needed, leave the space blank.

Example: A sundial can be __*an*__ attractive addition to _____ backyard gardens.

(1) Sundials take many forms, and they have come __*a*__ long way from their origins. (2) Today's backyard sundials usually feature __*a*__ small, circular table where __*a*__ triangular fin casts __*a*__ shadow. (3) Two hundred years ago, however, __*the*__ most popular sundials were small enough to be carried in __*a*__ pocket. (4) Pocket sundials were used instead of _____ watches until __*the*__ 1800s even though __*the*__ first watch was made in 1504. (5) It took watchmakers centuries to get __*the*__ tiny parts inside __*a*__ watch to run smoothly. (6) For this reason, __*a*__ rich European during __*the*__ Renaissance might have bought __*a*__ watch as __*a*__ fancy toy but used __*a*__ pocket sundial to tell time. (7) Pocket sundials are certainly __*a*__ thing of __*the*__ past, but larger sundials continue to be built for __*a*__ variety of purposes. (8) __*A*__ large sundial is often much more than __*an*__ attractive decoration for __*a*__ garden. (9) It might be __*a*__ sophisticated timekeeper, __*an*__ architectural wonder, or __*a*__ symbol. (10) For example, at __*the*__ Jantar Mantar observatory in Jaipur, India, __*a*__ three-hundred-year-old disk dial tells time as accurately as __*a*__ cell phone equipped with GPS. (11) At __*a*__ university in Hong Kong, __*a*__ red, flame-shaped sundial is a startling sculpture for __*the*__ main entrance to its campus. (12) And in California, __*a*__ bridge that spans __*the*__

Sacramento River is held up by _____*an*_____ enormous sundial. (13) This "Sundial Bridge" was built to represent _____*the*_____ relationship between _____ humans and _____ nature. (14) As these examples show, we remain fascinated by _____*the*_____ precision, simplicity, and beauty of sundials even though we no longer need _____*the*_____ sun to help us tell time.

33f Negative Statements and Questions

Negative Statements

Teaching Tip
Refer students to 18c for more on helping verbs.

To form a negative statement, add the word *not* directly after the first helping verb of the complete verb.

> Global warming has been getting worse.
>
> Global warming has <u>not</u> been getting worse.

Teaching Tip
Tell students that if a sentence includes the word *some* (*I have* <u>*some*</u> *money*), when it is turned into a negative statement, *any* replaces *some* (*I don't have* <u>*any*</u> *money*).

When there is no helping verb, a form of the verb *do* must be inserted before *not*.

> Automobile traffic contributes to pollution.
>
> Automobile traffic <u>does not</u> contribute to pollution.

Teaching Tip
Refer students to 26c for information on subject-verb agreement with the verb *do*.

However, if the main verb is *am, is, are, was,* or *were,* do not insert a form of *do* before *not*: *Harry was late. Harry was <u>not</u> late.*

Remember that when *do* is used as a helping verb, the form of *do* used must match the tense and number of the original main verb. Note that in the negative statement above, the main verb loses its tense and appears in the base form (*contribute,* not *contributes*).

Questions

Teaching Tip
If a statement includes more than one helping verb (*The governor* <u>*will*</u> <u>*be*</u> *working on the budget*), move only the *first* helping verb when you form a question (<u>*Will*</u> *the governor* <u>*be*</u> *working on the budget?*).

To form a question, move the helping verb that follows the subject to the position directly before the subject.

> The governor <u>is</u> trying to compromise.
>
> <u>Is</u> the governor trying to compromise?
>
> The governor <u>is</u> working on the budget.
>
> <u>Is</u> the governor working on the budget?

The same rule applies even when the verb is in the past or future tense.

> The governor <u>was</u> trying to lower state taxes.
>
> <u>Was</u> the governor trying to lower state taxes?
>
> The governor <u>will</u> try to get reelected.
>
> <u>Will</u> the governor try to get reelected?

As with negatives, when the verb does not include a helping verb, you must supply a form of *do*. To form a question, put the correct form of *do* directly before the subject.

The governor <u>works</u> hard.

<u>Does</u> the governor <u>work</u> hard?

The governor <u>improved</u> life in his state.

<u>Did</u> the governor <u>improve</u> life in his state?

However, if the main verb is *am, is, are, was,* or *were,* do not insert a form of *do* before the verb. Instead, move the main verb to before the subject: *Harry was late.* <u>Was</u> *Harry late?*

Note: The helping verb never comes before the subject if the subject is a question word, such as *who* or *which.*

<u>Who</u> is talking to the governor?

<u>Which</u> bills have been vetoed by the governor?

> **Teaching Tip**
> Tell students that if a sentence includes the word *some* (*He had <u>some</u> money*), when it is turned into a question, *any* replaces *some* (*Did he have <u>any</u> money?*).

PRACTICE

33-7 Rewrite each of the following sentences in two ways: first, turn the sentence into a question; then, rewrite the original sentence as a negative statement.

Example: Her newest album is selling as well as her first one.

Question: Is her newest album selling as well as her first one?

Negative statement: Her newest album is not selling as well as her first one.

1. Converting metric measurements to the system used in the United States is difficult.

   Question: Is converting metric measurements to the system used in the
   United States difficult?

   Negative statement: Converting metric measurements to the system used in the
   United States is not difficult.

> **Teaching Tip**
> Students may need help with past tense sentences, where verbs will change form in questions and negative statements.

2. The early frost damaged some crops.

   Question: Did the early frost damage any crops?

   _____

   Negative statement: The early frost did not damage any crops.

   _____

3. That family was very influential in the early 1900s.

   Question: Was that family very influential in the early 1900s?

   _____

Negative statement: _That family was not very influential in the early 1900s._

4. Most stores in malls are open on Sundays.

Question: _Are most stores in malls open on Sundays?_

Negative statement: _Most stores in malls are not open on Sundays._

5. Choosing the right gift is a difficult task.

Question: _Is choosing the right gift a difficult task?_

Negative statement: _Choosing the right gift is not a difficult task._

6. Most great artists are successful during their lifetimes.

Question: _Are most great artists successful during their lifetimes?_

Negative statement: _Most great artists are not successful during their lifetimes._

7. The lawyer can verify the witness's story.

Question: _Can the lawyer verify the witness's story?_

Negative statement: _The lawyer cannot verify the witness's story._

8. American cities are as dangerous as they were thirty years ago.

Question: _Are American cities as dangerous as they were thirty years ago?_

Negative statement: _American cities are not as dangerous as they were thirty years ago._

9. The British royal family is loved by most of the British people.

Question: _Is the British royal family loved by most of the British people?_

Negative statement: _The British royal family is not loved by most of the British people._

10. Segregation in the American South ended with the Civil War.

Question: _Did segregation in the American South end with the Civil War?_

Negative statement: _Segregation in the American South did not end with the Civil War._

33g Verb Tense

In English, a verb's form must indicate when an action took place (for instance, in the past or in the present). Always use the appropriate tense of the verb even if the time is obvious or if the sentence includes other indications of time (such as *two years ago* or *at present*).

Teaching Tip
Refer students to Chapters 29 and 30 for more on verb tense.

INCORRECT   Albert Einstein emigrate from Germany in 1933.

CORRECT   Albert Einstein emigrated from Germany in 1933.

33h Stative Verbs

Stative verbs usually tell that someone or something is in a state that will not change, at least for a while.

Hiro <u>knows</u> American history very well.

Most English verbs show action, and these action verbs can be used in the progressive tenses. The **present progressive** tense consists of the present tense of *be* plus the present participle (*I am going*). The **past progressive** tense consists of the past tense of *be* plus the present participle (*I was going*). Unlike most verbs, however, stative verbs are rarely used in the progressive tenses.

INCORRECT   Hiro is knowing American history very well.

CORRECT   Hiro knows American history very well.

FYI

Stative Verbs

Verbs that are stative—such as *know, understand, think, believe, want, like, love,* and *hate*—often refer to mental states. Other stative verbs include *be, have, need, own, belong, weigh, cost,* and *mean*. Certain verbs of sense perception, like *see* and *hear*, are also stative even though they can refer to momentary events as well as to unchanging states.

Many verbs have more than one meaning, and some of these verbs are active with one meaning but stative with another. An example is the verb *weigh*.

ACTIVE   The butcher <u>weighs</u> the meat.

STATIVE   The meat <u>weighs</u> three pounds.

In the first sentence above, the verb *weigh* means "to put on a scale"; it is active, not stative. In the second sentence, however, the same verb means "to have weight," so it is stative, not active. It would be unacceptable to say "The meat is weighing three pounds," but "The butcher is weighing the meat" would be correct.

PRACTICE

33-8 In each of the following sentences, circle the verb or verbs. Then, correct any problems with stative verbs by crossing out the incorrect verb tense and writing the correct verb tense above the line. If the verb is correct, write *C* above it.

Example: Police officers ~~are knowing~~ *know* that fingerprint identification
C
(is) one of the best ways to catch criminals.

1. As early as 1750 B.C., ancient Babylonians (were signing) *C* their identities with fingerprints on clay tablets.

2. By 220 A.D., the Chinese (were becoming) *C* aware that ink fingerprints (could identify) *C* people.

3. However, it (was) *C* not until the late 1800s that anyone ~~was believing~~ *believed* that criminal identification (was) *C* possible with fingerprints.

4. Today, we (know) *C* that each person ~~is having~~ *has* unique patterns on the tips of his or her fingers.

5. When police (study) *C* a crime scene, they (want) *C* to see whether the criminals (have left) *C* any fingerprint evidence.

6. There (is) *C* always a layer of oil on the skin, and police ~~are liking~~ *like* to use it to get fingerprints.

7. Crime scene experts ~~are often seeing~~ *often see* cases where the criminals ~~are touching~~ *touch* their hair and (pick up) *C* enough oil to leave a good fingerprint.

8. The police ~~are needing~~ *need* to judge whether the fingerprint evidence (has been damaged) *C* by sunlight, rain, or heat.

9. In the courtroom, juries often (weigh) fingerprint evidence before they
   ~~are deciding~~ *decide* on their verdict.

10. The FBI (is collecting) millions of fingerprints, which police depart-
    ments (can compare) with the fingerprints they (find) at crime scenes.

33i   Modal Auxiliaries

A **modal auxiliary** (such as *can, may, might,* or *must*) is a helping verb that
is used with another verb to express ability, possibility, necessity, intent,
obligation, and so on. In the following sentence, *can* is the modal auxiliary,
and *imagine* is the main verb.

> I <u>can</u> imagine myself in Hawaii.

Modal auxiliaries usually intensify the dominant verb's meaning:

> I <u>must</u> run as fast as I can.
> You <u>ought to</u> lose some weight.

Teaching Tip
Refer students to 18c for more
on helping verbs.

Modal Auxiliaries

can	ought to
could	shall
may	should
might	will
must	would

Modal auxiliaries are used in the following situations:

- To express physical ability

  > I can walk faster than my brother.

- To express the possibility of something occurring

  > He might get the job if his interview goes well.

- To express or request permission

  > May I use the restroom in the hallway?

- To express necessity

  > I must get to the train station on time.

- To express a suggestion or advice

  > To be healthy, you should [or ought to] exercise and eat balanced
  > meals.

Teaching Tip
Students should understand
the definition of modal auxiliary
verbs as expressions of will,
probability, permission, and
obligation. Students should
memorize the list of modals.

Teaching Tip
Show students how using the
wrong modal might be
received by a reader or
listener. For example, explain
the differences among *you will,
you can,* and *you ought.*

- To express intent

    I will try to study harder next time.

- To express a desire

    Would you please answer the telephone?

PRACTICE
33-9   In the exercise below, circle the correct modal auxiliary.

Example: (May/Would) you help me complete the assignment?

1. It doesn't rain very often in Arizona, but today it looks like it (can/ might).

2. I know I (will/ought to) call my aunt on her birthday, but I always find an excuse.

3. Sarah (should/must) study for her English exam, but she prefers to spend time with her friends.

4. John (can/would) be the best person to represent our class.

5. Many people believe they (could/should) vote in every election.

6. All students (will/must) bring two pencils, a notebook, and a dictionary to class every day.

7. (Would/May) you show me the way to the post office?

8. I (could/should) not ask for more than my health, my family, and my job.

9. Do you think they (could/can) come back tomorrow to finish the painting job?

10. A dog (should/might) be a helpful companion for your disabled father.

33j   Gerunds

A **gerund** is a verb form ending in -*ing* that acts as a noun.

   Reading the newspaper is one of my favorite things to do on Sundays.

   Just like a noun, a gerund can be used as a subject, a direct object, a subject complement, or the object of a preposition:

■ A gerund can be a subject.

> Playing tennis is one of my hobbies.

■ A gerund can be a direct object.

> My brother influenced my racing.

■ A gerund can be a subject complement.

> The most important thing is winning.

■ A gerund can be the object of a preposition.

> The teacher rewarded him for passing.

**PRACTICE
33-10** To complete the sentences below, fill in the blanks with the gerund form of the verb provided in parentheses.

Example: _____Typing_____ (type) is a skill that used to be taught in high school.

1. _____Eating_____ (eat) five or six smaller meals throughout the day is healthier than eating two or three big meals.

2. In the winter, there is nothing better than _____skating_____ (skate) outdoors on a frozen pond.

3. The household task I dread the most is _____cleaning_____ (clean).

4. The fish avoided the net by _____swimming_____ (swim) faster.

5. _____Quitting_____ (quit) is easier than accomplishing a goal.

6. Her parents praised her for _____remembering_____ (remember) their anniversary.

7. Her favorite job is _____organizing_____ (organize) her files.

8. I did not like his _____singing_____ (sing).

9. For me, _____cooking_____ (cook) is relaxing.

10. The best way to prepare for the concert is by _____practicing_____ (practice).

33k Placing Modifiers in Order

Adjectives and other modifiers that come before a noun usually follow a set order.

Required Order

■ Determiners always come first in a series of modifiers: *these fragile glasses*. The determiners *all* or *both* always precede any other determiners: *all these glasses*.

■ If one of the modifiers is a noun, it must come directly before the noun it modifies: *these wine glasses*.

■ Descriptive adjectives are placed between the determiners and the noun modifiers: *these fragile wine glasses*. If there are two or more descriptive adjectives, the following order is preferred.

Preferred Order

■ Adjectives that show the writer's attitude generally precede adjectives that merely describe: *these lovely fragile wine glasses*.

■ Adjectives that indicate size generally come early: *these lovely large fragile wine glasses*.

PRACTICE
33-11
Arrange each group of modifiers in the correct order, and rewrite the complete phrase in the blank.

Example: (annual, impressive, the, publisher's) report

the publisher's impressive annual report
_____

1. (brand-new, a, apartment, high-rise) building

   a brand-new high-rise apartment building
   _____

2. (gifted, twenty-five-year-old, Venezuelan, this) author

   this gifted twenty-five-year-old Venezuelan author
   _____

3. (successful, short-story, numerous) collections

   numerous successful short-story collections
   _____

4. (her, all, intriguing, suspense) novels

   all her intriguing suspense novels
   _____

5. (publisher's, best-selling, the, three) works

   the publisher's three best-selling works
   _____

6. (main, story's, two, this) characters

   this story's two main characters
   _____

7. (young, a, strong-willed) woman

   a strong-willed young woman
   _____

8. (middle-aged, attractive, the, British) poet

the attractive middle-aged British poet

9. (exquisite, wedding, an, white) gown

an exquisite white wedding gown

10. (extravagant, wedding, an) reception

an extravagant wedding reception

33l Choosing Prepositions

A **preposition** introduces a noun or pronoun and links it to other words in the sentence. The word the preposition introduces is called the **object** of the preposition.

A preposition and its object combine to form a **prepositional phrase**: _on the table, near the table, under the table._

I thought I had left the book <u>on</u> the table or somewhere <u>near</u> the table, but I found it <u>under</u> the table.

The prepositions _at, in,_ and _on_ sometimes cause problems for non-native speakers of English. For example, to identify the location of a place or an event, you can use _at, in,_ or _on._

- The preposition _at_ specifies an exact point in space or time.

    The museum is <u>at</u> 1000 Fifth Avenue. Let's meet there <u>at</u> 10:00 tomorrow morning.

- Expanses of space or time are treated as containers and therefore require _in._

    Women used to wear long skirts <u>in</u> the early 1900s.

- _On_ must be used in two cases: with names of streets (but not with exact addresses) and with days of the week or month.

    We will move into our new office <u>on</u> 18th Street either <u>on</u> Monday or <u>on</u> March 12.

33m Prepositions in Familiar Expressions

Many familiar expressions end with prepositions. Learning to write clearly and **idiomatically**—following the conventions of written English—means learning which preposition is used in such expressions. Even native speakers of English sometimes have trouble choosing the correct preposition.

The sentences that follow illustrate idiomatic use of prepositions in various expressions. Note that sometimes different prepositions are used with the same word. For example, both *on* and *for* can be used with *wait* to form two different expressions with two different meanings (*He waited on their table*; *She waited for the bus*). Which preposition you choose depends on your meaning. (In the list that follows, pairs of similar expressions that end with different prepositions are bracketed.)

EXPRESSION WITH PREPOSITION	SAMPLE SENTENCE
acquainted with	During orientation, the university offers workshops to make sure that students are <u>acquainted with</u> its rules and regulations.
addicted to	I think Abby is becoming <u>addicted to</u> pretzels.
agree on (a plan or objective)	It is vital that all members of the school board <u>agree on</u> goals for the coming year.
agree to (a proposal)	Striking workers finally <u>agreed to</u> the terms of management's offer.
angry about or at (a situation)	Taxpayers are understandably <u>angry about</u> (or <u>at</u>) the deterioration of city recreation facilities.
angry with (a person)	When the mayor refused to hire more police officers, his constituents became <u>angry with</u> him.
approve of	Amy's adviser <u>approved of</u> her decision to study in Guatemala.
bored with	Salah got <u>bored with</u> economics, so he changed his major to psychology.
capable of	Hannah is a good talker, but she is not <u>capable of</u> acting as her own lawyer.
consist of	The deluxe fruit basket <u>consisted of</u> five pathetic pears, two tiny apples, a few limp bunches of grapes, and one lonely kiwi.
contrast with	Coach Headley's relaxed style <u>contrasts</u> sharply <u>with</u> Coach Pauley's more formal approach.
convenient for	The proposed location of the new day-care center is <u>convenient for</u> many families.
deal with	Many parents and educators believe it is possible to <u>deal with</u> the special needs of autistic children in a regular classroom.
depend on	Children <u>depend on</u> their parents for emotional as well as financial support.
differ from (something else)	A capitalist system <u>differs from</u> a socialist system in its view of private ownership.
differ with (someone else)	When Miles realized that he <u>differed with</u> his boss on most important issues, <u>he handed in his</u> resignation.
emigrate from	My grandfather and his brother <u>emigrated from</u> the part of Russia that is now Ukraine.

grateful for (a favor)	If you can arrange an interview next week, I will be very <u>grateful for</u> your time and trouble.
grateful to (someone)	Jerry Garcia was always <u>grateful to</u> his loyal fans.
immigrate to	Many Cubans want to leave their country and <u>immigrate to</u> the United States.
impatient with	Keshia often gets <u>impatient with</u> her four younger brothers.
interested in	Tomiko had always been <u>interested in</u> computers, so no one was surprised when she became a Web designer.
interfere with	College athletes often find that their dedication to sports <u>interferes with</u> their schoolwork.
meet with	I hope I can <u>meet with</u> you soon to discuss my research project.
object to	The defense attorney <u>objected to</u> the prosecutor's treatment of the witness.
pleased with	Most of the residents are <u>pleased with</u> the mayor's crackdown on crime.
protect against	Nobel Prize–winner Linus Pauling believed that large doses of vitamin C could <u>protect</u> people <u>against</u> the common cold.
reason with	When two-year-olds have tantrums, it is nearly impossible to <u>reason with</u> them.
reply to	If no one <u>replies to</u> our ad within two weeks, we will advertise again.
responsible for	Should teachers be held <u>responsible for</u> their students' low test scores?
similar to	The blood sample found at the crime scene was remarkably <u>similar to</u> one found in the suspect's residence.
specialize in	Dr. Casullo is a dentist who <u>specializes in</u> periodontal surgery.
succeed in	Lisa hoped her MBA would help her <u>succeed in</u> a business career.
take advantage of	Some consumer laws are designed to prevent door-to-door salespeople from <u>taking advantage of</u> buyers.
wait for (something to happen)	Many parents of teenagers experience tremendous anxiety while <u>waiting for</u> their children to come home at night.
wait on (in a restaurant)	We sat at the table for twenty minutes before someone <u>waited on</u> us.
worry about	Why <u>worry about</u> things you cannot change?

FYI

Using Prepositions in Familiar Expressions

Below is a list of familiar expressions that have similar meanings. They are often used in the same contexts.

acquainted with, familiar with
addicted to, hooked on
angry with (a person), upset
  with
bored with, tired of
capable of, able to
consist of, have, contain,
  include
deal with, address (a problem)
depend on, rely on
differ from (something else),
  be different from
differ with (someone else),
  disagree
emigrate from, move from
  (another country)
grateful for (a favor),
  thankful for
immigrate to, move to
  (another country)

interested in, fascinated by
interfere with, disrupt
meet with, get together with
object to, oppose
pleased with, happy with
protect against, guard
  against
reply to, answer
responsible for, accountable for
similar to, almost the
  same as
succeed in, attain success in
take advantage of, use an
  opportunity to
wait for (something to
  happen), expect
wait on (in a restaurant),
  serve

PRACTICE

33-12 In the following passage, fill in each blank with the correct preposition.

Example: Like other struggling artists, writers often make a living

working ___*in*___ restaurants and waiting ___*on*___ customers.

(1) Most writers, even those who succeed ___*in*___ the literary world,

need day jobs to help pay ___*for*___ food and rent. (2) Many ___*of*___

them work ___*in*___ related fields—for example, ___*at*___ bookstores,

___*at*___ publishing houses, or ___*at*___ newspapers. (3) Some take

advantage ___*of*___ their talents and devote themselves ___*to*___ teach-

ing others ___*about*___ language and literature. (4) For example, ___*in*___

the 1990s, *Harry Potter* author J. K. Rowling worked as a teacher ___*in*___

Portugal and ___*in*___ Britain. (5) ___*In*___ the 1960s and 70s, students ___*at*___ Howard University ___*in*___ Washington, D.C., could enroll ___*in*___ classes taught ___*by*___ Nobel Prize–winner Toni Morrison. (6) Other writers work ___*in*___ fields unrelated ___*to*___ writing. (7) For instance, poet William Carlos Williams was a medical doctor who wrote poetry only ___*in*___ the evenings. (8) Science fiction writer Isaac Asimov worked ___*at*___ Boston University ___*in*___ the department ___*of*___ biochemistry. (9) Occasionally, an aspiring writer has friends and family who approve ___*of*___ his or her goals, and he or she can depend ___*on*___ them ___*for*___ financial help. (10) However, many family members, wanting to protect young writers ___*from*___ poverty, try to encourage them to focus ___*on*___ other goals.

33n Prepositions in Phrasal Verbs

A **phrasal verb** consists of two words, a verb and a preposition, that are joined to form an idiomatic expression. Many phrasal verbs are **separable**. This means that a direct object can come between the verb and the preposition. However, some phrasal verbs are **inseparable**; that is, the preposition must always come immediately after the verb.

> **Teaching Tip**
> You may want to mention that in some phrasal verbs, the second word is not a preposition but an adverb: *run across*, *speak up*.

Separable Phrasal Verbs

In many cases, phrasal verbs may be split, with the direct object coming between the two parts of the verb. When the direct object is a noun, the second word of the phrasal verb can come either before or after the object.

In the sentences below, *fill out* is a phrasal verb. Because the object of the verb *fill out* is a noun (*form*), the second word of the verb can come either before or after the verb's object.

CORRECT Please fill out the form.

CORRECT Please fill the form out.

When the object is a pronoun, however, these phrasal verbs must be split, and the pronoun must come between the two parts of the verb.

INCORRECT Please fill out it.

CORRECT Please fill it out.

> ### Some Common Separable Phrasal Verbs
>
> | | | | |
> |---|---|---|---|
> | ask out | give away | put back | throw away |
> | bring up | hang up | put on | try out |
> | call up | leave out | set aside | turn down |
> | carry out | let out | shut off | turn off |
> | drop off | make up | take down | wake up |
> | fill out | put away | think over | |
>
> Remember, when the object of the verb is a pronoun, these phrasal verbs must be split, and the pronoun must come between the two parts (for example, *take it down, put it on, let it out,* and *make it up*).

Inseparable Phrasal Verbs

Some phrasal verbs, however, cannot be separated; that is, the preposition cannot be separated from the verb. This means that a direct object cannot come between the verb and the preposition.

> **INCORRECT**   Please go the manual over carefully.

> **CORRECT**   Please go over the manual carefully.

Notice that in the correct sentence above, the direct object (*manual*) comes right after the preposition (*over*).

> ### Some Common Inseparable Phrasal Verbs
>
> | | | |
> |---|---|---|
> | come across | run across | show up |
> | get along | run into | stand by |
> | go over | see to | |

PRACTICE

33-13   In each of the following sentences, look closely at the phrasal verb, and decide whether the preposition is placed correctly in the sentence. If it is, write *C* in the blank after the sentence. If the preposition needs to be moved, edit the sentence.

Example: People who live in American suburbs are often surprised

to come across wild animals in their neighborhoods. _____*C*_____

1. In one case, a New Jersey woman was startled when a hungry bear

   woke up her ^*up* from a nap one afternoon. _____

2. She called the police, hung up the phone, and ran for her life. ___*C*___

3. Actually, although it is a good idea to stay ^*away* from bears ~~away~~, most wild bears are timid. _____

4. When there is a drought, people are more likely to run into bears and other wild animals. ___*C*___

5. The amount of blueberries and other wild fruit that bears eat usually drops ^*off* in dry weather ~~off~~. _____

6. Bears need to put on weight before the winter, so they may have to find food in suburban garbage cans. ___*C*___

7. It is a good idea for families to go ^*over* their plans ~~over~~ to safeguard their property against bears. _____

8. People should not leave pet food out overnight, or else their dog may find that a hungry bear has eaten its dinner. ___*C*___

9. If people have a bird feeder in the yard, they should put ~~away~~ it ^*away* during the autumn. _____

10. As the human population grows, more and more houses are built in formerly wild areas, so bears and people have to learn to get along with each other. ___*C*___

TEST · Revise · Edit

Look back at your response to the Write First activity on page 548. TEST what you have written. Then, revise and edit your work, paying special attention to the grammar and usage issues discussed in this chapter.

EDITING PRACTICE

Read the following student essay, which includes errors in the use of subjects, nouns, articles and determiners, and stative verbs, as well as errors with prepositions in idiomatic expressions. Check each underlined word or phrase. If it is not used correctly, write in any necessary changes. If the underlined word or phrase is correct, write *C* above it. The title of the essay has been edited for you.

in
How to Succeed ~~on~~ Multinational Business

on
Success in multinational business often depends <u>in</u> the ability to understand

from
other countries' cultures. Understanding how cultures <u>differ to</u> our own, however,

this   *it*
is only one key to <u>these</u> success. Also, <u>is</u> crucial that businesses learn to adapt to

^Ethnocentrism   *the*
different cultures. <u>The ethnocentrism</u> is the belief that one's own culture has <u>a</u> best

it   *C*
way of doing things. In international business, <u>is</u> necessary to <u>set aside</u> this belief.

use
A company cannot <u>be using</u> the same methods or sell the same products overseas

as it does at home. Though making these changes requires a lot of work, companies

markets   *C*
that choose to adjust to new <u>market</u> are usually <u>happy with</u> their decision.

There are
<u>It is</u> many aspects of a country that must be understood before <u>successful</u>

C   *C*   *against*
<u>international business</u> can be <u>carried out</u>. To protect itself <u>from</u> legal errors, a

company needs to understand the country's legal system, which may be very

It may
different from its home country's legal system. <u>May be</u> necessary to get licenses

to   *C*
to export products <u>onto</u> other countries. The role of <u>women</u> is also likely to be

different; without knowing this, businesspeople might unintentionally offend

many
people. Also, <u>much</u> personal interactions in other countries may give the wrong

impression to someone who is inexperienced. For example, in Latin American

often stand
countries, people <u>are often standing</u> close together and touch each other when

they are talking. Americans may feel uncomfortable in such a situation <u>unless</u>

they
<u>understand</u> it.

C
To <u>succeed in</u> international business, companies <u>are also needing</u> to understand

also need

what people buy and why. To avoid problems, a company that wants to sell

some
its product internationally <u>it</u> should do <u>a few</u> market research. For example, when

in   *^the company*
McDonald's opened restaurants <u>on</u> India, <u>realized</u> that beef burgers would not work

McDonald's in Egypt

Business meeting in Kuwait

in a country where many people believe that cows are sacred. Instead, burgers

were made from ground chickens. For India's many vegetarians, McDonald's created
chicken.

several different vegetable patty. McDonald's understood that both the religious
patties.

and cultural characteristic of India had to be considered if its new restaurants
characteristics

were going to succeed.

    Looking to attract new customer in today's international market, companies they
customers

are noticing a growing demand for *halal* goods and services. The word *halal* indicates
C

an object or action that is permissible by Islamic law. Businesses are realizing
C

that world's Muslims depend in companies to provide acceptable *halal* foods, banks,
the   *on*

hotels, magazines, and other services. Nestlé, Kentucky Fried Chicken, Subway, LG,

and Nokia are just a few of the well-known companies that have been successfully

remaking their products to appeal in Muslim consumers. Because these high-
to

quality items also appeal to non-Muslims, many of this companies are discovering
these

that meeting cultural needs and desires are simply good business.
is

    Over time, the marketplace is becoming more global. In those setting, individuals
C   *this*

from numerous cultures come together. To take advantage from opportunities
of

and perform effectively, an international company must hire people with the right

experiences. To deal with other cultures, multinational companies inside today's
experience.   *C*   *in*

global market must have good informations and show other cultures the highest
information

respects.
respect.

COLLABORATIVE ACTIVITIES

1. Working in a small group, make a list of ten prepositional phrases that
   include the prepositions *above, around, at, between, from, in, on, over,
   under,* and *with.* Use appropriate nouns as objects of these prepositions, and use as many modifying words as you wish. (Try, for example, to write something like *above their hideous wedding portrait,* not
   just *above the picture.*)

2. Exchange lists with another group. Still working collaboratively, compose a list of ten sentences, each including one of the other group's ten
   prepositional phrases. Give your list of ten sentences to another group.

3. Working with this new list of ten sentences, substitute a different prepositional phrase for each one that appears in a sentence. Make sure
   each sentence still makes sense.

> **Teaching Tip**
> Collaborative Activity 1 is
> an effective review. It can
> also be fun, especially if
> students use a lot of modifying
> words.

review checklist

Grammar and Usage for ESL Writers

☐ In almost all cases, English sentences must state their subjects. (See 33a.)

☐ In English, most nouns add -*s* to form plurals. Always use a form that indicates that a noun is plural. (See 33b.)

☐ English nouns may be count nouns or noncount nouns. A count noun names one particular thing or a group of particular things (*a teacher, oceans*). A noncount noun names something that cannot be counted (*gold, sand*). (See 33c.)

☐ Determiners are adjectives that identify rather than describe the nouns they modify. Determiners may also indicate amount or number. (See 33d.)

☐ The definite article *the* and the indefinite articles *a* and *an* are determiners that indicate whether the noun that follows is one readers can identify (*the book*) or one they cannot yet identify (*a book*). (See 33e.)

☐ To form a negative statement, add the word *not* directly after the first helping verb of the complete verb. To form a question, move the helping verb that follows the subject to the position directly before the subject. (See 33f.)

☐ A verb's form must indicate when an action took place. (See 33g.)

☐ Stative verbs indicate that someone or something is in a state that will not change, at least for a while. Stative verbs are rarely used in the progressive tenses. (See 33h.)

☐ A modal auxiliary is a helping verb that expresses ability, possibility, necessity, intent, obligation, and so on. (See 33i.)

☐ A gerund is a verb form ending in -*ing* that is always used as a noun. (See 33j.)

☐ Adjectives and other modifiers that come before a noun usually follow a set order. (See 33k.)

☐ The prepositions *at*, *in*, and *on* sometimes cause problems for nonnative speakers of English. (See 33l.)

☐ Many familiar expressions end with prepositions. (See 33m.)

☐ A phrasal verb consists of two words, a verb and a preposition, that are joined to form an idiomatic expression. (See 33n.)

Read the following student essay, which includes errors in the use of verbs, nouns, pronouns, adjectives, and adverbs, as well as ESL errors. Make any changes necessary to correct the basic grammar of the sentences. The first sentence has been edited for you.

The Mystery of the Bermuda Triangle

The Bermuda Triangle is an area in the Atlantic Ocean also know [known] as the Devil's Triangle. Its size, between 500,000 and 1.5 million square miles, depends on who [whom] you are believing [believe]. Strange events happen there.

During the past century, more than fifty ships and twenty airplanes have disappeared to these [in this] area. According to some people, a mysterious force causes ships and planes to vanish in the Bermuda Triangle. Everyone who hears about the mystery has to decide for themselves [himself or herself] what to believe. However, according to the U.S. Coast Guard, the explanations are not mysterious.

Map of the Bermuda Triangle

The stories about odd these [odd] occurrences they may have started as early as 1492. When Columbus sailed through the area, him [he] and his crew seen [saw] unusual lights in the sky. In addition, his compass reacted strangely. Now is [it] believed that the lights came from a meteor that crashed into the ocean. The peculiar compass readings were probably cause from [caused by] the fact that in this area, magnetic compasses point toward true north rather than magnetic north. These [This] variation can cause navigators to sail off course.

The modern Bermuda Triangle legend started in 1945, when Flight 19, compose [composed] of five U.S. Navy Avenger torpedo bombers, disappeared while on a routine training mission. Rescue [A rescue] plane that has [had] been sent to search for them also disappeared. Six aircraft and twenty-seven man [men] vanished. Not only were their lifes [lives] lost, but no bodies were ever found. Were [Was] a mysterious force responsible? Although the events themselves seem strange, there are several good explanation. [explanations.] First, all the crew members except his [their] leader were trainees. It is quite possibly [possible] that they flied [flew] through a magnetic storm or that the leader's compass was not working. If so, they would have become confused of [about] their location. Radio transmissions were unreliable because of a bad weather and a broken receiver in one of the planes.

One of the torpedo bombers that vanished in the Bermuda Triangle in 1945

The crew leader was not functioning very ~~good.~~ *well.* The leader ~~telled~~ *told* his pilots to head east; he ~~thinked~~ *thought* that they were over the Gulf of Mexico. However, they were flying up the Atlantic coastline, so his instructions sent ~~him~~ *them* further out to sea. If the planes crashed into the ocean at night, it is not likely there would have been any survivors. No wreckage was ever ~~recover.~~ *recovered.*

After Flight 19 disappeared, ~~storys start~~ *stories started* to appear about the events that ~~have~~ *had* occurred. The odd compass readings, the problems with radio transmissions, and the missing wreckage ~~lead~~ *led* to strange tales. Some people believed that the missing ships and planes were taken by UFOs (unidentified flying objects) to a different dimension. Others thought that those ~~whom~~ *who* disappeared were kidnapped ~~from~~ *by* aliens from other planets. However, there are ~~most~~ *more* logical explanations. The fact that magnetic compasses point toward true north in this area is now well known. It is also well known that the weather patterns in the southern Atlantic and Caribbean ~~is~~ *are* unpredictable. In addition, human error may have been involved. For these ~~reason,~~ *reasons,* the tales of the Bermuda Triangle are clearly science fiction, not fact.

Missing Ship Recalls 1918 Disappearance

Newspaper headline

Coast Guard Hunting Tanker With 43 Men

Newspaper headline

unit

8

Understanding Punctuation, Mechanics, and Spelling

REVISING
AND EDITING
YOUR
WRITING

34 Using Commas

write first

One of these pictures shows public housing in disrepair; one shows new affordable housing units. Write a paragraph or two about ideal affordable housing. Where should complexes for low-income families be located? What kinds of buildings should they consist of? What facilities and services should be offered to residents?

A **comma** is a punctuation mark that separates words or groups of words within sentences. In this way, commas keep ideas distinct from one another.

In earlier chapters, you learned to use a comma between two simple sentences (independent clauses) linked by a coordinating conjunction to form a compound sentence.

Some people are concerned about climate change, but others are not.

You also learned to use a comma after a dependent clause that comes before an independent clause in a complex sentence.

Although bears in the wild can be dangerous, hikers can take steps to protect themselves.

In addition, commas are used to set off directly quoted speech or writing from the rest of the sentence.

John F. Kennedy said, "Ask not what your country can do for you; ask what you can do for your country."

As you will learn in this chapter, commas have several other uses as well.

34a Commas in a Series

Use commas to separate all elements in a **series** of three or more words, phrases, or clauses.

Leyla, Zack, and Kathleen campaigned for Representative Lewis.

Leyla, Zack, or Kathleen will be elected president of Students for Lewis.

Leyla made phone calls, licked envelopes, and ran errands for the campaign.

Leyla is president, Zack is vice president, and Kathleen is treasurer.

FYI

Using Commas in a Series

Newspapers and magazines usually omit the comma before the coordinating conjunction in a series. However, in college writing, you should always use a comma before the coordinating conjunction.

Leyla, Zack, and Kathleen worked on the campaign.

Exception: Do not use *any* commas if all the items in a series are separated by coordinating conjunctions.

Leyla or Zack or Kathleen will be elected president of Students for Lewis.

PRACTICE

34-1   Edit the following sentences for the use of commas in a series. If the sentence is correct, write *C* in the blank.

Examples

Costa Rica produces bananas, cocoa, and sugarcane. _____*C*_____

The pool rules state that there is no running/ or jumping/ or diving.

_____

1. The musician plays guitar, bass, and drums. _____

2. The organization's goals are feeding the hungry, housing the homeless, and helping the unemployed find work. _____

3. *The Price Is Right, Let's Make a Deal,* and *Jeopardy!* are three of the longest-running game shows in television history. _____*C*_____

4. In native Hawaiian culture, yellow was worn by the royalty, red was worn by priests, and a mixture of the two colors was worn by others of high rank. _____

5. The diary Anne Frank kept while her family hid from the Nazis is insightful, touching, and sometimes humorous. _____

6. A standard bookcase is sixty inches tall, forty-eight inches wide, and twelve inches deep. _____

7. Most coffins manufactured in the United States are lined with bronze, or copper, or lead. _____

8. Young, handsome, and sensitive, Leonardo DiCaprio was the 1990s answer to the 1950s actor James Dean. _____

9. California's capital is Sacramento, its largest city is Los Angeles, and its oldest settlement is San Diego. _____

10. Watching television, playing video games, and riding a bicycle are some of the average ten-year-old boy's favorite pastimes. _____*C*_____

34b   Commas with Introductory Phrases and Transitional Words and Phrases

Introductory Phrases

Use a comma to set off an **introductory phrase** from the rest of the sentence.

> <u>In the event of a fire</u>, proceed to the nearest exit.
> <u>Walking home</u>, Nelida decided to change her major.
> <u>To keep fit</u>, people should try to exercise regularly.

PRACTICE

34-2   Edit the following sentences for the use of commas with introductory phrases. If the sentence is correct, write *C* in the blank.

Examples

From professionals to teenagers, many athletes have used steroids. _____

Regulated by the Drug Enforcement Administration, steroids are a controlled substance and can be legally obtained only with a prescription. __*C*__

(1) In the past few years, many Olympic athletes have been disqualified because they tested positive for banned drugs. _____ (2) At the 2008 Beijing Games, organizers adopted the slogan "Zero Tolerance for Doping." __*C*__ (3) In the past, banned steroids were the most common cause of positive drug tests. _____ (4) In recent years, other banned substances have also been used. _____ (5) For example, athletes have tested positive for male hormones and human growth hormones. __*C*__ (6) Among track and field athletes, doping has been especially common. _____ (7) In some cases, athletes' drug use was not uncovered until the games were long over. _____ (8) More than seven years after winning five medals at the 2000 Sydney Olympics, runner Marion Jones admitted to having used banned drugs. __*C*__ (9) Having witnessed many scandals and disappointments, today's fans are suspicious of extraordinary athletic feats. _____ (10) For instance, many suspected record-breaking sprinter Usain Bolt of doping at the 2008 Beijing Olympics. __*C*__

Transitional Words and Phrases

Also use commas to set off **transitional words or phrases**, whether they appear at the beginning, in the middle, or at the end of a sentence.

> In fact, Thoreau spent only one night in jail.
>
> He was, of course, bailed out by a friend.
>
> He did spend more than two years at Walden Pond, however.

Teaching Tip
Remind students that when they use a transitional word or phrase to join two complete sentences, they must use a semicolon and a comma: *Thoreau spent only one night in jail; however, he spent more than two years at Walden Pond.*

FYI

Using Commas in Direct Address

Always use commas to set off the name of someone whom you are addressing (speaking to) directly, whether the name appears at the beginning, in the middle, or at the end of a sentence.

> Molly, come here and look at this.
>
> Come here, Molly, and look at this.
>
> Come here and look at this, Molly.

PRACTICE
34-3   Edit the following sentences for the use of commas with transitional words and phrases. If the sentence is correct, write *C* in the blank.

Example: Eventually, most people build a personal credit history.

(1) Often, establishing credit can be difficult. _____ (2) College students, for example, often have no credit history of their own, especially if their parents pay their bills. _____ (3) Similarly, some married women have no personal credit history. _____ (4) In fact, their credit cards may be in their husbands' names. _____ (5) As a result, they may be unable to get their own loans. __*C*__ (6) Of course, one way to establish credit is to apply for a credit card at a local department store. _____ (7) Also, it is relatively easy to get a gas credit card. __*C*__ (8) It is important to pay these credit card bills promptly, however. _____ (9) In addition, having checking and savings accounts can help to establish financial reliability. _____ (10) Finally, people who want to establish a credit history can sign an apartment lease and pay the rent regularly to show that they are good credit risks. __*C*__

Teaching Tip
Refer students to 19c for lists of frequently used transitional words and phrases.

34c   Commas with Appositives

Use commas to set off an **appositive**—a word or word group that identifies, renames, or describes a noun or a pronoun.

> I have visited only one country, Canada, outside the United States. (*Canada* is an appositive that identifies the noun *country*.)

> Carlos Santana, leader of the group Santana, played at Woodstock in 1969. (*Leader of the group Santana* is an appositive that identifies *Carlos Santana*.)

> A really gifted artist, he is also a wonderful father. (*A really gifted artist* is an appositive that describes the pronoun *he*.)

FYI

Using Commas with Appositives

Most appositives are set off by commas, whether they fall at the beginning, in the middle, or at the end of a sentence.

> A dreamer, he spent his life thinking about what he could not have.

> He always wanted to build a house, a big white one, overlooking the ocean.

> He finally built his dream house, a log cabin.

PRACTICE

34-4   Underline the appositive in each of the following sentences. Then, check each sentence for the correct use of commas to set off appositives, and add any missing commas. If the sentence is correct, write *C* in the blank.

> **Example:** Wendy Kopp, a student at Princeton University, developed the Teach For America program to help minority students get a better education. _____

1. Guglielmo Marconi, a young Italian inventor, sent the first wireless message across the Atlantic Ocean in 1901. _____

2. A member of the boy band 'N Sync, Justin Timberlake went on to establish a successful career as a solo musician and actor. _____

3. HTML, hypertext markup language, is the set of codes used to create Web documents. _____

4. William Filene, founder of Filene's Department Store, invented the "bargain basement." _____ *C* _____

5. Known as NPR, National Public Radio presents a wide variety of programs. _____

6. On the southwest coast of Nigeria lies Lagos, a major port. _____

7. Home of the 2008 Olympics, Beijing continues to have serious problems with its air quality. _____ *C* _____

8. Lightning, a strong electrical charge, can be both beautiful and dangerous. _____

9. A plant that grows on mountains and in deserts, the fern is surprisingly adaptable. _____ *C* _____

10. Golf, a game developed in Scotland, is very popular in the United States. _____

34d Commas with Nonrestrictive Clauses

Clauses are often used to add information within a sentence. In some cases, you need to add commas to set off these clauses; in other cases, commas are not required.

Use commas to set off **nonrestrictive clauses**, clauses that are not essential to a sentence's meaning. Do not use commas to set off **restrictive clauses**.

- A **nonrestrictive clause** does *not* contain essential information. Nonrestrictive clauses are set off from the rest of the sentence by commas.

  Telephone calling-card fraud, which cost consumers and phone companies four billion dollars last year, is increasing.

Here, the clause between the commas (underlined) provides extra information to help readers understand the sentence, but the sentence would still communicate the same idea without this information.

  Telephone calling-card fraud is increasing.

- A **restrictive clause** contains information that is essential to a sentence's meaning. Restrictive clauses are *not* set off from the rest of the sentence by commas.

  Many rock stars who recorded hits in the 1950s made little money from their songs.

In the sentence above, the clause *who recorded hits in the 1950s* supplies specific information that is essential to the idea the sentence is communicating: it tells readers which group of rock stars made little money. Without the clause, the sentence does not communicate the same idea because it does not tell which rock stars made little money.

Many rock stars made little money from their songs.

Compare the meanings of the following pairs of sentences with nonrestrictive and restrictive clauses.

NONRESTRICTIVE   Young adults, <u>who text while driving</u>, put themselves and others in danger. (This sentence says that all young adults text while driving and all pose a danger.)

RESTRICTIVE   Young adults <u>who text while driving</u> put themselves and others in danger. (This sentence says that only those young adults who text and drive pose a danger.)

NONRESTRICTIVE   Student loans, <u>which are based on need</u>, may not be fair to middle-class students. (This sentence says that all student loans are based on need and all may be unfair to middle-class students.)

RESTRICTIVE   Student loans <u>that are based on need</u> may not be fair to middle-class students. (This sentence says that only those student loans that are based on need may be unfair to middle-class students.)

FYI

Which, That, and Who

■ *Which* always introduces a nonrestrictive clause.

The job, <u>which had excellent benefits</u>, did not pay well. (clause set off by commas)

■ *That* always introduces a restrictive clause.

He accepted the job <u>that had the best benefits</u>. (no commas)

■ *Who* can introduce either a restrictive or a nonrestrictive clause.

RESTRICTIVE   Many parents <u>who work</u> feel a lot of stress. (no commas)

NONRESTRICTIVE   Both of my parents, <u>who have always wanted the best for their children</u>, have worked two jobs for years. (clause set off by commas)

PRACTICE
34-5   Edit the following sentences so that commas set off all nonrestrictive clauses. (Remember, commas are *not* used to set off restrictive clauses.) If a sentence is correct, write C in the blank.

Example: A museum exhibition that celebrates the Alaska highway tells the story of its construction. ____*C*____

Teaching Tip
Have students do Practice 34-5 in groups. (Fewer papers allow you more time for careful grading.) Students can also form groups to look over the graded assignment.

(1) During the 1940s, a group of African-American soldiers who defied the forces of nature and human prejudice were shipped to Alaska. ____*C*____ (2) They built the Alaska highway, which stretches twelve hundred miles across Alaska. _____ (3) The troops who worked on the highway have received little attention in most historical accounts. ____*C*____ (4) The highway, which cut through some of the roughest terrain in the world, was begun in 1942. _____ (5) The Japanese had just landed in the Aleutian Islands, which lie west of the tip of the Alaska Peninsula. _____ (6) Military officials, who oversaw the project, doubted the ability of the African-American troops. _____ (7) As a result, they made them work under conditions, that made construction difficult. _____ (8) The troops who worked on the road proved their commanders wrong by finishing the highway months ahead of schedule. ____*C*____ (9) In one case, white engineers, who surveyed a river, said it would take two weeks to bridge. _____ (10) To the engineers' surprise, the soldiers who worked on the project beat the estimate. ____*C*____ (11) A military report that was issued in 1945 praised them. ____*C*____ (12) It said the goals that the African-American soldiers achieved would be remembered through the ages. ____*C*____

34e Commas in Dates and Addresses

Dates

Use commas in dates to separate the day of the week from the month and the day of the month from the year.

> The first Cinco de Mayo we celebrated in the United States was Tuesday, May 5, 1998.

Teaching Tip
Ask each student to write her or his birth date and address on the board. Have the class check comma usage.

When a date that includes commas does not fall at the end of a sentence, place a comma after the year.

> Tuesday, May 5, 1998, was the first Cinco de Mayo we celebrated in the United States.

Addresses

Use commas in addresses to separate the street address from the city and the city from the state or country.

> The office of the famous fictional detective Sherlock Holmes was located at 221b Baker Street, London, England.

When an address that includes commas falls in the middle of a sentence, place a comma after the state or country.

> The office at 221b Baker Street, London, England, belonged to the famous fictional detective Sherlock Holmes.

PRACTICE

34-6   Edit the following sentences for the correct use of commas in dates and addresses. Add any missing commas, and cross out any unnecessary commas. If the sentence is correct, write *C* in the blank.

Examples

June 3, 1988, is the day my parents were married. _____

Their wedding took place in Santiago, Chile. _____

1. The American Declaration of Independence was approved on July 4, 1776. _____

2. The Pelican Man's Bird Sanctuary is located at 1705 Ken Thompson Parkway, Sarasota, Florida. _____

3. At 175 Carlton Avenue, Brooklyn, New York, is the house where Richard Wright began writing *Native Son*. _____

4. I found this information in the February 12, 1994, issue of the *New York Times*. _____

5. The Mexican hero Father Miguel Hidalgo y Costilla was shot by a firing squad on June 30, 1811. ____*C*____

6. In the Palacio de Gobierno at Plaza de Armas, Guadalajara, Mexico, is a mural of the famous revolutionary. _____

7. The Pueblo Grande Museum is located at 1469 East Washington Street, Phoenix, Arizona. _____

8. Brigham Young led the first settlers into the valley that is now Salt Lake City, Utah, in 1847. _____ *C*

9. St. Louis Missouri was the birthplace of writer Maya Angelou, but she spent most of her childhood in Stamps Arkansas. _____

10. Some records list the writer's birthday as May 19 1928 while others indicate she was born on April 4 1928. _____

34f Unnecessary Commas

In addition to knowing where commas are required, it is also important to know when *not* to use commas.

■ Do not use a comma before the first item in a series.

> INCORRECT   *Duck Soup* starred, Groucho, Chico, and Harpo Marx.
>
> CORRECT   *Duck Soup* starred Groucho, Chico, and Harpo Marx.

Teaching Tip
Remind students to use commas between items in a series. Refer them to 34a.

■ Do not use a comma after the last item in a series.

> INCORRECT   Groucho, Chico, and Harpo Marx, starred in *Duck Soup*.
>
> CORRECT   Groucho, Chico, and Harpo Marx starred in *Duck Soup*.

■ Do not use a comma between a subject and a verb.

> INCORRECT   Students and their teachers, should try to respect one another.
>
> CORRECT   Students and their teachers should try to respect one another.

■ Do not use a comma before the coordinating conjunction that separates the two parts of a compound predicate.

> INCORRECT   The transit workers voted to strike, and walked off the job.
>
> CORRECT   The transit workers voted to strike and walked off the job.

Teaching Tip
Remind students that they *should* use a comma before a coordinating conjunction that links independent clauses in a compound sentence: *The transit workers voted to strike, and they walked off the job.*

■ Do not use a comma before the coordinating conjunction that separates the two parts of a compound subject.

> INCORRECT   The transit workers, and the sanitation workers voted to strike.
>
> CORRECT   The transit workers and the sanitation workers voted to strike.

Teaching Tip
Remind students that not every *and* and *but* is preceded by a comma.

■ Do not use a comma to set off a restrictive clause.

> INCORRECT People, who live in glass houses, should not throw stones.
>
> CORRECT People who live in glass houses should not throw stones.

■ Finally, do not use a comma before a dependent clause that follows an independent clause.

> INCORRECT He was exhausted, because he had driven all night.
>
> CORRECT He was exhausted because he had driven all night.

PRACTICE

34-7 Some of the following sentences contain unnecessary commas. Edit to eliminate unnecessary commas. If the sentence is correct, write *C* in the blank following it.

Example: Both the Dominican Republic/ and the republic of Haiti occupy the West Indian island of Hispaniola. _____

1. The capital of the Dominican Republic/ is Santo Domingo. _____

2. The country's tropical climate, generous rainfall, and fertile soil/ make the Dominican Republic suitable for many kinds of crops. _____

3. Some of the most important crops are/ sugarcane, coffee, cocoa, and rice. _____

4. Mining is also important to the country's economy/ because the land is rich in many ores. _____

5. Spanish is the official language of the Dominican Republic, and Roman Catholicism is the state religion. ____*C*____

6. In recent years, resort areas have opened/ and brought many tourists to the country. _____

7. Tourists who visit the Dominican Republic/ remark on its tropical beauty. _____

8. Military attacks/ and political unrest have marked much of the Dominican Republic's history. _____

9. Because the republic's economy has not always been strong, many Dominicans have immigrated to the United States. ____*C*____

10. However, many Dominican immigrants maintain close ties to their home country/ and return often to visit. _____

TEST · Revise · Edit

Look back at your response to the Write First activity on page 583. TEST what you have written. Then, make the following additions.

1. Add a sentence that includes a series of three or more words or word groups.

2. Add introductory phrases to two of your sentences.

3. Add an appositive to one of your sentences.

4. Add a transitional word or phrase to one of your sentences (at the beginning, in the middle, or at the end).

5. Add a nonrestrictive clause to one of your sentences.

When you have made all the additions, revise and edit your work, carefully checking your use of commas.

EDITING PRACTICE

Read the following student essay, which includes errors in comma use. Add commas where necessary between items in a series and with introductory phrases, transitional words and phrases, appositives, and non-restrictive clauses. Cross out any unnecessary commas. The first sentence has been edited for you. *Answers may vary.*

Maxine Hong Kingston

Brave Orchid

One of the most important characters in *The Woman Warrior*, Maxine Hong Kingston's autobiographical work, is Brave Orchid, Kingston's mother. Brave Orchid was a strong woman, but not a happy one. Through Kingston's stories about her mother, readers learn a lot about Kingston herself.

Readers are introduced to Brave Orchid, a complex character, as an imaginative storyteller, who tells her daughter vivid tales of China. As a young woman, she impresses her classmates with her intelligence. She is a traditional woman. However, she is determined to make her life exactly what she wants it to be. Brave Orchid strongly believes in herself; still, she considers herself a failure.

In her native China, Brave Orchid trains to be a midwife. The other women in her class envy her independence, brilliance, and courage. One day, Brave Orchid bravely confronts the Fox Spirit, and tells him he will not win. First of all, she tells him she can endure any pain that he inflicts on her. Next, she gathers together the women in the dormitory to burn the ghost away. After this event, the other women admire her even more.

Working hard, Brave Orchid becomes a midwife in China. After coming to America, however, she cannot work as a midwife. Instead, she works in a Chinese laundry, and picks tomatoes. None of her classmates in China would have imagined this outcome. During her later years in America, Brave Orchid becomes a woman, who is overbearing and domineering. She bosses her children around, she tries to ruin her sister's life, and she criticizes everyone and everything around her. Her daughter, a straight-A student, is the object of her worst criticism.

Brave Orchid's intentions are good. Nevertheless she devotes her energy to the wrong things. She expects the people around her to be as strong as she is. Because she bullies them however she eventually loses them. In addition she is too busy criticizing her daughter's faults to see all her accomplishments. Brave Orchid an independent woman and a brilliant student never achieves her goals. She is hard on the people around her because she is disappointed in herself.

Map of China

COLLABORATIVE ACTIVITIES

1. Bring a homemaking, sports, or fashion magazine to class. Working in a small group, look at the people pictured in the ads. In what roles are men most often depicted? In what roles are women presented? Identify the three or four most common roles for each sex, and give each kind of character a descriptive name—*jock* or *mother*, for example.

2. Working on your own, choose one type of character from the list your group made in Collaborative Activity 1. Then, write a paragraph in which you describe this character's typical appearance and habits. Refer to the magazine pictures to support your characterization.

3. Collaborating with other members of your group, write two paragraphs, one discussing how men are portrayed in ads and one discussing how women are portrayed.

4. Circle every comma in the paragraph you wrote for Collaborative Activity 2. Then, work with your group to explain why each comma is used. If no one in your group can explain why a particular comma is used, cross it out.

review checklist

Using Commas

☐ Use commas to separate all elements in a series of three or more words or word groups. (See 34a.)

☐ Use commas to set off introductory phrases and transitional words and phrases from the rest of the sentence. (See 34b.)

☐ Use commas to set off appositives from the rest of the sentence. (See 34c.)

☐ Use commas to set off nonrestrictive clauses. (See 34d.)

☐ Use commas to separate parts of dates and addresses. (See 34e.)

☐ Avoid unnecessary commas. (See 34f.)

preview

In this chapter, you will learn to

- use apostrophes to form contractions (35a)
- use apostrophes to form possessives (35b)
- revise incorrect use of apostrophes (35c)

write first

Certain jobs have traditionally been considered "men's work," and others have been viewed as "women's work." Although the workplace has changed considerably in recent years, some things have remained the same. Write a paragraph or two about the tasks that are considered "men's work" and "women's work" at your job or in your current household. Be sure to give examples of the responsibilities you discuss. (*Note:* Contractions, such as *isn't* or *don't*, are acceptable in this informal response.)

An **apostrophe** is a punctuation mark that is used in two situations: to form a contraction and to form the possessive of a noun or an indefinite pronoun.

35a Apostrophes in Contractions

A **contraction** is a word that uses an apostrophe to combine two words. The apostrophe takes the place of omitted letters.

> I <u>didn't</u> (*did not*) realize how late it was.
>
> <u>It's</u> (*it is*) not right for cheaters to go unpunished.

Teaching Tip
Be sure your students understand that even though contractions are used in speech and writing, they are not acceptable in most business or college writing situations. (You may allow students to use contractions in first-person essays.)

Frequently Used Contractions

I + am = I'm	are + not = aren't
we + are = we're	can + not = can't
you + are = you're	do + not = don't
it + is = it's	will + not = won't
I + have = I've	should + not = shouldn't
I + will = I'll	let + us = let's
there + is = there's	that + is = that's
is + not = isn't	who + is = who's

Teaching Tip
Remind students that this list does not include every contraction. For example, other personal pronouns (*she, he, they*) can also be combined with forms of *be* and *have*. (They will need to know this to do Practice 35-1.)

PRACTICE

35-1 In the following sentences, add apostrophes to contractions if needed. If the sentence is correct, write *C* in the blank.

Example: ~~Whats~~ *What's* the deadliest creature on earth? _____

(1) Bacteria and viruses, which we ~~cant~~ *can't* see without a microscope, kill many people every year. _____ (2) When we speak about the deadliest creatures, however, usually we ~~were~~ *we're* talking about creatures that cause illness or death from their poison, which is called venom. _____ (3) After ~~your~~ *you're* bitten, stung, or stuck, how long does it take to die? _____ (4) The fastest killer is a creature called the sea wasp, but it isn't a wasp at all. ___*C*___ (5) The sea wasp is actually a fifteen-foot-long jellyfish, and although ~~its~~ *it's* not aggressive, it can be deadly. _____ (6) People who've gone swimming off the coast of Australia have encountered this creature. ___*C*___ (7) While jellyfish found off the Atlantic coast of the United States can sting, they ~~arent~~ *aren't* as dangerous as the sea wasp, whose venom is

ESL Tip
Nonnative speakers often misplace or omit apostrophes in contractions. Spend extra time checking their work.

deadly enough to kill sixty adults. _____ (8) A person whos been stung by a sea wasp has anywhere from thirty seconds to four minutes to get help or die. _____ (9) Oddly, it's been found that something as thin as pantyhose worn over the skin will prevent these stings. ___C___ (10) Also, theres an antidote to the poison that can save victims. _____

35b   Apostrophes in Possessives

Possessive forms of nouns and pronouns show ownership. Nouns and indefinite pronouns do not have special possessive forms. Instead, they use apostrophes to indicate ownership.

Singular Nouns and Indefinite Pronouns

To form the possessive of **singular nouns** (including names) and **indefinite pronouns**, add an apostrophe plus an *s*.

> Cesar Chavez's goal (*the goal of Cesar Chavez*) was justice for American farm workers.
>
> The strike's outcome (*the outcome of the strike*) was uncertain.
>
> Whether it would succeed was anyone's guess (*the guess of anyone*).

FYI

Singular Nouns Ending in *-s*

Even if a singular noun already ends in *-s,* add an apostrophe plus an *s* to form the possessive.

> The class's next assignment was a research paper.
>
> Dr. Ramos's patients are participating in a clinical trial.

Plural Nouns

Most plural nouns end in *-s.* To form the possessive of **plural nouns ending in *-s*** (including names), add just an apostrophe (not an apostrophe plus an *s*).

> The two drugs' side effects (*the side effects of the two drugs*) were quite different.
>
> The Johnsons' front door (*the front door of the Johnsons*) is red.

Teaching Tip
Tell students that possessive pronouns have special forms, such as *its* and *his*, and that these forms never include apostrophes. Refer them to 31g.

Teaching Tip
Refer students to 26f and 31e for more on indefinite pronouns.

Teaching Tip
Tell students that most nouns form the plural by adding *-s.* Refer them to 31b for a list of frequently used irregular plurals.

Some irregular noun plurals do not end in -*s*. If a plural noun does not end in -*s*, add an apostrophe plus an *s* to form the possessive.

The <u>men's</u> room is right next to the <u>women's</u> room.

PRACTICE

35-2   Rewrite the following phrases, changing the noun or indefinite pronoun that follows *of* to the possessive form. Be sure to distinguish between singular and plural nouns.

Examples

the mayor of the city   *the city's mayor*

the uniforms of the players   *the players' uniforms*

1. the video of the singer   *the singer's video*

2. the scores of the students   *the students' scores*

3. the favorite band of everybody   *everybody's favorite band*

4. the office of the boss   *the boss's office*

5. the union of the players   *the players' union*

6. the specialty of the restaurant   *the restaurant's specialty*

7. the bedroom of the children   *the children's bedroom*

8. the high cost of the tickets   *the tickets' high cost*

9. the dreams of everyone   *everyone's dreams*

10. the owner of the dogs   *the dogs' owner*

35c Incorrect Use of Apostrophes

Be careful not to confuse a plural noun (*boys*) with the singular possessive form of the noun (*boy's*). Never use an apostrophe with a plural noun unless the noun is possessive.

Termites can be dangerous <u>pests</u> [not *pest's*].

The <u>Velezes</u> [not *Velez's*] live on Maple Drive, right next door to the <u>Browns</u> [not *Brown's*].

Also remember not to use apostrophes with possessive pronouns that end in -*s*: *theirs* (not *their's*), *hers* (not *her's*), *its* (not *it's*), *ours* (not *our's*), and *yours* (not *your's*).

Be especially careful not to confuse possessive pronouns with sound-alike contractions. Possessive pronouns never include apostrophes.

POSSESSIVE PRONOUN	CONTRACTION
The dog bit its master.	It's (*it is*) time for breakfast.
The choice is theirs.	There's (*there is*) no place like home.
Whose house is this?	Who's (*who is*) on first base?
Is this your house?	You're (*you are*) late again.

PRACTICE

35-3 Check the underlined words in the following sentences for correct use of apostrophes. If a correction needs to be made, cross out the word and write the correct version above it. If the noun or pronoun is correct, write *C* above it.

Example: The president's *(C)* views were presented after several other speaker's *(speakers)* first presented their's *(theirs)*.

1. Parent's *(Parents)* should realize that when it comes to disciplining children, the responsibility is there's *(theirs)*.

2. It's *(C)* also important that parents offer praise for a child's *(C)* good behavior.

3. In it's *(its)* first few week's *(weeks)* of life, a dog is already developing a personality.

4. His and her's *(hers)* towels used to be popular with couple's *(couples)*, but it's *(C)* not so common to see them today.

5. All the Ryan's *(Ryans)* spent four year's *(years)* in college and then got good jobs.

6. From the radio came the lyrics "You're *(C)* the one who's *(whose)* love I've been waiting for."

7. If you expect to miss any class's *(classes)*, you will have to make arrangements with someone who's *(C)* willing to tell you you're *(your)* assignment.

8. No other school's *(C)* cheerleading squad tried as many stunts as our's *(ours)* did.

9. Surprise test's *(tests)* are common in my economics teacher's *(C)* class.

10. Jazz's *(C)* influence on many mainstream musician's *(musicians)* is one of the book's *(C)* main subject's *(subjects)*.

TEST · Revise · Edit

Look back at your response to the Write First activity on page 598. TEST what you have written. Then, revise and edit your work, checking to make sure you have used apostrophes correctly in possessive forms and contractions. (Remember, because this is an informal exercise, contractions are acceptable.)

EDITING PRACTICE

Read the following student essay, which includes errors in the use of apostrophes. Edit it to eliminate errors by crossing out incorrect words and writing corrections above them. (Note that this is an informal response paper, so contractions are acceptable.) The first sentence has been edited for you.

The Women of Messina

In William ~~Shakespeares'~~ *Shakespeare's* play *Much Ado about Nothing*, the women of Messina, whether they are seen as love objects or as ~~shrew's,~~ *shrews,* have very few options. A ~~womans~~ *woman's* role is to please a man. She can try to resist, but she will probably wind up giving in.

The ~~plays~~ *play's* two women, Hero and Beatrice, are very different. Hero is the obedient one. ~~Heroes~~ *Hero's* cousin, Beatrice, tries to challenge the rules of the ~~mans~~ *man's* world in which she lives. However, in a place like Messina, even women like Beatrice find it hard to get the respect that should be ~~their's.~~ *theirs.*

Right from the start, we are drawn to Beatrice. ~~Shes~~ *She's* funny, she has a clever comment for most ~~situation's,~~ *situations,* and she always speaks her mind about other ~~peoples~~ *people's* behavior. Unlike Hero, she tries to stand up to the men in her life, as we see in her and ~~Benedicks~~ *Benedick's* conversations. But even though Beatrice's intelligence is obvious, she often mocks herself. ~~Its~~ *It's* clear that she doesn't have much self-esteem. In fact, Beatrice ~~is'nt~~ *isn't* the strong woman she seems to be.

Ultimately, Beatrice does get her man, and she will be happy—but at what cost? ~~Benedicks'~~ *Benedick's* last ~~word's~~ *words* to her are "Peace! I will stop your mouth." Then, he kisses her. The kiss is a symbolic end to their bickering. It is also the mark of ~~Beatrices~~ *Beatrice's* defeat. She has lost. Benedick has silenced her. Now, she will be Benedick's wife and do what he wants her to do. Granted, she will have more say in her marriage than Hero will have in ~~her's,~~ *hers,* but she is still defeated.

~~Shakespeares~~ *Shakespeare's* audience might have seen the ~~plays~~ *play's* ending as a happy one. For contemporary ~~audience's,~~ *audiences,* however, the ending is disappointing. Even Beatrice, the most rebellious of ~~Messinas~~ *Messina's* women, finds it impossible to achieve anything of importance in this male-dominated society.

William Shakespeare

Shakespeare's Globe Theater

603

COLLABORATIVE ACTIVITIES

1. Working in a group of four and building on your individual responses to the Write First exercise at the beginning of the chapter, consider which specific occupational and professional roles are still associated largely with men and which are associated primarily with women. Make two lists, heading one "women's jobs" and one "men's jobs."

2. Now, work in pairs, with one pair of students in each group concentrating on men and the other pair on women. Write a paragraph that attempts to justify why the particular jobs you listed should or should not be restricted to one gender. In your discussion, list the various qualities men or women possess that qualify (or disqualify) them for particular jobs. Use possessive forms whenever possible—for example, *women's energy* (not *women have energy*).

3. Bring to class a book, magazine, or newspaper whose style is informal—for example, a romance novel, *TV Guide*, your school newspaper, or even a comic book. Working in a group, circle every contraction you can find on one page of each publication, and substitute for each contraction the words it combines. Are your substitutions an improvement? (You may want to read a few paragraphs aloud before you reach a conclusion.)

review checklist

Using Apostrophes

☐ Use apostrophes to form contractions. (See 35a.)

☐ Use an apostrophe plus an *s* to form the possessive of singular nouns and indefinite pronouns, even when a noun ends in -*s*. (See 35b.)

☐ Use an apostrophe alone to form the possessive of plural nouns ending in -*s*, including names. If a plural noun does not end in -*s*, add an apostrophe plus an *s*. (See 35b.)

☐ Do not use apostrophes with plural nouns unless they are possessive. Do not use apostrophes with possessive pronouns. (See 35c.)

36 Understanding Mechanics

preview

In this chapter, you will learn to
- capitalize proper nouns (36a)
- punctuate direct quotations (36b)
- set off titles (36c)
- use hyphens correctly (36d)
- abbreviate words correctly (36e)
- use numerals and spelled-out numbers (36f)
- use minor punctuation marks correctly (36g)

write first

This picture shows a familiar scene from the classic 1939 film *The Wizard of Oz*. Write a paragraph or two describing a memorable scene from your favorite movie. Begin by giving the film's title and listing the names of the major stars and the characters they play. Then, tell what happens in the scene, quoting a few words of dialogue, if possible.

36a Capitalizing Proper Nouns

A **proper noun** names a particular person, animal, place, object, or idea. Proper nouns are always capitalized. The list that follows explains and illustrates specific rules for capitalizing proper nouns.

<table>
<tr><td>

Teaching Tip
Tell students that the words *black* and *white* are generally not capitalized when they name racial groups. However, *African American* and *Caucasian* are always capitalized.

</td></tr>
</table>

■ Always capitalize names of **races, ethnic groups, tribes, nationalities, languages, and religions**.

> The census data revealed a diverse community of Caucasians, African Americans, and Asian Americans, with a few Latino and Navajo residents. Native languages included English, Korean, and Spanish. Most people identified themselves as Catholic, Protestant, or Muslim.

■ Capitalize names of **specific people and the titles that accompany them**. In general, do not capitalize titles used without a name.

> In 1994, President Nelson Mandela was elected to lead South Africa.
>
> The newly elected fraternity president addressed the crowd.

■ Capitalize names of **specific family members and their titles**. Do not capitalize words that identify family relationships, including those introduced by possessive pronouns.

> The twins, Aunt Edna and Aunt Evelyn, are Dad's sisters.
>
> My aunts, my father's sisters, are twins.

■ Capitalize names of **specific countries, cities, towns, bodies of water, streets, and so on**. Do not capitalize words that do not name specific places.

> The Seine runs through Paris, France.
>
> The river runs through the city.

■ Capitalize names of **specific geographical regions**. Do not capitalize such words when they specify direction.

> William Faulkner's novels are set in the South.
>
> Turn right at the golf course, and go south for about a mile.

■ Capitalize names of **specific buildings and monuments**. Do not capitalize general references to buildings and monuments.

> He drove past the Liberty Bell and looked for parking near City Hall.
>
> He drove past the monument and looked for a parking space near the building.

■ Capitalize names of **specific groups, clubs, teams, and associations**. Do not capitalize general references to such groups.

> The Teamsters Union represents workers who were at the stadium for the Republican Party convention, the Rolling Stones concert, and the Phillies-Astros game.

The union represents workers who were at the stadium for the political party's convention, the rock group's concert, and the baseball teams' game.

■ Capitalize names of **specific historical periods, events, and documents**. Do not capitalize nonspecific references to periods, events, or documents.

> The Emancipation Proclamation was signed during the Civil War, not during Reconstruction.

> The document was signed during the war, not during the postwar period.

■ Capitalize **names of businesses, government agencies, schools, and other institutions**. Do not capitalize nonspecific references to such institutions.

> The Department of Education and Apple Computer have launched a partnership project with Central High School.

> A government agency and a computer company have launched a partnership project with a high school.

■ Capitalize **brand names**. Do not capitalize general references to kinds of products.

> While Jeff waited for his turn at the Xerox machine, he drank a can of Coke.

> While Jeff waited for his turn at the copier, he drank a can of soda.

Teaching Tip
Tell students that trade names that have been part of the language for many years—*nylon* and *aspirin*, for example—are no longer capitalized.

■ Capitalize **titles of specific academic courses**. Do not capitalize names of general academic subject areas, except for proper nouns—for example, a language or a country.

> Are Introduction to American Government and Biology 200 closed yet?

> Are the introductory American government course and the biology course closed yet?

ESL Tip
Use direct feedback when marking the work of nonnative speakers. Correct any incorrect usage of capitalized or non-capitalized trade names.

■ Capitalize **days of the week, months of the year, and holidays**. Do not capitalize the names of seasons.

> The Jewish holiday of Passover usually falls in April.

> The Jewish holiday of Passover falls in the spring.

PRACTICE

36-1 Edit the following sentences, capitalizing letters or changing capitals to lowercase where necessary.

Example: The third-largest City in the united states is chicago, illinois.

(1) Located in the midwest on lake Michigan, chicago is an important port city, a rail and highway hub, and the site of o'hare international

Teaching Tip
Have students do Practice 36-1 in pairs.

airport, one of the Nation's busiest. (2) The financial center of the city is Lasalle street, and the lakefront is home to Grant park, where there are many Museums and monuments. (3) To the North of the city, soldier field is home to the chicago bears, the city's football team, and wrigley field is home to the chicago cubs, a national league Baseball Team. (4) In the mid-1600s, the site of what is now Chicago was visited by father jacques marquette, a catholic missionary to the ottawa and huron tribes, who were native to the area. (5) By the 1700s, the city was a trading post run by john kinzie. (6) The city grew rapidly in the 1800s, and immigrants included germans, irish, italians, poles, greeks, and chinese, along with african americans who migrated from the south. (7) In 1871, much of the city was destroyed in one of the worst fires in united states history; according to legend, the fire started when mrs. O'Leary's Cow kicked over a burning lantern. (8) Today, Chicago's skyline has many Skyscrapers, built by businesses like the john hancock company, sears, and amoco. (9) I know Chicago well because my Mother grew up there and my aunt jean and uncle amos still live there.

(10) I also got information from the Chicago Chamber of Commerce when I wrote a paper for introductory research writing, a course I took at Graystone high school.

36b Punctuating Direct Quotations

A **direct quotation** shows the *exact* words of a speaker or writer. Direct quotations are always placed in quotation marks.

A direct quotation is usually accompanied by an **identifying tag**, a phrase (such as "she said") that names the person being quoted. In the following sentences, the identifying tag is underlined.

Lauren said, "My brother and Tina have gotten engaged."

A famous advertising executive wrote, "Don't sell the steak; sell the sizzle."

When a quotation is a complete sentence, it begins with a capital letter and ends with a period (or a question mark or exclamation point). When a quotation falls at the end of a sentence (as in the two examples above) the period is placed *before* the quotation marks.

Teaching Tip
You may need to explain what an identifying tag is by literally pointing it out.

If the quotation is a question or an exclamation, the question mark or exclamation point is also placed *before* the quotation marks.

The instructor asked, "Has anyone read *Sula*?"

Officer Warren shouted, "Hold it right there!"

If the quotation itself is not a question or an exclamation, the question mark or exclamation point is placed *after* the quotation marks.

Did Joe really say, "I quit"?

I can't believe he really said, "I quit"!

FYI

Indirect Quotations

A direct quotation shows someone's *exact* words, but an **indirect quotation** simply summarizes what was said or written. Do not use quotation marks with indirect quotations.

DIRECT QUOTATION	Martin Luther King Jr. said, "I have a dream."
INDIRECT QUOTATION	Martin Luther King Jr. said that he had a dream.

Teaching Tip
Tell students that an indirect quotation is usually introduced by the word *that* (*She told me that she was cold*).

The rules for punctuating direct quotations with identifying tags are summarized below.

Identifying Tag at the Beginning

When the identifying tag comes *before* the quotation, it is followed by a comma.

Alexandre Dumas wrote, "Nothing succeeds like success."

Identifying Tag at the End

When the identifying tag comes at the *end* of a quoted sentence, it is followed by a period. A comma (or, sometimes, a question mark or an exclamation point) inside the closing quotation marks separates the quotation from the identifying tag.

"Life is like a box of chocolates," stated Forrest Gump.

"Is that so?" his friends wondered.

"That's amazing!" he cried.

Identifying Tag in the Middle

When the identifying tag comes in the *middle* of the quoted sentence, it is followed by a comma. The first part of the quotation is also followed by a

Teaching Tip
Remind students that they will be required to document direct and indirect quotations in college writing.

comma, placed inside the quotation marks. Because the part of the quotation that follows the identifying tag is not a new sentence, it does not begin with a capital letter.

"This is my life," Bette insisted, "and I'll live it as I please."

Identifying Tag between Two Sentences

When the identifying tag comes *between two* quoted sentences, it is preceded by a comma and followed by a period. (The second quoted sentence begins with a capital letter.)

"Producer Berry Gordy is an important figure in the history of music," Tony explained. "He was the creative force behind Motown records."

Teaching Tip
Have students write sentences from Practice 36-2 on the board. Review fragments, which can be caused by incorrect punctuation of tags. Refer students to Chapter 25.

PRACTICE

36-2 The following sentences contain direct quotations. First, underline the identifying tag. Then, punctuate the quotation correctly, adding capital letters as necessary.

Example: " Why Darryl asked " are teachers so strict about deadlines? "

1. We who are about to die salute you said the gladiators to the emperor.

2. When we turned on the television, the newscaster was saying ladies and gentlemen, we have a new president-elect.

3. The bigger they are said boxer John L. Sullivan the harder they fall.

4. Do you take Michael to be your lawfully wedded husband asked the minister.

5. Lisa Marie replied I do.

6. If you believe the *National Enquirer* my friend always says then you'll believe anything.

7. When asked for the jury's verdict, the foreperson replied we find the defendant not guilty.

8. I had felt for a long time that if I was ever told to get up so a white person could sit Rosa Parks recalled I would refuse to do so.

9. Yabba dabba doo Fred exclaimed this brontoburger looks great.

10. Where's my money Addie Pray asked you give me my money!

36c Setting Off Titles

Some titles are typed in *italics*. Others are enclosed in quotation marks. The following box shows how to set off different kinds of titles.

> ### Italics or Quotation Marks?
>
> **ITALICIZED TITLES**
>
> Books: *How the García Girls Lost Their Accents*
> Newspapers: *Miami Herald*
> Magazines: *People*
> Long poems: *John Brown's Body*
> Plays: *Death of a Salesman*
> Films: *The Rocky Horror Picture Show*
> Television or radio series: *Battlestar Galactica*
>
> **TITLES IN QUOTATION MARKS**
>
> Book chapters: "Understanding Mechanics"
> Short stories: "The Tell-Tale Heart"
> Essays and articles: "The Suspected Shopper"
> Short poems: "Richard Cory"
> Songs and speeches: "America the Beautiful"; "The Gettysburg Address"
> Individual episodes of television or radio series: "The Montgomery Bus Boycott" (an episode of the PBS series *Eyes on the Prize*)

FYI

Capital Letters in Titles

Capitalize the first letters of all important words in a title. Do not capitalize an **article** (*a, an, the*), a **preposition** (*to, of, around*, and so on), the *to* in an infinitive, or a **coordinating conjunction** (*and, but,* and so on)—unless it is the first or last word of the title or subtitle (*On the Road*; "To an Athlete Dying Young"; *No Way Out*; *And Quiet Flows the Don*).

PRACTICE

36-3 Edit the following sentences, capitalizing letters as necessary in titles.

Example: *New york times* best-seller *three cups of tea* is about
Greg Mortenson's work building schools in Pakistan and Afghanistan.

1. When fans of the television show *lost* voted for their favorite episodes, "through the looking glass," "the shape of things to come," and "the incident" were in the top ten.

2. In 1948, Eleanor Roosevelt delivered her famous speech "the struggle for human rights" and published an article titled "toward human rights throughout the world."

3. Before being elected president, Barack Obama wrote and published two books: *dreams from my father* and *the audacity of hope.*

4. English actor Daniel Craig plays secret agent James Bond in the films *casino royale* and *quantum of solace.*

5. *janis joplin's greatest hits* includes songs written by other people, such as "piece of my heart," as well as songs she wrote herself, such as "mercedes benz."

PRACTICE 36-4 In the following sentences, underline titles to indicate italics or place them in quotation marks. (Remember that titles of books and other long works are italicized, and titles of stories, essays, and other shorter works are enclosed in quotation marks.)

Example: An article in the <u>New York Times</u> called "Whoopi Goldberg Joins <u>The View</u>" talks about a television talk show hosted by women.

1. Oprah Winfrey publishes a magazine called <u>O</u>.

2. At the beginning of most major American sporting events, the crowd stands for "The Star Spangled Banner."

3. People who want to purchase new cars often compare the different models in <u>Consumer Reports</u> magazine.

4. U2's song "Pride (in the Name of Love)" was written about Martin Luther King Jr.

5. Edgar Allan Poe wrote several mysterious short stories, two of which are called "The Tell-Tale Heart" and "The Black Cat."

6. The popular Broadway show <u>Fela!</u> was based on the life of the Nigerian musician Fela Kuti.

7. Lance Armstrong, who won the Tour de France bicycle race, wrote a book about his fight with cancer called It's Not about the Bike.

8. In a college textbook called Sociology: A Brief Introduction, the first chapter is titled The Essence of Sociology.

36d   Hyphens

A hyphen has two uses: to divide a word at the end of a line and to join words in compounds.

- Use a **hyphen** to divide a word at the end of a line. If you need to divide a word, divide it between syllables. (Check your dictionary to see how a word is divided into syllables.) Never break a one-syllable word, no matter how long it is.

    When the speaker began his talk, all the people seated in the audi-torium grew very quiet.

- Use a hyphen in a **compound**—a word that is made up of two or more words.

    This theater shows first-run movies.

Teaching Tip
Remind students that when they type, a long word will automatically be carried over to the next line.

PRACTICE
36-5   Add hyphens to join words in compounds in the following sentences.

Example: The course focused on nineteenth century American literature.

1. The ice skating rink finally froze over.

2. We should be kind to our four legged friends.

3. The first year students raised money for charity.

4. The under prepared soldiers were at a real disadvantage.

5. The hand carved sculpture looked like a pair of doves.

36e   Abbreviations

An **abbreviation** is a shortened form of a word. Although abbreviations are generally not used in college writing, it is acceptable to abbreviate the following.

■ Titles—such as Mr., Ms., Dr., and Jr.—that are used along with names

■ a.m. and p.m.

■ BC and AD (in dates such as 43 BC)

■ Names of organizations (NRA, CIA) and technical terms (DNA). Note that some abbreviations, called **acronyms**, are pronounced as words: AIDS, FEMA.

Keep in mind that it is *not* acceptable to abbreviate days of the week, months, names of streets and places, names of academic subjects, or titles that are not used along with names.

PRACTICE

36-6 Edit the incorrect use of abbreviations in the following sentences.

    Example: In leap years, ~~Feb.~~ has twenty-nine days. *(February)*

1. The ~~dr.~~ diagnosed a case of hypertension. *(doctor)*

2. ~~Nov.~~ 11 is a federal holiday. *(November)*

3. Derek registered for ~~Eng.~~ literature and a ~~psych~~ elective. *(English) (psychology)*

4. The museum was located at the corner of Laurel ~~Ave.~~ and Neptune ~~St.~~ *(Avenue) (Street.)*

5. The clinic is only open ~~Tues.~~ through ~~Thurs.~~ and every other ~~Sat.~~ *(Tuesday) (Thursday) (Saturday.)*

36f Numbers

In college writing, most numbers are spelled out (*forty-five*) rather than written as numerals (*45*). However, numbers more than two words long are always written as **numerals** (*4,530*, not *four thousand five hundred thirty*).

In addition, you should use numerals in the following situations.

DATES	January 20, 1976
ADDRESSES	5023 Schuyler Street
EXACT TIMES	10:00 (If you use *o'clock*, spell out the number: *ten o'clock*)
PERCENTAGES AND DECIMALS	80% 8.2
DIVISIONS OF BOOKS	Chapter 3 Act 4 Page 102

Note: Never begin a sentence with a numeral. Use a spelled-out number, or reword the sentence so the numeral does not come at the beginning.

PRACTICE

36-7 Edit the incorrect use of numbers in the following sentences.

Example: The population of the United States is over ~~three~~ *300*
~~hundred~~ million.

1. Only 2̬ students in the 8̬ o'clock lecture were late. *two* *eight*

2. More than ~~seventy-five percent~~ of the class passed the exit exam. *75%*

3. Chapter ~~six~~ begins on page 873. *6*

4. The wedding took place on October ~~twelfth~~ at 7:30. *12th*

5. Meet me at ~~Sixty-five~~ Cadman Place. *65*

36g Using Minor Punctuation Marks

The Colon

- Use a **colon** to introduce a quotation.

  Our family motto is a simple one: "Accept no substitutes."

- Use a colon to introduce an explanation, a clarification, or an example.

  Only one thing kept him from climbing Mt. Everest: fear of heights.

- Use a colon to introduce a list.

  I left my job for four reasons: boring work, poor working conditions, low pay, and a terrible supervisor.

The Dash

Use **dashes** to set off important information.

  She parked her car—a red Firebird—in a towaway zone.

Parentheses

Use **parentheses** to enclose material that is relatively unimportant.

  The weather in Portland (a city in Oregon) was overcast.

Teaching Tip
Tell students that when a colon introduces a quotation, an example, or a list, a complete sentence must precede the colon.

Teaching Tip
Tell students that all items in a list should be parallel. Refer them to Chapter 22.

Teaching Tip
Tell students that dashes give writing an informal tone and should therefore be used sparingly in college writing.

PRACTICE
36-8   Add colons, dashes, and parentheses to the following sentences where necessary.

Example: Megachurches (those with more than two thousand worshippers at a typical service) have grown in popularity since the 1950s. *Answers may vary.*

1. Megachurches—though they are Protestant—are not always affiliated with the main Protestant denominations.

2. Services in megachurches are unique: preaching may be accompanied by contemporary music and video presentations.

3. Although many of these churches are evangelical (actively recruiting new members), people often join because of friends and neighbors.

4. Megachurches tend to keep their members because they encourage a variety of activities—for example, hospitality committees and study groups.

5. Worshippers say that their services are upbeat: full of joy and spirituality.

6. Megachurches—in nearly all cases—use technology to organize and communicate with their members.

7. The largest of these churches—with ten thousand members—would be unable to function without telecommunications.

8. Some even offer services in a format familiar to their younger members: the podcast.

9. Critics of megachurches (and there are some) believe they take up too much tax-exempt land.

10. Other critics fear that smaller churches—already struggling to keep members—will lose worshippers to these huge congregations and eventually have to close.

TEST · **Revise** · **Edit**

Look back at your response to the Write First activity on page 605.
TEST what you have written.

 If you have quoted any dialogue from the film you wrote about, try varying the placement of the identifying tags you have used. If you did not include any lines of dialogue, try adding one or two. Then, add an example or list to your writing, introducing this new material with a colon. Make sure that a complete sentence comes before the colon.

 Finally, revise and edit your work, paying special attention to the issues covered in this chapter.

Man dying of the plague, fourteenth or fifteenth century

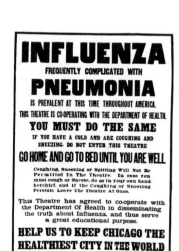

Public health quarantine poster for 1918 flu epidemic

EDITING PRACTICE

Read the following student essay, which includes errors in capitalization and punctuation and in the use of direct quotations and titles. Correct any errors you find. The first sentence has been edited for you.

Answers may vary.

A Threat to Health

Pandemics are like Epidemics, only more widespread, perhaps even spreading throughout the World. In a pandemic, a serious Disease spreads very easily. In the past, there have been many pandemics. In the future, in spite of advances in Medicine, there will still be pandemics. In fact, scientists agree that not every pandemic can be prevented, so pandemics will continue to be a threat.

Probably the best-known pandemic is the bubonic plague. It killed about one-third of the Population of europe during the middle ages. Some areas suffered more than others. According to Philip ziegler's book the black Death, at least half the people in florence, Italy, died in one year. Many years later, in 1918, a flu pandemic killed more than 50 million people worldwide, including hundreds of thousands in the United states.

Unfortunately, pandemics have not disappeared. AIDS, for example, is a current pandemic. Philadelphia the 1993 movie starring denzel washington and tom hanks is still one of the most moving depictions of the heartbreak of AIDS. The rate of AIDS infection is over 30 percent in parts of africa, and the disease continues to spread on other Continents as well. So far, efforts to find an AIDS vaccine have failed. Dr. anthony s. Fauci discussed recent AIDS research on NPR's series All things considered in a program called Search for an HIV vaccine expands.

Although some pandemic diseases, such as Smallpox, have been wiped out by Vaccination, new pandemics remain a threat. Many viruses and Bacteria change in response to treatment, so they may become resistant to Vaccination and Antibiotics. Also, with modern transportation, a disease can move quickly from Country to Country. For example, the disease known as severe acute respiratory syndrome (SARS) began in china but was spread to other countries by travelers.

Hundreds died as a result of the SARS pandemic between November 2002 and july^J 2003. Birds also remain a threat because they can transmit disease. It is obviously impossible to prevent birds from flying from one country to another. Markos kyprianou,^K health commissioner^C of the European union,^U has said that I am^{he was} concerned that birds in Turkey have been found with the bird flu Virus.^v He said, "There is a direct relationship with viruses found in Russia, Mongolia, and china.^C" If this Virus^v changes so that it can move easily from birds to Humans,^h bird flu could become the next pandemic.

Public Health^h Officials^o are always on the lookout for diseases with three characteristics[:] they are new, they are dangerous, and they are very contagious. Doctors try to prevent them from becoming Pandemics.^p However, they continue to warn that some Pandemics^p cannot be prevented.

Mother wearing mask to protect herself against SARS

COLLABORATIVE ACTIVITIES

1. Work in a small group to list as many items in each of the following five categories as you can: planets, islands, bands, automobile models, sports teams. Be sure all your items are proper nouns, and use capital letters where necessary. Then, write five original sentences, using one proper noun from each category in each sentence. When you are finished, exchange papers with another group, and check for correct use of capital letters.

2. Imagine that you and the other members of your group are the nominations committee for this year's Emmy, Oscar, or Grammy Awards. Work together to compile a list of categories and several nominees for each category, deciding as a group when to use capital letters.

   Trade lists with another group. From each category, select the individual artist or work you believe deserves to win. Write a sentence about each winner, explaining why each is the best in its category.

   When you have finished, exchange papers with another group. Check one another's papers for correct use of capitals, quotation marks, and underlining.

3. Working in pairs, write a conversation between two characters, real or fictional, who have very different positions on a particular issue. Place all direct quotations within quotation marks, and include identifying tags that clearly indicate which character is speaking. (Begin a new paragraph each time a new person speaks.)

   Exchange your conversation with another pair, and check their work to see that directly quoted speech is set within quotation marks and that capital letters and other punctuation are used correctly.

review checklist

Understanding Mechanics

- Capitalize proper nouns. (See 36a.)

- Always place direct quotations within quotation marks. (See 36b.)

- In titles, capitalize all important words. Use italics or quotation marks to set off titles. (See 36c.)

- Use a hyphen to divide a word at the end of a line or to join words in compounds. (See 36d.)

- Abbreviate titles used with names, a.m. and p.m., BC and AD, names of organizations, and technical terms. (See 36e.)

- Use numerals for numbers more than two words long and in certain other situations. (See 36f.)

- Use colons, dashes, and parentheses to set off material from the rest of the sentence. (See 36g.)

37 Understanding Spelling

preview

In this chapter, you will learn to
- become a better speller (37a)
- know when to use *ie* and *ei* (37b)
- understand prefixes (37c) and suffixes (37d)
- identify commonly confused words (37e)

write first

In an effort to improve discipline and boost self-esteem, a number of elementary schools across the country have begun requiring students to wear uniforms. Write about whether or not you think elementary school students should be required to wear uniforms such as the ones in this picture.

37a   Becoming a Better Speller

Improving your spelling may take time, but the following steps can make this task a lot easier.

1. **Use a spell checker**. When you write on a computer, always use your spell checker. It will correct most misspelled words and also identify many typos, such as transposed or omitted letters. Keep in mind, however, that spell checkers do not identify typos that create other words (*then/than*, *form/from*, or *big/beg*, for example) or words that you have used incorrectly (*their/there* or *its/it's*, for example).
2. **Proofread carefully**. Even if you have used a spell checker, always proofread your papers for spelling before you hand them in.
3. **Use a dictionary**. As you proofread your papers, circle words whose spellings you are unsure of. After you have finished your draft, look up these words in a print or online dictionary.
4. **Keep a personal spelling list**. Write down all the words you misspell. Whenever your instructor returns one of your papers, look for misspelled words—usually circled and marked *sp*. Add these to your personal spelling list.
5. **Look for patterns in your misspelling**. Do you consistently misspell words with *ei* combinations? Do you have trouble forming plurals? Once you figure out which errors you make most frequently, you can take steps to eliminate them.
6. **Learn the basic spelling rules**. Memorize the spelling rules in this chapter, especially those that apply to areas in which you are weak. Remember that each rule can help you spell many words correctly.
7. **Review the list of commonly confused words in 37e**. If you have problems with any of these word pairs, add them to your personal spelling list.
8. **Use memory cues**. Memory cues help you remember how to spell certain words. For example, remembering that *definite* contains the word *finite* will help you remember that *definite* is spelled with an *i*, not an *a*.
9. **Learn to spell some of the most frequently misspelled words**. Identify any words on the list below that give you trouble, and add them to your personal spelling list.

Frequently Misspelled Words

across	calendar	describe	finally
all right	cannot	develop	forty
a lot	careful	disappoint	fulfill
already	careless	early	generally
argument	cemetery	embarrass	government
beautiful	certain	entrance	grammar
becoming	conscience	environment	harass
beginning	definite	everything	height
believe	definitely	exercise	holiday
benefit	dependent	experience	integration

intelligence	occurrences	receive	tomatoes
interest	occurring	recognize	truly
interfere	occurs	reference	until
judgment	personnel	restaurant	usually
loneliness	possible	roommate	Wednesday
medicine	potato	secretary	weird
minute	potatoes	sentence	window
necessary	prejudice	separate	withhold
noticeable	prescription	speech	woman
occasion	privilege	studying	women
occur	probably	surprise	writing
occurred	professor	tomato	written

FYI

Vowels and Consonants

Knowing which letters are vowels and which are consonants will help you understand the spelling rules presented in this chapter.

Vowels: a, e, i, o, u

Consonants: b, c, d, f, g, h, j, k, l, m, n, p, q, r, s, t, v, w, x, z

The letter *y* may be considered either a vowel or a consonant, depending on how it is pronounced. In *young, y* acts as a consonant because it has the sound of *y;* in *truly,* it acts as a vowel because it has the sound of *ee.*

> **Teaching Tip**
> Discuss the fact that English spelling is complex and unpredictable. Mention that many languages have more regular spelling than English does.

Because English pronunciation is not always a reliable guide for spelling, most people find it useful to memorize some spelling rules.

37b *ie* and *ei*

Memorize this rule: *i* comes before *e* except after *c,* or when the *ei* sound is pronounced *ay.*

> **Teaching Tip**
> Have students memorize spelling rules. Test them on these rules.

I BEFORE *E*	EXCEPT AFTER *C*	OR WHEN *EI* IS PRONOUNCED *AY*
ach<u>ie</u>ve	c<u>ei</u>ling	<u>ei</u>ght
bel<u>ie</u>ve	conc<u>ei</u>ve	fr<u>ei</u>ght
fr<u>ie</u>nd	dec<u>ei</u>ve	n<u>ei</u>ghbor
		w<u>ei</u>gh

Note that there are some exceptions to the "*i* before *e*" rule. Because these exceptions follow no pattern, you must memorize them.

ancient	either	leisure	seize
caffeine	foreign	neither	species
conscience	height	science	weird

PRACTICE

37-1   Proofread the underlined words in the following sentences for correct spelling. If a correction needs to be made, cross out the incorrect word, and write the correct spelling above it. If the word is spelled correctly, write *C* above it.

　　　　　　　　　　　　　　　　　C　　*receive*
Example:　It was a <u>relief</u> to <u>recieve</u> the good news.

　　　　　　　　weigh
1. Be sure to <u>wiegh</u> the pros and cons before making important decisions,

　　　　　　　　　　　　　　　　　　　C
　　particularly those involving <u>friends</u>.

　　　　　　　　　C　　　　　　　　　　　　　　　　*achieve*
2. When your <u>beliefs</u> are tested, you may be able to <u>acheive</u> a better

　　understanding of yourself.

　　　　　　　C　　　　　　　　*deceive*　　　　　　　　　*believing*
3. In our <u>society</u>, many people <u>decieve</u> themselves into <u>beleiving</u> that they

　　are better than everyone else.

　　Chiefly
4. <u>Cheifly</u> because they have been lucky, they have reached a certain

　　C
　　<u>height</u> in the world.

　　　　　　　　　　　　　　　　　　　　　　　　C　*veins*
5. They think that the blood running through <u>their</u> <u>viens</u> makes them

　　　　　　　　　C
　　belong to a higher <u>species</u> than the average person.

37c   Prefixes

A **prefix** is a group of letters added at the beginning of a word that changes the word's meaning. Adding a prefix to a word never affects the spelling of the original word.

dis + service = disservice	pre + heat = preheat
un + able = unable	un + natural = unnatural
co + operate = cooperate	over + rate = overrate

PRACTICE

37-2   Write in the blank the new word that results when the specified prefix is added to each of the following words.

Example:　dis + respect = _disrespect_

1. un + happy = _____unhappy_____   6. non + negotiable = _____nonnegotiable_____

2. tele + vision = _____television_____   7. im + patient = _____impatient_____

3. pre + existing = _____preexisting_____   8. out + think = _____outthink_____

4. dis + satisfied = _____dissatisfied_____   9. over + react = _____overreact_____

5. un + necessary = _____unnecessary_____   10. dis + solve = _____dissolve_____

37d   Suffixes

A **suffix** is a group of letters added to the end of a word that changes the word's meaning or its part of speech. Adding a suffix to a word can change the spelling of the original word.

Words Ending in Silent -*e*

If a word ends with a silent (unpronounced) -*e*, drop the *e* if the suffix begins with a vowel.

DROP THE *E*

hope + <u>ing</u> = hoping   dance + <u>er</u> = dancer

continue + <u>ous</u> = continuous   insure + <u>able</u> = insurable

EXCEPTIONS

change + able = changeable   courage + ous = courageous

notice + able = noticeable   replace + able = replaceable

Keep the *e* if the suffix begins with a consonant.

KEEP THE *E*

hope + <u>ful</u> = hopeful   bore + <u>dom</u> = boredom

excite + <u>ment</u> = excitement   same + <u>ness</u> = sameness

EXCEPTIONS

argue + ment = argument   true + ly = truly

judge + ment = judgment   nine + th = ninth

PRACTICE

37-3   Write in the blank the new word that results from adding the specified suffix to each of the following words.

Examples

insure + ance = _____insurance_____

love + ly = _____lovely_____

1. lone + ly = _lonely_
2. use + ful = _useful_
3. revise + ing = _revising_
4. desire + able = _desirable_
5. true + ly = _truly_

6. microscope + ic = _microscopic_
7. nine + th = _ninth_
8. indicate + ion = _indication_
9. effective + ness = _effectiveness_
10. arrange + ment = _arrangement_

Words Ending in -y

When you add a suffix to a word that ends in -y, change the y to an i if the letter before the y is a consonant.

CHANGE Y TO I

beauty + ful = beautiful   busy + ly = busily
try + ed = tried   friendly + er = friendlier

EXCEPTIONS

■ If the suffix starts with an i, keep the y.

cry + ing = crying   baby + ish = babyish

■ When you add a suffix to certain one-syllable words, keep the y.

shy + er = shyer   dry + ness = dryness

■ Keep the y if the letter before the y is a vowel.

KEEP THE Y

annoy + ance = annoyance   enjoy + ment = enjoyment
play + ful = playful   display + ed = displayed

EXCEPTIONS

day + ly = daily   say + ed = said
gay + ly = gaily   pay + ed = paid

PRACTICE
37-4   Write in the blank the new word that results from adding the specified suffix to each of the following words.

Examples

study + ed = _studied_

employ + ment = _employment_

1. happy + ness = _happiness_
2. convey + or = _conveyor_

3. deny + ing = _denying_
4. carry + ed = _carried_

5. ready + ness = _readiness_   8. twenty + eth = _twentieth_

6. annoy + ing = _annoying_   9. cry + ed = _cried_

7. destroy + er = _destroyer_   10. lonely + ness = _loneliness_

Doubling the Final Consonant

When you add a suffix that begins with a vowel—for example, *-ed, -er,* or *-ing*—sometimes you need to double the final consonant in the original word. Do this (1) if the last three letters of the word have a consonant-vowel-consonant (cvc) pattern *and* (2) if the word has one syllable (or if the last syllable is stressed).

Teaching Tip
Refer students to the FYI box in 37a for more information on vowels and consonants.

FINAL CONSONANT DOUBLED

drum	+	ing	=	drumming	(cvc—one syllable)
bat	+	er	=	batter	(cvc—one syllable)
pet	+	ed	=	petted	(cvc—one syllable)
commit	+	ed	=	committed	(cvc—stress is on last syllable)
occur	+	ing	=	occurring	(cvc—stress is on last syllable)

FINAL CONSONANT NOT DOUBLED

answer	+	ed	=	answered	(cvc—stress is not on last syllable)
happen	+	ing	=	happening	(cvc—stress is not on last syllable)
act	+	ing	=	acting	(no cvc)

Teaching Tip
As a homework assignment, have students think of other examples to add to the suffix lists in this section.

PRACTICE

37-5 Write in the blank the new word that results from adding the specified suffix to each of the following words.

Examples

rot + ing = _rotting_

narrow + er = _narrower_

1. flip + ed = _flipped_   6. open + er = _opener_

2. shop + er = _shopper_   7. unzip + ed = _unzipped_

3. rest + ing = _resting_   8. trap + ed = _trapped_

4. combat + ed = _combatted_   9. refer + ing = _referring_

5. reveal + ing = _revealing_   10. omit + ed = _omitted_

37e Commonly Confused Words

Accept/Except *Accept* means "to receive something." *Except* means "with the exception of" or "to leave out or exclude."

> "I <u>accept</u> your challenge," said Alexander Hamilton to Aaron Burr.

> Everyone <u>except</u> Darryl visited the museum.

Affect/Effect *Affect* is a verb meaning "to influence." *Effect* is a noun meaning "result."

> Carmen's job could <u>affect</u> her grades.

> Overexposure to sun can have a long-term <u>effect</u> on skin.

All ready/Already *All ready* means "completely prepared." *Already* means "previously, before."

> Serge was <u>all ready</u> to take the history test.

> Gina had <u>already</u> been to Italy.

Brake/Break *Brake* is a noun that means "a device to slow or stop a vehicle." *Break* is a verb meaning "to smash" or "to detach" and sometimes a noun meaning either "a gap" or "an interruption" or "a stroke of luck."

> Peter got into an accident because his foot slipped off the <u>brake</u>.

> Babe Ruth thought no one would ever <u>break</u> his home run record.

> The baseball game was postponed until there was a <u>break</u> in the bad weather.

Buy/By *Buy* means "to purchase." *By* is a preposition meaning "close to," "next to," or "by means of."

> The Stamp Act forced colonists to <u>buy</u> stamps for many public documents.

> He drove <u>by</u> but did not stop.

> He stayed <u>by</u> her side all the way to the hospital.

> Malcolm X wanted "freedom <u>by</u> any means necessary."

PRACTICE
37-6 Proofread the underlined words in the following sentences for correct spelling. If a correction needs to be made, cross out the incorrect word, and write the correct spelling above it. If the word is spelled correctly, write *C* above it.

Example: We must ~~except~~ *accept* the fact that the human heart can <u>break</u>. *C*

1. The <u>affects</u> *effects* of several new AIDS drugs have <u>all ready</u> *already* been reported.

2. *Consumer Reports* gave high ratings to the <u>breaks</u> *brakes* on all the new cars tested <u>accept</u> *except* one.

3. Advertisements urge us to ~~by~~ *buy* a new product even if we <u>already</u> *C* own a

   similar item.

4. If you ~~except~~ *accept* the charges for a collect telephone call, you will probably

   have to ~~brake~~ *break* your piggy bank to pay their bill.

5. Cigarette smoking <u>affects</u> *C* the lungs <u>by</u> *C* creating deposits of tar that

   make breathing difficult.

Conscience/Conscious *Conscience* is a noun that refers to the part of the mind that urges a person to choose right over wrong. *Conscious* is an adjective that means "aware" or "deliberate."

> After he cheated at cards, his <u>conscience</u> started to bother him.
>
> As she walked through the woods, she became <u>conscious</u> of the hum of insects.
>
> Elliott made a <u>conscious</u> decision to stop smoking.

Everyday/Every day *Everyday* is a single word that means "ordinary" or "common." *Every day* is two words that mean "occurring daily."

> *Friends* was a successful comedy show because it appealed to <u>everyday</u> people.
>
> <u>Every day</u>, the six friends met at the Central Perk café.

Fine/Find *Fine* means "superior quality" or "a sum of money paid as a penalty." *Find* means "to locate."

> He sang a <u>fine</u> solo at church last Sunday.
>
> Demi had to pay a <u>fine</u> for speeding.
>
> Some people still use a willow rod to <u>find</u> water.

Hear/Here *Hear* means "to perceive sound by ear." *Here* means "at or in this place."

> I moved to the front so I could <u>hear</u> the speaker.
>
> My great-grandfather came <u>here</u> in 1883.

Its/It's *Its* is the possessive form of *it*. *It's* is the contraction of *it is* or *it has*.

> The airline canceled <u>its</u> flights because of the snow.
>
> <u>It's</u> twelve o'clock, and we are late.
>
> Ever since <u>it's</u> been in the accident, the car has rattled.

Teaching Tip
Students often use *it's* instead of *its*. Read aloud a sentence containing this error, replacing the contraction with the two words it stands for (for example, *The baby fell out of it is high chair*). The error should be immediately apparent.

PRACTICE
37-7 Proofread the underlined words in the following sentences for correct spelling. If a correction needs to be made, cross out the incorrect word, and write the correct spelling above it. If the word is spelled correctly, write *C* above it.

                                       C   *everyday*
Example:　~~It's~~ often difficult for celebrities to adjust to ~~every day~~ life.

Here
1. ~~Hear~~ at Simonson's Fashions, we try to make our customers feel that

   every day
   ~~everyday~~ is a sale day.

               fine   *it's*
2. My uncle was a ~~find~~ person, and ~~its~~ a shame that he died so young.

                             C   *conscience*
3. That inner voice you ~~hear~~ is your ~~conscious~~ telling you how you should

   behave.

         everyday   *find*
4. In the ~~every day~~ world of work and school, it can be hard to ~~fine~~ the

   time to relax and enjoy life.

                     conscious   *its*
5. By the time I became ~~conscience~~ of the cracked pipe, ~~it's~~ leak had done

   a lot of damage.

Know/No/Knew/New　*Know* means "to have an understanding of" or "to have fixed in the mind." *No* means "not any," "not at all," or "not one." *Knew* is the past tense form of the verb *know*. *New* means "recent or never used."

> I <u>know</u> there will be a lunar eclipse tonight.
>
> You have <u>no</u> right to say that.
>
> He <u>knew</u> how to install a <u>new</u> light switch.

Lie/Lay　*Lie* means "to rest or recline." The past tense of *lie* is *lay*. *Lay* means "to put or place something down." The past tense of *lay* is *laid*.

> Every Sunday, I <u>lie</u> in bed until noon.
>
> They <u>lay</u> on the grass until it began to rain, and then they went home.
>
> Tammy told Carl to <u>lay</u> his cards on the table.
>
> Brooke and Cassia finally <u>laid</u> down their hockey sticks.

Loose/Lose　*Loose* means "not fixed or rigid" or "not attached securely." *Lose* means "to mislay" or "to misplace."

> In the 1940s, many women wore <u>loose</u>-fitting pants.
>
> I never gamble because I hate to <u>lose</u>.

Passed/Past　*Passed* is the past tense of the verb *pass*. It means "moved by" or "succeeded in." *Past* is a noun or an adjective meaning "earlier than the present time."

> The car that <u>passed</u> me was doing more than eighty miles an hour.
>
> David finally <u>passed</u> his driving test.
>
> The novel was set in the <u>past</u>.
>
> The statement said that the bill was <u>past</u> due.

Peace/Piece　*Peace* means "the absence of war" or "calm." *Piece* means "a part of something."

The British prime minister tried to achieve <u>peace</u> with honor.

My <u>peace</u> of mind was destroyed when the flying saucer landed.

"Have a <u>piece</u> of cake," said Marie.

PRACTICE

37-8 Proofread the underlined words in the following sentences for correct spelling. If a correction needs to be made, cross out the incorrect word, and write the correct spelling above it. If the word is spelled correctly, write *C* above it.

Example: Although the soldiers stopped fighting, a *peace* ~~piece~~ treaty was

never signed.

1. Because he was late for the job interview, he was afraid he would *lose* ~~loose~~

his chance to work for the company.

2. While she *lay* ~~laid~~ down for a nap, her children cooked dinner and cleaned

the house.

3. There will be *no* ~~know~~ wool sweaters on sale before the holidays.

4. The *C* past chair of the committee left a lot of unfinished business.

5. The broken knife found in the trash turned out to be a *piece* ~~peace~~ of the

murder weapon.

Principal/Principle *Principal* means "first" or "highest" or "the head of a school." *Principle* means "a law or basic assumption."

She had the <u>principal</u> role in the movie.

I'll never forget the day the <u>principal</u> called me into his office.

It was against his <u>principles</u> to lie.

Quiet/Quit/Quite *Quiet* means "free of noise" or "still." *Quit* means "to leave a job" or "to give up." *Quite* means "actually" or "very."

Jane looked forward to the <u>quiet</u> evenings at the lake.

Sammy <u>quit</u> his job and followed the girls into the parking lot.

"You haven't <u>quite</u> got the hang of it yet," she said.

After practicing all summer, Tamika got <u>quite</u> good at tennis.

Raise/Rise *Raise* means "to elevate" or "to increase in size, quantity, or worth." The past tense of *raise* is *raised*. *Rise* means "to stand up" or "to move from a lower position to a higher position." The past tense of *rise* is *rose*.

Carlos <u>raises</u> his hand whenever the teacher asks for volunteers.

They finally <u>raised</u> the money for the down payment.

The crowd <u>rises</u> every time their team scores a touchdown.

Kim <u>rose</u> before dawn so she could see the eclipse.

Sit/Set *Sit* means "to assume a sitting position." The past tense of *sit* is *sat*. *Set* means "to put down or place" or "to adjust something to a desired position." The past tense of *set* is *set*.

I usually <u>sit</u> in the front row at the movies.

They <u>sat</u> at the clinic waiting for their names to be called.

Elizabeth <u>set</u> the mail on the kitchen table and left for work.

Every semester I <u>set</u> goals for myself.

Suppose/Supposed *Suppose* means "to consider" or "to assume." *Supposed* is both the past tense and the past participle of *suppose*. *Supposed* also means "expected" or "required." (Note that when *supposed* has this meaning, it is always followed by *to*.)

<u>Suppose</u> researchers were to find a cure for cancer.

We <u>supposed</u> the movie would be over by ten o'clock.

You were <u>supposed</u> to finish a draft of the report by today.

Teaching Tip
Remind students not to drop the *d* of *supposed* before *to*: He is <u>supposed</u> to study, not He is <u>suppose</u> to study.

PRACTICE
37-9

Proofread the underlined words in the following sentences for correct spelling. If a correction needs to be made, cross out the incorrect word, and write the correct spelling above it. If the word is spelled correctly, write *C* above it.

Example: Boarding the plane took <u>quite</u> [*C*] a long time because of the security process.

1. Jackie was <u>suppose</u> [*supposed*] to mow the lawn and trim the bushes last weekend.

2. It is important to <u>sit</u> [*set*] the computer in a place where the on-off switch can be reached.

3. If you <u>raise</u> [*C*] the window, a pleasant breeze will blow into the bedroom.

4. The <u>principle</u> [*principal*] reason for her <u>raise</u> [*rise*] to the position of <u>principal</u> [*C*] of the school was hard work.

5. We were all told to <u>sit</u> [*C*] and wait for the crowd to become <u>quite</u> [*quiet*].

Teaching Tip
Teach students how to use mnemonic devices to remember spellings. (For example, *their* refers to ownership, and so does *heir*; *there* refers to location, and so does *here*.)

Their/There/They're *Their* is the possessive form of the pronoun *they*. *There* means "at or in that place." *There* is also used in the phrases *there is* and *there are*. *They're* is the contraction of "they are."

They wanted poor people to improve <u>their</u> living conditions.

I put the book over <u>there</u>.

<u>There</u> are three reasons I will not eat meat.

<u>They're</u> the best volunteer firefighters I've ever seen.

Then/Than *Then* means "at that time" or "next in time." *Than* is used in comparisons.

He was young and naive <u>then</u>.

I went to the job interview and <u>then</u> stopped off for coffee.

My dog is smarter <u>than</u> your dog.

Threw/Through   *Threw* is the past tense of *throw. Through* means "in one side and out the opposite side" or "finished."

Satchel Paige <u>threw</u> a baseball more than ninety-five miles an hour.

It takes almost thirty minutes to go <u>through</u> the tunnel.

"I'm <u>through</u>," said Clark Kent, storming out of Perry White's office.

To/Too/Two   *To* means "in the direction of." *Too* means "also" or "more than enough." *Two* denotes the numeral 2.

During spring break, I am going <u>to</u> Disney World.

My roommates are coming <u>too</u>.

The microwave popcorn is <u>too</u> hot to eat.

"If we get rid of the Tin Man and the Cowardly Lion, the <u>two</u> of us can go to Oz," said the Scarecrow to Dorothy.

Use/Used   *Use* means "to put into service" or "to consume." *Used* is both the past tense and past participle of *use. Used* also means "accustomed." (Note that when *used* has this meaning, it is followed by *to*.)

I <u>use</u> a soft cloth to clean my glasses.

"Hey! Who <u>used</u> all the hot water?" he yelled from the shower.

Marisol had <u>used</u> all the firewood during the storm.

After two years in Alaska, they got <u>used</u> to the short winter days.

Teaching Tip
Remind students not to use the informal spelling *thru* for *through*.

PRACTICE

37-10   Proofread the underlined words in the following sentences for correct spelling. If a correction needs to be made, cross out the incorrect word, and write the correct spelling above it. If the word is spelled correctly, write *C* above it.

Example: Because of good nutrition, people are taller ~~then~~ ^*than*^ they ~~use~~ ^*used*^ to be in the past.

1. The power went out in the dorms, and many students <u>then</u> ^*C*^ went <u>too</u> ^*to*^ the library to study.

2. Whenever he <u>through</u> ^*threw*^ out the trash, he walked <u>threw</u> ^*through*^ the backyard on his way <u>two</u> ^*to*^ the alley.

3. Get your tickets before <u>their</u> ^*they're*^ all gone.

4. I <u>use</u> ^*used*^ to think that my ancestors all came from northern Europe, but I recently learned that some <u>used</u> ^*C*^ to live in South Africa.

5. The countries that signed the peace treaty have not lived up to <u>they're</u> ^{*their*}

responsibilities.

Weather/Whether   *Weather* refers to temperature, humidity, precipitation, and so on. *Whether* is used to introduce alternative possibilities.

The *Farmer's Almanac* says that the <u>weather</u> this winter will be severe.

<u>Whether</u> or not this prediction will be correct is anyone's guess.

Where/Were/We're   *Where* means "at or in what place." *Were* is the past tense of *are*. *We're* is the contraction of "we are."

<u>Where</u> are you going, and <u>where</u> have you been?

Charlie Chaplin and Mary Pickford <u>were</u> popular stars of silent movies.

<u>We're</u> doing our back-to-school shopping early this year.

Whose/Who's   *Whose* is the possessive form of *who*. *Who's* is the contraction of either "who is" or "who has."

My roommate asked, "<u>Whose</u> book is this?"

"<u>Who's</u> there?" squealed the second little pig as he leaned against the door.

<u>Who's</u> been blocking the driveway?

Your/You're   *Your* is the possessive form of *you*. *You're* is the contraction of "you are."

"You should have worn <u>your</u> running shoes," said the hare as he passed the tortoise.

"<u>You're</u> too kind," said the tortoise sarcastically.

PRACTICE

37-11   Proofread the underlined words in the following sentences for correct spelling. If a correction needs to be made, cross out the incorrect word, and write the correct spelling above it. If the word is spelled correctly, write *C* above it.

Example: As citizens, <s><u>were</u></s> ^{*we're*} all concerned with <u>where</u> ^{*C*} our country is

going.

1. The police are attempting to discover <u>who's</u> ^{*whose*} fingerprints <u>were</u> ^{*C*} left at

the scene of the crime.

2. Cancer does not care <u>weather</u> ^{*whether*} <u>your</u> ^{*you're*} rich or poor, young or old.

3. Santa Fe, <u>were</u> ^{*where*} I lived for many years, has better <u>weather</u> ^{*C*} than New

Jersey has.

4. Whenever we listen to politicians debate, *we're* were likely to be wondering *who's* whose telling the truth.

5. You should take *C* your time before deciding *whether* weather to focus *C* your energy on school or on work.

TEST · Revise · Edit

Look back at your response to the Write First activity on page 621. TEST what you have written. Then, revise and edit your work, paying particular attention to any spelling errors you found after spell-checking and proofreading.

EDITING PRACTICE

Read the following student essay, which includes spelling errors. Identify the words you think are misspelled; then, look them up in a dictionary. Finally, cross out each incorrectly spelled word, and write the correct spelling above the line. The first sentence has been edited for you.

The Guardian Angels

The Guardian Angels are volunteers ~~who's~~ *whose* aim is to promote public ~~saftey~~ *safety*. ~~Organizzed~~ *Organized* in New York City in 1979, the Angels ~~originaly~~ *originally* got together to fight crime on New York's subways. ~~Unnarmed,~~ *Unarmed,* they ~~patroled~~ *patrolled* the streets, hoping to prevent violence before it happened. Since ~~than,~~ *then,* the group has expanded ~~it's~~ *its* reach to include other cities and other methods of violence prevention. The ~~organizetion~~ *organization* now has chapters in more than 100 cities all over the world, and in addition to doing ~~there~~ *their* Safety Patrols, the Guardian Angels offer youth programs and promote Internet safety.

All Guardian Angel patrollers are volunteers who ~~recieve~~ *receive* training in first aid and CPR. Before going out on the streets, they also learn how to communicate ~~effectively~~ *effectively* and resolve conflicts ~~piecefully~~ *peacefully*. Their distinctive red jackets and red berets make them ~~noticable~~ *noticeable* ~~whereever~~ *wherever* they go. When they first appeared more than thirty years ago, the Safety Patrols ~~rised quiet~~ *raised quite* a stir. Many ~~goverment~~ *government* officials ~~where~~ *were* opposed to them. Today, however, many chapters are welcomed by local police and city ~~leadders,~~ *leaders,* who ~~except~~ *accept* that ~~buy~~ *by* trying to prevent ~~nieghborhood~~ *neighborhood* violence, the Angels are providing a ~~usefull~~ *useful* service.

From the ~~begining,~~ *beginning,* the Guardian Angels have ~~tryed~~ *tried* to include young people in their programs. Founder Curtis Sliwa ~~beleives~~ *believes* that his organization gives urban youth a positive way to be involved in ~~there~~ *their* communities. Although people under 16 ~~can not~~ *cannot* join the Safety Patrols, the Guardian Angels have groups specifically designed for young teenagers and children. ~~Accordding~~ *According* to the organization's Web site, the Urban Angels program offers 12- to 16-year-olds an alternative to gangs and drugs. Urban Angels learn about violence prevention ~~threw~~ *through* working with peers on community-service projects. The Junior Angels program is ~~suppose~~ *supposed* to give 7- to

find
11-year-olds a way to build self-esteem and fine a sense of purpose. Junior Angels

resolve ^
also learn about nonviolent ways to ressolve conflicts.

^
In 1995, to detect online threats and to educate people about the risks of

created *new*
the Internet, the Guardian Angels creatted a knew group, the CyberAngels. These
^   ^

harassment,
Angels aim to teach people how to protect themselves from online harasment,
^

identity theft, computer viruses, and other online dangers. This group is also

interested   *recognize*   *particular*
intrested in helping parents and schools to reconize the particlar problems
^   ^   ^

children face when they spend time online and to protect children from Internet

a lot   *arguing*
threats. Often, parents spend alot of time argueing with their children about
^   ^

advise
appropriate limits on Internet use. The CyberAngels advice parents about how to
^

interfering
monitor use effectively without interferring too much in their children's lives.
^

there   *everything*
Although they're are people who do not approve of evrything the Guardian
^   ^

honorable.
Angels do, most acknowledge that the Angels' aims are honorible. These
^

volunteers are committed to understanding and improving their own communities.

In addition, the Guardian Angels have shown they can change with the times.

developed   *useful*   *it's*
Because they have developped a diverse range of usefull programs, its likely they
^   ^   ^

will be around for years to come.

COLLABORATIVE ACTIVITIES

1. Working in pairs, compare responses to the Write First activity on page 621. How many misspelled words did each of you find? How many errors did you and your partner have in common?

2. Are there any patterns of misspelling in your Write First activities? What types of spelling errors seem most common?

3. Collaborate with your partner to make a spelling list for the two of you, and then work with other groups to create a spelling list for the whole class. When you have finished, determine which types of errors are most common.

review checklist

Understanding Spelling

☐ Follow the steps to becoming a better speller. (See 37a.)

☐ Remember the following rules:

☐ *I* comes before *e*, except after *c* or in any *ay* sound. (See 37b.)

☐ Adding a prefix to a word never affects the word's spelling. (See 37c.)

☐ Adding a suffix to a word may change the word's spelling. (See 37d.)

☐ When a word ends with silent *e,* drop the *e* if the suffix begins with a vowel. Keep the *e* if the suffix begins with a consonant. (See 37d.)

☐ When you add a suffix to a word that ends with a *y,* change the *y* to an *i* if the letter before the *y* is a consonant. Keep the *y* if the letter before the *y* is a vowel. (See 37d.)

☐ When you add a suffix that begins with a vowel—for example, *-ed, -er,* or *-ing*—sometimes you need to double the final consonant in the original word. Do this (1) if the last three letters of the word have a consonant-vowel-consonant (cvc) pattern *and* (2) if the word has one syllable (or if the last syllable is stressed). (See 37d.)

☐ Learn to spell the most commonly confused words. (See 37e.)

EDITING PRACTICE: SENTENCES

Read the following sentences, which contain errors in punctuation, mechanics, and spelling. Identify the sentences that need to be corrected, and edit the faulty sentences. Some sentences have more than one error.

1. There are ~~fourty~~ *forty* ~~restuarants~~ *restaurants* within 5 *five* miles of my house but the most popular place is: *,* Golden Crown *,* a Chinese buffet.

2. Mr *.* Glass *,* my middle school ~~principle~~ *principal,* retired last year; *,* after he turned 65. *sixty-five.*

3. Mike has lived in Chicago *,* Illinois *,* since he was born on ~~Aug. eleventh~~ *August 11,* 1986.

4. When we moved into our new apartment *,* *"* Tony said, *,* ~~their~~ *"there* were ~~alot~~ *a lot* of ants in the kitchen *,* and the front door lock ~~didnt~~ *didn't* work. *"*

5. There are several ways ~~too~~ *to* keep a computer secure; *:* install spam blocking software *,* change your email ~~adress~~ *address* frequently *,* and keep ~~your're~~ *your* real name a secret.

6. What kind of ~~vaccum~~ *vacuum* cleaner is ~~Jins~~ *Jin's* grandmother using. *?*

7. ~~Its~~ *It's* clear that the clerk at the registration desk *,* one of the first people guests see when they check in *,* needs better ~~comunication~~ *communication* skills.

8. Stan and his wife spent part of their ~~Summer~~ *summer* vacation in Philadelphia, visiting Constitution ~~center~~ *Center,* and ~~independance hall.~~ *Independence Hall.*

9. At first, readers thought that in his book *The Painted Bird*, ~~writter~~ *writer* Jerzy Kosinski was ~~discribeing~~ *describing* his own ~~dificult~~ *difficult* life as a young boy in Nazi-occupied ~~poland~~ *Poland,* but now ~~they're~~ *there* are doubts about ~~weather~~ *whether* he ever had those ~~experiances~~ *(experiences* or even wrote the book himself. *)*

10. Lenders say that families should spend no more ~~then~~ *than* 35 percent of ~~there~~ *their* total income on housing, but many ~~familyies~~ *families* are spending almost 50 percent.

You can use this exercise to get students ready for the multi-error editing practice that follows.

639

EDITING PRACTICE: ESSAY

Read the following student essay, which contains errors in the use of punctuation, mechanics, and spelling. Identify the sentences that need to be corrected, and edit the faulty sentences. (Underline to indicate italics where necessary.) The first sentence has been edited for you.

Answers will vary.

Telenovelas

What is the most-watched kind of television program in Spanish-speaking countries? It's the telenovela, a Spanish-language soap opera. Televised in the prime evening hours, telenovelas started in the early 1950s and are still popular today. In fact, more telenovelas are shown in Central America and South America than any other type of TV drama. In a 1998 study, more than half the population of Latin American countries said that they watch these shows. Telenovelas are different from American soap operas in the way they are planned and scheduled. Also, they don't have the same kind of plots. Telenovelas' popularity can be seen in their Web sites and by their growth in countries that do not speak Spanish.

Telenovelas are quite different from American Soap Operas. In the United States, there have been some evening soap opera dramas (*dallas* and *dynasty* are good examples), but they have usually been televised once a week; however, telenovelas usually appear Monday through Friday. In the United States, soap operas generally continue for months and years, until viewers stop watching and ratings fall. The writers of an american soap opera do not know how the plot will develop or when it will end. In contrast, telenovelas are usually completely planned at the beginning. In general, a telenovela continues for about eight months, and then it is finished. A new telenovela takes its place.

The plots may seem weird to American viewers. In a typical telenovela, the beautiful heroine is a girl who has no money but has a good heart. The hero—a rich handsome man—rejects his rich but evil girlfriend in favor of the heroine. Eventually, the heroine may turn out to be the secret child of a wealthy family. The unhappy villains may wind up in the cemetery, and the heroine and her hero will live happily ever after. Other telenovelas occur in the past or may deal with modern social problems such as drug abuse, or predjudice. Some telenovelas are really cereal comedies and are more like American sitcoms.

Telenovelas are becomeing more and more popular. There are even Web sites dedicated to popular telenovelas and there actors. For example viewers can go to the Web site called topnovelas to access plot summaries lists of the most popular shows and downloads of episodes. Although telenovelas started in Spanish-speaking countries they have spread to other countries. The first telenovela to be translated into another language was "The Rich Cry too" (Los Ricos También Lloran) which was first produced in Mexico in nineteen seventy-nine and was brought to, China, the Soviet Union and the United States. Other places where telenovelas are popular include the following countries; france israel japan, malaysia Singapore and indonesia.

The popularity of the telenovela in the United states is only partly a reflection of its' millions of spanish speaking people. While it is true that networks want hispanic viewers it is also true that the format and subject matter truely interrest English-speaking viewers. Its quite possable that the once a week format of most american TV shows may be a thing of the past and that telenovelas in English will soon appear every night.

38 Reading Critically

Reading is essential in all your college courses. To get the most out of your reading, you should approach the books, articles, and Web pages you read in a practical way, always asking yourself what information they can offer you. You should also approach assigned readings critically, just as you approach your own writing when you revise.

Reading critically does not mean challenging or arguing with every idea, but it does mean wondering, commenting, questioning, and judging. Most of all, it means being an active rather than a passive reader. Being an **active reader** means participating in the reading process: approaching a reading assignment with a clear understanding of your purpose, previewing a selection, highlighting and annotating it, and perhaps outlining it—all *before* you begin to respond in writing to what you have read.

To gain an understanding of your **purpose**—your reason for reading—you should start by answering some questions.

QUESTIONS ABOUT YOUR PURPOSE

- Why are you reading?
- Will you be expected to discuss what you are reading? If so, will you discuss it in class or in a conference with your instructor?
- Will you have to write about what you are reading? If so, will you be expected to write an informal response (for example, a journal entry) or a more formal one (for example, an essay)?
- Will you be tested on the material?

Once you understand your purpose, you are ready to begin reading.

38a Previewing

Your first step is to *preview* the material you have been assigned to read. When you **preview**, you try to get a sense of the writer's main idea and key supporting points as well as the general emphasis of the passage. You can begin by focusing on the title, the first paragraph (which often contains a thesis statement or overview), and the last paragraph (which often contains a summary of the writer's points). You should also look for clues to content and emphasis in other **visual signals** (headings, boxes, and so on) as well as in **verbal signals** (the words and phrases the writer uses to indicate which points are stressed and how ideas are arranged).

Previewing: Visual Signals

- Look at the title.
- Look at the opening and closing paragraphs.
- Look at each paragraph's first sentence.
- Look at headings.
- Look at *italicized* and **boldfaced** words.
- Look at numbered lists.
- Look at bulleted lists (like this one).
- Look at graphs, charts, tables, photographs, and so on.

- Look at any information that is boxed.
- Look at any information that is in color.

Previewing: Verbal Signals

- Look for phrases that signal emphasis ("The *primary* reason"; "The *most important* idea").
- Look for repeated words and phrases.
- Look for words that signal addition (*also, in addition, furthermore*).
- Look for words that signal time sequence (*first, after, then, next, finally*).
- Look for words that identify causes and effects (*because, as a result, for this reason*).
- Look for words that introduce examples (*for example, for instance*).
- Look for words that signal comparison (*likewise, similarly*).
- Look for words that signal contrast (*unlike, although, in contrast*).
- Look for words that signal contradiction (*however, on the contrary*).
- Look for words that signal a narrowing of the writer's focus (*in fact, specifically, in other words*).
- Look for words that signal summaries or conclusions (*to sum up, in conclusion*).

Teaching Tip
You may want to review the use of transitional words and phrases to convey different meanings. Refer students to 3d, and have them do Practice 24-6.

When you have finished previewing, you should have a general sense of what the writer wants to communicate.

PRACTICE

38-1 "No Comprendo" ("I Don't Understand") is a newspaper article by Barbara Mujica, a professor of Spanish at Georgetown University in Washington, D.C. In this article, which was published in the *New York Times*, Mujica argues against bilingual education (teaching students in their native language as well as in English).

In preparation for class discussion and for other activities that will be assigned later in this chapter, preview the article. As you read, try to identify the writer's main idea and key supporting points, and then write them on the lines that follow the article on page 648.

Teaching Tip
Direct students' attention to this essay's title, thesis statement, topic sentences, and opening and closing paragraphs.

No Comprendo

Last spring, my niece phoned me in tears. She was graduating from high school and had to make a decision. An outstanding soccer player, she was offered athletic scholarships by several colleges. So why was she crying? 1

My niece came to the United States from South America as a child. Although she had received good grades in her schools in Miami, she spoke English with a heavy accent, and her comprehension and writing skills were deficient. She was afraid that once she left the Miami environment, she would feel uncomfortable and, worse still, have difficulty keeping up with class work. 2

Programs that keep foreign-born children in Spanish-language class- 3
rooms for years are only part of the problem. During a visit to my niece's
former school, I observed that all business, not just teaching, was conducted
in Spanish. In the office, secretaries spoke to the administrators and the
children in Spanish. Announcements over the public-address system were
made in an English so fractured that it was almost incomprehensible.

I asked my niece's mother why, after years in public schools, her 4
daughter had poor English skills. "It's the whole environment," she replied.
"All kinds of services are available in Spanish or Spanglish.[1] Sports and
after-school activities are conducted in Spanglish. That's what the kids
hear on the radio and in the street."

Until recently, immigrants made learning English a priority. But even 5
when they didn't learn English themselves, their children grew up speaking it. Thousands of first-generation Americans still strive to learn English,
but others face reduced educational and career opportunities because they
have not mastered this basic skill they need to get ahead.

According to the 1990 census, 40 percent of the Hispanics born in the 6
United States do not graduate from high school, and the Department of
Education says that a lack of proficiency in English is an important factor
in the drop-out rate.

People and agencies that favor providing services only in foreign 7
languages want to help people who do not speak English, but they may be
doing these people a disservice by condemning them to a linguistic ghetto
from which they cannot easily escape.

And my niece? She turned down all of her scholarship opportunities, 8
deciding instead to attend a small college in Miami, where she will never
have to put her English to the test.

Writer's main idea

Because Hispanics are not being encouraged to learn English, their opportunities

are limited.

Key supporting points

1. *Writer's niece is afraid to go to college away from Miami.*

2. *Foreign-born students are kept in Spanish-language classes.*

3. *Many services are provided in Spanish.*

4. *Many Hispanics do not graduate from high school.*

38b Highlighting

After previewing the assigned material, read through it carefully, *highlighting* as you read. **Highlighting** means using underlining and symbols to
identify key ideas. This active reading strategy will help you understand
the writer's ideas and make connections among them when you reread.

---

1. A mixture of Spanish and English.

Be selective; don't highlight too much. Remember, you will eventually be rereading every highlighted word, phrase, and sentence—so highlight only the most important, most useful information.

> ### Using Highlighting Symbols
>
> - <u>Underline</u> key ideas—for example, topic sentences.
> - Box or circle words or phrases you want to remember.
> - Place a check mark (✓) or star (∗) next to an important idea.
> - Place a double check mark (✓✓) or double star (∗∗) next to an especially significant idea.
> - Draw lines or arrows to connect related ideas.
> - Put a question mark (?) beside a word or idea that you need to look up.
> - Number the writer's key supporting points or examples.

FYI

Knowing What to Highlight

You want to highlight what's important—but how do you *know* what's important? As a general rule, you should look for the same **visual signals** you looked for when you did your previewing. Many of the ideas you will need to highlight will probably be found in material that is visually set off from the rest of the text—opening and closing paragraphs, lists, and so on.

Also, continue to look for **verbal signals**—words and phrases like *however, therefore, another reason, the most important point,* and so on—that often introduce key points. Together, these visual and verbal signals will give you clues to the writer's meaning and emphasis.

Here is how one student highlighted an excerpt from a newspaper column, "Barbie at Thirty-Five" by Anna Quindlen.

But consider the recent study at the University of Arizona investigating the <u>attitudes of white and black teenage girls toward body image</u>. The ∗ attitudes of the white girls were a nightmare. Ninety percent expressed ✓ <u>dissatisfaction with their own bodies</u>, and many said they saw dieting as a kind of all-purpose panacea. "I think the reason I would diet would be to gain self-confidence," said one. "I'd feel like it was a way of getting control," said another. And they were curiously united in their description of the perfect girl. She's 5 feet 7 inches, weighs just over 100 pounds, has long legs and flowing hair. The researchers concluded, "The ideal girl was a living manifestation of the Barbie doll."

While white girls described an impossible ideal, black teenagers talked about appearance in terms of style, attitude, pride, and personality. White respondents talked "thin," black ones "shapely." Seventy percent of the black teenagers said they were satisfied with their weight, and there was ✓ little emphasis on dieting. "We're all brought up and taught to be realistic about life," said one, "and we don't look at things the way you want them to be. You look at them the way they are."

The student who highlighted the passage above was preparing to write an essay about eating disorders. Because the passage included no visual signals apart from the paragraph divisions, she looked carefully for verbal signals.

The student began her highlighting by underlining and starring the writer's main idea. She then boxed the names of the two key groups the passage compares—*white girls* and *black teenagers*—and underlined two phrases that illustrate how the attitudes of the two groups differ (*dissatisfaction with their own bodies* and *satisfied with their weight*). Check marks in the margin remind the student of the importance of these two phrases, and arrows connect each phrase to the appropriate group of girls.

The student also circled three related terms that characterize white girls' attitudes—*perfect girl, Barbie doll,* and *impossible ideal*—drawing lines to connect them. Finally, she circled the unfamiliar word *panacea* and put a question mark above it to remind herself to look up the word's meaning.

PRACTICE

38-2   Review the highlighted passage on pages 649–50. How would your own highlighting of this passage be similar to or different from the sample student highlighting?

PRACTICE

38-3   Reread "No Comprendo" (pp. 647–48). As you reread, highlight the article by underlining and starring main ideas, boxing and circling key words, checkmarking important points, and drawing lines and arrows to connect related ideas. Be sure to circle each unfamiliar word and to put a question mark above it.

38c Annotating

As you highlight, you should also *annotate* what you are reading. **Annotating** a passage means reading critically and making notes—of questions, reactions, reminders, and ideas for writing or discussion—in the margins or between the lines. (If you run out of room on the page, you can use sticky notes.) Keeping an informal record of ideas as they occur to you will prepare you for class discussion and for writing.

As you read, asking the following questions will help you make useful annotations.

Teaching Tip
Encourage students to write notes in the margin as they read, even if a thought seems irrelevant. Such notes are often useful for class discussion.

Questions for Critical Reading

- What is the writer saying? What do you think the writer is suggesting or implying? What makes you think so?
- What is the writer's purpose (his or her reason for writing)?
- What kind of audience is the writer addressing?
- Is the writer responding to another writer's ideas?
- What is the writer's main idea?
- How does the writer support his or her points? Does the writer use facts? Opinions? Both?
- What kind of supporting details and examples does the writer use?
- Does the writer include enough supporting details and examples?
- What pattern of development does the writer use to arrange his or her ideas? Is this pattern the best choice?
- Does the writer seem well informed? Reasonable? Fair?
- Do you understand the writer's vocabulary?
- Do you understand the writer's ideas?
- Do you agree with the points the writer is making?
- How are the ideas presented in this reading selection like (or unlike) those presented in other selections you have read?

Teaching Tip
Refer students to 2b for more on purpose and audience.

Teaching Tip
Refer students to Chapter 16 for more on patterns of essay development.

The following passage, which reproduces the student's highlighting from pages 649–50, also illustrates her annotations.

But consider the recent study at the University of Arizona investigating the attitudes of white and black teenage girls toward body image. The attitudes of the white girls were a nightmare. Ninety percent expressed dissatisfaction with their own bodies, and many said they saw dieting as

= cure-all

Need for control,
perfection. Why?
Media? Parents?

Barbie doll
= plastic, unreal

"Thin" vs. "shapely"
Only 30% dissatisfied—
but 90% of white girls

a kind of all-purpose panacea. "I think the reason I would diet would be to gain self-confidence," said one. "I'd feel like it was a way of getting control," said another. And they were curiously united in their description of the perfect girl. She's 5 feet 7 inches, weighs just over 100 pounds, has long legs and flowing hair. The researchers concluded, "The ideal girl was a living manifestation of the Barbie doll."

While white girls described an impossible ideal, black teenagers talked about appearance in terms of style, attitude, pride, and personality. White respondents talked "thin," black ones "shapely." Seventy percent of the black teenagers said they were satisfied with their weight, and there was little emphasis on dieting. "We're all brought up and taught to be realistic about life," said one, "and we don't look at things the way you want them to be. You look at them the way they are." vs. Barbie doll (= unrealistic)

overgeneralization?

In her annotations, this student wrote down the meaning of the word *panacea*, put the study's conclusions and the contrasting statistics into her own words, and recorded questions she intended to explore further.

PRACTICE
38-4   Reread "No Comprendo" (pp. 647–48). As you reread, refer to the Questions for Critical Reading (p. 651), and use them to guide you as you write down your own thoughts and questions in the margins of the article. Note where you agree or disagree with the writer, and briefly explain why. Quickly summarize any points you think are particularly important. Take time to look up any unfamiliar words you have circled and to write brief definitions. Think of these annotations as your preparation for discussing the article in class and eventually writing about it.

PRACTICE
38-5   Trade workbooks with another student, and read over his or her highlighting and annotating of "No Comprendo." How are your written responses similar to the other student's? How are they different? Do your classmate's responses help you see anything new about the article?

Teaching Tip
Ask students to consider whether they believe "No Comprendo" includes any biased assumptions about Hispanics or about bilingual education.

38d   Outlining

Outlining is another technique you can use to help you understand a reading assignment. Unlike a **formal outline**, which follows strict conventions, an **informal outline** enables you to record a passage's ideas in the order in which they are presented. After you have made an informal outline of a passage, you should be able to see the writer's emphasis (which ideas are more important than others) as well as how the ideas are related.

Teaching Tip
Tell students that formal outlines can help them keep track of ideas in long essays or research papers. Refer them to 13f and 17f for examples of formal outlines.

FYI

Constructing an Informal Outline

To construct an informal outline, follow these guidelines:

1. Write or type the passage's main idea at the top of a sheet of paper. (This will remind you of the writer's focus and help keep your outline on track.)

2. At the left margin, write down the most important idea of the first body paragraph or first part of the passage.

3. Indent the next line a few spaces, and list the examples or details that support this idea. (You can use your computer's Tab key to help you set up your outline.)

4. As ideas become more specific, indent further. (Ideas that have the same degree of importance are indented the same distance from the left margin.)

5. Repeat the process with each body paragraph or part of the passage.

The student who highlighted and annotated the excerpt from Anna Quindlen's "Barbie at Thirty-Five" (pp. 649–50 and 651–52) made the following informal outline to help her understand the writer's ideas.

Teaching Tip
Refer students to 2f and 13f for additional examples of informal outlines.

Main idea: Black and white teenage girls have very different attitudes about their body images.

White girls dissatisfied
    90% dissatisfied with appearance
    Dieting = cure-all
        –self-confidence
        –control
    Ideal = unrealistic
        –tall and thin
        –Barbie doll

Black girls satisfied
    70% satisfied with weight
    Dieting not important
    Ideal = realistic
        –shapely
        –not thin

PRACTICE

38-6 Working on your own or in a small group, make an informal outline of "No Comprendo" (pp. 647–48). Refer to your highlighting and annotations as you construct your outline. When you have finished, check to make certain your outline accurately represents the writer's emphasis and the relationships among her ideas.

38e Summarizing

Once you have highlighted, annotated, and outlined a passage, you may want to *summarize* it to help you understand it better. A **summary** retells, *in your own words*, what a passage is about. A summary condenses a passage, so it leaves out all but the main idea and perhaps the key supporting points. A summary omits supporting examples and details, and it does *not* include your own ideas or opinions.

To summarize a reading assignment, follow these guidelines:

1. Review your outline.

2. Consulting your outline, restate the passage's main idea *in your own words*.

3. Consulting your outline, restate the passage's key supporting points. Add transitional words and phrases between sentences where necessary.

4. Reread the original passage to make sure you have not left out anything significant.

Note: To avoid accidentally using the exact language of the original, do not look at the passage while you are writing your summary. If you want to use a distinctive word or phrase from the original passage, put it in quotation marks.

The student who highlighted, annotated, and outlined the excerpt from "Barbie at Thirty-Five" (pp. 649–53) wrote the following summary.

> As Anna Quindlen reports in "Barbie at Thirty-Five," a University of Arizona study found that black and white teenage girls have very different attitudes about their body images. Almost all white girls said they were dissatisfied with their appearance. To them, the "perfect girl" would look like a Barbie doll (tall and very thin). Quindlen sees this attitude as unrealistic. Black girls in the study, however, were generally happy with their weight. They did not say they wanted to be thin; they said they wanted to be "shapely."

PRACTICE

38-7 Write a brief summary of "No Comprendo" (pp. 647–48). Use your outline to guide you, and keep your summary short and to the point. Your summary should be about one-quarter to one-third the length of the original article.

38f Writing a Response Paragraph

Once you have highlighted and annotated a reading selection, you are ready to write about it—perhaps in a **response paragraph** in which you record your informal reactions to the writer's ideas.

Because a response paragraph is informal, no special guidelines or rules govern its format or structure. As in any paragraph, however, you should include a topic sentence, support the topic sentence with examples and details, use complete sentences, and link sentences with appropriate transitions. In a response paragraph, informal style and personal opinions are acceptable.

The student who highlighted, annotated, outlined, and summarized the Quindlen passage wrote the following response paragraph.

> Why are white and black girls' body images so different? Why do black girls think it's okay to be "shapely" while white girls want to be thin? Maybe it's because music videos and movies and fashion magazines show so many more white models, all half-starved, with perfect hair and legs. Or maybe white girls get different messages from their parents or from the people they date. Do white and black girls' attitudes about their bodies stay the same when they get older? And what about <u>male</u> teenagers' self-images? Do white and black <u>guys</u> have different body images too?

The process of writing this paragraph was very helpful to the student. The questions she asked suggested some interesting ideas that she could explore in class discussion or in a more fully developed piece of writing.

PRACTICE

38-8 Write a response paragraph expressing your reactions to "No Comprendo" (pp. 647–48) and to the issue of bilingual education.

38g Reading in the Classroom, in the Community, and in the Workplace

In college, in your life as a citizen of your community, and in the workplace, you will read material in a variety of different formats—for example, textbooks, newspapers, Web pages, and job-related memos, letters, emails, and reports.

Teaching Tip
Refer students to Chapters 2 and 3 for more on writing a paragraph.

Teaching Tip
Remind students that contractions are acceptable here only because this is an informal paragraph.

Although the active reading process you have just reviewed can be applied to all kinds of material, various kinds of reading require slightly different strategies during the previewing stage. One reason for this is that different kinds of reading may have different purposes: to present information, to persuade, and so on. Another reason is that the various documents you read are aimed at different audiences, and different readers require different signals about content and emphasis. For these reasons, you need to look for different kinds of verbal and visual signals when you preview different kinds of reading material.

Reading Textbooks

Much of the reading you do in college is in textbooks (like this one). The purpose of a textbook is to present information, and when you read a textbook, your goal is to understand that information. To do this, you need to figure out which ideas are most important as well as which points support those key ideas and which examples illustrate them.

checklist

Reading Textbooks

Look for the following features as you preview:

- [ ] **Boldfaced** and *italicized* words, which can indicate terms to be defined

- [ ] Boxed checklists or summaries, which may appear at the ends of sections or chapters

- [ ] Bulleted or numbered lists, which may list key reasons or examples or summarize important material

- [ ] Diagrams, charts, tables, graphs, photographs, and other visuals that illustrate the writer's points

- [ ] Marginal quotations and definitions

- [ ] Marginal cross-references

- [ ] Web links

PRACTICE
38-9

Using the checklist above as a guide, preview the following page from the textbook *Technical Communication*, Ninth Edition (2009), by Michael Markel. When you have finished, highlight and annotate the page.

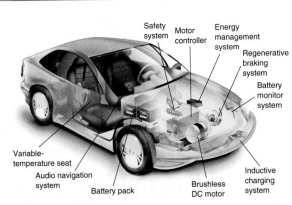

Safety system
Motor controller
Energy management system
Regenerative braking system
Battery monitor system
Variable-temperature seat
Audio navigation system
Battery pack
Brushless DC motor
Inductive charging system

The batteries are red. The warm red contrasts effectively with the cool green of the car body.

Figure 12.6 Colors Have Clear Associations for Readers

In using color in graphics and page design, keep these principles in mind:

- *Take advantage of any symbolic meanings colors may already have.* In American culture, for example, red signals danger, heat, or electricity; yellow signals caution; and orange signals warning. Using these warm colors in ways that depart from their familiar meanings could be confusing. The cooler colors—blues and greens—are more conservative and subtle. (Figure 12.6 illustrates these principles.) Keep in mind, however, that different cultures interpret colors differently.

- *Be aware that color can obscure or swallow up text.*

▷ **In This Book**
For more about cultural patterns, see Ch. 5, p. 96.

If you are using print against a colored background, you might need to make the type a little bigger, because color makes text look smaller.

Text printed against a white background looks bigger than the same size text printed against a colored background. White letters counteract this effect.

Is this text the same size?	Is this text the same size?

This line of type appears to reach out to the reader.
This line of type appears to recede into the background.

CHOOSING THE APPROPRIATE KIND OF GRAPHIC

Graphics used in technical documents fall into two categories: tables and figures. Tables are lists of data, usually numbers, arranged in columns. Figures are everything else: graphs, charts, diagrams, photographs, and the like. Typically, tables and figures are numbered separately: the first table in a document is Table 1; the first figure is Figure 1. In documents of more than one chapter (like this book), the graphics are usually numbered within each chapter. That is, Figure 3.2 is the second figure in Chapter 3.

Reading News Articles

As a student, as an employee, and as a citizen, you read school, community, local, and national newspapers in print and online. Like textbooks, news articles communicate information. In addition, newspapers also publish editorials (which aim to persuade) as well as feature articles (which may be designed to entertain as well as to inform).

Many people read news articles online rather than in print form. If this is what you usually do, keep in mind that newspaper Web pages tend to be very busy and crowded, so you may have to work hard to distinguish important information from not-so-important material. For example, a

Teaching Tip
Tell students that many newspapers can be found online.

news article that you read online may be surrounded by advertising and include links to irrelevant (and potentially distracting) material—such as Facebook pages. For this reason, it is very important to read online material with care.

checklist

Reading News Articles

Look for the following features as you preview:

☐ Headlines

☐ **Boldfaced** headings within articles

☐ Labels like *editorial, commentary,* or *opinion,* which indicate that an article communicates the writer's own views

☐ Brief biographical information at the end of an opinion piece

☐ Phrases or sentences in **boldface** (to emphasize key points)

☐ The article's first sentence, which often answers the questions *who, what, why, where, when,* and *how*

☐ The **dateline**, which tells you the date and the city the writer is reporting from

☐ Photographs

☐ In print news articles, related articles that appear on the same page—for example, boxed information and **sidebars**, short articles that provide additional background on people and places mentioned in the article

☐ In online news articles, links to related articles, reader comments, and other useful material

Teaching Tip
You may want to tell students that an *op-ed piece* expresses the opinion of an individual writer who may not be associated with the publication's full-time staff. "Op-ed" stands for *opposite editorial* because of its traditional position opposite the editorial page in the newspaper.

PRACTICE

38-10 Using the checklist above as a guide, preview the excerpt from an online news article shown on pages 659–60. Then, highlight and annotate it.

HOME PAGE   TODAY'S PAPER   VIDEO   MOST POPULAR   TIMES TOPICS

The New York Times

U.S.

WORLD   U.S.   N.Y. / REGION   BUSINESS   TECHNOLOGY   SCIENCE   HEALTH   SPORTS   OPINION

POLITICS   EDUCATION   BAY AREA   CHICAGO   TEXAS

As Bullies Go Digital, Parents Play Catch-Up

By JAN HOFFMAN
Published: December 4, 2010

Ninth grade was supposed to be a fresh start for Marie's son: new school, new children. Yet by last October, he had become withdrawn. Marie prodded. And prodded again. Finally, he told her.

 Enlarge This Image

In sixth grade, Sierra received a text message identifying her as the slashed figure in the drawing above.

Poisoned Web

Trying to Provide a Safety Net

This is the second in a series of articles on Internet bullying.

· Go to Previous Article in Series

Online Safety Resources for Families

Family Online Safety Institute

Connect Safely

Connect Safely: Parents' Guide to Facebook

Commonsense Media: Cyberbullying Tips

Stop Cyberbullying: Guide to Reporting Abuses

iKeepSafe.org

WebWiseKids

RECOMMEND

TWITTER

COMMENTS (184)

SIGN IN TO E-MAIL

PRINT

SINGLE PAGE

REPRINTS

SHARE

"The kids say I'm saying all these nasty things about them on Facebook," he said. "They don't believe me when I tell them I'm not on Facebook."

But apparently, he was.

Marie, a medical technologist and single mother who lives in Newburyport, Mass., searched Facebook. There she found what seemed to be her son's page: his name, a photo of him grinning while running — and, on his public wall, sneering comments about teenagers he scarcely knew.

Someone had forged his identity online and was bullying others in his name.

Students began to shun him. Furious and frightened, Marie contacted school officials. After expressing their concern, they told her they could do nothing. It was an off-campus matter.

But Marie was determined to find out who was making her son miserable and to get them to stop. In choosing that course, she would become a target herself. When she and her son learned who was behind the scheme, they would both feel the sharp sting of betrayal. Undeterred, she would insist that the culprits be punished.

(continued on next page)

(continued from previous page)

Related

A Range of Options for a Victim's Parents (December 5, 2010)

Times Topic: Cyberbullying

🔍 Enlarge This Image

Richard Perry/The New York Times

WORDS OF WARNING Jill Brown of Generation Text speaks to parents about cyberbullying. A friend snubbed her for trying to intervene in an online incident.

🏳 Readers' Comments

Readers shared their thoughts on this article.

Read All Comments (184) »

It is difficult enough to support one's child through a siege of schoolyard bullying. But the lawlessness of the Internet, its potential for casual, breathtaking cruelty, and its capacity to cloak a bully's identity all present slippery new challenges to this transitional generation of analog parents.

Desperate to protect their children, parents are floundering even as they scramble to catch up with the technological sophistication of the next generation.

Like Marie, many parents turn to schools, only to be rebuffed because officials think they do not have the authority to intercede. Others may call the police, who set high bars to investigate. Contacting Web site administrators or Internet service providers can be a daunting, protracted process.

When parents know the aggressor, some may contact that child's parent, stumbling through an evolving etiquette in the landscape of social awkwardness. Going forward, they struggle with when and how to supervise their adolescents' forays on the Internet.

Marie, who asked that her middle name and her own nickname for her son, D.C., be used to protect his identity, finally went to the police. The force's cybercrimes specialist, Inspector Brian Brunault, asked if she really wanted to pursue the matter.

"He said that once it was in the court system," Marie said, "they would have to prosecute. It could probably be someone we knew, like a friend of D.C.'s or a neighbor. Was I prepared for that?"

Marie's son urged her not to go ahead. But Marie was adamant. "I said yes."

Parental Fears

One afternoon last spring, Parry Aftab, a lawyer and expert on cyberbullying, addressed seventh graders at George Washington Middle School in Ridgewood, N.J.

"How many of you have ever been cyberbullied?" she asked.

The hands crept up, first a scattering, then a thicket. Of 150 students, 68 raised their hands. They came forward to offer rough tales from social networking sites, instant messaging and texting. Ms. Aftab stopped them at the 20th example.

Then she asked: How many of your parents know how to help you?

A scant three or four hands went up.

Cyberbullying is often legally defined as repeated harassment online, although in popular use, it can describe even a sharp-elbowed, gratuitous swipe. Cyberbullies themselves resist easy categorization: the anonymity of the Internet gives cover not only to schoolyard-bully types but to victims themselves, who feel they can retaliate without getting caught.

But online bullying can be more psychologically savage than schoolyard bullying. The Internet erases inhibitions, with adolescents often going further with slights online than in person.

Reading on the Job

In your workplace, you will be called on to read memos, letters, emails, and reports. These documents, which may be designed to convey information or to persuade, are often addressed to a group rather than to a single person. (Note that the most important information is often presented *first*—in a subject line or in the first paragraph.)

checklist ——————————————

Reading on the Job

Look for the following features as you preview:

☐ Numbered or bulleted lists of tasks or problems (numbers indicate the order of the items' importance)

☐ In an email, links to the Web

☐ In a memo or an email, the person or persons addressed

☐ In a memo or an email, the subject line

☐ In a memo or a report, headings that might highlight key topics or points

☐ The first and last paragraphs and the first sentence of each body paragraph, which often contain key information

☐ **Boldfaced**, underlined, or *italicized* words

PRACTICE
38-11
Read the memo on page 662. What is the writer's purpose? What is the most important piece of information she wants to communicate? Highlight and annotate the memo, and then write a two-sentence summary of it.

Memorandum

To: Clark F. Davis, Executive Director
From: Lucia Ramos, Director, Drug and Alcohol Program
Re: Lisa Williams, candidate for Case Manager position

Attached is the résumé of Ms. Lisa Williams, who is applying for the position of Case Manager in our drug treatment program.

Ms. Williams is well qualified for this position. She has a BA from LaSalle University, where she majored in sociology and criminal justice; she has met the requirements for the Certified Addiction Counselor (CAC) certificate; and she has worked as an administrative assistant in an engineering firm. In addition, she projects a very professional image.

In some ways, Ms. Williams is overqualified for the position, but I believe that the experience she will get as a Case Manager will make her valuable to the further development of our drug and alcohol program. She will be able to take on the role of counselor during worker absences as well as provide a backup in case of the departure of the current drug and alcohol coordinator.

I believe Ms. Williams will contribute a great deal to our program, and I recommend that we offer her the position.

CC: Cynthia Logue, Human Resources Director

review checklist

Reading Critically

- [ ] Preview the material. (See 38a.)
- [ ] Highlight the material. (See 38b.)
- [ ] Annotate the material. (See 38c.)
- [ ] Outline the material. (See 38d.)
- [ ] Summarize the material. (See 38e.)
- [ ] Write a response paragraph. (See 38f.)
- [ ] Use active reading strategies in the classroom, in the community, and in the workplace. (See 38g.)

39 Readings for Writers

preview

In this chapter, you will learn to react critically to essays by professional writers.

The following nineteen essays by professional writers offer interesting material to read, react to, think critically about, discuss, and write about. In addition, these essays illustrate some of the ways you can organize ideas in your own writing.

The essays in this chapter use the nine patterns of development you learned about in Units 1 through 3 of this book: exemplification, narration, description, process, cause and effect, comparison and contrast, classification, definition, and argument. Of course, these patterns are not your only options for arranging ideas in essays; in fact, many essays combine several patterns of development. Still, understanding how each of these nine patterns works will help you choose the most effective organization strategy when you are writing for a particular purpose and audience.

In this chapter, two essays by professional writers illustrate each pattern of development. (For argument, three model essays are included.) Each essay is preceded by a short **headnote**, an introduction that tells you something about the writer and suggests what to look for as you read. Following each selection are five sets of questions. (Questions that you can work on in collaboration with other students are marked with an **asterisk** [*].)

Teaching Tip
Refer students to Chapters 4 through 12 for information on using various patterns for developing paragraphs and to Chapter 16 for information on writing essays that use these patterns of development.

- **Reacting to the Reading** questions suggest guidelines for previewing, highlighting, and annotating the essay.
- **Reacting to Words** questions focus on the writer's language.
- **Reacting to Ideas** questions encourage you to respond critically to the writer's ideas and perhaps to consider his or her audience or purpose.
- **Reacting to the Pattern** questions ask you to consider how ideas are arranged within the essay and how they are connected to one another.
- **Writing Practice** suggestions give you opportunities to explore writing ideas and organizational strategies related to the chapter's readings.

As you read each of the following essays, **preview**, **highlight**, and **annotate** it to help you understand the writer's ideas and emphasis. (See pp. 646–52 for advice on previewing, highlighting, and annotating.) Then, read the essay again carefully in preparation for class discussion and writing.

Teaching Tip
Refer students to Chapter 38 for more on previewing, highlighting, and annotating.

39a Exemplification

Teaching Tip
Refer students to 16a for more on how to write an exemplification essay.

An **exemplification** essay uses specific examples to support a thesis statement. The two selections that follow, "Don't Call Me a Hot Tamale" by Judith Ortiz Cofer and "Around the World, Women Are on the Move" by Richard Rodriguez, are examples of exemplification essays.

DON'T CALL ME A HOT TAMALE

Judith Ortiz Cofer

Teaching Tip
Remind students to familiarize themselves with the end-of-essay questions before they read the essay.

Award-winning poet, novelist, and essayist Judith Ortiz Cofer often writes about her experiences as a Latina—a Hispanic woman—living in a non-Hispanic culture. In 1998, Cofer received the Christ-Janner Award in Creative Research from the University of Georgia, where she is now professor of English and Creative Writing. In "Don't Call Me a Hot Tamale," an excerpt from her book *The Latin Deli: Prose and Poetry* (1993), she discusses how being Puerto Rican has affected her in the world beyond Puerto Rico. As you read, note how her examples illustrate the stereotypes she encounters in reaction to both her heritage and her gender.

On a bus to London from Oxford University, where I was earning some graduate credits one summer, a young man, obviously fresh from a pub, approached my seat. With both hands over his heart, he went down on his knees in the aisle and broke into an Irish tenor's rendition of "Maria" from *West Side Story*. I was not amused. "Maria" had followed me to London, reminding me of a prime fact of my life: You can leave the island of Puerto Rico, master the English language, and travel as far as you can, but if you're a Latina, especially one who so clearly belongs to Rita Moreno's[1] gene pool, the island travels with you.

ESL Tip
In choosing essays to assign, consider the nonnative-speaking students in your class. For example, assigning an essay by a Latino writer may help draw in students whose first language is Spanish.

Growing up in New Jersey and wanting most of all to belong, I lived in two completely different worlds. My parents designed our life as a microcosm of their *casas* on the island—we spoke in Spanish, ate Puerto Rican food bought at the *bodega*, and practiced strict Catholicism complete with Sunday mass in Spanish.

I was kept under tight surveillance by my parents, since my virtue and modesty were, by their cultural equation, the same as their honor. As teenagers, my friends and I were lectured constantly on how to behave as proper *señoritas*. But it was a conflicting message we received, since our Puerto Rican mothers also encouraged us to look and act like women by dressing us in clothes our Anglo schoolmates and their mothers found too "mature" and flashy. I often felt humiliated when I appeared at an American friend's birthday party wearing a dress more suitable for a semiformal. At Puerto Rican festivities, neither the music nor the colors we wore could be too loud.

I remember Career Day in high school, when our teachers told us to come dressed as if for a job interview. That morning, I agonized in front of my closet, trying to figure out what a "career girl" would wear, because the only model I had was Marlo Thomas[2] on TV. To me and my Puerto Rican girlfriends, dressing up meant wearing our mother's ornate jewelry and clothing.

At school that day, the teachers assailed us for wearing "everything at once"—meaning too much jewelry and too many accessories. And it was painfully obvious that the other students in their tailored skirts and silk blouses thought we were hopeless and vulgar. The way they looked at us was a taste of the cultural clash that awaited us in the real world, where prospective employers and men on the street would often misinterpret our tight skirts and bright colors as a come-on.

It is custom, not chromosomes, that leads us to choose scarlet over pale pink. Our mothers had grown up on a tropical island where the natural environment was a riot of primary colors, where showing your skin was one way to keep cool as well as to look sexy. On the island, women felt freer to dress and move provocatively since they were protected by the traditions and laws of a Spanish/Catholic system of morality and machismo, the main rule of which was: *You may look at my sister, but if you touch her I will kill you.* The extended family and church structure provided them with a circle of safety on the island; if a man "wronged" a girl, everyone would close in to save her family honor.

Off-island, signals often get mixed. When a Puerto Rican girl who is dressed in her idea of what is attractive meets a man from the mainstream

---

1. A Puerto Rican actress, dancer, and singer. She is well known for her role in the movie musical *West Side Story*, a version of Shakespeare's *Romeo and Juliet* featuring Anglos and Puerto Ricans in New York City.
2. Star of a 1966–71 television comedy about a young woman living on her own in New York City.

culture who has been trained to react to certain types of clothing as a sexual signal, a clash is likely to take place. She is seen as a Hot Tamale, a sexual firebrand. I learned this lesson at my first formal dance when my date leaned over and painfully planted a sloppy, overeager kiss on my mouth. When I didn't respond with sufficient passion, he said in a resentful tone: "I thought you Latin girls were supposed to mature early." It was only the first time I would feel like a fruit or vegetable—I was supposed to *ripen*, not just grow into womanhood like other girls.

These stereotypes, though rarer, still surface in my life. I recently stayed at a classy metropolitan hotel. After having dinner with a friend, I was returning to my room when a middle-aged man in a tuxedo stepped directly into my path. With his champagne glass extended toward me, he exclaimed, "Evita!"[3]   8

Blocking my way, he bellowed the song "Don't Cry for Me, Argentina." Playing to the gathering crowd, he began to sing loudly a ditty to the tune of "La Bamba"[4]—except the lyrics were about a girl named Maria whose exploits all rhymed with her name and gonorrhea.   9

I knew that this same man—probably a corporate executive, even worldly by most standards—would never have regaled a white woman with a dirty song in public. But to him, I was just a character in his universe of "others," all cartoons.   10

Still, I am one of the lucky ones. There are thousands of Latinas without the privilege of the education that my parents gave me. For them every day is a struggle against the misconceptions perpetuated by the myth of the Latina as whore, domestic worker or criminal.   11

Rather than fight these pervasive stereotypes, I try to replace them with a more interesting set of realities. I travel around the U.S. reading from my books of poetry and my novel. With the stories I tell, the dreams and fears I examine in my work, I try to get my audience past the particulars of my skin color, my accent or my clothes.   12

I once wrote a poem in which I called Latinas "God's brown daughters." It is really a prayer, of sorts, for communication and respect. In it, Latin women pray "in Spanish to an Anglo God / with a Jewish heritage," and they are "fervently hoping / that if not omnipotent, / at least He be bilingual."   13

Reacting to the Reading

1. Underline the essay's thesis statement.
2. In the margins of the essay, number the examples Cofer uses to support this thesis.

Reacting to Words

*1. Define these words: *tamale* (title), *rendition* (paragraph 1), *microcosm* (2), *ornate* (4), *assailed* (5), *riot* (6), *machismo* (6), *firebrand* (7), *regaled* (10), *perpetuated* (11), *pervasive* (12), *omnipotent* (13). Can you suggest a synonym for each word that will work in the essay?

3. Eva Perón, wife of Juan Perón, president of Argentina in the 1940s and 1950s. She is the subject of the musical *Evita*.
4. A song with Spanish lyrics popular in the late 1950s.

2. What does the phrase *hot tamale* suggest to you? What do you think Cofer intends it to suggest? Can you think of another word or phrase that might be more effective?

Reacting to Ideas

*1. Cofer states her thesis in paragraph 1: "You can leave the island of Puerto Rico, master the English language, and travel as far as you can, but if you're a Latina, . . . the island travels with you." Restate this thesis in your own words. Do you think this statement applies only to Latinas or to members of other ethnic groups as well? Explain.

2. How, according to Cofer, are the signals sent by dress and appearance interpreted differently in Puerto Rico and "off-island" (paragraph 7)? How does this difference create problems for Cofer? Do you think there is anything she can do to avoid these problems?

Teaching Tip
Remind students to answer all questions in complete sentences.

Reacting to the Pattern

1. What examples does Cofer use to support her thesis? Do you think she supplies enough examples to convince readers that her thesis is reasonable?

2. Cofer begins her essay with an example. Do you think this is an effective opening strategy? Why or why not? How else might she have begun her essay?

3. All of Cofer's examples are personal experiences. Are they as convincing as statistics or examples from current news articles would be? Are they *more* convincing? Explain.

Writing Practice

1. What positive examples can you think of to counteract the stereotype of the Latina as "whore, domestic worker or criminal" (paragraph 11)? Write a letter to a television network in which you propose the addition of several different Latina characters to actual programs in which they might appear.

2. What do you think Cofer can do to avoid being stereotyped? Write an essay that gives examples of specific things she might do to change the way others see her. In your thesis, state why she should (or should not) make these changes.

3. Do you think others stereotype you because of your heritage—or because of your age, your gender, your dress, or where you live? Write an essay in which you discuss some specific instances of such stereotyping.

Teaching Tip
Before assigning Writing Practice 2, discuss with the class whether or not they believe Cofer *should* take steps to change how others see her. (You can also have this discussion after students finish the assignment.)

AROUND THE WORLD, WOMEN ARE ON THE MOVE

Richard Rodriguez

Richard Rodriguez, a Mexican-American writer whose work explores the issues of class, race, and ethnicity, is best known for his autobiographical trilogy, which includes *Hunger of Memory* (1982), *Days of Obligation:*

Teaching Tip
Remind students to familiarize themselves with the end-of-essay questions before they read the essay.

An Argument with My Mexican Father (1992), and *Brown: The Last Discovery of America* (2002). In 1997, Rodriguez won a Peabody Award, one of television's highest honors, for the essays on American life that he contributes regularly to PBS's *NewsHour*. "Around the World, Women Are on the Move" first aired on *NewsHour* in 2009. As you read, consider how Rodriguez moves from examples of the gender revolution in America to examples from around the world.

In 1996, President Bill Clinton appointed Madeleine Albright as Secretary of State. Because of Madeleine Albright, because of Condoleezza Rice who came soon after, because of Hillary Clinton, we scarcely mark the gender revolution that has taken place in just over a decade. Today, the diplomatic face of America is a woman's face. [1]

All over the world, women and girls are on the move. In Pakistani and Afghan villages, girls make their way to school, sometimes furtively, wary of boys or men who might splash them with acid for daring to learn to read and to write. In the last half-century, hundreds of thousands of Mexican women have left their villages to find jobs in America or to work in Mexican border town assembly plants. In Ciudad Juárez, hundreds of women who ventured into the world alone have been murdered. The world remains a dangerous place for women. [2]

Even so, at U.S. colleges, female students are signing up for study-abroad programs by a 2-to-1 ratio over males. Indeed, female students, many the daughters and granddaughters of women who did not assume college in their lives, now outnumber male students on American campuses. [3]

In American legend, as in so many of the world's myths, it is the young man who leaves home to find gold or slay the dragon. Lewis and Clark are paradigmatic American explorers, blazing a trail from St. Louis to the Pacific Coast. But as it happened, they were led up the Missouri River and across the Rockies by a Shoshone Indian. Her name was Sacagawea. [4]

In the Americas, there were other stories like hers, native women who became go-betweens, translators, even lovers of the foreign. In colonial Virginia, Pocahontas left her tribe to marry an Englishman, and she traveled with him to London to become a figure in history. In Mexico, male history still reviles Doña Marina, La Malinche, as a sexual traitor. She was an Indian woman who became the lover of the Spaniard Cortés. Marina conspired with Cortés against the Aztecs who had imprisoned her own tribe. [5]

What are we to make of these stories of women moving among cultures and conflict? Today we have the story of Kansas-born Ann Dunham, an anthropologist, whose son is now president of the United States. In interviews, Barack Obama describes his mother as searching but also reckless. Her life was a series of journeys. In Hawaii, white Ann Dunham married a black Kenyan. When their marriage failed, he returned to Africa, which for him was the known world. She ventured outward to Muslim Indonesia. [6]

In American homes when marriages fail, it is usually the husband who disappears. Women become the head of the family, responsible for instilling in sons as well as daughters the meaning of adulthood. Professional [7] athletes, movie stars, convicts, presidents all testify to the importance of single mothers. At last summer's Olympics, the world saw Michael Phelps emerge from the pool after each event to search the crowd for his mother.

The news this evening is of failing male oligarchies on Wall Street. The news this evening is of tribal chieftains at war with modernity. The news is of religious leaders who forbid the ordination of women, even as they stumble from one diplomatic gaffe to another.   8

Throughout history, the world has been largely governed by men. When the male order falters and fails—as it seems now—we would make a mistake if we assumed the world was collapsing. All over the world, millions of women are valiantly venturing far from custom, little girls are walking across the desert to school.   9

Reacting to the Reading

1. Underline the thesis statement of this essay, and place an asterisk [*] in the margin beside it.
2. Put a check mark beside the example that you think most convincingly supports Rodriguez's thesis.

ESL Tip
Have native- and nonnative-speaking students work in groups or in pairs to discuss the exercises before they write their answers.

Reacting to Words

*1. Define these words: *furtively* (paragraph 2), *instilling* (7), *oligarchies* (8), *ordination* (8), *gaffe* (8), *falters* (9), *valiantly* (9). Can you suggest a synonym for each word that will work in the essay?
2. What different meanings could the expression "on the move" (title) have? Which meaning do you think Rodriguez wants to communicate?

Teaching Tip
Students might need help defining words. With nonnative-speaking students, consider going over the definitions in class before assigning the reading.

Reacting to Ideas

1. What failures does Rodriguez suggest men have been responsible for? How does he expect women to solve the problems men have created? Do you think he is right to expect this?
*2. In paragraph 2, Rodriguez says that despite their advances, "The world remains a dangerous place for women." How does he support this statement? Can you give additional examples?
*3. How does paragraph 6, which focuses on President Obama's mother, support Rodriguez's thesis? Do you think the material about single mothers (7) provides good support for his thesis?

Teaching Tip
Remind students to answer all questions in complete sentences.

Reacting to the Pattern

*1. Rodriguez gives many examples to support his thesis. Which examples do you find most convincing? Which do you find least convincing? Why?
2. How are the kinds of examples Rodriguez gives in paragraph 2, paragraph 3, and paragraphs 4–5 different? In other words, why are these different kinds of examples grouped together?

Writing Practice

1. Write an exemplification essay called "In My Family, Women Are on the Move." Support your thesis with specific examples of achievements by the women in your family. You may focus on one example in each body paragraph, or you can combine several related examples in some of your paragraphs.

2. In paragraph 3, Rodriguez presents some information about the progress made by college women. Write an exemplification essay in which you develop this idea further, illustrating the advances and achievements of female students at your school.

39b Narration

Teaching Tip
Refer students to 16b for more on how to write a narrative essay.

A **narrative** essay tells a story by presenting a series of events in chronological order. In the first of the two essays that follow, "The Sanctuary of School," Lynda Barry tells a story about home and family. In the second essay, "My Half-Baked Bubble," Joshuah Bearman recounts an experience from his elementary school days.

THE SANCTUARY OF SCHOOL

Lynda Barry

Teaching Tip
Remind students to familiarize themselves with the end-of-essay questions before they read the essay.

In her many illustrated works—including graphic novels, comic books, and a weekly cartoon strip, "Ernie Pook's Comeek," which appears in a number of newspapers and magazines—Lynda Barry looks at the world through the eyes of children. Her characters remind adult readers of the complicated world of young people and of the clarity with which they see social situations. In "The Sanctuary of School," first published in the *Baltimore Sun* in 1992, Barry tells a story from her own childhood. As you read this essay, note how Barry relates her personal experience to a broader issue.

I was 7 years old the first time I snuck out of the house in the dark. It was winter and my parents had been fighting all night. They were short on money and long on relatives who kept "temporarily" moving into our house because they had nowhere else to go.   1

My brother and I were used to giving up our bedroom. We slept on the couch, something we actually liked because it put us that much closer to the light of our lives, our television.   2

At night when everyone was asleep, we lay on our pillows watching it with the sound off. We watched Steve Allen's mouth moving. We watched Johnny Carson's mouth moving.[1] We watched movies filled with gangsters shooting machine guns into packed rooms, dying soldiers hurling a last grenade and beautiful women crying at windows. Then the sign-off finally came and we tried to sleep.   3

1. Steve Allen and Johnny Carson were late-night television hosts.

The morning I snuck out, I woke up filled with a panic about needing to get to school. The sun wasn't quite up yet but my anxiety was so fierce that I just got dressed, walked quietly across the kitchen and let myself out the back door.

4

It was quiet outside. Stars were still out. Nothing moved and no one was in the street. It was as if someone had turned the sound off on the world.

5

I walked the alley, breaking thin ice over the puddles with my shoes. I didn't know why I was walking to school in the dark. I didn't think about it. All I knew was a feeling of panic, like the panic that strikes kids when they realize they are lost.

6

That feeling eased the moment I turned the corner and saw the dark outline of my school at the top of the hill. My school was made up of about 15 nondescript portable classrooms set down on a fenced concrete lot in a rundown Seattle neighborhood, but it had the most beautiful view of the Cascade Mountains. You could see them from anywhere on the playfield and you could see them from the windows of my classroom— Room 2.

7

I walked over to the monkey bars and hooked my arms around the cold metal. I stood for a long time just looking across Rainier Valley. The sky was beginning to whiten and I could hear a few birds.

8

In a perfect world my absence at home would not have gone unnoticed. I would have had two parents in a panic to locate me, instead of two parents in a panic to locate an answer to the hard question of survival during a deep financial and emotional crisis.

9

But in an overcrowded and unhappy home, it's incredibly easy for any child to slip away. The high levels of frustration, depression and anger in my house made my brother and me invisible. We were children with the sound turned off. And for us, as for the steadily increasing number of neglected children in this country, the only place where we could count on being noticed was at school.

10

"Hey there, young lady. Did you forget to go home last night?" It was Mr. Gunderson, our janitor, whom we all loved. He was nice and he was funny and he was old with white hair, thick glasses and an unbelievable number of keys. I could hear them jingling as he walked across the playfield. I felt incredibly happy to see him.

11

He let me push his wheeled garbage can between the different portables as he unlocked each room. He let me turn on the lights and raise the window shades and I saw my school slowly come to life. I saw Mrs. Holman, our school secretary, walk into the office without her orange lipstick on yet. She waved.

12

I saw the fifth-grade teacher Mr. Cunningham, walking under the breezeway eating a hard roll. He waved.

13

And I saw my teacher, Mrs. Claire LeSane, walking toward us in a red coat and calling my name in a very happy and surprised way, and suddenly my throat got tight and my eyes stung and I ran toward her crying. It was something that surprised us both.

14

It's only thinking about it now, 28 years later, that I realize I was crying from relief. I was with my teacher, and in a while I was going to sit at my desk, with my crayons and pencils and books and classmates all around me, and for the next six hours I was going to enjoy a thoroughly secure,

15

warm and stable world. It was a world I absolutely relied on. Without it, I don't know where I would have gone that morning.

Mrs. LeSane asked me what was wrong and when I said "Nothing," she seemingly left it at that. But she asked me if I would carry her purse for her, an honor above all honors, and she asked if I wanted to come into Room 2 early and paint.   16

She believed in the natural healing power of painting and drawing for troubled children. In the back of her room there was always a drawing table and an easel with plenty of supplies, and sometimes during the day she would come up to you for what seemed like no good reason and quietly ask if you wanted to go to the back table and "make some pictures for Mrs. LeSane." We all had a chance at it—to sit apart from the class for a while to paint, draw and silently work out impossible problems on 11 × 17 sheets of newsprint.   17

Drawing came to mean everything to me. At the back table in Room 2, I learned to build myself a life preserver that I could carry into my home.   18

We all know that a good education system saves lives, but the people of this country are still told that cutting the budget for public schools is necessary, that poor salaries for teachers are all we can manage and that art, music and all creative activities must be the first to go when times are lean.   19

Before- and after-school programs are cut and we are told that public schools are not made for baby-sitting children. If parents are neglectful temporarily or permanently, for whatever reason, it's certainly sad, but their unlucky children must fend for themselves. Or slip through the cracks. Or wander in a dark night alone.   20

We are told in a thousand ways that not only are public schools not important, but that the children who attend them, the children who need them most, are not important either. We leave them to learn from the blind eye of a television, or to the mercy of "a thousand points of light"[2] that can be as far away as stars.   21

I was lucky. I had Mrs. LeSane. I had Mr. Gunderson. I had an abundance of art supplies. And I had a particular brand of neglect in my home that allowed me to slip away and get to them. But what about the rest of the kids who weren't as lucky? What happened to them?   22

By the time the bell rang that morning I had finished my drawing and Mrs. LeSane pinned it up on the special bulletin board she reserved for drawings from the back table. It was the same picture I always drew—a sun in the corner of a blue sky over a nice house with flowers all around it.   23

Mrs. LeSane asked us to please stand, face the flag, place our right hands over our hearts and say the Pledge of Allegiance. Children across the country do it faithfully. I wonder now when the country will face its children and say a pledge right back.   24

Reacting to the Reading

1. Underline passages that describe Barry's home life in negative terms and her school life in positive terms.
2. In the margins of the essay, note the specific features of the two places (home and school) that are contrasted.

ESL Tip
Have native- and nonnative-speaking students work in groups or in pairs to discuss the exercises before they write their answers.

2. Phrase used by former president George Herbert Walker Bush to promote volunteerism.

Reacting to Words

*1. Define these words: *nondescript* (paragraph 7), *fend* (20). Can you suggest a synonym for each word that will work in the essay?

2. Look up the word *sanctuary* in a dictionary. Which of the listed definitions do you think comes closest to Barry's meaning?

Teaching Tip
Students may need help defining words. With nonnative-speaking students, consider going over the definitions in class before assigning the reading.

Reacting to Ideas

1. In paragraph 10, Barry characterizes herself and her brother as "children with the sound turned off." What do you think she means?

2. List the ways in which Barry's home and school worlds are different.

*3. What is the main point of Barry's essay—the idea that she wants to convince readers to accept? Is this idea actually stated in her essay? If so, where? If not, do you think it should be?

Teaching Tip
Remind students to answer all questions in complete sentences.

Reacting to the Pattern

1. Paragraphs 9–10 and 19–22 interrupt Barry's story. What purpose do these paragraphs serve? Do you think the essay would be more effective if paragraphs 9 and 10 came earlier? If paragraphs 19–22 came after paragraph 24? Explain.

2. What transitional words and phrases does Barry use to move readers from one event to the next? Do you think her essay needs more transitions? If so, where should they be added?

Writing Practice

1. Did you see elementary school as a "sanctuary" or as something quite different? Write a narrative essay that conveys to readers what school meant to you when you were a child.

2. In addition to school, television was a sanctuary for Barry and her brother. Did television watching (or some other activity) serve this function for you when you were younger? Is there some activity that fills this role now? In a narrative essay, write about your own "sanctuary."

3. What role does college play in your life? Write an article for your school newspaper in which you use narration to tell what school means to you now that you are an adult.

MY HALF-BAKED BUBBLE

Joshuah Bearman

Joshuah Bearman is a freelance writer and editor whose work has appeared in *Rolling Stone, Harper's, Wired*, the *New York Times Magazine, The Believer*, and *McSweeney's.* He also contributes frequently to Chicago Public Radio's *This American Life.* In "My Half-Baked Bubble," an op-ed article that appeared in the *New York Times* in 2009, Bearman writes about a

Teaching Tip
Remind students to familiarize themselves with the end-of-essay questions before they read the essay.

fondly remembered childhood experience. As you read, note that he begins and ends his article with quotations, and uses a humorous tone to engage readers in his story.

"Sardines are better than candy," my father said. "They're oily, but nutritious!" Easy for him to say. I was 8 and had just moved to a new, fancier school. The socioeconomic shift was most apparent to me in the cafeteria, where there was a wide disparity between my lunch and everyone else's. Ours was a Spartan household: no chocolate, cookies or extraneous sugar. For us, Rice Krispies cereal was supposed to be some kind of special indulgence.

My childhood happened to coincide with that historic moment in the early '80s when the full ingenuity of modern science was brought to bear on lunch snacks. Fruit roll-ups had just hit the scene. Capri Sun was like quicksilver-cocooned astronaut juice with a cool dagger straw. Chocolate pudding came in palm-sized cups!

My dad was a physicist, so I thought he should know the formula for turning our flavorless Rice Krispies into Rice Krispie treats. And yet he packed me the same lunch day after day: one peanut butter and jelly sandwich, one apple, one box of raisins. When I complained, he solved the problem (and taught me a lesson) by giving me sardines instead. As if that was an upgrade.

So I became the weird kid in the corner, opening a tin of sardines, like a hobo—when I managed not to lose the key, that is. "Stick with sardines," my dad said. "Cheap sweets are empty promises."

But they didn't seem so empty to me. Every day at lunchtime the cafeteria turned into an informal marketplace. My classmates laid out their wares on one of the big tables, displaying a panoply of forbidden processed delights. While I was busy trying to open my indestructible sardine can with a sharp rock, a brisk trading economy was under way.

"I am so bored with my Chunky," a luckier boy would say, considering the options before him. "Maybe I'll give Mr. E. L. Fudge a try!" And with a quick swap, the deal was done.

I must admit, it was a fairly efficient market. Everyone got what he wanted. Except for me. My sardines had zero value as trading currency. With no way into this economy, I had to watch from the sidelines.

Until one day, out of the depths of my isolation, I developed what you might call a creative business prospectus.

I'm not sure how I came up with this idea, but what I told my classmates was this: my mom is an expert baker, and at the end of the year she always bakes this incredible cake, the best cake ever, for me and my best friends at school. It's coming, this wonderful cake. Can you picture it in your mind? It will be a great day. But in the meantime, I said, I will let you in on this special opportunity! If you give me, say, your Cheetos now, you can stake a claim on this fantastic pending cake. Like a deposit. One Hostess cupcake equals one share.

Just like that, I became a market maker, peddling delicious cake futures.

And people were buying! First came a round of vanguard investors. Then others followed, figuring they had to get in on the ground floor with this cake deal. From there it went wide. My table in the lunchroom became the hot new trading floor. The bell would ring and my classmates would line up with their items, eager to buy in.

At the beginning, of course, I figured I could really persuade my mom to bake such a cake, and so I'd dutifully record all the trading "transactions" in my Trapper Keeper. Twinkie = one piece of cake. Chunky = half-a-piece. Fruit roll-up = two pieces. Watermelon-flavored Jolly Rancher?! I don't even want that. Zero pieces! I was setting the terms! It was like a dream come true.

Soon enough, however, the market was spiraling out of control. I started allowing customized cake shares. My Trapper Keeper ledger kept growing, and getting more complicated. The records described a wildly fantastic cake: hundreds of layers, rising to the heavens in all different flavors—chocolate mousse on top of meringue on top of half angel food and half red velvet. I was drunk with power, the creator of a bizarre lunchroom derivatives bubble.

Had anyone thought about it, it would have been clear that my mother, no matter how skilled a baker, could not fulfill my debts. But no one thought about it. We were all in too deep. I had to let the ledger keep growing.

The thing was, we all wanted to believe in this cake. For my investors, it was pragmatic: people were already into this cake for, like, 14 bags of Doritos, and they couldn't just walk away from the whole idea. So they kept pouring more Doritos in and hoping for the best. Even I sort of believed in it—and I could see the numbers. I too was deluded, imagining the hero's welcome I would receive when my mom and I eventually wheeled this amalgamated baked colossus into the schoolyard. I couldn't face the truth.

This was the mutually reinforcing psychology that allowed the cake futures market to continue. Just like the Dutch tulip mania.[1] Or the South Sea Bubble.[2] Or the American housing market. We were trafficking in dreams. Is there anything wrong with that?

The answer, as we all know, is yes—there is something wrong with that. Like all bubbles, mine couldn't last forever. Eventually, someone was going to blow the whistle.

Spencer. Spencer was both good at math and jealous; he'd always done well by the original cafeteria economy. Since everyone had been lured over to the fancy new derivatives guy, the old trading table had sat empty, and it was Spencer, Mr. Fundamentals, who did a back-of-the-napkin calculation to demonstrate how irrational our exuberance was. If you look at the numbers, he pointed out, my cake would defy the laws of physics.

At first no one wanted to believe him. If Spencer wants to be left out of the glorious new cake era, everyone thought, then, hey, fine by us. But then Spencer won a few people over with his sober analysis. And then a few more. And just as quickly as confidence in the cake was built, it eroded. We crossed the crash threshold and, overnight, belief in the cake evaporated. My classmates knew that the ledger was a sham, and they were not getting their investments back. The Fritos, Nutter Butters, Hostess pies—they were all gone, good snacks after bad.

---

1. Seventeenth-century economic crash associated with sudden collapse (after wildly inflated prices) of the tulip-bulb market.
2. Eighteenth-century economic disaster caused by stock speculation.

The bigger the bubble, the harder the fall. I was an outsider before, but now I was a pariah. The old snack economy quietly rebuilt itself, and I was back to knocking my sardine can against the monkey bars out in the playground.

20

When my dad found out about my mischief, I got a lecture. It was one big "I told you so," because, well, he had told me so. "Stick with the sardines," he'd said. "Cheap sweets are empty promises."

21

Reacting to the Reading

1. Put a check mark next to each passage that quotes Bearman's father.

2. In economic terms, what is a bubble? Write a useful definition of *bubble* in the margin beside paragraph 3. (Be sure your definition is appropriate for the context.)

ESL Tip
Have native- and nonnative-speaking students work in groups or in pairs to discuss the exercises before they write their answers.

Teaching Tip
Students may need help defining words. With nonnative-speaking students, consider going over the definitions in class before assigning the reading.

Reacting to Words

*1. Define these words: *disparity* (1), *Spartan* (1), *panoply* (5), *vanguard* (11), *deluded* (15), *eroded* (19), *sham* (19), *pariah* (20). Can you suggest a synonym for each word that will work in the essay?

*2. What does the expression *half-baked* mean? What two meanings does it have in the title of this essay?

3. Bearman compares his experiences in his school cafeteria to stock-market speculation, using words like "transactions" (12) and "derivatives" (13). List other words and phrases used here that suggest financial activity. What are the advantages and disadvantages of using this kind of vocabulary here?

Reacting to Ideas

Teaching Tip
Remind students to answer all questions in complete sentences.

*1. Why did Bearman first decide to develop his "creative business prospectus" (8)? Why did his idea get out of hand?

*2. In paragraphs 4 and 21, Bearman quotes his father, who says, "Cheap sweets are empty promises." Do you think this sentence is the essay's thesis? If not, what alternative thesis statement would you suggest? Is there another sentence in the essay that might serve as a thesis?

Reacting to the Pattern

*1. Although this essay is a narrative, Bearman also uses other patterns to develop his ideas. Where does he use description? Where does he use exemplification?

2. In paragraph 8, with the phrase, "Until one day, . . ." Bearman begins his story. What transitional words and phrases does he use to move readers from one event to the next? List as many as you can.

Writing Practice

1. Write a narrative essay about a time when your parents' advice turned out to be valuable. What lesson did you learn? Be sure to quote your parents' specific words of advice.

2. In paragraph 4, Bearman describes himself as "the weird kid in the corner." Write a narrative essay about a time in your childhood when you were an outsider. What did you do to fit in?

3. Retell Bearman's narrative as a fairy tale directed at elementary school children. Begin with "Once upon a time, . . ." use third-person (*Joshuah*, *he*, *the boy*), and use the sentence "Cheap sweets are empty promises" as the tale's moral.

39c   Description

A **descriptive** essay tells what something looks, sounds, smells, tastes, or feels like. It uses details to give readers a clear, vivid picture of a person, place, or object. In "Fish Cheeks," Amy Tan describes a family meal. In "Rice," Jhumpa Lahiri describes her father as well as his *pulao*, a rice dish.

> **Teaching Tip**
> Refer students to 16c for more on how to write a descriptive essay.

FISH CHEEKS

Amy Tan

Born in California shortly after her parents immigrated there from China, Amy Tan started writing at an early age. Author of the best-selling novel *The Joy Luck Club* (1989) and the more recent *Saving Fish from Drowning* (2006), Tan is known for exploring Chinese-American mother-daughter relationships. In "Fish Cheeks," originally published in 1987 in *Seventeen* magazine, Tan describes her family's Christmas dinner and the lessons she learns about sharing and appreciating her Chinese heritage. As you read, note how her descriptions reflect her mixed feelings about the dinner.

> **Teaching Tip**
> Remind students to familiarize themselves with the end-of-essay questions before they read the essay.

1   I fell in love with the minister's son the winter I turned fourteen. He was not Chinese, but as white as Mary in the manger. For Christmas I prayed for this blond-haired boy, Robert, and a slim new American nose.

2   When I found out that my parents had invited the minister's family over for Christmas Eve dinner, I cried. What would Robert think of our shabby *Chinese* Christmas? What would he think of our noisy *Chinese* relatives who lacked proper American manners? What terrible disappointment would he feel upon seeing not a roasted turkey and sweet potatoes but *Chinese* food?

3   On Christmas Eve I saw that my mother had outdone herself in creating a strange menu. She was pulling black veins out of the backs of fleshy prawns. The kitchen was littered with appalling mounds of raw food: a slimy rock cod with bulging fish eyes that pleaded not to be thrown into a pan of hot oil. Tofu, which looked like stacked wedges of rubbery white sponges. A bowl soaking dried fungus back to life. A plate of squid, their backs crisscrossed with knife markings so they resembled bicycle tires.

4   And then they arrived—the minister's family and all my relatives in a clamor of doorbells and rumpled Christmas packages. Robert grunted hello, and I pretended he was not worthy of existence.

Dinner threw me deeper into despair. My relatives licked the ends of their   5
chopsticks and reached across the table, dipping them into the dozen or so
plates of food. Robert and his family waited patiently for platters to be passed
to them. My relatives murmured with pleasure when my mother brought out
the whole steamed fish. Robert grimaced. Then my father poked his chopsticks just below the fish eye and plucked out the soft meat. "Amy, your
favorite," he said, offering me the tender fish cheek. I wanted to disappear.

At the end of the meal my father leaned back and belched loudly,   6
thanking my mother for her fine cooking. "It's a polite Chinese custom to
show you are satisfied," explained my father to our astonished guests. The
minister managed to muster up a quiet burp. I was stunned into silence
the rest of the night.

After everyone had gone, my mother said to me, "You want to be the   7
same as American girls on the outside." She handed me an early gift. It
was a miniskirt in beige tweed. "But inside you must always be Chinese.
You must be proud you are different. Your only shame is to have shame."

And even though I didn't agree with her then, I knew that she   8
understood how much I had suffered during the evening's dinner. It
wasn't until many years later—long after I had gotten over my crush on
Robert—that I was able to fully appreciate her lesson and the true purpose behind our particular menu. For Christmas Eve that year, she had
chosen all my favorite meals.

Reacting to the Reading

*1. Circle all the adjectives in this essay that convey a negative impression—
for example, *shabby* and *terrible* in paragraph 2.

2. In the margins, write brief annotations explaining what these negative
words add to the essay.

Reacting to Words

*1. Define these words: *appalling* (3), *clamor* (4), *grimaced* (5). Can you
suggest a synonym for each word that will work in the essay?

2. Look carefully at each use of the word *Chinese* in this essay. What does
the word suggest in each case? Does it suggest something positive,
negative, or neutral?

Reacting to Ideas

1. Tan is very nervous about the encounter between her family and Robert's. What do you think she is really afraid of?

*2. What does Tan's mother mean by "Your only shame is to have shame" (7)?

3. Why does Tan's mother give her the tweed miniskirt?

Reacting to the Pattern

*1. In paragraph 2, Tan asks, "What would Robert think of our shabby
Chinese Christmas?" How does this question help to establish the dominant impression Tan wants to convey?

ESL Tip
Have native- and nonnative-
speaking students work in
groups or in pairs to discuss
the exercises before they write
their answers.

Teaching Tip
Students may need help defining
words. With nonnative-speaking
students, consider going over
the definitions in class before
assigning the reading.

Teaching Tip
Remind students to answer
all questions in complete
sentences.

2. In paragraph 3, Tan describes the food that was served; in paragraphs 5 and 6, she describes the people. How do the descriptive details she chooses support the essay's dominant impression?

3. Is this essay primarily a subjective or an objective description? Explain.

Writing Practice

1. Describe a family meal of your own—either a typical breakfast, lunch, or dinner or a "company" or holiday meal.

2. Describe the Tan family's meal from Robert's point of view. What does he see? How does the scene (and the food) look to him?

RICE

Jhumpa Lahiri

Born in London to Bengali Indian parents and raised in the United States, Jhumpa Lahiri is a writer whose first short story collection, *Interpreter of Maladies* (1999), won the 2000 Pulitzer Prize for Fiction and whose first novel, *The Namesake* (2003), was made into a popular film. In her fiction, Lahiri examines the culture shock Indian immigrants experience when they move to America. Lahiri's "Rice" first appeared in *The New Yorker* magazine in 2009. As you read, consider the kinds of details Lahiri includes to give readers a clear picture of her father and the way he makes his famous *pulao*.

Teaching Tip
Remind students to familiarize themselves with the end-of-essay questions before they read the essay.

My father, seventy-eight, is a methodical man. For thirty-nine years, he has had the same job, cataloguing books for a university library. He drinks two glasses of water first thing in the morning, walks for an hour every day, and devotes almost as much time, before bed, to flossing his teeth. "Winging it" is not a term that comes to mind in describing my father. When he's driving to new places, he does not enjoy getting lost.

In the kitchen, too, he walks a deliberate line, counting out the raisins that go into his oatmeal (fifteen) and never boiling even a drop more water than required for tea. It is my father who knows how many cups of rice are necessary to feed four, or forty, or a hundred and forty people. He has a reputation for *andaj*—the Bengali word for "estimate"—accurately gauging quantities that tend to baffle other cooks. An oracle of rice, if you will.

But there is another rice that my father is more famous for. This is not the white rice, boiled like pasta and then drained in a colander, that most Bengalis eat for dinner. This other rice is pulao, a baked, buttery, sophisticated indulgence, Persian in origin, served at festive occasions. I have often watched him make it. It involves sautéing grains of basmati in butter, along with cinnamon sticks, cloves, bay leaves, and cardamom pods. In go halved cashews and raisins (unlike the oatmeal raisins, these must be golden, not black). Ginger, pulverized into a paste, is incorporated, along with salt and sugar, nutmeg and mace, saffron threads if they're available, ground turmeric if not. A certain amount of water is added, and the rice simmers until most of the water evaporates. Then it is spread out in a baking tray. (My father prefers disposable aluminum ones, which he recycled long before recycling laws were passed.) More water is flicked on top with his fingers, in the ritual and cryptic manner of Catholic priests. Then the tray, covered with foil, goes into the oven, until the rice is cooked through and not a single grain sticks to another.

Despite having a superficial knowledge of the ingredients and the technique, I have no idea how to make my father's pulao, nor would I ever dare attempt it. The recipe is his own, and has never been recorded. There has never been an unsuccessful batch, yet no batch is ever identical to any other. It is a dish that has become an extension of himself, that he has perfected, and to which he has earned the copyright. A dish that will die with him when he dies.   4

In 1968, when I was seven months old, my father made pulao for the first time. We lived in London, in Finsbury Park, where my parents shared the kitchen, up a steep set of stairs in the attic of the house, with another Bengali couple. The occasion was my *annaprasan*, a rite of passage in which Bengali children are given solid food for the first time; it is known colloquially as a *bhath*, which happens to be the Bengali word for "cooked rice." In the oven of a stove no more than twenty inches wide, my father baked pulao for about thirty-five people. Since then, he has made pulao for the *annaprasans* of his friends' children, for birthday parties and anniversaries, for bridal and baby showers, for wedding receptions, and for my sister's Ph.D. party. For a few decades, after we moved to the United States, his pulao fed crowds of up to four hundred people, at events organized by Prabasi, a Bengali cultural institution in New England, and he found himself at institutional venues—schools and churches and community centers—working with industrial ovens and stoves. This has never unnerved him. He could probably rig up a system to make pulao out of a hot-dog cart, were someone to ask.   5

There are times when certain ingredients are missing, when he must use almonds instead of cashews, when the raisins in a friend's cupboard are the wrong color. He makes it anyway, with exacting standards but a sanguine hand.   6

When my son and daughter were infants, and we celebrated their *annaprasans*, we hired a caterer, but my father made the pulao, preparing it at home in Rhode Island and transporting it in the trunk of his car to Brooklyn. The occasion, both times, was held at the Society for Ethical Culture, in Park Slope. In 2002, for my son's first taste of rice, my father warmed the trays on the premises, in the giant oven in the basement. But by 2005, when it was my daughter's turn, the representative on duty would not permit my father to use the oven, telling him that he was not a licensed cook. My father transferred the pulao from his aluminum trays into glass baking dishes, and microwaved, batch by batch, rice that fed almost a hundred people. When I asked my father to describe that experience, he expressed no frustration. "It was fine," he said. "It was a big microwave."   7

Reacting to the Reading

1. Underline all the adjectives Lahiri uses to describe her father. Are these words primarily positive or negative?
2. Write a one-sentence definition of *pulao* in the margin beside paragraph 3.

Reacting to Words

*1. Define these words: *methodical* (1), *oracle* (2), *indulgence* (3), *cryptic* (3), *sanguine* (6). Can you suggest a synonym for each word that will work in the essay?

*2. Suggest an alternative one-word title for this essay.

Teaching Tip
Students may need help defining words. With nonnative-speaking students, consider going over the definitions in class before assigning the reading.

Reacting to Ideas

*1. Do you think the subject of this essay is really rice (as its title suggests), or do you think the real subject is Lahiri's father? Explain.

2. What role has *pulao* played in Lahiri's life? What do you think it means to her now?

Teaching Tip
Remind students to answer all questions in complete sentences.

Reacting to the Pattern

1. Lahiri describes both *pulao* and ordinary white rice. How are they different?

2. Is this a subjective or an objective description? Explain.

*3. What dominant impression does this essay give readers of Lahiri's father? Of his rice?

Writing Practice

1. Write a subjective description of a food you loved when you were a child. Try to describe the smell, taste, and feel of the food as well as its appearance.

2. Write an essay about a friend or family member with whom you associate a particular food or meal. Include descriptions of that person engaged in eating or in preparing the food.

3. How have your tastes in food changed since you were a child? Describe the foods that defined each stage of your life. Your thesis should convey how (and perhaps why) your preferences changed over time.

39d Process

A **process** essay explains the steps in a procedure, telling how something is (or was) done. In "Slice of Life," Russell Baker gives a set of instructions for carving a turkey. In "My First Conk," Malcolm X explains the process he went through to straighten his hair.

Teaching Tip
Refer students to 16d for more on how to write a process essay.

SLICE OF LIFE

Russell Baker

Pulitzer Prize–winning columnist and author Russell Baker was known for his keen political insight and sharp social commentary. He was also known for being funny. The source of much of Baker's humor is his deadpan approach,

Teaching Tip
Remind students to familiarize themselves with the end-of-essay questions before they read the essay.

in which he pretends to be completely serious. In "Slice of Life," first published in the *New York Times* in 1974, Baker uses this approach to turn what seems to be a straightforward set of instructions into a humorous discussion of a holiday ritual. As you read, think about your family's Thanksgivings.

How to carve a turkey: 1

Assemble the following tools—carving knife, stone for sharpening carving knife, hot water, soap, wash cloth, two bath towels, barbells, meat cleaver. If the house lacks a meat cleaver, an ax may be substituted. If it is, add bandages, sutures, and iodine to above list. 2

Begin by moving the turkey from the roasting pan to a suitable carving area. This is done by inserting the carving knife into the posterior stuffed area of the turkey and the knife-sharpening stone into the stuffed area under the neck. 3

Thus skewered, the turkey may be lifted out of the hot grease with relative safety. Should the turkey drop to the floor, however, remove the knife and stone, roll the turkey gingerly into the two bath towels, wrap them several times around it and lift the encased fowl to the carving place. 4

You are now ready to begin carving. Sharpen the knife on the stone and insert it where the thigh joins the torso. If you do this correctly, which is improbable, the knife will almost immediately encounter a barrier of bone and gristle. This may very well be the joint. It could, however, be your thumb. If not, execute a vigorous sawing motion until satisfied that the knife has been defeated. Withdraw the knife and ask someone nearby, in as testy a manner as possible, why the knives at your house are not kept in better carving condition. 5

Exercise the biceps and forearms by lifting barbells until they are strong enough for you to tackle the leg joint with bare hands. Wrapping one hand firmly around the thigh, seize the turkey's torso in the other hand and scream. Run cold water over hands to relieve pain of burns. 6

Now, take a bath towel in each hand and repeat the above maneuver. The entire leg should snap away from the chassis with a distinct crack, and the rest of the turkey, obedient to Newton's law[1] about equal and opposite reactions, should roll in the opposite direction, which means that if you are carving at the table the turkey will probably come to rest in someone's lap. 7

Get the turkey out of the lap with as little fuss as possible, and concentrate on the leg. Use the meat cleaver to sever the sinewy leather which binds the thigh to the drumstick. 8

If using the alternate, ax method, this operation should be performed on a cement walk outside the house in order to preserve the table. 9

Repeat the above operation on the turkey's uncarved side. You now have two thighs and two drumsticks. Using the wash cloth, soap and hot water, bathe thoroughly and, if possible, go to a movie. Otherwise, look each person in the eye and say, "I don't suppose anyone wants white meat." 10

If compelled to carve the breast anyhow, sharpen the knife on the stone again with sufficient awkwardness to tip over the gravy bowl on the person who started the stampede for white meat. 11

While everyone is rushing about to mop the gravy off her slacks, hack at the turkey breast until it starts crumbling off the carcass in ugly chunks. 12

1. Sir Isaac Newton, seventeenth-century physicist and mathematician known for formulating the laws of gravity and light and for inventing calculus.

The alternative method for carving white meat is to visit around the neighborhood until you find someone who has a good carving knife and borrow it, if you find one, which is unlikely.

13

This method enables you to watch the football game on neighbors' television sets and also creates the possibility that somebody back at your table will grow tired of waiting and do the carving herself.

14

In this case, upon returning home, cast a pained stare upon the mound of chopped white meat that has been hacked out by the family carving knife and refuse to do any more carving that day. No one who cares about the artistry of carving can be expected to work upon the mutilations of amateurs, and it would be a betrayal of the carver's art to do so.

15

Reacting to the Reading

1. Number the steps in the process.
2. Underline or star the cautions and warnings Baker provides for readers.

Reacting to Words

*1. Define these words: *sutures* (paragraph 2), *gingerly* (4), *encased* (4), *torso* (5), *execute* (5), *testy* (5), *chassis* (7). Can you suggest a synonym for each word that will work in the essay?
2. In paragraph 14, Baker uses *herself* to refer to *somebody*. What is your reaction to this pronoun use? What other options did Baker have? Why do you think he chose to use *herself*?

Reacting to Ideas

1. This process is not intended to be taken seriously or followed exactly. How can you tell?
*2. Referring to your response to the first Reacting to the Reading question, list the steps in Baker's process of carving a turkey. Then, cross out all nonessential or humorous material. Are the instructions that remain logically ordered? Clear? Accurate?

Reacting to the Pattern

1. How do you know that this essay is a set of instructions and not an explanation of a process?
*2. Do you think the phrase "How to carve a turkey" is an adequate introduction for this essay? What other kind of introduction might Baker have written?
3. Review the various cautions and warnings that you identified in the second Reacting to the Reading question. Are they all necessary? Explain.

Writing Practice

1. Write a new introductory paragraph for this essay. Then, turn Baker's instructions into a straightforward process explanation, deleting any material you consider irrelevant to your purpose. Be sure to include all necessary articles (*a, an, the*) and transitions.

ESL Tip
Have native- and nonnative-speaking students work in groups or in pairs to discuss the exercises before they write their answers.

Teaching Tip
Students may need help defining words. With nonnative-speaking students, consider going over the definitions in class before assigning the reading.

Teaching Tip
You may want to refer students to 31e for further explanation of pronoun options.

Teaching Tip
Remind students to answer all questions in complete sentences.

Teaching Tip

When students write process essays, they often use very simple subject-verb-object sentences. Remind students to vary their sentence structure. Refer them to Chapter 20 if necessary.

2. List the steps in a recipe for preparing one of your favorite dishes. Then, expand your recipe into an essay, adding transitions and cautions and reminders. Finally, add opening and closing paragraphs that describe the finished product and tell readers why the dish is worth preparing.

3. Write an essay that explains to your fellow students how you juggle the demands of family, work, and school in a typical day. Organize your essay either as a process explanation or as a set of instructions.

MY FIRST CONK

Malcolm X

Malcolm X (1925–1965) was an influential leader of the 1960s civil rights movement in the United States. Jailed as a young man, he continued his education in prison and later became a charismatic member of the religious organization Nation of Islam. In "My First Conk," from *The Autobiography of Malcolm X* (1964), Malcolm X explains how he had his hair styled to look like a white man's because he, like many African Americans at the time, was ashamed of his natural hair. As you read, consider the importance of the burning sensation that is part of the "conking" process and how it illustrates his emotional pain.

Teaching Tip

Remind students to familiarize themselves with the end-of-essay questions before they read the essay.

Shorty soon decided that my hair was finally long enough to be conked. He had promised to school me in how to beat the barber shops' three- and four-dollar price by making up congolene, and then conking ourselves.   1

I took the little list of ingredients he had printed out for me, and went to a grocery store, where I got a can of Red Devil lye, two eggs, and two medium-sized white potatoes. Then at a drugstore near the poolroom, I asked for a large jar of vaseline, a large bar of soap, a large-toothed comb and a fine-toothed comb, one of those rubber hoses with a metal spray-head, a rubber apron, and a pair of gloves.   2

"Going to lay on that first conk?" the drugstore man asked me. I proudly told him, grinning, "Right!"   3

Shorty paid six dollars a week for a room in his cousin's shabby apartment. His cousin wasn't at home. "It's like the pad's mine, he spends so much time with his woman," Shorty said. "Now, you watch me—"   4

He peeled the potatoes and thin-sliced them into a quart-sized Mason fruit jar, then started stirring them with a wooden spoon as he gradually poured in a little over half the can of lye. "Never use a metal spoon; the lye will turn it black," he told me.   5

A jelly-like, starchy-looking glop resulted from the lye and potatoes, and Shorty broke in the two eggs, stirring real fast—his own conk and dark face bent down close. The congolene turned pale-yellowish. "Feel the jar," Shorty said. I cupped my hand against the outside, and snatched it away. "Damn right, it's hot, that's the lye," he said. "So you know it's going to burn when I comb it in—it burns bad. But the longer you can stand it, the straighter the hair."   6

He made me sit down, and he tied the string of the new rubber apron tightly around my neck, and combed up my bush of hair. Then, from the big vaseline jar, he took a handful and massaged it hard all through my hair and into the scalp. He also thickly vaselined my neck, ears and forehead.   7

"When I get to washing out your head, be sure to tell me anywhere you feel any little stinging," Shorty warned me, washing his hands, then pulling on the rubber gloves, and tying on his own rubber apron. "You always got to remember that any congolene left in burns a sore into your head."

The congolene just felt warm when Shorty started combing it in. But then my head caught fire. 8

I gritted my teeth and tried to pull the sides of the kitchen table together. The comb felt as if it was raking my skin off. 9

My eyes watered, my nose was running. I couldn't stand it any longer; I bolted to the washbasin. I was cursing Shorty with every name I could think of when he got the spray going and started soap lathering my head. 10

He lathered and spray-rinsed, lathered and spray-rinsed, maybe ten or twelve times, each time gradually closing the hot-water faucet, until the rinse was cold, and that helped some. 11

"You feel any stinging spots?" 12

"No," I managed to say. My knees were trembling. 13

"Sit back down, then. I think we got it all out okay." 14

The flame came back as Shorty, with a thick towel, started drying my head, rubbing hard. *"Easy, man, easy!"* I kept shouting. 15

"The first time's always worst. You get used to it better before long. You took it real good, homeboy. You got a good conk." 16

When Shorty let me stand up and see in the mirror, my hair hung down in limp, damp strings. My scalp still flamed, but not as badly; I could bear it. He draped the towel around my shoulders, over my rubber apron, and began again vaselining my hair. 17

I could feel him combing, straight back, first the big comb, then the fine-tooth one. 18

Then, he was using a razor, very delicately, on the back of my neck. Then, finally, shaping the sideburns. 19

My first view in the mirror blotted out the hurting. I'd seen some pretty conks, but when it's the first time, on your *own* head, the transformation, after the lifetime of kinks, is staggering. 20

The mirror reflected Shorty behind me. We both were grinning and sweating. And on top of my head was this thick, smooth sheen of shining red hair—real red—as straight as any white man's. 21

How ridiculous I was! Stupid enough to stand there simply lost in admiration of my hair now looking "white," reflected in the mirror in Shorty's room. I vowed that I'd never again be without a conk, and I never was for many years. 22

This was my first really big step toward self-degradation: when I endured all of that pain, literally burning my flesh to have it look like a white man's hair. I had joined that multitude of Negro men and women in America who are brainwashed into believing that the black people are "inferior"—and white people "superior"—that they will even violate and mutilate their God-created bodies to try to look "pretty" by white standards. 23

Look around today, in every small town and big city, from two-bit catfish and soda-pop joints into the "integrated" lobby of the Waldorf-Astoria, and you'll see conks on black men. And you'll see black women wearing these green and pink and purple and red and platinum-blonde wigs. They're all more ridiculous than a slapstick comedy. It makes you wonder if the Negro has completely lost his sense of identity, lost touch with himself. 24

You'll see the conk worn by many, many so-called "upper class"   25
Negroes, and, as much as I hate to say it about them, on all too many
Negro entertainers. One of the reasons that I've especially admired some
of them, like Lionel Hampton and Sidney Poitier, among others, is that
they have kept their natural hair and fought to the top. I admire any Negro
man who has never had himself conked, or who has had the sense to get
rid of it—as I finally did.

I don't know which kind of self-defacing conk is the greater shame—   26
the one you'll see on the heads of the black so-called "middle class" and
"upper class," who ought to know better, or the one you'll see on the heads
of the poorest, most downtrodden, ignorant black men. I mean the legal-
minimum-wage ghetto-dwelling kind of Negro, as I was when I got my
first one. It's generally among these poor fools that you'll see a black ker-
chief over the man's head, like Aunt Jemima; he's trying to make his conk
last longer, between trips to the barbershop. Only for special occasions is
this kerchief-protected conk exposed—to show off how "sharp" and "hip"
its owner is. The ironic thing is that I have never heard any woman, white
or black, express any admiration for a conk. Of course, any white woman
with a black man isn't thinking about his hair. But I don't see how on earth
a black woman with any race pride could walk down the street with any
black man wearing a conk—the emblem of his shame that he is black.

To my own shame, when I say all of this, I'm talking first of all about   27
myself—because you can't show me any Negro who ever conked more
faithfully than I did. I'm speaking from personal experience when I say of
any black man who conks today, or any white-wigged black woman, that
if they gave the brains in their heads just half as much attention as they
do their hair, they would be a thousand times better off.

Reacting to the Reading

1. In the margins of the essay, number the steps in the process Malcolm X describes.
2. What purpose do paragraphs 22–27 serve? In the margin beside these paragraphs, summarize them in one or two sentences.

Reacting to Words

*1. Define these words: *staggering* (20), *vowed* (22), *self-degradation* (23), *multitude* (23), *mutilate* (23), *slapstick* (24), *self-defacing* (26), *downtrod-den* (26), *emblem* (26). Can you suggest a synonym for each word that will work in the essay?
2. Exactly what is a conk? Write an objective one-sentence definition that explains what the word means.

Reacting to Ideas

*1. What process is Malcolm X explaining here? What is his motive for explaining this process?
2. Where does Malcolm X mention the pain and discomfort of the pro-cess? Why do you think he includes these negative details?

*3. What is Malcolm X's first impression of his finished conk? What does he now think of this reaction?

4. What does Malcolm X mean when he says that a black man with a conk is wearing "the emblem of his shame that he is black" (26)?

Reacting to the Pattern

1. What is the first step in the process? Where does the process end?

2. How can you tell this is a process explanation and not a set of instructions?

3. What materials and equipment are needed for this process? If Malcolm X doesn't expect his readers to perform the process themselves, why does he tell them what items are needed?

4. What cautions does Shorty give Malcolm X? What other cautions do you think should be given to people who are about to conk their hair?

Writing Practice

1. Write an essay explaining a distasteful process that you have experienced. In your essay, try to convince readers that this process should be changed (or eliminated).

2. Write a process essay explaining the daily routine you follow in a job you hold (or held). Include a thesis statement that tells readers how you feel about the job.

3. Write a process essay in which you explain how to perform a particular task at a job—for example, how to keep a potential customer on the phone during a sales call, how to service a piece of equipment, or how to stock shelves in a convenience store.

39e Cause and Effect

A **cause-and-effect** essay identifies causes or predicts effects; sometimes, it does both. In "How Facebook Is Making Friending Obsolete," Julia Angwin considers how Facebook has changed the nature of friendship. In "The Seat Not Taken," John Edgar Wideman considers the possible motives of train passengers who choose not to sit beside him.

Teaching Tip
Refer students to 16e for more on how to write a cause-and-effect essay.

HOW FACEBOOK IS MAKING FRIENDING OBSOLETE

Julia Angwin

Raised in Silicon Valley by parents who both worked in technology, Angwin acquired an interest in digital technology at an early age. Before taking up her current post at the *Wall Street Journal* as a technology editor and columnist, Angwin covered technology at the *San Francisco Chronicle*. In 2009, she published the book *Stealing MySpace*, which examines the cultural phenomenon of MySpace and other social-networking sites. In "How Facebook Is Making

Teaching Tip
Remind students to familiarize themselves with the end-of-essay questions before they read the essay.

Friending Obsolete," first published in the *Wall Street Journal* in 2009, Angwin comments on the potential consequences of Facebook's efforts to make it harder to keep profiles private. As you read, consider your own feelings about Facebook and privacy.

1   "Friending" wasn't used as a verb until about five years ago, when social networks such as Friendster, MySpace and Facebook burst onto the scene.

2   Suddenly, our friends were something even better—an audience. If blogging felt like shouting into the void, posting updates on a social network felt more like an intimate conversation among friends at a pub.

3   Inevitably, as our list of friends grew to encompass acquaintances, friends of friends and the girl who sat behind us in seventh-grade homeroom, online friendships became devalued.

4   Suddenly, we knew as much about the lives of our distant acquaintances as we did about the lives of our intimates—what they'd had for dinner, how they felt about Tiger Woods and so on.

5   Enter Twitter with a solution: no friends, just followers. These one-way relationships were easier to manage—no more annoying decisions about whether to give your ex-boyfriend access to your photos, no more fussing over who could see your employment and contact information.

6   Twitter's updates were also easily searchable on the Web, forcing users to be somewhat thoughtful about their posts. The intimate conversation became a talent show, a challenge to prove your intellectual prowess in 140 characters or less.

7   This fall, Twitter turned its popularity into dollars, inking lucrative deals to allow its users' tweets to be broadcast via search algorithms on Google and Bing.

8   Soon, Facebook followed suit with deals to distribute certain real-time data to Google and Bing. (Recall that despite being the fifth-most-popular Web site in the world, Facebook is barely profitable.) Facebook spokesman Barry Schnitt says no money changed hands in the deals but says there was "probably an exchange of value."

9   Just one catch: Facebook had just "exchanged" to Google and Microsoft something that didn't exist.

10   The vast majority of Facebook users restrict updates to their friends, and do not expect those updates to appear in public search results. (In fact, many people restrict their Facebook profile from appearing at all in search results.)

11   So Facebook had little content to provide to Google's and Bing's real-time search results. When Google's real-time search launched earlier this month, its results were primarily filled with Twitter updates.

12   Coincidentally, Facebook presented its 350 million members with a new default privacy setting last week. For most people, the new suggested settings would open their Facebook updates and information to the entire world. Mr. Schnitt says the new privacy suggestions are an acknowledgement of "the way we think the world is going."

13   Facebook Chief Executive Mark Zuckerberg led by example, opening up his previously closed profile, including goofy photos of himself curled up with a teddy bear.

14   Facebook also made public formerly private info such as profile pictures, gender, current city and the friends list. (Mr. Schnitt suggests that users are free to lie about their hometown or take down their profile

picture to protect their privacy; in response to users' complaints, the friends list can now be restricted to be viewed only by friends.)

Of course, many people will reject the default settings on Facebook and keep on chatting with only their Facebook friends. (Mr. Schnitt said more than 50% of its users had rejected the defaults at last tally.) 15

But those who want a private experience on Facebook will have to work harder at it: if you inadvertently post a comment on a friend's profile page that has been opened to the public, your comment will be public too. 16

Just as Facebook turned friends into a commodity, it has likewise gathered our personal data—our updates, our baby photos, our endless chirping birthday notes—and readied it to be bundled and sold. 17

So I give up. Rather than fighting to keep my Facebook profile private, I plan to open it up to the public—removing the fiction of intimacy and friendship. 18

But I will also remove the vestiges of my private life from Facebook and make sure I never post anything that I wouldn't want my parents, employer, next-door neighbor or future employer to see. You'd be smart to do the same. 19

We'll need to treat this increasingly public version of Facebook with the same hard-headedness that we treat Twitter: as a place to broadcast, but not a place for vulnerability. A place to carefully calibrate, sanitize and bowdlerize our words for every possible audience, now and forever. Not a place for intimacy with friends. 20

Reacting to the Reading

1. In the margin beside paragraph 4, write down some additional examples of things people can learn about their "distant acquaintances" on social-networking sites.

2. In the margin beside paragraphs 5 and 6, list the differences between Facebook and Twitter.

Reacting to Words

*1. Define these words: *void* (2), *prowess* (6), *calibrate* (20), *bowdlerize* (20). Can you suggest a synonym for each word that will work in the essay?

*2. Write a one-sentence definition of the verb *to friend*.

Reacting to Ideas

*1. Angwin claims that online friendships have been "devalued" (3). What does she mean? Do you agree with her? Why or why not?

*2. How, according to Angwin, is Facebook "making friending obsolete"? In your opinion, is Facebook also making *friendship* obsolete—or at least changing its meaning?

Reacting to the Pattern

1. What actions has Facebook taken to make its information more and more public? What led to these actions? What has been the result of these actions?

2. Is this essay's emphasis on causes, on effects, or on both causes and effects? Explain.

Writing Practice

1. Angwin plans to open her Facebook profile to the public. Would you do—or have you already done—the same? Why or why not? Write a cause-and-effect essay in which you give your reasons for making your profile public—or your reasons for keeping it private.

2. How would your life change if you lost access to social networking? Write an essay explaining the possible results of this loss of access.

THE SEAT NOT TAKEN

John Edgar Wideman

John Edgar Wideman has published numerous books, both fiction and nonfiction, as well as articles in publications such as the *New York Times,* the *New Yorker*, *Vogue*, *Emerge*, and *Esquire*. Wideman has received the O. Henry Award, the American Book Award for Fiction, the Lannan Literary Fellowship for Fiction, the PEN/Faulkner Award for Fiction (twice—the first person so honored), and a MacArthur Fellowship. He is currently professor of Africana Studies and English at Brown University. In "The Seat Not Taken," an op-ed article first published in the *New York Times* in 2010, Wideman reflects on his weekly train commute and raises questions about the motives his fellow commuters have for not sitting in the empty seat beside him. As you read, think about how you would react in Wideman's situation.

Teaching Tip
A reading such as "The Seat Not Taken" may create some racial tension in the classroom. Before assigning the reading, decide whether you are ready to handle students' possible reactions.

Teaching Tip
Remind students to familiarize themselves with the end-of-essay questions before they read the essay.

At least twice a week I ride Amtrak's high-speed Acela train from my home in New York City to my teaching job in Providence, R.I. The route passes through a region of the country populated by, statistics tell us, a significant segment of its most educated, affluent, sophisticated and enlightened citizens. 1

Over the last four years, excluding summers, I have conducted a casual sociological experiment in which I am both participant and observer. It's a survey I began not because I had some specific point to prove by gathering data to support it, but because I couldn't avoid becoming aware of an obvious, disquieting truth. 2

Almost invariably, after I have hustled aboard early and occupied one half of a vacant double seat in the usually crowded quiet car, the empty place next to me will remain empty for the entire trip. 3

I'm a man of color, one of the few on the train and often the only one in the quiet car, and I've concluded that color explains a lot about my experience. Unless the car is nearly full, color will determine, even if it doesn't exactly clarify, why 9 times out of 10 people will shun a free seat if it means sitting beside me. 4

Giving them and myself the benefit of the doubt, I can rule out excessive body odor or bad breath; a hateful, intimidating scowl; hip-hop clothing; or a hideous deformity as possible objections to my person. Considering also the cost of an Acela ticket, the fact that I display no visible indications of religious preference and, finally, the numerous external signs of middle-class membership I share with the majority of the passengers, color appears to be a sufficient reason for the behavior I have recorded. 5

Of course, I'm not registering a complaint about the privilege, conferred upon me by color, to enjoy the luxury of an extra seat to myself. I relish the opportunity to spread out, savor the privacy and quiet and work or gaze at the scenic New England woods and coast. It's a particularly appealing perk if I compare the train to air travel or any other mode of transportation, besides walking or bicycling, for negotiating the mercilessly congested Northeast Corridor. Still, in the year 2010, with an African-descended, brown president in the White House and a nation confidently asserting its passage into a postracial era, it strikes me as odd to ride beside a vacant seat, just about every time I embark on a three-hour journey each way, from home to work and back.

I admit I look forward to the moment when other passengers, searching for a good seat, or any seat at all on the busiest days, stop anxiously prowling the quiet-car aisle, the moment when they have all settled elsewhere, including the ones who willfully blinded themselves to the open seat beside me or were unconvinced of its availability when they passed by. I savor that precise moment when the train sighs and begins to glide away from Penn or Providence Station, and I'm able to say to myself, with relative assurance, that the vacant place beside me is free, free at last, or at least free until the next station. I can relax, prop open my briefcase or rest papers, snacks or my arm in the unoccupied seat.

But the very pleasing moment of anticipation casts a shadow, because I can't accept the bounty of an extra seat without remembering why it's empty, without wondering if its emptiness isn't something quite sad. And quite dangerous, also, if left unexamined. Posters in the train, the station, the subway warn: if you see something, say something.

Reacting to the Reading

1. Circle the words in this essay that refer specifically to race. Do you think Wideman should have included more references to his own race (and to the races of his fellow passengers) in this essay? Why or why not?

2. In the margin beside paragraph 5, list a few reasons you might have for not wanting to sit next to someone on a train.

Reacting to Words

*1. Define these words: *disquieting* (2), *shun* (4), *bounty* (8). Can you suggest a synonym for each word that will work in the essay?

2. In paragraph 1, Wideman suggests that his fellow passengers are some of the United States' "most educated, affluent, sophisticated and enlightened citizens." What impression does he intend to convey by using these words to characterize the other passengers?

Reacting to Ideas

*1. Why does Wideman see the empty seat beside him as not simply sad but also dangerous? Do you think he is right to see it this way, or do you think he is overreacting? Explain your views.

*2. Why does Wideman close the essay with "if you see something, say something" (8)? In what context(s) does this sentence usually appear these days? What is the "something" that Wideman wants people to say in this case?

ESL Tip
Have native- and nonnative-speaking students work in groups or in pairs to discuss the exercises before they write their answers.

Teaching Tip
Students may need help defining words. With nonnative-speaking students, consider going over the definitions in class before assigning the reading.

Teaching Tip
Remind students to answer all questions in complete sentences.

Reacting to the Pattern

*1. This essay focuses on examining causes. What do you think might be the *effects* (on Wideman and on society in general) of the behavior Wideman describes?

2. Write a one-sentence thesis statement for this essay, including at least one word or phrase (for example, *because*, *for this reason*, or *as a result*) that indicates it is a cause-and-effect essay.

Writing Practice

1. How do you account for the empty seat beside Wideman on so many train trips? Do you agree with his analysis of the situation, or can you think of other explanations that he has not considered? Write a cause-and-effect essay responding to Wideman's article and its reflections on race.

2. What kinds of people would you try to avoid sitting next to on a train? Why? Do you see your objections as reasonable, or do you think some of your objections might be considered prejudice? Write an essay in which you explain your objections as clearly and thoughtfully as possible.

39f Comparison and Contrast

Teaching Tip
Refer students to 16f for more on how to write a comparison-and-contrast essay.

Teaching Tip
Before beginning this section, review the difference between point-by-point and subject-by-subject comparison. Refer students to 16f.

Teaching Tip
Remind students to familiarize themselves with the end-of-essay questions before they read the essay.

A **comparison-and-contrast** essay explains how two things are alike or how they are different; sometimes, it discusses both similarities and differences. In "The Twin Revolutions of Lincoln and Darwin," Steven Conn compares two important historical figures. In "Men Are from Mars, Women Are from Venus," John Gray compares men and women.

THE TWIN REVOLUTIONS OF LINCOLN AND DARWIN

Steven Conn

Steven Conn is a professor of American cultural and intellectual history and director of the Public History Program at Ohio State University. He is the author of five books, most recently *Do Museums Still Need Objects?* (2009). In "The Twin Revolutions of Lincoln and Darwin," which first appeared in the *Philadelphia Inquirer* in 2009, Conn compares the lives of two seemingly unrelated historical figures—Abraham Lincoln and Charles Darwin. As you read, note any points of comparison that you find surprising.

Abraham Lincoln, the Great Emancipator, has been much on our minds recently. Today, exactly 200 years after Lincoln's birth, Barack Obama's presidency is one fulfillment of the work Lincoln started.   1

Lincoln shares his birthday with Charles Darwin, the other Great Emancipator of the 19th century. In different ways, each liberated us from tradition.   2

Charles Darwin and Abraham Lincoln were exact contemporaries. Both were born on Feb. 12, 1809—Darwin into a comfortable family in Shropshire, England; Lincoln into humble circumstances on the American frontier.   3

They also came to international attention at virtually the same moment. Darwin published his epochal book, *On the Origin of Species*, in 1859. The following year, Lincoln became the 16th president of the United States. Also in 1860, Harvard botanist Asa Gray wrote the first review of Darwin's book to appear in this country.

4

Lincoln and Darwin initiated twin revolutions. One brought the Civil War and the emancipation of roughly four million slaves; the other, a new explanation of the natural world. Lincoln's war transformed the social, political and racial landscape in ways that continue to play out. Darwin transformed our understanding of biology, paving the way for countless advances in science, especially medicine.

5

With his powerful scientific explanation of the origins of species, Darwin dispensed with the pseudoscientific assertions of African American inferiority. In this way, Darwin provided the scientific legitimacy for Lincoln's political and moral actions.

6

The two revolutions shared a commitment to one proposition: that all human beings are fundamentally equal. In this sense, both Lincoln and Darwin deserve credit for emancipating us from the political and intellectual rationales for slavery.

7

For Lincoln, this was a political principle and a moral imperative. He was deeply ambivalent about the institution of slavery. As the war began, he believed that saving the Union, not abolishing slavery, was the cause worth fighting for. But as the war ground gruesomely on, he began to see that ending slavery was the only way to save the Union without making a mockery of the nation's founding ideals.

8

This is what Lincoln meant when he promised, in the 1863 Gettysburg Address, that the war would bring "a new birth of freedom." He was even more emphatic about it in his second inaugural address, in 1865. Slavery could not be permitted to exist in a nation founded on the belief that we are all created equal.

9

Darwin, for his part, was a deeply committed abolitionist from a family of deeply committed abolitionists. Exposed to slavery during his travels in South America, Darwin wrote, "It makes one's blood boil." He called abolishing slavery his "sacred cause." In some of his first notes about evolution, he railed against the idea that slaves were somehow less than human.

10

For Darwin, our shared humanity was a simple biological fact. Whatever variations exist among the human species—what we call *races*—are simply the natural variations that occur within all species. Like it or not, in a Darwinian world we are all members of one human family. This truth lay at the center of Darwin's science and his abolitionism.

11

That understanding of human equality—arrived at from different directions and for different reasons—helps explain the opposition to the revolutions unleashed by Lincoln and Darwin. It's also why many Americans—virtually alone in the developed world—continue to deny Darwinian science.

12

Many white Southerners never accepted Lincoln's basic proposition about the political equality of black Americans. In the years after the Civil War and Reconstruction, they set up the brutal structures and rituals of segregation. All of the elaborate laws, customs and violence of the segregated South served to deny the basic truth that all Americans are created equal. Most Northerners, meanwhile, didn't care much about the "Southern problem."

13

No wonder, then, that many Americans simply rejected Darwin's insights out of hand. Slavery and segregation rested on the assumption that black Americans were not fully human. Darwinian science put the lie to all that. 14

Lincoln insisted on equality as a political fact: Darwin demonstrated it as a biological fact. In their shared commitment to human equality, each in his own realm, these two Great Emancipators helped us break free from the shackles of the past. 15

Reacting to the Reading

1. Underline this essay's thesis statement. In the margin, paraphrase this thesis.
2. In the margins of the essay, label the content of each paragraph *Lincoln* or *Darwin*.

Reacting to Words

*1. Define these words: *Emancipator* (1), *epochal* (4), *imperative* (8), *ambivalent* (8), *emphatic* (9), *abolitionist* (10), *shackles* (15). Can you suggest a synonym for each word that will work in the essay?
*2. What exactly does Conn mean when he calls Lincoln and Darwin "these two Great Emancipators" (15)?

Reacting to Ideas

1. How are Lincoln and Darwin alike? What are their "twin revolutions"? How are these revolutions similar?
2. How are Lincoln and Darwin different? In Conn's view, is it their similarities or their differences that are most significant?
3. Why, according to Conn, were so many people opposed to both Lincoln's and Darwin's ideas?

Reacting to the Pattern

*1. Is this a point-by-point or a subject-by-subject comparison? How can you tell?
2. Does Conn make the same points about the two men he focuses on, or does he discuss some points for one man and not for the other? If the points he presents do not match exactly, do you see this as a problem?
3. What specific words and phrases does Conn use in this essay to introduce similarities and differences? (For example, in paragraph 7, he uses the word *both*.) Do you think he needs more words and phrases like these to make his points of comparison or contrast clear? If so, where?

Writing Practice

1. Write a comparison-and-contrast essay in which you compare and/or contrast two historical figures or fictional characters. In your thesis statement, be sure to communicate the significance of the central parallel or contrast you identify.

2. Write a comparison-and-contrast essay in which you compare and/or contrast your life before and after an important personal or historical event. What changed for you, and what remained the same?

MEN ARE FROM MARS, WOMEN ARE FROM VENUS

John Gray

Marriage counselor, seminar leader, and author John Gray has written a number of books that examine relationships between men and women. His best-known book, *Men Are from Mars, Women Are from Venus* (1992), suggests that men and women are at times so different that they might as well come from different planets. In the following excerpt from this book, Gray contrasts the different communication styles that he believes are characteristic of men and women. As you read, consider whether Gray's comparison oversimplifies the gender differences he discusses.

The most frequently expressed complaint women have about men is that men don't listen. Either a man completely ignores [a woman] when she speaks to him, or he listens for a few beats, assesses what is bothering her, and then proudly puts on his Mr. Fix-It cap and offers her a solution to make her feel better. He is confused when she doesn't appreciate this gesture of love. No matter how many times she tells him that he's not listening, he doesn't get it and keeps doing the same thing. She wants empathy, but he thinks she wants solutions.   1

The most frequently expressed complaint men have about women is that women are always trying to change them. When a woman loves a man she feels responsible to assist him in growing and tries to help him improve the way he does things. She forms a home-improvement committee, and he becomes her primary focus. No matter how much he resists her help, she persists—waiting for any opportunity to help him or tell him what to do. She thinks she's nurturing him, while he feels he's being controlled. Instead, he wants her acceptance.   2

These two problems can finally be solved by first understanding why men offer solutions and why women seek to improve. Let's pretend to go back in time, where by observing life on Mars and Venus—before the planets discovered one another or came to Earth—we can gain some insights into men and women.   3

Martians value power, competency, efficiency, and achievement. They are always doing things to prove themselves and develop their power and skills. Their sense of self is defined through their ability to achieve results. They experience fulfillment primarily through success and accomplishment.   4

Everything on Mars is a reflection of these values. Even their dress is designed to reflect their skills and competence. Police officers, soldiers, businessmen, scientists, cab drivers, technicians, and chefs all wear uniforms or at least hats to reflect their competence and power.   5

They don't read magazines like *Psychology Today*, *Self*, or *People*. They are more concerned with outdoor activities, like hunting, fishing, and racing cars. They are interested in the news, weather, and sports and couldn't care less about romance novels and self-help books.   6

They are more interested in "objects" and "things" rather than people and feelings. Even today on Earth, while women fantasize about romance, men fantasize about powerful cars, faster computers, gadgets, gizmos, and new more powerful technology. Men are preoccupied with the "things" that can help them express power by creating results and achieving their goals.

7

Achieving goals is very important to a Martian because it is a way for him to prove his competence and thus feel good about himself. And for him to feel good about himself he must achieve these goals by himself. Someone else can't achieve them for him. Martians pride themselves in doing things all by themselves. Autonomy is a symbol of efficiency, power, and competence.

8

Understanding this Martian characteristic can help women understand why men resist so much being corrected or being told what to do. To offer a man unsolicited advice is to presume that he doesn't know what to do or that he can't do it on his own. Men are very touchy about this, because the issue of competence is so very important to them.

9

Because he is handling his problems on his own, a Martian rarely talks about his problems unless he needs expert advice. He reasons: "Why involve someone else when I can do it by myself?" He keeps his problems to himself unless he requires help from another to find a solution. Asking for help when you can do it yourself is perceived as a sign of weakness.

10

However, if he truly does need help, then it is a sign of wisdom to get it. In this case, he will find someone he respects and then talk about his problem. Talking about a problem on Mars is an invitation for advice. Another Martian feels honored by the opportunity. Automatically he puts on his Mr. Fix-It hat, listens for a while, and then offers some jewels of advice.

11

This Martian custom is one of the reasons men instinctively offer solutions when women talk about problems. When a woman innocently shares upset feelings or explores out loud the problems of her day, a man mistakenly assumes she is looking for some expert advice. He puts on his Mr. Fix-It hat and begins giving advice; this is his way of showing love and of trying to help.

12

He wants to help her feel better by solving her problems. He wants to be useful to her. He feels he can be valued and thus worthy of her love when his abilities are used to solve her problems.

13

Once he has offered a solution, however, and she continues to be upset it becomes increasingly difficult for him to listen because his solution is being rejected and he feels increasingly useless.

14

He has no idea that by just listening with empathy and interest he can be supportive. He does not know that on Venus talking about problems is not an invitation to offer a solution.

15

Venusians have different values. They value love, communication, beauty, and relationships. They spend a lot of time supporting, helping, and nurturing one another. Their sense of self is defined through their feelings and the quality of their relationships. They experience fulfillment through sharing and relating.

16

Everything on Venus reflects these values. Rather than building highways and tall buildings, the Venusians are more concerned with living together in harmony, community, and loving cooperation. Relationships are more important than work and technology. In most ways their world is the opposite of Mars.

17

They do not wear uniforms like the Martians (to reveal their competence). On the contrary, they enjoy wearing a different outfit every day, according to how they are feeling. Personal expression, especially of their feelings, is very important. They may even change outfits several times a day as their mood changes. 18

Communication is of primary importance. To share their personal feelings is much more important than achieving goals and success. Talking and relating to one another is a source of tremendous fulfillment. 19

This is hard for a man to comprehend. He can come close to understanding a woman's experience of sharing and relating by comparing it to the satisfaction he feels when he wins a race, achieves a goal, or solves a problem. 20

Instead of being goal oriented, women are relationship oriented; they are more concerned with expressing their goodness, love, and caring. Two Martians go to lunch to discuss a project or business goal; they have a problem to solve. In addition, Martians view going to a restaurant as an efficient way to approach food: no shopping, no cooking, and no washing dishes. For Venusians, going to lunch is an opportunity to nurture a relationship, for both giving support to and receiving support from a friend. Women's restaurant talk can be very open and intimate, almost like the dialogue that occurs between therapist and patient. 21

On Venus, everyone studies psychology and has at least a master's degree in counseling. They are very involved in personal growth, spirituality, and everything that can nurture life, healing, and growth. Venus is covered with parks, organic gardens, shopping centers, and restaurants. 22

Venusians are very intuitive. They have developed this ability through centuries of anticipating the needs of others. They pride themselves in being considerate of the needs and feelings of others. A sign of great love is to offer help and assistance to another Venusian without being asked. 23

Because proving one's competence is not as important to a Venusian, offering help is not offensive, and needing help is not a sign of weakness. A man, however, may feel offended because when a woman offers advice he doesn't feel she trusts his ability to do it himself. 24

A woman has no conception of this male sensitivity because for her it is another feather in her hat if someone offers to help her. It makes her feel loved and cherished. But offering help to a man can make him feel incompetent, weak, and even unloved. 25

On Venus it is a sign of caring to give advice and suggestions. Venusians firmly believe that when something is working it can always work better. Their nature is to want to improve things. When they care about someone, they freely point out what can be improved and suggest how to do it. Offering advice and constructive criticism is an act of love. 26

Mars is very different. Martians are more solution oriented. If something is working, their motto is don't change it. Their instinct is to leave it alone if it is working. "Don't fix it unless it is broken" is a common expression. 27

When a woman tries to improve a man, he feels she is trying to fix him. He receives the message that he is broken. She doesn't realize her caring attempts to help him may humiliate him. She mistakenly thinks she is just helping him to grow. 28

ESL Tip

Have native- and nonnative-speaking students work in groups or in pairs to discuss the exercises before they write their answers.

Teaching Tip

Students may need help defining words. With nonnative-speaking students, consider going over the definitions in class before assigning the reading.

Teaching Tip

Remind students to answer all questions in complete sentences.

Reacting to the Reading

1. In marginal annotations, number the specific characteristics of men and women that Gray identifies.
2. Using these characteristics as a guide, make an informal outline for a point-by-point comparison.

Reacting to Words

*1. Define these words: *empathy* (paragraph 1), *nurturing* (2), *autonomy* (8), *unsolicited* (9). Can you suggest a synonym for each word that will work in the essay?
2. Do you think referring to men as Martians and women as Venusians is an effective strategy? What other contrasting labels might work?

Reacting to Ideas

1. Do you think Gray is serious? Why or why not?
*2. Do you think Gray's specific observations about men and women are accurate? Is he stereotyping men and women? Explain.
*3. Do you agree with Gray's general point that men and women seem to be from two different planets? Why or why not?

Reacting to the Pattern

1. This essay is a subject-by-subject comparison. How does Gray signal the movement from the first subject to the second subject? Why do you suppose he chose to write a subject-by-subject rather than a point-by-point comparison?
*2. If you were going to add a more fully developed conclusion to sum up this selection's points, what closing strategy would you use? Do you think the selection needs such a conclusion?

Writing Practice

1. Are young (or adolescent) boys and girls also from two different planets? Take a position on this issue, and support it in an essay using subject-by-subject comparison. In your thesis statement, try to account for the differences you identify between boys and girls.
2. Identify one general area in which you believe men's and women's attitudes, behavior, or expectations are very different—for example, dating, careers, eating habits, sports, housekeeping, or driving. Write a comparison-and-contrast essay (serious or humorous) that explores the differences you identify.
3. How are men and women portrayed in television dramas or sitcoms? Choose a program that has several well-developed male and female characters, and write an essay in which you contrast the men and the women in terms of their actions and their conversations.

39g   Classification

A **classification** essay divides a whole into parts and sorts various items into categories. In "How Your Body Works," humorist Dave Barry classifies various parts of the human body. On a more serious note, Scott Russell Sanders's "The Men We Carry in Our Minds" classifies the working men he has known.

HOW YOUR BODY WORKS

Dave Barry

Well-known humorist Dave Barry is a nationally syndicated newspaper columnist who wrote for the *Miami Herald* from 1983 to 2005 and won the Pulitzer Prize for commentary in 1988. Barry has also published several books, most recently *I'll Mature When I'm Dead: Dave Barry's Amazing Tales of Adulthood* (2010). In this excerpt from his book *Stay Fit and Healthy Until You're Dead* (2000), Barry uses his characteristic brand of humor to classify different parts of the body. As you read, think about how you learned the information he presents.

1   Your body is like a superbly engineered luxury automobile: if you use it wisely and maintain it properly, it will eventually break down, most likely in a bad neighborhood. To understand why this is, let's take a look inside this fascinating "machine" we call the human body.

2   Your body is actually made up of billions and billions of tiny cells, called "cells," which are so small that you cannot see them. Neither can I. The only people who can see them are white-coated geeks called "biologists." These are the people who wrote your high-school biology textbooks, in which they claimed to have found all these organs inside the Frog, the Worm, and the Perch. Remember? And remember how, in Biology Lab, you were supposed to take an actual dead frog apart and locate the heart, the liver, etc., as depicted in the elaborate color diagrams in the textbook?

3   Of course, when you cut it open, all you ever found was frog glop, because that is what frogs contain, as has been proven in countless experiments performed by small boys with sticks. So you did what biology students have always done: you pretended you were finding all these organs in there, and you copied the diagram out of the book, knowing full well that in real life a frog would have no use whatsoever for a liver.

4   Anyway, biologists tell us that the human body consists of billions of these tiny cells, which combine to form organs such as the heart, the kidney, the eyeball, the funny bone, the clavichord, the pustule, and the hernia, which in turn combine to form the body, which in turn combines with other bodies to form the squadron. Now let's take a closer look at the various fitness-related organs and see if we can't think of things to say about them.

The Skin

5   Your skin performs several vital functions. For example, it keeps people from seeing the inside of your body, which is repulsive, and it prevents

your organs from falling out onto the ground, where careless pedestrians might step on them. Also, without skin, your body would have no place to form large facial zits on the morning before your wedding.

But for fitness-oriented persons like yourself, the important thing about skin is that it acts as your Body's Cooling System. Whenever you exercise or get on an elevator, sweat oozes out of millions of tiny skin holes so it can evaporate and cool the area. Unfortunately, virtually all of these holes are located in your armpits, which is stupid. I mean, you hardly ever hear people complaining about having hot armpits. So what we seem to have here is one of those cases where Mother Nature really screwed up, like when she developed the concept of nasal hair.   6

The Muscle System

Your muscles are what enable you to perform all of your basic movements, such as bowling, sniping, pandering, carping, and contacting your attorney. Basically, there are two kinds of muscle tissue: the kind that people in advertisements for fitness centers have, which forms units that look like sleek and powerful pythons writhing just beneath the surface of the skin, and the kind you have, which looks more like deceased baby rabbits.   7

The beauty of muscle tissue, however, is that it responds to exercise. In a later chapter, we'll talk about how, using modern exercise equipment such as the Nautilus machine in a scientific workout program, you can stretch those pudgy little muscle tissues of yours to the point where you won't even be able to scream for help without the aid of powerful painkilling drugs.   8

The Skeletal System

How many bones do you think your skeletal system has? Would you say 50? 150? 250? 300? More than 300?   9

If you guessed 50, you're a real jerk. I would say it's around 250, but I don't really see why it's all that important. The only important part of your skeleton, for fitness purposes, is your knees.   10

Knees are God's way of telling mankind that He doesn't want us to do anything really strenuous. When we do, our knees punish us by becoming injured, as you know if you've ever watched professional football on television: 11

ANNOUNCER	The handoff goes to Burger; he's tackled at the six. . . . Uh oh! He's hurt!
COLOR COMMENTATOR	Looks like a knee injury, Bob, from the way that bone there is sticking out of his knee.
ANNOUNCER	Burger's teammates are bending over him. . . . Uh oh! Now *they're* down on the field!
COLOR COMMENTATOR	Looks like they've all injured their knees, too, Bob.
ANNOUNCER	Here comes the team physician, who is . . . Uh oh! Now *he's* down on the . . .

So one of the things we're going to stress in our fitness program is knee safety. We're going to get you so aware of this important topic that you won't even discuss racquetball over the telephone without first putting on knee braces the size of industrial turbines.

12

The Digestive System

Your digestive system is your body's Fun House, whereby food goes on a long, dark, scary ride, taking all kinds of unexpected twists and turns, being attacked by vicious secretions along the way, and not knowing until the last minute whether it will be turned into a useful body part or ejected into the Dark Hole by Mister Sphincter. You must be careful about what you eat, unless you want your body making heart valves out of things like bean dip.

13

The Central Nervous System

The central nervous system is your body's Messenger, always letting your brain know what's going on elsewhere in your body. "Your nose itches!" it tells your brain. Or, "Your foot is falling asleep!!" Or, "You're hungry!!!" All day long, your brain hears messages like these, thousands of them, hour after hour, until finally it deliberately rests your hand on a red-hot stove just for the pleasure of hearing your nervous system scream in pain.

14

Your Respiratory System

Your respiratory system takes in oxygen and gives off carbon monoxide, a deadly gas, by a process called "photosynthesis." This takes place in your lungs, yam-shaped organs in your chest containing millions of tiny little air sacs, called "Bernice." In a normal person, these sacs are healthy and pink, whereas in smokers they have the wretched, soot-stained, anguished look of the people fleeing Atlanta in *Gone with the Wind*. This has led many noted medical researchers to conclude that smoking is unhealthy, but we must weigh this against the fact that most of the people in cigarette advertisements are generally horse-riding, helicopter-flying hunks of major-league manhood, whereas your noted medical researchers tend to be pasty little wimps of the variety that you routinely held upside down over the toilet in junior high school.

15

The Circulatory System

This is, of course, your heart, a fist-sized muscle in your chest with a two-inch-thick layer of greasy fat clinging to it consisting of every Milky Way you ever ate. Your heart's job is to pump your blood, which appears to be nothing more than a red liquid but which, according to biologists (this should come as no surprise), is actually teeming with millions of organisms, some of them with tentacles so they can teem more efficiently.

16

The only organisms that actually belong in your blood are the red cells and the white cells. The red cells are your body's Room Service, carrying tiny particles of food and oxygen to the other organs, which snork them up without so much as a "thank you." The only reward the red cells get is iron in the form of prunes, which the other cells don't want anyway. If you don't eat enough prunes, your red cells get tired—a condition doctors call "tired blood"—and you have to lie down and watch "All My Children."

17

The white cells are your body's House Detectives. Most of the time they 18
lounge around the bloodstream, telling jokes and forming the occasional
cyst. But they swing into action the instant your body is invaded by one of
the many enemy organisms that can get into your bloodstream, these being
bacteria, viruses, rotifers, conifers, parameciums, cholesterol, tiny little lock-
jaw germs that dwell on the ends of all sharp objects, antacids, riboflavin,
and the plague. As soon as the white cells spot one of these, they drop whatever they're doing and pursue it on a wild and often hilarious chase through
your various organs, which sometimes results in damage to innocent tissue.
Eventually they catch the invader and tie its tentacles behind its back with
antibodies, which are the body's Handcuffs, and deport it via the bowel.

Of course this is just a brief rundown on your various organs and sys- 19
tems; in the short space I have here, it's very difficult for me to explain all
of your body's complexities and subtleties in any detail, or even get any
facts right. For more information, I suggest you attend Harvard Medical
School, which I believe is in Wisconsin.

Reacting to the Reading

1. What function do the headings serve in this essay? Would the essay
   work as well without them?
2. Next to the discussion of each category Barry identifies, write a one-
   sentence definition, based on the descriptions Barry provides.

Reacting to Words

*1. Define these words: *sniping* (paragraph 7), *pandering* (7), *carping* (7),
   teeming (16). Can you suggest a synonym for each word that will work
   in the essay?
*2. If you wanted to retitle this essay so it conveyed the idea of classifica-
   tion, what would you call it?
3. Barry's humorous essay is filled with slang terms, such as *glop* (3), *zits*
   (5), *jerk* (10), and *wimps* (15). Identify as many of these slang terms as
   you can. Do they seem appropriate here? Why or why not?

Reacting to Ideas

1. Do you think Barry is genuinely trying to be informative here, or is he
   just trying to entertain his readers? How can you tell?
*2. Barry uses a number of **analogies**—comparisons that explain unfamiliar items by comparing them to more familiar items—in this essay.
   For example, in paragraph 13, he says, "Your digestive system is your
   body's Fun House." Try to identify other analogies. Are they helpful in
   understanding his subject, or just amusing?

Reacting to the Pattern

1. What is the subject of this essay? Into what seven categories does Barry
   divide his subject? Can you think of any categories he does not discuss?
2. What, if anything, determines the order in which Barry presents his
   categories? Does this arrangement make sense to you? Would another
   order work as well?

3. Does Barry treat each category in the same way, or does he give more (or different) information about some categories?

Writing Practice

1. Rewrite this essay for an audience of elementary school students. Use your own words, and delete Barry's sarcastic comments and jokes; your purpose here is not to be funny or sarcastic but to explain seriously how the body's various systems work. Use Barry's categories, and try to give each category a new title; treat each category in similar terms. Include analogies and diagrams or other illustrations if you think they will be helpful to your audience.

2. Write a classification essay that gives readers an overview of this textbook. What are its major divisions? What kind of material is found in each category? Is any category more important than the others? (Use the table of contents on page xiii to help you organize your essay.)

THE MEN WE CARRY IN OUR MINDS

Scott Russell Sanders

Scott Russell Sanders is a professor of English and an essayist. His essays are personal reflections that include social and philosophical commentary and are often set in the Midwest, where he was born and raised. In "The Men We Carry in Our Minds," first published in the *Milkweed Chronicle* in 1984, Sanders reflects on the working lives of the men he knew when he was a boy and classifies them according to the kind of work they do. His essay discusses not only his boyhood impressions of the work these men did but also the direction his own professional life has taken. As you read, notice how Sanders moves from classifying men's work to comparing men's lives to women's lives.

Teaching Tip
Remind students to familiarize themselves with the end-of-essay questions before they read the essay.

The first men, besides my father, I remember seeing were black convicts and white guards, in the cottonfield across the road from our farm on the outskirts of Memphis. I must have been three or four. The prisoners wore dingy gray-and-black zebra suits, heavy as canvas, sodden with sweat. Hatless, stooped, they chopped weeds in the fierce heat, row after row, breathing the acrid dust of boll-weevil poison. The overseers wore dazzling white shirts and broad shadowy hats. The oiled barrels of their shotguns flashed in the sunlight. Their faces in memory are utterly blank. Of course those men, white and black, have become for me an emblem of racial hatred. But they have also come to stand for the twin poles of my early vision of manhood—the brute toiling animal and the boss.   1

When I was a boy, the men I knew labored with their bodies. They were marginal farmers, just scraping by, or welders, steelworkers, carpenters; they swept floors, dug ditches, mined coal, or drove trucks, their forearms ropy with muscle; they trained horses, stoked furnaces, built tires, stood on assembly lines wrestling parts onto cars and refrigerators. They got up before light, worked all day long whatever the weather, and when they came home at night they looked as though somebody had been whipping them. In the evenings and on weekends they worked on their own places, tilling gardens that were lumpy with clay, fixing broken-down cars, hammering on houses that were always too drafty, too leaky, too small.   2

The bodies of the men I knew were twisted and maimed in ways visible and invisible. The nails of their hands were black and split, the hands tattooed with scars. Some had lost fingers. Heavy lifting had given many of them finicky backs and guts weak from hernias. Racing against conveyor belts had given them ulcers. Their ankles and knees ached from years of standing on concrete. Anyone who had worked for long around machines was hard of hearing. They squinted, and the skin of their faces was creased like the leather of old work gloves. There were times, studying them, when I dreaded growing up. Most of them coughed, from dust or cigarettes, and most of them drank cheap wine or whiskey, so their eyes looked bloodshot and bruised. The fathers of my friends always seemed older than the mothers. Men wore out sooner. Only women lived into old age. **3**

As a boy I also knew another sort of men, who did not sweat and break down like mules. They were soldiers, and so far as I could tell they scarcely worked at all. During my early school years we lived on a military base, an arsenal in Ohio, and every day I saw GIs in the guardshacks, on the stoops of barracks, at the wheels of olive drab Chevrolets. The chief fact of their lives was boredom. Long after I left the Arsenal I came to recognize the sour smell the soldiers gave off as that of souls in limbo. They were all waiting—for wars, for transfers, for leaves, for promotions, for the end of their hitch—like so many braves waiting for the hunt to begin. Unlike the warriors of older tribes, however, they would have no say about when the battle would start or how it would be waged. Their waiting was broken only when they practiced for war. They fired guns at targets, drove tanks across the churned-up fields of the military reservation, set off bombs in the wrecks of old fighter planes. I knew this was all play. But I also felt certain that when the hour for killing arrived, they would kill. When the real shooting started, many of them would die. This was what soldiers were *for*, just as a hammer was for driving nails. **4**

Warriors and toilers: those seemed, in my boyhood vision, to be the chief destinies for men. They weren't the only destinies, as I learned from having a few male teachers, from reading books, and from watching television. But the men on television—the politicians, the astronauts, the generals, the savvy lawyers, the philosophical doctors, the bosses who gave orders to both soldiers and laborers—seemed as removed and unreal to me as the figures in tapestries. I could no more imagine growing up to become one of these cool, potent creatures than I could imagine becoming a prince. **5**

A nearer and more hopeful example was that of my father, who had escaped from a red-dirt farm to a tire factory, and from the assembly line to the front office. Eventually he dressed in a white shirt and tie. He carried himself as if he had been born to work with his mind. But his body, remembering the earlier years of slogging work, began to give out on him in his fifties, and it quit on him entirely before he turned sixty-five. Even such a partial escape from man's fate as he had accomplished did not seem possible for most of the boys I knew. They joined the Army, stood in line for jobs in the smoky plants, helped build highways. They were bound to work as their fathers had worked, killing themselves or preparing to kill others. **6**

A scholarship enabled me not only to attend college, a rare enough feat in my circle, but even to study in a university meant for the children of the rich. Here I met for the first time young men who had assumed from birth that they would lead lives of comfort and power. And for the first time **7**

I met women who told me that men were guilty of having kept all the joys and privileges of the earth for themselves. I was baffled. What privileges? What joys? I thought about the maimed, dismal lives of most of the men back home. What had they stolen from their wives and daughters? The right to go five days a week, twelve months a year, for thirty or forty years to a steel mill or a coal mine? The right to drop bombs and die in war? The right to feel every leak in the roof, every gap in the fence, every cough in the engine, as a wound they must mend? The right to feel, when the layoff comes or the plant shuts down, not only afraid but ashamed?

I was slow to understand the deep grievances of women. This was because, as a boy, I had envied them. Before college, the only people I had ever known who were interested in art or music or literature, the only ones who read books, the only ones who ever seemed to enjoy a sense of ease and grace were the mothers and daughters. Like the menfolk, they fretted about money, they scrimped and made-do. But, when the pay stopped coming in, they were not the ones who had failed. Nor did they have to go to war, and that seemed to me a blessed fact. By comparison with the narrow, ironclad days of fathers, there was an expansiveness, I thought, in the days of mothers. They went to see neighbors, to shop in town, to run errands at school, at the library, at church. No doubt, had I looked harder at their lives, I would have envied them less. It was not my fate to become a woman, so it was easier for me to see the graces. Few of them held jobs outside the home, and those who did filled thankless roles as clerks and waitresses. I didn't see, then, what a prison a house could be, since houses seemed to me brighter, handsomer places than any factory. I did not realize—because such things were never spoken of—how often women suffered from men's bullying. I did learn about the wretchedness of abandoned wives, single mothers, widows; but I also learned about the wretchedness of lone men. Even then I could see how exhausting it was for a mother to cater all day to the needs of young children. But if I had been asked, as a boy, to choose between tending a baby and tending a machine, I think I would have chosen the baby. (Having now tended both, I know I would choose the baby.)

So I was baffled when the women at college accused me and my sex of having cornered the world's pleasures. I think something like my bafflement has been felt by other boys (and by girls as well) who grew up in dirt-poor farm country, in mining country, in black ghettos, in Hispanic barrios, in the shadows of factories, in Third World nations—any place where the fate of men is as grim and bleak as the fate of women. Toilers and warriors. I realize now how ancient these identities are, how deep the tug they exert on men, the undertow of a thousand generations. The miseries I saw, as a boy, in the lives of nearly all men I continue to see in the lives of many—the body-breaking toil, the tedium, the call to be tough, the humiliating powerlessness, the battle for a living and for territory.

When the women I met at college thought about the joys and privileges of men, they did not carry in their minds the sort of men I had known in my childhood. They thought of their fathers, who were bankers, physicians, architects, stockbrokers, the big wheels of the big cities. These fathers rode the train to work or drove cars that cost more than any of my childhood houses. They were attended from morning to night by female helpers, wives and nurses and secretaries. They were never laid off, never short of cash at month's end, never lined up for welfare. These fathers made decisions that mattered. They ran the world.

The daughters of such men wanted to share in this power, this glory. 11
So did I. They yearned for a say over their future, for jobs worthy of their
abilities, for the right to live at peace, unmolested, whole. Yes, I thought,
yes yes. The difference between me and these daughters was that they saw
me, because of my sex, as destined from birth to become like their fathers,
and therefore as an enemy to their desires. But I knew better. I wasn't an
enemy, in fact or in feeling. I was an ally. If I had known, then, how to tell
them so, would they have believed me? Would they now?

Reacting to the Reading

1. In the margins of the essay, name and number the categories Sanders
   identifies. If he does not name a particular category, supply a suitable
   name.
2. Highlight the key ideas in paragraph 8. Then, write a one-sentence
   summary of this paragraph's ideas in the margin. Be sure to use your
   own words.

ESL Tip
Have native- and nonnative-
speaking students work in
groups or in pairs to discuss
the exercises before they write
their answers.

Reacting to Words

*1. Define these words: *sodden* (1), *acrid* (1), *overseers* (1), *tilling* (2), *finicky*
   (3), *toilers* (5), *savvy* (5), *expansiveness* (8), *undertow* (9), *yearned* (11).
   Can you suggest a synonym for each word that will work in the essay?
2. Suggest two or three alternative names for the categories *warriors*
   and *toilers* (5). Do you think any of your suggestions are better than
   Sanders's choices?

Teaching Tip
Students may need help defining
words. With nonnative-speaking
students, consider going over
the definitions in class before
assigning the reading.

Reacting to Ideas

1. When Sanders was young, what did he see as his destiny? How did he
   escape his fate? How else do you think he might have escaped?
2. What were the grievances of the women Sanders met at college? Why
   did Sanders have trouble understanding these grievances?
*3. Who do you believe has an easier life—men or women? Explain.

Teaching Tip
Remind students to answer
all questions in complete
sentences.

Reacting to the Pattern

1. What two types of men did Sanders know when he was young? How
   are they different? What do they have in common?
2. What kinds of men discussed in the essay do not fit into the two
   categories Sanders identifies in paragraphs 2 through 4? Why don't
   they fit?
*3. Sanders does not categorize the women he discusses. Can you think of
   a few categories into which these women could fit?

Writing Practice

1. Write a classification essay in which you identify and discuss three or
   four categories of workers (females as well as males) you observed in
   your community when you were growing up. In your thesis statement,

draw a conclusion about the relative status and rewards of these workers' jobs.

2. Consider your own work history as well as your future career. Write a classification essay in which you discuss your experience in several different categories of employment in the past, present, and future. Give each category a descriptive title, and include a thesis statement that sums up your progress.

3. Write an essay in which you categorize the workers in your current place of employment or on your college campus.

39h Definition

A **definition** essay presents an extended definition, using other patterns of development to move beyond a simple dictionary definition. In "Quinceañera," Julia Alvarez defines a coming-of-age ritual for Latinas. In "I Want a Wife," Judy Brady defines a family role.

QUINCEAÑERA

Julia Alvarez

Born in New York City to Dominican parents, Julia Alvarez has published numerous works of fiction and nonfiction, including poetry, children's stories, novels, and essays. One of her most famous books, *In the Time of the Butterflies* (1994), offers a fictionalized account of the tragic story of three sisters who became revolutionary leaders in the Dominican Republic under the dictatorship of Rafael Trujillo. (Alvarez's own family fled this regime in 1960.) As you read this excerpt from the nonfiction work *Once Upon a Quinceañera: Coming of Age in the USA* (2007), note how Alvarez uses her own childhood experiences to help her define a *quinceañera*.

What exactly is a *quinceañera*?   1

The question might soon be rhetorical in our quickly Latinoizing American culture. Already, there is a *Quinceañera* Barbie; *quinceañera* packages at Disney World and Las Vegas; an award-winning movie, *Quinceañera*; and for tots, *Dora the Explorer* has an episode about her cousin Daisy's *quinceañera*.   2

A *quinceañera* (the term is used interchangeably for the girl and her party) celebrates a girl's passage into womanhood with an elaborate, ritualized *fiesta* on her fifteenth birthday. (*Quince años*, thus *quinceañera*, pronounced: keen-seah-gnéer-ah.) In the old countries, this was a marker birthday: after she turned fifteen, a girl could attend adult parties; she was allowed to tweeze her eyebrows, use makeup, shave her legs, wear jewelry and heels. In short, she was ready for marriage. (Legal age for marriage in many Caribbean and Latin and Central American countries is, or until recently was, fifteen or younger for females, sixteen or older for males.) Even humble families marked a girl's fifteenth birthday as special, perhaps with a cake, certainly with a gathering of family and friends at which the *quinceañera* could now socialize and dance with young men. Upper-class   3 families, of course, threw more elaborate parties at which girls dressed up in long, formal gowns and danced waltzes with their fathers.

Somewhere along the way these fancier parties became highly ritual-   4
ized. In one or another of our Latin American countries, the *quinceañera* was crowned with a tiara; her flat shoes were changed by her father to heels; she was accompanied by a court of fourteen *damas* escorted by four-teen *chambelanes*, who represented her first fourteen years; she received a last doll, marking both the end of childhood and her symbolic readiness to bear her own child. And because our countries were at least nominally Catholic, the actual party was often preceded by a Mass or a blessing in church or, at the very least, a priest was invited to give spiritual heft to the *fiesta*. These celebrations were covered in newspapers, lavish spreads of photos I remember poring over as a little girl in the Dominican Republic, reassured by this proof that the desire to be a princess did not have to be shed at the beginning of adulthood, but could in fact be played out happily to the tune of hundreds upon thousands of Papi's *pesos*.

In the late sixties, when many of our poor headed to *el Norte*'s land of   5
opportunity, they brought this tradition along, and with growing economic power, the no-longer-so-poor could emulate the rich back home. The spin-offs grew (*quinceañera* cruises, *quinceañera* resort packages, *quinceañera* vid-eos and photo shoots); stories of where this *quinceañera* custom had come from proliferated (an ancient Aztec tradition, an import from European courts); further elaborations were added (Disney themes, special entrances, staged dance routines à la Broadway musicals); and in our Pan-Hispanic mixing stateside, the U.S. *quinceañera* adopted all the little touches of spe-cific countries to become a much more elaborate (and expensive) ceremony, exported back to our home countries. But rock-bottom, the U.S. *quinceañera* is powered by that age-old immigrant dream of giving the children what their parents had never been able to afford back where they came from.

In fact, the *quince* expression notwithstanding, many of us older first-   6
generation Latinas never had a *quinceañera*. There was no money back when we were fifteen, or we had recently arrived in the United States and didn't want anything that would make us stand out as other than all-American. Or we looked down our noses at such girly-girl fuss and said we didn't want a *quince* because we didn't understand that this was not just about us.

These cultural celebrations are also about building community in a   7
new land. Lifted out of the context of our home cultures, traditions like the *quinceañera* become malleable; they mix with the traditions of other cultures that we encounter here; they become exquisite performances of our ethnicities within the larger host culture while at the same time reaf-firming that we are not "them" by connecting us if only in spirit to our root cultures. In other words, this tradition tells a larger story of our transfor-mation into Latinos, a Pan-Hispanic group made in the USA, now being touted as the "new Americans."

Reacting to the Reading

ESL Tip
Have native- and nonnative-speaking students work in groups or in pairs to discuss the exercises before they write their answers.

1. Underline the formal (dictionary) definition of *quinceañera* that Alvarez includes in this essay. In the margin, rewrite this definition in your own words.

2. Circle all the Spanish words that Alvarez uses. If any of them are not famil-iar to you, look them up, and then write brief definitions in the margin.

Reacting to Words

*1. Define these words: *rhetorical* (paragraph 2), *ritualized* (4), *symbolic* (4), *nominally* (4), *heft* (4), *emulate* (5), *reaffirming* (7), *touted* (7). Can you suggest a synonym for each word that will work in the essay?

2. Alvarez uses a number of Spanish words in this essay, but she does not define them. Do you think she should have provided definitions? Why or why not?

Teaching Tip
Students may need help defining words. With non-native speaking students, consider going over the definitions in class before assigning the reading.

Reacting to Ideas

1. Do you think Alvarez expects her readers to be familiar with the term she is defining? How can you tell?

2. In paragraph 5, Alvarez explains how the *quinceañera* grew and changed as Latino families settled in the United States. What is her attitude toward these changes? For example, does she seem to suggest that they have somehow lessened the meaning of the ritual?

3. According to Alvarez, what is the value of the *quinceañera* for Latinas? For the culture of which they are a part?

Teaching Tip
Remind students to answer all questions in complete sentences.

Reacting to the Pattern

1. Where does Alvarez give information about the origin of the term *quinceañera*?

2. Where does Alvarez develop her definition with examples? Where does she use description? Does she use any other patterns of development?

Writing Practice

1. Write a definition essay about a coming-of-age ritual that is significant in your own community, culture, or religion. Assume that your readers are not familiar with the ritual you are discussing, and develop your definition with exemplification and description. (You can also use comparison and contrast if you think explaining your ritual by showing how it is like a more familiar practice will be helpful to your readers.)

2. Write a definition essay about a coming-of-age ritual with which you are familiar. Develop your definition primarily through narration—by telling the story of your own introduction to this ritual.

I WANT A WIFE

Judy Brady

Judy Brady helped found the Toxic Links Coalition, an organization dedicated to exposing the dangers of environmental toxins and their impact on public health. She was also an activist in the women's movement, and her classic essay "I Want a Wife" was published in the first issue of *Ms.* magazine (1971). As you read, note how Brady uses examples to support her definition of a wife.

Teaching Tip
Remind students to familiarize themselves with the end-of-essay questions before they read the essay.

I belong to that classification of people known as wives. I am A Wife. And, not altogether incidentally, I am a mother.

Not too long ago a male friend of mine appeared on the scene fresh from a recent divorce. He had one child, who is, of course, with his ex-wife. He is looking for another wife. As I thought about him while I was ironing one evening, it suddenly occurred to me that I, too, would like to have a wife. Why do I want a wife?

I would like to go back to school so that I can become economically independent, support myself, and, if need be, support those dependent upon me. I want a wife who will work and send me to school. And while I am going to school I want a wife to take care of my children. I want a wife to keep track of the children's doctor and dentist appointments. And to keep track of mine, too. I want a wife to make sure my children eat properly and are kept clean. I want a wife who will wash the children's clothes and keep them mended. I want a wife who is a good nurturant attendant to my children, who arranges for their schooling, makes sure that they have an adequate social life with their peers, takes them to the park, the zoo, etc. I want a wife who takes care of the children when they are sick, a wife who arranges to be around when the children need special care, because, of course, I cannot miss classes at school. My wife must arrange to lose time at work and not lose the job. It may mean a small cut in my wife's income from time to time, but I guess I can tolerate that. Needless to say, my wife will arrange and pay for the care of the children while my wife is working.

I want a wife who will take care of *my* physical needs. I want a wife who will keep my house clean. A wife who will pick up after my children, a wife who will pick up after me. I want a wife who will keep my clothes clean, ironed, mended, replaced when need be, and who will see to it that my personal things are kept in their proper place so that I can find what I need the minute I need it. I want a wife who cooks the meals, a wife who is a *good* cook. I want a wife who will plan the menus, do the necessary grocery shopping, prepare the meals, serve them pleasantly, and then do the cleaning up while I do my studying. I want a wife who will care for me when I am sick and sympathize with my pain and loss of time from school. I want a wife to go along when our family takes a vacation so that someone can continue to care for me and my children when I need a rest and change of scene.

I want a wife who will not bother me with rambling complaints about a wife's duties. But I want a wife who will listen to me when I feel the need to explain a rather difficult point I have come across in my course of studies. And I want a wife who will type my papers for me when I have written them.

I want a wife who will take care of the details of my social life. When my wife and I are invited out by my friends, I want a wife who will take care of the babysitting arrangements. When I meet people at school that I like and want to entertain, I want a wife who will have the house clean, will prepare a special meal, serve it to me and my friends, and not interrupt when I talk about things that interest me and my friends. I want a wife who will have arranged that the children are fed and ready for bed before my guests arrive so that the children do not bother us. I want a wife who takes care of the needs of my guests so that they feel comfortable, who makes sure that they have an ashtray, that they are passed the hors d'oeuvres, that they are offered a second helping of the food, that their wine glasses are replenished when necessary, that their coffee is served to them as they like it. And I want a wife who knows that sometimes I need a night out by myself.

I want a wife who is sensitive to my sexual needs, a wife who makes love passionately and eagerly when I feel like it, a wife who makes sure that I am satisfied. And, of course, I want a wife who will not demand sexual attention when I am not in the mood for it. I want a wife who assumes the complete responsibility for birth control, because I do not want more children. I want a wife who will remain sexually faithful to me so that I do not have to clutter up my intellectual life with jealousies. And I want a wife who understands that *my* sexual needs may entail more than strict adherence to monogamy. I must, after all, be able to relate to people as fully as possible.   7

If, by chance, I find another person more suitable as a wife than the wife I already have, I want the liberty to replace my present wife with another one. Naturally, I will expect a fresh new life; my wife will take the children and be solely responsible for them so that I am left free.   8

When I am through with school and have a job, I want my wife to quit working and remain at home so that my wife can more fully and completely take care of a wife's duties.   9

My God, who *wouldn't* want a wife?   10

Reacting to the Reading

1. Review all the characteristics of a wife that Brady mentions. Then, in the margin, write a one-sentence definition of *wife* that summarizes these characteristics.

2. In the margin beside paragraph 10, answer Brady's concluding question.

ESL Tip
Have native- and nonnative-speaking students work in groups or in pairs to discuss the exercises before they write their answers.

Reacting to Words

*1. Define these words: *nurturant* (3), *peers* (3), *hors d'oeuvres* (6), *replenished* (6), *adherence* (7), *monogamy* (7). Can you suggest a synonym for each word that will work in the essay?

*2. Brady repeats the word *wife* over and over in her essay. Can you think of other words she could have used instead? How might using these words change her essay?

Teaching Tip
Students may need help defining words. With nonnative-speaking students, consider going over the definitions in class before assigning the reading.

Reacting to Ideas

1. How do you define *wife*? Is your idea of a wife different from Brady's? If so, exactly what is the difference?

2. What central point or idea do you think Brady wants to communicate to her readers? Does she ever actually state this idea? If not, do you think she should?

*3. Brady's essay was written in 1971. Does her idea of a wife seem dated, or does it still seem accurate to you?

Teaching Tip
Remind students to answer all questions in complete sentences.

Reacting to the Pattern

1. Does Brady include a formal definition of *wife* anywhere in her essay? If so, where? If not, do you think she should?

*2. Brady develops her definition with examples. What are some of her most important examples?

3. Besides exemplification, what other patterns of development does Brady use to develop her definition?

Writing Practice

1. Assume you are Brady's husband and feel unjustly attacked by her essay. Write her a letter in which you define *husband*, using as many examples as you can to show how overworked and underappreciated you are.

2. Write an essay in which you define your ideal teacher, parent, spouse, or boss.

Teaching Tip
Refer students to 16i for more on how to write an argument essay.

Teaching Tip
Before you begin this unit, you may want to review the difference between an inductive argument and a deductive argument. Refer students to 16i.

39i   Argument

An **argument** essay takes a stand on one side of a debatable issue, using facts, examples, and expert opinion to persuade readers to accept a position. The writers of the three essays that follow—Mary Sherry in "In Praise of the F Word," Oprah Winfrey in "Dnt Txt N Drv," and Steven Pinker in "Mind over Mass Media"—try to convince readers to accept their positions or at least to acknowledge that they are reasonable.

IN PRAISE OF THE F WORD

Mary Sherry

Mary Sherry is a writer and an adult literacy educator. "In Praise of the F Word," which was first published in the "My Turn" column of *Newsweek* in 1991, argues that it is good for students to fail once in a while because it motivates them to continue to do their best work. As you read Sherry's essay, think about how persuasive her argument is, noting the facts and examples she uses to support her claims.

Teaching Tip
Remind students to familiarize themselves with the end-of-essay questions before they read the essay.

Tens of thousands of 18-year-olds will graduate this year and be handed meaningless diplomas. These diplomas won't look any different from those awarded their luckier classmates. Their validity will be questioned only when their employers discover that these graduates are semiliterate.   1

Eventually a fortunate few will find their way into educational-repair shops—adult-literacy programs, such as the one where I teach basic grammar and writing. There, high-school graduates and high-school dropouts pursuing graduate-equivalency certificates will learn the skills they should have learned in school. They will also discover they have been cheated by our educational system.   2

As I teach, I learn a lot about our schools. Early in each session I ask my students to write about an unpleasant experience they had in school. No writers' block here! "I wish someone would have had made me stop doing drugs and made me study." "I liked to party and no one seemed to   3 care." "I was a good kid and didn't cause any trouble, so they just passed me along even though I didn't read and couldn't write." And so on.

I am your basic do-gooder, and prior to teaching this class I blamed the poor academic skills our kids have today on drugs, divorce and other impediments to concentration necessary for doing well in school. But, as I rediscover each time I walk into the classroom, before a teacher can expect students to concentrate, he has to get their attention, no matter what distractions may be at hand. There are many ways to do this, and they have much to do with teaching style. However, if style alone won't do it, there is another way to show who holds the winning hand in the classroom. That is to reveal the trump card of failure.

I will never forget a teacher who played that card to get the attention of one of my children. Our youngest, a world-class charmer, did little to develop his intellectual talents but always got by. Until Mrs. Stifter.

Our son was a high-school senior when he had her for English. "He sits in the back of the room talking to his friends," she told me. "Why don't you move him to the front row?" I urged, believing the embarrassment would get him to settle down. Mrs. Stifter looked at me steely-eyed over her glasses. "I don't move seniors," she said. "I flunk them." I was flustered. Our son's academic life flashed before my eyes. No teacher had ever threatened him with that before. I regained my composure and managed to say that I thought she was right. By the time I got home I was feeling pretty good about this. It was a radical approach for these times, but, well, why not? "She's going to flunk you," I told my son. I did not discuss it any further. Suddenly English became a priority in his life. He finished out the semester with an A.

I know one example doesn't make a case, but at night I see a parade of students who are angry and resentful for having been passed along until they could no longer even pretend to keep up. Of average intelligence or better, they eventually quit school, concluding they were too dumb to finish. "I should have been held back," is a comment I hear frequently. Even sadder are those students who are high-school graduates who say to me after a few weeks of class, "I don't know how I ever got a high-school diploma."

Passing students who have not mastered the work cheats them and the employers who expect graduates to have basic skills. We excuse this dishonest behavior by saying kids can't learn if they come from terrible environments. No one seems to stop to think that—no matter what environments they come from—most kids don't put school first on their list unless they perceive something is at stake. They'd rather be sailing.

Many students I see at night could give expert testimony on unemployment, chemical dependency, abusive relationships. In spite of these difficulties, they have decided to make education a priority. They are motivated by the desire for a better job or the need to hang on to the one they've got. They have a healthy fear of failure.

People of all ages can rise above their problems, but they need to have a reason to do so. Young people generally don't have the maturity to value education in the same way my adult students value it. But fear of failure, whether economic or academic, can motivate both. Flunking as a regular policy has just as much merit today as it did two generations ago. We must review the threat of flunking and see it as it really is—a positive teaching tool. It is an expression of confidence by both teachers and parents that the students have the ability to learn the material presented to them. However, making it work again would take a dedicated, caring conspiracy between teachers and parents. It would mean facing the tough reality that passing kids who haven't learned the material—while it might save them grief for the short term—dooms them to long-term illiteracy. It would mean that teachers would have to follow through on their threats, and parents would have to stand behind them, knowing their children's best interests are indeed at stake. This means no more doing Scott's assignments for him because he might fail. No more passing Jodi because she's such a nice kid.

This is a policy that worked in the past and can work today. A wise   11
teacher, with the support of his parents, gave our son the opportunity to succeed—or fail. It's time we return this choice to all students.

Reacting to the Reading

1. Highlight the passage in which Sherry states her thesis.
2. Next to the passage, write a marginal note that explains why you think Sherry places her thesis there. Where else could she have stated her thesis? Would it have been more or less effective in this location? Why?

Reacting to Words

*1. Define these words: *semiliterate* (paragraph 1), *equivalency* (2), *distractions* (4), *trump card* (4), *flustered* (6), *composure* (6), *priority* (6), *perceive* (8), *motivated* (9), *merit* (10), *conspiracy* (10). Can you suggest a synonym for each word that will work in the essay?
*2. What does Sherry mean in paragraph 10 when she says, "Flunking as a regular policy has just as much merit today as it did two generations ago"?

Reacting to Ideas

1. Who or what does Sherry blame for the "meaningless diplomas" (1) that are being issued each year? What other reasons for this situation can you think of?
2. How does the experience Sherry's son had in high school convince her that the threat of failure is a "positive teaching tool" (10)?
*3. Do you agree with Sherry's point that if students do not have "a healthy fear of failure" (10), they will not be motivated to work? Explain.

Reacting to the Pattern

*1. Is Sherry's argument inductive or deductive? Explain. (For a discussion of these two types of argument, see page 287.)
2. What evidence does Sherry use to support her thesis? Does she present enough evidence? What other kinds of evidence should she have presented?
3. Does Sherry address arguments against her position? If so, where? What opposing arguments can you think of? How would you refute them?

Writing Practice

1. Write an argument essay that presents your opinion about using flunking as a teaching tool. Support your thesis with information from your own experience and observations. Be sure to state your position clearly and to include specific examples to support your thesis.

2. Choose a social or political issue you feel strongly about. Write an email to the editor of your local newspaper in which you take a stand on this issue.

DNT TXT N DRV

Oprah Winfrey

One of the most famous and successful women in the world today, Oprah Winfrey has made her mark as a television host, actress, producer, and philanthropist. She began her career in radio and television broadcasting and in 1985 won an Academy Award nomination for Best Supporting Actress for her role in the film *The Color Purple*. The following year, Winfrey began her twenty-five-year run as host of *The Oprah Winfrey Show*, eventually building a media empire that included the magazine *O: The Oprah Magazine* and OWN, the Oprah Winfrey television network. In "Dnt Txt N Drv," first published in the op-ed section of the *New York Times* in 2010, Winfrey makes the argument that texting while driving is an unfortunate but avoidable cause of many fatal car accidents. As you read, try to determine Winfrey's primary purpose in writing the article. Consider, too, the effect of her powerful final sentence.

Teaching Tip
Remind students to familiarize themselves with the end-of-essay questions before they read the essay.

When I started out as a TV reporter in Nashville in 1973, a death from drunken driving was big news. One person killed by a drunken driver would lead our local broadcast. Then, as the number of drunken driving deaths across the country continued to rise, the stakes for coverage got even higher. One death wasn't good enough anymore. Two deaths—that would warrant a report. Then a whole family had to die before the news would merit mention at the top of the broadcast. The country, all of us, had gotten used to the idea of drunken driving. I just kept thinking: How many people have to die before we "get it"? 1

Fortunately, we did get it, and since 1980, the number of annual traffic fatalities due to drunken driving has decreased to under 15,500 from more than 30,000. But in recent years, another kind of tragic story has begun to emerge with ever greater frequency. This time, we are mourning the deaths of those killed by people talking or sending text messages on their cellphones while they drive. 2

Earlier this month, I visited Shelley and Daren Forney, a couple in Fort Collins, Colo., whose 9-year-old daughter, Erica, was on her bicycle, just 15 pedals from her front door, when she was struck and killed by a driver who was distracted by a cellphone. I think about Erica's death and how senseless and stupid it was—caused by a driver distracted by a phone call that just couldn't wait. 3

Sadly, there are far too many stories like hers. At least 6,000 people were killed by distracted drivers in 2008, according to the National Highway Traffic Safety Administration, and the number is rising. A lot of good work already is happening to try to change this. President Obama signed 4 an executive order banning texting while driving on federal business. Transportation Secretary Ray LaHood is pushing for tougher laws and more enforcement. States are passing laws, too. Local groups are gaining strength, spurred by too many deaths close to home.

But we are hesitant to change. I saw this firsthand when I instituted 5 a policy at my company that forbids employees from using their phones for company business while driving. I heard countless stories about how hard it was for people to stop talking and texting while driving. Everyone is busy. Everyone feels she needs to use time in the car to get things done. But what happened to just driving?

It was difficult for my employees to adjust, but they have. Life is more 6 precious than taking a call or answering an e-mail message. Because even though we think we can handle using our cellphone in the car, the loss of thousands of lives has shown we can't.

So many issues that we have to deal with seem beyond our control: 7 natural disasters, child predators, traffic jams. Over the years, I've done shows on just about all of them. But this is a real problem we can do something about and get immediate results. All we have to do is hang up or switch off. It really is that simple. Once we do that, not another son or daughter will have to die because someone was on the phone and behind the wheel—and just not paying attention.

So starting from the moment you finish this article, and in the days, 8 weeks and years that follow, give it up. Please. And to those who feel like this is asking too much, think about your own child just 15 pedals from your front door. Struck down.

Reacting to the Reading

1. Underline Winfrey's thesis statement.
2. In the margin beside the thesis statement, rewrite it in your own words.

Reacting to Words

*1. Define these words: *warrant* (paragraph 1), *merit* (1), *emerge* (2), *frequency* (2), *distracted* (3), *executive order* (4), *enforcement* (4), *hesitant* (5), *predators* (7). Can you think of a synonym for each word that will work in the essay?
2. What does the title of this essay suggest to you? Why do you think Winfrey chose this title?

Reacting to Ideas

1. Winfrey begins her essay with an anecdote about her time as a TV reporter in Nashville. Why does she begin this way? Would another introductory strategy have been more effective? Explain.
*2. List other potentially distracting activities that people routinely perform as they drive. Do you think texting is more or less dangerous than these activities?
3. In her conclusion, Winfrey begs people to stop texting as they drive. Do you think her highly emotional appeal is appropriate? Is it effective?

ESL Tip
Have native- and nonnative-speaking students work in groups or in pairs to discuss the exercises before they write their answers.

Teaching Tip
Students may need help defining words. With nonnative-speaking students, consider going over the definitions in class before assigning the reading.

Teaching Tip
Remind students to answer all questions in complete sentences.

Reacting to the Pattern

1. Does Winfrey consider her audience to be friendly, hostile, or neutral? How can you tell?

2. Where in her essay does Winfrey introduce opposing arguments? Do you think she addresses them in enough detail? Explain.

3. Winfrey relies primarily on examples from her own experience as evidence. What are the advantages and disadvantages of this strategy? What other kinds of evidence does she use?

Writing Practice

1. Many states prohibit texting while driving. Write a letter to the National Highway Traffic Safety Administration arguing for or against this policy. Like Winfrey, use examples from your own experience to support your thesis.

2. Assume that you are an employee at Winfrey's company, Harpo Productions, and that you have been told that you cannot use your cell phone for company business while you drive. Write an email to Winfrey telling her why you disagree or agree with this decision.

3. Many high schools do not allow students to carry cell phones anywhere on school property. Assume that you are the parent of a high school student who is not permitted to carry a cell phone. Write a letter either to your child or to his or her principal in which you argue for or against this rule. (Be sure to refute the main arguments against your thesis.)

MIND OVER MASS MEDIA

Steven Pinker

Steven Pinker is a psychology professor at Harvard whose research on visual cognition and the psychology of language has won numerous awards. Pinker has written several prize-winning books, including *The Language Instinct* (1994), *How the Mind Works* (1997), and *The Blank Slate* (2002), and he frequently contributes to publications such as the *New York Times* and the *New Republic*. His latest book is *The Stuff of Thought: Language as a Window into Human Nature* (2007). In 2004, *Time* magazine included Pinker on its list of "The 100 Most Influential People in the World Today." In "Mind over Mass Media," first published in 2010 in the *New York Times*, Pinker argues against the common belief that mass media necessarily have negative effects on our brains and cognitive abilities. As you read this article, consider how Pinker uses facts and examples to persuade his audience.

Teaching Tip
Remind students to familiarize themselves with the end-of-essay questions before they read the essay.

New forms of media have always caused moral panics: the printing press, newspapers, paperbacks and television were all once denounced as threats to their consumers' brainpower and moral fiber.   1

So too with electronic technologies. PowerPoint, we're told, is reducing discourse to bullet points. Search engines lower our intelligence, encouraging us to skim on the surface of knowledge rather than dive to its depths. Twitter is shrinking our attention spans.   2

But such panics often fail basic reality checks. When comic books were accused of turning juveniles into delinquents in the 1950s, crime was falling to record lows, just as the denunciations of video games in the 1990s coincided with the great American crime decline. The decades of television, transistor radios and rock videos were also decades in which I.Q. scores rose continuously.   3

For a reality check today, take the state of science, which demands high levels of brainwork and is measured by clear benchmarks of discovery. These days scientists are never far from their e-mail, rarely touch paper and cannot lecture without PowerPoint. If electronic media were hazardous to intelligence, the quality of science would be plummeting. Yet discoveries are multiplying like fruit flies, and progress is dizzying. Other activities in the life of the mind, like philosophy, history and cultural criticism, are likewise flourishing, as anyone who has lost a morning of work to the Web site Arts & Letters Daily can attest.   4

Critics of new media sometimes use science itself to press their case, citing research that shows how "experience can change the brain." But cognitive neuroscientists roll their eyes at such talk. Yes, every time we learn a fact or skill the wiring of the brain changes; it's not as if the information is stored in the pancreas. But the existence of neural plasticity does not mean the brain is a blob of clay pounded into shape by experience.   5

Experience does not revamp the basic information-processing capacities of the brain. Speed-reading programs have long claimed to do just that, but the verdict was rendered by Woody Allen after he read "War and Peace" in one sitting: "It was about Russia." Genuine multitasking, too, has been exposed as a myth, not just by laboratory studies but by the familiar sight of an S.U.V. undulating between lanes as the driver cuts deals on his cellphone.   6

Moreover, as the psychologists Christopher Chabris and Daniel Simons show in their new book "The Invisible Gorilla: And Other Ways Our Intuitions Deceive Us," the effects of experience are highly specific to the experiences themselves. If you train people to do one thing (recognize shapes, solve math puzzles, find hidden words), they get better at doing that thing, but almost nothing else. Music doesn't make you better at math, conjugating Latin doesn't make you more logical, brain-training games don't make you smarter. Accomplished people don't bulk up their brains with intellectual calisthenics; they immerse themselves in their fields. Novelists read lots of novels, scientists read lots of science.   7

The effects of consuming electronic media are also likely to be far more limited than the panic implies. Media critics write as if the brain takes on the qualities of whatever it consumes, the informational equivalent of "you are what you eat." As with primitive peoples who believe that eating fierce animals will make them fierce, they assume that watching quick cuts in rock videos turns your mental life into quick cuts or that reading bullet points and Twitter postings turns your thoughts into bullet points and Twitter postings.   8

Yes, the constant arrival of information packets can be distracting or addictive, especially to people with attention deficit disorder. But distraction is not a new phenomenon. The solution is not to bemoan technology but to develop strategies of self-control, as we do with every other temptation in life. Turn off e-mail or Twitter when you work, put away your BlackBerry at dinner time, ask your spouse to call you to bed at a designated hour.   9

And to encourage intellectual depth, don't rail at PowerPoint or Google. It's not as if habits of deep reflection, thorough research and rigorous reasoning ever came naturally to people. They must be acquired in special institutions, which we call universities, and maintained with constant upkeep, which we call analysis, criticism and debate. They are not granted by propping a heavy encyclopedia on your lap, nor are they taken away by efficient access to information on the Internet.

10

The new media have caught on for a reason. Knowledge is increasing exponentially; human brainpower and waking hours are not. Fortunately, the Internet and information technologies are helping us manage, search and retrieve our collective intellectual output at different scales, from Twitter and previews to e-books and online encyclopedias. Far from making us stupid, these technologies are the only things that will keep us smart.

11

Reacting to the Reading

1. Where does Pinker state his thesis? Why do you think he chooses to state it where he does?

2. Underline any statements in this essay with which you disagree. In the margins, briefly explain why.

Reacting to Words

*1. Define these words: *media* (paragraph 1), *denounced* (1), *fiber* (1), *discourse* (2), *delinquents* (3), *denunciations* (3), *coincided* (3), *benchmarks* (4), *flourishing* (4), *cognitive* (5), *neuroscientists* (5), *pancreas* (5), *neural* (5), *plasticity* (5), *revamp* (6), *undulating* (6), *calisthenics* (7), *immerse* (7), *equivalent* (8), *bemoan* (9), *rail* (10), *exponentially* (11). Can you suggest a synonym for each word that will work in the essay? For which words were you unable to find a synonym? Why?

2. What does the term *new media* (5) suggest to you? Does it suggest something positive or negative? Explain.

Reacting to Ideas

1. In paragraph 3, Pinker talks about "reality checks." What are the reality checks he is referring to? According to him, what is the reality check for new media?

2. Critics of new media say that they can actually change the brain. How does Pinker respond to this charge?

*3. Do you think that Pinker is too optimistic about the advantages of new media? What disadvantages does he fail to consider?

Reacting to the Pattern

1. Is Pinker's argument inductive, deductive, or a combination of the two? (For a discussion of the two types of argument, see page 287.)

2. In paragraph 7, Pinker mentions a book written by the psychologists Christopher Chabris and Daniel Simons. How does he use their ideas to support his thesis?

*3. Where does Pinker introduce opposing arguments? How effectively does he refute them?

Writing Practice

1. Do you think that the Internet and other information technologies make us stupid(er) or make us smart(er)—or neither? Write an argument essay in which you answer this question.

2. Write a proposal to your school's president arguing for or against the idea that all incoming students should be required to buy a computer. Make sure your proposal has a clearly stated thesis, and support your points with examples from your own experience.

3. Write an editorial for your school's newspaper in which you take a stand on the issue of whether online classes are better or worse than traditional classes. Do online classes enable students to take full advantage of new technology, or do they shortchange students by depriving them of a classroom experience?

Acknowledgments

Picture Acknowledgments

1 YinYang/iStockphoto; **21T** Rene Sheret/Getty Images; **21B** Bill Aron/PhotoEdit; **46** Richard Ross/Photodisc/Getty Images; **67** vm/iStockphoto; **76** Created by the Kaplan Thaler Group; **77** From *One! Hundred! Demons!* by Lynda Barry. Copyright © 2002 by Lynda Barry. Published by Sasquatch Books and used with permission; **86** Digital Vision/Getty Images; **87** Alejandro Soto/iStockphoto; **96** Frank Siteman; **97** EuToch/iStockphoto; **108** Photofest; **109** lana13r/iStockphoto; **120** ManoAfrica/iStockphoto; **121L** James Devaney/Getty Images; **121R** John Shearer/Getty Images; **134T** Dennis Macdonald/Photolibrary; **134B** Richard Pasley/Stock Boston; **135** Chuck Savage/Corbis; **144** egal/iStockphoto; **145** Emily Behrendt; **155TL** Jupiter Images/Comstock Premium/Alamy; **155TR** Jose Luis Pelaez, Inc./Blend Images/Getty Images; **155BL** Rachel Epstein/The Image Works; **155BR** Michael Newman/PhotoEdit; **156** Win McNamee/Getty Images; **170** Giannina Amato, Creative Director and Copywriter; **173** Denis Sinyakov/Reuters; **205** Ken Reid/Getty Images; **206** David Young-Wolff/PhotoEdit; **208** OkCupid; **218** Photofest; **226T** Joseph Sohm/Visions of America/Corbis; **226B** Mark Kelley/Getty Images; **229** David Young-Wolff/PhotoEdit; **327** Courtesy of EBSCO Publishing, Inc.; **328** *Spanglish* by Ilan Stavans. Copyright © 2008 by Ilan Stavans. Reproduced with permission of ABC-CLIO, LLC.; **329** Elianne Ramos, Vice-Chair of Communications & PR, LATISM; **333** AP Photo/Kathy Willens; **342T** Mark Savage/Corbis; **342B** Reuters/Bill Davilla/Landov; **344** Stephen Ferry/Getty Images; **345** The Weinstein Company/The Kobal Collection; **356** University of Texas Libraries; **357** SuperStock; **359** Eric Fowke/PhotoEdit; **368** Greg Martin/SuperStock; **371** Senator John Heinz History Center; **388T** Bloomberg/Getty Images; **388B** Dennis Hallinan/Alamy; **389** The Advertising Archives; **391** vasiliki/iStockphoto; **397T** AP Photo/Harpo Productions, George Burns; **397B** Chris Hartlove; **400** Amanda Clement/Photodisc/Getty Images; **411T** Chris Ware/Getty Images; **411B** Library of Congress; **412** 3M Co.; **413T** John Madere/Corbis; **413B** Don Smetzer/PhotoEdit; **414** Ryan McGinnis/Alamy; **417** David Young-Wolff/PhotoEdit; **429T** King Features Syndicate, Inc.; **429B** AF archive/Alamy; **431** Erick W. Rasco/Getty Images; **454** ACA Galleries, New York; **465** Masterfile Corporation; **466T** AP Photo/Donna McWilliam; **466M** AP Photo/Robert E. Klein; **466B** John Madere/Corbis; **468** David Young-Wolff/PhotoEdit; **474** AP Photo/Kathy Willens; **484** Photofest; **485T** AP Photo/Seth Wenig; **485B** Bobby Bank/Getty Images; **487T** Park Street/PhotoEdit; **487B** Kim Steel/Photographer's Choice/Getty Images; **488** Pamela Chen/Syracuse Newspapers/The Image Works; **491** AP Photo; **498T** AP Photo/Jennifer Graylock; **498B** CRC Health Group; **500** Paramount Classics/courtesy Everett Collection; **512** Photofest; **535T** AP Photo/Paul Sakuma; **535B** Toby Burrows/Digital Vision/Getty Images; **538** Amy Etra/PhotoEdit; **546T** University of Texas Libraries; **546B** Abbas/Magnum Photos; **548** Christie's Images/SuperStock; **576T** Stuart Franklin/Magnum Photos; **576B** James Smalley/Photolibrary; **579T** GraphicMaps.com; **579B** AP Photo; **583T** Mario Tama/Getty Images; **583B** Joshua Lutz/Redux Pictures; **596** AP Photo/Eric Risberg; **597** University of Texas Libraries; **598** Tony Freeman/PhotoEdit; **603T** Library of Congress; **603B** Art Resource, NY; **605** Photofest; **618T** The British Library/HIP/The Image Works; **618B** National Library of Medicine; **619** Reuters/Bill Davilla/Landov; **621** Image Source/Getty Images; **660** The New York Times/Redux Pictures

Text Acknowledgments

Julia Alvarez. "Quinceañera." From *Once Upon a Quinceañera: Coming of Age in the USA*, by Julia Alvarez. Copyright © 2007 by Julia Alvarez. Published by Plume, an imprint of The Penguin Group (USA), Inc., and in hardcover by Viking. By permission of Susan Bergholz Literary Services, New York, NY, and Lamy, NM. All rights reserved.

Julia Angwin. "How Facebook Is Making Friending Obsolete." December 15, 2009. From *The Wall Street Journal* by Dow Jones & Company. Copyright © 2009. Reproduced with permission of Dow Jones & Company, Inc., via Copyright Clearance Center.

Russell Baker. "Slice of Life." From *The New York Times*, November 24, 1974. Copyright © 1974 by The New York Times. All rights reserved. Used by permission and protected by the Copyright Laws of the United States. The printing, copying, redistribution, or retransmission of the Material without express written permission is prohibited. [www.nytimes.com]

Brooks Barnes. Excerpt from "A Star Idolized and Haunted, Michael Jackson Dies at 50." From *The New York Times*, June 26, 2009. Copyright © 2009 by The New York Times. All rights reserved. Used by permission and protected by the Copyright Laws of the United States. The printing, copying, redistribution, or retransmission of the Material without express written permission is prohibited. [www.nytimes.com]

Dave Barry. "How Your Body Works." From *Stay Fit and Healthy Until You're Dead* by Dave Barry. Copyright © 1985 by Dave Barry. Reprinted by permission of Rodale Inc., Emmaus, PA 18098.

Lynda Barry. "The Sanctuary of School." From *The New York Times*, January 5, 1992. Copyright © 1992. Reprinted by permission of Darhansoff & Verrill Literary Agents.

Index

Note: Page numbers in **bold** type indicate pages where terms are defined.

Revision Symbols

This chart lists symbols that many instructors use to point out writing problems in student papers. Next to each problem is the chapter or section of *Writing First* where you can find help with that problem. If your instructor uses different symbols from those shown here, write them in the space provided.

YOUR INSTRUCTOR'S SYMBOL	STANDARD SYMBOL	PROBLEM
	adj	problem with use of adjective 32
	adv	problem with use of adverb 32
	agr	agreement problem (subject-verb) 26 agreement problem (pronoun-antecedent) 31d, 31e
	apos	apostrophe missing or used incorrectly 35
	awk	awkward sentence structure 27, 28
	cap or triple underline [example]	capital letter needed 36a
	case	problem with pronoun case 31g, 31h
	cliché	cliché 23d
	coh	lack of paragraph coherence 3d
	combine	combine sentences 21c
	cs	comma splice 24
	d or wc	diction (poor word choice) 23
	dev	lack of paragraph development 3b
	frag	fragment 25
	fs	fused sentence 24
	ital	italics or underlining needed 36c
	lc or diagonal slash [Example]	lowercase; capital letter not needed 36a
	para or ¶	indent new paragraph 2a
	pass	overuse of passive voice 27c
	prep	nonstandard use of preposition 33m, 33n
	ref	pronoun reference not specific 31e
	ro	run-on sentence 24
	shift	illogical shift 27
	sp	incorrect spelling 37
	tense	problem with verb tense 29, 30
	trans	transition needed 3d
	unity	paragraph not unified 3a
	w	wordy, not concise 23b
	//	problem with parallelism 22
	⟨,⟩	problem with comma use 34
	⟨;⟩	problem with semicolon use 19b, 19c
	⟨" "⟩	problem with quotation marks 36b, 36c
	⊂ *[ex ample]*	close up space
	∧	insert
	⸝ *[exaample]*	delete
	∼ *[words example]*	reversed letters or words
	X	obvious error
	✓	good point, well put
	# *[examplewords]*	add a space